CONTENTS

PREFACE

Business organizations and corporate law is a subject offered in nearly every paralegal program in the country. This text is designed to provide students with a thorough understanding of the subject, offered in a style designed to enhance student retention. This book explores the basic concepts of business, from sole proprietorships to corporations. *Business Organizations and Corporate Law* works hard to strike a balance between theory, which is a necessary intellectual building block for any course as in-depth as business organizations or corporation law, and practical applications of this knowledge, which helps students make a connection with the material. In this way, this text creates a middle ground between the books currently available for paralegal students. This book explores not only the various models of business organizations, but also all the critical roles played by the paralegal and legal team in creating and maintaining those business organizations.

▶ FEATURES OF THE TEXT

The text has numerous features that take advantage of the varying learning styles that students apply to learning. Based on the recognition that students who apply their newly acquired knowledge often retain it much better than those who do not, this text requires students to apply the knowledge that they have gained. Each chapter has practical examples of business organizational models in action and also relies heavily on the abundant information to be found on the Internet.

- Each chapter analyzes the elements of business organizational models from sole proprietorships to the intricacies of corporate law.
- Significant cases are excerpted and explored in great detail.
- Web sites for further research and/or discussion are provided at the end of each chapter.
- Step-by-step analysis of the creation of various business types is presented.
- Chapter discussions are based on actual business problems.
- Numerous scenarios and practical examples are offered to bring home the issues discussed in each chapter.
- Each chapter presents a synopsis of important issues in "Getting to the Basics" and "Key Points."

- Practical assignments are given, based on real-world problems business people and attorneys face on a daily basis.
- Each chapter presents numerous sidebars addressing a wide variety of issues.
- The end-of-chapter exercises, hands-on assignments, and practical applications emphasize the theoretical concepts presented in the text.
- The material is also topical, including discussions about ethical concerns for legal professionals, especially those raised by e-mail, insider trading, the Internet, and e-commerce.

Key Features of Each Chapter

Each chapter has numerous features that are designed to assist the student in acquiring a solid footing in the topic of business organizations. These chapter-specific features include:

- learning objectives stated at the beginning of each chapter

The learning objectives for the chapter are stated clearly and succinctly at the beginning of each chapter. These learning objectives help the student and the instructor focus on the critical issues for each chapter and provide the student with a method for evaluating the student's mastery of the material.

- terms and legal vocabulary defined immediately for the student

The first time a key word or legal term is mentioned in the text, a definition of it appears in the margin. This helps students grasp the meaning without breaking into the flow of the reading by having to turn to the glossary.

- exhibits that illustrate crucial points and capitalize on different student learning styles

The author provides numerous exhibits to develop certain points from the material. This feature takes advantage of the different learning styles among students, allowing those geared to a more visual learning style the opportunity to absorb the material appropriately.

- numerous scenarios to help students develop their understanding of the material

The author uses hypothetical questions and other scenarios to illustrate the points under discussion in each chapter. These scenarios also provide an excellent foundation for classroom discussion.

- case law that explores topics raised in the chapter

Each chapter contains one complete appellate case, taken from state and federal jurisdictions nationwide, that show how the topics discussed in the chapter are applied in the legal arena. The author also includes a question section at the end of the case that is directed to specific issues in the case.

- "Getting to the Basics"

Each chapter contains several entries entitled "Getting to the Basics," which encapsulate the material under discussion and provide a handy reference for students as they review the material to prepare for assignments or examinations.

- ■ "Key Points"

In order to further assist students in comprehension of the material, the author has provided another feature called "Key Points," which addresses the central issue in each section. This feature helps to illuminate important issues under discussion and provide an additional study tool for students.

- ■ "Legal Checklists," based on actual activities carried out by attorneys and paralegals in creating various business structures.

Checklists provided in each chapter act as a guideline for the student. The checklists are based on material raised in the chapter and help focus the student on critical aspects of each chapter.

- ■ Numerous sidebars

Each chapter also contains numerous sidebars. These explore aspects of the text in greater detail, explaining various features of businesses and legal issues related to various types of business structures.

- ■ "Ethics File"

Ethics is crucial for any legal professional. Each chapter explores an important ethical question and explains the relevance of ethical systems for the day-to-day practice of law.

- ■ End-of-chapter questions, activities, and assignments to increase student comprehension and retention of the concepts presented in the chapter

End-of-chapter exercises include Applying Chapter Concepts, Review Questions, and Questions for Reflection to assist the student in continuing to apply the concepts presented in the chapter.

- ■ Web sites for further research and/or discussion

At the end of each chapter is an extensive list of Web resources focusing on the issues raised in that chapter. Students are provided links to various governmental and other Web sites that help them expand on the discussion in the text and also allow them to get in-depth on any particular issue that suits them.

- ■ Appendices containing a complete set of uniform acts

The Appendices A–C contain the text of the Uniform Partnership Act, the Uniform Limited Partnership Act, and the Uniform Limited Liability Company Act.

- ■ Secretary of state Web sites

A complete set of Web sites for all 50 states and territories is provided in Appendix D. This aids students in applying the general materials in the text to their specific state law.

- ■ Glossary containing definitions of all terms used in the text

All of the terms and phrases defined throughout the text are also provided in a comprehensive glossary.

▶ PEDAGOGY

The text is written in clearly presented language that engages the student, keeps the reader's interest, and presents information in a variety of styles to take advantage of different learning styles. Each new concept is presented in a multilayer fashion, first presenting the basic concepts and then adding greater complexity once the intellectual foundation is laid. Charts and diagrams are provided to illustrate concepts as they are discussed and to provide the instructor with additional material for class discussion. Sidebars, tables, and interviews are also presented to supplement the chapter information in a different format for students who may not fully grasp the concepts on initial presentation. Finally, practical, hands-on assignments and discussion questions are presented to reiterate and emphasize the concepts. This allows for greater comprehension and retention by the student. The author fills the text with a balance of theoretical discussions and practical examples, all presented in a well-written, enjoyable style.

▶ NON-GENDER-SPECIFIC LANGUAGE

In recognition of the impact of gender-specific language, the author has adopted the following convention in the text: each even-numbered chapter uses "he" in general discussions and examples, while the odd-number chapters use "she" for the same purposes.

▶ SUPPLEMENTAL TEACHING MATERIALS

▪ Instructor's Manual with Test Bank

This is available both in print and on-line at http://www.westlegalstudies.com in the Instructor's Lounge under Resource. Written by the author of the text, the *Instructor's Manual* provides the following features:

- ▪ suggested syllabi and lesson plans
- ▪ annotated outlines for each chapter
- ▪ answers to all end-of-chapter questions
- ▪ Test Bank

The test bank includes a variety of test questions, including:

- ▪ essay questions (five per chapter)
- ▪ short answer (ten per chapter)
- ▪ multiple choice (twenty-five per chapter)
- ▪ true-false (ten per chapter)
- ▪ On-line Companion™

The Online Companion™ Web site can be found at http://www.
westlegalstudies.com in the Resource section of the Web site. The On-
Line Companion™ contains the following:

- additional cases
- questions
- scenarios
- Web sites
- PowerPoint slides

Web page

Come visit our Web site at http://www.westlegalstudies.com, where
you will find valuable information specific to this book, such as hot links
and sample materials to download, as well as other West Legal Studies
products.

Westlaw®

West's on-line computerized legal research system offers students
"hands-on" experience with a system commonly used in law offices.
Qualified adopters can receive ten free houses of Westlaw®. Westlaw® can
be accessed with Macintosh and IBM PC and compatibles. A modem is
required.

Please note the internet resources are of a time-sensitive nature and
URL addresses may often change or be deleted.

Contact us at westlegalstudies@delmar.com

ACKNOWLEDGMENTS

The author would like to thank the following people for their assistance in creating this book: Deborah Bevans, Melissa Riveglia, and Pamela Fuller.

The author and Thomson Delmar Learning would also like to thank the following reviewers for their valuable comments and suggestions:

Pamela Goetsch
David N. Myers University
Cleveland, Ohio

Judith Maloney
Long Island University
Brookville, New York

Kristine Mullendore
Grand Valley State University
Grand Rapids, Michigan

Beth Pless
Northeast Wisconsin Technical College
Green Bay, Wisconsin

ABOUT THE AUTHOR

Neal Bevans is a former private attorney and Assistant District Attorney in Atlanta, Georgia. A veteran of over 150 trials, Mr. Bevans has tried every major felony from rape, murder, and narcotics to armed robbery. One of his cases was televised nationally on Court TV *(Georgia v. Mobley)*. He has been a college instructor for over ten years. He is a writer of fiction and nonfiction material, and he is the author of *Criminal Law and Procedure for the Paralegal* and *Business Law: A Hands On Approach*. He has published numerous magazine articles about many aspects of the legal field. He is a former contributing columnist to *Legal Assistant Today* magazine.

Chapter 1

INTRODUCTION TO BUSINESS ORGANIZATIONS

Chapter Objectives

Upon completion of this chapter, you should be able to:

- Explain why the choice of business entity is so important.
- Describe the differences between various types of business organizations.
- Define the difference between a sole proprietorship and other business models.
- Explain the role of the legal team in helping to create a new business.
- Describe the importance of licenses, permits, and other governmental regulations for a new business.

INTRODUCTION

Business is the lifeblood of a capitalist society. At one time or another we have all considered going into business. Every day, millions of people in the United States buy goods from businesses. They pay with the money that they have made working in other businesses. The tax dollars generated by these businesses help support a government infrastructure that is unrivaled in the modern world. We are a nation of businesses.

This is a book devoted to the concepts of business and business organizations. Businesses can be as simple as a sole proprietorship or as complex as a multinational corporation. The choice of business organization can often mean the difference between a successful business and one that fails.

We will explore a wide range of business types in this text. After beginning with the relatively straightforward issues involved in sole proprietorship, we will then examine some of the preliminary issues in forming other types of businesses, from general partnerships to corporations.

One of the most important aspects of any business decision is the extent of liability of the person running the business. In this chapter, we will explore the concepts related to sole proprietorships. This form of business has the least legal protection of any type of business organization. In fact, many of the other business organizational models were developed expressly as a consequence of the liabilities that fall on the shoulders of a sole proprietorship. When we speak of legal liability, what are we actually saying? Legal liability is the extent of personal assets that a business owner may have to liquidate in order to pay a legal claim.

THE IMPORTANCE OF BUSINESS TYPE

What business model to use is one of the most important questions that a business owner must answer. If the owner chooses poorly, he or she can open the business up to unlimited liability. The owner's personal assets might be seized to satisfy a judgment. On the other hand, a business model that has too much complexity will stifle the owner's initiative and creativity.

LEGAL CHECKLIST

FACTORS IN CHOOSING A BUSINESS ORGANIZATIONAL STRUCTURE

❑ WHO WILL OWN THE BUSINESS?

❑ WHAT DEGREE OF FORMALITY IS REQUIRED TO CREATE THE BUSINESS STRUCTURE?

❑ WHAT IS THE OWNER'S INCOME TAX SITUATION?

❑ HOW DIFFICULT WILL IT BE TO ACQUIRE ADDITIONAL INVESTMENTS?

 GETTING TO THE BASICS

Deciding on the form of business can have a profound impact on the success of the business.

◢ OVERVIEW OF BUSINESS ORGANIZATIONAL MODELS

In the next few paragraphs, we will profile the various types of business organizations, from sole proprietorships to corporations, as a way of introducing these models. In future chapters, we will expand on each of the organizations.

SOLE PROPRIETORSHIPS

A **sole proprietorship** is a business that is owned and run by a single individual. It is one of the simplest business forms to create and to dissolve. Sole proprietorships are the alter egos of their owners. These business owners have little protection for their personal assets, but they do enjoy favorable tax treatment. They can, for instance, pass business losses through on their individual income taxes to reduce their annual tax burden. We will discuss sole proprietorships in much greater detail in chapter 3.

sole proprietorship One of the most basic business models; a business run by a single individual, where all profits and losses are passed through on the individual's income tax returns and where the individual has little or no liability protection.

PARTNERSHIPS

A **partnership** consists of two or more people working together in a joint business venture. Partnerships have several obvious advantages over sole proprietorships. First, there are more people to share the load. Partners can bring additional financial and other resources to bear for the good of the business. However, with these greater resources come more limitations. The partners must consult with one another before making business decisions, and all partners face the possibility of losing their personal assets in a judgment against the partnership.

partnership A form of business where two or more persons conduct a business together, sharing both profits and losses.

Formation of a Partnership

The decision to form a partnership can be as simple as two people deciding to go into business together. General partnerships, as opposed to limited partnerships, limited liability companies, and the myriad of other business models, have few legal requirements. In almost all circumstances, there is no legal reason for a written partnership agreement. Instead, the parties might simply decide to pool their assets and share in the profits.

> **Scenario 1–1. Southern Bella**
> Ginger Frank and Carrie Westall formed a partnership two years ago. Their business, Southern Bella, sells a wide variety of knickknacks, soaps, and linens.
> Like many business partners, they were friends first. They had worked together at another retail establishment and then decided to open their own business.
> They came up with estimates about how much money they would need to make every day to cover their expenses, and like many new

business owners, they drastically underestimated how much money they would need to run their business.

As with many business partners, their plan was informal. The entire plan was written out on two pages.

In chapter 4, we will examine exactly how a general partnership is formed and how partnership agreements are created and also provide an opportunity for hands-on applications, such as drafting a partnership agreement for Southern Bella.

LIMITED PARTNERSHIPS

limited partnership A business model that shields some of the partners' personal assets by creating a form of limited liability. Limited partners enjoy limited liability, while the general partners have little or no protection from liability concerns.

limited liability A legal concept that, when used in the context of business, refers to the protection of an investor's personal assets. Potential loss is limited to the total amount invested in the venture, not the investor's total personal assets.

A **limited partnership** combines the basics of a typical partnership with the concept of limited liability. We will explore limited liability in much greater detail in a future chapter, but a word about it here is also appropriate. When a person enjoys limited liability, it means that his or her personal assets are never in danger, no matter how large a judgment is entered against the business. Sole proprietorships and partnerships are always concerned about liability issues. A judgment could easily affect the owners' personal assets. But a limited partnership is protected by a statutorily created scheme called **limited liability.** In limited liability business arrangements, the most that a person can lose is her total investment. Limited liability protects personal assets from forfeiture and therefore encourages people to invest in businesses that they might otherwise avoid.

A limited partnership enjoys some measure of limited liability protection. In a limited partnership, there is a general partner who serves the same function, and has the same unlimited liability, as the partner in a general partnership, but there are also individuals who are labeled "limited partners." These partners contribute money to the business, but have no direct say in how the business is run. They enjoy limited liability.

LIMITED LIABILITY COMPANIES

limited liability company A limited liability company is a cross between a partnership and a corporation, owned by members who may manage the company directly or delegate to officers or managers who are similar to a corporation's directors.

The **limited liability company** (LLC) is a relatively recent invention. They resemble limited partnerships but have legal protections that are similar to those of a corporation. As in limited partnerships, investors in LLCs enjoy limited liability. However, the day-to-day business of an LLC is run more like a corporation. We discuss LLC's in much greater detail in chapter 6.

Formation of a Limited Liability Company

Scenario 1–2. Fiction Addiction

Fiction Addiction is a used-book store that also sells books online. Owned and operated by Jill McFarlane, the store has bookshelves from floor to ceiling containing books on a dizzying variety of topics. Besides offering Internet sales, the store also boasts a feature not seen in most bookstores: a spunky kitten named Miles. Jill, like many business owners, had thought about opening up her own business for years.

For Jill, extensive research and planning were the keys to success. Unlike the ladies who created Southern Bella, Jill put together a detailed business plan. Although none of the numbers on her plan turned out to be accurate, the general overview for the business was correct.

Jill found that starting up the business required attention to detail. Unlike Southern Bella, which opted for a general partnership, Jill registered as a limited liability company. In chapter 6, we will examine limited liability companies, as well as other forms of limited liability enterprises, in greater detail.

CORPORATIONS

Corporations are another form of business that is authorized by state statute. A corporation is a form of business that is in many ways unique. A corporation is much more than another business model. A corporation is considered to be an artificial person. This "person" can own other businesses, enter into partnerships, pay taxes, and do many of the activities that we would associate with a sole proprietor. Investors in a corporation enjoy the full range of limited liability, but the real strength of a corporation goes beyond that concept. A corporation has both substantial protection and substantial freedom.

A corporation has several distinct advantages over other types of businesses. As we will see in chapter 7, a corporation not only is protected by limited liability, but also has the power to own property in its own right. Corporations function in ways that other business models would find difficult if not impossible.

There are many different types of corporate structures, such as nonprofit corporations, subchapter S corporations, service corporations, and professional corporations. We will examine these and many other corporate structures beginning in chapter 7 and continuing to the end of the text.

corporation A creature of statute; corporations are considered to be artificial persons; investors enjoy limited liability; corporations may own property, pay taxes, and carry out many of the activities traditionally associated with natural persons.

Professional Corporations

In chapter 7, we will examine the many different types of corporate structures. One such arrangement is the professional corporation. These are business structures that are offered to specific types of professions only. For instance, doctors and lawyers, and certain others, are permitted to form a **professional corporation.** Similar to limited liability companies, these corporations offer professionals the chance to pool resources and to protect the personal assets of their members.

Formation of a Corporation

Creating a corporation requires careful attention to detail and a solid understanding of your state's laws. When we discuss the creation, running, and

professional corporation A special corporate structure reserved for individuals who can practice their profession only after receiving a license from the state.

termination of corporations, state law will be of paramount concern. As we explore the issues surrounding corporations, we will also examine applicable statutes and emphasize practical applications of those statutes, including review of available law, analysis of cases and statutes relevant to corporate law and actual experience in creating a corporation. See Exhibit 1–1.

Scenario 1–3. Fulenwider Enterprises, Inc.

Michael Fulenwider has been in the restaurant business since he was eighteen years old. His father bought a Kentucky Fried Chicken franchise in 1965, and the entire family went to work there. Eventually, the single store became two, then three, then a dozen.

Fulenwider eventually took over all of the stores, handling the books and payroll and ordering supplies. As his family acquired other restaurants, including Burger King, Subway, and Taco Bell franchises, he realized that his family needed to form a corporation to protect their personal assets.

He formed Fulenwider Enterprises, Inc., and hired a large staff to keep track of complicated real estate transactions, payroll taxes, social security employee payments, and a whole host of federal, state, and local legal issues. Forming a corporation solved certain problems, but also created others. For instance, his corporation is required to file taxes on its profits. The corporation, not the family, owns the restaurants, and that imposes some restraint on what individual family members can do with the properties. We will examine the advantages and disadvantages of corporations in chapter 7.

Exhibit 1–1. The questions that often arise in forming a corporation

> ❏ Who will record corporate minutes?
> ❏ How does the corporation acquire a corporate seal?
> ❏ Should the company issue stock certificates?
> ❏ What should the corporate bylaws state?
> ❏ How does the company acquire a business checking account?
> ❏ Are there any issues regarding patents?
> ❏ Are there any issues regarding copyrights?
> ❏ How easy will it be to borrow money?
> ❏ Should the company arrange for unemployment insurance?

The Role of the Legal Team in Creating a Business

Throughout this text, we will examine not only the theoretical issues involved in creating, maintaining, and dissolving businesses, but also the practical issues that legal professionals must face on a day-to-day basis. We will examine the role of both attorneys and paralegals in advising clients and in analyzing cases and statutes, and the practical applications of business theory. In the next few paragraphs, we will explore the types of actions taken by law firms in general and paralegals in particular in helping business owners create their businesses and continue to run them within applicable state and federal laws.

Business people often seek legal advice for many different issues. As a paralegal in a business firm, you will be called upon to engage in a wide variety of activities to help create a business. The paralegal's role is extensive in a corporate law practice, including interviewing clients, drafting documents, researching applicable laws, working with government officials, and paying close attention to detail in creating final forms of important state and federal documents. One example of the kind of research that a paralegal might conduct in a case involves something as simple as the company name.

Registering the Company Name

Suppose that you have a client named John Doe who wants to open up a business as a trainer of exotic animals. He claims that he can train any type of animal. He boasts that he has even trained deer to star in wilderness movies. He could call his business "John Doe, Animal Trainer," but he doesn't like the sound of it. Instead, he wants to name his business Doe-A-Deer Company. However, this company name raises an immediate issue.

In most states, when a person wishes to name a business something other than his real name, he must apply with the state for a "fictitious name" certification. Such a registration is required whenever the business name does not contain the actual name of the business owner. Many times, these registrations must be submitted to the state secretary of state's office.

As a legal professional, one of your first duties may be to contact the secretary of state's office and determine whether there are already any other businesses with this name. If so, John Doe will not be able to use it. He will have to develop a different name.

Acquiring a Web Site

Although many business owners arrange Web sites themselves, more and more are turning to law firms to do it for them. Part of the service offered by the firm might include registering a "domain name" with the Internet Corporation for Assigned Names and Numbers (ICANN). We will discuss this organization in greater detail in future chapters.

Searching for a Trademark

In addition to issues surrounding the company name, there are also additional issues regarding trademarks. The client may wish to use a particular emblem as a symbol for his business. In the case of Doe-A-Deer Company, the client wishes to use the image of a deer's head and antlers with "Doe-A-Deer" appearing to dangle from the points of the antlers. If the client wishes to register this as a trademark for his company, the firm must conduct a trademark search in order to ensure that no other company has already registered the same or a substantially similar image. The actual search usually falls to the paralegal.

Obtaining Licenses and Permits

New business owners are often ignorant of the many different types of business licenses and permits that are required to run a business. For instance, local ordinances may require business licenses or other permits to run specific types of businesses. If the business will be run out of the client's home, there is also the issue of zoning permits. If the zoning certification does not permit the type of business that the client wishes to run, then a request for zoning variance may be required. In addition to business licenses, a wide variety of other types of permits and certifications may be required. See Exhibit 1–2.

Exhibit 1–2. Some of the state licenses and certifications that a sole proprietor may need to obtain

❏ business licenses
❏ health inspections
❏ fire inspections
❏ special permits
❏ dangerous substances
❏ selling food to the public
❏ special licenses to run businesses such as:
  ▪ real estate firms
  ▪ contracting
  ▪ hair dresser/barber
  ▪ dry cleaning
(Federal licenses might also be required)

Interviewing Clients

Throughout this text, we will address some of the important skills that any paralegal must acquire in order to be effective when working with business clients. Perhaps the most important of these skills is the ability to interview clients and gather as much detail as possible. Many clients have a natural tendency to shield or shade certain facts in a way that puts them in as good a light as possible. This is especially true for clients who have encountered trouble running their businesses and are now considering declaring bankruptcy or otherwise terminating their business. They may be embarrassed or humiliated. They may also feel that the full facts paint them in a bad light. One of the many skills you will develop throughout this text is the ability to dig for the facts and develop the full story to get the best possible result for the client.

CASE LAW: *Suing a Sole Proprietor*

Yellow Book of NY L.P. v. Dimilia, 188 Misc.2d 489, 729 N.Y.S.2d 286
(N.Y.Dist.Ct.,2001)
Kenneth L. Gartner, J.

The defendant, an $11,000.00 per year house cleaner residing in Section 8 housing in the Suffolk County town of Westhampton Beach, sought to have vacated the $3,000.00 default judgment entered against her by the plaintiff, a publisher of a Yellow Pages directory. The judgment was for an admittedly unpaid fee for advertising concededly published by the plaintiff on behalf of an entity known as The Rug Nurse.

By prior decision, this Court deferred action on the defendant's motion pending a hearing on three specified factual issues raised by the parties' papers.

The plaintiff now moves for reargument, asserting that plaintiff's motion should be denied without the necessity for a factual hearing. For the following reasons, the plaintiff's motion for reargument is granted, but on reargument the prior determination is adhered to.

In the prior decision, this Court determined that one factual issue had been raised because the defendant has disputed the service alleged by the plaintiff's process server. The process server attests that service was made upon an individual identified as the defendant's daughter, Sue Dimilia. The defendant, however, asserts that "no one in my household was ever served a paper regarding this matter. The paper was served to a Sue Dimilia. There is no such person at that address."

In the prior decision, this Court observed that, as held by the Appellate Division in Chase Manhattan Bank, N.A. v. Carlson, 113 A.D.2d 734, 735, 493 N.Y.S.2d 339 (2d Dep't 1985), if service were in fact improper, dismissal would be required whether or not a meritorious defense had been stated:

Absent proper service of the summons, a default judgment is a nullity and once it is shown that proper service was not effected, the judgment must be unconditionally vacated. The existence or lack of a meritorious defense is irrelevant to the question of whether a judgment should be vacated for lack of personal jurisdiction.

The plaintiff, in its current papers, asserts without citing any authority that this determination was "improper" because an affidavit was filed by the plaintiff "which clearly indicates that the defendant was sufficiently served with process according to the mandates of the CPLR." This contention is without merit.

This Court determined (and the defendant agrees) that if (as the summons and complaint in this action indicate) The Rug Nurse is not a corporation but rather, a d/b/a of the individual defendant, individual liability will lie and the defendant, having conceded that advertising charges were incurred by The Rug Nurse and have not been paid, would have no defense, since a sole proprietor bears unlimited liability for the venture's undertakings. However, this Court determined that if The Rug Nurse is in fact a corporate party, rather than a sole proprietorship, no liability would lie, since the single signature line utilized on the plaintiff's form contracts is ambiguous, and thus, in light of the mandate that form contracts be construed against the drafters, is insufficient to personally bind the individual signatory on behalf of a corporate party. This is particularly the case on the instant facts where, as observed by the Supreme Court, Nassau County, in Yellow Book Co., Inc. v. Williams, N.Y.L.J.,

(continued)

CASE LAW: *Suing a Sole Proprietor* (continued)

the signatories are largely "unsophisticated, non-legal-trained individuals running small businesses...." A factual issue is thus presented as to whether The Rug Nurse is indeed a sole proprietorship or some other form of entity.

A reading of the two page agreement involved herein reveals that it clearly and unambiguously made the defendant individually liable thereon. Under the circumstances, the defendant's attempt to avoid personal responsibility was properly rejected.

A hearing must therefore be held as directed in this Court's prior decision.

CASE QUESTIONS

1. Why does the defendant claim that there was no proper service of process in this case?
2. What is the significance of the fact that The Rug Nurse is not a corporation?
3. If the court determines that The Rug Nurse is a corporation, what effect does this have on the service of process in this case?
4. Explain the court's ruling that The Rug Nurse has unlimited liability.

CASE LAW: *Does Budgetary Control Equal Ownership?*

Coastal Corp. v. Torres, 133 S.W.3d 776 (2004)
Before Chief Justice VALDEZ and Justices HINOJOSA and RODRIGUEZ.

OPINION

Opinion by Justice RODRIGUEZ.

This is a personal injury case that involves a refinery explosion caused by a defect in a pressure vessel. Appellees, Daniel Torres, William Bourland, and David Natividad, asserted a negligence claim against appellant, The Coastal Corporation (Coastal). Following a jury trial, the trial court entered judgment against Coastal. By five issues, Coastal contends appellees' theory of recovery is not recognized in Texas; the evidence is legally and factually insufficient to support such theory, if recognized; the trial court erred in admitting expert testimony; the award of actual damages is excessive; and prejudgment interest on future damages should not have been awarded. We reverse and render.

I. BACKGROUND

An explosion occurred in May 1999 at a Corpus Christi refinery owned and operated by Coastal Refining & Marketing, Inc. (Coastal Refining). A pressure vessel ruptured, releasing a large amount of naphtha that found an ignition source and exploded. Appellees, who were Coastal Refining employees, received serious injuries in the accident. The rupture occurred as a result of the vessel's walls thinning from internal corrosion.

Appellees sued appellant for negligence and gross negligence alleging that "through central budgetary authority exercised by Coastal's corporate officers in Houston, Texas, Coastal . . . assumed control over maintenance, turnaround, and inspection matters at the plant." In response to a broad-form negligence question, the jury found Coastal's negligence proximately caused appellees' injuries. [The court's charge to the jury stated]:

In order to find negligence on the part of The Coastal Corporation, you must find all of the following: (1) The Coastal Corporation had the right to control the budget and/or expenditures of Coastal Refining & Marketing, Inc.; (2) The Coastal Corporation exercised that right of control through a person who was acting as a director, officer, employee or agent of The Coastal Corporation; and (3) The Coastal Corporation's exercise of that control amounted to negligence.

The jury answered, "Yes," as to each appellee and awarded actual damages totaling $122.5 million.

By its first issue, Coastal challenges appellees' theory of liability in this case. It contends Texas does not recognize a cause of action against a parent company for negligent control of the budget of its subsidiary. Because appellees have waived any premises liability, Coastal argues that appellees are left with theories of recovery that have no support in Texas law.

II. ANALYSIS

Appellees assert that Coastal's duty arises from traditional and mainstream principles of tort law. Coastal, however, contends Texas courts have not accepted any theory of recovery urged by appellees.

A. Negligent Control of Subsidiary's Budget

Appellees complain of Coastal's actions in allegedly taking control of the safety budget and expenditures for the refinery and imposing policies that created strict procedures over its subsidiary's access to funds. Because Coastal was allegedly negligent through its own conduct in creating that management scheme and in withholding funds for inspectors and safety maintenance, appellees contend Coastal is liable.

Appellees assert Texas case law provides the mainstream duty that Coastal owed appellees, that being a duty arising from its alleged negligent control over budgets and expenditures. Relying on *Redinger v. Living, Inc.,* 689 S.W.2d 415, 417-18

(Tex.1985), and cases following *Redinger,* to support their control-based liability theory, appellees contend Coastal, by limiting expenditures, controlled and influenced its subsidiary in a way that directly resulted in appellees' injuries. The facts, however, underlying the *Redinger* line of cases are distinguishable from the present facts.

In *Redinger,* the court reviewed supervisory control over construction work that caused the injury, an activity conducted on the premises. *See id. Redinger* adopted section 414 of the Restatement (Second) of Torts, which imposes liability based on control of another's work activities. Section 414 provides:

One who entrusts work to an independent contractor, but who retains control of any part of the work, is subject to liability for physical harm to others for whose safety the employer owes a duty to exercise reasonable care, which is caused by his failure to exercise his control with reasonable care.

From the *Redinger* line of cases, it is apparent that liability is imposed when there is specific control over the activity that caused the accident.

In the present case, appellees assert negligent control of the budget, not negligent control over details of specific operational activities. We cannot conclude the cited authority provides support for appellees' argument. Because appellees have provided us with no authority, and we find none, where a Texas court has imposed liability against a parent company, under mainstream principles of tort law, for negligent control of such remote conduct as budgeting activities, we conclude appellees' control-based negligence theory of recovery fails.

B. Affirmative Conduct/Undertaking Liability

Coastal also challenges the viability of any affirmative conduct theory of recovery appellees now argue on appeal.

Appellees assert Coastal's tort duty flows from the mainstream duty rule that a party must use reasonable care in its affirmative conduct. Appellees construe the affirmative conduct about which they complain as Coastal's choice of a business management plan that allegedly gave Coastal control over

(continued)

CASE LAW: *Does Budgetary Control Equal Ownership?* *(continued)*

expenditures and budgets. They describe this theory as one closely akin to an "undertaking liability."

The Texas Supreme Court discussed the undertaking theory of liability in *Torrington Co. v. Stutzman*, 46 S.W.3d 829, 837 (Tex.2000). The *Torrington* court concluded undertaking liability requires the submission of the following specific duty predicates:

(1) [the defendant] undertook to perform services that it knew or should have known were necessary for the plaintiffs' protection, (2) the defendant failed to exercise reasonable care in performing those services, and either (3) a third party charged with protecting the plaintiffs relied upon the defendant's performance, or (4) the defendant's performance increased the plaintiffs' risk of harm.

While the trial court's charge in *Torrington* included the usual definitions of "negligence," "ordinary care," and "proximate cause," it gave the jury no further instructions or definitions applicable to the negligence question. *Id.* Because the charge did not submit the necessary duty predicates for a voluntary undertaking claim, and because neither plaintiff nor the court of appeals had the guidance of *Torrington* at the time the case was tried, the supreme court remanded the undertaking claim to the trial court. *Id.* at 841.

The elements of an undertaking theory are dictated by section 324A of the Restatement (Second) of Torts, which covers the situation in which one undertakes to perform a service to another that is for the protection of the plaintiff as a third party.

In the present case, the above duty predicates were not submitted in the trial court's charge. Unlike *Torrington,* however, the court's charge did include the following predicates which appellees assert gave rise to a legal duty: (1) Coastal had the right to control the budget and/or expenditures of Coastal Refining & Marketing, Inc.; and (2) Coastal exercised that right of control through a person who was acting as a director, officer, employee or agent of Coastal.

Appellees assert these elements were submitted in an effort to prove that, by refusing to budget necessary funds, Coastal chose to control the "safety duty" that the refinery owed its employees. However, the actions about which appellees complain are not affirmative actions of control undertaken to provide services to protect another. Appellees are complaining of refusals or failures to budget. This is the antithesis of an affirmative course of action. Accordingly, we conclude Coastal's alleged actions do not comprise affirmative conduct akin to an affirmative undertaking pursued for the benefit of the injured person. Moreover, appellees have provided us with no authority, and we find none, where a Texas court has, under mainstream principles of tort law, construed a parent company's refusal or failure to budget as an affirmative undertaking and imposed liability against a parent company. Thus, appellees' affirmative conduct theory also fails.

Accordingly, the judgment of the trial court is reversed and rendered that appellees take nothing.

CASE QUESTIONS

1. What are the allegations raised by the employees regarding the extent of control over operations by the parent company?

2. How does the parent company's control over the budget of its subsidiary affect its liability for an explosion on the premises?

3. How did the parent company, according to the appellees, maintain its control of the facility where the explosion occurred?

4. Does the court agree with the premise raised by the employees who were injured in the explosion? Explain.

5. What argument do the appellees make concerning the parent company's choice of business model, and is this argument successful?

Ethics File

Throughout this book, we will examine specific ethical issues that arise in the formation, existence, and termination of businesses. Legal professionals must abide by their own ethical standards, ensure that clients abide by them as well, and ensure that the legal services provided to business clients meet the highest ethical standards. Not only is this good practice, but it also has practical consequences. Legal professionals who abide by ethical standards are less likely to become involved in legal malpractice actions brought by former clients. Following ethical standards is also a way of improving society's view of the legal profession as a whole. Finally, ethical considerations are also a matter of common sense. When everyone obeys the rules, it is easier to get things done. At the conclusion of each of the future chapters, we will examine specific ethical issues that arise from the chapter materials. You should be prepared to discuss these various ethical concerns not only in class and discussion, but also on future assignments and tests.

SUMMARY

In this chapter, we have seen that some of the preliminary questions that a prospective business owner must answer include not only questions about financing, inventory, and purchasing, but also the choice of business model. A sole proprietorship offers unique advantages for a business owner. It gives the owner a great deal of flexibility and efficiency. A sole proprietor is under no obligation to run his or her business ideas through a board of directors or other controlling individuals. A sole proprietor can implement changes in the business structure faster than any other type of business model. However, a sole proprietorship also has distinct disadvantages, including the legal liability of the business owner. Because a sole proprietorship is so intertwined with the business owner's personal finances, losses from the business can result in a declaration of personal bankruptcy. On top of that, there is also the issue of legal liability. Sole proprietors face unlimited liability in civil suits brought against them. This chapter also introduces some of the basic foundational questions surrounding other types of business models. Each of those business models will be explored in future chapters.

HELPFUL WEB SITES

Business.gov
http://www.business.gov/

American Bar Association—Business Law Section
http://www.abanet.org/buslaw/blt/

Findlaw.com for Small Business
http://smallbusiness.findlaw.com/

Stanford Journal of Law, Business and Finance
http://sjlbf.stanford.edu/

Small Business Administration
http://www.sba.gov/businesslaw/index.html

KEY TERMS

corporation

limited liability

limited liability company

limited partnership

partnership

professional corporation

sole proprietorship

APPLYING CHAPTER CONCEPTS

1. Locate a sole proprietor in your area and ask this person some questions. For instance, what prompted this person to start a business in the first place? Did the sole proprietor consider other business models? Ask the sole proprietor about the advantages and disadvantages of running a business. How do these answers compare with the chapter material?

2. Based on what you learned in this chapter, if you were going to set up business as a sole proprietor, how would you handle such issues as financing and legal liability?

3. Visit the Small Business Administration (*http://www.sba.gov*) Web site and summarize the information and links that can be found there.

4. Contact your local government and ask about requirements for business licenses and permits to run the following types of businesses:
    - an attorney's office
    - a certified public accountant's office
    - a paralegal firm
    - a pharmacy

REVIEW QUESTIONS

1. What is the difference between a sole proprietor and other forms of business?

2. What are some of the specific concerns for a sole proprietor?

3. Explain the concept of unlimited liability.

4. What are some of the ways that a sole proprietor can protect his or her assets?

5. Why is it important for a sole proprietor to understand the law regarding business licenses and permits?

6. Why is trademark such an important issue for a sole proprietor?

7. What are some specific activities carried out by paralegals and attorneys in assisting business owners?

8. Prepare a checklist of questions that should be asked of a new client who is seeking to create a new business as a sole proprietor.

9. Why is the choice of business organization so important?

10. What are the advantages of a sole proprietorship?

11. What are the disadvantages of a sole proprietorship?

12. What are some of the legal questions that a sole proprietor should resolve before starting his or her business?

13. What is the significance of this chapter's critical case?

14. How does a sole proprietorship differ from a general partnership?

15. What is a corporation?

QUESTIONS FOR REFLECTION

1. Given the fact that sole proprietorships face unlimited liability and have other disadvantages, why do business owners continue to adopt this model?

2. Do business owners have a knowledge gap when it comes to the legal implications of business? Explain your answer.

 For additional resources visit our Web site at *http://www.westlegalstudies.com*

Chapter 2

PRINCIPALS AND AGENTS

Chapter Objectives

Upon completion of this chapter, you should be able to:

- Explain the duties that an agent owes to a principal.
- Explain the legal implications of a principal-agency relationship.
- Define how a principal-agency relationship is created.
- Explain the principal's duties to an agent.
- Explain an agent's duties to third parties and others outside the principal-agency relationship.

▶ INTRODUCTION

In this chapter, we will examine the principal-agency relationship. This relationship is based on a simple premise: that one person represents the interests of another. However, this simple relationship can spawn some complicated issues. We will begin our discussion of the principal-agency relationship first by exploring why such a relationship is necessary, then by examining how it is created; we will then move on to the duties owed by the participants to one another. Finally, we will define the ways that an agency relationship is terminated.

▶ NECESSITY FOR AN AGENCY RELATIONSHIP

There are times when persons, or corporations, are unwilling or unable to conduct business on their own behalf. A company might be unwilling to

agent The person who acts for the principal; agents receive their authority to act from a principal and may undertake business relationships and commitments on behalf of the principal.

principal The person for whom the agent acts; the principal receives the benefit of the agent's actions and is bound by the agent's actions on his or her behalf.

agency A legally recognized, fiduciary relationship where one person acts on behalf of another. Agents act under the authority, consent, and control of principals.[1]

announce its interest in a sale for fear of driving up the price. In these situations, an **agent** may be the best person to carry out the negotiations. A real estate agent, for example, knows the market better than a home seller, and can probably get a better price for the house than the seller. Attorneys, who often act as agents for their clients, can use their experience and knowledge to resolve legal matters for their clients. In these and many other situations individuals and companies select an agent to work for them. The person who hires an agent is referred to as the **principal.** The principal-agent relationship has existed in one form or another for thousands of years. While we will not be exploring the extensive history of the law of **agency** in this book, we will devote the entirety of this chapter to the subject. The reason for this is that almost all business transactions involve agency relationships at some point or other. Whether it is an agent negotiating the purchase of real estate for a principal, a person handling delicate negotiations between major companies, or an attorney acting on behalf of a client, an understanding of agency law is critical for all legal professionals.

GETTING TO THE BASICS

Agency relationships are necessary where the principal wishes to remain unknown or where the agent has skill, education, and training that exceeds that of the principal.

Scenario 2–1. Tump Towers
Donald Tump, a well-known celebrity and multimillionaire, has recently become interested in purchasing a tract of land in your state. He is considering building a resort there. However, Tump has learned over the years that every time he announces his intention of purchasing property, the price rises dramatically. Tump would prefer to have someone else negotiate the transaction for him. He doesn't want this person to let anyone know that he is really the purchaser.

His solution? Hire an agent to negotiate the purchase for him.

THE BASICS OF THE AGENCY RELATIONSHIP

The basic premise upon which the law of agency rests is that principals carry out actions through agents that they would have done themselves. Agents are, therefore, an extension of the principals. An agent's authority to act derives from the principal's rights. If the principal lacks capacity, so does the agent.[2]

Because agents derive their authority from principals, it is an absolute requirement that the principal have the ability to control the agent's actions.

Agents, in essence, are stand-ins for the principal. As we will see later in this chapter, agents may have expressed authority to act (where the principal specifically states the terms of the agent's authority) or implied authority (where the agent has the implied authority to carry out the transaction, but no other authority).[3] As far as the law is concerned, an agent is merely a substitute for the principal.[4]

KEY POINT

Agents act on behalf of the principal; they derive their authority from the principal.

COMPONENTS OF AN AGENCY RELATIONSHIP

An agency is created when the principal engages an agent to act on his or her behalf. The agent works for the principal and is empowered, to a degree, to negotiate and enter into binding agreements in the name of the principal. An agent's authority flows directly from the principal. Given the nature of an agency relationship and the fact that an agent can legally bind a principal to any of a number of business relationships, most principals and agents spell out the parameters of their agreement with great specificity. One such example of a principal-agency agreement is the brokerage agreement entered into by a home seller and a real estate broker. Real estate brokers act as agents for the homeowner, who is, obviously, the principal. But there are many other types of agency relationships.

> **Scenario 2–2. The Vintage Motorcycle**
> Danny has always wanted a vintage motorcycle called the Flying Valley Stomper. Danny's friend, Maria, knows a man who has a 1934 Flying Valley Stomper that he might be willing to sell. However, the man doesn't want to deal with anyone except Maria. Danny meets with Maria and gives her some money. He tells her, "No matter what, don't go over $2000 on the sale price." Is Maria an agent?
>
> **Answer:** Yes. The moment that Maria begins acting on behalf of Danny, she becomes his agent, even though neither one of them ever uses the term agency, agent, or principal. Maria is acting on Danny's behalf to negotiate the purchase of the motorcycle. She even has specific instructions about the maximum amount she may pay for the motorcycle. Maria is an agent; Danny is a principal.

CREATION OF AN AGENCY RELATIONSHIP

The most common way to create an agency relationship is through the express agreement of the parties. Normally, this agreement is spelled out in writing, where the principal specifies the types of actions that the agent will carry out and the extent of the agent's responsibilities. The agent will also want his or her method of compensation spelled out in equally clear detail. See Exhibit 2–1.

Exhibit 2–1. Points to consider when forming an agency relationship

> ❏ agreement of the parties
> ❏ contract
> ❏ operation of law

Agreement of the Parties

The most common way to create an agency relationship is by the express agreement of the parties. One person solicits another to act on his or her behalf. This person becomes the principal, while the other is classified as an agent. Inherent in the idea of creating an agency relationship is the principal's control, to some degree, of the agent's actions. A principal must have the capacity to set limits for an agent's activities on his or her behalf. These limitations are normally set out in the agreement. The best way to ensure that the agent and principal are in agreement about the features of their arrangement is to put it in writing.

KEY POINT

Agency relationships are usually created by the express, intentional actions of the parties.

Contract

Although an oral agreement to create an agency relationship is adequate, many parties opt for a more rigid approach and put the extent of the agency agreement on paper. A written contract solves many of the problems that an oral agreement either does not address or never considers. Written agreements also have the benefit of clarifying the parties' intentions and alleviate many questions that may surface during the agency relationship.

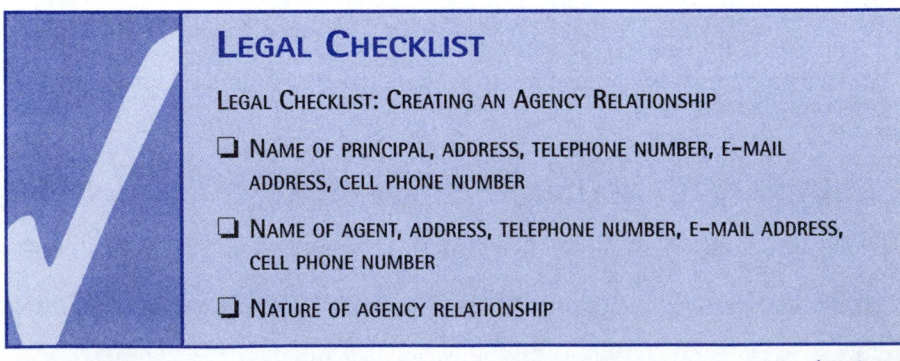

LEGAL CHECKLIST

LEGAL CHECKLIST: CREATING AN AGENCY RELATIONSHIP

❏ NAME OF PRINCIPAL, ADDRESS, TELEPHONE NUMBER, E-MAIL ADDRESS, CELL PHONE NUMBER

❏ NAME OF AGENT, ADDRESS, TELEPHONE NUMBER, E-MAIL ADDRESS, CELL PHONE NUMBER

❏ NATURE OF AGENCY RELATIONSHIP

(continued)

- ❏ THIS ARRANGEMENT IS CREATED FOR THE EXPRESS PURPOSE
  OF _____

- ❏ THE AGENT HAS THE FOLLOWING AUTHORITY GRANTED FROM THE
  PRINCIPAL:
  - ▪ TO NEGOTIATE TERMS
  - ▪ TO SIGN DOCUMENTS ON BEHALF OF PRINCIPAL
  - ▪ TO LEGALLY BIND PRINCIPAL TO SPECIFIC TYPES OF AGREEMENTS

- ❏ AGENT'S DUTIES
  - ▪ THE AGENT HAS THE FOLLOWING EXPRESS DUTIES, AUTHORITY FOR
    WHICH IS EXPRESSLY GRANTED BY THE PRINCIPAL: _____.
  - ▪ AGENT WILL DEVOTE APPROXIMATELY _____ HOURS PER WEEK TO
    FURTHER PRINCIPAL'S INTERESTS.
  - ▪ PRINCIPAL HAS THE RIGHT TO CONTROL SPECIFIC ACTIONS BY AGENT,
    INCLUDING:

    _____
    _____
    _____

- ❏ AGENCY TERMINATION
  - ▪ THE AGENCY RELATIONSHIP BEGINS ON _____ AND WILL
    END ON _____.

- ❏ AGENT'S COMPENSATION
  - ▪ AGENT WILL BE COMPENSATED BY
    - ▪ HOURLY WAGE
    - ▪ COMMISSION BASED ON SALE PRICE
    - ▪ CONTINGENCY FEE
    - ▪ FINDER'S FEE
    - ▪ COMPENSATION IN THE FORM OF PERSONAL PROPERTY

- ❏ REIMBURSEMENT
  - ▪ AGENT IS ENTITLED TO REIMBURSEMENT OF EXPENSES ASSOCIATED
    WITH AGENCY RELATIONSHIP, TO AN AMOUNT OF
    $_____.

- ❏ TERMINATION OF AGENCY RELATIONSHIP
  - ▪ PRINCIPAL MAY TERMINATE THIS RELATIONSHIP AT ANY TIME BY
    GIVING NOTICE TO THE AGENT AS FOLLOWS:

    _____.

- ❏ PRINCIPAL WILL PAY ANY OUTSTANDING REIMBURSEMENTS AND AGENT
  FEES EARNED UP TO THE POINT OF TERMINATION.

- ❏ SUBAGENTS
  - ▪ AGENT IS AUTHORIZED TO APPOINT SUBAGENTS TO CONDUCT
    SPECIFIC ACTIVITIES.
  - ▪ AGENT WILL COMPENSATE SUBAGENTS OUT OF HER OWN FEE.

(continued)

❑ DUTIES THAT AGENT OWES PRINCIPAL
■ OBEDIENCE: AGENT WILL ABIDE BY ALL DIRECTIONS AND ORDERS OF THE PRINCIPAL.
■ LOYALTY: AGENT SHALL NOT ENGAGE IN SELF-DEALING OR BECOME INVOLVED IN A BUSINESS THAT COMPETES WITH PRINCIPAL'S BUSINESS.
■ CONFIDENTIALITY: AGENT WILL NOT DIVULGE TRADE SECRETS.

❑ AGENT'S LIMITATIONS
■ AGENT IS SPECIFICALLY AUTHORIZED TO CONDUCT THE FOLLOWING NEGOTIATIONS ON BEHALF OF THE PRINCIPAL: _____.
■ AGENT IS NOT AUTHORIZED TO DO THE FOLLOWING: _____.

❑ AGENT'S ACCOUNTING
■ AGENT WILL ACCOUNT FOR ALL TIME SPENT ON THE PROJECT BY SUBMITTING BIWEEKLY REPORTS PROVIDING DETAILED ENTRIES AND EXPLANATIONS OF ACTIONS TAKEN AND TIME SPENT ON THESE ACTIVITIES.

❑ RENEWAL OF AGENCY RELATIONSHIP
■ PRINCIPAL AND AGENT MAY, BY MUTUAL AGREEMENT, RENEW THE AGENCY RELATIONSHIP FOR SUBSEQUENT VENTURES.

❑ LAW APPLICABLE TO AGENCY RELATIONSHIP
■ THE LAW OF THE STATE OF FLORIDA SHALL GOVERN THIS AGENCY AGREEMENT.

❑ DATE:

❑ SIGNATURES:

_____   _____
PRINCIPAL   AGENT[5]

estoppel A legal doctrine that prevents a person from denying facts or suggestions that his or her conduct has suggested.

Operation of Law

Although the most common method to create an agency is by the express intentions of the parties, there are situations where an agency will be recognized and enforced even when the parties dispute that such an agreement exists. Agency relationships can be created by operation of law in several different contexts. The most common method is by a court decree that a particular relationship amounted to an agency relationship, even when the parties deny it. This is referred to as agency by **estoppel**.

Agency by estoppel is closely tied to the issue of the agent's authority, discussed in the next section. The issue of agency by estoppel arises in situations where third parties rely on the representations of a person purporting to be the agent of another, or by the apparent relationship between two parties who appear to be principal and agent. When the principal helps create the impression that the agent has such authority, then the law of estoppel prevents the principal from denying.

agency by estoppel A court decree that an agency relationship existed because the parties involved created that impression and a third party had no reason to doubt the arrangement.

 GETTING TO THE BASICS

Courts occasionally create an agency relationship even where the parties dispute that one exists; they do this in order to avoid injustice to a third party.

Scenario 2–3. Gadgets, Inc.

Sam has opened negotiations to purchase an electronics franchise called Gadgets, Inc. The president of Gadgets, Inc., is Norton. Sam has hinted that he represents Nakomoto, Inc., a large Japanese corporation that has been buying up smaller electronics companies in recent years. Norton has actually met a representative from Nakomoto, Inc. at a lunch where Sam was also present. The Nakomoto representative pointed at Sam and said, "He's our guy when it comes to mergers and acquisitions." Norton decides to sell his business, but only later learns that Sam had no agency agreement with Nakomoto and that now the corporation is disputing aspects of the sale agreement. Can Norton rely on agency by estoppel to enforce the sale?

Answer: Based on the statement by the Nakomoto representative, Norton was reasonable in reaching a conclusion that Sam had authority to act on behalf of that corporation. Sam should be successful in claiming agency by estoppel.

Limitation on Agency by Estoppel Theory

There are important limitations on the use of estoppel to create an agency relationship. For example, the person seeking to use the theory must show that he or she had no knowledge of the true nature of the relationship between the parties. If the person knew, or could by reasonable diligence have discovered, that there was no agency relationship between the parties, then the estoppel will not be granted.

CHARACTERIZATION OF AN AGENCY RELATIONSHIP

One of the problems with a term such as "agency" is that it can be construed in many different ways. Agency relationships can encompass an enormous variety of business relationships. Because the term is so general, we must

Sidebar

"Estoppels are equitable in nature. They were created by a court of equity in order to promote justice and to prevent a party from benefiting by his own misleading representations, but it seems to be well settled that an estoppel will not operate against a person who stands by and allows another to deal with his property when the person sought to be estopped has no knowledge of his interest in the property."[6]

resort to language that is more specific and helpful. One way of pinpointing an agency relationship is by classifying the agent in terms of the agent's authority.

Distinguishing Agency from Other Relationships

It is important to understand both what an agency is and what it is not. Many relationships recognized in creating and running a business do not amount to agency relationships. Under these relationships, neither party would be able to negotiate contracts or otherwise bind the other party to agreements.

Borrowers and Lenders

Lenders and borrowers are not in an agency relationship. Lenders review credit applications and underwrite loans to prospective borrowers. Lenders are not permitted to engage in transactions that bind the borrower. Similarly, the borrower is not authorized to enter into contracts on behalf of the lender. In many ways, these parties operate at arm's length, each with its own agenda and with its own particular concerns.

Independent Contractors

An independent contractor is not an agent for anyone. By its very definition, an independent contractor makes up his or her own mind about how a particular job should be carried out, what tools should be used, when and where the job should be completed. Independent contractors operate with little or no supervision and therefore are not considered to be agents for others. They are responsible only for themselves.

Business Partners

An interesting question arises in a typical business partnership: Are the partners agents for one another? The question can become complicated by the partnership agreement. In general, partners can be agents for other partners, but only in limited aspects. As we will see later in this chapter, there are three different classifications of agents and partners are often classified as special agents, not general agents. Partners can enter into agreements that bind other partners, but their authority only extends to the context of their business. A business partner cannot, for example, bind the other partners to a separate venture that was never discussed by the partnership. Business partners also cannot force their partners to become legally obligated for a particular partner's personal obligations.

Employer-Employee

There are times when an employee meets the minimum requirements to be considered an agent for the employer. The question in such cases revolves around the responsibilities that the employer entrusts to the employee. If the employee can negotiate on behalf of the employer, accept payments, and sign agreements binding the employer, then the employee is an agent and the employee will be held to the standard imposed on all agents. Consider the case of *Bermudez v. Ruiz*.

CASE LAW: *Is a Truck Driver an Agent?*
Bermudez v. Ruiz, 185 A.D.2d 212, 586 N.Y.S.2d 258
(N.Y.A.D. 1 Dept.,1992)

MEMORANDUM DECISION

Order and judgment (one paper) of the Supreme Court, Bronx County (Douglas McKeon, J.), entered August 8, 1991, which granted defendant Marba Furniture's motion for summary judgment dismissing the complaint and all cross-claims against it, unanimously reversed, on the law, without costs, and the complaint and cross-claims reinstated.

Plaintiff commenced this action to recover damages for personal injuries sustained by her son on February 24, 1986 when he was struck by a truck owned and operated by defendant Ramon Ruiz, who was engaged in making a furniture delivery for defendant Marba Furniture.

Supreme Court determined that, as a matter of law, Ruiz was an independent contractor and not an agent of Marba. In reaching this conclusion, the court relied on the fact that Ruiz owned and insured his own delivery truck, employed his own helper, paid for all repair costs of the vehicle, and decided the time (but not the date) and manner of delivery. Ruiz received a weekly payment from Marba Furniture based upon the number and type of pieces delivered without any Social Security or income taxes withheld.

The facts of this matter are not distinguishable from those of cases in which the Court of Appeals has found that whether the operator of a delivery vehicle is an agent or independent contractor is a question for the trier of fact. In *Johnson v. R.T.K. Petroleum Co.*, 289 N.Y. 101, 44 N.E.2d 6, *reh. denied* 289 N.Y. 646, 44 N.E.2d 619, the owner of a truck, used exclusively for the past year to deliver gasoline for the corporate defendant, struck and injured the plaintiff. The court held that it was error for the appellate court, in reversing the judgment of the Trial Justice against the corporate defendant, to find that the truck owner was an independent contractor. The Court of Appeals stated, "The nature of the relationship existing was a question of fact which the trier of the facts resolved in favor of the plaintiff." (*Id.*, at 104, 44 N.E.2d 6.) Although the driver in that case stated that the company could "fire" him if it was dissatisfied with his services, nothing in the record before us indicates that Marba Furniture could not discontinue its use of the delivery service provided by Ramon Ruiz at any time.

In *Bratt v. Midland Asphalt Corp.*, 8 N.Y.2d 963, 204 N.Y.S.2d 191, 168 N.E.2d 855, the owner of a "hired" truck, hauling asphalt for the Jamestown Macadam Company at a rate of 80 cents a ton, struck plaintiffs' automobile head on. Where the company arranged the deliveries, even though no income or social security taxes were withheld from the payments made to the truckers, the nature of the relationship between the company and the truck owner was held to be a question of fact.

The general rule is stated in *Felice v. St. Agnes Hosp.*, 65 A.D.2d 388, 396, 411 N.Y.S.2d 901 2d Dept, Titone, J.: "Whether a person is an 'employee' or an 'independent contractor' is an ultimate fact to be determined from the evidence itself." The evidence in this matter does not permit resolution of this issue upon the record. Ruiz was employed as a delivery driver by Marba until June, 1985 when new management instituted the procedure of hiring trucks to make the company's deliveries. Although it is alleged that Ruiz could perform work for other

(continued)

CASE LAW: *Is a Truck Driver an Agent?* *(continued)*

companies, it is undisputed that he continued to make deliveries exclusively for Marba. Delivery dates were arranged directly by Marba with its customers. Drivers received a list of deliveries to be made each day from the warehouse manager, and the only paperwork used in the course of delivery was that furnished by the company.

We note that a letter, proffered by Marba as a "contract", indicating Ruiz's status as an independent contractor, bears only his signature and was submitted without any authentication. Moreover, at his deposition, Ruiz testified that he had never signed any contract with Marba establishing that he was an independent contractor.

Accordingly, whether defendant Marba Furniture exercised a sufficient degree of direction and control over defendant Ruiz to constitute an agency relationship is a question of fact for resolution at trial (*Garcia v. Herald Tribune Fresh Air Fund*, 51 A.D.2d 897, 380 N.Y.S.2d 676). N.Y.A.D. 1 Dept.,1992.

CASE QUESTIONS

1. Why does the court examine the details of the arrangement between Ruiz and Marba Furniture?

2. Why is the determination of Ruiz's status as an independent contractor or an employee important from the perspective of an agency relationship?

3. In civil and criminal cases, the judge is considered the final arbiter on questions of law, while the jury makes the final determination on facts. In this case, what determination did the jury make about the relationship between Ruiz and Marba Furniture?

4. If the jury determines that Ruiz is an employee and therefore an agent of Marba Furniture, what consequence does this have on the underlying suit brought by Bermudez, who was struck by a truck driven by Ruiz?

 GETTING TO THE BASICS

There are times when employees are considered to be agents for their employers.

Insurance Agents and Insured

Insurance agents are usually considered to be agents, but only of their customers, the individuals insured under policies. They are not agents for the insurance company and cannot bind the company to agreements or even accept service of process for lawsuits filed against insurance companies.[7]

LIABILITY ISSUES IN AGENCY RELATIONSHIPS

One of the most important questions that arises in agency relationships is the principal's legal responsibility for the actions carried out by the agent. If the agent can bind the principal to contracts, can the agent also bind the principal in other ways? For instance, what happens when the agent commits a tort while in the service of the principal? At least one court doctrine will transfer liability for the action through the agent to the principal, binding the principal as though he or she had committed the action.

Respondeat Superior

The doctrine of **respondeat superior** is an ancient doctrine, originally created when slavery was still legal. Under that theory, the acts committed by a slave could be imputed to the master. Respondeat superior survived the abolition of slavery in the United States and continues to be applied in situations where employees or agents commit actions on behalf of principals. When these actions result in physical, financial, or emotional damage to third parties, that person is permitted to bring suit not only against the employee/agent, but also the employer/principal.

respondeat superior (Latin) "Let the master respond"; a legal theory that imposes legal liability on an employer for the actions of the employee, when the employee is carrying out his duties for the employer.

THE EXTENT OF THE AGENCY RELATIONSHIP

A principal may appoint an agent to handle any transaction that the principal was legally capable of carrying out. The theory of agency relationships is that the agent's authority flows from the principal, and therefore the principal must have the power to act. In essence, the principal transfers his or her capacity to the agent. When the principal lacks some legal requirement, such as capacity, the agent cannot receive it, and the agency relationship is void. Obviously, an agency relationship that entertains the notion of committing a crime or violating public policy is invalid and cannot be enforced. Examples of such relationships would include an agency relationship to negotiate the purchase of narcotics or to charge usurious interest rates.

CLASSIFICATION OF AGENCY BY THE AGENT'S AUTHORITY

We can classify the agency relationship by the nature of the agent's authority. For instance, an agent may have

- actual authority
- express authority
- apparent authority
- implied authority

Actual Authority

Actual authority refers to the specific instructions, rights, and parameters granted to the agent from the principal. Because courts take a dim view of an agency relationship where the agent is authorized to take any action, agency law often focuses on the precise nature of the agent's authority. Just how far can an agent go on behalf of a principal? That is the question that actual authority seeks to answer. Actual authority refers to powers that the principal has delegated or conferred on the agent. Consider the facts in Scenario 2–2. What actual authority did Maria have? If we review the conversation between

actual authority The authority legally conferred on the agent by the principal.

express authority The authority specifically conferred on the agent by the principal, either orally or in writing.

Danny and Maria, then Danny specifically authorized Maria to make a bid on the motorcycle, but only up to a specific amount. That amount was $2000. Danny has not given Maria any authority to exceed that amount. Maria's actual authority is limited to bidding up to $2000 to purchase the motorcycle.

Actual authority comes in three different forms: express authority, implied authority, and apparent authority.

Express Authority

Express authority refers to the statements and agreements between the principal and agent. In written agreements, this authority may be explained in exhaustive detail. In other agency relationships, the express authority may be very limited, such as the arrangement between Danny and Maria. However, express authority has limitations. If an agent were limited to express authority only, then the agent might not be able to do his or her job effectively. Consider Scenario 2–3.

> **Scenario 2–3. The Vintage Motorcycle, Part Two**
>
> When Maria arrives to negotiate the purchase of the motorcycle, she finds that Bruno, the owner, has already sold the bike. Maria is disappointed because she knows how much Danny wanted to purchase it. Before she leaves, Bruno points out another bike. This one is a 1938 Valley Stomper and isn't in as good a shape as the one that Maria came to buy. Can Maria negotiate the purchase of this bike, as long as she doesn't exceed Danny's set amount of $2000?
>
> **Answer:** No. Maria's authority derives from the conversation that she had with Danny. He was specific about wanting a vintage motorcycle and also very specific about wanting the 1934 Flying Valley Stomper. This motorcycle is not a 1934 and is not in as good a condition as the one that Danny wanted. Danny did not authorize Maria to buy a different bike, and therefore she has no authority to do so. Maria should return to Danny, tell him the bad news, and then mention the other motorcycle.

It is precisely because of the limiting nature of express authority that the concept of implied authority was created.

Implied Authority

There are times when an agent's express authority does not conform to the reality of the situation. This is where the concept of implied authority enters the picture.

implied authority An agent's authority to act that is not expressed by the principal, but is assumed by both parties to be present.

If you look up a definition of **implied authority,** you usually see some reference to it as a form of actual authority. What this means is that there are some actions that the agent is allowed to take even though they were not detailed in the original principal-agency relationship, because common sense dictates that the agent would have these powers. In the scenario we have been developing with Danny and Maria, Danny's express authority was very limited. The only express authority he provided was that Maria could bid up to $2000. However, this arrangement assumes some powers that Danny hasn't mentioned. For one thing, Maria obviously has the authority to bind Danny to the sale, if she can arrange to purchase the motorcycle for an amount less than or equal to the agreed-upon amount. Just as obviously, Maria has the right to pay over the money in exchange for the title to the motorcycle. None of these details were set out between Danny and Maria; they are simply assumed. Implied authority fills in the gaps left out between the parties.

Apparent Authority

Apparent authority differs from implied authority in a very important way. Implied authority is the authority that the principal obviously intended that the agent should have. In the scenario with Danny and Maria, Danny obviously intended for Maria to have the power to negotiate with Bruno and even to bind Danny to the transaction if they arrived at an appropriate sale price. Apparent authority, on the other hand, does not derive from the express agreement of the principal and agent, or even by the assumed powers granted by the principal to the agent. Apparent authority derives from the perceptions of others.

When a principal creates an impression that someone is empowered to act on his or her behalf, when, in reality, that person has no such authorization, the courts will intervene and supply the missing elements of the agency relationship. Courts have created the doctrine of apparent authority in order to prevent principals from escaping the obligations that they have created. Under this theory, a principal will be bound by the authority that he or she apparently transferred to the agent, even if this transfer was never actually completed. Consider Scenario 2–4.

> ### Scenario 2–4. Talk to My People
>
> Mad Mel is a well-known movie actor. One day, as he is trying to have lunch at a restaurant downtown, Mel is besieged by a writer who claims to have a guaranteed hit on his hands. He wants Mel to buy the movie rights. Mel, who just wants to be left alone, tells the writer, "Talk to my people. See what you can arrange." Mel motions casually in the general direction of Toby, who is also sitting in the restaurant, trying to eat his lunch. Toby has no connection to Mad Mel, other than the fact that he is a movie producer. The writer approaches Toby, and they negotiate a movie deal for $10 million. Later, the writer seeks to enforce this agreement on Mel. Mel counters that Toby had no authority to act as an agent for him, and therefore, Mel has no obligation to the writer. Will Mel win?
>
> **Answer:** Probably not. Mel has given the writer the impression that Toby is one of "his people" and also given the impression that Toby has the apparent authority to negotiate for him. Because there was no way that the writer could have known that Toby had no such authority, the courts may very well rule that Toby had apparent authority.

In order to evaluate whether or not apparent authority has been created, courts have devised tests that apply to fact situations in individual cases. For instance, courts use the reasonable, prudent person test to evaluate apparent authority. Under this test, if a reasonably prudent person, in view of the principal's conduct, would naturally suppose the agent had a specific type of authority, then the jury is allowed to presume that the agent did have it.[9]

apparent authority The authority created when a principal leaves another with the impression that someone is his or her agent, when, in fact, that is not true.

Exhibit 2–2. General Power of Attorney

General Power of Attorney

I, John Doe, residing at 123 Maple Lane, Anytown, PL 003300, hereby appoint Mary Doe of 123 Maple Lane, Anytown, PL 003300, as my Attorney-in-Fact ("Agent").

If my Agent is unable to serve for any reason, I designate Darryl Doe, of 456 Elm Street, Anytown, PC 003300, as my successor Agent.

By this document, I hereby revoke and cancel any and all general powers of attorney previously entered into by me.

Agent shall have full power and authority to act on my behalf. The Agent's power to act on my behalf is authorized by me and extends to the management and conduct of all business, legal, and other affairs and to exercise all legal rights in and on my behalf. Agent's powers shall include, but are not limited to, the authority to

1. Open, maintain, or close bank accounts of whatever type or description in any lending institute. Such authority shall extend to the right of Agent to sign my name to appropriate documents. Such signatures shall have the same binding effect as if they had been signed by me.
2. Sell, exchange, buy, invest, or reinvest any assets or property owned by me.
3. Purchase and/or maintain insurance, including life insurance upon my life or the life of any other appropriate person.
4. Recover any debts owed to me and take reasonable and necessary steps to collect such debts on my behalf, including instituting legal action to protect my interests.
5. Enter into binding contracts on my behalf.
6. Exercise all stock rights on my behalf as my proxy, including all rights with respect to stocks, bonds, debentures, or other investments.
7. Maintain and/or operate any business that I may own.
8. Employ professional and business assistance as may be appropriate, including attorneys, accountants, and real estate agents.
9. Prepare, sign, and file documents with any governmental body or agency, including, but not limited to, authorization to:
10. Sell, give away, or make gifts or donations of my assets to family members, friends, or charitable organizations. Agent is not authorized to transfer any title to any real or personal property to Agent.

This Power of Attorney shall be construed broadly as a General Power of Attorney. The listing of specific powers is not intended to limit or restrict the general powers granted in this Power of Attorney in any manner.

(continued)

Exhibit 2–2. General Power of Attorney *(continued)*

Any power or authority granted to my Agent under this document shall be limited to the extent necessary to prevent this Power of Attorney from causing: (i) my income to be taxable to my Agent, (ii) my assets to be subject to a general power of appointment by my Agent, and (iii) my Agent to have any incidents of ownership with respect to any life insurance policies that I may own on the life of Agent.

My Agent shall not be liable for any loss that results from a judgment error that was made in good faith. However, my Agent shall be liable for willful misconduct or the failure to act in good faith while acting under the authority of this Power of Attorney.

I authorize my Agent to indemnify and hold harmless any third party who accepts and acts under this document.

Agent shall be entitled to reasonable compensation for any services provided as my Agent. Agent shall be entitled to reimbursement of all reasonable expenses incurred in connection with this Power of Attorney.

This Power of Attorney shall become effective immediately and shall not be affected by my disability or lack of mental competence, except as may be provided otherwise by an applicable state statute. This is a Durable Power of Attorney. This Power of Attorney shall continue effective until my death. This Power of Attorney may be revoked by me at any time by providing written notice to my Agent.

So executed, this the _____ day of _____, 20_____.

_____
John Doe

Notary:
I hereby certify that the above signed individual did personally appear before me and execute the above document in my presence.

_____
Nora Notory

My commission expires on the _____ day of _____, 20_____.

GETTING TO THE BASICS

A general power of attorney authorizes an agent to carry on a wide range of activities for the principal.

AGENTS EXCEEDING THEIR AUTHORITY

What happens when agents exceed the authority that principals have given to them? Put another way, can agents bind principals to contracts and agreements for which they had no authority? Suppose, for example, that an agent is simply authorized to provide information to a particular buyer and then to relay any offers made by the buyer. However, when the buyer makes what the agent believes to be a particularly good offer, the agent accepts on behalf of the principal. The agent was not authorized to accept, and when the principal learns of this action, the principal would be within his rights to take action against the agent for exceeding the agent's authority. The principal could disavow the agreement and refuse to be bound by it. However, suppose that the principal agrees with the agent's actions, even while he acknowledges that the agent had no authority to act. In such a situation, the legal doctrine of ratification becomes important.

Ratification

ratification Confirmation of a prior act that may not have been authorized, but to which the principal agrees to be bound.

When an agent lacks authority for an action, but the principal agrees to abide by those actions, the principal is said to have ratified the agent's behavior. **Ratification** is important because it confers the principal's agreement on the earlier, unapproved action, and results in a legally binding agreement. However, an agent should not exceed his or her authority in the belief that the principal will later ratify the actions. The principal might just as easily declare the agent's actions to be invalid under their arrangement, and the result might well be catastrophic for the agent. In such a scenario, the agent could be liable to the principal and the buyer.

AGENT AS A FIDUCIARY TO THE PRINCIPAL

fiduciary A person, such as a guardian, who has an obligation to act with honesty, fair dealing, and trust for another. Fiduciaries must act in the best interests of their principals.

Agents are considered to have a **fiduciary** relationship to a principal. A fiduciary is someone who owes legal and ethical duties to act in the best interests of another person. We will encounter this term numerous times throughout this text. When a person is a fiduciary for another, it means that the person owes another person the obligation to act honestly and fairly. A fiduciary must act in that person's best interests. This obligation goes beyond the normal degree of honesty and fair dealing that we would expect from persons in a transaction. A fiduciary's obligation is first and foremost to the other person.

Many of the duties that agents owe to principals arise directly from the agent's role as a fiduciary.

AGENT'S DUTIES TO THE PRINCIPAL

Once the principal-agency relationship has been created, the law imposes specific duties that the agent owes to the principal. These duties are summarized in Exhibit 2–3.

Exhibit 2–3. Agent's duties to principal

❑ obedience
❑ care
❑ loyalty
❑ accounting

Obedience

An agent's first duty is to obey the instructions of the principal. The agent acts as the principal's representative, and the agent's obedience to the principal's directions is one of the core requirements of a principal-agency relationship. The principal 's instructions may be spelled out in detail, or the principal may simply rely on the education, training, and experience of the agent in bringing about the best possible result.

Skill, Care, and Diligence

While the agent is working for the principal, the agent has a duty of acting with diligence and due care in performing his or her duties. In fact, the agent will be held to the standard of what other reasonable and prudent agents in the same situation would have done. If the agent fails to exercise that degree of care, the principal may have an action against the agent for negligence.

Loyalty

Another core requirement of the agency relationship is the loyalty owed by the agent to the principal. An agent must always act in the best interests of the principal. This duty requires that when an agent is faced with a conflict of interest, such as when the interests of the agent and the interests of the principal are at cross-purposes, the agent should withdraw from representing the principal. The duty of loyalty also requires an agent to ensure that the interests of the principal are placed foremost in the business relationship. Later, when we discuss the specifics of a real estate broker's relationship with a homeowner, we will see that when a buyer confides relevant information to the broker, the broker is required to pass that information along to the homeowner/principal.

The duty of loyalty also requires that an agent avoid self-dealing. This is a term that refers to an agent using the principal-agency relationship to enrich himself at the expense of the principal.

Scenario 2–5. Avoiding Self-Dealing

While Bill Broker is representing Sal Seller, Bill learns that Sal is planning on buying some tracts of land across town. Sal is desperate to acquire these tracts and will pay almost any price to get them. Bill secretly purchases these tracts for a modest sum and then offers them to Sal at twice the price that he paid. Bill is using the information that he gained from his agency relationship to enrich himself at the expense of his principal. Such an action is a violation of the agency relationship and would open Bill up to civil action by Sal (and possible sanction by the Real Estate Board).

KEY POINT

Agents have ethical and legal obligations to their principals.

Accounting

Among the more mundane duties of the agent is the responsibility of keeping track of all financial arrangements between the agent and the principal. This duty of accounting extends to any financial arrangement, negotiation, earnest money, or other financial exchange that occurs within the confines of the principal-agency relationship.

AGENT'S DUTIES TO THIRD PARTIES

The rules change when the agent is dealing with a party other than the principal. An agent's duties to third parties include:

- the duty of honesty and fair dealing
- the duty not to commit fraud
- the duty to avoid negligent misrepresentation

The Duty of Honesty and Fair Dealing

An agent has a responsibility to deal with third parties in an honest and fair way. On a practical level, an agent must avoid deceptive trade practices and other unfair (or illegal) practices. This duty is also strongly connected with the second and third duties to third parties, the duties to avoid fraud and misrepresentation.

Duty Not to Commit Fraud

Fraud is a legal action that can be brought when an agent commits any act or fails to act in such a way that conceals material facts. The act must cause injury to the third party or give the agent an unjustified or unconscionable advantage. See Exhibit 2–4.

Exhibit 2–4. The legal elements of fraud

> Fraud involves proof of the following:
> ❏ The agent made a representation of a material fact or concealed a fact.
> ❏ The representation was false.
> ❏ The agent knew the representation was false.
> ❏ The agent made the representation with the intent that the other party would rely on it.
> ❏ The other party's reliance on the representation was reasonable under the circumstances.
> ❏ The other party suffered injury from his reliance on the representation.

Material Facts

One of the most important elements in a fraud action is proof that the representation involved a material fact. A **material fact** is a fact that is a central point in the agreement or a critical factor in the negotiations. When an agent states that he is representing a certain principal when in fact he is not, this is a material fact and will leave the agent open to a claim of fraud.

material fact A critical fact in the contract or negotiations; one that, if truthfully revealed, might abort the transaction.

Salesmanship and Puffing

The types of statements that salespersons make in discussing a sale usually do not qualify as fraud. It is not fraud to claim that "this house is the best on the market" or to say, "I don't know when I've seen a more beautiful motorcycle." These statements are commonly referred to as **puffing** and no reasonable person would believe that they are statements of actual fact. On the other hand, it is fraud to claim that a house has never suffered from roof damage when in fact it has, or that "this car has never been in an accident" when it has.

puffing Typical sales exaggerations about an item for sale; common sales statements that do not misrepresent material facts.

Duty to Avoid Negligent Misrepresentation

In many ways, negligent misrepresentation and fraud are quite similar. But there is one important exception. Fraud involves an intentional action. When an agent commits fraud, he or she is actively lying. In negligent misrepresentation, a statement is made without knowledge of its veracity or with reckless disregard for the truth. The important distinction between negligent misrepresentation and fraud is that an agent can be liable under negligent misrepresentation for a statement that the agent actually believed was true, but one that the agent did not verify. The elements of negligent misrepresentation are presented in Exhibit 2–5.

Exhibit 2–5. The legal elements of negligent misrepresentation

❏ The agent made a false statement.
❏ The agent believed that the statement was true.
❏ But the agent had no reasonable grounds for this belief or made the statement in reckless disregard of the truth.
❏ A third party suffered a financial loss because of reasonable reliance on this false statement.

TYPES OF AGENTS

There are three broad categories of agents. Each has its own peculiar limitations and powers. The categories of agents are:

- general
- universal
- special

General Agents

A general agent is one who is authorized to carry out all actions related to a particular series of transactions. General agents have general authority to act on behalf of the principal. They do have limits, however. For instance, their powers are limited to the series of transactions originally approved by the principal. They are not permitted to open a new series of transactions or to obligate the principal in a completely unrelated contract.

Universal Agents

Unlike general agents, universal agents may carry out any transaction on behalf of a principal. Universal agents have broad authority to engage in an entire series of transactions for the principal. An example of a universal agent is one who possesses a general power of attorney.

Special Agents

Special agents have the most limited authority of any of the three categories. They are authorized to carry out a specific transaction only. They are not authorized to negotiate other deals or involve themselves in any transaction other than the one to which they have been specifically assigned.

Agents for Service of Process

There is a final category of agency that is not normally mentioned in the context of principal-agency relationships. An agent for service of process is not an agent in the traditional sense of the word. This agent cannot, for example, negotiate for anyone or even bind another party to a contract. But agents for service of process do perform one vitally important role: they provide a person on whom legal pleadings can be served. When a plaintiff wishes to sue a corporation, the question often becomes, how does one serve a complaint on a company? The answer is that states require corporations and other types of business organizations to appoint specific individuals to act as agents for service of process. These agents are responsible for accepting pleadings and forwarding them to the corporation's officers for further action. For an example of this type of agency, see the case law excerpt at the end of this chapter.

▶ TYPES OF PRINCIPALS

The principal-agency relationship gives principals a great deal of freedom in the way that they structure their arrangement with the agent. We have already seen that the principal can control the agent's actions and can limit the agent's authority. But a principal can also limit others from learning his or her identity. We can summarize agency relationships by the extent to which others know of the principal's existence. For instance, principals can be classified as:

- disclosed principal
- partially disclosed principal
- undisclosed principal

DISCLOSED PRINCIPAL

A disclosed principal is someone who is known to all parties in the transaction. The principal's identity is not a secret, and neither is the fact that the agent is working for the principal.

PARTIALLY DISCLOSED PRINCIPAL

A partially disclosed principal arrangement permits the agent to inform others that the agent is representing another party, but does not authorize the agent to reveal the principal's identity.

UNDISCLOSED PRINCIPAL

In an undisclosed principal arrangement, the agent carries out all of the activities as though he or she were the principal. The agent does not reveal that another person is involved in the transaction, and as far as the other parties are concerned, the entire transaction involves only a single individual. After the transaction the agent will then transfer any rights obtained in the negotiation to the undisclosed principal.

◣ PRINCIPAL'S DUTY TO AGENT

So far, we have discussed the wide range of duties owed by agents to principals. However, the principal also has some responsibilities to the agent, even if they are light when compared to the duties of the agent to the principal.

A principal has the following duties to an agent:

- duty to compensate the agent
- duty not to unfairly injure the agent's reputation
- duty to cooperate

DUTY TO COMPENSATE THE AGENT

Among the more obvious duties owed by a principal to an agent is the duty to compensate the agent for services rendered. When the agent performs as agreed, the agent is due compensation for his or her services. A failure by the principal to pay the agent opens the principal up for a lawsuit to collect the agent's fees. This obligation to compensate the agent involves payment not only for services rendered, but also for the agent's expenses in carrying about his or her duties.

DUTY NOT TO UNFAIRLY INJURE THE AGENT'S REPUTATION

The principal is also under an obligation not to unfairly injure the agent's reputation. A principal is liable to an agent when the principal claims that the agent failed to adequately complete an assignment, when the agent actually did complete it in satisfactory fashion.

DUTY TO COOPERATE

Finally, the principal has a duty to cooperate with the agent as the agent attempts to carry out the principal's business. A principal is not permitted to throw obstructions in the agent's way as a means of avoiding paying the agent's compensation when he or she fails to complete the assignment. A direct corollary of this obligation is that a principal cannot terminate the relationship for unjust or frivolous reasons.

◣ TERMINATION OF AGENCY RELATIONSHIP

An agency relationship can terminate in any of several ways. These include:

- by stated term
- by implication
- by the passage of a reasonable period of time
- by agreement

■ by operation of law
■ by accomplishment of purpose

BY STATED TERM

Under this arrangement, the agency relationship has a specific duration. When the time expires, the agency ceases to exist. At that point, the agent no longer owes any duties to the principal.

BY IMPLICATION

Even when the agency agreement does not contain a specific provision setting out the date that it expires, the relationship may terminate by implication. For instance, the parties may have in mind a single transaction, and when that transaction is complete, the agency terminates, even though there was no wording in the agreement that provided for a termination date. In the scenario with Danny and Maria, Maria's authority terminates by implication when the sale of the motorcycle is concluded. Maria obviously does not have the power to negotiate the purchase of other types of vehicles on Danny's behalf.

BY THE PASSAGE OF A REASONABLE PERIOD OF TIME

Where the agreement provides no language for termination of the agency and there is also no clear termination by implication, courts will rule that an agency terminates after a reasonable period of time. Where the principal and agent have had no interaction for a long period, the courts will often rule that the arrangement has terminated. The definition of "reasonable time" depends on many factors, including the relationship between the parties, the types of transactions that they have been involved in, and any other relevant information.

BY AGREEMENT

The parties are also free to terminate the agency relationship on their own agreement. If neither wishes to continue the relationship, they can simply agree to terminate it.

BY OPERATION OF LAW

If the arrangement between the principal and agent has become illegal since it was first entered into, or if the situation between the parties has changed substantially, the court may intercede and abolish the agency relationship on its accord.

By Accomplishment of Purpose

Closely related to termination by implication, termination by accomplishment of purpose is a rule that provides that an agency clearly established to achieve a specific goal would be terminated when that goal is achieved.

Key Point

Agency relationships can terminate in a wide variety of ways.

Ethics File: Commingling Funds

One of the most common ethical violations in agency relationships occurs when an agent commingles funds belonging to the principal. When an agent handles the principal's funds, there is a certain temptation to borrow against these funds for the agent's personal use. This is referred to as commingling. Sometimes an agent gets into financial trouble, and the lure of the client's money is just too great. When an agent uses client funds for personal reasons, it is both an ethical violation and also may be a criminal act. Because an agent has fiduciary obligations to the principal, the agent is not permitted to use the principal's funds for personal reasons. Even when an agent borrows the principal's funds with the intention of replacing them before the principal is aware of it, this is still an ethical violation. All legal professionals must be attentive to the accounting duty owed by agents to principals and make sure that no one is commingling funds.

Case Law: *Is Notice to an Agent the Same as Notice to a Principal?*

Ledbetter v. Crudup[10]
HEIPLE, Justice

The plaintiff, Arlinda Ledbetter, was injured while on property owned by Lannie Crudup. Ledbetter sued Crudup and obtained a default judgment in the amount of $25,000, because of Crudup's failure to answer the complaint. Ledbetter, then, initiated a garnishment proceeding against Crudup's insurer, Illinois Founders Insurance Company (IFIC), the garnishee-appellee, in order to collect the judgment amount. IFIC filed its answers to the garnishment interrogatories stating that it was not in possession of any property or funds owing to Crudup. IFIC alleged, as a policy defense, that it had never received notice of the lawsuit and therefore, under the terms of the insurance contract, was not obligated to provide Crudup with insurance coverage in this case. In his statement, Crudup claimed that he delivered the summons and complaint to James Fox of the Baldwin Insurance Company (it was through James Fox that Crudup kept his coverage by IFIC current). It must be noted that Mr. Fox and Baldwin Insurance are not licensed agents of IFIC, but are brokers of IFIC insurance policies. IFIC filed a motion for summary judgment supported by the affidavit of Mr. Fox in which Mr. Fox denied having received the complaint and denied having sent the same to IFIC. The trial court resolved the conflict between the statements of Crudup and Fox in favor of Ledbetter by assuming that Crudup did deliver the complaint to Fox. However, the trial court found that the portion of Fox's statement wherein Fox claimed he did not forward the complaint to IFIC was undisputed. The court further found that Fox, a broker, was the agent of

Crudup and not the agent of IFIC for the receipt of notice. The trial court ruled in favor of IFIC's motion and Ledbetter appealed.

The issue before this court is whether the lower court erred in holding that notice to the broker, Fox, was not notice to the insurance Company, IFIC. Stated another way, the issue is whether, based upon the facts presented to the trial court, Mr. Fox was the agent of the insurance carrier or the agent of the insured for receipt of notice of the suit. If Mr. Fox acted on behalf of the insurance company, then the notice delivered to Mr. Fox would be considered as notice delivered to the insurance company.

The trial court correctly stated that it is the general rule that a broker is one who acts on behalf of the insured, and not on behalf of the carrier. (Section 490 of the Illinois Insurance Code, Ill.Rev.Stat.1981, ch. 73, par. 1065.37; *Lynn v. Village of West City* (1976), 36 Ill.App.3d 561, 564, 345 N.E.2d 172.) Nonetheless, the court below noted that there are two exceptions to the rule. One exception is custom. Courts have found an insurance company can be estopped from denying the authority of a broker to act on its behalf where the broker had acted in accordance with customary practices. A custom or usage becomes binding upon parties if it has been uniformly acquiesced in and applied by the parties for such a period of time so as to indicate that the custom was contemplated by the parties at the time formation of the contract was undertaken. A custom or usage should be established by the testimony of several witnesses. (*DeGraw v. State Security Ins. Co.* (1976), 40 Ill.App.3d 26, 34, 351 N.E.2d 302.) In the instant case, the lower court observed that Ledbetter simply did not present the court with any witnesses which could have established the existence of a custom that brokers are the agents of insurance companies for notice of a suit.

The other exception considered by the lower court is course of dealings between a broker and an insurance company. In *Boston Store of Chicago v. Hartford Accident and Indemnity Co.* (1922), 227 Ill.App. 192, 201, it is explained that sometimes the action of the company and its dealings with the broker create the relation of principal and agent between the company and the broker. This relation must be established by evidence of the dealings of the broker and the insurance company. On this issue, too, the trial court found an absence of evidence sufficient to establish an agency for notice of the suit.

Although not an issue on this appeal, it is worthwhile to note there is a third exception to the rule and that is a statutory exception. For example, the legislature has specifically made brokers the agent of the insurance carriers for the receipt of insurance premiums. Section 505 of the Illinois Insurance Code, Ill.Rev.Stat.1981, ch. 73, par. 1065.52. See also, *Davidson v. Comet Casualty Co.* (1980), 89 Ill.App.3d 720, 44 Ill.Dec. 943, 412 N.E.2d 19, wherein the court held that this provision does not make a broker the insurer's agent for the purpose of transmitting refunds to the insured.

After reviewing the record, this court must agree with the conclusions of the trial court. We find no evidence of a customary practice, applicable to the case at hand, of allowing brokers to be the agents of insurance companies for the receipt of notice of a suit. On the issue of course of dealing, Ledbetter, in his brief, points to statements of Crudup and Fox which suggest that Fox told Crudup to bring any notice of claims directly to Fox and that Fox would forward the notice to the insurance carrier. This is only evidence of the conduct of Fox. In order to establish an agency relationship in fact or by estoppel, it was incumbent upon Ledbetter to provide the trial court with evidence of informed acquiescence or conduct of IFIC sufficient to create an agency. (*Fredrich v. Wolf* (1943), 383 Ill. 638, 640, 50 N.E.2d 755; *Crittendon v. State Oil Co.* (1966), 78 Ill.App.2d 112, 117, 222 N.E.2d 561.) The trial court, being unable to find such evidence in the pleadings, statements and affidavits, properly found that Fox was not the agent of IFIC for the receipt of notice of the suit. Compare *Lynn v. Village of West City* (1976), 36 Ill.App.3d 561, 565, 345 N.E.2d 172 (no conduct on the part of the insurance carrier) with *American Home v. City of Granite City* (1978), 59 Ill.App.3d 656, 663, 16 Ill.Dec. 862, 375 N.E.2d 969 (statements of insurance company employee as to course of dealing of insurance company with the broker).

(continued)

CASE LAW: *Is Notice to an Agent the Same as Notice to a Principal?* (continued)

It is the opinion of this court that the conclusions of fact made by the trial court are supported by the record and that its finding that Mr. Fox was not the agent of IFIC for receipt of the notice of the suit was correct. Therefore, the decision of the trial court is affirmed.

AFFIRMED.

CASE QUESTIONS

1. What is the significance of the finding that Fox was an agent for the plaintiff, not the insurance company?

2. What reasoning did the court use to reach this conclusion?

3. What exceptions did the court note to the general rule that an insurance broker is an agent for the insured and not the insurance company?

4. What role does estoppel play in the court's decision?

5. What would Ledbetter have to prove in order to establish an agency by estoppel theory in this case?

SUMMARY

Agency relationships have existed in one form or another for thousands of years. The basic premise behind an agency relationship is that one person acts in the interest of another. An agent has a fiduciary obligation to the principal to act honestly and fairly. Agents have specific duties to principals, including the duty of loyalty, fairness, honesty, care, skill, and diligence. Principals also have duties to agents. A principal must compensate the agent for the actions that the agent carries out on his or her behalf. An agency relationship can be terminated by one of several methods, including the agreement of the parties, operation of law, and the accomplishment of the purpose of the agency.

HELPFUL WEB SITES

U.S. Department of Labor—Real Estate Brokers and Sales Agents
http://www.bls.gov

Legal Information Institute—Overview of Agency Law
http://www.law.cornell.edu

The Free Dictionary.com—Agency law
http://Encyclopedia.thefreedictionary.com

KEY TERMS

actual authority	fiduciary
agency	implied authority
agency by estoppel	material fact
agent	principal
apparent authority	puffing
estoppel	ratification
express authority	respondeat superior

APPLYING CHAPTER CONCEPTS

1. Contact a local real estate agent and ask this agent how he or she complies with the duties that all agents owe to principals. Does the agent require the principal, in this case the seller, to sign any disclosure forms or other forms in order to comply with the agent's duties to third parties?
2. Describe a situation in which you might become an agent for a friend.

REVIEW QUESTIONS

1. Why is a principal-agency relationship necessary?
2. What are some ways that a principal-agency relationship is created?
3. What duties does an agent owe to a principal?
4. What is a disclosed principal?
5. What is commingling funds?
6. How is an agency relationship terminated?
7. What is ratification?
8. What is the most common way that an agency relationship is created?
9. What is a fiduciary?
10. What is the significance of this chapter's crucial case?
11. What is the difference between express authority and implied authority?
12. What is apparent authority?
13. What is actual authority?
14. What is an undisclosed principal?
15. Can a principal order an agent to do some action that violates the law? Why or why not?

QUESTIONS FOR REFLECTION

1. Are the duties imposed on agents unfair? Should there be more give and take between principals and agents? Explain your answer.

2. Why are there different classifications of agents, such as general, universal, and special? What advantages or disadvantages do these categories create?

ENDNOTES

[1]CJS Agency § 1.

[2]*Doane Agr. Service, Inc. v. Coleman*, 254 F.2d 40 (6th Cir. 1958).

[3]*Gus Z. Lancaster's Stock Yards, Inc. v. Williams*, 37 N.C. App. 698, 246 S.E.2d 823 (1978).

[4]*In re Guardianship of Muriel K.*, 251 Wis. 2d 10, 640 N.W.2d 773 (2002).

[5]Adopted from AMJUR LF § 14:9 (Courtesy of West, a Thomson business).

[6]*Richey v. Miller*, 142 Tex. 274, 279, 177 S.W.2d 255, 256 (Tex. 1944).

[7]*State Sec. Ins. Co. v. Burgos*, 145 Ill.2d 423, 583 N.E.2d 547, 164 Ill.Dec. 631 (Ill.,1991).

[8]*Columbia Broadcasting System, Inc. v. Stokely-Van Camp, Inc.*, 522 F.2d 369 (2d Cir. 1975).

[9]*State Sec. Ins. Co. v. Burgos*, 145 Ill.2d 423, 583 N.E.2d 547 (Ill.,1991).

[10]114 Ill.App.3d 401, 449 N.E.2d 265, 70 Ill.Dec. 391 (Ill.App. 3 Dist.,1983).

Chapter 3

SOLE PROPRIETORSHIPS

Chapter Objectives

Upon completion of this chapter, you should be able to:

- List and explain the features of a sole proprietorship.
- Describe why a person would choose to be a sole proprietor.
- Explain the tax consequences of sole proprietorships.
- Describe the advantages and disadvantages of sole proprietorships.
- Explain the important federal, state, and local rules that come into play when a person decides to open a business.

INTRODUCTION

In this chapter we will examine the most basic form of business organization: the sole proprietorship. Unlike all other business models, the sole proprietorship's greatest strength is also its greatest weakness. The sole proprietor relies on his or her own finances, skill, and resources to conduct a business. The business is the sole proprietor's alter ego. This business model offers several advantages over other types of business organizational schemes, but also suffers from several distinct drawbacks. We will examine all of these features in this chapter.

SOLE PROPRIETORSHIP

A sole proprietorship is the most basic, and in many ways the simplest, type of business organization. A sole proprietorship is a business run by a single individual. This individual is often both the owner and the only employee. Although we will see that a sole proprietorship faces many types of legal liabilities that other types of business organizational models do not encounter, there are some distinct advantages to a sole proprietorship. One of these advantages is freedom. A sole proprietor is free of any other influence in deciding how to run his or her business. A sole proprietor does not answer to shareholders or to other partners. A single person makes all of the business decisions. If the owner wishes to change the course of the business, he or she can do so immediately, without referring to anyone else. Although this is somewhat of an oversimplification of sole proprietorship, no one could argue the point that a sole proprietorship has fewer legal constraints than any other type of business.

GETTING TO THE BASICS

Sole proprietorships are the easiest type of business to create.

CONCERNS AND ISSUES FOR SOLE PROPRIETORSHIPS

With the freedom of action that comes with sole proprietorship, there are also many potential problems and concerns. For one thing, there is the issue of financing.

Financing Problems

Although a sole proprietorship is free of many of the constraints faced by all other types of business organizational models, one of the biggest problems facing any sole proprietorship is financing. Sole proprietors must rely on their own financial resources to run their businesses. Unfortunately, this often means that their businesses are undercapitalized. They do not have sufficient financial resources to draw on to expand their business, and they are often faced with a classic "Catch-22" situation. They make enough money to pay their creditors, but not enough money to expand their business. Because their credit worthiness is closely tied to their personal assets, which may already be stretched to the maximum, they find themselves unable to borrow any more money to build up their business. In fact, most new businesses fail because of lack of available capital.

In addition to concerns about capitalization and financing, there are other concerns for a sole proprietorship.

When there is only a single individual running a business, the business's greatest advantage is also its greatest weakness: if the owner becomes tired, sick, or otherwise unable to carry on the business, the business will fail. There is usually no one else who can take over the business, even for short periods of time.

Scenario 3–1. Maria's Web Design Business
Maria is considering opening up a Web design company. She plans on marketing herself to local businesses and individuals to help them develop their Web pages. She plans on working on the business at night and on the weekends until she can generate enough money from her new business to quit her day job and devote herself full time to her new business. What concerns does Maria have?

 ## GETTING TO THE BASICS

Business financing for sole proprietors is tied to the owner's personal credit.

THE ADVANTAGES OF SOLE PROPRIETORSHIPS

Many people have dreamed of running their own business. Often, they see themselves as immediately successful, applying a minimum amount of effort for a maximum amount of profits. Although the reality is often quite different, many sole proprietors enjoy the fact that they have no boss to answer to. They can set their own hours and their own schedule, and this degree of freedom is difficult to find in any other type of occupation. The sole proprietor has total control of the course of the business and can decide, without reference to others, which direction to take the business in or when and how to end the business, if he or she chooses to do so. See Exhibit 3–1.

KEY POINT

For sole proprietors, the issue often boils down to protecting personal assets.

Exhibit 3–1. Advantages of sole proprietorships

❏ It is the easiest form of business organization to create.
❏ The owner has complete control over the business.
❏ All profits go directly to the owner.
❏ Tax losses can be itemized on individual income tax return.

Organization of the Business

Unlike the case with other business models, there is little or no organization that must go into creating a sole proprietorship. The business owner may be required to obtain a business license, but very little else in the way of public documents is required to open a sole proprietorship. In fact, many business owners find themselves in a business almost by default. What begins as an interest transforms into a hobby that then becomes a business.

Complete Control

Sole proprietors enjoy one particular advantage that is not seen in any other business model: they have complete control over the way that the business is run. Sole proprietors can decide when to open for the day, when to close, and how to run their daily activities, all without interference or control from others. However, this advantage comes at a price. Because the sole proprietor is, in effect, the business, when he or she is unavailable, no commerce can be conducted. The sole proprietor must be present in order to carry out activities, and this can exhaust a single individual over time. Saying that a sole proprietor has complete control also oversimplifies some of the realities of running a business. When the sole proprietor owes money to creditors, they may have substantial influence over the course of the business. They may, for instance, refuse to deliver any additional product until they are paid. They may refuse to extend credit to a sole proprietor. Creditors even have the option of forcing a sole proprietor into bankruptcy. Any of these actions can have a profound impact on the continued existence of the sole proprietor's business.

> **Scenario 3–2. Maria's Web Design Business, Part Two**
>
> After several months of running her Web design business, Maria has realized that although she can make some money designing Web pages, there are so many good software packages out there that can essentially do the same thing that she should seriously consider retooling her business and putting her emphasis on some other aspect of the Web. Instead of designing Web pages, she will now create a package that allows businesses to track visitors and also create a system that allows customers to order items easily and conveniently. Is Maria required to inform anyone about her change of direction?

KEY POINT

Sole proprietors have complete control over the course and direction of their businesses.

Profits

Sole proprietors also have the advantage of being able to take all profits from the business. They are not required to share the profits with others, such as partners or shareholders. Instead, they may use the profits to reimburse their personal funds and even use business profits to pay personal debts. Because there is no legal separation between a sole proprietor and the business, there is no impediment to using profits for personal reasons. Of course, a sole proprietor cannot attempt to shield profits or disguise the source of funds in order to defraud taxing agencies.

Tax Advantages

Sole proprietorships also carry with them certain tax advantages. Because the sole proprietor and the business are interchangeable, a sole proprietor's business losses can be passed through to his or her personal income tax return as losses. These business losses can offset gains for the year and lower the sole proprietor's overall tax burden.

Scenario 3–3. Sally's Scrapbooking Business

Sally has wanted to open her own business for years. She's been an avid scrapbooker for years and has decided to turn her hobby into a business. What should be her first step towards opening her own business?

Answer: Sally should review her financial situation. Where will she get the money to open and run her business? How much money will she need? What financial resources does she have? Will she be able to borrow money from friends or family? Can she borrow against the equity in her home? These are all questions that she should answer before considering any other issues in creating her own business.

 ## GETTING TO THE BASICS

> Sole proprietors can "pass through" losses from their business to their personal income tax returns.

THE DISADVANTAGES OF SOLE PROPRIETORSHIPS

One of the biggest disadvantages to a sole proprietor is his or her unlimited liability. We discussed the concept of limited liability in chapter 1. There, we saw that many business models help to protect the personal assets of investors and others by creating a separation between money invested to run a business and the individual's personal assets. In later chapters, we will explore limited liability in many different contexts, from limited liability companies to corporations. But there is no issue about limited liability for sole proprietors; they do not have it.

For sole proprietors, unlimited liability is the rule. What unlimited liability means is that when a sole proprietor is sued or otherwise becomes responsible for a legal claim, not only the business assets can be seized by creditors, but also the sole proprietors' personal assets as well. A sole proprietor might well lose all of his or her personal assets to satisfy a judgment. Creditors might obtain judgments and seize personal assets to satisfy them, or the sole proprietor might declare bankruptcy and lose many of these assets. Either situation is fraught with difficulties and legal implications, and this is one of the main reasons that individuals give for not going into business on their own.

There are ways for sole proprietors to limit their total loss. For instance, sole proprietors may be able to obtain insurance coverage that will help pay any judgments assessed. However, insurance usually covers the sole proprietor's personal assets, not the business assets. Creditors will still be able to seize business assets to pay a judgment. In such a case, the business will inevitably fail. See Exhibit 3–2.

Exhibit 3–2. Disadvantages of sole proprietorships

> ❏ personal commitment
> ❏ financial commitment
> ❏ limited existence of business (it dies when the sole proprietor dies)
> ❏ personal liability for business debts and judgments

Personal Commitment

One of the aspects of running a business that many people ignore is the sheer investment of time. Starting a commercial enterprise from scratch is a daunting task and demands huge personal commitment on the part of the sole proprietor. Without that commitment, the business is doomed to failure. However, because the sole proprietor has only himself or herself to rely on, the business will suffer if the owner becomes ill or otherwise incapacitated. There is literally no one else who can do what the sole proprietor can do.

Financial Commitment

Most businesses fail because they are undercapitalized. Starting a business requires enough capital to pay for items such as: rent, utilities, phone service, insurance, inventory, supplies, displays, and a wide variety of other expenses that most novice business people never consider. As a result, the money that the sole proprietor has set aside to start the business usually runs out much sooner than planned. That leaves sole proprietors with a critical problem: they must raise additional capital or risk losing whatever business they have already established. The only way to do that is to borrow money, and lenders may not be willing to extend credit.

Obtaining Credit

Sole proprietors often rely on their personal savings and credit in order to start a new business. Business loans are usually not an option for a new business. Traditional lenders are reluctant to provide funds for an unproven business. Sole proprietors often fall back on their personal credit: charging items to their personal credit cards and borrowing money against their homes or other personal assets. Unfortunately, when these assets have been used up, there may not be any other sources. Without enough capital to keep the business running, it will fail.

Scenario 3–4. Jack's Car-Detailing Business

Jack wants to open a car-detailing business. He will accept appointments over the phone and visit clients at their homes, where he will clean up their cars, inside and out. However, in order to maximize his efficiency, he should have some equipment, such as buffers and high-speed vacuum cleaners, that would make his job faster and easier. Jack can't afford to purchase them outright. What are some of Jack's potential sources for borrowing money to purchase these items?

Limited Existence

Unlike other business forms, a sole proprietorship exists only as long as the individual owner does. On the owner's death, the business ceases to exist. Because there is no distinction between the sole proprietor's personal and business assets, the business proceeds will be distributed through the sole proprietor's estate as would any other personal property. There is no provision that allows the business to continue when the owner dies or is otherwise incapable of continuing.

Personal Liability

Time commitments, financial strain, and limited existence are all important disadvantages for sole proprietorships, but the biggest disadvantage is the owner's **personal liability**. As with any business venture, a sole proprietor can be sued, and when a judgment is obtained against the business, the business owner must pay it. Of course, if the sole proprietor dies, the chance for recovery against him or her dies as well. Consider "Case Law: Suing a Sole Proprietorship."

personal liability The liability that a sole proprietor has for all business related debts and judgments; sole proprietorships do not have the protection of limited liability.

KEY POINT

One of the biggest disadvantages of sole proprietorships is the personal liability of the owner.

CASE LAW: *Suing a Sole Proprietorship*
Borah v. Monumental Life Ins. Co.[1]

MEMORANDUM AND ORDER

SCHILLER, J.

Plaintiffs Bishnu Borah, M.D. ("Borah") and Bishnu C. Borah, M.D., P.C. ("Borah, M.D.") bring this action alleging RICO violations, violations of the New Jersey Racketeering Act and the New Jersey Consumer Fraud Act, fraud, negligent misrepresentation, breach of fiduciary duty, respondeat superior, and conspiracy. Presently before the Court is the motion of Defendant Sea Nine Associates ("Sea Nine") to dismiss. For the reasons below, this Court grants the motion.

BACKGROUND

The following allegations are taken from the Complaint and accepted as true for purposes of the instant motion. Borah practices medicine through Borah, M.D. The numerous Defendants in this action

(continued)

CASE LAW: *Suing a Sole Proprietorship* (continued)

are insurance companies, insurance salespersons, financial services companies, and financial planners who have engaged in a scheme to induce Plaintiffs to participate in a program of life insurance known as Continuous Group ("C-Group") life insurance. Various Defendants marketed the C-Group life insurance through Voluntary Employee Benefit Associations ("VEBA"). Although these VEBA plans were presented as tax-deductible options in which medical corporations, like Borah, M.D., could participate, Defendants knew that contributions to the plan were not tax-deductible. Despite the fact that the IRS expressly took no position on the issue, Defendants deceived employers into believing that the IRS had ruled that contributions to VEBAs were tax-deductible. Beginning in 1990, Defendants engaged in deceptive conduct that led Plaintiffs to contribute over $100,000 to the VEBA program, contributions that have subsequently been lost.

Defendant Steven Ross engaged in the business of selling insurance and insurance-related products. At the time Plaintiffs filed the Complaint, Ross was deceased. Defendant Sea Nine was a sole proprietorship operated by Ross in California that designed, marketed, and sold insurance and insurance-related products, as well as administrative services related to the business of insurance and other benefit-related plans. Sea Nine has continued operations since Ross' death.

DISCUSSION

Defendant Sea Nine moves to dismiss on the grounds that it cannot be sued because it was a sole proprietorship whose sole proprietor, Ross, died. Therefore, the claims against Sea Nine hinge upon its status as a sole proprietorship. According to the Complaint, Sea Nine is a sole proprietorship operated by Ross in California. A sole proprietorship is "a business in which one person owns all the assets, owes all the liabilities, and operates in his or her personal capacity." BLACK'S LAW DICTIONARY 1427 (8th ed. 2004); *see also Ladd v. Scudder Kemper Invs., Inc.,* 433 Mass. 240, 243, 741 N.E.2d 47 (2001) (providing definitions of sole proprietorship that all rec-

ognize that a single individual owns the business). The capacity to sue or be sued is set out in Federal Rule of Civil Procedure 17(b), which directs that, the capacity of an individual . . . to sue or be sued shall be determined by the law of the individual's domicile. The capacity of a corporation to sue or be sued shall be determined by the law under which it was organized. In all other cases capacity to sue or be sued shall be determined by the law of the state in which the district court is held. . . .

FED. R. CIV. P. 17(b) (2005). Therefore, under Rule 17(b), the capacity of Sea Nine to sue or be sued is determined with reference to Pennsylvania law. *See* FED. R. CIV. P. 17(b) ("In all other cases capacity to sue or be sued shall be determined by the law of the state in which the district court is held. . . .") Under Pennsylvania law, a sole proprietorship is not legally separate from its owner. *The Glidden Co., Inc. v. Dept. of Labor & Indus.,* 700 A.2d 555, 558 (Pa.Commw.Ct. 1997) ("A sole proprietorship has no existence separate and apart from its owner.") As Sea Nine has no legal existence apart from its owner, Steven Ross, it cannot be sued separately and must be dismissed from this action. *See Cashco Oil Co. v. Moses,* 605 F.Supp. 70, 71 (N.D.Ill. 1985) (dismissing sole proprietorship from action because it had no separate legal existence apart from owner and could not be sued along with owner under the relevant applicable law). The individual owner remains personally liable for all of the business' obligations. "Doing business under another name does not create an entity distinct from the person operating the business; the firm name and the sole proprietor's name are but two names for one person." 65 C.J.S. *Names* § 14 (2004).

Apparently relying on the conclusion that a sole proprietorship has no existence separate from its owner, Sea Nine urges the Court to apply California law under Rule 17(b). (Mem. of Law in Support of Mot. of Sea Nine Assoc. to Dismiss the Compl. at 4.) The choice of law issue is academic however, because under California law a sole proprietorship is also not legally separate from its owner. Burger v. Kuimelis, *325 F.Supp.2d 1026, 1033 (N.D.Cal.2004);* see also Providence Wash. Ins. Co. v. Valley Forge Ins. Co., *Cal.Rptr.2d 192, 194 (Cal.Ct.App.1992) ("A sole proprietorship is not a legal entity itself. Rather, the term refers to a natural person who directly owns the business. . . .")*

It is also clear that "a dead man cannot be a party to an action and any such attempted proceeding is completely void and of no effect." Plaintiffs obviously recognize this fact, as they have consented to the dismissal of their claims against Ross. It is undisputed that Sea Nine Associates was a sole proprietorship operated by Ross. As a sole proprietorship is not a legal entity apart from the sole proprietor, and an action cannot be brought against a dead man, the claims against Sea Nine must be dismissed.

Plaintiffs argue that, nonetheless, Sea Nine may have incorporated after Ross' death and thus may be sued separately. To support this position, Plaintiffs have attached a verification and letter to their response to Sea Nine's motion to dismiss. This material does not aid Plaintiffs' argument for two reasons. First, the Court may not consider these documents in assessing the motion to dismiss. *See Arizmendi v. Lawson,* 914 F.Supp. 1157, 1160-61 (E.D.Pa. 1996) (in resolving a motion to dismiss, a court may properly look beyond the complaint to matters of public record including court files, records and letters of official actions or decisions of government agencies and administrative bodies, documents referenced and incorporated in the complaint and documents referenced in the complaint or essential to a plaintiff's claim which are attached to a defendant's motion); *see also Kuromiya v. U.S.,* 37 F.Supp.2d 717, 730-31 (E.D.Pa. 1999) (refusing to consider attached documents not central to complaint). Second, regardless of the current status of Sea Nine, Plaintiffs sued it as a sole proprietorship, which was not a separate entity apart from Ross. Plaintiffs sued Sea Nine as a sole proprietorship despite the fact that the sole proprietor had died and they may not now treat it otherwise to avoid dismissal of their case against Sea Nine.

CONCLUSION

For the above stated reasons, the motion of Sea Nine to dismiss is granted.

CASE QUESTIONS

1. What grounds does Sea Nine allege in requesting the court to dismiss the plaintiff's complaint?

2. How does this court define "sole proprietorship"?

3. Why does the court refer readers to Federal Rule of Civil Procedure 17(b), capacity to be sued?

4. Does Sea Nine have an existence that is separate from Stephen Ross? Why or why not?

5. What action did the plaintiffs take in order to avoid a contention that a dead man cannot be sued?

6. What argument do the plaintiffs offer to overcome the assumption that a right to sue a sole proprietor dies with the owner?

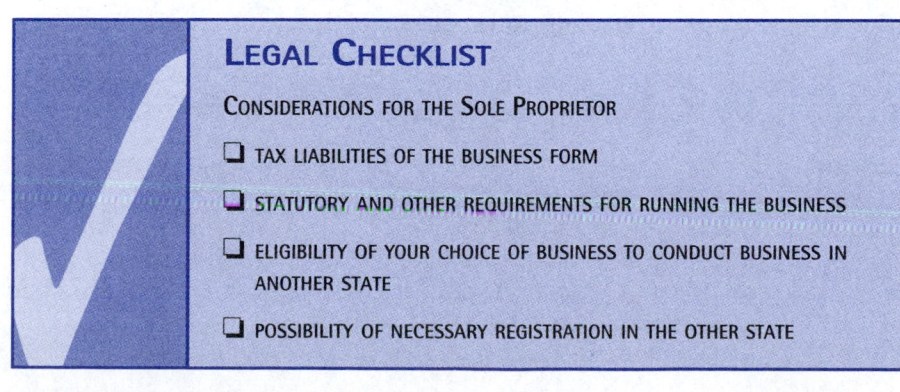

LEGAL CHECKLIST

CONSIDERATIONS FOR THE SOLE PROPRIETOR

❏ TAX LIABILITIES OF THE BUSINESS FORM

❏ STATUTORY AND OTHER REQUIREMENTS FOR RUNNING THE BUSINESS

❏ ELIGIBILITY OF YOUR CHOICE OF BUSINESS TO CONDUCT BUSINESS IN ANOTHER STATE

❏ POSSIBILITY OF NECESSARY REGISTRATION IN THE OTHER STATE

DISSOLUTION OF A SOLE PROPRIETORSHIP

In later chapters we will see that dissolving or terminating a business often becomes quite complicated. This is not the case with sole proprietorships. A sole proprietor may simply terminate the business at his or her whim. Generally speaking, on the death of the sole proprietor, the business dissolves. Sole proprietorships also terminate with the personal bankruptcy of the owner.

▶ GETTING TO THE BASICS

There are very few steps required to dissolve a sole proprietorship.

REGULATORY CONCERNS FOR SOLE PROPRIETORSHIPS

Sidebar

Sole proprietors may be able to take advantage of a home-office tax deduction, which allows them to deduct expenses related to keeping a business office in their homes.

For sole proprietors, at least as far as the Internal Revenue Service is concerned, there is no difference between personal income and business income. All income is treated the same. The business income and any other personal income of the sole proprietor will be lumped together and taxed as a single unit. If the business shows a loss, the sole proprietor can "pass through" this loss on his or her personal income tax return and often receive a tax break.

KEY POINT

In a sole proprietorship, the character of the business is the character of the owner.

However, this is not to minimize the tax and regulatory consequences of owning and running a business. Sole proprietorships have numerous important local, state, and federal filings that must be completed in order to keep the business operating within applicable law. In this section, we will address federal income tax concerns for sole proprietorships, state issues, and then local requirements.

FEDERAL TAX CONCERNS FOR THE SOLE PROPRIETORS

According to IRS regulations, a sole proprietor is a business owned by one individual. It does not exist separately from the owner, and therefore the tax liability of the business and the tax liability of the owner are the same. The IRS requires sole proprietors to file profit and losses from their businesses on Form 1040 schedule C. Other forms may also be required, such as Schedule SE, Self-Employment Tax. See Exhibits 3–3 and 3–4.

Exhibit 3–3. IRS 1040, Schedule C

**SCHEDULE C
(Form 1040)**

Department of the Treasury
Internal Revenue Service

Profit or Loss From Business
(Sole Proprietorship)

▶ Partnerships, joint ventures, etc., must file Form 1065 or 1065-B.

▶ Attach to Form 1040 or 1041. ▶ See Instructions for Schedule C (Form 1040).

OMB No. 1545-0074

2004

Attachment
Sequence No. **09**

Name of proprietor

Social security number (SSN)

A Principal business or profession, including product or service (see page C-2 of the instructions)

B Enter code from pages C-7, 8, & 9 ▶

C Business name. If no separate business name, leave blank.

D Employer ID number (EIN), if any

E Business address (including suite or room no.) ▶ ....
City, town or post office, state, and ZIP code

F Accounting method: **(1)** ☐ Cash **(2)** ☐ Accrual **(3)** ☐ Other (specify) ▶ ....

G Did you "materially participate" in the operation of this business during 2004? If "No," see page C-3 for limit on losses ☐ Yes ☐ No

H If you started or acquired this business during 2004, check here . . . . ▶ ☐

Part I **Income**

1	Gross receipts or sales. **Caution.** If this income was reported to you on Form W-2 and the "Statutory employee" box on that form was checked, see page C-3 and check here . . . . ▶ ☐	**1**	
2	Returns and allowances	**2**	
3	Subtract line 2 from line 1	**3**	
4	Cost of goods sold (from line 42 on page 2)	**4**	
5	**Gross profit.** Subtract line 4 from line 3	**5**	
6	Other income, including Federal and state gasoline or fuel tax credit or refund (see page C-3)	**6**	
7	**Gross income.** Add lines 5 and 6 . . . . ▶	**7**	

Part II **Expenses.** Enter expenses for business use of your home **only** on line 30.

8	Advertising	**8**		19 Pension and profit-sharing plans	**19**	
9	Car and truck expenses (see page C-3)	**9**		20 Rent or lease (see page C-5):		
10	Commissions and fees	**10**		a Vehicles, machinery, and equipment	**20a**	
11	Contract labor (see page C-4)	**11**		b Other business property	**20b**	
12	Depletion	**12**		21 Repairs and maintenance	**21**	
13	Depreciation and section 179 expense deduction (not included in Part III) (see page C-4)	**13**		22 Supplies (not included in Part III)	**22**	
				23 Taxes and licenses	**23**	
				24 Travel, meals, and entertainment:		
14	Employee benefit programs (other than on line 19)	**14**		a Travel	**24a**	
15	Insurance (other than health)	**15**		b Meals and entertainment		
16	Interest:			c Enter nondeductible amount included on line 24b (see page C-5)		
a	Mortgage (paid to banks, etc.)	**16a**		d Subtract line 24c from line 24b	**24d**	
b	Other	**16b**		25 Utilities	**25**	
17	Legal and professional services	**17**		26 Wages (less employment credits)	**26**	
18	Office expense	**18**		27 Other expenses (from line 48 on page 2)	**27**	

28	**Total expenses** before expenses for business use of home. Add lines 8 through 27 in columns . ▶	**28**	
29	Tentative profit (loss). Subtract line 28 from line 7	**29**	
30	Expenses for business use of your home. Attach **Form 8829**	**30**	
31	**Net profit or (loss).** Subtract line 30 from line 29.		
	• If a profit, enter on **Form 1040, line 12,** and **also** on **Schedule SE, line 2** (statutory employees, see page C-6). Estates and trusts, enter on Form 1041, line 3.	**31**	
	• If a loss, you **must** go to line 32.		
32	If you have a loss, check the box that describes your investment in this activity (see page C-6).		
	• If you checked 32a, enter the loss on **Form 1040, line 12,** and **also** on **Schedule SE, line 2** (statutory employees, see page C-6). Estates and trusts, enter on Form 1041, line 3.	**32a** ☐ All investment is at risk.	
	• If you checked 32b, you **must** attach **Form 6198.**	**32b** ☐ Some investment is not at risk.	

For Paperwork Reduction Act Notice, see Form 1040 instructions. Cat. No. 11334P **Schedule C (Form 1040) 2004**

(continued)

Exhibit 3–3. IRS 1040, Schedule C *(continued)*

Schedule C (Form 1040) 2004   Page **2**

Part III   **Cost of Goods Sold** (see page C-6)

33   Method(s) used to
      value closing inventory: **a** ☐ Cost   **b** ☐ Lower of cost or market   **c** ☐ Other (attach explanation)

34   Was there any change in determining quantities, costs, or valuations between opening and closing inventory? If
      "Yes," attach explanation . . . .   ☐ Yes   ☐ No

35   Inventory at beginning of year. If different from last year's closing inventory, attach explanation . . | 35 |

36   Purchases less cost of items withdrawn for personal use   . . . . | 36 |

37   Cost of labor. Do not include any amounts paid to yourself . . . . | 37 |

38   Materials and supplies . . . . | 38 |

39   Other costs . . . . | 39 |

40   Add lines 35 through 39 . . . . | 40 |

41   Inventory at end of year . . . . | 41 |

42   **Cost of goods sold.** Subtract line 41 from line 40. Enter the result here and on page 1, line 4 . . | 42 |

Part IV   **Information on Your Vehicle.** Complete this part **only** if you are claiming car or truck expenses on
line 9 and are not required to file Form 4562 for this business. See the instructions for line 13 on page
C-4 to find out if you must file Form 4562.

43   When did you place your vehicle in service for business purposes? (month, day, year) ▶ . . . . . . /. . . . . . . /. . . . . . .

44   Of the total number of miles you drove your vehicle during 2004, enter the number of miles you used your vehicle for:

 a   Business . . . .   **b** Commuting . . . .   **c** Other . . . .

45   Do you (or your spouse) have another vehicle available for personal use?. . . . .   ☐ Yes   ☐ No

46   Was your vehicle available for personal use during off-duty hours? . . . .   ☐ Yes   ☐ No

47a   Do you have evidence to support your deduction? . . . .   ☐ Yes   ☐ No

  b   If "Yes," is the evidence written? . . . .   ☐ Yes   ☐ No

Part V   **Other Expenses.** List below business expenses not included on lines 8–26 or line 30.

48   **Total other expenses.** Enter here and on page 1, line 27 . . . . | 48 |

Schedule C (Form 1040) 2004

Exhibit 3–4. IRS 1040, Schedule C-EZ

| SCHEDULE C-EZ
(Form 1040)

Department of the Treasury
Internal Revenue Service | **Net Profit From Business**
(Sole Proprietorship)
▶ Partnerships, joint ventures, etc., must file Form 1065 or 1065-B.
▶ Attach to Form 1040 or 1041. ▶ See instructions on back. | OMB No. 1545-0074
2004
Attachment
Sequence No. 09A |

Name of proprietor | Social security number (SSN)

Part I   General Information

You May Use Schedule C-EZ Instead of Schedule C Only If You:

- Had business expenses of $5,000 or less.
- Use the cash method of accounting.
- Did not have an inventory at any time during the year.
- Did not have a net loss from your business.
- Had only one business as a sole proprietor.

And You:

- Had no employees during the year.
- Are not required to file **Form 4562,** Depreciation and Amortization, for this business. See the instructions for Schedule C, line 13, on page C-4 to find out if you must file.
- Do not deduct expenses for business use of your home.
- Do not have prior year unallowed passive activity losses from this business.

A   Principal business or profession, including product or service | B Enter code from pages C-7, 8, & 9 ▶

C   Business name. If no separate business name, leave blank. | D Employer ID number (EIN), if any

E   Business address (including suite or room no.). Address not required if same as on Form 1040, page 1.

City, town or post office, state, and ZIP code

Part II   Figure Your Net Profit

1   **Gross receipts. Caution.** If this income was reported to you on Form W-2 and the "Statutory employee" box on that form was checked, see **Statutory Employees** in the instructions for Schedule C, line 1, on page C-3 and check here . . . . ▶ ☐ | 1

2   **Total expenses** (see instructions). If more than $5,000, you **must** use Schedule C. . . . . | 2

3   **Net profit.** Subtract line 2 from line 1. If less than zero, you **must** use Schedule C. Enter on **Form 1040, line 12,** and **also** on **Schedule SE, line 2.** (Statutory employees **do not** report this amount on Schedule SE, line 2. Estates and trusts, enter on Form 1041, line 3.) . . . . . | 3

Part III   **Information on Your Vehicle.** Complete this part **only** if you are claiming car or truck expenses on line 2.

4   When did you place your vehicle in service for business purposes? (month, day, year) ▶ .... / .... / ....

5   Of the total number of miles you drove your vehicle during 2004, enter the number of miles you used your vehicle for:

a Business .... b Commuting .... c Other ....

6   Do you (or your spouse) have another vehicle available for personal use? . . . . ☐ Yes ☐ No

7   Was your vehicle available for personal use during off-duty hours? . . . . ☐ Yes ☐ No

8a Do you have evidence to support your deduction? . . . . ☐ Yes ☐ No

b If "Yes," is the evidence written? . . . . ☐ Yes ☐ No

For Paperwork Reduction Act Notice, see Form 1040 instructions.   Cat. No. 14374D   Schedule C-EZ (Form 1040) 2004

KEY POINT

Sole proprietors have important IRS documents that must be completed every year.

Employees

If the sole proprietor has employees, then in addition to paying their salaries, the owner must also comply with Internal Revenue Service requirements by making the correct withholdings from each employee's pay. These include FICA (Federal Insurance Contributions Act), which requires withholdings of 12.4 percent of an employee's earned income up to an annual limit. These payments are directed to the Social Security Administration. Another 3 percent must be paid into Medicare. In addition to FICA and Medicare, there may be issues regarding unemployment insurance. See Exhibit 3–5.

Spouses as Employees

Some sole proprietors hire their spouses to work as employees in their businesses. When they do, they raise specific tax issues. For instance, if the spouse is truly an employee (someone who receives directions and orders from the owner), then the sole proprietor must pay Social Security and Medicare withholding taxes for the employee. On the other hand, if the spouse is actually a partner (someone with equal authority to run the business), then the business income must be reported as that of a general partnership.

Employer Identification Number

employer identification number A number issued by the Internal Revenue Service, it identifies tax accounts held by businesses, including sole proprietorships, partnerships, corporations, and many others; required on many tax and other business filings.

An **employer identification number** (EIN) is also known as a federal tax identification number and is required for almost all types of business filings. (It is usually required to purchase products at wholesale prices, as well). This number is required for any of a number of transactions, including filing for unemployment insurance, workers' compensation, Medicare, FICA, and other withholdings.

STATE REQUIREMENTS

States also have income tax filing requirements that are similar, but not identical, to federal laws. Sole proprietors must be aware of these requirements and file all appropriate documentation with the state to avoid any fees or penalties.

Exhibit 3–5. IRS Form 940 Employer's Annual Federal Unemployment Tax Return

Form **940**

Department of the Treasury
Internal Revenue Service (99)

Employer's Annual Federal Unemployment (FUTA) Tax Return

► **See the separate Instructions for Form 940 for information on completing this form.**

OMB No. 1545-0028

2004

T	
FF	
FD	
FP	
I	
T	

You must complete this section. ►

Name (as distinguished from trade name)

Trade name, if any

Address (number and street)

Calendar year

Employer identification number (EIN)

City, state, and ZIP code

A Are you required to pay unemployment contributions to only one state? (If "No," skip questions B and C.) ☐ Yes ☐ No

B Did you pay all state unemployment contributions by January 31, 2005? ((1) If you deposited your total FUTA tax when due, check "Yes" if you paid all state unemployment contributions by February 10, 2005. (2) If a 0% experience rate is granted, check "Yes." (3) If "No," skip question C.) . . . . ☐ Yes ☐ No

C Were all wages that were taxable for FUTA tax also taxable for your state's unemployment tax? . . . . ☐ Yes ☐ No

D Did you pay all wages in a state other than New York? . . . . ☐ Yes ☐ No

If you answered "No" to any of these questions, you must file Form 940. If you answered "Yes" to all the questions, you may file Form 940-EZ, which is a simplified version of Form 940. (Successor employers, see **Special credit for successor employers** in the separate instructions.) You can get Form 940-EZ by calling 1-800-TAX-FORM (1-800-829-3676) or from the IRS website at **www.irs.gov.**

If you will not have to file returns in the future, check here (see **Who Must File** in the separate instructions) **and complete and sign the return** . . . . ► ☐

If this is an Amended Return, check here (see **Amended Returns** in the separate instructions) . . . . ► ☐

Part I	Computation of Taxable Wages

1 Total payments (including payments shown on lines 2 and 3) during the calendar year for services of employees **1**

2 Exempt payments. (Explain all exempt payments, attaching additional sheets if necessary.) ► --------------------------------- **2**

3 Payments of more than $7,000 for services. Enter only amounts over the first $7,000 paid to each employee (see separate instructions). Do not include any exempt payments from line 2. The $7,000 amount is the federal wage base. Your state wage base may be different. **Do not use your state wage limitation** **3**

4 Add lines 2 and 3 . . . . **4**

5 **Total taxable wages** (subtract line 4 from line 1) . . . . ► **5**

6 Additional tax resulting from credit reduction for unpaid advances to the State of New York. Enter the wages included on line 5 for New York and multiply by .003. (See the separate Instructions for Form 940.) Enter the credit reduction amount here and in Part II, line 5: New York wages _____ x .003 = ... ► **6**

Be sure to complete both sides of this form, and sign in the space provided on the back.

For Privacy Act and Paperwork Reduction Act Notice, see separate instructions. ▼ **DETACH HERE** ▼ Cat. No. 11234O Form **940** (2004)

Form **940-V**

Department of the Treasury
Internal Revenue Service

Payment Voucher

Use this voucher only when making a payment with your return.

OMB No. 1545-0028

2004

Complete boxes 1, 2, and 3. Do not send cash, and do not staple your payment to this voucher. Make your check or money order payable to the "United States Treasury." Be sure to enter your employer identification number (EIN), "Form 940," and "2004" on your payment.

1 Enter your employer identification number (EIN).

2 **Enter the amount of your payment.** ►

Dollars	Cents

3 Enter your business name (individual name for sole proprietors).

Enter your address.

Enter your city, state, and ZIP code.

(continued)

Exhibit 3–5. IRS Form 940 Employer's Annual Federal Unemployment Tax Return *(continued)*

Form 940 (2004)   Page **2**

Name   Employer identification number (EIN)

Part II   **Tax Due or Refund**

1   Gross FUTA tax. (Multiply the wages from Part I, line 5, by .062) **1**

2   Maximum credit. (Multiply the wages from Part I, line 5, by .054) . . | **2** |

3   Computation of tentative credit (**Note:** *All taxpayers must complete the applicable columns.*)

(a) Name of state	(b) State reporting number(s) as shown on employer's state contribution returns	(c) Taxable payroll (as defined in state act)	(d) State experience rate period From	To	(e) State experience rate	(f) Contributions if rate had been 5.4% (col. (c) x .054)	(g) Contributions payable at experience rate (col. (c) x col. (e))	(h) Additional credit (col. (f) minus col.(g)) If 0 or less, enter -0-.	(i) Contributions paid to state by 940 due date

3a | Totals . . . ▶

3b   **Total tentative credit** (add line 3a, columns (h) and (i) only—for late payments, also see the instructions for Part II, line 3) . . . . ▶   **3b**

4   **Credit:** Enter the smaller of the amount from Part II, line 2 or line 3b; or the amount from the worksheet on page 7 of the separate instructions **4**

5   Enter the amount from Part I, line 6 . . . .   **5**

6   **Credit allowable** (subtract line 5 from line 4). If zero or less, enter "-0-" **6**

7   **Total FUTA tax** (subtract line 6 from line 1). If the result is over $100, also complete Part III   **7**

8   Total FUTA tax deposited for the year, including any overpayment applied from a prior year . .   **8**

9   **Balance due** (subtract line 8 from line 7). Pay to the "United States Treasury." If you owe more than $100, see **Depositing FUTA Tax** on page 3 of the separate instructions . . . . . ▶   **9**

10   **Overpayment** (subtract line 7 from line 8). Check if it is to be: ☐ **Applied to next return** or ☐ **Refunded** . . . . ▶   **10**

Part III   **Record of Quarterly Federal Unemployment Tax Liability** (Do not include state liability.) **Complete only if line 7 is over $100.** See page 7 of the separate instructions.

Quarter	First (Jan. 1–Mar. 31)	Second (Apr. 1–June 30)	Third (July 1–Sept. 30)	Fourth (Oct. 1–Dec. 31)	Total for year
Liability for quarter					

Third-Party Designee   Do you want to allow another person to discuss this return with the IRS (see separate instructions)? ☐ **Yes.** Complete the following.   ☐ **No**

Designee's name ▶   Phone no. ▶ ( )   Personal identification number (PIN)

Under penalties of perjury, I declare that I have examined this return, including accompanying schedules and statements, and, to the best of my knowledge and belief, it is true, correct, and complete, and that no part of any payment made to a state unemployment fund claimed as a credit was, or is to be, deducted from the payments to employees.

Signature ▶   Title (Owner, etc.) ▶   Date ▶

Form **940** (2004)

BUILDING PERMITS, BUSINESS LICENSES, AND OTHER CONCERNS

In addition to federal and state concerns, a sole proprietor must also comply with all local ordinances, rules, and regulations. These can be summarized as three broad categories.

- building permits
- business licenses
- miscellaneous governmental regulations

Building Permits

Whenever a new business involves construction, a building permit must be obtained and filed with local authorities. Failure to file for a building permit may result in fines and the refusal of local authorities to grant public access to the building. See Exhibit 3–6.

Exhibit 3–6. Building permit application, California

PLANNING & DEVELOPMENT

Permit Service Center
2120 Milvia Street, Berkeley, CA 94704
Main Tel: 510.981.7500 TDD: 510.981.7474 Fax: 510.981.7505
Schedule Inspections: 510.981.7444 Building Inspectors: 510.981.7440
Email: Planning@ci.berkeley.ca.us

BUILDING PERMIT APPLICATION

SHADED AREAS FOR STAFF USE ONLY

Please note: **Electrical, Mechanical, and Plumbing elements require separate applications.**

APPLICATION # _____ APN # _____ Use Permit#_____

STREET ADDRESS/ UNIT #(if applicable)

TOTAL PROJECT SQUARE FEET | **＊ VALUATION ($)**

The valuation used in computing the Building Permit fee shall be the total replacement value of all construction work for which the permit is issued, as well as all finished work, painting, roofing, electrical, plumbing, heating, air conditioning, elevators, fire extinguishing systems and any other permanent equipment. **BMC SECTION 19.28.100**

APPLICATION GROUP:
☐ NEW ☐ ADD ☐ DEMO>DEM ☐ REMODEL>REM ☐ REPAIR>REP ☐ SEISMIC ☐ GRADING
☐ OTHER (Describe below)

Fire Zone: 1☐ 2☐ 3☐	Alquist Priolo: Yes☐ No☐	Flood Zone: A☐ B☐ C ☐
Liquefaction Zone: Yes☐ No☐		Landslide Area: Yes☐ No☐
Creek on the Parcel: Yes☐ No☐		Work in the Right of Way: Yes☐ No☐

DESCRIBE SCOPE OF WORK:

Additional Permits Required: ☐ Electrical ☐ Mechanical ☐ Plumbing ☐ Other_____

	Construction Type	Occupancy Code	Square Footage	#Residential Units	# Stories
EXISTING					
PROPOSED					

Property Owner Name	Phone#	**Applicant/Contact Person**	Phone#
Address		Address	
City, ST	Zip Code	City, ST	Zip Code

Contractor's Company Name		**State Lic#**	**Bus Lic#**
Address			Phone#
City, ST			ZIP Code

Business Licenses

Whenever a person decides to run a business within a particular county, he or she must obtain a business license. These licenses normally cost less than $100 and are assessed by local governments for the privilege of running a business within the geographic limits of the city or county.

Miscellaneous Governmental Regulations

Beyond building permits and business licenses, a sole proprietor may have numerous other administrative obligations. For instance, before opening a retail establishment, the sole proprietor must have the premises inspected by a heath or fire inspector. Businesses that plan to sell food to the public must pass other inspections. These businesses are also subject to periodic reinspection.

Zoning Regulations

Zoning rules limit the ways that structures can be used. Many cities and towns have zoning regulations that limit use to particular types of use, such as residential, commercial, industrial, or agricultural.

Health Inspections

New businesses are subject to periodic inspections. Any business that deals regularly with the public will be inspected by local governmental agencies. Inspectors may review food preparation areas, restroom facilities, and any other area that poses a potential health risk to customers or other members of the public.

Safety Inspections

Businesses are also subject to safety inspections, often in the form of a visit from the local fire department. These visits are designed to make sure that all fire suppression technology, including fire extinguishers, smoke detectors, and ceiling sprinklers, are in working order. Fire inspectors are authorized to issue citations for any nonworking devices. They may also insist that exit doors remain unlocked during business hours and that escape routes remain free of obstructions.

Ethics File: Tax Evasion

One of the temptations sole proprietors face is to underreport (or fail to report) taxes collected as part of retail sales. When businesses run into financial trouble, the owners often see taxes collected as a short-term bonus that may help defray other costs. Many owners plan on repaying the tax at a later time. Some sole proprietors underreport their taxable income as a way of evading the true tax that they are legally obligated to pay. Some even go so far as to fail to report income at all. In either situation, the business owner is subject to criminal fines and potential prison time when the IRS discovers that the sole proprietor has failed to correctly report taxable income.

CASE LAW: *Insurance Issues for Sole Proprietors*

Koehlke v. Clay Street Inn, Inc.[2]
William M. O'Neill, J.

Plaintiff-appellant, Jennifer Koehlke ("Koehlke"), appeals the judgment of the Ashtabula County Court of Common Pleas, which granted summary judgment in favor of appellee, The Cincinnati Insurance Company ("Cincinnati").

On May 16, 1998, Koehlke was involved in a single car accident while riding as a passenger in her own vehicle. The car was driven by Jose Marte. Koehlke sustained serious injuries while Marte was not injured. Marte was insured through a policy issued by Nationwide Insurance Company. Koehlke's vehicle was also insured under another policy through Nationwide. Koehlke subsequently settled with Nationwide for the tortfeasor's liability in the amount of $251,246.83. Koehlke executed a release at that time with Nationwide which expressly stated that no subrogation rights were reserved.

At the time of the accident, Koehlke was employed as a manager at the Clay Street Inn, Inc. ("Clay Street"). Clay Street maintained a commercial general liability policy issued from Cincinnati. Clay Street purchased the insurance when the status of the business was a sole proprietorship. Thus, the declarations page denotes the insured as "Shelly J. Koehlke-Stark d.b.a. Clay Street Inn." The effective dates of the policy are from October 7, 1996 through October 7, 1999. Subsequent to the initiation of the policy, but prior to the accident, Shelly J. Koehlke-Stark filed papers of incorporation and formed Clay Street Inn, Inc. on February 11, 1997.

On October 5, 2001, Koehlke filed the instant declaratory judgment action in an effort to recover uninsured/underinsured motorist (UM/UIM) coverage through Clay Street's commercial general liability policy pursuant to the *Scott-Pontzer* theory of liability. Cincinnati has maintained that

the instant lawsuit was its first notice of either Koehlke's claim, or the change in Clay Street's business status.

On September 16, 2002, Koehlke filed a motion for partial summary judgment on the issue of liability with damages to be determined. Cincinnati filed its motion in opposition and a cross-motion for summary judgment on October 16, 2002. On December 5, 2002, the trial court entered judgment, denying Koehlke's motion for partial summary judgment and granting Cincinnati's motion for summary judgment. Koehlke ultimately filed this timely appeal, citing two assignments of error:

Koehlke's first assignment of error is:
"The trial court erred in granting the cross motion for summary judgment for defendant-appellee."

Regarding a motion for summary judgment, the moving party has the burden of establishing that there is no genuine issue of material fact, that the moving party is entitled to judgment as a matter of law, and that reasonable minds, construing the evidence in favor of the nonmoving party, can come to but one conclusion which is adverse to the nonmoving party.

In her first assignment of error, Koehlke contends that the trial court erred by "confusing the language of the policy concerning the policy's terms with the **status** of the named insured." (Emphasis in original.)

Cincinnati asserts that Koehlke never raised the issue regarding whether Cincinnati can avoid coverage due to a change in the business status of the insured at the lower court and is, therefore, precluded from making those arguments for the first time on appeal. However, a review of the record reveals that in Koehlke's reply to Cincinnati's brief in opposition to Koehlke's motion for summary judgment and

(continued)

CASE LAW: *Insurance Issues for Sole Proprietors* (continued)

cross-motion for summary judgment, she argued that the insurance policy did not require that Cincinnati be notified of a change in Clay Street's business structure. Koehlke makes ostensibly the same argument here in her first assignment of error.

Koehlke contends that the trial court erred in holding that the policy language required Clay Street to notify Cincinnati that it had changed its business status. When interpreting the terms of a contract, courts are to give terms and phrases in the contract their plain and ordinary meaning. Where the terms of a contract are clear and unambiguous, its interpretation is a matter of law.

The language in question in the instant case is the policy provision designated "changes." That clause states, in its entirety:

"This policy contains all the agreements between you and us concerning the insurance afforded. The first Named Insured shown in the Declarations is authorized to make changes in the terms of this policy with our consent. This policy's terms can be amended or waived only by endorsement issued by us and made a part of this policy."

Koehlke contends that the language does not require the insured to notify the insurance company of a change in business status but, rather, that the insurer has a responsibility to keep itself notified of changes in the business status of its insureds. Koehlke further states that the essence of the insurance policy would not change regardless if the insured were a sole proprietorship or a corporation.

The trial court held that the business status issue was dispositive to the ultimate outcome. The court held that the *Scott-Pontzer* theory of liability does not apply in this situation because Clay Street was a sole proprietorship at the time the policy was issued. Thus, under the policy in question, the court held that, as the insured listed is "Shelly J. Koehlke, d.b.a. Clay Street Inn" and further delineates it as an "INDIVIDUAL" policy, "there is no ambiguity in the definition of who is an insured person, as there is when the named insured is a corporation." Therefore, the trial court held *Scott-Pontzer* would not apply and plaintiff would not be insured under the policy.

The trial court further held that the language in the "changes" clause does not provide for unilateral changes to the policy but requires consent and a written endorsement by the insurer. Thus, the trial court held, without consent and a written endorsement, the insured under the policy remains the sole proprietorship, not a corporation.

This court has held that a sole proprietorship has no legal identity separate from the individual named in the policy and, therefore, *Scott-Pontzer* does not apply. Here, as in *Herschell,* the declarations page listed the insured as the individual sole proprietor followed by the d.b.a. designation. This court held that "unlike a corporation, a sole proprietorship does not have an identity separate from the individual who owns it. When 'd.b.a.' (doing business as) is used, there is no legal distinction between the individual and the business entity since it is merely a descriptive of the person who does business under some other name."

Here, unlike in *Herschell,* the sole proprietorship was transformed into a corporation prior to Koehlke's accident. However, despite the change in the business status, Cincinnati never received notice of the change in status and continued to provide sole proprietorship coverage. We find Koehlke's argument, placing the onus on Cincinnati to monitor its insureds to detect changes in circumstances, to be untenable. To do so would render the "changes" clause in the provision meaningless. Shelley J. Koehlke, as the sole proprietor and an insured under the policy, was required by the language in the policy to notify Cincinnati of the change in her business status. Her failure to abide by the terms of the policy should not result in a finding that the insurer is now liable under the *Scott-Pontzer* theory for an insured that it still recognized under the applicable policy as a sole proprietorship.

Based on the foregoing, we find Koehlke's assignment of error to be without merit, and the judgment of the trial court is affirmed.

CASE QUESTIONS

1. Explain the basic facts of this case.
2. What impact does the defendant's business status have on the ultimate issues in the case?

3. Koehlke required to notify the insurance company about the change in status from a sole proprietorship to a corporation? Why or why not?
4. Why does the court rule that the burden of informing the insurance company about a change from sole proprietorship to a corporation falls on the insured?

SUMMARY

Sole proprietorships are the simplest form of business model. They are easy to set up and maintain. As far as the law is concerned, there is no difference between the sole proprietor and the owner. The sole proprietorship offers the advantage of flexibility for the business owner by giving him or her the option of engaging in nearly any type of business and the flexibility to decide how the business will be run. However, the flexibility and independence of a sole proprietorship comes at a cost. Sole proprietorships have distinct disadvantages, including financing problems, time and resource commitments, and the inability of the business owner to protect personal assets from creditor judgments or bankruptcy.

HELPFUL WEB SITES

The Official Business Link to the U.S. Government
http://www.business.gov

Business search engine
http://www.business.com

Small Business Administration
http://www.sba.gov

KEY TERMS

employer identification number

personal liability

APPLYING CHAPTER CONCEPTS

Contact your local government and gather information about the following issues.

- Where does a new business owner apply in order to obtain a business license?
- If the business is a retail establishment, what fees, inspections, or assessments are required before the business can be opened?
- If the business will be serving food to the public, what health inspections are required?
- If the client intends to change a retail store into a restaurant, is a building permit required? If so, where does the client go to obtain a building permit?

REVIEW QUESTIONS

1. Explain why a sole proprietorship is simple to create and maintain.
2. What tax advantages does a sole proprietorship offer?
3. What are some of the financial concerns facing sole proprietors?
4. What organizational steps must a sole proprietor go through in order to begin his or her new business?
5. Explain the cash-flow arrangement in a sole proprietorship.
6. The text mentions that sole proprietors have complete control over their businesses, but also shows that there are some practical limitations. Discuss these limitations.
7. Describe the tax advantages of sole proprietorships.
8. Why are the time and personal commitments considered to be disadvantages in the sole proprietorship?
9. Why is it difficult for new businesses to obtain financing and credit?
10. One of the disadvantages of a sole proprietorship is the fact that it has limited existence. What does this phrase mean?
11. Explain the personal liability that a sole proprietor has in his or her business.
12. Is it possible to sue a sole proprietorship after the owner is dead? Explain.
13. What steps are required to dissolve a sole proprietorship?
14. What Internal Revenue Service forms are required in order to track profits and losses from a sole proprietorship?
15. What are some of the sole proprietor's concerns when hiring employees?

QUESTIONS FOR REFLECTION

1. What, in your opinion, is the biggest advantage of being a sole proprietor? What is the biggest disadvantage?

2. Statistics show that most new businesses fail in their first year. Why? Is it because of lack of finances, poor management, or some other reason? What is your opinion?

ENDNOTES

[1] 2005 WL 351040, 3 (E.D.Pa., 2005).

[2] 2003 WL 22290888, 4 (Ohio App. 11 Dist., 2003).

Chapter 4

GENERAL PARTNERSHIPS

Chapter Objectives

Upon completion of this chapter, you should be able to:

- Explain the basic organization of a general partnership.
- Define the advantages and disadvantages of a general partnership.
- Describe how a general partnership is formed.
- Explain the significance of the Uniform Partnership Act.
- Describe how a general partnership is terminated.

▶ INTRODUCTION

In this chapter, we will examine the role of **general partnerships** as a business model. Partnerships bring several distinct advantages to the everyday world of business that sole proprietors cannot match. General partners can pool their resources and share profits and losses. Historically, partnership was considered to be a contractual arrangement between two or more parties. However, with the adoption of the Uniform Partnership Act, partnership has come to be seen as something more than a contract. Where the UPA has been enacted, general partnership has come to resemble a hybrid between a contract and a form of business entity. In this chapter we will explore the creation, management, and dissolution of a general partnership.

general partnership An unincorporated business organization co-owned by two or more persons that is run for profit.

THE NATURE OF A PARTNERSHIP

At its core, a partnership is a contractual agreement between two or more persons to conduct a business. Because the law considers a partnership to be, first and foremost, a contract, the basic principles of contract law apply.

A partnership consists of two or more people working together in a joint business venture. Partnerships have several obvious advantages over sole proprietorships. First of all, there are more people to share the load. Partners can bring additional financial and other resources to bear for the good of the business. However, with these greater resources come more limitations. The partners must consult with one another before making business decisions, and all partners face the possibility of losing their personal assets in a judgment against the partnership. We refer to this arrangement as a general partnership in order to distinguish it from a limited partnership, discussed in the next chapter.

◼ THE MINIMUM REQUIREMENTS OF A PARTNERSHIP

Because a general partnership is essentially a contract, the partners must meet all of the minimum requirements of any legally binding contract.[1] These elements include:

- ◼ mutual assent or meeting of the minds
- ◼ capacity
- ◼ consideration
- ◼ legality
- ◼ running a business for profit

KEY POINT

Partnerships must meet the same requirements as a contract.

MUTUAL ASSENT

mutual assent The meeting of the minds of the parties to the contract; a general agreement as to the details of the arrangement between the contracting parties.

For a partnership agreement to be binding on all parties, there must be a meeting of the minds, or **mutual assent** as to the details of the arrangement. Like any contract, the parties to a partnership agreement must be in agreement about the details of the partnership. When there is a dispute about whether a partnership agreement was created, courts will always look to the intent of all parties at the time that the purported agreement was created. In many ways, this is the same inquiry that the court would make in any disputed contract. The court will ask, "What was the intent of the parties at the time that the partnership agreement was executed?" If that intent is not clear, then the court is more likely to rule that no partnership agreement exists. If, on the other hand, the parties' intentions are clear, the court will rule that an agreement exists, even if one of the parties has had second thoughts afterwards. Consider Scenario 4–1.

Scenario 4–1. Shooting the Breeze

Dale and Juan are talking one evening in a bar. Dale has a landscape business, and Juan owns a tree removal business. They are both having trouble keeping up with customer demands. Juan says, "Hey, wouldn't it be great if we could team up? You could do the landscaping; I could do the trees. We could even afford to hire some extra people on big jobs."

Dale likes the idea. Unfortunately, he gets a call and has to leave. On the way out, Dale says, "Juan, that's a great idea. Let's talk about the details tomorrow."

The next day, Juan bids on a large job and tells the customer that he now has a partner. Later, when Dale learns that Juan has told others that he and Juan are now partners, he disputes this. "That was just talk," Dale says. Juan, on the other hand, says that they formed a partnership agreement. Juan sues Dale when Dale refuses to work on the new job. How is the court likely to rule in this case?

Answer: The court will rule that no partnership agreement existed. How can we be sure? If we view a partnership agreement as we would any other contract, then there is no meeting of the minds or mutual assent about the details of this contract. There isn't even an agreement about sharing of profits or losses, or any other issues. Dale's contention that they were just talking through an idea is an accurate assessment.

CAPACITY

Capacity is a party's ability to know and understand the terms of the contract. A person lacks capacity when he or she is acting under the influence of alcohol or other drugs. Mentally incompetent persons also lack capacity. Children also lack the capacity to enter into a contract. Under the law in most states, a child is anyone under the age of 18. Because partnership is rooted so firmly in contract law, individuals who lack capacity to enter into a contract also lack the capacity to enter into a partnership agreement.

capacity A person's ability to know and understand not only the terms of the contract, but also the legal obligation incurred.

CONSIDERATION

Consideration is a contract requirement that stipulates that both parties must give up something of value to obtain something of value in the agreement. Consideration isn't usually an issue in partnership agreements, where both parties are obviously surrendering something of value. A partner is giving up the right to make independent decisions and the right to take all of the profits. In exchange for giving up these rights, the partner gains the right to share in profits from the new business. However, if a partner does not incur some form of detriment or advantage from the arrangement, it may not be a valid partnership agreement.

consideration Bargained-for exchange in a contract; a requirement that all parties to a contract surrender something of value in exchange for receiving something of value.

LEGALITY

legality The requirement that a contract have, as its purpose, a goal that is legitimate and not barred by any statute or common law provision.

Legality is a requirement of all contracts, including partnership agreements. A partnership that is formed for the purpose of carrying out an illegal enterprise is not valid. There is a simple reason for this rule. If it did not exist, then a court would be put in the bizarre situation of attempting to enforce the terms of a partnership agreement for illegal purposes. In order to avoid this sticky problem, courts refuse to enforce any contracts, including partnership agreements, that have an illegal purpose. For an example, see Case Law: Is a Wife Liable to Her Husband's Partner?

KEY POINT

A person who cannot enter into a contract cannot enter into a partnership agreement.

BUSINESS RUN FOR PROFIT

Besides the basic contractual components, a general partnership agreement must also meet other requirements. One of those requirements is that the business must be run to earn profits.

In addition to basic contract requirements, a general partnership must also be set up to make a profit. The purpose of the business must be to make money. Nonprofit organizations do not qualify as partnerships. Even if the business doesn't actually make money, a business may still qualify as a partnership if the members set out to make a profit.[2]

ADVANTAGES OF GENERAL PARTNERSHIPS

The advantages of a partnership are obvious: With two or more people, the business can expand and serve more customers. Partners can also contribute more financial resources than a single individual. A second person in the business sometimes helps to balance the personality of the other person. Where one partner is bold, the other may be cautious. The partner may also contribute talents and skills not possessed by the other partner.

DISADVANTAGES OF GENERAL PARTNERSHIPS

unlimited liability A concept that places all of a person's personal assets within reach of a civil judgment.

Like sole proprietorships, general partners also suffer from one major disadvantage: **unlimited liability.** A general partner's personal assets could be seized to pay a judgment, sometimes putting the general partnership in a precarious situation. The partners need their personal resources to run the business, but risk losing them because of a business problem. This shortcoming, found in both sole proprietorships and general partnerships, was one of the motivating factors behind the creation of a new type of business entity: the limited partnership, which we will discuss in the next chapter.

In addition to financial and liability issues, the death of a general partner often dissolves the partnership. Although a partnership agreement may anticipate the death of a partner and make provisions to allow the business to continue after this event, in practical terms that may be impossible.

▶ TYPES OF PARTNERSHIPS

There are many different types of partnerships. The different forms give partners different rights and obligations. They include the two most popular forms of partnerships:

general
limited

But in addition to these classifications, there are also other partnership arrangements, including:

partnership associations
mining partnerships
sub-partnerships

GENERAL PARTNERSHIPS

The two basic classifications for partnerships are general and limited. A general partnership is an agreement between two or more persons to run a business for profit. In this arrangement, all partners are liable for business debts, and their personal assets may be subject to judgments. The Uniform Partnership Act was originally created to provide a framework for these types of partnerships. General partnerships can take on many different forms, from a simple two-person partnership to a huge, multilevel arrangement. However, the basic components remain the same: partners pool financial and other resources to spread the risk of running a business.

LIMITED PARTNERSHIPS

Limited partnerships are creatures of statute and provide the business owners with limited liability. Partners in limited partnerships can protect their personal assets and are generally not subject to creditors and business judgments. We will discuss limited partnerships in greater detail in the next chapter.

PARTNERSHIP ASSOCIATIONS

Partnership associations are another recent innovation in the area of partnership law. Like limited partnerships, partnership associations attempt to shield the partners from some or all liability for business debts and judgments. We will examine partnership associations in greater detail in the next chapter.

MINING PARTNERSHIPS

Some states give special status to partnerships created for specific purposes, such as mining. Mining partnerships, like limited partnerships and partnership associations, give the partners some protection and were created as a way of encouraging individuals to take on particular risky ventures, such as mining.

SUB-PARTNERSHIPS

Sub-partnerships come into existence when a partnership engages in an agreement with a non-partner to split profits. This new individual would be classified not as a partner, but as a sub-partner. The individual does not have the rights and obligations of the general partnership, but does have limited rights. A sub-partnership might be created for a specific venture. Rather than grant partnership status to the new individual, the general partnership would simply create a temporary sub-partnership with the third party. This would prevent the third party from receiving profits from the general partnership's other business holdings, but would entitle him or her to profits from a particular venture.

CASE LAW: *Is a Wife Liable to Her Husband's Partner?*

Morrison v. Dickey[3]
COBB, J.

This was an action by Mrs. Morrison against Dickey to recover a sum of money which she alleged had been wrongfully appropriated by Dickey to the payment of her husband's debt. The jury found in favor of the defendant, and the plaintiff assigns error upon the overruling of her motion for a new trial.

Mrs. Morrison was the owner of a business which was conducted by her husband in his name. Her ownership was not disclosed to the world, nor was there anything to indicate to those who dealt with Morrison that he was not the owner of the business. Dickey, while ignorant of Mrs. Morrison's ownership, bought from Morrison a half interest in the business. This sale

was made, if not with the approval, certainly without the disapproval, of Mrs. Morrison. Morrison and Dickey purchased a machine, which, if not necessary, was adapted to and useful in the business they were carrying on, and was actually used in that business. The contract for the purchase price was signed, not by the partnership, but by Morrison and Dickey individually. Suit was brought upon this contract, and judgment obtained against Morrison and Dickey as individual joint promisors. Up to this point it seems that Dickey was still in ignorance of the fact that the business into which he had been admitted as a partner with Morrison was in reality the business of Morrison's wife, but this fact was subsequently disclosed to him. Dickey, having ascertained that Mrs. Morrison was the real owner of the business, negotiated with her for the purchase of her remaining one-half interest; and an agreement was reached by which Mrs. Morrison sold this interest to Dickey for the sum of $2,500, $1,000 of which was to be paid in cash. The stipulation in the contract with reference to the remaining $1,500 was in the following words: "The balance of the amount, being fifteen hundred dollars, I hereby give and convey to him, my said husband, J. J. Morrison, for the affection I have for him, together with some compensation for his long service in it. Of course he can do as he pleases with that, provided I get one thousand dollars or its equivalent." Dickey assumed all debts and liabilities of the firm. Morrison agreed with Dickey that the $1,500 above referred to should be left in the latter's hands, to be appropriated first to the payment of one-half of the judgment against Dickey and Morrison above referred to, and the remainder, so far as necessary, to the payment of one-half of the other debts of the firm. Dickey subsequently paid the balance due on the judgment, and it is claimed by Mrs. Morrison that this payment was made from the proceeds of the business in which her money had been placed by her husband, and therefore that one-half of this money paid on this judgment was hers, and should have been paid to her, and the payment of it by Dickey on her husband's debt was illegal, and she was entitled to recover the amount from him; it being also claimed that the arrangement by which $1,500 of the purchase money of her remaining interest in the business should be left in the hands of her husband, and the subsequent arrangement between Dickey and her husband that this sum should be appropriated in part to the payment of the judgment, was merely a scheme or device to use her money for the purpose of paying her husband's debt. No partnership relation existed between Mrs. Morrison and Dickey prior to the time that he knew that the business was owned by her. The partnership up to that time was one composed of Dickey and Morrison. The relation created by a partnership agreement is one founded so essentially upon mutual confidence that there can be no such thing in the law as a part-

nership between persons unless the persons are known to each other, and each has an opportunity to determine whether that relation shall be formed between them. Partnership is founded upon agreement and consent, and there can be no consent to the formation of a partnership with a person who is not known. 1 Bates on Part. § 158; 22 Am. & Eng. Enc. Law (2d Ed.) 15. The relation which existed between Morrison and his wife after Dickey had been admitted as a partner into the business carried on by Morrison was in the nature of a subpartnership, which made Morrison and his wife partners as between themselves; and as such they assumed all of the responsibilities that would be incident to a partnership created between two persons, where one furnished the capital, and the other the skill and labor, necessary in carrying out the enterprise. 1 Bates on Part. §§ 164, 169. How profits between themselves as members of this subpartnership would be divided would be immaterial, and therefore the mere fact that Mrs. Morrison was to receive the entire profits of the business thus carried on in her husband's name for her benefit would not deprive the business relationship between them of the essential elements of a subpartnership. It is now the settled law of this state that husband and wife may lawfully engage in business as partners. Ellis v. Mills, 99 Ga. 490, 27 S. E. 740. But this relation existing between Morrison and his wife as to each other would not make the wife a partner in the business carried on by Dickey and Morrison, nor would she be liable for the debts of that partnership; but she would be liable for any debts which might be considered as debts of the subpartnership existing between herself and her husband. 1 Bates on Part. §§ 168, 169; 22 Am. & Eng. Enc. Law (2d Ed.) 17. Mrs. Morrison therefore could not have been held bound on the contract for the purchase of the machine above referred to, as this purchase was made before the fact of her interest in the business came to the knowledge of Dickey, and therefore before there could have been, in law, any partnership relation existing between them. But Morrison was bound not only by virtue of the partnership relation existing between himself and Dickey, but by the express terms of the contract itself. When Dickey discovered that Mrs. Morrison

(continued)

CASE LAW: *Is a Wife Liable to Her Husband's Partner?* (continued)

was the real owner of the business which he had formerly carried on as a partner of her husband, he had a right to deal with her as such owner, by either admitting her into the partnership, or by purchasing from her her interest therein. The contract, therefore, between Dickey and Mrs. Morrison, by which he purchased her remaining one-half interest in the business, was valid and lawful, and after this purchase he became the owner of the entire business. It was lawful for him to pay her $1,000, and agree to pay her $1,500 in the future, and it was also lawful for her to make a gift of the latter amount to her husband. This is the legal effect of the contract upon its face, and, if the gift became complete, it was immaterial for what purposes her husband used the money which was the subject of the gift. He might use it for the purpose of paying his debts, and the subsequent agreement between him and Dickey that a portion of the money given to him should be applied by Dickey to the judgment against Morrison and himself was a transaction free from legal infirmity. Morrison would then be paying his own debt with his own money, and not with the money of his wife. In addition to this, while Mrs. Morrison was not at all bound by the judgment against Morrison and Dickey, and not in any way liable upon the contract which was the foundation of that judgment, this liability of Morrison and Dickey was one of the liabilities of the partnership between them; and, when Mrs. Morrison saw fit to disclose her ownership of the business, and Dickey saw proper to recognize her as a partner, she then took her position for the first time as a partner in the business with Dickey, and she then became liable, upon an accounting as to the affairs of the partnership, to account to her partner for all claims or demands which, as between the partners, would be lawful charges against the partnership business; and, if the partnership had gone into liquidation, there would have been, in an accounting between the partners, no legal obstacle in the way of Dickey insisting that the money expended for the machine should be treated, as between him and Mrs.

Morrison, as a liability of the firm, and one for which she should account for one-half. This is true notwithstanding the fact that at the time the machine was purchased, when her ownership of the business was not known to Dickey, she gave her husband special instructions not to purchase the machine; it appearing that the machine was actually purchased and used in carrying on the business of the partnership. Take still another view of the matter. The subpartnership or relation in the nature thereof, existing between Mrs. Morrison and her husband, rendered her liable to account to her husband for all legitimate and necessary expenses incurred in realizing or attempting to realize profits from the partnership between him and Dickey; and, if the purchase of the machine was necessary or proper for the conduct of the business, and was actually used in the business, before Mrs. Morrison could demand from her husband the profits of the business she would have to account to him for the amount for which he rendered himself liable on account of such purchase. Her protest against its purchase would not avail her as an excuse for not so accounting, if the profits claimed by her were the result of the business in which the machine had been actually used.

So that it seems to us that, under any view of the law and facts of the case, no other legal judgment could have been rendered than one in favor of the defendant. There is nothing in the case to authorize a finding that the transaction was a mere scheme or device to use Mrs. Morrison's money for the purpose of paying her husband's debt. It was either the use of her money to pay a liability which Dickey would have a right to claim against her when she admitted her ownership, and accepted position as a partner with him, or it was a payment by Morrison of his debt with his money, title to which he had derived by a voluntary gift from his wife, or the payment of a sum which Mrs. Morrison would have been bound to pay in an accounting with her husband. While the instructions of the judge are not at all in accord with some of the principles above laid down, still, under the undisputed facts of the case, the verdict for the defendant was demanded, and any errors committed in charging the jury were harmless.

Judgment affirmed. All the Justices concur.

1. Why does the court rule that Dickey was not a partner with Mrs. Morrison until her ownership was revealed?

2. According the court, can a person form a partnership with someone that he or she does not know? Why?

3. How does the court explain the concept of sub-partnership?

4. Who was in a sub-partnership with Mrs. Morrison? Explain.

5. How does Mrs. Morrison's gift to her husband affect the debts owed by the partnership?

THE NATURE OF A PARTNER

Because partnership is based, at least in part, on contract law, all partners must have the legal ability to enter into a contract. The Uniform Partnership Act provides that a partner may also be another business entity, such as a corporation. Under this definition, a person, even an artificial person such as a corporation, can be a partner. A general partnership can consist of two or more human beings, or any combination of human beings, other general partnerships, and corporations, all pooling their resources to run a particular business for profit. As you can imagine, the situation can become very complicated when a general partnership comprises persons and other businesses, some of which may be protected by limited liability in some contexts, but not others.

Silent Partners

A **silent partner** is someone who contributes money or something else of value, while the other partner contributes labor to the enterprise. Silent partners usually have no hand in running the day-to-day operations of the business. Instead, they allow the other partner to manage the company, while they share in the profits (and losses). When a person is a silent partner, his or her name does not normally appear on the business sign, letterhead, or other identifying information.[4]

silent partner A partner who takes no part in the management or day-to-day running of the general partnership.

Spouses as Partners

Under the old common law rules, a husband and wife could not be partners. The simple reason was that the law considered married couples to be a single entity. Because a partnership required at least two separate persons, common law prohibited partnerships between husbands and wives. However, the Uniform Partnership Act takes a different view on the subject. Recognizing that husbands and wives are now recognized as two separate people in almost all aspects of the law, the UPA updated the spouse-partnership rule. Under the UPA, husbands and wives can be partners.[5]

Classifications of Partners

Partnership agreements may provide that some individuals are designated as "senior" partners, while others are referred to as "junior" partners. These designations make some impact on the way that profits are distributed, but as far as the legalities are concerned, a partner is a partner. Whether the partner is labeled "senior," "managing," or "contributing," the law imposes the same duties and obligations on each. They all face the same potential liability under a general partnership, no matter what the partnership chooses to call each owner.

▶ LAWS THAT APPLY TO PARTNERSHIPS

Because general partnerships have existed for centuries, this business model, like sole proprietorship, has been heavily influenced by common law. However, each state had its own rules about the creation, maintenance, and dissolution of general partnerships, and this often raised concerns. What happens when the partners are located in different states? Which state law applies? Under the old common law rules, unless there was some provision in the partnership agreement that provided for a different result, the general partnership would be bound by the laws of the state where it was created. Whenever a dispute arose about the partnership, even one that encompassed the entire country, that original state's laws would apply. However, this rule actually created more problems than it solved. Some states did not recognize specific types of general partnerships, and others refused to apply another state's laws to a business that was run within its own boundaries. The answer to this problem was the Uniform Partnership Act.

THE UNIFORM PARTNERSHIP ACT

The Uniform Partnership Act has been a feature of partnership law for decades. It creates a framework that seeks to minimize state law differences in partnership law. The UPA takes the position that a partnership is a form of business entity and not merely a creature of contract law. In addition to making the law on general partnership more uniform across the nation, the UPA creates a special property category: **tenancy by partnership.** This is a legally recognized form of ownership in which title to personal and real property is held in the name of the partnership, not in the names of the individual partners. The UPA also creates a framework for creating a partnership.

tenancy by partnership A legally recognized estate where general partners hold title to all real and personal property associated with the business.

CREATION OF A PARTNERSHIP UNDER THE UPA

In most situations, forming a general partnership is a simple matter. The partners simply agree to be bound to one another in a business and to pledge their financial assets for the business. Although many partners write out a general partnership agreement, in most situations it is not required. An example of a general partnership agreement is provided in this chapter.

The partners are free to negotiate any arrangement of duties, profits, and losses among themselves. In most states, there are only two types of partnerships: general partnerships and limited partnerships. We will address limited partnerships in the next chapter.

THE PARTNERSHIP AGREEMENT

The **partnership agreement** can contain any provision that the partners wish. The law is very fluid on this point. Partners are even free to create provisions contrary to the **Uniform Partnership Agreement** and common law theories. They are not free, however, to create a partnership that has illegal provisions. Courts will attempt to implement the terms of the partnership agreement, even when the clauses are difficult to understand. See Exhibit 4–1.

partnership agreement The contract that sets out the duties, responsibilities, and benefits of the persons who have agreed to enter into a partnership with one another.

Uniform Partnership Agreement A model act designed as a guideline for state legislation for partnership law.

Exhibit 4–1. Partnership Agreement (Courtesy of West, a Thomson business)

Partnership agreement made on _____ [date], between _____ of _____ [address], _____ [city], _____ County, _____ [state], and _____, of _____ [address], _____ [city], _____ County, _____ [state] (the "partners").

In consideration of the mutual covenants contained in this agreement, the partners form a partnership in accordance with the Uniform Partnership Act of _____ [state], on the terms and conditions set forth below:

ARTICLE ONE.
NAME, PURPOSE AND PLACE OF BUSINESS

The name of the partnership shall be _____. The business to be carried on by the partnership is that of _____. The principal place of business of the partnership shall be located at _____ [address], _____ [city], _____ County, _____ [state], and at such other places as may be mutually agreed on by the parties.

ARTICLE TWO.
DURATION

The partnership shall begin on _____ [date], and shall continue until dissolved by mutual agreement of the parties.

(continued)

Exhibit 4–1. Partnership Agreement (Courtesy of West, a Thomson business) *(continued)*

ARTICLE THREE.
CAPITAL CONTRIBUTIONS

The capital of the partnership is to be $_____. Each partner is to contribute the following amounts:

Name	Amount
_____	$_____
_____	$_____
_____	$_____

The contributions of all partners must be made to the partnership on or before _____ [date], or this agreement shall be void and of no effect.

ARTICLE FOUR.
SHARING PROFITS AND LOSSES

Each of the partners shall share in the profits and losses of the business on the following basis: _____ [specify in detail].

ARTICLE FIVE.
SERVICES OF PARTNERS

Each of the partners shall give his or her undivided time and attention to the business and shall use the utmost endeavors to promote the interests of the partnership.

ARTICLE SIX.
BOOKS OF ACCOUNT

Books of account of the transactions of the partnership shall be kept at the principal place of business, and shall be available at all times for inspection by any partner. Each partner shall cause to be entered on the books an accurate account of all the partner's dealings, receipts, and expenditures for or on account of the partnership.

ARTICLE SEVEN.
ANNUAL ACCOUNTING AND INVENTORY

In the month of _____ of each year, a full and complete inventory of stock shall be taken, and a complete statement of the condition of the partnership shall be made, and an accounting between the partners shall be had. The profits or losses of the preceding year shall then be divided and paid or distributed. The fiscal

(continued)

Exhibit 4–1. Partnership Agreement (Courtesy of West, a Thomson business) *(continued)*

year of the partnership shall begin on the _____ day of _____ [month] of each year.

ARTICLE EIGHT.
WITHDRAWALS FOR LIVING EXPENSES

Each of the partners shall be permitted to draw from the funds of the partnership $_____ per _____ [month or as the case may be] for the partner's living expenses. The sums so drawn shall be charged to the partner and at the annual accounting, shall be charged against that partner's share of the profits. If the partner's share of the profits does not equal the sum so drawn, the partner shall at once become obligated to pay the deficiency to the partnership. The deficiency shall draw interest at the rate of _____% per year until paid.

ARTICLE NINE.
MANAGEMENT AND AUTHORITY

Partners shall have equal rights in the management and conduct of the partnership. Decisions shall be by majority vote.

ARTICLE TEN.
RESTRICTIONS ON POWERS OF PARTNERS

None of the partners shall become obligated as surety for any other person, or lend, spend or give any part of the partnership property, or draw or accept any bill, note, or other security in the name of the partnership, except in the due course of partnership business, without the consent of all the partners.

ARTICLE ELEVEN.
RETIREMENT

Any of the partners may retire from the partnership at the expiration of any fiscal year on giving the other partners _____ days' written notice of the partner's intention to do so.

ARTICLE TWELVE.
CONTINUATION OR TERMINATION

A. Election by Partners. On the dissolution of the partnership by reason of death, withdrawal, or other act of any partner before the termination of the term specified below, the remaining partners may continue the business. In the event the remaining partners so elect to

(continued)

Exhibit 4–1. Partnership Agreement (Courtesy of West, a Thomson business) *(continued)*

continue, they shall have the right to purchase the interest of the other partner by paying to that partner or the legal representative of the partner the value of the interest, in the manner set forth below:

1. *Appointment of Appraisers.* The partners electing to continue the business shall appoint one individual as an appraiser and the withdrawing partner or the legal representative of the deceased or incapacitated partner shall appoint one individual as an appraiser. The appraisers so appointed shall determine the value of the assets of the partnership, and the partners electing to continue the business shall pay to the withdrawing partner or legal representative of the partner _____ [fraction or percentage] of the amount so determined. The withdrawing partner or the legal representative shall execute such documents as may be necessary to convey the partner's interest in the partnership to the other partners.

2. *Additional Appraiser in Event of Disagreement.* In the event the appraisers are unable to agree on the value of the assets of the partnership within _____ [days] after their appointment, they shall select and designate one additional appraiser for this purpose whose appraisement shall be binding on all parties. If any appraiser should become unable or unwilling to serve, a substitute shall be appointed by the person originally selecting the appraiser. If the two appraisers first appointed shall be unable to agree on a third appraiser, the third appraiser shall be appointed by _____.

B. Rights and Obligations of Continuing Partners. The partners continuing the business shall assume all of the legal obligations of the partnership and shall indemnify the withdrawing partner or the legal representative of a partner against all liability on those obligations. _____ [If desired, add: The partners continuing the business may continue to use the partnership name.]

ARTICLE THIRTEEN.
DISSOLUTION

In the event that all the partners agree to dissolve the partnership, the business shall be wound up, the debts paid, and the surplus divided among the partners according to their respective interests.

(continued)

Exhibit 4–1. Partnership Agreement (Courtesy of West, a Thomson business) *(continued)*

> ### ARTICLE FOURTEEN.
> ### AMENDMENTS
>
> This agreement, except with respect to vested rights of partners, may be amended at any time by a majority vote as measured by the interest in the sharing of profits and losses.
>
> The parties have executed this agreement at _____ [designate place of execution] on the day and year first above written.
>
> **[Signatures]**[6]

*Am. Jur. LF § 194:19.

No Requirement for Written Agreement

In most situations, there is no requirement that the partnership agreement be in writing. Businesses have been run for years with no written agreement between partners. As long as the basic agreement takes into account the minimum requirements of a contract, then there is a binding partnership agreement, even if it is never reduced to writing.

 GETTING TO THE BASICS

> Although there is no requirement that a partnership agreement be reduced to writing, it is a good practice and can help avoid misunderstandings early on in the process.

Terms of the Partnership Agreement

Obviously, the partnership agreement will set out the basic issues, such as how profits and losses will be distributed between the partners. Other provisions might include the duration of the partnership, property rights in the personal property contributed to the partnership, and any other term that the partners deem to be important. The establishment of a partnership relationship does not depend on equal contributions by the partners. In fact, one partner may contribute all of the start-up capital, while the other partner contributes only his or her efforts and labor. Courts have been very liberal in permitting partners to arrange their affairs as they see fit. Consider Scenario 4–2.

Scenario 4–2. N&L Lawn Association

Ned is nineteen years old and has been running a lawn business for a few months to save money for college. He has done so well that he needs help. Although Ned would like to have one of his friends work with him, Ned's mother suggests that Ned should talk to his sister, Lisa. She is eighteen, and as much as Ned would hate to admit it, she is a good worker. Ned also suspects that some of his friends would slack off and not get the work done. Swallowing his objections, he works out the following agreement with his sister:

> *"I, Ned, agree to work with you, Lisa, to run N&L Lawn Association. We will split the profits 60-40. I'll get 60% of whatever we make; you'll get 40%. I'll run the mower and you'll do the trim work, like running the weed whacker and trimming bushes and stuff."*

(Signed) Ned

(Signed) Lisa

Is this a partnership agreement?

Answer: Absolutely. Ned and Lisa are now partners in a business to make money. All of the requirements for a partnership agreement are met.

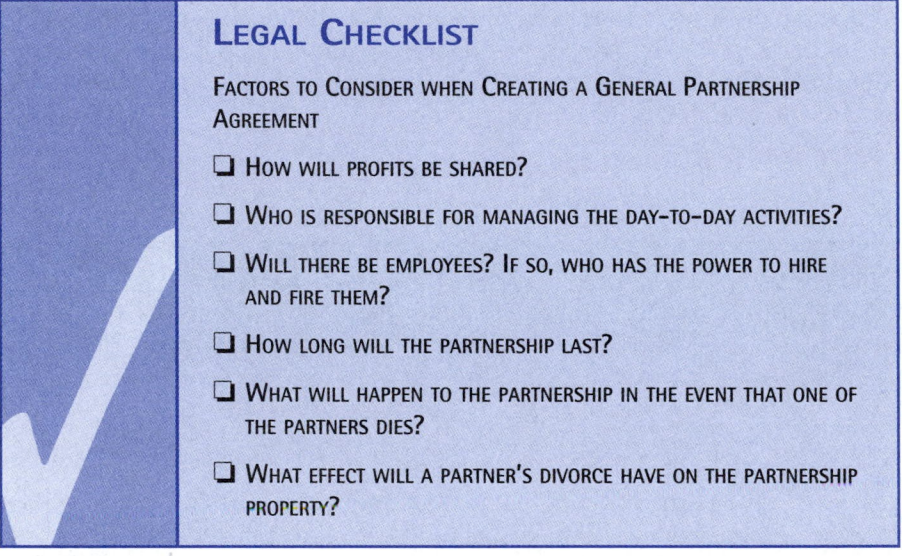

LEGAL CHECKLIST

FACTORS TO CONSIDER WHEN CREATING A GENERAL PARTNERSHIP AGREEMENT

❑ HOW WILL PROFITS BE SHARED?

❑ WHO IS RESPONSIBLE FOR MANAGING THE DAY-TO-DAY ACTIVITIES?

❑ WILL THERE BE EMPLOYEES? IF SO, WHO HAS THE POWER TO HIRE AND FIRE THEM?

❑ HOW LONG WILL THE PARTNERSHIP LAST?

❑ WHAT WILL HAPPEN TO THE PARTNERSHIP IN THE EVENT THAT ONE OF THE PARTNERS DIES?

❑ WHAT EFFECT WILL A PARTNER'S DIVORCE HAVE ON THE PARTNERSHIP PROPERTY?

TRANSFER OF PARTNERSHIP PROPERTY INTERESTS

During the course of a partnership, some partners may wish to transfer their interests to someone outside the original agreement, essentially creating a new member of the partnership. Partners may wish to buy out other partners, dwindling the size of the partnership, and some partners may wish to retire from the partnership entirely. All of these situations create potential problems for the partnership. For instance, there is a common law rule that holds that a general partnership is automatically terminated when any of the original partners dies or otherwise withdraws from the partnership. There are also provisions that provide that the addition of a new partner may terminate the old partnership and create a new one in its place. Because of these difficulties, the Uniform Partnership Act provides mechanisms that allow a partnership to continue to exist on the death or retirement of a partner and also allow partnership interests to be transferred to others. See Exhibit 4–2.

Exhibit 4–2. Transfer of partner's transferable interest

(a) A transfer, in whole or in part, of a partner's transferable interest in the partnership:

(1) is permissible;
(2) does not by itself cause the partner's dissociation or a dissolution and winding up of the partnership business; and
(3) does not, as against the other partners or the partnership, entitle the transferee, during the continuance of the partnership, to participate in the management or conduct of the partnership business, to require access to information concerning partnership transactions, or to inspect or copy the partnership books or records.

(b) A transferee of a partner's transferable interest in the partnership has a right:

(1) to receive, in accordance with the transfer, distributions to which the transferor would otherwise be entitled;
(2) to receive upon the dissolution and winding up of the partnership business, in accordance with the transfer, the net amount otherwise distributable to the transferor; and
(3) to seek under Section 801(6) a judicial determination that it is equitable to wind up the partnership business.*

---

*Uniform Partnership Act 1997 § 503. By permission of the National Conference of Comissioners on Uniform State Law.

INVOLUNTARY PARTNERSHIP

Although courts sometimes impose a contract where none exists, that is never the case with partnerships. When a person enters a contract, she does so of her own free will. Courts will not impose partnership agreements on individuals; they enter the agreement voluntarily or not at all. The main reason for this requirement is the entire purpose of creating a general partnership in the first place: A partnership is an agreement between individuals to pool resources to achieve a common goal. Therefore, the law does not have a provision for the creation of an "involuntary" partnership. All members must enter the business enterprise voluntarily and with full knowledge of the details of their business transaction.

NAMING OF THE PARTNERSHIP

In most situations, the name of the partnership must contain the name of at least one of the partners. The partnership name is important, because the business builds its reputation with the public on the name, and if the partners wish to sell the business, the name is part of the goodwill that makes up the sale price. Although the Uniform Partnership Act does not impose any naming restrictions, most states have regulations that require a business to use the name of an owner or to register a fictitious name with the state. Although a partnership agreement can stipulate that the firm will continue using a partner's name after he or she retires, most states have laws that require the firm to stop using the name when the partner dies. See Exhibit 4–3.

Exhibit 4–3. Fictitious name registration—general partnership

FILING FEES:
INITIAL CERTIFICATE $50.00
AMENDED CERTIFICATE $25.00
CANCEL $25.00

PRINT CLEARLY

PARTNERSHIP FICTITIOUS NAME

Check the appropriate action: • Initial Certificate   • Amended Certificate   • Cancel

Oklahoma Secretary of State, 2300 N. Lincoln Blvd., Room 101, State Capitol Building, Oklahoma City, OK 73105-4897
Telephone (405)-521-3912

The undersigned, hereby submits the following fictitious name certificate pursuant to Title 54, Oklahoma Statutes, Sections 81, 84 or 84.1:

1.   The fictitious name to be registered:

_____

2.   The partnership was formed under the laws of the State/Country of _____

3.   The names in full of all the members **and** their resident street addresses:

NAME   **RESIDENCE STREET ADDRESS**

_____
(Use attachment if necessary)

4.   The physical office address of the partnership:

_____

(continued)

Exhibit 4–3. Fictitious name registration—general partnership *(continued)*

<u>**MUST BE SIGNED BY AT LEAST TWO PARTNERS**</u>

_____   _____
Print Name of Partner   Signature of Partner

_____   _____
Print Name of Partner   Signature of Partner

_____   _____
Print Name of Partner   Signature of Partner

_____   _____
Print Name of Partner   Signature of Partner

(SOS FORM 107-06/2001)

▶ PARTNERSHIP LIABILITY CONCERNS

Another feature of partnership is that each partner has **joint and several liability** for the debts incurred by any of the other partners. This means that if one partner assumes a debt, all partners assume it. Partners are also liable for the torts committed by any of the other partners. This is also true of business transactions. One partner can bind all of the other partners when he or she negotiates with third parties.[6]

joint and several liability When two or more persons are liable for the actions of either.

▶ GETTING TO THE BASICS

Partners are liable for the actions of the other partners.

SUING A PARTNERSHIP

Because partners share in profits, losses, and the day-to-day management of the business, each partner is liable for the actions of the other partners, at least for the actions carried out within the scope of the business. When a party has a claim against the partnership, **service of process** on one of the partners is sufficient notice for all partners. If the partner fails to inform the other partners about the suit and the partnership fails to file a response to the complaint, a **default judgment** may be obtained against all of the partners.

service of process The service of a civil claim, such as a complaint for damages, on the defendant in the suit.

default judgment A judgment for the full amount requested in the complaint when the defendant fails to file an answer to the complaint.

TERMINATING THE PARTNERSHIP

A partnership can be terminated by any of a number of means. They include:

- by agreement
- by contractual terms
- by bankruptcy
- by death of a partner

By Agreement

The partners are allowed to reach an agreement to end the partnership at any time that they see fit. Although there are provisions controlling how the partnership is dissolved, especially in regard to paying off creditors, partnerships are voluntary agreements, and they can be dissolved when the parties agree.

By Contract Terms

Partnerships can be created with provisions that they will exist only for a stated period of time. Although most partnership agreements leave the termination date open-ended, either form is valid. Partners may have very good reasons for limiting the term of the partnership to a specific time frame, such as five years. When a partnership agreement has a specified date for termination, then barring any modification of the agreement, it terminates on that date.

By Bankruptcy

When the partnership goes into Chapter 7 bankruptcy, the business assets are liquidated and the partnership is dissolved. However, if the business goes through Chapter 11 repayment, the partnership may emerge from bankruptcy with its structure intact.

By Death of a Partner

Unless a provision is inserted in the partnership agreement that makes some alternate arrangements, the partnership terminates on the death of any of the partners. There may be a good reason to insert a clause in the partnership agreement that permits the business to continue running after the death of the one of the partners, such as being able to continue using partnership accounts, but there must be a provision in the agreement that spells out this right.

DISSOLVING THE PARTNERSHIP

When the partners decide to dissolve the business, the partnership does not terminate immediately. Instead, the law requires a period of "winding up" that allows the partnership to pay off its outstanding debts and to make disbursements of profits. Winding up refers to the entire process of paying off outstanding debts, settling civil cases, reimbursing partners and employees for out-of-pocket expenses, and, finally, distributing profits. When a partnership has a net gain once all outstanding claims have been satisfied, this profit will be distributed among the partners according to the partnership agreement. This is the point where the internal designations of senior or junior partner can have a huge impact. A senior partner is entitled to a larger percentage of the pool of profits than is a junior partner. Of course, if there are no funds remaining after the winding up of business, then partners may be jointly and severally liable for any unpaid debts.

Ethics File: When Partners Steal

We addressed the issue of fiduciaries in the last chapter. Like agents, partners are fiduciaries for one another. When someone is a fiduciary, the law imposes on that person a duty to act honestly and fairly for the benefit of someone else. Because general partners must act in the best interests of the other partners, if any partner is stealing from the business, that partner is violating a basic obligation to the other partners. Proof that a partner is stealing from the business could be sufficient grounds to remove that partner from the partnership. However, the issue becomes cloudy when a partnership is being dissolved and there is no clear provision in the partnership agreement about what to do with the partnership property. Similarly, problems can arise when there is no clear agreement about how profits and losses will be shared among the partners. This is why having a partnership agreement in writing can be extremely important to businesses. Legal professionals should always avoid even the appearance of helping a partner take property or cash from the business that the partner is not entitled to receive.

CASE LAW: *Illegal Partnership?*

Williams v. Burrus[7]
ANDERSEN, Judge.

This is an appeal from a judgment of the trial court holding that a contract relating to the operation of a restaurant and cocktail lounge is illegal and refusing to enforce it.

The plaintiff, Paul J. Williams, sued the defendants, Richard Burrus and wife, for dissolution of a partnership between Williams and Burrus and for an accounting and distribution to Williams of his claimed share of the partnership assets.

Williams and Burrus had entered into a written agreement on March 22, 1974, to purchase the Skagit Inn Restaurant in Mount Vernon. The restaurant, later known as the Maple Leaf Three, had a class H liquor license. The agreement provided in substance that Williams would put up certain property as collateral for a bank loan to assist Burrus in purchasing the business. The agreement also was to the effect that the business was to be in Burrus' name and Burrus alone would apply for a transfer of the liquor license without revealing Williams' interest in the business. At the time, Williams was known to be unacceptable to the Washington State Liquor Control Board as a licensee.

Following a trial to the court, the trial court found that the Defendant Richard Burrus or Plaintiff and Defendant making a joint application would in all probability have not received a Class H license if disclosure had been made of the foregoing partnership agreement or financial interest of the Plaintiff. The Court further finds the Plaintiff and Defendants entered into the partnership agreement dated March 22, 1974, for an illegal purpose to conceal the interest of the Plaintiff Paul Williams in the purchase of the business and exposing the name of Defendant Richard Burrus as the sole owner, knowing at the time that the identity of Plaintiff Paul Williams as a partner, co-owner, or investor would in all probability cause a rejection by the liquor board of the application for the Class H liquor license. The Court further finds that

(continued)

CASE LAW: *Illegal Partnership?* *(continued)*

this concealment was a joint effort on the part of Plaintiff and Defendants to enter into an illegal relationship for an illegal purpose and accordingly finds the partnership of Plaintiff and Defendants to be an illegal partnership.

Finding of fact No. 3 (part).

The trial court then concluded that the agreement between the parties being illegal was unenforceable and dismissed the complaint of the plaintiff Williams.

One central issue is presented.

Did the trial court err in refusing to grant the plaintiff any relief?

Courts will not assist in the dissolution of an illegal partnership or entertain an action for an accounting or distribution of its assets. The trial court's decision was not erroneous.

Where, as here, no error is assigned to the findings of fact, our review is limited to determining whether the challenged conclusions of law are supported by the findings. Jordin v. Vauthiers, 89 Wash.2d 725, 728, 575 P.2d 709 (1978).

No state retail liquor license of any kind can be issued to a partnership unless all of the members thereof are qualified to obtain a license, and no licenseholder can allow any other person to use such a license.

Furthermore, a partnership is dissolved by any event which makes it unlawful for the business of the partnership to be carried on or for the members to carry it on in partnership. RCW 25.04.310(3).

The issue of illegality may be raised at any time. Waring v. Lobdell, 63 Wash.2d 532, 533-34, 387 P.2d 979 (1964).

Under the general rule that the courts will not aid either party to an illegal agreement where a partnership is formed to carry out an illegal business or to conduct a lawful business in an illegal manner, the courts will refuse to aid any of the parties thereto in an action against the other. Brower v. Johnson, 56 Wash.2d 321, 324-25, 352 P.2d 814 (1960); 59 Am.Jur. 2d Partnership s 24 (1971); 68 C.J.S. Partnership S 7

(1950). The present case is not one wherein the promise sued upon is only remotely or collaterally related to the illegal transaction and not illegal in and of itself. See Sherwood & Roberts-Yakima, Inc. v. Cohan, 2 Wash.App. 703, 710-17, 469 P.2d 574 (1970) and cases therein discussed. The trial court did not err in deciding as it did.

Plaintiff's further claim that the trial court erred in refusing his request to reopen the case in order to present additional evidence is likewise not well taken. Such a motion is addressed to the sound discretion of the trial court. Rogers Walla Walla, Inc. v. Ballard, 16 Wash.App. 81, 90, 553 P.2d 1372 (1976). The proffered evidence was that the defendant had taken an inconsistent position, that the contract was not illegal, at an administrative hearing before the Liquor Control Board. Such evidence was cumulative only and the trial court did not abuse its discretion by denying the motion to reopen. Rogers Walla Walla, Inc. v. Ballard, supra. On that same basis, the plaintiff was not entitled to a new trial on the ground that such evidence constituted newly discovered evidence. Simpson Timber Co. v. Ljutic Indus., Inc., 1 Wash.App. 631, 638-39, 463 P.2d 243 (1969).

Affirmed.

CASE QUESTIONS

1. What was the basic partnership agreement between Burrus and Williams?

2. According to the court, what was the illegal purpose of this partnership?

3. When may the issue of illegality be raised in a partnership?

4. Why does the court refuse to enforce the partnership agreement between Burrus and Williams?

5. According to the court, what role does a court play when it discovers that a partnership agreement is illegal?

SUMMARY

General partnerships have several distinct advantages over the sole proprietorship model that we discussed in chapter 1. Individual business owners can pool their resources and take advantage of each other's expertise in expanding their business. Partners function as fiduciaries to one another, keeping the best interests of the business in mind as they negotiate their business deals. Traditionally, partnership was seen as a contractual relationship, but in more recent times, especially with the adoption of the Uniform Partnership Act, general partnerships have come to be seen as a hybrid between contract law and a business entity. This hybrid model allows general partnerships to own property in their own right under tenancy by partnership. General partnerships are created by the consent of the parties and exist as long as the parties desire. Partnerships terminate on the death of the partner, by voluntary agreement, and by other means.

HELPFUL WEB SITES

Uniform Partnership Act
http://www.law.upenn.edu

Delaware Uniform Partnership Act
http://www.delcode.state.de.us/title6

KEY TERMS

capacity	partnership agreement
consideration	service of process
default judgment	silent partner
general partnership	tenancy by partnership
joint and several liability	Uniform Partnership Agreement
legality	unlimited liability
mutual assent	

APPLYING CHAPTER CONCEPTS

You have decided that you want to open a paralegal firm with another paralegal, who is also a good friend of yours. Draft a general partnership agreement that anticipates the following:

- the way profits and losses will be shared in the partnership
- the ownership of personal property

- the effect of a partner's death on the general partnership
- any other provisions you think are important

REVIEW QUESTIONS

1. Is a general partnership agreement required to be in writing? Why or why not?
2. Explain the concept of tenancy by partnership.
3. Explain some of the ways that a partnership is created.
4. What duties do general partners owe one another?
5. What is the Uniform Partnership Act?
6. What is the effect of the negotiation where only one partner agrees to be bound to a contract, without the consent or knowledge of the other partners?
7. Who is responsible for running the day-to-day activities of a general partnership?
8. What is a "silent partner"?
9. What are some of the methods for terminating a general partnership?
10. What does the term "winding up" mean when it is applied to general partnerships?
11. What features should a written general partnership agreement contain?
12. Is a partnership a contract, or is it some other form of legal arrangement? Explain your answer.
13. What effect does a finding of illegality have on the partnership?
14. Explain the court's decision in this chapter's "Case law: Illegal Partnership."
15. What are the rules governing how partners may name their business?

QUESTIONS FOR REFLECTION

1. Can you frame an argument that a general partnership should be considered solely a creature of statute, like corporations, rather than a hybrid between statutes and contract law?
2. Why was it necessary to adopt the Uniform Partnership Act?
3. What details in Scenario 4–1, involving Juan and Dale, would have changed the court's ruling? Would it have helped if Juan had been more specific? What additional information can you add to the scenario to change the result?

ENDNOTES

[1]*Heck & Paetow Claim Service, Inc. v. Heck,* 93 Wis. 2d 349, 286 N.W.2d 831 (1980).

[2]*Chocknok v. State, Commercial Fisheries Entry Com'n,* 696 P.2d 669 (Alaska 1985).

[3]50 S.E. 175 (Ga. 1905).

[4]*Dinkelspeel v. Lewis,* 50 Wyo. 380, 65 P.2d 246 (1937).

[5]*Matter of Ward,* 6 B.R. 93 (Bankr. M.D. Fla. 1980).

[6]*First American Title Ins. Co. v. Lawson,* 351 N.J. Super. 407, 798 A.2d 661 (App. Div. 2002).

[7]20 Wash.App. 494, 581 P.2d 164 (Wash.App. 1978).

Chapter 5

LIMITED PARTNERSHIPS

Chapter Objectives

Upon completion of this chapter, you should be able to:

- Explain the concept of limited liability as it applies to the organization and function of a limited partnership.
- Describe the internal organization of a limited partnership.
- Distinguish between general partnerships and limited partnerships.
- Explain the role of state statutes in the creation of limited partnerships.
- Describe the requirements placed on limited partnerships in naming and running the day-to-day operation of the business.

▶ INTRODUCTION

Up to this point, our discussions of business entities have focused on the assets and abilities that the owners bring to the business. However, sole proprietorships and general partnerships suffer from one important limitation: unlimited liability. Both forms of business leave the individual owner susceptible to business debts and judgments that could wipe out their personal assets. The possibility of losing personal assets discourages investors. After all, who would be willing to invest in any business where the potential downside could be the loss of your financial assets? Limited partnerships were the first type of business structure designed to remedy this shortcoming.

A limited partnership takes the basic arrangement found in a general partnership and adds the protection of limited liability. Unlike sole proprietorships and general partnerships, limited partnerships are the first example we have addressed in this text where state statutes create the basic framework for the business. Prior to this point, sole proprietorships and general partnerships were both creatures that had existed in one form or another for centuries and continue to have relatively few statutory restrictions. But this is not true of limited partnerships.

KEY POINT

Under limited liability, a person who qualifies as a limited partner limits his or her maximum possible legal obligation to the total amount of investment in the business.

LIMITED PARTNERSHIPS

In a limited partnership, the business is structured in such a way that there are general partners, who have the same role (and the same liability) as partners in a general partnership, and there are limited partners, who do not face liability for business debts. These partners limit their losses to the amount of their investment in the business, thus making them limited partners. These partners cannot control day-to-day operations of the business, but are shielded by limited liability. General partners perform the same duties in this business structure as they do in general partnerships, but they have a bigger pool of assets to draw upon.

Unlike other business entities, limited partnerships are strictly creatures of statute. They have no common law history to draw upon. Every state has a separate statute authorizing the creation, operation, and termination of limited partnerships.

GETTING TO THE BASICS

In a limited partnership, general partners fulfill the same roles and perform the same duties as they do in a general partnership; they also face personal liability. Limited partners are protected by limited liability.

LIMITED PARTNERSHIPS' AUTHORIZATION BY STATE STATUTES

Because limited partnerships are creatures of statute, not of case law, old common law cases and interpretations do not apply to limited partnerships as they often do to general partnerships. Research on the law of limited partnerships should concentrate on state statutes and the cases that apply them, rather than on the large body of case law devoted to partnership issues. In many ways, limited partnerships have more in common with corporations than they do with general partnerships. In many ways, a limited partnership is a hybrid between the legal structures of general partnerships and corporations. Partnership law, after all, developed out of the legal consequences that occurred when two sole proprietors decided to combine assets. Corporations, as we will see in future chapters, are entirely creatures of statute and actually classified as artificial persons. Like corporations, limited partnerships are created by statutes, which authorize the creation, operation, and termination of limited partnerships. See Exhibit 5–1.

Exhibit 5–1. New York's statute authorizing the creation of limited partnerships

---

§91. Formation

(1) Two or more persons desiring to form a limited partnership shall

    (a) Sign and acknowledge or swear to a certificate, which shall state.

        I. The name of the partnership.
        II. The character of the business.
        III. The location of the principal place of business.
        IV. The name and place of residence of each member; general and limited partners being respectively designated.
        V. The term for which the partnership is to exist.
        VI. The amount of cash and a description of and the agreed value of the other property contributed by each limited partner.
        VII. The additional contributions, if any, agreed to be made by each limited partner and the times at which or events on the happening of which they shall be made.
        VIII. The time, if agreed upon, when the contribution of each limited partner is to be returned.
        IX. The share of the profits or the other compensation by way of income which each limited partner shall receive by reason of his contribution.
        X. The right, if given, of a limited partner to substitute an assignee as contributor in his place, and the terms and conditions of the substitution.
        XI. The right, if given, of the partners to admit additional limited partners.
        XII. The right, if given, of one or more of the limited partners to priority over other limited partners, as to contributions

---

(continued)

Exhibit 5–1. New York's statute authorizing the creation of limited partnerships
(continued)

> or as to compensation by way of income, and the nature of such priority.
>
> XIII. The right, if given, of the remaining general partner or partners to continue the business on the death, retirement or insanity of a general partner, and
>
> XIV. The right, if given, of a limited partner to demand and receive property other than cash in return for his contribution.
>
> (b) File the certificate in the office of the county clerk of the county in which the principal office of such partnership is located. Immediately after the filing of the certificate, a copy of the same or a notice containing the substance thereof, shall be published once in each week for six successive weeks, in two newspapers of the county in which such original certificate is filed, to be designated by the county clerk, one of which newspapers shall be a newspaper published in the city or town in which the principal place of business is intended to be located, if a newspaper be published therein; or, if no newspaper is published therein, in the newspaper nearest thereto, and proof of such publication by the affidavit of the printer or publisher of each of such newspapers must be filed with the original certificate.*

*McKinney's Consolidated Laws of New York Ann., Partnership Law § 91.

 GETTING TO THE BASICS

Limited partnerships are really a hybrid between general partnerships and corporations.

UNIFORM LIMITED PARTNERSHIP ACT

Uniform Limited Partnership Act
A model act that serves as a guideline for state legislation governing limited partnership.

There has been a long history of uniform acts related to limited partnerships in the United States. The first of these acts, the **Uniform Limited Partnership Act,** was created in 1916. Other versions have followed. There have been major revisions to the Uniform Limited Partnership Act in 1976, 1985, and 2001. Each of these acts has sought to correct mistakes and omissions in previous acts. However, the basic formulation of limited partnership remains the same: general partners manage the business, limited partners share the profits and losses of the business but have no input on day-to-day management.

 ### Getting to the Basics

Most states define a limited partnership as a business comprising of one or more general partners, who manage the business and remain personally liable, and one of more limited partners, who enjoy limited liability.

Sidebar

The 2001 revision of the Uniform Limited Partnership Act was created as a complete legislative packet; it could be adopted wholesale by state legislatures, without reference to other statutes or enabling acts.

Differences between Limited Partnerships and General Partnerships

The most important difference between general partnerships and limited partnerships is the issue of **limited liability.** General partners always face the risk of losing their personal assets in the event that the business goes into bankruptcy or is assessed with a large judgment. Limited partners face no such impediment. The extent of a limited partner's liability is the investment. In the event of a business bankruptcy or civil judgment, the most that the limited partner can lose is the amount of money invested in the business. However, with this protection come limitations. Unlike general partners, limited partners are prohibited from taking an active role in the business. They cannot manage the day-to-day affairs, negotiate contracts, or hire and fire employees. All of those rights remain vested in the general partner.

limited liability A legal concept that, when used in the context of business, refers to the protection of an investor's assets. Potential loss is limited to the total amount invested in the venture, not the investor's total assets.

 ### Getting to the Basics

Limited partners do not have the power or authority to bind the business to contracts, handle day-to-day business affairs, or participate in the management of the business.

One way of explaining the rights of the general partner in a limited partnership is to say that the general partner in a limited partnership operates in almost exactly the same way that the general partner would in a regular partnership. The partner faces extensive liability, but counterbalances that with the right to conduct the business relatively free from interference by anyone except other general partners. General partners are free to make decisions affecting the course of the business and do not have to seek approval from the limited partners. However, unlike the case with general partnerships, there is a larger pool of investors. A business can have dozens, or even hundreds, of limited partners. This expands the potential assets of a company far beyond what is seen in a typical general partnership. Although many commentators have said that a limited partnership is a hybrid between a general partnership and a corporation, many would argue that this business model has more in common with corporate principles than general partnership law. In many ways, a limited partner resembles a shareholder in a corporation. Both enjoy protection under limited liability, and both are barred from running the day-to-day operations of the business.[1]

ADVANTAGES OF LIMITED PARTNERSHIPS

The advantage of a limited partnership is that it provides a vehicle for individuals to invest money in a business without the threat of personal liability for business losses and debts. Limited partners share in both profits and losses of the business, but only to the extent of their investment. Unlike general partners, limited partners cannot be sued for business debts or held liable for actions carried out by the business. In exchange for this protection, limited partners are prohibited from running the day-to-day operations of the business or from dictating business policies and decisions to the general partners. Besides providing a vehicle for profits, the limited partnership structure also has important advantages when it comes to personal income taxes.

Tax Consequences of Limited Partnerships

Limited partners are permitted to "pass through" business losses on their personal income tax returns. Because the limited partner is not considered a separate legal entity, like a corporation, individual partners pay income taxes on business profits. This means that if the business shows a loss for a particular year, this loss may be reflected on the individual partner's income tax return, giving the partner a paper loss that might actually improve the limited partner's overall tax liability for the year.

KEY POINT

> Limited partnerships can have important tax consequences.

The Limited Partner's Contribution

In order to enter into a limited partnership agreement, the limited partner must invest in the company. This investment is normally referred to as a **contribution.** The extent of the contribution reflects the percentage of the limited partner's rights to profits from the enterprise. For instance, a minimum contribution might be set at $1,000. This contribution equals 1 percent ownership in the partnership. This would entitle the limited partner to 1 percent of the profits, should any occur.

Although a limited partner's contribution usually comes in the form of a cash investment, the law allows other types of contribution. For instance, a limited partner can contribute property or services in lieu of a cash investment in the business. The Uniform Limited Partnership Act is liberal on the topic of what constitutes a contribution, so long as the contribution consists of something of value.[2] Why would a partnership allow someone to invest something other than cash in the business? Consider Scenario 5–1.

Scenario 5–1. Maria's Van

A group of friends is considering opening a catering business. They decide to form a general partnership. They will each contribute money to the enterprise, but soon they realize that they don't have enough money to purchase a van that will help them buy supplies and deliver the food to events. Another friend named Maria has a van, but no interest in getting involved in the business. The partners approach her with a proposition: Maria can be a limited partner, and her van will constitute her contribution to the business. They set a value on the van and determine that the van is worth 10 percent of any profits that they make on the business. They have the makings of a limited partnership. Assuming that they complete the appropriate filings with the state, they can run their business as a limited partnership, with Maria as the sole limited partner.

Scenario 5–2. The Renegotiated Agreement

Ingrid enters into an agreement with several other partners to run a company that provides business advice to local firms. Under the partnership agreement, Ingrid is forbidden to engage in any negotiations on behalf of the partnership or to purchase items for the partnership without the full consent of the other partners. Later, her partners renegotiate the partnership agreement, excluding her from all business dealings. Has Ingrid become a limited partner?

Answer: No. Because limited partnerships must be created by express provisions in an agreement, as well as filings done with the state, they cannot be created by implication or assumption on the part of the parties. They must be created by strict adherence to statutory guidelines. This means that Ingrid is not a limited partner unless the parties all agree to form a limited partnership.[3]

► CREATION OF A LIMITED PARTNERSHIP

As we saw in the previous chapter, general partnerships can be created under a variety of means. For instance, a general partnership may be created by implication, informal agreement, or even, under certain circumstances, judicial intervention. None of these methods can be used to create a limited partnership. Instead, a limited partnership comes into existence only after the strict statutory guidelines have been complied with. The most important of the statutory requirements is the **certificate of limited partnership.**

certificate of limited partnership
An official filing with the state, setting out the organizational details of the limited partnership.

Scenario 5–3. The Neglected Certificate

Four individuals decide to create a limited partnership. Two will act as general partners, while the other two will act as limited partners. After their negotiations, they write up a memorandum of understanding, but fail to file the certificate of limited partnership with the state. Have they successfully created a limited partnership?

Answer: No. Because limited partnerships come into existence only after a certificate of limited partnership has been filed with the state, until that document is filed, no limited partnership exists. Even though the parties clearly intended to enter into a limited partnership, their failure to follow the correct procedures will result in a ruling that no limited partnership was created.[4]

THE CERTIFICATE OF LIMITED PARTNERSHIP

All states require that any business considering operating as a limited partnership must file appropriate documentation with the state. One of the most important of these documents is the certificate of limited partnership. See Exhibit 5–2. State governments require the following minimum information in the certificate of limited partnership:

- the name of the limited partnership
- the street and mailing address of the agent for service of process
- the street and mailing address of the designated office of the limited partnership
- the name, street and mailing addresses of all general partners

Naming of a Limited Partnership

Different states have different approaches to the names that can be used in limited partnerships. The most common limitations for naming limited partnerships include:

- Limited partnerships cannot contain the name of a limited partner.
- Limited partnerships can bear the name of a general partner.
- The name of the partnership must include the words "limited partnership" or the letters "LP" or "L.P."
- Limited partnerships cannot use a name that is substantially similar to a preexisting business.

Reserving a Name

In most states, the secretary of state office allows businesses to reserve names for a period of 120 days prior to filing the certificate of limited partnership. In this way, a business can prevent others from taking the name that the business intends to use.[5] However, different states follow different rules when it comes to reserving names and the length of time that a particular name can be reserved.

Exhibit 5–2. Certificate of limited partnership, Missouri

State of Missouri
Robin Carnahan, Secretary of State

Corporations Division
P.O. Box 778 / 600 W. Main Street, Rm 322
Jefferson City, MO 65102

Certificate of Limited Partnership
(Submit with filing fee of $105.00)

The undersigned general partner(s) for the purpose of forming a limited partnership under the Missouri Uniform Limited Partnership Law state the following:

1. The name of the limited partnership is (must include "L.P.", "LP", or "Limited Partnership" in the name):

    _____

2. The name and address of the limited partnership's initial registered agent in this state is:

    _____

    Name   *Street Address*   *(P.O. Box may only be used in addition to a physical street address)*   *City/State/Zip*

3. The name and mailing address of each general partner is (if G.P. is a Corporation, this Certificate must be signed below by an authorized person. Also, include the state of domestication):

    _____

    _____

    Name   *Street Address*   *City/State/Zip*

4. The events, if any, on which the limited partnership is to dissolve or the number of years the limited partnership is to continue, which may be any number or perpetual: _____

5. Any other matters the general partners want to include (may attach additional pages):

    _____

6. The effective date of this document is the date it is filed by the Secretary of State of Missouri, unless you indicate a future date, as follows:

    _____

    Date may not be more than 90 days after the filing date in this office

Please see next page

┌───┐
│ Name and address to return filed document: │
│   │
│ Name: _____   │
│ Address: _____   │
│ City, State, and Zip Code: _____   │
└───┘

LP- 41 (01/05)

(continued)

Exhibit 5–2. Certificate of limited partnership, Missouri *(continued)*

In Affirmation thereof, the facts stated above are true and correct:
(The undersigned understands that false statements made in this filing are subject to the penalties provided under Section 575.040, RSMo)

Signed by all general partners

_____
        Signature   *Printed Name*   *Date*

_____
        Signature   *Printed Name*   *Date*

_____
        Signature   *Printed Name*   *Date*

_____
        Signature   *Printed Name*   *Date*

LP- 41 (01/05)

Agent for Service of Process

An **agent for service of process** is a person or business that the limited partnership designates in its certificate to accept service of process. This means that if anyone wishes to sue the business, they will have a specific person designated to receive the pleadings. This is a common provision for more complex business organizational models, where it may not be easy to identify the persons who actually own the business. When we spoke of sole proprietors and general partners, a person who wished to bring suit against them would simply complete service of process on the business owners. However, when dealing with limited partnerships, limited liability companies, and especially with corporations, it would be extremely difficult to identify the correct person to be served so that the lawsuit can commence. Requiring these types of businesses to appoint a registered agent solves the problem. Service on this person is deemed service on the entire business.

Because a limited partnership enjoys the protections of limited liability, limited partners cannot be served with lawsuits seeking redress against the partnership. Instead, the limited partnership must designate an agent who will receive the pleadings. Service on this agent constitutes service on the business entity and triggers the deadlines that must be complied with by both sides to the action. As we saw in previous chapters, when suit is filed against general partnerships or sole proprietors, pleadings may simply be served on the business owners. However, from this point forward, as we discuss increasingly more complicated business entities and structures, we will see that almost all of these business entities are required to nominate an agent for service of process. This information must also be filed with the state. Before bringing suit against a limited partnership, a law firm must look up this information in order to verify the agent's name and address.

agent for service of process An individual authorized by a company to accept source of pleadings on behalf of the company.

Individuals Who Qualify as an Agent for Service of Process

An agent for service of process can be an individual who is a resident of the state or may be another form of business, such as a corporation, which is authorized to do business in the state. Regardless of the identity of the agent, the agent's address must be listed in the certificate of limited partnership so that the agent can be located and served with the appropriate paperwork.

Designated Office Address

In addition to selecting an agent for service of process, a limited partnership must also provide information to the state about the location of the main office for the partnership. This business address is where the partnership records are maintained. The reason for requiring this information with the certificate of limited partnership is so that if the state wishes to review the limited partnership records, it will know where to go to find them.

The General Partners

In addition to naming the limited partnership, identifying an agent for service of process, and maintaining records at a designated location, the certificate of limited partnership must also identify the general partners. These partners must be listed by name and address.

Individuals Who Qualify as a General Partner

One interesting feature of limited partnerships is that a single person may be both a general partner and a limited partner at the same time. A person might decide to invest in the business as a limited partner while also running the business as a general partner. However, such an arrangement does not protect the general partner to any greater degree than it would protect any other general partner. Even where a single person is both a limited partner and a general partner, he or she would face unlimited liability for business debts and judgments.

When the certificate is presented and the state has determined that the certificate is in substantial compliance with state law, the certificate is filed and a limited partnership is created. In most states, the office responsible for maintaining these records is the secretary of state's office.

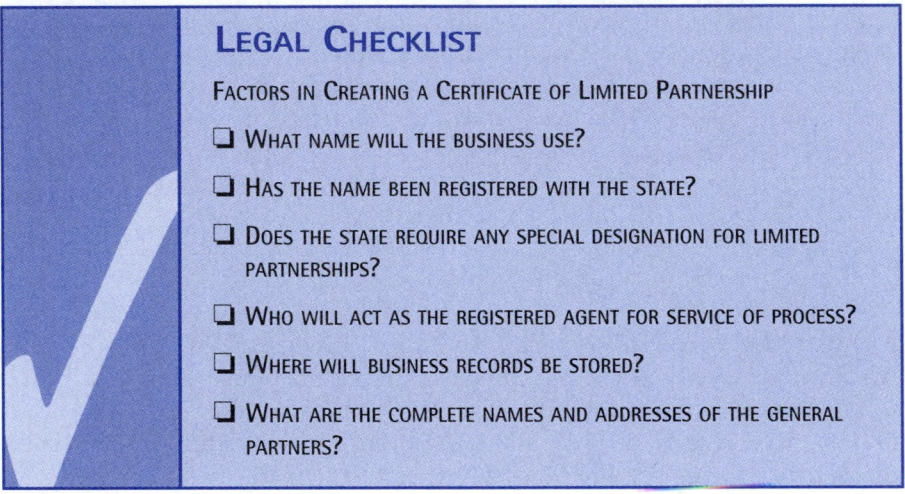

LEGAL CHECKLIST

FACTORS IN CREATING A CERTIFICATE OF LIMITED PARTNERSHIP

❑ WHAT NAME WILL THE BUSINESS USE?

❑ HAS THE NAME BEEN REGISTERED WITH THE STATE?

❑ DOES THE STATE REQUIRE ANY SPECIAL DESIGNATION FOR LIMITED PARTNERSHIPS?

❑ WHO WILL ACT AS THE REGISTERED AGENT FOR SERVICE OF PROCESS?

❑ WHERE WILL BUSINESS RECORDS BE STORED?

❑ WHAT ARE THE COMPLETE NAMES AND ADDRESSES OF THE GENERAL PARTNERS?

▶ LIMITED PARTNERSHIP AGREEMENTS

Filing a certificate of limited partnership status with the state is only the beginning in creating a limited partnership. The individuals involved in the business will also draft an agreement among themselves to determine things such as who will be the general partners, how the business will be run, and how profits and losses will be shared among general and limited partners. These issues will be addressed in the **limited partnership agreement.**

As with every other aspect of a limited partnership, state law governs the agreement. However, most state statutes allow the parties great flexibil-

limited partnership agreement A contract between the general and limited partners setting out their rights, duties and obligations.

ity in drafting specific provisions of the agreement. Statutes take a hands-off approach about most details in the limited partnership agreement, allowing the parties to negotiate their terms to suit their own business concerns. The parties are free to negotiate any terms that they like, as long as their agreement does not run counter to the law, public policy, or the established parameters of the partners' rights and obligations. Consider Scenario 5–4.

Scenario 5–4. Dream Seeds Productions

A group of individuals has created a limited partnership entitled Dream Seeds Productions, which plans on creating major motion pictures. Although their partnership agreement has many typical features, one provision allows limited partners to negotiate contracts with other production companies. Does this clause affect the legality of the limited partnership agreement?

Answer: yes. A limited partnership agreement is a very flexible document, but cannot contravene law, public policy, or the basic arrangement in a limited partnership. Limited partners are, by statutory definition, barred from carrying out day-to-day activities in the business. The practical result of allowing a limited partner to conduct negotiations for the business is to remove the partner's limited liability and to make him or her a general partner.[6]

CONSTRUCTION OF THE LANGUAGE IN A LIMITED PARTNERSHIP AGREEMENT

The language used to create the actual agreement is subject to the same rules of construction as any other business document. Words are given their normal and everyday meaning. When presented with the agreement, the courts will attempt to resolve any ambiguities by determining the parties' intent, when that can be ascertained. Courts are free to refer to other documents in order to determine specific provisions or to clear up cloudy or confusing provisions.[7] As a result, the actual language used to create a limited partnership agreement can be very simple and direct. There is no requirement that such agreements contain legal expressions, such as "party of the first part."

 GETTING TO THE BASICS

Limited partnership agreements are contracts between the partners and are construed like any other contract.

When the limited partnership agreement does contain ambiguities that cannot be interpreted by the courts, the ambiguity is construed against the party who created the contract. If the agreement was drafted by one of the general partners, or the partner's attorney, then the ambiguous language will be interpreted against that partner.[8] This is a rule that runs throughout contract disputes and is the court's way of encouraging the business parties to get adequate legal advice before setting up a business organization.

ELEMENTS OF A LIMITED PARTNERSHIP AGREEMENT

What are the basic elements that a limited partnership agreement should contain? Although these agreements can contain an amazing quantity of detail, limited partnership agreements can also be very basic. At its simplest, the agreement should list:

- the duties and responsibilities of general partners
- remedies available for breach of those duties
- qualification as a limited partner
- distribution of profits and losses
- classification of contributions
- partnership meetings
- dissolution and winding up

Duties and Responsibilities of General Partners

General partners in a limited partnership run the business. However, beyond simply being required to handle the day-to-day affairs of the business, general partners owe fiduciary duties to the other partners, both general and limited. When a partner has a fiduciary duty, it means that he or she must act in the best interests of the others partners and the business. The fiduciary duty begins when the limited partnership is created and continues through to dissolution and winding up of the business. Among the fiduciary duties owed by general partners to the other partners are:

- duty to act in good faith
- duty of fairness
- duty of loyalty

Duty to Act in Good Faith

General partners must act in good faith towards the other partners. This means that general partners must not attempt to personally enrich themselves at the expense of the business. They cannot, for example, take money from the business without the permission of the others partners. They cannot liquidate assets and pocket the money. They must, in all of their dealings, keep the best interests of the business and partners foremost in their minds. They cannot, for example, engage in **self-dealing**.

self-dealing When persons put their own interests ahead of those of the business to which they owe a fiduciary duty.

Self-dealing is the practice of using information, assets, or other company property to personally enrich the partner. The duty of good faith requires that the partners keep all of the other partners informed and not engage in practices that profit the partner at the expense of the business.

Duty of Fairness

The duty of fairness is closely tied to the duty to act in good faith. A general partner must act fairly towards other partners. This duty sometimes applies to third parties, as well, but a partner's true obligation of fairness is to the business in general and the other partners in particular.

Duty of Loyalty

Partners are not permitted to act in ways that hurt the business. Partners must be loyal to one another and avoid practices that put the individual's interests ahead of the company's interests.

KEY POINT

In a limited partnership, general partners owe fiduciary duties to both general and limited partners.

Remedies for Breach of Fiduciary Duty

The limited partnership agreement can, and often does, contain specific remedies that the partners have against the offending partner. The remedies available to limited partnerships are similar to the ones that are available in a general partnership. The parties can dissolve the partnership. They can also file suit against the partner, asking the court to rule that the general partner's unauthorized personal gain should be seized and redistributed among the partners. In such a situation, courts often rely on the **constructive trust doctrine,** holding that the partner who misappropriated funds, or acted to enrich himself at the expense of the business, acquired these funds as a trust for the business. The amount held in trust can then be distributed among the partners, as it should have been in the first place. This essentially gives the court the power to order the misbehaving partner to pay restitution to the other partners. The partner may also be subject to civil damages. These damages can include the actual damages suffered by the business, as well as punitive damages.[9]

constructive trust doctrine The theory that a partner who acquires profits for his or her own enrichment holds such funds for the benefit of the company as a whole and can be ordered to return such funds to the other partners.

 GETTING TO THE BASICS

A general partner's fiduciary duty can be summarized as a moral and ethical duty to act in the best interests of the partnership, to avoid negligent or reckless conduct in business practices, and to avoid breaking the law.[10]

Distribution of Profits

One of the most important elements of the limited partnership agreement is the issue of distributing profits. The partners are free to negotiate any distribution that they like, but most agreements call for several tiers of disbursements, with one type of distribution going to the general partners and another going to the limited partners. The profits distributed among the limited partners are generally determined by each limited partner's percentage of ownership in the business. Obviously, the method used to distribute profits (or pass through losses) will be heavily influenced by tax concerns for the individual partners.

Classification of Contributions

Other details that are usually found in a limited partnership agreement include provisions for classifications of contributions made by both general and limited partners. We have already seen that contribution refers to the property transferred into the partnership. Classifying this contribution, especially as to its monetary value, becomes important when the limited partnership is dissolved. A partner may be entitled to return of specific property or remuneration of actual value of any contribution.

Partnership Meetings

The limited partnership agreement will also contain provisions for partnership meetings. These meetings are vitally important for both general and limited partners because they set protocols and establish the direction of the business. The meeting is also where the official decision to terminate the partnership is made. As a result, limited partnership agreements contain provisions setting the date, time, and place for partner meetings as well as the methods that the business must use in order to notify partners of upcoming meetings.

Dissolution of a Limited Partnership

Limited partnerships can terminate in any of a number of ways. The partnership agreement might contain a specific date for dissolution or specify that the partnership will terminate when a certain event occurs, such as the sale of a tract of land, the final production of a movie, or the discovery of oil. See Exhibit 5–3.

Courts may also dissolve the limited partnership, under the doctrine of **judicial dissolution.** A court might take this action when it becomes clear that the limited partnership is a sham, or in violation of the law, or justice requires a finding that the business is terminated. Some states also have provisions that allow the Secretary of State to dissolve a limited partnership that has failed to pay appropriate fees and taxes or failed to file an annual report with that office.[11]

judicial dissolution A court's determination that a company should be dissolved for the good of the partners or creditors or because the business has engaged in illegal activities.

Winding up Business Affairs

Just as we saw with general partnerships, the dissolution of a limited partnership only occurs after a period of "winding up" the business affairs. This period includes finalizing any payments, accepting shipments, reconciling

Exhibit 5–3. Limited partnership certificate of dissolution, California

State of California
Secretary of State

LIMITED PARTNERSHIP
CERTIFICATE OF DISSOLUTION

IMPORTANT – Read instructions before completing this form

NOTE: THIS CERTIFICATE OF DISSOLUTION (LP-3) MUST BE FILED IN ORDER TO DISSOLVE YOUR LIMITED PARTNERSHIP. YOU MUST ALSO FILE A CERTIFICATE OF CANCELLATION (LP-4/7) IN ORDER TO CANCEL YOUR CERTIFICATE OF LIMITED PARTNERSHIP (LP-1) AND NOT INCUR FURTHER LIABILITY FOR TAX AS A LIMITED PARTNERSHIP.

This Space For Filing Use Only

1. SECRETARY OF STATE FILE NUMBER	2. NAME OF LIMITED PARTNERSHIP

3. EFFECTIVE DATE OF DISSOLUTION: MONTH   DAY   YEAR

4. THE EVENT CAUSING THE DISSOLUTION OF THIS LIMITED PARTNERSHIP IS:

A. ☐ IT IS THE TIME SPECIFIED IN THE PARTNERSHIP AGREEMENT FOR DISSOLUTION.

B. ☐ THE EVENTS FOR DISSOLUTION THAT ARE SPECIFIED IN THE PARTNERSHIP AGREEMENT HAVE OCCURRED.

C. ☐ WRITTEN CONSENT OF ALL GENERAL PARTNERS AND A MAJORITY IN INTEREST OF THE LIMITED PARTNER(S).

D. ☐ THERE ARE NO GENERAL PARTNERS TO CONTINUE THE BUSINESS OF THE LIMITED PARTNERSHIP.

E. ☐ ENTRY OF A DECREE OF JUDICIAL DISSOLUTION UNDER SECTION 15682.

5. OTHER INFORMATION THE PARTNERS FILING THE CERTIFICATE OF DISSOLUTION DETERMINE TO INCLUDE: (ATTACH ADDITIONAL PAGES IF NECESSARY)

6. I DECLARE THAT I AM THE PERSON WHO EXECUTED THIS INSTRUMENT, WHICH EXECUTION IS MY ACT AND DEED.

SIGNATURE OF AUTHORIZED PERSON   POSITION OR TITLE OF AUTHORIZED PERSON

TYPE OR PRINT NAME OF AUTHORIZED PERSON   DATE

SIGNATURE OF AUTHORIZED PERSON   POSITION OR TITLE OF AUTHORIZED PERSON

TYPE OR PRINT NAME OF AUTHORIZED PERSON   DATE

SIGNATURE OF AUTHORIZED PERSON   POSITION OR TITLE OF AUTHORIZED PERSON

TYPE OR PRINT NAME OF AUTHORIZED PERSON   DATE

LP-3 (REV. 03/2005)   Approved by Secretary of State

accounts receivable, and any other routine business matters. Once all creditors have been paid, the partners are free to distribute the remaining assets among themselves according to the terms of the limited partnership agreement. See Exhibit 5–4.

Exhibit 5–4. Limited partnership agreement (Courtesy of West, a Thomson business)

LIMITED PARTNERSHIP AGREEMENT

Agreement of limited partnership made on _____ [date], between _____ [A.B.], of _____ [address], _____ [city], _____ County, _____ [state], _____ ("general partner"), and _____ [C.D.], of _____ [address], _____ [city], _____ County, _____ [state], and _____ [E.F.], of _____ [address], _____ [city], _____ County, _____ [state] ("limited partners").

RECITALS

A. General and limited partners desire to enter into the business of _____.

B. General partner desires to manage and operate the business.

C. Limited partners desire to invest in the business and limit their liabilities.

In consideration of the matters described above, and of the mutual benefits and obligations set forth in this agreement, the parties agree as follows:

ARTICLE ONE.
GENERAL PROVISIONS

The limited partnership is organized pursuant to the provisions of _____ [cite statute] of _____ [state], and the rights and liabilities of the general and limited partners shall be as provided in that statute, except as otherwise stated in this agreement.

ARTICLE TWO.
NAME OF PARTNERSHIP

The name of the partnership shall be _____ (the "partnership").

ARTICLE THREE.
BUSINESS OF PARTNERSHIP

The purpose of the partnership is to engage in the business of _____.

(continued)

Exhibit 5–4. Limited partnership agreement (Courtesy of West, a Thomson business) *(continued)*

ARTICLE FOUR.
PRINCIPAL PLACE OF BUSINESS

The principal place of business of the partnership shall be at _____ [address], _____ [city], _____ County, _____ [state]. The partnership shall also have other places of business as from time to time shall be determined by general partner.

ARTICLE FIVE.
CAPITAL CONTRIBUTION OF GENERAL PARTNER

General partner shall contribute $_____ to the original capital of the partnership. The contribution of general partner shall be made on or before _____ [date]. If general partner does not make _____ [his or her] entire contribution to the capital of the partnership on or before that date, this agreement shall be void. Any contributions to the capital of the partnership made at that time shall be returned to the partners who have made the contributions.

ARTICLE SIX.
CAPITAL CONTRIBUTIONS OF LIMITED PARTNERS

The capital contributions of limited partners shall be as follows:

Name   Amount
_____ $_____
_____ $_____

Receipt of the capital contribution from each limited partner as specified above is acknowledged by the partnership. No limited partner has agreed to contribute any additional cash or property as capital for use of the partnership.

ARTICLE SEVEN.
DUTIES AND RIGHTS OF PARTNERS

General partner shall diligently and exclusively apply _____ [himself or herself] in and about the business of the partnership to the utmost of _____ [his or her] skill and on a full-time basis.

General partner shall not engage directly or indirectly in any business similar to the business of the partnership at any time during the term of this agreement without obtaining the written approval of all other partners.

(continued)

Exhibit 5–4. Limited partnership agreement (Courtesy of West, a Thomson business) *(continued)*

General partner shall be entitled to _____ days' vacation and _____ days' sick leave in each calendar year, commencing with the calendar year _____. If general partner uses sick leave or vacation days in a calendar year in excess of the number specified above, the effect on _____ [his or her] capital interest and share of the profits and losses of the partnership for that year shall be determined by a majority vote of limited partners.

No limited partner shall have any right to be active in the conduct of the partnership's business, nor have power to bind the partnership in any contract, agreement, promise, or undertaking.

ARTICLE EIGHT.
SALARY OF GENERAL PARTNER

General partner shall be entitled to a monthly salary of $_____ for the services rendered by general partner. The salary shall commence on _____ [date], and be payable on the _____ day of each subsequent month. The salary shall be treated as an expense of the operation of the partnership business and shall be payable whether or not the partnership shall operate at a profit.

ARTICLE NINE.
LIMITATIONS ON DISTRIBUTION OF PROFITS

General partner shall have the right, except as provided below, to determine whether from time to time partnership profits shall be distributed in cash or shall be left in the business, in which event the capital account of all partners shall be increased.

In no event shall any profits be payable for a period of _____ months until _____% of those profits have been deducted to accumulate a reserve fund of $_____ over and above the normal monthly requirements of working capital. This accumulation is to enable the partnership to maintain a sound financial operation.

ARTICLE TEN.
PROFITS AND LOSSES FOR LIMITED PARTNERS

Limited partners shall be entitled to receive a share of the annual net profits equivalent to their share in the capitalization of the partnership.

Limited partners shall each bear a share of the losses of the partnership equal to the share of profits to which each limited

(continued)

Exhibit 5–4. Limited partnership agreement (Courtesy of West, a Thomson business) *(continued)*

partner is entitled. The share of losses of each limited partner shall be charged against the limited partner's capital contribution.

Limited partners shall at no time become liable for any obligations or losses of the partnership beyond the amounts of their respective capital contributions.

ARTICLE ELEVEN.
PROFITS AND LOSSES FOR GENERAL PARTNER

After provisions have been made for the shares of profits of limited partners, all remaining profits of the partnership shall be paid to general partner. After giving effect to the share of losses chargeable against the capital contributions of limited partners, the remaining partnership losses shall be borne by general partner.

ARTICLE TWELVE.
BOOKS OF ACCOUNT

There shall be maintained during the continuance of this partnership an accurate set of books of account of all transactions, assets, and liabilities of the partnership. The books shall be balanced and closed at the end of each year, and at any other time on reasonable request of the general partner. The books are to be kept at the principal place of business of the partnership and are to be open for inspection by any partner at all reasonable times. The profits and losses of the partnership and its books of account shall be maintained on a fiscal year basis, terminating annually on
_____ [month and day], unless otherwise determined by general partner.

ARTICLE THIRTEEN.
SUBSTITUTIONS, ASSIGNMENTS, AND ADMISSION
OF ADDITIONAL PARTNERS

General partner shall not substitute a partner in _____ [his or her] place, or sell or assign all or any part of general partner's interest in the partnership business without the written consent of limited partners.

Additional limited partners may be admitted to this partnership on terms that may be agreed on in writing between general partner and the new limited partners. The terms so stipulated shall constitute an amendment to this partnership agreement.

(continued)

Exhibit 5–4. Limited partnership agreement (Courtesy of West, a Thomson business) *(continued)*

No limited partner may substitute an assignee as a limited partner in _____ [his or her] place; but the person or persons entitled by rule or by intestate laws, as the case may be, shall succeed to all the rights of limited partner as a substituted limited partner.

ARTICLE FOURTEEN.
TERMINATION OF INTEREST OF LIMITED PARTNER; RETURN OF CAPITAL CONTRIBUTION

The interest of any limited partner may be terminated by (1) dissolution of the partnership for any reason provided in this agreement; (2) the agreement of all partners; or (3) the consent of the personal representative of a deceased limited partner and the partnership.

On the termination of the interest of a limited partner there shall be payable to that limited partner, or the limited partner's estate, as the case may be, a sum to be determined by all partners, which sum shall not be less than _____ times the capital account of the limited partner as shown on the books at the time of the termination, including profits or losses from the last closing of the books of the partnership to the date of the termination, when the interest in profits and losses terminated. The amount payable shall be an obligation payable only out of partnership assets, and at the option of the partnership, may be paid within _____ years after the termination of the interest, provided that interest at the rate of _____% shall be paid on the unpaid balance.

ARTICLE FIFTEEN.
BORROWING BY PARTNER

In case of necessity as determined by a majority vote of all partners, a partner may borrow up to $_____ from the partnership. Any such loan shall be repayable at _____ [describe terms of repayment], together with interest at the rate of _____% per year.

ARTICLE SIXTEEN.
TERM OF PARTNERSHIP AND DISSOLUTION

The partnership term commences on _____[date], and shall end on (1) the dissolution of the partnership by operation of law; (2) the dissolution of the partnership at any time designated by general partner; or (3) the dissolution of the partnership at the close of the month following the qualification and appointment of the personal representative of deceased general partner.

(continued)

Exhibit 5–4. Limited partnership agreement (Courtesy of West, a Thomson business) *(continued)*

ARTICLE SEVENTEEN.
PAYMENT FOR INTEREST OF DECEASED GENERAL PARTNER

In the event of the death of general partner there shall be paid out of the partnership's assets to decedent's personal representative for decedent's interest in the partnership a sum equal to the capital account of decedent as shown on the books at the time of the decedent's death, adjusted to reflect profits or losses from the last closing of the books of the partnership to the day of the decedent's death.

ARTICLE EIGHTEEN.
AMENDMENTS

This agreement, except with respect to vested rights of partners, may be amended at any time by a majority vote as measured by the interest and the sharing of profits and losses.

ARTICLE NINETEEN.
BINDING EFFECT OF AGREEMENT

This agreement shall be binding on the parties to the agreement and their respective heirs, executors, administrators, successors, and assigns.

The parties have executed this agreement at _____[designate place of execution] the day and year first above written.

[Signatures]*

*Am. Jur. LF § 194:664.

Ethics File: Partners' Fiduciary Duty

Because general partners owe fiduciary duties to other partners in a limited partnership arrangement, anyone who works closely with such partnerships should always be ready to advise partners about particular behaviors that could result in serious problems for the business. For instance, if it becomes clear that one partner is removing money from the company without the knowledge or permission of the other partners, the remaining partners should be informed at once. Any delay could have drastic consequences for the company.

CASE LAW: *When a Limited Partnership Is Not a Limited Partnership*

Saulnier v. Fanaras Enterprises, Inc.[12]
THAYER, Justice.

This is an appeal of the Superior Court's (Dickson, J.) ruling that the parties failed to form a limited partnership and that the only contractual relationship formed by them was that of mortgagor-mortgagee. We reverse and remand for dissolution and an accounting.

While employed by Fanaras Enterprises, Inc. (Fanaras Enterprises), Richard Saulnier approached Joseph Fanaras, the sole shareholder of Fanaras Enterprises, about a loan of $40,000 so that Saulnier could purchase a gravel pit. On January 9, 1986, Fanaras loaned $40,000 to Richard and Rose Saulnier, who took title to the gravel pit as tenants in common. On the same day, the Saulniers signed a promissory note, a mortgage on the gravel pit securing the note, a document entitled "limited partnership agreement," and a document entitled "security agreement interest in limited partnership." The limited partnership was to be named Stepping Stone Materials. Fanaras Enterprises was designated as the general partner and the Saulniers were to be the limited partners. The limited partnership agreement executed by the parties provided that the partnership was organized under Massachusetts law, and that the principal place of business was to be in Salisbury, Massachusetts, where Fanaras Enterprises was located. The parties executed a certificate of limited partnership on the same day that the other instruments were executed. The certificate was submitted to the Massachusetts Secretary of State on January 13, 1986.

From March 1986 to June 1986, Mr. Saulnier, in his role as an employee of Fanaras Enterprises, loaded gravel from the pit for use in Fanaras Enterprises' construction activities in Massachusetts. Equipment owned by Fanaras Enterprises was brought to the gravel pit to expedite loading. Because of increased truck traffic on local roads, the Town of Lee, through a temporary agreement, imposed restrictions on Fanaras Enterprises' transfer of gravel. When the agreement with the town expired on June 27, 1986, the equipment was removed from the pit, and

the pit ceased to be a source of gravel for Fanaras Enterprises. In September 1986, Mr. Saulnier paid off the $40,000 loan with interest. In December 1986, Mr. Saulnier was laid off as an equipment operator by Fanaras Enterprises.

By the spring of 1987, Mr. Saulnier began operating the gravel pit himself and purchased an adjacent parcel of land to provide another access route for trucks to enter the pit. In April 1987, the Saulniers filed a petition for dissolution of the purported partnership and for an accounting from Fanaras Enterprises for profits earned from the gravel pit operations during 1986. In October 1988, Fanaras Enterprises brought a separate petition for an accounting, imposition of a constructive trust, assessment of damages, permanent injunction, and other legal and equitable relief based on the Saulniers' alleged wrongful ouster of the general partner and improper diversion of partnership proceeds. The superior court consolidated the actions.

At issue in the dispute between the parties is the money received by the Saulniers from proceeds of the sale of gravel since 1987. At trial, the Saulniers advanced the position that the limited partnership never came into existence because the purported general partner did not make the required capital contribution to the partnership when it loaned money to the Saulniers in their personal capacity.

The trial court agreed, finding that despite the professed intent of all the parties involved, they failed to create a partnership. We review this finding according to our customary standard of review: "Findings and rulings of the trial court must be sustained unless they are lacking in evidential support or tainted by error of law." Burnham v. Downing, 125 N.H. 293, 296, 480 A.2d 128, 130 (1984).

Testimony at trial showed that the limited partnership agreement provided that the general partner would make a loan to Stepping Stone Materials. Fanaras Enterprises, however, made no loan to Stepping Stone Materials; instead, Fanaras Enterprises loaned $40,000 to the Saulniers in their personal capacity. The limited partnership agreement provided that the "General Partner Fanaras Enterprises shall diligently apply himself in and about the business of the Partnership to the utmost of his skill," yet no attempt was made to sell gravel to members of the public until after the Saulniers paid off the mortgage on the gravel pit. All of the gravel removed from the pit, but for one small sale, was used by Fanaras Enterprises. Moreover, although the limited partnership agreement provided that an accurate set of books or accounts for all transactions would be maintained by the general partner, no books or financial records for Stepping Stone Materials were kept except for a shoebox full of loading slips for gravel removed by Fanaras Enterprises. These facts, however, do not relate to the formation of a limited partnership, but instead are relevant as to whether there was a breach of the partnership agreement once the partnership was formed.

The defendants, Fanaras Enterprises and Stepping Stone Materials, argue that the existence of the limited partnership agreement signed by the parties, along with other manifestations of the parties' intent, is enough to sustain a finding that a limited partnership had been established. The defendants miss the mark with this argument because the intent of the parties to form a limited partnership means nothing if the parties do not comply with the statutory requirements for formation.

Limited partnerships did not exist at common law; they are statutory creatures that must be formed and conducted in substantial compliance with the statutes authorizing such a business relationship. Metzger v. New Century Oil & Gas Supply, 230 Ill.App.3d 679, 171 Ill.Dec. 698, 594 N.E.2d 1218, 1231 (1992) (substantial compliance with detailed filing requirements is needed to form limited partnership); Voudouris v. Walter E. Heller & Co., 560 S.W.2d 202, 207 (Tex.Ct.App.1977) (limited partnership failed to become effective because certificate not filed). Accordingly, given the agreement as to the parties' intent, the question before us is whether the parties substantially complied with the statutes governing the formation of limited partnerships. See Dominion Nat. Bk. v. Sundowner Jt. V., 50 Md.App. 145, 157, 436 A.2d 501, 507-08 (1981) (despite "understanding and intent" of appellees to form limited partnership, valid partnership not created where no compliance with statutory requirements).

The limited partnership agreement executed by the parties provided that the limited partnership was to be organized pursuant to Massachusetts law, and therefore, we will apply Massachusetts law to the substantive question of whether the parties formed a limited partnership. Waite v. Sylvester, 131 N.H. 663, 667, 560 A.2d 619, 621 (1989). Massachusetts General Law chapter 109 governs the formation of limited partnerships. At the time the parties executed the certificate of limited partnership, Mass.Gen.Laws.Ann. ch. 109, § 8(a) (West 1990) provided that in order to form a limited partnership, two or more persons must have executed a certificate including thirteen required pieces of information. Section 8(b) of chapter 109 provides:

"A limited partnership is formed at the time of the filing of the certificate of limited partnership in the office of the secretary of state or at any later time specified in the certificate of limited partnership if, in either case, there has been substantial compliance with the requirements of this section."

When the secretary of state determines that the certificate conforms to the law, the certificate is marked "filed" and time-stamped. Mass.Gen.Laws Ann. ch. 109, § 13(a)(1) (West 1990). Our review of the certificate of limited partnership executed by the parties and submitted to the Massachusetts Secretary of State reveals that the required information is contained therein and the certificate is marked "filed" and time-stamped on January 13, 1986. Therefore, under the law of Massachusetts, Stepping Stone Materials, Ltd. was formed on that date. We hold that the trial court's decision is not supported by the evidence and remand for the trial court to dissolve the limited partnership and perform an accounting, and for such further proceedings as may be consistent with this opinion.

Reversed and remanded for further proceedings consistent with this opinion.

(continued)

CASE LAW: *When a Limited Partnership Is Not a Limited Partnership* (continued)

CASE QUESTIONS

1. Explain the basic partnership agreement between the parties in this case.
2. Explain the contention regarding the Saulniers' alleged wrongful ouster of a partner.
3. What is the significance of the fact that the general partner never provided capital to the limited partnership?
4. According to the court, which is more controlling, the limited partnership agreement or the compliance with state statutes to form a limited partnership? Explain.
5. Was a limited partnership ever formed, and if so, what effect does that ruling have on the ultimate issues in the case?

CASE LAW: *Agency and Limited Partnership Rights*

In re Estate of Capuzzi[13]

The issue presented is whether the death of the principal revokes his agent's order to transfer limited partnership shares when all necessary actions by the agent were completed before the principal's death, but the transfer was not yet completed by a third party. We hold that an agent's actions are not revoked by the death of the principal when the agent has completed all actions necessary for the transaction before the principal's death. Therefore, we reverse the decision of the Court of Appeals and affirm the decision of the trial court granting the petitioners summary disposition.

FACTS

Decedent, Eugene T. Capuzzi, M.D., owned shares in a limited partnership. Dr. Capuzzi's will divided that interest equally among his three children, Michael, Eugene Jr., and Christina. A few days before his death, Dr. Capuzzi directed Michael to transfer the limited partnership shares to his sons, Michael and Eugene, Jr., petitioners in this case. Michael was acting as Dr. Capuzzi's agent pursuant to a durable power of attorney agreement. The agreement gave Michael "full power and authority to do and perform every act and thing whatsoever requisite and necessary to be done." The transfer would eliminate Christina's interest in the limited partnership shares; Christina is the respondent in this case. Michael contacted the limited partnership on August 10, 1998, and again on August 11, 1998, and he directed that the shares be transferred pursuant to the power of attorney and Dr. Capuzzi's wishes. Dr. Capuzzi died on August 14, 1998. On August 19, 1998, the limited partnership sent Michael a letter stating that Dr. Capuzzi's death had revoked the power of attorney and, therefore, the transfer could not be completed. During probate proceedings, petitioners objected to the shares passing under the will. The probate court granted summary disposition for petitioners. The Court of Appeals reversed and remanded, holding that the transfer of the shares could not be completed because Dr. Capuzzi's death immediately revoked the power of attorney.

ANALYSIS

It is a longstanding legal principle that a duly authorized agent has the power to act and bind the principal to the same extent as if the principal acted.

A power of attorney provides the agent with all the rights and responsibilities of the principal as outlined in the agreement. In effect, the agent stands in the shoes of the principal.

It is also well-settled that the death of the principal revokes the authority of the agent, unless the agency is coupled with an interest. Any act done by the agent after the principal dies cannot affect the estate. This is true even if an agent performed some of the acts necessary in a single transaction but not all of them. If an agent is in the midst of a transaction when the principal dies, the transaction cannot continue, regardless of the principal's previously stated wishes.

However, when an agent has completed all necessary actions and all that is left is for a third party to act to complete the transaction, we hold that the principal's death has no effect on the validity of the transaction and does not relieve the requirement on the *third party* to act. This is because the *agent's* actions were complete at the time of the principal's death. Notably, if a third party requires additional information to confirm that the agent has the authority to act or if, for example, the third party requires completion of an additional form indicating power of attorney, then the agent has obviously *not completed all actions necessary for the transaction.* If the principal dies before the agent meets the third party's requirements, then the third party is not required to follow the directive of the agent. This is because all necessary actions have not been completed by the agent before the principal dies.

When all necessary actions have been completed, just as the third party would be required to follow the directive of the principal, the third party is also required to follow the directive of the agent. Although the agent's authority to act terminates when the principal dies, actions completed before the termination no longer require the agent to exercise authority. Therefore, the principal's death does not revoke already completed actions by the agent.

In this case, in accord with Dr. Capuzzi's wishes and acting as Dr. Capuzzi's agent pursuant to a durable power of attorney, Michael contacted the third party and directed that the shares be transferred. Just as Dr. Capuzzi had the authority to compel the third party to transfer the shares, Michael, as Dr. Capuzzi's agent, possessed the same authority. Once he ordered the third party to transfer the shares, this concluded the agent's actions that were necessary to complete the transaction. All that remained was for the third party to act. Again, in this case, the agent did all that was required to transfer the shares. The failure to transfer the shares was solely the result of the third party's delay and had nothing to do with the third party's internal procedures or concerns that the agent did not have the proper authority.

Notably, the agent acted on behalf of the principal *before* the agent's authority was revoked by the principal's death and, thus, there was nothing precluding the third party from relying on the agent's authority. Because there was nothing prohibiting the agent from ordering the transfer when he did, that is, while the principal was still alive, there was nothing prohibiting the third party from acting pursuant to the validly given order. The third party's authority to transfer the shares does not depend on the agent's authority to act on behalf of the principal at the time of the transfer of the shares; rather, it depends on the agent's authority to act *at the time the agent ordered the shares to be transferred.* Therefore, because the agent properly exercised his authority while the principal was still alive, the third party was not excused from acting on the agent's authority.

Although M.C.L. § 700.497 has been repealed, we are aware that it was in effect at the time of the agent's order to transfer the shares. M.C.L. § 700.497(1) stated, in pertinent part, the following:

> *The death of a principal who has executed a power of attorney in writing, durable or otherwise, does not revoke or terminate the agency of the attorney in fact, agent, or other person who, without actual knowledge of the death, acts in good faith under the power of attorney or agency. An action so taken, unless otherwise invalid or unenforceable, binds the principal and the principal's heirs, devisees, and personal representatives.*

> *In brief, M.C.L. § 700.497(1) stated that the death of a principal who had executed a written*

(continued)

CASE LAW: *Agency and Limited Partnership Rights* (continued)

power of attorney did not terminate the agency of the attorney in fact, agent, or other person who acted under the power of attorney or agency in good faith without knowledge of the death. M.C.L. § 700.497(1) is not germane to this case because the principal's agent acted before the principal died.

Also, M.C.L. § 700.497(2) stated the following:

In the absence of fraud, an affidavit executed by the attorney in fact or agent stating that he or she did not have, at the time of doing an act pursuant to the power of attorney, actual knowledge of the revocation or termination of the power of attorney by death, disability, or incompetence is conclusive proof of the nonrevocation or nontermination of the power at that time. If the exercise of the power requires execution and delivery of any instrument that is recordable, the affidavit when authenticated for record is likewise recordable.

This section essentially stated that an affidavit executed by the attorney in fact or agent stating that he did not have knowledge of the principal's death at the time of doing the act in question is conclusive proof of nontermination of the power at that time and the act must be enforced. Thus, if, unknown to the agent, the principal died, the agent's act must be enforced nonetheless once the agent files an affidavit. The third party could not rebut such an affidavit and would have no authority or basis to refuse to carry out the agent's order. Of course, this section is not applicable to the facts of this case because when the agent completed his act the principal was still alive. And this section is not applicable to the third party because the statute only applied to the attorney in fact or agent and the third party in this case is neither. However, it is important to note that M.C.L. § 700.497(2) mandated that the actions of an agent be enforced when the agent was unaware of

the principal's death at the time of the act in question; therefore, actions taken by an agent, at the principal's behest, when the principal was still *alive* are certainly enforceable. If we were to hold to the contrary, the actions of a third party could revoke the completed acts of an agent. This would circumvent the intent of the principal and allow a third party's actions to control. A third party's delay, whether intentional or not, should not be allowed to thwart the principal's wishes when the principal's agent has completed all necessary actions before the principal's death. Further, to find that an agent had the authority to order the transfer of the shares but that the third party did not have to follow the order would render the agent's authority a nullity.

CONCLUSION

We hold that an agent's completed actions are not revoked by the death of the principal when all necessary actions have been taken by the agent before the principal's death. Accordingly, we reverse the decision of the Court of Appeals and affirm the decision of the trial court.

CASE QUESTIONS

1. What is the issue in this case?

2. What action did the limited partnership take in regard to the request by the agent to transfer shares to the deceased's two children?

3. According to the court, what authority does an agent have prior to the death of a principal?

4. Why is the distinction about the completion of the agent's actions before the death of the principal important, especially regarding third parties?

5. What is the court's conclusion, and what effect does this ruling have on Christina's claim to her father's assets?

SUMMARY

The limited partnership is the first type of business entity we have discussed in this book that enjoys the protection of limited liability. Limited liability means that the most a party can lose in a particular business transaction is the amount of his or her investment. Limited partnerships are creatures of statute, not of common law. The Uniform Limited Partnership Act has been adopted in all states and provides a mechanism for creating a limited partnership. Before a limited partnership can be created, the appropriate documents must be completed and filed with the state. Once the documents have been filed, a limited partnership has specific features. For instance, a limited partnership consists of one or more general partners and one or more limited partners. The general partners have the same duties and obligations as general partners in any other type of partnership, namely, running the day-to-day operation of the business, making business decisions, and hiring and firing employees. However, limited partners have no such authority. In exchange for receiving the protection of limited liability, limited partners have no say in the day-to-day operation of the business. Limited partners are not permitted to control the actions of the general partners. General partners in a limited partnership are not protected by limited liability any more than general partners in any other type of business. Limited partnerships can dissolve by their own terms or by judicial interaction. Once the partnership is dissolved, there is a period of winding up business affairs before profits can be distributed to the partners.

HELPFUL WEB SITES

New York Secretary of State Limited Partnership Filings
http://www.dos.state.ny.us/corp/lpfile.html

North Carolina Department of Secretary of State
http://www.secretary.state.nc.us

KEY TERMS

agent for service of process

certificate of limited partnership

constructive trust doctrine

contribution

judicial dissolution

limited liability

limited partnership agreement

self-dealing

Uniform Limited Partnership Act

APPLYING CHAPTER CONCEPTS

1. Limited partnerships are often used as investment vehicles or to acquire investment capital for a risky business venture. Locate limited partnerships in your area that have been created for the express purpose of engaging in a speculative business practice, such as oil exploration, making a movie, or buying real estate to develop. Once you've located this limited partnership, answer some basic questions.
   - What does it cost to become a limited partner?
   - What are the potential profits?
   - What provisions or disclaimers do general partners and limited partners express in the materials advertising limited partnerships?

REVIEW QUESTIONS

1. What is limited liability?
2. How is a limited partnership different from a general partnership?
3. Is there a common law of limited partnerships? Why or why not?
4. What is the Uniform Limited Partnership Act?
5. What is the basic definition of a limited partnership?
6. How is the role of a general partner different in a limited partnership than in a general partnership?
7. What rights does a limited partner have in running the day-to-day business?
8. What are some of the advantages of a limited partnership over a general partnership?
9. Explain the tax consequences of passing through profits and losses from a limited partnership.
10. What is a certificate of limited partnership?
11. What types of information are normally contained in a certificate of limited partnership?
12. Besides identification of the partners, what other important items of information are required in a certificate of limited partnership?
13. What are some of the rules and limitations on naming a limited partnership?
14. How can a company considering creating a limited partnership reserve the name before the partnership is formed?
15. What types of considerations go into drafting a limited partnership agreement?
16. What are the rules regarding construing language in a limited partnership agreement?

17. What duties do general partners owe limited partners?

18. Is a general partner a fiduciary of a limited partner? Explain your answer.

19. What are some of the considerations that partners face before distributing profits from a limited partnership?

20. Explain some of the ways that a limited partnership can be dissolved.

21. What are some of the concerns in winding up a limited partnership?

QUESTION FOR REFLECTION

1. If you were considering creating a new business, would you opt for a sole proprietorship, a general partnership, or a limited partnership? Would your choice of business model depend on the type of business you were planning on creating? Explain.

ENDNOTES

[1]*Energy Investors Fund, L.P. v. Metric Constructors, Inc.,* 351 N.C. 331, 525 S.E.2d 441 (2000).

[2]Revised Uniform Limited Partnership Act § 101 (1976 version).

[3]*Odom v. Slavik,* 703 F.2d 212 (6th Cir. 1983).

[4]*Saulnier v. Fanaras Enterprises, Inc.,* 136 N.H. 565, 618 A.2d 841 (1992).

[5]Revised Uniform Limited Partnership Act § 103 (1976 Revision).

[6]*Westminster Properties, Inc. v. Atlanta Associates,* 250 Ga. 841, 301 S.E.2d 636 (1983).

[7]*First Bank & Trust Co. v. Cannon,* 164 Ga. App. 449, 297 S.E.2d 349 (1982).

[8]*SI Management L.P. v. Wininger,* 707 A.2d 37 (Del. 1998).

[9]*Washington Medical Center, Inc. v. Holle,* 573 A.2d 1269 (D.C. 1990).

[10]Uniform Limited Partnership Act § 408(c) (2001).

[11]Uniform Limited Partnership Act § 809(b) (2001).

[12]136 N.H. 565, 618 A.2d 841 (N.H. 1992).

[13]470 Mich. 399, 684 N.W.2d 677†(Mich. 2004).

 For additional resources visit our Web site at *http://www.westlegalstudies.com*

Chapter 6

LIMITED LIABILITY COMPANIES

Chapter Objectives

Upon completion of this chapter, you should be able to:

- Explain the basic organization of a limited liability company.
- Describe the advantages that a limited liability company offers over other business models.
- Describe the process of creating a limited liability company.
- Define the roles of the members and managers of limited liability companies.
- Explain the process of dissolving a limited liability company.

▶ INTRODUCTION

The limited liability company (LLC) is a relatively recent phenomenon. In our discussions about both partnerships and limited partnerships, we have seen that these business structures have existed for decades, and in some cases for centuries. However, limited liability companies are creatures of the latter half of the 20th century. The first limited liability company statute was proposed in Wyoming in 1977.[1] With Wyoming's success, other states followed suit. By the end of the 20th century nearly every state had some form of limited liability company statute.

This new form of business offered obvious advantages over general partnerships, limited partnerships, and, to a certain extent, corporations. In this chapter, we will explore this newest type of business organization model and explain the advantages it enjoys over many other types of businesses.

managers The persons responsible for the day-to-day operation of a limited liability company.

members The persons who invest in a limited liability company.

KEY POINT

Limited liability companies have existed only since the early 1980s.

NATURE OF A LIMITED LIABILITY COMPANY?

The popularity of the limited liability company is due to the fact that it is essentially a hybrid between corporations and partnerships, with all of the advantages of a limited partnership and none of its disadvantages.

As we saw in the previous chapter, a limited partnership is the first type of business model we have discussed that enjoys the protection of limited liability. Investors in a business know that the most that they can lose in a venture is the amount of their contribution. However, limited partnerships also have general partners. These general partners still face unlimited liability. They may lose their personal assets. There are individuals willing to take this risk because of the potential profits from a business and also because both general and limited partners can pass through profits and losses on their individual income tax returns. The limited liability company was designed as a vehicle to keep the attractions of a limited partnership while avoiding its downside: liability for the general partners.

Under a limited liability company arrangement, none of the owners face the specter of unlimited liability. Their personal assets are not in danger. This removes the last obstacle to investment: the risk of loss for the day-to-day managers of the business.

GETTING TO THE BASICS

Limited liability companies offer the advantages of limited partnerships with none of the disadvantages.

ORGANIZATION OF A LIMITED LIABILITY COMPANY

Limited liability companies share many organizational elements with limited partnerships. However, there are some important differences. For one thing, limited liability companies do not have general partners. Instead, the persons responsible for the day-to-day management of the business are referred to as **managers**. The investors in the business are called **members**. The members have voting rights about business decisions and are permitted to take an active role in the operation of the business. Another unique feature of limited liability companies is that the managers may also be members. Because they all enjoy the protection of limited liability, there is no practical reason to bar managers from also investing in the business as members. There's also no requirement that a manager must be a member. Limited liability companies offer a great deal of flexibility in the organization and operation of business.

Limited liability companies also resemble corporations in that members own a percentage of the company, but the company itself has a separate existence. What we mean by separate existence is that limited liability companies can, in certain situations, act like individuals. For example, limited liability companies can own property. As we will see in our discussions on corporations, in the next chapter, something as simple as owning property in the company's name is a radical departure from business practices in the past.

KEY POINT

A limited liability company has at least one member who has membership interest in the company. Managers control the business. Managers are permitted to be members.

Members of a limited liability company retain the right to vote on changes in the operating agreement and to set limits on the addition of new members into the company. We will explore the issue of operating agreements in greater detail later in this chapter.

As we saw in the last chapter, limited partners can be secure in the knowledge that their personal liability extends only to the amount of their contribution to the business. The same rule applies in limited liability companies. An individual member's liability is again restricted to the amount of his or her contribution to the business. Just as in limited partnerships, contributions to limited liability companies can come in the form of cash or services.

Members of limited liability companies face no personal liability for the company's debts, judgments, or other assessments. These must be paid out of the company's funds. However, unlike in limited partnerships, managers are also protected by limited liability.

ADVANTAGES OF LIMITED LIABILITY COMPANIES

As we will see in the next chapter, limited liability companies have a very similar structure to that of a corporation. A corporation is owned by shareholders and managed by officers. The shareholders are protected by limited liability. The corporate structure has great advantages over almost all other types of business models, except limited liability companies. In fact, limited liability companies enjoy certain advantages over the corporate model. For one thing, the way that taxes are assessed against limited liability companies is different from the method used to assess taxes against corporations. Limited liability companies offer great flexibility to their owners and protection for everyone involved in the enterprise. This puts them head and shoulders above limited partnerships, which still have general partners who face personal liability. However, one could easily argue that the best advantage of a limited liability company structure is the tax benefit.

 GETTING TO THE BASICS

> The biggest advantage of the limited liability company is that there are no general partners who remain personally liable for any debts or judgments incurred by the business. All members are protected by limited liability.

Tax Advantages of the LLC

Perhaps the single most important motivating factor in creating a limited liability company is the pass-through feature of tax treatment. Just as in limited partnerships, members can deduct business losses on their personal income taxes. This arrangement is a powerful incentive for individuals to create a limited liability company. If the business suffers an economic loss, this loss can be reflected on the individual member's income tax returns. This can have a substantial impact on a member's tax liability in any given year. This loss can offset gains made in other business ventures. That, by itself, would be enough to make one consider creating a limited liability company. However, the tax advantages, coupled with the protections of limited liability, make this a very attractive business form.

When limited liability companies were originally created, no one was sure how the Internal Revenue Service would perceive this new business organization. Would it, for instance, tax it as a corporation? The issue of corporate taxation is complex, but it basically boils down to double taxation. The company pays taxes in its own right, and individual shareholders (the owners) pay taxes on any losses or gains they have realized. What made limited liability companies so intriguing was that there was a possibility that there would only be one level of taxation. Business gains and losses would be passed through to the company's members. However, there was no guarantee that the IRS would agree that limited liability companies fell into this category. The IRS might just as easily rule that limited liability companies are similar to corporations and therefore subject to double taxation.

The issue concerning the taxation of limited liability companies was resolved in 1988 and legitimized limited liability companies as a business structure. The IRS ruled that limited liability companies should be taxed like limited partnerships rather than as corporations. Under that ruling, as long as a limited liability company meets certain prerequisites, it will be taxed in exactly the same way as a limited partnership. The advantages of a limited liability company over a limited partnership became obvious. Business owners could still enjoy limited liability and pass through profits and losses on their individual income tax returns, and there would be no general partners to face personal liability for business debts. Is it any wonder that limited liability companies are far more popular than limited partnerships? See Exhibit 6–1.

Exhibit 6–1. Internal Revenue Service ruling on the tax consequences of forming a limited liability company

Published: September 2, 1988

ISSUE

Whether a Wyoming limited liability company, none of whose members or designated managers are personally liable for any debts of the company, is classified for federal tax purposes as an association or as a partnership.

FACTS

M was organized as a limited liability company pursuant to the provisions of the Wyoming Limited Liability Company Act (Act). The purpose of M is to acquire, own, and operate improved real property. M has 25 members, including A, B, and C.

The Act provides that a limited liability company may be managed by a designated manager or managers, or by its members. If the limited liability company is managed by its members, management authority is vested in its members in proportion to their capital contributions to the company. M is managed by its designated managers, A, B, and C.

Under the Act, neither the members nor the designated managers of a limited liability company are liable for any debts, obligations, or liabilities of the limited liability company.

The Act also provides that the interest of a member in a limited liability company is part of the personal estate of the member; however, each member can assign or transfer the member's respective interest in the limited liability company only upon the unanimous written consent of all the remaining members. In the event that the remaining members fail to approve the assignment or transfer, the assignee or transferee has no right to participate in the management or become a member of the limited liability company. However, the assignee or transferee is entitled to receive the share of profits or other compensation and the return of contributions to which the transferring member would otherwise be entitled.

A limited liability company formed under the Act is dissolved upon the occurrence of any of the following events: (1) when the period fixed for the duration of the company expires; (2) by the unanimous written consent of all the members; or (3) by the death, retirement, resignation, expulsion, bankruptcy, dissolution of a member or

(continued)

Exhibit 6–1. Internal Revenue Service ruling on the tax consequences of forming a limited liability company *(continued)*

occurrence of any other event that terminates the continued membership of a member, unless the business of the company is continued by the consent of all the remaining members under a right to do so stated in the articles of organization of the company. Under M's articles of organization, the business of M is continued by the consent of all the remaining members.

LAW AND ANALYSIS

Section 7701(a)(2) of the Internal Revenue Code provides that the term 'partnership' includes a syndicate, group, pool, venture, or other unincorporated organization, through or by means of which any business, financial operation, or venture is carried on, and which is not a trust or estate or a corporation.

Section 7701(a)(3) of the Code provides that the term 'corporation' includes associations, joint-stock companies, and insurance companies.

Section 301.7701-2(a)(1) of the regulations sets forth the following basic characteristics of a corporation: (1) associates, (2) an objective to carry on business and divide the gains therefrom, (3) continuity of life, (4) centralization of management, (5) liability for corporate debts limited to corporate property, and (6) free transferability of interests. Whether a particular organization is to be classified as an association must be determined by taking into account the presence or absence of each of these corporate characteristics. In addition to the six major characteristics, other factors may be found in some cases which may be significant in classifying an organization as an association, a partnership, or a trust.

Section 301.7701-2(a)(3) of the regulations provides that if an unincorporated organization possesses more corporate characteristics than noncorporate characteristics, it constitutes an association taxable as a corporation.

In interpreting section 301.7701-2 of the regulations, the Tax Court, in Larson v. Commissioner, 66 T.C. 159 (1976), acq., 1979-1 C.B. 1, concluded that equal weight must be given to each of the four corporate characteristics of continuity of life, centralization of management, limited liability, and free transferability of interests.

Section 301.7701-2(b)(1) of the regulations provides that if the death, insanity, bankruptcy, retirement, resignation, or expulsion of any member will cause a dissolution of the organization, continuity of life does not exist.

(continued)

Exhibit 6–1. Internal Revenue Service ruling on the tax consequences of forming a limited liability company *(continued)*

Under the Act, unless the business of M is continued by the consent of all the remaining members, M is dissolved upon the death, retirement, resignation, expulsion, bankruptcy, dissolution of a member or occurrence of any other event that terminates the continued membership of a member in the company. If a member ceases to be a member of M for any reason, the continuity of M is not assured, because all remaining members must agree to continue the business. Consequently, M lacks the corporate characteristic of continuity of life.

Under the Act, a limited liability company has the discretion to be managed either by a designated manager or managers, or to be managed by its members. Because M is managed by its designated managers, A, B, and C, M possesses the corporate characteristic of centralized management.

Section 301.7701-2(d)(1) of the regulations provides that an organization has the corporate characteristic of limited liability if under local law there is no member who is personally liable for the debts of, or claims against, the organization. Personal liability means that a creditor of an organization may seek personal satisfaction from a member of the organization to the extent that the assets of such organization are insufficient to satisfy the creditor's claim.

Under the Act, neither the managers nor the members of M are personally liable for its debts and obligations. Consequently, M possesses the corporate characteristic of limited liability.

M lacks the corporate characteristic of free transferability of interests. M has associates and an objective to carry on business and divide the gains therefrom. In addition, M possesses the corporate characteristic of centralized management and limited liability. M does not, however, possess the corporate characteristics of continuity of life and free transferability of interests.

HOLDING

M has associates and an objective to carry on business and divide the gains therefrom, but lacks a preponderance of the four remaining corporate characteristics. Accordingly, M is classified as a partnership for federal tax purposes.*

*Rev. Rul. 88-76, 1988-2 C.B. 260, 1988-38 I.R.B. 1, 1988 WL 546801 (IRS RRU).

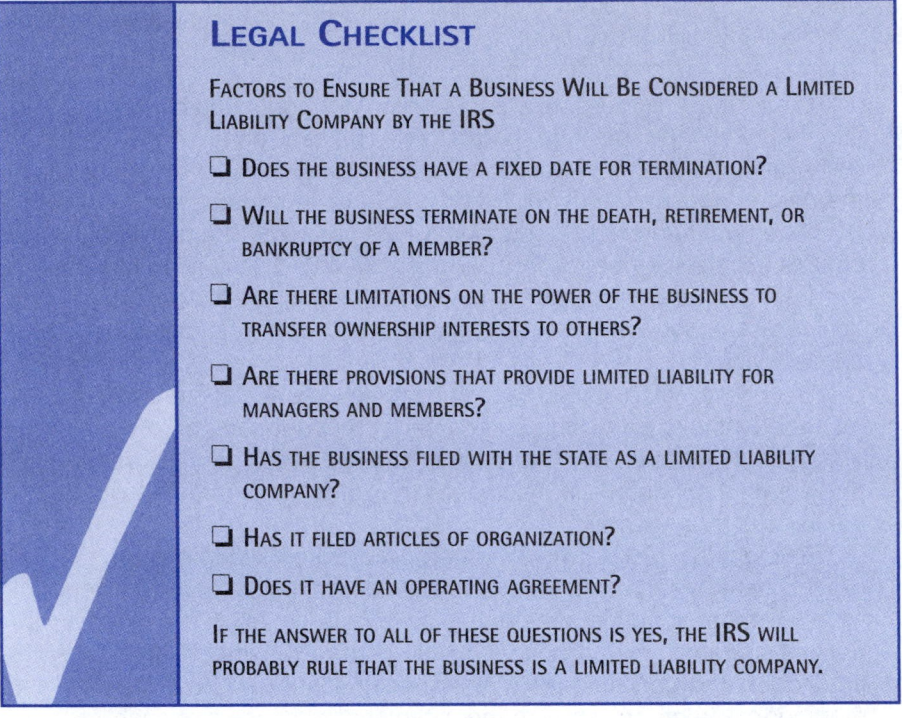

LEGAL CHECKLIST

FACTORS TO ENSURE THAT A BUSINESS WILL BE CONSIDERED A LIMITED LIABILITY COMPANY BY THE IRS

❏ DOES THE BUSINESS HAVE A FIXED DATE FOR TERMINATION?

❏ WILL THE BUSINESS TERMINATE ON THE DEATH, RETIREMENT, OR BANKRUPTCY OF A MEMBER?

❏ ARE THERE LIMITATIONS ON THE POWER OF THE BUSINESS TO TRANSFER OWNERSHIP INTERESTS TO OTHERS?

❏ ARE THERE PROVISIONS THAT PROVIDE LIMITED LIABILITY FOR MANAGERS AND MEMBERS?

❏ HAS THE BUSINESS FILED WITH THE STATE AS A LIMITED LIABILITY COMPANY?

❏ HAS IT FILED ARTICLES OF ORGANIZATION?

❏ DOES IT HAVE AN OPERATING AGREEMENT?

IF THE ANSWER TO ALL OF THESE QUESTIONS IS YES, THE IRS WILL PROBABLY RULE THAT THE BUSINESS IS A LIMITED LIABILITY COMPANY.

IRS Entity Classifications

In 1996, the IRS again revisited the issue of limited liability companies and corporations. Under the traditional analysis, set out in the legal checklist, a company's official tax status was governed by its various components. That often made for contradictory findings from one jurisdiction to another. These days, the IRS follows a more simplified approach: Under the new rules, the business organizers can choose their business type, and as long as it qualifies under state law, the IRS will treat it by its own classification. Under this rule, a company that calls itself a limited liability company and is organized and registered under state law as an LLC will be taxed as one.

▶ CREATION OF A LIMITED LIABILITY COMPANY

Because limited liability companies became so popular and were enacted in so many different states at approximately the same time, there is a greater diversity among the states for this type of business organization than for any of the others we have discussed so far. Depending on the state, the regulations concerning the creation and day-to-day operation and dissolution of limited liability companies can vary considerably. Added to that, many states enacted tax legislation to encourage companies to form their limited liability companies in their states. Delaware has long been a state favorable to corporations and, starting the 1990s, the venue of choice for forming limited liability companies. States such as Delaware and Wyoming have streamlined their application process and statutes that authorize the creation of limited liability companies.

LIMITED LIABILITY COMPANIES AS CREATURES OF STATUTES

Before considering creating a limited liability company, the business owners should spend time reviewing statutes that authorize the creation of these businesses. There is no common law of limited liability companies. This business structure derives exclusively from state statutes, and the statutes must be closely followed in order to create a viable limited liability company. It turns out that creating a limited liability company, in most states, is a relatively simple process involving filing appropriate documentation, such as the articles of organization and name reservation forms. In addition, the parties will also wish to draft an operating agreement. See Exhibit 6–2.

KEY POINT

Like corporations and limited partnerships, limited liability companies are creatures of statute.[5]

The Uniform Limited Liability Company Act

Like its predecessors, the Uniform Partnership Act and the Uniform Limited Partnership Act, the Uniform Limited Liability Company Act grew out of a need for a uniform system of creating, maintaining, and dissolving a limited liability company. As the prefatory notes state, "the allure of the limited liability company is its unique ability to bring together in a single business organization the best features of all other business forms—properly structured, its owners obtain both a corporate-styled liability shield and the pass-through tax benefits of a partnership. General and limited partnerships do not offer their partners a corporate-styled liability shield. Corporations, including those having made a Subchapter Selection, do not offer their shareholders all the pass-through tax benefits of a partnership. All state limited liability company acts contain provisions for a liability shield and partnership tax status."[6]

FILING REQUIREMENTS

Limited liability companies are formed first by filing the appropriate documentation with the state secretary of state office. One piece of this documentation is the application to reserve a specific name. In addition to that filing, most states require limited liability companies to file a copy of their articles of organization.

Exhibit 6–2. Powers of limited liability companies (Wyoming)

(a) Each limited liability company organized and existing under this act may:

   (i) Sue and be sued, complain and defend, in its name;

   (ii) Purchase, take, receive, lease or otherwise acquire, own, hold, improve, use and otherwise deal in and with real or personal property, or an interest in it, wherever situated;

   (iii) Sell, convey, mortgage, pledge, lease, exchange, transfer and otherwise dispose of all or any part of its property and assets;

   (iv) Lend money to and otherwise assist its members, managers and employees;

   (v) Purchase, take, receive, subscribe for or otherwise acquire, own, hold, vote, use, employ, sell, mortgage, lend, pledge or otherwise dispose of, and otherwise use and deal in and with shares or other interests in or obligations of other limited liability companies, domestic or foreign corporations, associations, general or limited partnerships or individuals, or direct or indirect obligations of the United States or of any government, state, territory, governmental district or municipality or of any instrumentality of it;

   (vi) Make contracts and guarantees and incur liabilities, borrow money at such rates of interest as the limited liability company may determine, issue its notes, bonds and other obligations and secure any of its obligations by mortgage or pledge of all or any part of its property, franchises and income;

   (vii) Lend money for its proper purposes, invest and reinvest its funds and take and hold real property and personal property for the payment of funds so loaned or invested;

   (viii) Conduct its business, carry on its operations and have and exercise the powers granted by this act in any state, territory, district or possession of the United States, or in any foreign country;

   (ix) Elect or appoint managers, officers, employees and agents of the limited liability company, and define their duties and authority, which may include authority also delegated to the members or managers under W.S. 17-15-117 and 17-15-118, and fix their compensation.*

*Wyoming Stat. §17-15-104.

Reserving a Company Name

All states have provisions that allow a prospective company to reserve a company name before they officially file for limited liability company status. This application reserves the name and prevents others from using it before the company has completed its application process. See Exhibit 6–3.

Exhibit 6–3. Application for reservation of name of limited liability company

APPLICATION FOR RESERVATION OF NAME
OF LIMITED LIABILITY COMPANY

Wyoming Secretary of State   Phone (307) 777-7311/7312
The Capitol Building, Room 110   Fax (307) 777-5339
200 W. 24th Street   E-mail: corporations@state.wy.us
Cheyenne, WY 82002-0020

       Pursuant to W.S. 17-15-105(d), and according to the rules promulgated by the Secretary of State of Wyoming, a person may reserve a name for a limited liability company for a one hundred twenty (120) day period, by delivering an application to the Secretary of State for filing.

1.   Name of applicant: _____

2.   Address of applicant: _____

        _____

3.   Proposed name to be reserved: _____

        _____

Date: _____   Signed: _____

Filing Fee: $50.00

llnamres - Revised: 9/2003

Naming Restrictions on a Limited Liability Company

When naming a limited liability company, the official name must contain the words "limited liability company" or the abbreviation "LLC," although some states do allow for additional designations. These naming limitations are similar to those imposed on limited partnerships and serve the same purpose: to put the public on notice that it is dealing with a company that enjoys the protections of limited liability. See Exhibit 6–4.

Exhibit 6–4. Naming limitations on limited liability companies

> (a) The words "limited liability company," or its abbreviations "LLC" or "L.L.C.," "limited company," or its abbreviations "LC" or "L.C.," "Ltd. liability company," "Ltd. liability co." or "limited liability co." shall be included in the name of every limited liability company formed under the provisions of this act and, in addition, the limited liability company name may not:
>
>   (i) Contain a word or phrase which indicates or implies that it is organized for a purpose other than one (1) or more of the purposes contained in its articles of organization;
>
>   (ii) Be the same as, or deceptively similar to, any trademark or service mark registered in this state and shall be distinguishable upon the records of the secretary of state from other business names as provided in W.S. 17-16-401.*

*Wyoming Stat. §17-15-105.

ARTICLES OF ORGANIZATION

articles of organization The document that sets out the organization, powers, duration, day-to-day operation, and eventual dissolution of a limited liability company.

Like the certificate of limited partnership mentioned in the last chapter, the **articles of organization** set out the details of the limited liability company. For instance, the articles will list the names of the agent for service of process, the mailing address of the principal office of the company, the style of management, and any other matters that the owners feel they wish to make a part of the public record. See Exhibits 6–5 and 6–6.

OPERATING AGREEMENT

operating agreement The general business agreement between members and managers as to the function of a limited liability company.

The **operating agreement** forms the entire framework for all interactions between members in an LLC. The agreement sets out the many issues involved in creating, running, and eventually dissolving the business. Any operating agreement should address the following issues:

- finance and management
- members' percentage of interest in LLC

Exhibit 6–5. State of California limited liability company articles of organization form

---

State of California
Kevin Shelley
Secretary of State

LIMITED LIABILITY COMPANY
ARTICLES OF ORGANIZATION

A $70.00 filing fee must accompany this form.

IMPORTANT – Read instructions before completing this form.

File # _____

This Space For Filing Use Only

ENTITY NAME (End the name with the words "Limited Liability Company," "Ltd. Liability Co.," or the abbreviations "LLC" or "L.L.C.")

1. NAME OF LIMITED LIABILITY COMPANY

PURPOSE (The following statement is required by statute and may not be altered.)

2. THE PURPOSE OF THE LIMITED LIABILITY COMPANY IS TO ENGAGE IN ANY LAWFUL ACT OR ACTIVITY FOR WHICH A LIMITED LIABILITY COMPANY MAY BE ORGANIZED UNDER THE BEVERLY-KILLEA LIMITED LIABILITY COMPANY ACT.

INITIAL AGENT FOR SERVICE OF PROCESS (If the agent is an individual, the agent must reside in California and both Items 3 and 4 must be completed. If the agent is a corporation, the agent must have on file with the California Secretary of State a certificate pursuant to Corporations Code section 1505 and Item 3 must be completed (leave Item 4 blank).

3. NAME OF INITIAL AGENT FOR SERVICE OF PROCESS

4. IF AN INDIVIDUAL, ADDRESS OF INITIAL AGENT FOR SERVICE OF PROCESS IN CALIFORNIA   CITY   STATE   ZIP CODE

     CA

MANAGEMENT (Check only one)

5. THE LIMITED LIABILITY COMPANY WILL BE MANAGED BY:

☐ ONE MANAGER

☐ MORE THAN ONE MANAGER

☐ ALL LIMITED LIABILITY COMPANY MEMBER(S)

ADDITIONAL INFORMATION

6. ADDITIONAL INFORMATION SET FORTH ON THE ATTACHED PAGES, IF ANY, IS INCORPORATED HEREIN BY THIS REFERENCE AND MADE A PART OF THIS CERTIFICATE.

EXECUTION

7. I DECLARE I AM THE PERSON WHO EXECUTED THIS INSTRUMENT, WHICH EXECUTION IS MY ACT AND DEED.

_____   _____

SIGNATURE OF ORGANIZER   DATE

_____

TYPE OR PRINT NAME OF ORGANIZER

RETURN TO (Enter the name and the address of the person or firm to whom a copy of the filed document should be returned.)

8. NAME

FIRM

ADDRESS

CITY/STATE/ZIP

LLC-1 (REV 12/2004)   APPROVED BY SECRETARY OF STATE

Exhibit 6–6. Articles of organization

(1) In order to form a limited liability company, articles of organization of a limited liability company shall be executed and filed with the Department of State by one or more members or authorized representatives of the limited liability company. The articles of organization shall set forth:

(a) The name of the limited liability company.

(b) The mailing address and the street address of the principal office of the limited liability company.

(c) The name and street address of its initial registered agent for service of process in the state. The articles of organization shall include or be accompanied by the written statement required by s. 608.415.

(d) Any other matters that the members elect to include in the articles of organization.

(2) A limited liability company is formed at the time described in s. 608.409 if the person filing the articles of organization has substantially complied with the requirements of this section.

(3) The articles of organization shall be executed by at least one member or the authorized representative of a member.

(4) If the limited liability company is to be managed by one or more managers, the articles of organization may, but need not, include a statement that the limited liability company is to be a manager-managed company.

(5) The fact that articles of organization are on file with the Department of State is notice that the entity formed in connection with the filing of the articles of organization is a limited liability company formed under the laws of this state and is notice of all other facts set forth in the articles of organization.*

*California Corporations Code. §§17050–17062.

- members' rights and responsibilities
- members' voting power
- allocation of profits and losses
- rules for meetings and votes
- transfer issues

Although most of these issues are self-explanatory, the last category, transfer issues, bears some discussion. One of the limitations placed on limited liability companies is that interest in the company is not freely transferable to other individuals. When a member withdraws from a limited liability company, the business will be dissolved, unless there is some provision permitting it to continue. The operating agreement may set out some provisions that allow transfer of interest to other members, but as we saw in the IRS ruling, it is the limitations on the transfer of ownership interests that keep a limited liability company from receiving double taxation, and therefore those limitations must be strictly maintained.

Judicial Interpretation of Operating Agreements

Just as we have seen in other contexts, courts are often called upon to interpret the language in operating agreements in the same way that they must interpret the language in contracts and partnership agreements. When an operating agreement contains ambiguous or contradictory terms, courts must attempt to resolve these conflicts in such a way as to keep the company functioning.

Hiring attorneys to draft the operating agreement is one way of making sure that the operating agreement meets all of the minimum legal standards. However, this can be an expensive proposition because each agreement must be tailor-made to the facts and circumstances of the specific business. Very few operating agreements exist in a standardized form that would be applicable to the wide variety of business types that have adopted limited liability company models. See Exhibit 6–7.

Exhibit 6–7. Operating agreements under the Uniform Limited Liability Company Act

(a) Except as otherwise provided in subsection (b), all members of a limited liability company may enter into an operating agreement, which need not be in writing, to regulate the affairs of the company and the conduct of its business, and to govern relations among the members, managers, and company. To the extent the operating agreement does not otherwise provide, this [Act] governs relations among the members, managers, and company.

(b) The operating agreement may not:
   (1) unreasonably restrict a right to information or access to records under Section 408;
   (2) eliminate the duty of loyalty under Section 409(b) or 603(b)(3), but the agreement may:
      (i) identify specific types or categories of activities that do not violate the duty of loyalty, if not manifestly unreasonable; and
      (ii) specify the number or percentage of members or disinterested managers that may authorize or ratify, after full disclosure of all material facts, a specific act or transaction that otherwise would violate the duty of loyalty;

(continued)

Exhibit 6–7. Operating agreements under the Uniform Limited Liability Company Act
(continued)

> (3) unreasonably reduce the duty of care under Section 409(c) or 603(b)(3);
> (4) eliminate the obligation of good faith and fair dealing under Section 409(d), but the operating agreement may determine the standards by which the performance of the obligation is to be measured, if the standards are not manifestly unreasonable;
> (5) vary the right to expel a member in an event specified in Section 601(6);
> (6) vary the requirement to wind up the limited liability company's business in a case specified in Section 801(3) or (4); or
> (7) restrict rights of a person, other than a manager, member, and transferee of a member's distributional interest, under this [Act].*

*Uniform Limited Liability Company Act §103.

Unwritten or Nonexistent Operating Agreements

Given the importance of the operating agreement, it might seem odd to consider the fact that the laws authorizing limited liability companies do not actually require one. Most states opt for an approach that takes a very liberal view of what constitutes an operating agreement. For instance, some states have ruled that an agreement that was drafted when the business was a partnership might also suffice for a newly created limited liability company.[7]

Transfer of Interests

Modern law allows members to freely transfer their interests to others. For an example of a provision detailing how and when a member can transfer interest in an LLC, see Exhibit 6–8.

DISSOLUTION OF A LIMITED LIABILITY COMPANY

Limited liability companies can be dissolved by any of a number of actions. Many of the circumstances that will terminate a limited partnership are similar to those that bring about dissolution of a limited liability company. For instance, a limited liability company might have a specific life span. The company may have been created with a specific time period in mind. When that time period is up, the company will automatically dissolve. The company may have been formed with a specific purpose in mind, and when that purpose is satisfied, the operating agreement authorizes the termination of the

Exhibit 6–8. Operating agreement for limited liability company (Courtesy of West, a Thomson business)

OPERATING AGREEMENT
OF
_____, LLC

This Operating Agreement (this "Agreement") of _____ [Limited Liability Company or L.L.C. or LLC], a _____ [state] limited liability company (the "Company"), is adopted and entered into on _____ [date], by and among _____ and _____, as members (the "Members," which term includes any other persons who may become members of the Company in accordance with the terms of this Agreement and the Act) and the Company pursuant to and in accordance with the Limited Liability Company Law of the State of _____, as amended from time to time (the "Act"). Terms used in this Agreement which are not otherwise defined shall have the respective meanings given those terms in the Act.

In consideration of the matters described above, and of the mutual benefits and obligations set forth in this agreement, the parties agree as follows:

ARTICLE ONE
NAME

The name of the limited liability company under which it was formed is _____ [Limited Liability Company or L.L.C. or LLC].

ARTICLE TWO
TERM

_____ [The Company] shall dissolve on _____ (date) unless dissolved before such date in accordance with the Act.
or
The Company shall continue until dissolved in accordance with the Act.

ARTICLE THREE
MANAGEMENT

Management of the Company is vested in its Members, who will manage the Company in accordance with the Act. Any Member exercising management powers or responsibilities will be deemed to be a manager for purposes of applying the provisions of the Act, unless the context otherwise requires, and that Member will have and be subject to all of the duties and liabilities of a manager provided in

(continued)

Exhibit 6–8. Operating agreement for limited liability company (Courtesy of West, a Thomson business) *(continued)*

the Act. The Members will have the power to do any and all acts necessary or convenient to or for the furtherance of the purposes of the Company set forth in this Agreement, including all powers of Members under the Act.

ARTICLE FOUR
PURPOSE

The purpose of the Company is to engage in any lawful act or activity for which limited liability companies may be formed under the Act and to engage in any and all activities necessary or incidental to these acts.

ARTICLE FIVE
MEMBERS

The names and the business, residence or mailing address of the members are as follows:

Name   Address

_____ _____

_____ _____

_____ _____

ARTICLE SIX
CAPITAL CONTRIBUTIONS

The Members have contributed to the Company the following amounts, in the form of cash, property or services rendered, or a promissory note or other obligation to contribute cash or property or to render services:

Member   Amount of Capital Contribution

_____ $_____

_____ $_____

_____ $_____

ARTICLE SEVEN
ADDITIONAL CONTRIBUTIONS

No member is required to make any additional capital contribution to the Company.

(continued)

Exhibit 6–8. Operating agreement for limited liability company (Courtesy of West, a Thomson business) *(continued)*

ARTICLE EIGHT
ALLOCATION OF PROFITS AND LOSSES

The Company's profits and losses will be allocated in proportion to the value of the capital contributions of the Members.

ARTICLE NINE
DISTRIBUTIONS

Distributions shall be made to the Members at the times and in the aggregate amounts determined by the Members. Such distributions shall be allocated among the Members in the same proportion as their then capital account balances.

ARTICLE TEN
WITHDRAWAL OF MEMBER

A Member may withdraw from the Company in accordance with the Act.

ARTICLE ELEVEN
ASSIGNMENTS

A Member may assign in whole or part his or her membership interest in the Company; provided, however, an assignee of a membership interest may not become a Member without the vote or written consent of at least a majority in interest of the Members, other than the Member who assigns or proposes to assign his or her membership interest.

ARTICLE TWELVE
ADMISSION OF ADDITIONAL MEMBERS

One or more additional Members of the Company may be admitted to the Company with the vote or written consent of a majority in interest of the Members (as defined in the Act).

ARTICLE THIRTEEN
LIABILITY OF MEMBERS

The members do not have any liability for the obligations or liabilities of the Company, except to the extent provided in the Act.

(continued)

Exhibit 6–8. Operating agreement for limited liability company (Courtesy of West, a Thomson business) *(continued)*

ARTICLE FOURTEEN
EXCULPATION OF MEMBER-MANAGERS

A Member exercising management powers or responsibilities for or on behalf of the Company will not have personal liability to the Company or its members for damages for any breach of duty in that capacity, provided that nothing in this Article shall eliminate or limit: (i) the liability of any Member-Manager if a judgment or other final adjudication adverse to him or her establishes that his or her acts or omissions were in bad faith or involved intentional misconduct or a knowing violation of law, or that he or she personally gained in fact a financial profit or other advantage to which he or she was not legally entitled, or that, with respect to a distribution to Members, his or her acts were not performed in accordance with Section _____ of the Act; or (ii) the liability of any Member-Manager for any act or omission prior to the date of first inclusion of this paragraph in this Agreement.

ARTICLE FIFTEEN
GOVERNING LAW

This Agreement shall be governed by, and construed in accordance with, the laws of the State of _____, all rights and remedies being governed by those laws.

ARTICLE SIXTEEN
INDEMNIFICATION

To the fullest extent permitted by law, the Company shall indemnify and hold harmless, and may advance expenses to, any Member, manager or other person, or any testator or intestate of such Member, manager or other person (collectively, the "Indemnitees"), from and against any and all claims and demands whatsoever; provided, however, that no indemnification may be made to or on behalf of any Indemnitee if a judgment or other final adjudication adverse to such Indemnitee establishes: (i) that his or her acts were committed in bad faith or were the result of active and deliberate dishonesty and were material to the cause of action so adjudicated; or (ii) that he or she personally gained in fact a financial profit or other advantage to which he or she was not legally entitled. The provisions of this section shall continue to afford protection to each Indemnitee regardless of whether he or she remains a Member, manager, employee or agent of the Company.

(continued)

Exhibit 6–8. Operating agreement for limited liability company (Courtesy of West, a Thomson business) *(continued)*

ARTICLE SEVENTEEN
TAX MATTERS

The Members of the Company and the Company intend that the Company be treated as a partnership for all income tax purposes, and will file all necessary and appropriate forms in furtherance of that position.

In witness, the parties have executed this agreement the day and year first above written.

[Signatures]*

---

*Am. Jur. LF §167A:9.

company. The withdrawal of a member will also trigger the dissolution of the limited liability company. There are usually provisions in the operating agreement that allow the members to expel one of their own for a specific reason and thus keep the limited liability company functioning. See Exhibit 6–9.

Exhibit 6–9. Dissolution of limited liability company

(a) A limited liability company organized under this chapter shall be dissolved upon the occurrence of any of the following events:
  (i)   When the period fixed for the duration of the limited liability company shall expire;
  (ii) By the unanimous written agreement of all members; or
  (iii) Upon the death, retirement, resignation, expulsion, bankruptcy, dissolution of a member or occurrence of any other event which terminates the continued membership of a member in the limited liability company, unless the business of the limited liability company is continued by the consent of all the remaining members under a right to do so stated in the articles of organization of the limited liability company.
(b) As soon as possible following the occurrence of any of the events specified in this section effecting the dissolution of the limited liability company, the limited liability company shall execute a statement of intent to dissolve in such form as shall be prescribed by the secretary of state.*

---

*Wyoming Stat. §17-15-123.

Members can be removed from the company by the votes of the other members. A member may lose his or her membership for any of the following reasons:

- filing of a personal bankruptcy
- death
- declaration of mental incompetence

Consequences of Member Withdrawal

When a member withdraws from a limited liability company, he or she is entitled to return of the original contribution. In this context, contribution consists of the monetary investment that the member made in the business. Contribution can also come in the form of services provided, property transferred, or anything else of value. The rules about contribution to limited liability companies are virtually interchangeable with the rules that we discussed in the previous chapter concerning contributions to limited partnerships. See Exhibit 6–10.

Exhibit 6–10. Distributions on withdrawal from a limited liability company

On any event of withdrawal of a member, except as otherwise provided in an operating agreement, the withdrawn member and the withdrawn member's personal representatives, successors and assigns do not have the right to receive any distribution by reason of the withdrawal but do have the rights of an assignee of the withdrawn member's interest in the limited liability company to receive distributions with respect to the member's interest during any continuation of the business of the limited liability company and during and on completion of winding up less any damages recoverable against the withdrawn member if the event of withdrawal violated an operating agreement.*

*Arizona Stat. A.R.S. §29-707.

Ethics File: Fiduciary Duties Owed by Members and Managers of Limited Liability Companies

Oddly enough, most of the states that provide a wealth of detail about the creation of limited liability companies provide few, if any, rules when it comes to the fiduciary and ethical duties that members owe one another. The patchwork of legislation has led to variations in fiduciary responsibilities among members and managers. Because of this, members of limited liability companies must be aware that the state of law regarding fiduciary obligations between the members is in this state of flux. It may well be that, in the future, courts will more clearly define the fiduciary obligations and ethical duties that members owe one another and to third parties. This is another example of why it's important to remain familiar with changes in law and stay updated on changes in statutes and case law regarding business organizations.

CASE LAW: *Controlling Former Members of Limited Liability Companies*

Advanced Orthopedics, L.L.C. v. Moon[8]
GOTHARD, Judge.

This is an appeal of a trial court decision which granted summary judgments in favor of plaintiff and third party defendant. For the following reasons, we affirm.

FACTS

On November 20, 1992, Byron Heath ("Heath") and John E. Moon ("Moon") established a prosthetic and orthotic services business in the Parish of Jefferson, State of Louisiana, called Advanced Orthopedics, L.L.C. ("Advanced"). Pursuant to LSA-R.S. 12:1301, et seq., Heath filed Advanced's Articles of Organization and an Initial Report with the Louisiana Secretary of State's Office. On November 25, 1992, the secretary of state issued a certificate of organization, recognizing Advanced as a Limited Liability Company ("L.L.C.") and authorizing Advanced to transact business as an L.L.C.

Thereafter, Advanced, under the management of Heath and Moon, began providing prosthetic and orthotic services to the community. By June of 1993, Moon and Heath were having difficulties in managing Advanced together. Negotiations for a potential buy-out were held, but to no avail. By November of 1993, Moon had opened his own prosthetic and orthotic services business, Moon Orthopedics. After setting up his new business, and upon the advice of his own counsel, Moon resigned from Advanced.

On November 29, 1993, Advanced filed a "petition for permanent injunction and damages" against Moon, alleging that Moon violated his fiduciary duties to Advanced during the time that he was setting up his competing business, and requesting an injunction to prevent Moon from soliciting Advanced's patients and compelling him to return certain "patient records, posting registers, library references, supplier catalogues, and all equipment not originally contributed by him to the L.L.C. as his capital contribution."

On December 13, 1993, the trial court granted a preliminary injunction in favor of Advanced, enjoining Moon from soliciting any patients of Advanced or using any of Advanced's records without prior written consent. Moon thereafter answered Advanced's petition and filed a third party demand against Heath, alleging Heath "fraudulently enticed" Moon to become a manager of Advanced and that Heath violated his fiduciary duty to Advanced by his "non-participation" which resulted "in the constructive expulsion of John E. Moon as a manager member of Advanced Orthopedics, L.L.C." Moon also filed a reconventional demand against Advanced for refusing "to account to John E. Moon for his membership interest prior to or following his withdrawal from Advanced Orthopedics, L.L.C. "

It defies logic to believe that one party's non-participation in a business would result in the constructive expulsion of another party.

On July 11, 1994, Advanced and Heath filed motions for summary judgment on Moon's reconventional demand and third party demand against them. On September 2, 1994, Moon amended his original answer to the suit, alleging that Advanced "was not a legally formed limited liability company," or, alternatively, when Moon did not sign a proposed operating agreement, "he effectively withdrew from the L.L.C. resulting in mandatory dissolution by operation of law pursuant to Louisiana Revised Statute 12:1334(3)."

On September 7, 1994, a hearing on the motions for summary judgment was held. On September 13, 1994, the trial court granted both motions for summary judgment and dismissed Moon's reconventional demand and third party demand with prejudice.

Moon thereafter brought this appeal, alleging that: 1) "The district court erred in holding that there

(continued)

CASE LAW: *Controlling Former Members of Limited Liability Companies* (continued)

existed no genuine issue of material fact in dispute relative to the subjective intent of the parties to form a limited liability company;" and 2) "In the alternative, the district court erred as a matter of law in determining that there were no genuine issues of material fact in dispute as to John Moon's right to a capital contribution distribution."

ANALYSIS

In Moon's first assignment of error, he argues that he did not have the subjective intent to form an L.L.C. with Heath, and that therefore, a material fact is still in dispute. We disagree. During the year that Moon participated in the management of Advanced, he never questioned its viability as an L.L.C. He testified in his deposition that he reviewed informational materials regarding L.L.C.s prior to Advanced's inception and that he knew that he and Heath were operating their business as an L.L.C. Furthermore, LSA-R.S. 12:1304B provides in pertinent part that "[t]he certificate of organization shall be conclusive evidence of the fact that the limited liability company has been duly organized . . ." Advanced clearly provided enough evidence to the trial court to support its argument that an L.L.C. was formed and operating. The burden then shifted to Moon to present evidence that material facts were still at issue, and he could no longer rest on the allegations and denials contained in his pleadings. Durrosseau, supra.

On appeal, Moon argues that he did not adequately understand the concept of an L.L.C. and that because he did not sign a proposed operating agreement, he rejected the formation of an L.L.C. These arguments fail to place material issues of fact in dispute. Attaining a certain level of understanding regarding L.L.C.s is not a prerequisite to the formation of and participation in one. Further, we are aware of no requirement in the law that an L.L.C. have an operating agreement to be viable.

After a thorough review of the record, we cannot find any support for Moon's assertion that somehow he did not have the subjective intent to form an L.L.C. with Heath.

Moon's second assignment of error, that the trial court erred by finding that he is not entitled to any reimbursement for a capital contribution from Advanced, likewise lacks merit. Moon testified in his deposition that he agreed with Heath that each of them would contribute $10,000.00 to start up their business. However, since Moon did not have the money, Heath agreed to contribute the full $20,000.00 and be reimbursed for Moon's $10,000.00 in the future. Moon argues on appeal that the trial court erred by finding that Moon was not entitled to any reimbursement for a capital contribution because he did not make a contribution in cash. He asserts that pursuant to LSA-R.S. 12:1321, a capital contribution does not have to be in the form of cash, and that he made capital contributions to Advanced via his past experience, good will, services rendered and equipment he contributed, "which assisted this business in its infancy."

While it is true that capital contributions do not have to be in the form of cash, Moon has offered no proof to support his assertion that he made non-cash capital contributions to Advanced. There is no evidence in the record that Heath and Moon agreed that Moon would make a non-cash capital contribution, nor is there any evidence that Moon did so on his own volition. The only evidence in the record regarding capital contributions is Moon's deposition testimony that he put up nothing. Standing alone, Moon's assertion that he made non-cash capital contributions is insufficient to overcome his burden of proof for the purposes of a summary judgment. La.Code Civ.Proc. art. 967.

Lastly, in Advanced's brief, counsel for Advanced requests that, pursuant to U.R.C.A. rule 2-12.4, counsel for Moon be punished and sanctioned for contempt of court for making "[i]nsulting, abusive, discourteous, and irrelevant matter or criticism of opposing counsel . . ." The portion of Moon's brief which counsel for Advanced finds offensive is a three sentence statement where counsel for Moon calls into question counsel for Advanced's propriety in purportedly representing both Advanced and Moon at the same time. While superfluous and not relevant to the issues before us today, we do not find that counsel for Moon's comments rise to the level required for punishment for contempt of court under rule 2-12.4.

> *In reference to an October of 1993 letter sent by counsel for Advanced to Moon regarding his involvement in both Advanced and his newly formed competing company, Moon Orthopedics, Moon's brief states: "Ironically, the legal advise [sic] given to Moon was given to him by Raymond P. Ladouceur, attorney for Byron Heath, as well as attorney for Advanced Orthopedics. In light of this fact, one must question the propriety of Mr. Ladouceur's involvement as counsel for opposing parties in this particular case. It is apparent that Mr. Ladouceur should have disqualified himself from the representation in this particular case."*

For the foregoing reasons, the trial court's September 13, 1994 judgment, granting summary judgment in favor of Advanced Orthopedics, L.L.C., dismissing the reconventional demand of John E. Moon with prejudice; and granting summary judgment in favor of Byron Heath, dismissing the reconventional demand of John E. Moon with prejudice, is hereby affirmed.

AFFIRMED.

CASE QUESTIONS

1. What are the allegations that Advanced Orthopedics, L.L.C. brought against Moon?

2. What is the basis of Moon's claim for "fraudulent enticement" to become a manager of the limited liability company?

3. Explain Moon's allegation that the limited liability company was not properly formed.

4. What does the court rule about Moon's contention about the viability of the limited liability company he formed with Heath?

5. According to the court, did Moon make non-cash contributions to the business?

CASE LAW: *When a Limited Liability Company Has Only One Member*

In re Paul J. Ferrigan Revocable Trust [9]
PER CURIAM.

Respondents-appellants Ferrigan, Ferrigan, Wrobel, and Robinson appeal as of right from an order of the probate court interpreting decedent's estate documents, which consist of a will, a trust, an amendment to the trust, and an operating agreement for a limited liability company (LLC). We affirm.

This appeal involves the interpretation of decedent's estate documents, as well as the applicable statutes. If the language is unambiguous, "the proper role of a court is simply to apply the terms of the statute to the circumstances in a particular case." *Veenstra v. Washtenaw Country Club*, 466 Mich. 155, 159-160; 645 NW2d 643 (2002). "As in the context of statutory interpretation, the core purpose of interpreting wills is to give effect to the drafter's intent, limited only by applicable law," and to that end, the

(continued)

CASE LAW: *When a Limited Liability Company Has Only One Member* (continued)

relevant documents are to be read as a whole and harmonized if possible, but plain language should not be overscrutinized. *In re Estate of Bem*, 247 Mich.App 427, 433-434; 637 NW2d 506 (2001). Trust documents are construed according to the same rules applicable to wills. *In re Maloney Trust*, 423 Mich. 632, 639; 377 NW2d 791 (1985). Proper interpretation of a contract is also a question of law reviewed de novo with the goal being to determine and carry out the parties' intent. *Klapp v United Ins Group Agency, Inc*, 468 Mich. 459, 463, 473; 663 NW2d 447 (2003).

The first question on appeal is whether the operating agreement for Ferrigan Farm, LLC, is valid. We find that it is not.

Decedent was the only member of the LLC when the operating agreement was executed on August 9, 2001. At the time, MCL 450.4102(2)(n) defined "operating agreement" to require more than one member in the LLC. 2000 PA 336. However, 2002 PA 686 amended the statute to allow operating agreements for companies with only one member. MCL 450.4102(2)(q). Simultaneously, the Legislature also enacted MCL 450.4215, which states, "An operating agreement of a limited liability company that has 1 member is not unenforceable because only 1 person is a party to the operating agreement." Thus, the question before us is whether the operating agreement became valid by operation of the statutory changes.

In determining whether a statute should apply retroactively, the intent of the Legislature governs, but statutes are presumed to be prospective absent a clear indication to the contrary. *Frank W Lynch & Co v. Flex Technologies, Inc*, 463 Mich. 578, 583; 624 NW2d 180 (2001). We see nothing in the language of the statute that indicates that the Legislature intended for it to apply retroactively. *Id.* at 584. ("Most instructive is the fact that the Legislature included no express language regarding retroactivity."). Additionally, although "in Michigan, a legislative analysis is a feeble indicator of legislative intent and is therefore a generally unpersuasive tool of statutory construction," *Id.*

at 587, we nevertheless note that legislative analysis of the public act indicates a desire to clarify that a single person was thereafter authorized to enter into an agreement with himself despite the apparently illogical nature of doing so. Enrolled Analysis SB 1418, p 5. A remedial statute might be retroactive, but legislation such as this that affects substantive rights is not remedial. *Frank W Lynch & Co, supra* at 585. Thus, every indication is that the Legislature did not intend 2002 PA 686 to apply retroactively.

Respondents-appellants further argue that MCL 450.5102 allows retroactive application of any changes in the law. That section states, "This act may be supplemented, altered, amended, or repealed by the legislature, and every limited liability company subject to this act is bound by the changes." On its face, § 5102 only states that LLCs will be required to comply with any changes the Legislature makes to the MLLCA. As with 2002 PA 686, it contains no retrospective language. We therefore decline to find it a general-purpose statute designed to make any changes to the entire act automatically retroactive.

In the absence of any specific language stating that 2002 PA 686 was to be applied retroactively, considering the fact that it is not remedial in nature, and, notwithstanding its minimally probative nature, we conclude that it was not intended to reanimate invalid operating agreements. The operating agreement here was invalid when it was executed, and it remained that way.

Respondents-appellants argue that the operating agreement should constitute a valid governing document akin to bylaws even if it is not a valid statutory operating agreement. Operating agreements are intended to function as the LLC equivalent of bylaws in a corporation. Moreover, the Michigan Limited Liability Company Act (MLLCA), MCL 450.4101 *et. seq.*, does not provide for any governing documents other than operating agreements. Although members are free to contract with each other, such documents would only be enforceable against the contracting parties. Thus, only an actual, valid, statutory operating agreement may be used as a governing document for a LLC under the MLLCA. Petitioner was not a party to the operating agreement here. Thus, the operating agreement was not a valid governing document binding on petitioner under the MLLCA.

Respondents-appellants next argue that the amendment to the trust created a mandatory gift that requires petitioner to transfer decedent's farm into the LLC and distribute it to the seven beneficiaries. We disagree.

The relevant original trust language was as follows:

5.2 Specific Gifts. Trustee shall make the following distributions from principal:

none at this time

If any above-named individual does not survive Settlor, or if any above-named organization is not in existence at Settlor's death, such gift or gifts shall fail if there is no substitute beneficiary named. Trustee shall make the distributions at such reasonable times as Trustee deems advisable. No interest shall be paid on any of these gifts. Absent a problem in construing this paragraph, a beneficiary who receives a distribution only under this paragraph is to be informed only of that specific gift and is not to receive any inventory, accounting, or information about gifts to other beneficiaries.

The amendment then provided as follows:

Pursuant to the right reserved to me under the provisions of the above Trust, I amend that Trust as follows:

I amend Article V, 5.2 Specific Gifts, by authorizing the following gift:

It is my intention that all my Farm property remaining at my death, currently consisting of 159 acres (in 4 deeds) located in Woodhull Township, Shiawassee County, Michigan, be transferred to my limited liability company, Ferrigan Farm, LLC, and that said limited liability company then be distributed according to Article V, 5.4 "Balance of Property", of this Trust.

The word "shall" is unambiguously mandatory. *Roberts v. Mecosta Co Gen Hosp*, 466 Mich. 57, 65; 642 NW2d 663 (2002). However, to "authorize" refers to

granting authority, permission, or approval, so it is not mandatory. See *Random House Webster's College Dictionary* (1997) and Black's Law Dictionary (7th ed). The plain language of the amendment therefore permits the gift of the farm to the LLC but does not require it.

" 'The intent of the testator is the cardinal rule in the construction of wills, and if that intent can be clearly conceived, and it is not contrary to some positive rule of law, it must prevail.' " *Foster v. Stevens*, 146 Mich. 131, 136; 109 NW 265 (1906), quoting *Finlay v. King's Lessee*, 28 U.S. (3 Pet) 346, 363; 7 L Ed 701 (1830). That intention is to be determined by reading the relevant documents as a whole. *In re Ives' Estate*, 182 Mich. 699, 704; 148 NW 727 (1914).

When the amendment is read as a whole, respondents-appellants' argument that it was intended to augment, rather than replace, § 5.2 in the trust is clearly correct. It states that it is an amendment, and it specifies no deletions or replacements. Thus, the language "Trustee shall make the following distributions from principal" in the original trust was unchanged by the amendment. Accordingly, when the trust and trust amendment are read together as a single instrument, the result is that the trust states that the trustee *shall* make "no gifts at this time" and *may* make one gift of the farm. Thus, the trust amendment creates a precatory gift only.

MCL 450.4504 states that membership in an LLC is personal property. Decedent's membership would pass into the trust through his will as a piece of intangible personal property. Thus, in an indirect sense, petitioner would be the only member, albeit only in her capacity as trustee and personal representative, with the sole fiduciary responsibility for managing that membership as a business interest under § 6.23 of the trust. Respondents-appellants cite to MCL 450.4401(a) for the proposition that petitioner must also be a manager, but managers, not members, manage the LLC, so MCL 450.4401 explicitly does not apply. Under MCL 450.4502(4)(a), the members may authorize dissolution of the company. MCL 450.4801(c) states that this may be done "upon the unanimous vote of all members entitled to vote." Because she is functionally the only member, she is authorized to do so by herself.

(continued)

CASE LAW: *When a Limited Liability Company Has Only One Member* (continued)

Because petitioner is not obligated to distribute the LLC or place the farm into it, the LLC may remain unfunded and valueless. Under § 7.14 of the trust, petitioner may abandon an asset that is valueless or otherwise not beneficial to the trust. Thus, the trial court correctly found petitioner authorized to dissolve the LLC or abandon it.

Affirmed.

CASE QUESTIONS

1. What is the issue in this case?
2. Is the operating agreement for the limited liability company in this case legally enforceable? Why or why not?
3. What is the significance that the decedent was the only member of the limited liability company?
4. Did the change in the law apply retroactively? Explain.
5. What is the argument that an operating agreement is analogous to bylaws? How does the court rule on this argument?

SUMMARY

Limited liability companies are a relatively recent phenomenon. Most states adopted limited liability company statutes in the 1980s and 1990s as a means to offer a new business model. Limited liability companies offer several advantages over other types of business structures. In a limited liability company, there are no general partners. Instead, all members are protected by limited liability. This is a great advantage over the limited partnership model, which grants limited liability protection to only certain individuals. Limited liability companies offer some of the same advantages as limited partnerships. For instance, business profits and losses are "passed through" on the individual owner's income tax returns. This avoids the problem of double taxation, where the business and the individual owners must each file a separate income tax return.

Limited liability companies are organized with managers and members. Managers run the day-to-day operation of the business, while members enjoy the profits from the business. Members may contribute to the business in the form of cash or other valuable consideration, and they will be rewarded with profit sharing commensurate with the percentage of their contribution. In limited liability companies, managers may also be members. This means that all of the participants are protected by limited liability coverage.

Limited liability companies are organized in operating agreements that set out the rights and responsibilities of all members. In order to be recognized as a limited liability company, the business must file appropriate documentation with the state. This documentation includes not only a notice that the business intends to operate as a limited liability company, but also articles of organization. These articles are the bylaws for how the business will be run.

Limited liability companies can terminate in several different ways. The operating agreement may set a specific date for termination of the business, or the company may terminate upon the death or bankruptcy of a member. Limited liability companies have great flexibility in their day-to-day operation, but they do have some limitations. For instance, the business must contain the words "limited liability company" or the abbreviation "LLC" in order to be considered a valid legal entity.

HELPFUL WEB SITES

Iowa Secretary of State—Limited Liability Companies
http://www.sos.state.ia.us/business/llc.html

California Business Portal
http://www.ss.ca.gov/business/llc/llc_formsfees.htm

Wyoming Secretary of State—How to Form a Limited Liability Company
http://soswy.state.wy.us/corporat/llc.htm

KEY TERMS

articles of organization   members

managers   operating agreement

APPLYING CHAPTER CONCEPTS

Locate a local limited liability company. What type of business does it conduct? When was it formed? What information can you glean from state records about this particular limited liability company?

REVIEW QUESTIONS

1. What advantages do limited liability companies offer over partnerships and limited partnerships?
2. When did limited liability companies become popular in the United States?
3. What was the first state to introduce legislation to authorize the creation of limited liability companies?
4. What are the tax advantages of limited liability companies?
5. How are limited liability companies organized?

6. Who runs the day-to-day operation of the limited liability company?

7. How does someone become a member of a limited liability company?

8. What filing requirements do most states impose on companies seeking limited liability company status?

9. What are articles of organization?

10. What typical features must articles of organization contain?

11. What are the naming restrictions on limited liability companies?

12. What are some of the ways that a limited liability company can be dissolved?

13. Explain the holding in this chapter's Case Law.

14. What is the significance of the Uniform Limited Liability Company Act?

15. Are limited liability companies similar to limited partnerships? Explain.

QUESTION FOR REFLECTION

With the advantages offered by limited liability companies, why would a new business opt to follow some other type of business model, such as a limited partnership or a general partnership?

ENDNOTES

[1] *Lieberman v. Wyoming.com LLC*, 11 P.3d 353 (Wyo. 2000).

[2] 41 Case W. Res. L. Rev. 387.

[3] *PB Real Estate, Inc. v. DEM II Properties*, 719 A.2d 73, 74 (Conn. App. Ct. 1998).

[4] Jonathan R. Macey, *The Limited Liability Company: Lessons for Corporate Law*, 73 Wash.U.L.Q. 433, 434 (1995).

[5] *Harbison v. Strickland*, 2004 WL 2367837 (Ala. 2004).

[6] Prefatory Notes, (1996).

[7] *Goldstein v. Tonkin*, 974 S.W.2d 543 (Mo. App. 1998). Uniform Limited Liability Corporations Act.

[8] 656 So.2d 1103 (La.App. 5 Cir. 1995).

[9] 2005 WL 2372082 4 (Mich.App. 2005).

 For additional resources visit our Web site at *http://www.westlegalstudies.com*

Chapter 7

THE RISE OF THE CORPORATION

Chapter Objectives

Upon completion of this chapter, you should be able to:

- Describe the basic structure of a corporation.
- List and describe the features that corporations have in common.
- Describe the historical development of corporations in the United States.
- Explain the significance of the Sherman Antitrust Act and the Federal Trade Commission on modern corporate law.
- Define the differences between various types of corporations.

▶ INTRODUCTION

In this chapter we will explore the foundations of corporate structure, discussing not only how corporations came into existence, but also how they are classified and how they function. We will see how corporate business structures contributed to the rise of the American economy in the 1800s and have helped to maintain the superiority of the American economy into the 21st century. But first, we must answer a more basic question: What is a corporation?

NATURE OF A CORPORATION

At its simplest, a corporation is an artificial person. Unlike all other business models, the corporation has rights similar to that of a human being. A corporation can own property, pay taxes, exist for an indefinite period, sue, and be sued.[1] In 1819, the United States Supreme Court defined a corporation as an artificial being that is invisible and untouchable, and it exists only in the theory of the law.[2] The definition has expanded considerably since that time.

First and foremost, a corporation is a creature created by statute.[3] Its existence, authority to act, and dissolution are all controlled by statutory law. What makes corporations so unusual is that unlike other forms of business, such as partnerships or sole proprietorships, corporations have a separate identity from the people who created them.[4] Statutes give corporations the power to own property, pay taxes, and do many of the actions we would normally associate with a human being. Even when the original creators die or leave the company, the corporation will continue to exist. Obviously, a corporation can function only through its agents, directors, and officers, but it is important that, unlike the case with many of the other business models we have discussed so far, the identity of these individuals is not important. They can come and go, but the corporation will continue to exist as long as there is someone who can act on its behalf.

 ### GETTING TO THE BASICS

Corporations are not simply a different form of partnership. They are artificial persons who can own property, pay taxes, hire employees, and engage in business.[5]

CORPORATIONS' LIMITED LIABILITY

We have discussed the concept of limited liability at several points throughout this book already, but it is the corporation that first adopted this important protection. Business models such as limited partnerships and limited liability companies are all latecomers to the game. Corporations have existed in one form or another for centuries. These other business types were created based on the example set by corporations. Just as we have seen with limited partnerships and limited liability companies, corporate stockholders are not personally liable for the acts or obligations of the corporation. They are protected by limited liability.[6]

KEY POINT

A corporation gets its power to act as an artificial person from state statutes that authorize its creation.

Although a corporation qualifies as an artificial person, it obviously must act through its employees, agents, officers, and directors.[7] These individuals are important members of a corporation, but the corporation exists separately from them. When it owns property, it does so in its own name. A corporation consists of **shareholders,** who own the corporation, **officers,** who carry out the day-to-day activities of the business, and **directors,** who decide on long-term policies and initiatives for the corporation. We will discuss the role of these individuals in much greater detail in chapter 8. If the individual members change, the corporation remains the same.[8] This accounts for the fact that many major corporations have long outlasted the individuals who originally created them.

ELEMENTS OF A CORPORATION

A legally constituted corporation has some basic elements. For instance, a corporation can:

- exist perpetually
- sue or be sued
- acquire and hold property in its own right
- make laws that regulate its own behavior[9]

Corporations Have Perpetual Existence

Corporations do not die. They have no set expiration date. They could, conceivably, exist forever. This does not mean that every corporation that has ever been created is still in existence today. As we will see in later chapters, corporations can terminate through bankruptcy, dissolution, or other actions. However, unlike other business ventures, corporations are not created with a termination date in mind.

Corporations Can Sue or Be Sued

A corporation can hire attorneys to bring suit against other individuals. Like a human being, a corporation can sue for violation of a contract or almost any other action. Similarly, they can also be sued. When a corporation is sued, and the suit is successful, the corporation's assets may be seized to satisfy the judgment. However, the personal assets of the individual shareholders, officers, and directors are not subject to seizure.

Corporations Can Own Property

Unlike most other business types, corporations can own property in their own right. When we have discussed sole proprietorships, general partnerships, and other business models, individuals who comprise the business almost always held title to property. A partner might have title to property and contribute that property to the business, but title remains vested in the individual. Although there are now provisions that allow other business types to hold title to property, this concept originated with corporations. In its own way, this was considered to be one of the more controversial and innovative approaches to corporate structure.

shareholder A person who owns shares in a corporation.

officer An individual hired or selected by a board of directors who has specific authority, such as the ability to bind the corporation to contracts and other agreements.

director Individuals who set policy and long-term goals for corporations.

Corporate Bylaws and Articles of Incorporation

Like limited partnerships and limited liability companies, corporations operate on agreements that set out the nature and scope of the business. The document that creates the basic structure of the corporation is the **articles of incorporation,** discussed in detail in chapter 8. A corporation can also establish bylaws that control the day-to-day operations of the business and establish policies for such things as negotiating contracts, hiring employees, disbursing funds, and many other issues.

articles of incorporation The document that frames the creation, organization, day-to-day operation, sale of assets, identity of registered agent, and dissolution of a corporation.

► A SHORT HISTORY OF CORPORATIONS IN THE UNITED STATES

Law is a conservative business. Innovations in legal thought often lag far behind innovations in society. However, when it comes to corporation law, this is not true. In the early 1800s, corporate law was a minor legal subspecialty, with relatively little influence. However, by 1870, the law of corporations had taken a commanding presence in the legal field, and it has remained so ever since. The reason for this is simple: corporate structure allowed entrepreneurs and capitalists the best structure to amass enormous wealth and property.[10]

Corporations became such a powerful vehicle that many in society began to worry about this concentration of power in the hands of so few. A relatively small clique of men controlled the bulk of the American economy and could, with relative ease, bring it to its knees.[11] The growing power of men such as Andrew Carnegie and J. P. Morgan led to a dangerous concentration of power that they were more than ready to use. These men, and the corporations that they controlled, maintained a stranglehold on the American economy.

Huge corporations, such as United States Steel Corporation or the Standard Oil Company, established monopolies in various industries. These monopolies engaged in unfair and deceptive trade practices, crippled competitors, and essentially set whatever price they wished for the products that they sold. Their power was such that men such as J. P. Morgan had more money than the United States treasury. Morgan even underwrote the federal government's budget during a financial crisis in the late 1800s. With the dawn of a new century, these huge corporations became targets for men, such as Theodore Roosevelt, who wished to break up the power of the monopolies.

MONOPOLIES

monopoly A company's absolute, or near absolute, control over an industry or business area.

In the famous Parker Brothers board game, creating a **monopoly** is a good thing. But in real life, monopolies can cause huge problems for society. When a person or company has a monopoly, it controls all aspects of a particular industry. It can force consumers to pay any price it wishes, especially when the monopoly is in an area such as oil production, where heating oil means the difference between having a comfortable winter or freezing to death. Monopolies can engage in practices such as "cutthroat competition," where they lower the prices of their goods to a point that no one else could compete. Then, when competitors have either been bought up or gone out of business, the monopoly can raise prices as high as it likes.

Whether called "trusts" or "monopolies" the basic idea was the same: a small group of individuals would completely take over a particular industry and dictate transportation, supply, and labor costs, while simultaneously wiping out all competitors. The mantra of these businessmen seemed to be "bigger is better."

The federal government was slow to regulate these industries. In the period immediately after the Civil War, neither the court system nor the Congress offered any restrictions on the rapid expanse of railroad, oil, steel, and other businesses. However, all of that began to change in the late 1800s and early 1900s. The earliest legislation to recognize the growing danger of monopolies was the Sherman Antitrust Act.

THE SHERMAN ANTITRUST ACT

The **Sherman Antitrust Act** was passed in 1890 in response to a growing antitrust movement across the country. Individuals had begun to complain about the power—and the practices—of many of these huge corporations.

The purpose of the Sherman act was to prevent many of the practices that corporations were then engaging in. The act specifically prohibited cutthroat competition and any other practice that sought to "restrain trade or commerce."[12] The primary goal of the act was to stop practices that destroyed competition. A corporation could still engage in competitive practices, but could not seek to wipe out the competition through engaging in industrial espionage, setting up dummy companies, forcing related businesses to stop working with the competition, and many of the other practices that corporations used at the time.[13] The act recognizes that competition is good for society, even if it isn't necessarily good for the profits of huge, multinational corporations.

> **Sherman Antitrust Act** One of the first federal legislative attempts to regulate the power of corporations in the United States.

 GETTING TO THE BASICS

The Sherman Antitrust Act was one of the first statutes designed to protect consumers and the general public from the power of huge corporations.[14]

The passage of the Sherman Antitrust Act was the first step by the federal government to restrict the power of corporations and a tentative step towards lower prices, better products, and advancements in production methods.[15]

Within a few years of its creation, the act was put to the test in the famous *The Standard Oil Company* case.

U.S. v. The Standard Oil Company

The Standard Oil Company was created by John and William Rockefeller in 1870 and swiftly established itself as a monopoly in oil production. Over the next three decades, Standard Oil bought up or wiped out nearly all of its competitors, using tactics that were at best questionable and were at worst illegal. In 1911, the U.S. government brought suit against Standard Oil under the Sherman Antitrust Act. The result of that hard-fought legal battle was a disbanding of the Standard Oil Corporation into smaller, less dangerous companies.[16]

The legacy of the Standard Oil case, and the Sherman Antitrust Act, remains with us today. The Federal Trade Commission, which carries out the modern job of investigating and challenging monopolies, was established in 1914 and continues to be one of the most important governmental agencies related to corporations. It maintains an antitrust division, which oversees mergers, acquisitions, and practices by leading corporations in this country. It has the power to break up companies that have engaged in unfair practices or have established monopolies in certain areas. See Exhibit 7–1.

Exhibit 7–1. 15 U.S.C.A. § 1. Commerce and trade

Chapter 1. Monopolies and Combinations in Restraint of Trade

Trusts, etc., in restraint of trade illegal; penalty

Every contract, combination in the form of trust or otherwise, or conspiracy, in restraint of trade or commerce among the several States, or with foreign nations, is declared to be illegal. Every person who shall make any contract or engage in any combination or conspiracy hereby declared to be illegal shall be deemed guilty of a felony, and, on conviction thereof, shall be punished by fine not exceeding $100,000,000 if a corporation, or, if any other person, $1,000,000, or by imprisonment not exceeding 10 years, or by both said punishments, in the discretion of the court.

CASE LAW: *Price Fixing by Corporations?*

State Oil Co. v. Khan[17]
Justice O'CONNOR delivered the opinion of the Court.

Under § 1 of the Sherman Act, 26 Stat. 209, as amended, 15 U.S.C. § 1, "[e]very contract, combination ···, or conspiracy, in restraint of trade" is illegal. In Albrecht v. Herald Co., 390 U.S. 145, 88 S.Ct. 869, 19 L.Ed.2d 998 (1968), this Court held that vertical maximum price fixing is a per se violation of that statute. In this case, we are asked to reconsider that decision in light of subsequent decisions of this Court. We conclude that Albrecht should be overruled.

I

Respondents, Barkat U. Khan and his corporation, entered into an agreement with petitioner, State Oil Company, to lease and operate a gas station and convenience store owned by State Oil. The agreement provided that respondents would obtain the station's gasoline supply from State Oil at a price equal to a suggested retail price set by State Oil, less a margin of 3.25 cents per gallon. Under the agreement, respondents could charge any amount for gasoline sold to the station's customers, but if the price charged was higher than State Oil's suggested retail price, the excess was to be rebated to State Oil. Respondents could sell gasoline for less than State Oil's suggested retail price, but any such decrease would reduce their 3.25 cents-per-gallon margin.

About a year after respondents began operating the gas station, they fell behind in lease payments. State Oil then gave notice of its intent to terminate the agreement and commenced a state court proceeding to evict respondents. At State Oil's request, the state court appointed a receiver to operate the gas station. The receiver operated the station for several months without being subject to the price restraints in respondents' agreement with State Oil. According to respondents, the receiver obtained an overall profit margin in excess of 3.25 cents per gallon by lowering the price of regular-grade gasoline and raising the price of premium grades.

Respondents sued State Oil in the United States District Court for the Northern District of Illinois, alleging in part that State Oil had engaged in price fixing in violation of § 1 of the Sherman Act by preventing respondents from raising or lowering retail gas prices. According to the complaint, but for the agreement with State Oil, respondents could have charged different prices based on the grades of gasoline, in the same way that the receiver had, thereby achieving increased sales and profits. State Oil responded that the agreement did not actually prevent respondents from setting gasoline prices, and that, in substance, respondents did not allege a violation of antitrust laws by their claim that State Oil's suggested retail price was not optimal.

The District Court found that the allegations in the complaint did not state a per se violation of the Sherman Act because they did not establish the sort of "manifestly anticompetitive implications or pernicious effect on competition" that would justify per se prohibition of State Oil's conduct. Subsequently, in ruling on cross-motions for summary judgment, the District Court concluded that respondents had failed to demonstrate antitrust injury or harm to competition. The District Court held that respondents had not shown that a difference in gasoline pricing would have increased the station's sales; nor had they shown that State Oil had market power or that its pricing provisions affected competition in a relevant market. Accordingly, the District Court entered summary judgment for State Oil on respondents' Sherman Act claim.

The Court of Appeals for the Seventh Circuit reversed. 93 F.3d 1358 (1996). The court first noted that the agreement between respondents and State Oil did indeed fix maximum gasoline prices by making it "worthless" for respondents to exceed the suggested retail prices. After reviewing legal and economic aspects of price fixing, the court concluded that State Oil's pricing scheme was a per se antitrust violation under Albrecht v. Herald Co., supra. Although the Court of Appeals characterized Albrecht as "unsound when decided" and "inconsistent with later decisions" of this Court, it felt constrained to follow that decision. 93 F.3d, at 1363. In light of Albrecht and Atlantic Richfield Co. v. USA Petroleum Co., 495 U.S. 328, 110 S.Ct. 1884, 109 L.Ed.2d 333 (1990) (ARCO), the court found that respondents could have suffered antitrust injury from not being able to adjust gasoline prices.

We granted certiorari to consider two questions, whether State Oil's conduct constitutes a per se violation of the Sherman Act and whether respondents are entitled to recover damages based on that conduct. 519 U.S. 1107, 117 S.Ct. 941, 136 L.Ed.2d 831 (1997).

(continued)

CASE LAW: *Price Fixing by Corporations?* *(continued)*

II

A

Although the Sherman Act, by its terms, prohibits every agreement "in restraint of trade," this Court has long recognized that Congress intended to outlaw only unreasonable restraints. As a consequence, most antitrust claims are analyzed under a "rule of reason," according to which the finder of fact must decide whether the questioned practice imposes an unreasonable restraint on competition, taking into account a variety of factors, including specific information about the relevant business, its condition before and after the restraint was imposed, and the restraint's history, nature, and effect.

Some types of restraints, however, have such predictable and pernicious anticompetitive effect, and such limited potential for procompetitive benefit, that they are deemed unlawful per se. Per se treatment is appropriate "[o]nce experience with a particular kind of restraint enables the Court to predict with confidence that the rule of reason will condemn it." Thus, we have expressed reluctance to adopt per se rules with regard to "restraints imposed in the context of business relationships where the economic impact of certain practices is not immediately obvious."

Albrecht involved a newspaper publisher who had granted exclusive territories to independent carriers subject to their adherence to a maximum price on resale of the newspapers to the public. Influenced by its decisions in Socony-Vacuum, Kiefer-Stewart, and Schwinn, the Court concluded that it was per se unlawful for the publisher to fix the maximum resale price of its newspapers. The Court acknowledged that "[m]aximum and minimum price fixing may have different consequences in many situations," but nonetheless condemned maximum price fixing for "substituting the perhaps erroneous judgment of a seller for the forces of the competitive market."

Albrecht was animated in part by the fear that vertical maximum price fixing could allow suppliers to discriminate against certain dealers, restrict the services that dealers could afford to offer customers, or disguise minimum price fixing schemes. The Court rejected the notion (both on the record of that case and in the abstract) that, because the newspaper publisher "granted exclusive territories, a price ceiling was necessary to protect the public from price gouging by dealers who had monopoly power in their own territories."

B

Thus, our reconsideration of Albrecht's continuing validity is informed by several of our decisions, as well as a considerable body of scholarship discussing the effects of vertical restraints. Our analysis is also guided by our general view that the primary purpose of the antitrust laws is to protect interbrand competition. "Low prices," we have explained, "benefit consumers regardless of how those prices are set, and so long as they are above predatory levels, they do not threaten competition." Our interpretation of the Sherman Act also incorporates the notion that condemnation of practices resulting in lower prices to consumers is "especially costly" because "cutting prices in order to increase business often is the very essence of competition."

So informed, we find it difficult to maintain that vertically imposed maximum prices could harm consumers or competition to the extent necessary to justify their per se invalidation. As Chief Judge Posner wrote for the Court of Appeals in this case:

"As for maximum resale price fixing, unless the supplier is a monopsonist he cannot squeeze his dealers' margins below a competitive level; the attempt to do so would just drive the dealers into the arms of a competing supplier. A supplier might, however, fix a maximum resale price in order to prevent his dealers from exploiting a monopoly position. . . . [S]uppose that State Oil, perhaps to encourage . . . dealer services . . . has spaced its dealers sufficiently far apart to limit competition among them (or even given each of them an exclusive territory); and suppose further that Union 76 is a sufficiently distinctive and popular brand to give the dealers in it at least a modicum of monopoly power. Then State Oil might want to place a ceiling on the dealers' resale prices in order to prevent them from exploiting that monopoly powerfully. It would do this not out of disinterested malice, but in its commercial self-interest. The higher the price at which gasoline is resold, the smaller the volume sold, and so the lower the profit to the supplier if the higher profit per gallon at the higher price is being snared by the dealer."

We recognize that the Albrecht decision presented a number of theoretical justifications for a per se rule against vertical maximum price fixing. But criticism of those premises abounds. The Albrecht decision was grounded in the fear that maximum price fixing by suppliers could interfere with dealer freedom.

The Albrecht Court also expressed the concern that maximum prices may be set too low for dealers to offer consumers essential or desired services. 390 U.S., at 152-153, 88 S.Ct., at 872-874. But such conduct, by driving away customers, would seem likely to harm manufacturers as well as dealers and consumers, making it unlikely that a supplier would set such a price as a matter of business judgment. In addition, Albrecht noted that vertical maximum price fixing could effectively channel distribution through large or specially advantaged dealers. It is unclear, however, that a supplier would profit from limiting its market by excluding potential dealers. Further, although vertical maximum price fixing might limit the viability of inefficient dealers, that consequence is not necessarily harmful to competition and consumers.

Finally, Albrecht reflected the Court's fear that maximum price fixing could be used to disguise arrangements to fix minimum prices, which remain illegal per se. Not only are the potential injuries cited in Albrecht less serious than the Court imagined, the per se rule established therein could in fact exacerbate problems related to the unrestrained exercise of market power by monopolist-dealers. Indeed, both courts and antitrust scholars have noted

that Albrecht's rule may actually harm consumers and manufacturers.

We do not intend to suggest that dealers generally possess sufficient market power to exploit a monopoly situation. Such retail market power may in fact be uncommon. Nor do we hold that a ban on vertical maximum price fixing inevitably has anticompetitive consequences in the exclusive dealer context.

[9] After reconsidering Albrecht's rationale and the substantial criticism the decision has received, however, we conclude that there is insufficient economic justification for per se invalidation of vertical maximum price fixing. That is so not only because it is difficult to accept the assumptions underlying Albrecht, but also because Albrecht has little or no relevance to ongoing enforcement of the Sherman Act. Moreover, neither the parties nor any of the amici curiae have called our attention to any cases in which enforcement efforts have been directed solely against the conduct encompassed by Albrecht's per se rule.

In any event, the history of various legislative proposals regarding price fixing seems neither clearly to support nor to denounce the per se rule of Albrecht. Respondents are of course free to seek legislative protection from gasoline suppliers of the sort embodied in the Petroleum Marketing Practices Act, 92 Stat. 322, 15 U.S.C. § 2801 et seq. For the reasons we have noted, however, the remedy for respondents' dispute with State Oil should not come in the form of a per se rule affecting the conduct of the entire marketplace.

There remains the question whether respondents are entitled to recover damages based on State Oil's conduct. Although the Court of Appeals noted that "the district judge was right to conclude that if the rule of reason is applicable, Khan loses,"93 F.3d, at 1362, its consideration of this case was necessarily premised on Albrecht's per se rule. Under the circumstances, the matter should be reviewed by the Court of Appeals in the first instance. We therefore vacate the judgment of the Court of Appeals and remand the case for further proceedings consistent with this opinion.

It is so ordered.

(continued)

CASE LAW: *Price Fixing by Corporations?* *(continued)*

1. The plaintiffs in this case claimed that their oil and gas supplier was engaging in violations of the Sherman Antitrust Act. What are their precise allegations?

2. Explain the wholesale/retail arrangement between State Oil Co. and Khan.

3. According to the Court, is vertical price fixing per se illegal? Why or why not?

4. Why did the Court decide to overturn the *Albrecht* decision?

5. Are all restraints of trade illegal under the Sherman act? Why or why not?

▶ PUBLIC AND PRIVATE CORPORATIONS

public corporation A corporation formed to carry out some function or service traditionally associated with state or federal government.

private corporation A corporation organized to carry out a private purpose, such as earning profits or administering a private charity.

Corporations can be broken down into two general types: **public corporations** and **private corporations**. Public corporations are closely associated with governmental agencies. Private corporations are in the business of making money, or carrying out some private concern, such as charity work. When we use the term "public corporation," we must make a distinction between corporations that carry out a public, or governmental, function and "publicly traded corporations." A publicly traded corporation is one that sells its shares on the open market. Although the two terms sound similar, there is no connection between public corporations and publicly traded corporations.

Because corporations are creatures of state law, states are free to create as many different types of corporations as they see fit. Over time, this flexibility of approach has resulted in a wide variety of corporate models.

PUBLIC CORPORATIONS

Public corporations further government affairs. They are often created by special state legislation. Examples of public corporations include corporations that have been set up to:

- care for state property, such as parks and wildlife sanctuaries
- promote education, such as colleges, universities, and schools
- provide for urban renewal[18]
- provide low-cost housing[19]

KEY POINT

In general, any corporation can be classified into one of two categories: public or private.

The distinction between public and private corporations is important. Public corporations are usually not bound by the same set of rules and statutes as are private corporations. Public corporations are often given special tax treatment and other benefits that private corporations do not receive. Public corporations, after all, are designed to carry out a public purpose and do receive some benefit for this function.

 GETTING TO THE BASICS

Public corporations are set up to carry out a governmental function; private corporations are created to carry out individual desires, such as making money or carrying out a specific agenda.

QUASI-PUBLIC CORPORATIONS

Some corporations that were not originally classified as public corporations can become de facto public corporations because of the service that they provide. Consider Scenario 7–1. When a private corporation becomes, for all intents and purposes, a public corporation, it is referred to as a **quasi-public corporation.** A good example of this type of corporation is the public service corporation.

Public service corporations were not originally created to serve as public corporations, but have received a special commission, or made a unique arrangement with the government to provide a service. Examples of quasi-public corporations include:

- telephone companies
- electric companies
- companies that provide ambulance and other emergency services

quasi–public corporation A company that was originally created as a private corporation, but after taking on a governmental function, has been reclassified.

> **Scenario 7–1. The Garbage Guy**
>
> David's Garbage Service, Inc., has been running a garbage service in the rural part of the county for years. He has several garbage trucks that run regular routes for customers. This year, the county had a severe budget shortfall and has decided to disband its garbage service and offer a contract to David's company to collect trash throughout the entire county. David wants to know if this arrangement will make him a quasi-public corporation. What should our firm tell him?
>
> **Answer:** Because David has entered into a contract to provide the exclusive service to county residents for an action that is traditionally associated with the government, that is, trash collection, David's Garbage Service, Inc., meets the requirements to be considered a quasi-public corporation.

NONPROFIT CORPORATIONS

nonprofit corporation A corporation specifically created for a purpose other than generating income; for example, charity.

A third type of corporate arrangement, the **nonprofit corporation** (or not-for-profit corporation) may also qualify as a public corporation. Nonprofits actually fall somewhere between public corporations and private corporations. Depending on how they are organized, they might be considered as either. Nonprofit corporations are generally designed for a public purpose or for charity. Whatever their purpose, nonprofit corporations must meet one very important requirement: they cannot distribute profits to members. If none of the income generated by the corporation is distributed among its shareholders, officers, or directors, then it is a nonprofit corporation.[20] See Exhibit 7–2.

When a corporation is classified as a nonprofit, it receives special advantages. For instance, nonprofit corporations pay few taxes. But there are other advantages, as well. They also receive special treatment in the following areas:

- unemployment insurance breaks
- special protections in bankruptcy
- reduced Social Security obligations
- special protections in the areas of copyright, antitrust, and customs, among many others

Given these special considerations, nonprofits work to ensure that their status does not change. If the government reclassifies a nonprofit as a for-profit, all of those protections disappear. Nonprofit corporations can make money; they simply cannot distribute the earnings to their members. Instead, the money earned must be devoted towards the corporation's stated purpose. If not, then the government may declare the corporation to be a private, for-profit enterprise and tax it accordingly.[21] Nonprofit corporations can pay their employees a reasonable salary for their activities. Most states also prohibit these corporations from issuing stock.[22] See Exhibit 7–3.

Sidebar

In some cases, a nonprofit corporation may also qualify as a public corporation.

Sidebar

Nonprofit corporations are very common. Some sources state that they comprise nearly 20% of all corporations currently in existence.[23]

Scenario 7–2. Mario's Quick Oil Change & Lube, Inc.

Last year, Mario started a new business. He purchased a truck and advertised "on the spot" oil changes and lubrication service for cars. He will drive his truck to a customer's car and complete the service right there. However, Mario has not made any money at this business. In fact, every month since he opened the business, he has lost money.

Mario has come to our firm and wants to have his corporation reclassified as a nonprofit so that he can take advantage of the special tax treatment. Does Mario's business qualify as a nonprofit?

Answer: No. Failing to make a profit is not the same thing as running a nonprofit corporation. If a corporation consistently loses money, it does not change its classification into nonprofit status. The corporation must be specifically designed to be a nonprofit in order to enjoy the benefits given to such corporations.

Exhibit 7–2. Articles of incorporation for not-for-profit corporation, Illinois

---

FORM **NFP 102.10** (rev. Dec. 2003)
ARTICLES OF INCORPORATION
General Not For Profit Corporation Act

Jesse White, Secretary of State
Department of Business Services
Springfield, IL 62756
217-782-9522
www.cyberdriveillinois.com

Remit payment in the form of a cashier's
check, certified check, money order or
Illinois attorney's or C.P.A.'s check
payable to Secretary of State.

_____ File #_____ Filing Fee: $50   Approved: _____

–– –– Submit in duplicate –– –– Type or Print clearly in black ink –– –– Do not write above this line –– ––

Article 1.   Name of Corporation: _____

Article 2.   Name and Address of Initial Registered Agent and Registered Office:

   Registered Agent_____
                        First Name   Middle Name   Last Name

   Registered Office_____
                        Number   Street   Suite No. (P.O. Box alone is unacceptable)

                           _____IL_____
                               City   ZIP Code   County

Article 3.   The first Board of Directors shall be _____ in number, their Names and Addresses being as follows:
                                                   Not less than three

Director Name	Street Address	City	State	ZIP Code

Article 4.   Purposes for which the corporation is organized:

(continued on back)

Printed by authority of the State of Illinois. September 2005 – 10M – C 157.14

(continued)

Exhibit 7–2. Articles of incorporation for not-for-profit corporation, Illinois *(continued)*

Article 4. (continued)

Is this corporation a Condominium Association as established under the Condominium Property Act? (check one)
☐ Yes ☐ No

Is this corporation a Cooperative Housing Corporation as defined in Section 216 of the Internal Revenue Code of 1954? (check one)
☐ Yes ☐ No

Is this corporation a Homeowner's Association, which administers a common-interest community as defined in subsection (c) of Section 9-102 of the Code of Civil Procedure? (check one)
☐ Yes ☐ No

Article 5. Other provisions (attach additional pages if needed):

Article 6. Names & Addresses of Incorporators
The undersigned incorporator(s) hereby declare(s), under penalties of perjury, that the statements made in the foregoing Articles of Incorporation are true.

Dated _____ , _____
                 Month & Day   Year

Signatures and Names	**Post Office Address**
1. _____ Signature	1. _____ Street
_____ Name (please print)	City/Town State ZIP
2. _____ Signature	2. _____ Street
_____ Name (please print)	City/Town State ZIP
3. _____ Signature	3. _____ Street
_____ Name (please print)	City/Town State ZIP
4. _____ Signature	4. _____ Street
_____ Name (please print)	City/Town State ZIP
5. _____ Signature	5. _____ Street
_____ Name (please print)	City/Town State ZIP

Signatures must be in BLACK INK on the original document.
Carbon copies, photocopies or rubber stamped signatures may only be used on the duplicate copy.

- If a corporation acts as incorporator, the name of the corporation and the state of incorporation shall be shown and the execution shall be by a duly authorized corporate officer. Please print name and title under the officer's signature.
- The registered agent cannot be the corporation itself.
- The registered agent may be an individual, resident in Illinois, or a domestic or foreign corporation, authorized to act as a registered agent.
- The registered office may be, but need not be, the same as its principal office.
- A corporation that is to function as a club, as defined in Section 1-3.24 of the "Liquor Control Act" of 1934, must insert in its purpose clause a statement that **it will comply with the State and local laws and ordinances relating to alcoholic liquors.**

(For inserts use 8 1/2 x 11 white paper)

Printed by authority of the State of Illinois. September 2005 – 10M – C 157.14

Exhibit 7–3. Examples of nonprofit corporations

- ❑ veterans' organizations
- ❑ Fraternal Order of Police
- ❑ Boy Scouts of America
- ❑ parent-teacher associations
- ❑ religious organizations
- ❑ charities*

*19 *Fletcher Cyclopedia of Private Corp.* § 2:15 West Group, 1931.

DETERMINATION OF A CORPORATION'S STATUS

Public or private? How do you determine one from the other? The simple way to distinguish a public from a private corporation is to examine its charter and articles of organization. What is the purpose of the corporation? Is it designed to make money or to carry out a governmental service? Will it distribute profits to its members or use those profits exclusively to provide a service? The answers to these questions will determine whether a corporation is public or private.

PRIVATE CORPORATIONS

A private corporation consists of the features that we outlined at the beginning of this chapter. They have shareholders, directors, and officers. They can exist perpetually. Private corporations pay taxes on earnings; they can sue and be sued. As far as the law is concerned, they are artificial persons. A private corporation is organized around its articles of incorporation and comes into existence when it satisfies all statutory requirements and files the appropriate documentation with the state.[24] In later chapters, we will examine the many different forms that private corporations can take. However, in this general discussion of private corporations, there is one type that should be addressed: closely held corporations.

Closely Held Corporation

A **closely held corporation** has few members. In other settings, the business could just as easily be organized as a partnership. Closely held corporations have a small number of stockholders; all or nearly all of the stockholders take an active role in the business and there is no ready market for the corporations stock, even if someone were willing to sell it.[25]

In many ways, closely held corporations resemble partnerships, at least to the extent that there are only a few individuals involved in the enterprise. However, even a closely held corporation still derives its authority from statutes, not the agreement among the owners. As such, closely held corporations must still file with the state. They must also abide by statutory regulations. See Exhibits 7–4 and 7–5.

closely held corporation A small company owned and managed by shareholders.

Exhibit 7–4. Minnesota Statutes Annotated. Business corporations: Definitions

> 302A.011. Definitions
>   "Closely held corporation" means a corporation which does not have more than 35 shareholders.*

*Minnesota Statutes Annotated § 302A.011.

KEY POINT

Closely held corporations operate more like partnerships than traditional corporations.

Exhibit 7–5. Elements of a closely held corporation

> Most states will rule that a closely held corporation has been created when:
> ❑ There is no ready market for the company's stock.
> ❑ All or nearly all of the stockholders participate in the management, direction, and operations of the corporation.*
> ❑ All stockholders are concentrated in one geographic area.**
> ❑ The company has filed as a closely held corporation.

*Am. Jur. Corporations §38.
**111 A.L.R. 5th 207.

Importance of the Distinction of "Closely Held" Corporation

The designation of "closely held" corporation was important because under traditional corporate law analysis, small corporations might run into trouble with state corporate laws. For instance, corporate statutes require that board members must act independently, that statutory provisions regarding corporate minutes and meetings must be complied with, and that specific types of filings must be made periodically. A corporation that failed to meet these obligations faced the possibility of judicial dissolution. This harsh rule led many state legislatures to amend their corporate statutes to include a looser definition of corporation, or to enact closely held corporate company provisions that allowed what was essentially a general partnership to form as a corporation.[27]

Sub-Chapter S Corporations

In 1986, the tax structure for corporations was changed, and the corporate structure became even more attractive. For instance, if a corporation organizes as a "sub-chapter S" (referring to the tax code that authorized the designation), a shareholder avoids the infamous double taxation often seen in other corporate models. In traditional corporations, a corporation must pay taxes on its profits, and if it passes some of these profits on to its shareholders in the form of dividends, then the shareholders must also pay income tax on the dividends. Sub-chapter S designation avoids double taxation by allowing corporations to pass profits directly to shareholders, who then declare them as income. The pass-through provisions of a sub-chapter S corporation make it a very popular corporate structure. These days, there are additional corporate models that have other tax advantages.

Sidebar

Some of the strict limitations on sub-chapter S corporations were lifted in 1997 with new tax legislation. For instance, the maximum number of shareholders was expanded from 35 to 75, and charitable organizations were also allowed to hold limited interests in sub-chapter S corporations.

PROFESSIONAL CORPORATIONS

The final type of corporation we will discuss in this chapter is the professional corporation. Under the original corporate statutes, a corporation was prevented from practicing a profession.[28] However, this meant that attorneys, doctors, and other professionals could not organize their businesses to receive the protection that corporate standing brought. All states have revised their corporate rules to allow the creation of a "professional corporation," sometimes called a "professional association."[29] Under these rules, individuals who must be licensed by the state before they can practice are allowed to join into a corporate structure. This opens up this valuable business model to attorneys, accountants, doctors, and others.[30] See Exhibit 7–6.

Exhibit 7–6. Defining professional service corporations (Florida)

The term "professional service" means any type of personal service to the public which requires as a condition precedent to the rendering of such service the obtaining of a license or other legal authorization. By way of example and without limiting the generality thereof, the personal services which come within the provisions of this act are the personal services rendered by certified public accountants, public accountants, chiropractic physicians, dentists, osteopathic physicians, physicians and surgeons, doctors of medicine, doctors of dentistry, podiatric physicians, chiropodists, architects, veterinarians, attorneys at law, and life insurance agents.*

*Florida Statutes §621.03.

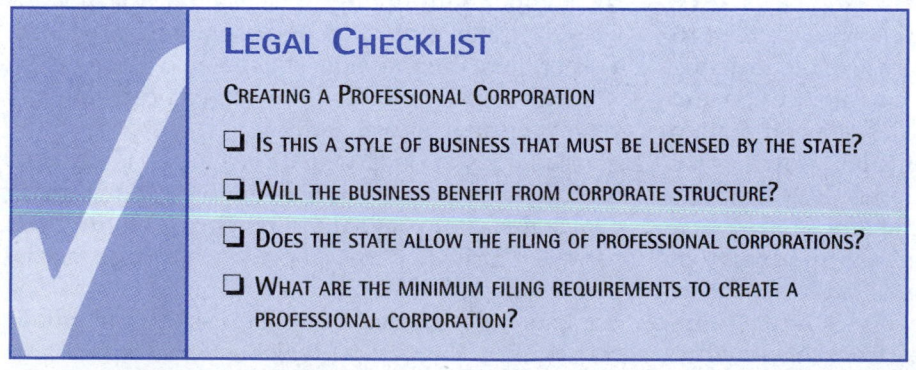

LEGAL CHECKLIST

CREATING A PROFESSIONAL CORPORATION

❏ IS THIS A STYLE OF BUSINESS THAT MUST BE LICENSED BY THE STATE?

❏ WILL THE BUSINESS BENEFIT FROM CORPORATE STRUCTURE?

❏ DOES THE STATE ALLOW THE FILING OF PROFESSIONAL CORPORATIONS?

❏ WHAT ARE THE MINIMUM FILING REQUIREMENTS TO CREATE A PROFESSIONAL CORPORATION?

Ethics File: Creating a Corporation as a Sham

Some unscrupulous individuals see the corporate structure as a way to avoid taking responsibility for certain actions. For instance, some individuals may wish to create a sham non-profit corporation that will disguise profits, property, and other assets and hide them (at least temporarily) from the IRS. Legal professionals should avoid any situation where the client is attempting to create a corporation for an unlawful purpose, especially as a way to defraud the government or hide assets in a divorce or other action. Not only is assisting a client in such an endeavor unethical, it may also be illegal.

CASE LAW: *Administrative Dissolution of a Corporation*

State v. Sunset Ditch Co.[31]
MABRY, Justice.

Suit was brought by the State of New Mexico, plaintiff-appellee, against defendant-appellant corporation, and others named as officers thereof, to declare the corporation dissolved for failure to comply with the statute concerning annual reports, and to enjoin the corporation from functioning as such. From a decree in plaintiff's favor the defendants prosecute this appeal. The parties may hereinafter, at times, be referred to as "the State" and "the Company," respectively.

The Company was organized on Feb. 3, 1903, for the purpose of operating a ditch and irrigation works and supplying water to a certain area in Grant county [sic], New Mexico, from the Rio Gila. The articles of incorporation recite that the capital stock of the corporation was to be $50,000, divided into 200 shares at par value of $25 per share. It was incorporated under C. 12, Laws 1887, secs. 468-492, Comp.Laws 1897. The chapter title of the enactment relates to "the formation of companies for the purpose of constructing irrigating and other canals and the colonization and improvement of lands." The articles of incorporation appear to follow the requirements laid down in the statute authorizing such corporations. The Company contends that it was never operated for profit, that it paid no dividends, that it derived revenue only from assessments against water users and that arising from water served by its ditches. Stock in the Company was issued and transferred from time to time,

but whether such stock transfers in all cases were related to the land benefited, the record does not clearly disclose.

The corporation has continued to function to the time of this suit. No annual report was ever filed by the Company, and the State Corporation Commission on Feb. 19, 1940, by certificate, declared and held the corporation to be dissolved as of June 14, 1921, for violation of C. 185, Laws 1921, also hereinafter to be noticed.

The challenge to the trial court's finding of fact to the effect that the defendant Company, organized and registered as a corporation on Feb. 3, 1903, never filed any annual reports nor paid the required fees, is without merit. Whether the Company's charter was, or could be, dissolved ipso facto by Chap. 185, Laws of 1921, becomes the one important question presented. If the statute be self-executing, it may not become important, although a decision on this point is passed, whether the order of dissolution by the State Corporation Commission was entered on June 14, 1921, the effective date of the act, or nearly twenty years thereafter, as was the case.

The question posed under Point 2 is, likewise, without merit. If we can hold that the Company in question was organized and authorized to do business as a private corporation this question is disposed of; and we can, and must, so hold. The Company was obviously either a private or public corporation. The statutes which we deal with in this connection make no other classification. The Company was governed by the general corporation law.

Those corporations are public which are created for public purposes only, connected with the administration of the government, and the interests and franchises of which are the exclusive property and domain of the government itself. Private corporations are created for private as distinguished from purely public purposes, and they are not in contemplation of law public because it may have been supposed by the legislature that their establishment would promote either directly or consequentially the public interest. A railroad corporation, though engaged in a quasi-public business, is a private corporation, and the fact that the state owns a portion of the stock does not change its character. The character of a corporation as public or private is determined solely by the terms of its charter and the general law under which it was organized.

The Company concedes that the act of 1905, C. 79, refers to irrigation companies, but contends that the vague and limited manner of reference thereto robs it of much of its force. With this principle we do not agree.

We look only to its articles of incorporation to determine whether the Company was organized for profit. The question is not whether the corporation, after being organized for such purpose, made a profit or even undertook to do so. The charter becomes the guide in distinguishing such corporations from ones organized solely for religious, charitable or benevolent purposes. We do not look to any specific acts, or results flowing from an exercise of its corporate powers, to determine the character of the corporation or the purposes for which it was organized. Obviously, a corporation organized, as was this one, with capital stock divided into shares and sold and assigned in the course of doing business, was a private corporation organized for profit.

It may be true that it is not possible to give a precise and satisfactory definition of a public, as distinguished from a private, corporation; yet, the corporation with which we are now dealing could not reasonably be said to fall under any other classification but that of private.

Under the above standards we cannot escape the conclusion that appellant Company was a private, as distinguished from a public, corporation, and that the 1921 act in question would apply to it, if it can be said that under the law, and notwithstanding the constitutional objections relied upon, it was required to file an annual report. Annual reports are required of every corporation except those not organized for profit.

Thus appraising the corporation the State contends that by the Laws of 1905, C. 79, § 48(1), Sec. 54-236, Comp.1941, it was required to file annual reports; and, upon the failure to so do, the 1921 act provided such corporation "be and the same [is] hereby declared to be dissolved." The record before us is silent upon the question of notice having been given under this statute, and we must assume none was given. The State contends that no particular significance is to be attached to the act, in any event. And, it is doubtless correct. The case must rest upon the much more narrow and simple question touching the constitutionality of the Laws of 1921, C. 185, as it applies to appellant.

Therefore, the Company being a private corporation, as distinguished from a public one, upon the passage of Laws 1921, C. 185, did it become subject to the terms of the act? The pertinent part of this statute provides: "Section 1. That all private corporations organized under the laws of the Territory of New Mexico which have refused or neglected to file the annual reports required by law in the office of the State Corporation Commission of New Mexico, be and the same are hereby declared to be dissolved, and the State Corporation Commission is hereby authorized and directed to strike the names of all such corporations from its index of live corporations."

It cannot be doubted that a duty may be imposed upon corporations requiring them to make and file annual, or other, reports. Such legislation is upheld as the proper exercise either of the legislative reserved power over corporate charters, or as proper exercise of the police power which cannot be surrendered in any event.

As we understand it, appellant does not question the right of the state to require annual reports of

(continued)

CASE LAW: *Administrative Dissolution of a Corporation* (continued)

corporations, whether organized under territorial or state laws, and regardless of whether there has been by charter, or by legislation or constitutional provision, a specific reservation of power to appropriately amend or alter either the laws or charter under which such corporations began to operate. But, it does properly urge, that any such requirement must be reasonably implemented with procedure which would not, by omitting notice or hearing or an opportunity to correct the default when not made in bad faith, completely destroy the corporation; particularly under the circumstances here present where there may be entertained some doubt whether appellant corporation is amenable to the general corporation laws and therefore required to make such reports, in any event.

If our holding upon the points which are the basis of our decision as herein pointed out did not bear the clear imprint of logical reasoning and we felt constrained to look further for support of our holding, the rule generally, although not universally, accepted, to the effect that in cases where no public detriment is involved a statute providing for forfeiture in case of abuse of its corporate powers or of failure to perform some such statutory duty as making and filing annual reports, will be liberally construed, would, doubtless, compel that liberal application of the statute here.

Provision for forfeiture of corporate rights and privileges relating to filing annual reports must be strictly construed, since forfeitures are not favored.

"Corporations are protected, as a rule, from the retroactive operation of laws. Where such provision is not afforded by constitutional authority, the courts, on principles of natural justice, will so construe all laws, including constitutional provisions, as intended to be prospective in their operations, unless a retroactive operation is clearly indicated." It has been held that the defense that plaintiff corporation filed no proper annual report with the Secretary of State, being technical, should not be unnecessarily extended.

It is said in Thompson on Corporations (3rd Ed.) Sec.2947, page 684, citing specific authority: "It is not every failure to perform the duty imposed upon a corporation that will work a forfeiture of its franchise. There must be some plain abuse of power by which the corporation fails to fulfill the design and purpose of its organization, and the acts of misuser or non-user must relate to matters which are of the essence of the contract between the state and the corporation, and they must be wrongful and repeated. There must be something more than accidental negligence, or excess of power, or mere mistake in the mode of exercising it".

We hold that, within the constitutional interdiction, and as to appellant, equal protection of the law has been denied and the obligation of contract has been impaired.

The trial court was in error in giving judgment for the state, holding appellant corporation to have been dissolved and in enjoining the stockholders, agents, servants, attorneys of the company, and others from acting as a corporation.

The judgment is therefore reversed, with instructions to trial court to reinstate the cause upon the docket, set aside its judgment and decree of injunction heretofore made and entered, and to give judgment for appellant company.

And, it is so ordered.

CASE QUESTIONS

1. Why did the state seek to declare the Sunset Ditch Co. as an invalid corporation?

2. How does the court in this case define the difference between public and private corporations?

3. What document does the court refer to in order to decide whether the company was a public or private corporation?

4. What is the significance of the company's failure to file annual reports?

5. Why did the court rule in favor of the corporation?

SUMMARY

A corporation is an artificial person that has the right to own property, hire employees, bring lawsuits, and pay taxes. Corporations are the product of state legislation. Corporations have existed in one form or another for centuries. Until the mid-1800s, corporations were an insignificant subspecialty of law. However, with the arrival of the Industrial Revolution, corporations took on a much more important role in the American economy. By the end of the 1800s, huge, multinational corporations not only came to dominate industry, but also the American legal system as well. Society began to see corporations as a threat, and Congress responded with the Sherman Antitrust Act, among other legislation. That act prohibited cutthroat competition and many of the other unfair practices that corporations were using to wipe out their competitors. The creation of the Federal Trade Commission and its antitrust division firmly established the role of the federal government in regulating corporations.

Modern corporations have mutated into many different types. Public corporations are institutions devoted to governmental projects or policies. Private corporations, on the other hand, are engaged in businesses and usually run for profit. A type of private corporation, the closely held corporation, resembles a partnership in many ways. Nonprofit corporations carry out charities and are not allowed to distribute profits to their members. Corporations are unlike most other types of business models in that they provide complete protection to owners and investors in the form of limited liability. As such, they are a powerful organizational model and are very effective in carrying out business transactions.

HELPFUL WEB SITES

Federal Trade Commission
http://www.ftc.gov

Florida Division of Corporations
http://www.sunbiz.org/

Illinois Secretary of State Online Corporate Database
http://www.cyberdriveillinois.com/

KEY TERMS

articles of incorporation	nonprofit corporation
closely held corporation	officer
director	private corporation
monopoly	public corporation

quasi-public corporation   Sherman Antitrust Act

shareholder

APPLYING CHAPTER CONCEPTS

Visit your secretary of state's Web site and answer the following questions.

- What type of information is listed there about private corporations?
- Are there any provisions for reserving a corporate name?
- Does the Web site maintain a list of downloadable forms for businesses considering incorporation?
- What are the fees required to incorporate a business?

REVIEW QUESTIONS
---

1. What is the definition of a corporation?
2. How did the Industrial Revolution contribute to the reinvigoration of corporate law?
3. List and explain the features that all corporations have in common.
4. What is the Sherman Antitrust Act?
5. What role does the Federal Trade Commission play in modern corporate law?
6. The chapter mentions that a corporation is considered to be an artificial person. What does this mean?
7. Why is it significant that corporations can own property in their own name?
8. What is a monopoly?
9. What is the significance of the Standard Oil Co. case?
10. What is a public corporation?
11. What is a quasi-public corporation?
12. What is the difference between a public corporation and a private corporation?
13. What is a closely held corporation?
14. What is a professional corporation?
15. What is the significance of this chapter's crucial Case Law?
16. Corporations are said to have "perpetual existence." What does this mean?
17. What functions are normally associated with quasi-public corporations?
18. What are the guidelines for nonprofit corporations to maintain their special status?

19. What are some examples of public corporations?
20. What is a professional corporation?

QUESTION FOR REFLECTION

Would the U.S. economy have developed as quickly during the Industrial Revolution if the corporate form had not been available? Suppose, for instance, that the only types of business models available were sole proprietorships and general partnerships. What effect would this have had on the early steel, railroad, shipping, and manufacturing businesses?

ENDNOTES

[1]Am.Jur. Corporations § 1.

[2]*Trustees of Dartmouth College v. Woodward*, 17 U.S. 518 (1819).

[3]*Woodale, Inc. v. Fidelity & Deposit Co.*, 378 F.2d 627 (8th Cir. 1967).

[4]18 Am. Jur. 2d § 42 (1985).

[5]*Gober v. Stubbs*, 682 So. 2d 430 (Ala. 1996).

[6]18 Am. Jur. 2d § 850 (1985).

[7]*State v. Luv Pharmacy, Inc.*, 118 N.H. 398, 388 A.2d 190 (1978).

[8]*Old Dominion Copper Mining & Smelting Co. v. Lewisohn*, 210 U.S. 206 (1908).

[9]*St. Lawrence University v. Trustees of Theological School of St. Lawrence University*, 20 N.Y.2d 317, 282 N.Y.2d 746 (1967).

[10]Lawrence Friedman, *A History of American Law* (New York: Simon and Schuster, 1973), p. 446.

[11]*United States v. Von's Grocery Co.*, 384 U.S. 270 (1966).

[12]*Appalachian Coals, Inc. v. United States*, 288 U.S. 344 (1933).

[13]*United States v. American Linseed Oil Co.*, 262 U.S. 371 (1923).

[14]*Spectrum Sports v. McQuillan*, 506 U.S. 447 (1993).

[15]*Clamp-All Corp. v. Cast Iron Soil Pipe Institute*, 851 F.2d 478 (1st Cir. 1988).

[16]Marc Winerman, *The Origins of the FTC: Concentration, Corporation, Control, and Competition*, 71 Antitrust L.J. 1 (2003).

[17]522 U.S. 3, 118 S.Ct. 275, 139 L.Ed.2d 199 (1997).

[18]*Schwartz v. Urban Redevelopment Authority of Pittsburgh*, 192 A.2d 371 (Pa. 1963).

[19]*Tumulty v. Jersey City*, 155 A.2d 148 (N.J. 1959).

[20]*Summers v. Cherokee Children & Family Services, Inc.*, 112 S.W.3d 486 (Tenn. 2002).

[21]*Summers v. Cherokee Children & Family Services, Inc.*, 112 S.W.3d 486 (Tenn. 2002).

[22]*Fletcher Cyclopedia of Private Corp.* § 2:15 West Group, 2006.

[23]*Fletcher Cyclopedia of Private Corp.* § 2:15 West Group, 2006.

[24]*Mackay v. New York, N.H. & H.R. Co.*, 82 Conn. 73, 72 A. 583 (1909).

[25]*Galler v. Galler*, 32 Ill.2d 16, 203 N.E.2d 577 (1964).

[26]Am. Jur. 2d § 2120.

[27]Dennis Karjala, *An Analysis of Close Corporation Legislation in the United States*, 21 Ariz. St. L.J. 663 (1989).

[28]Am. Jur. 2d § 2120.

[29]*Street v. Sugarman*, 202 So.2d 749 (D.C. Fla. 1967).

[30]*Vinall v. Hoffman*, 133 Ariz. 322, 651 P.2d 850 (1982).

[31]145 P.2d 219 (N.M. 1944).

Chapter 8

CREATING A CORPORATION

Chapter Objectives

Upon completion of this chapter, you should be able to:

- Explain the function of the Secretary of State's office in creating a corporation.
- Describe the function of articles of incorporation.
- Explain the role of promoters and incorporators in creating a corporation.
- Describe the organizational activities that must occur in order to create a valid corporation.
- Explain how state statutes govern the creation and organization of a corporation.

▶ INTRODUCTION

In this chapter, we will explore how corporations are created. Because this business entity is so closely tied to statutes—they owe their very existence to statutory authority—we will also examine statutes from different states that bear on the question of creating a statute.

In earlier chapters when we explored sole proprietorships and general partnerships, we encountered a rich heritage of common law. Cases and statutes have existed for hundreds of years to amplify the various issues involved in those business models. That is not the case with corporations. This business structure is statute-driven.[1] If a party fails to meet the statutory obligations, a court might rule that the corporation was never created, and therefore none of the benefits of the corporate scheme will accrue to the benefit of the company.

Corporations are created by authority of state statutes.

CREATION OF THE CORPORATION

One of the first questions that often arises when individuals are considering the creation of a corporation is where to locate it. When the corporation is small, the best choice is where a majority of the stockholders or business property will be located. However, when the corporation is large, and will be doing business in many states, the individuals who form the corporation might decide to take advantage of some of the state laws around the country that are specifically designed to be corporate-friendly. One such state is Delaware. Many years ago, the State of Delaware streamlined its statutes for creating and maintaining corporations. It also has favorable tax treatment for corporations organized there. Many other states have followed Delaware's example.

Once the question of where to organize the corporation is answered, the next question focuses on who can carry out the incorporation. Again, we must review state statutes for an answer about who has the authority to create a corporation. For instance, municipalities are not authorized to create corporations.[2] Individuals who lack the ability to enter into a contract are also forbidden to create corporations. Contractual ability is a prerequisite to organizing a corporation, and all of the following would be barred from creating one:

> infants (under the age of 18)
> intoxicated persons
> mentally incompetent persons

Beyond the legal abilities of the founders, there are other issues that must be addressed in creating a corporation. For instance, the corporate founders must comply with state law on all issues related to corporate structure. As we will see later in this chapter, those issues concern items such as articles of incorporation, bylaws, organizational meetings, and issuance of shares.

If we are to think about corporation statutes from the perspective of contract law, then the requirements of state law are conditions precedent to the creation of incorporation. These conditions must be complied with before corporate status will be recognized. The failure to live up to these conditions will justify forfeiture of corporate status.[3]

The rules that govern a corporation come from the following sources:

- state constitution
- state statutes authorizing the creation of corporations
- the articles of incorporation
- certificate of incorporation[4]

Each of the sources must be in agreement with the others. There is no provision, for example, that would allow a corporation to declare in its articles of incorporation that it will not follow applicable state law.[5]

DE FACTO CORPORATIONS

What happens when business owners fail to follow the applicable statutes? Suppose, for instance, that the documents filed to create the corporation have typographical errors or omissions? Put another way, what is the status of the business that behaves as though it is a corporation, when it has failed to meet all of the requirements of the state's corporation laws? Courts have wrestled with this question for years. In such a situation, the corporation would be referred to as a **de facto** corporation. If the parties can show a good-faith attempt to abide by the statutes, courts will rule the corporation to be de facto and may grant it most of the corporate benefits that accrue to any corporation under the state's laws. This recognition gives the de facto corporation an opportunity to correct the original errors. However, if the parties cannot show a good-faith attempt to abide by the law, courts are authorized to disregard corporate status entirely and make the business owners personally liable for all debts and judgments.[6] See Exhibit 8–1.

de facto (Latin) "in fact," an event that is true in fact, if not in law.

> **Sidebar**
>
> The old designations of corporations "de jure," "de facto," and "by estoppel" were generally abolished by modern statutes.[7]

KEY POINT

> A de facto corporation has not met all of the requirements set out by state statute but operates as though it has. Courts may grant it temporary status as a corporation.

 ### GETTING TO THE BASICS

> The rules about articles of incorporation are simple and straightforward: if they contain a fatal defect, a corporation is not authorized under the law.

Exhibit 8–1. Examples of de facto corporations

> ❏ There is a defect in the corporate papers.
> ❏ A general meeting was held instead of an organizational meeting.
> ❏ Corporate notes were not properly recorded.
> ❏ The certificate of incorporation contained errors.*

*Duck River Preservation Ass'n v. Tennessee Valley Auth., 410 F.Supp. 756 (E.D. Tenn. 1974).

CASE LAW: *Can a Gun Club Violate the Clean Water Act?*

Simsbury-Avon Preservation Society, LLC. v. Metacon Gun Club, Inc.[8]
Ruling On Defendant's Motion to Dismiss
Arterton, J.

The Simsbury-Avon Preservation Society and six individual members bring a five-count complaint against the Metacon Gun Club, alleging violations of the Resource Conservation and Recovery Act ("RCRA"), 42 U.S.C. § 6901 et seq., as amended, and the Clean Water Act ("CWA"), 33 U.S.C. § 1251 et seq. Defendant moves to dismiss the complaint on the grounds that the Simsbury-Avon Preservation Society ("Society") was not legally recognized by the Connecticut Secretary of State until after the present lawsuit was filed, and therefore does not have standing to maintain the suit.

FACTUAL BACKGROUND

The complaint alleges the following facts, which are presumed to be true for purposes of deciding this motion to dismiss.

The Metacon Gun Club has operated an outdoor shooting range in Simsbury, Connecticut, for the past fifteen years. "Members and guests are allowed to use shotguns, assault rifles, automatic weapons, anti-tank guns, and all other large and small firearms at the Site." The club is on Nod Road, which "runs alongside the Farmington River and separates the river from the Site. The Site is situated on an area of extensive wetlands and streams and is part of an area designated as a Flood Plain which becomes flooded many times during the year, but especially in the Spring." Bordering the firing range are a golf course, a riding stable, a State Police firing range, a private home and Talcott Mountain State Park.

The complaint alleges that "The Defendants' operations include the discharge of chromium, lead, lead shot, lead bullets, ammunition fragments, ammunition wadding and other ammunition to surface waters and to sediments and soils on the Site. Due to inadequate safety measures and the range of shot

from automatic rifles used by the Defendants, significant amounts of [these materials] are discharged into Talcott Mountain State Park."

Plaintiffs estimate that "thousands of pounds of lead" have been deposited on the defendant's land and adjacent areas since approximately 1980. This lead, they allege, has contaminated ground water and sediments on the site, and "directly contaminates the Farmington River several times each year when said river floods onto the Site." Plaintiffs further state that "analyses of soils, surface waters and sediments on the Site and on property adjacent to the Site show serious contamination from lead, well above" levels approved by the Connecticut Department of Environmental Protection. These levels of lead cause "damage to aquatic biota, birds and other wildlife" and can cause lead poisoning in children who use the shooting range and play on adjacent property. Plaintiffs allege that "Defendants have never conducted a clean-up operation of lead from shooting activities on the Site or on property adjacent to the Site."

The Society is comprised of homeowners who live adjacent to and near the Site. Three individual plaintiffs-Robert Patricelli, Greg Silpe and Gayle March-are residents of Simsbury, and three-Rinaldo Tedeschi, Diane Tedeschi and Sheldon Cherry-are residents of Avon. "Members of the Preservation Society depend upon water resources in the immediate vicinity of the Site and enjoy recreation activities and wildlife in the area." They allege that the "quality of the environment in the vicinity of the Site directly affects their health, recreational, aesthetic and environmental interests...."

Plaintiffs seek declaratory and injunctive relief as well as civil penalties of up to $25,000 per day for each violation under RCRA and CWA. Defendant now moves to dismiss all claims of the complaint.

DISCUSSION

A. STANDING OF SIMSBURY-AVON PRESERVATION SOCIETY

Defendant challenges the standing of the Society to bring suit in its own name and on behalf of its members. Defendant asserts that the "Plaintiff LLC was effectively formed and recognized by the Secretary of the State of Connecticut on May 18, 2004. At the time this suit was filed on May 13, 2004, however, the Plaintiff LLC did not legally exist." Defendant further argues that "because the plaintiff entity lacked standing to bring the lawsuit, adding individual plaintiffs does not cure the original defect."

The Court disagrees with defendant's contentions. Even if the Society were not officially incorporated until May 18, five days after the instant complaint was filed, the Society and its individual members have standing to sue. As Judge Beach held in a companion state case to this action, the Society was a de facto corporation on May 11, the date its articles of incorporation were first submitted, even if the paperwork was returned to its attorney due to a technicality (a missing address) two days later.

Additionally, the Society need not have adopted any particular corporate form in order to sue on behalf of its members, as long as its members also have individual standing to bring this action. "An association has standing to bring suit on behalf of its members when its members would otherwise have standing to sue in their own right, the interests at stake are germane to the organization's purpose, and neither the claim asserted nor the relief requested requires the participation of individual members in the lawsuit." Defendant does not argue that the Society's members lack individual standing, nor does defendant challenge the sufficiency of the allegations in the complaint that the six named plaintiffs, who are also members of the Society, live adjacent to the site, "depend upon water resources in the immediate vicinity of the Site and enjoy recreation activities and wildlife in the area," and "share a common concern about the quality of the environment in the vicinity. . . ." The Supreme Court has "held that environmental plaintiffs adequately allege injury in fact when they aver that they use the affected area and are persons 'for whom the aesthetic and recreational values of the area will be lessened' by the challenged activity." Under this standard, the individual plaintiffs in the present action have standing, and the Society has standing to represent its members. Defendant's motion to dismiss for lack of standing therefore is denied.

It is especially appropriate for an association to sue on behalf of its members where injunctive relief is sought, as in the present case. Warth v. Seldin, 422 U.S. 490, 515, 95 S.Ct. 2197, 45 L.Ed.2d 343 (1975) ("whether an association has standing to invoke the court's remedial powers on behalf of its members depends in substantial measure on the nature of the relief sought. If in a proper case the association seeks a declaration, injunction, or some other form of prospective relief, it can reasonably be supposed that the remedy, if granted, will inure to the benefit of those members of the association actually injured.").

Therefore defendant's motion to dismiss the remaining counts of the complaint for lack of notice is denied. Defendant does not move to dismiss plaintiff's remaining claims on their merits, and therefore Counts One, Three, Four and Five remain.

IT IS SO ORDERED.

CASE QUESTIONS

1. What allegations does the Simsbury-Avon Preservation Society raise against the Metacon Gun Club?

2. Who comprises the Society?

3. What grounds does the Gun Club use to challenge the action brought by the Society?

4. According to the court, was the Society a legally recognized corporation when it filed this action? Explain the significance of the court's reasoning.

5. Is there another reason why the Society would still have been allowed to bring its action against the Gun Club? Explain.

CORPORATE PURPOSE

In addition to complying with state statutes, it should go without saying that a corporation must be formed for a legal purpose. Courts will not recognize corporations that have been formed to conduct criminal enterprises. When a question arises as to what the purpose of a corporation is, courts will look to the articles of incorporation for guidance.[9] What most state statutes provide is that a corporation can be established for any purpose "not contrary to law."[10] Among the accepted reasons for creating a corporation is a desire to avoid personal liability, favorable tax treatment, or some other type of financial advantage.[11] For example, corporations can be established for any of the following reasons:

- to acquire the assets of another corporation
- to run a farm
- to conduct a lobbying business
- to conduct a profession, such as the practice of law or of medicine[12]

 GETTING TO THE BASICS

Corporations must be formed for a legal purpose.

The general rule about statutes authorizing corporate powers is that if the statute fails to list a particular power, a corporation is not allowed to assume it. Here, omission equates to lack of permission.[13]

THE ROLE OF THE STATE SECRETARY OF STATE'S OFFICE

When a business wishes to become a corporation, it must file appropriate documentation with the state's secretary of state's office. This office has many different responsibilities. For instance, this office is usually responsible for supervising state-based elections, maintaining the state archives, and registering charitable organizations. But the most important function of that office, at least for our purposes, is to maintain records related to corporations and other business structures. When persons want to form a corporation, they must file documentation with the secretary of state. See Exhibit 8–2.

Exhibit 8–2. Effect of filing in the secretary of state's office

> Upon the filing of the certificate of incorporation by the department of state, the corporate existence shall begin, and such certificate shall be conclusive evidence that all conditions precedent have been fulfilled and that the corporation has been formed.*

*N.Y. Corporate Law (McKinney 2006).

One of the first issues that a proposed corporation will consider is the selection of a corporate name.

NAME SELECTION

The secretary of state's office maintains a complete list of all corporations formed in the state and the names used by each. When a new corporation is created, it must use a unique name. Many secretary of state's offices offer online databases to help corporate organizers discover if a particular name is available. See "Helpful Web Sites" at the conclusion of this chapter.

The secretary of state's office is authorized to accept any name selected by the parties, as long as the name is not already in use. See Exhibit 8–3. In fact, there is even authority for the proposition that the office must register names for organizations or groups that might be offensive to some. Consider Scenario 8–1.

> **Scenario 8–1. Naming a Nonprofit Corporation**
>
> A group has gathered and desires to form a corporation to advocate for gay and lesbian rights. They have decided to name their nonprofit corporation "The Gay Activists Alliance, Inc." When they submit their articles of incorporation and application to the state secretary of state, the secretary refuses to grant recognition, insisting that the group call itself something less offensive to some citizens. The group files suit, alleging that they have the right to use the name they originally submitted. Who will win?
>
> **Answer:** The Gay Activists Alliance will be granted corporate recognition under that name. There is no provision in the statutes that authorizes the secretary of state to refuse to grant corporate status to groups that the secretary may not like, or that the secretary believes would violate public policy.

Reserving a Corporate Name

When a company is considering filing as a corporation, most states allow the company to reserve a name that it intends to use. The reservation period varies from state to state, but is usually 60–120 days. See Exhibit 8–4.

 GETTING TO THE BASICS

Corporations must apply for and receive permission from the secretary of state's office before they can use a particular name.

THE CORPORATE CHARTER

When the term "corporate charter" is used, it is not in reference to a particular document. Instead, the charter refers to all of the laws that bind a corporation. A corporation's charter is composed of its articles of incorporation and the state laws that govern the creation and activities of the corporation.

Exhibit 8–3. Name reservation request, Nevada Secretary of State's office

DEAN HELLER
Secretary of State
206 North Carson Street
Carson City, Nevada 89701-4299
(775) 684 5708
Website: secretaryofstate.biz

Name Reservation Request

I, _____, hereby request that the name

_____

_____

be reserved for the period of 90 days.

Please mail my confirmation to:

_____

_____

_____

_____

Notes:

_____

_____

_____

Filing fee: $25.00

This form must be accompanied by appropriate fee.

Nevada Secretary of State Name Reservation 200?
Revised on: 01/07/04

Exhibit 8–4. Reserving a corporate name, New York

Application to reserve a corporate name shall be delivered to the department of state. It shall set forth the name and address of the applicant, the name to be reserved and a statement of the basis under paragraph (a) or (b) for the application. The secretary of state may require the applicant to set forth in his application the nature of the activities to be conducted by the corporation. If the name is available for corporate use, the department of state shall reserve the name for the use of the applicant for a period of sixty days and issue a certificate of reservation.*

*N.Y. Corporate Law § 303 (McKinney, 2006).

Under this view, state law becomes an implied part of all corporate articles of incorporation.[14] This is one reason why the articles of incorporation are so important and why the second half of this chapter is devoted to exploring them in detail.

The corporate charter consists not only of applicable laws and the articles of incorporation, but also any agreements created while the corporation was being formed. This class of agreements is referred to as preincorporation agreements.

Preincorporation Agreements

A **preincorporation agreement** is a general term that refers to any type of contract related to the business structure or agreements that are created before the business is incorporated under state law. When the business owners enter into an agreement to create a corporation, this is classified as a preincorporation agreement. The agreement to incorporate often not only includes the details of how and when the corporation will be formed, but also specifies the financial arrangements and capital funding that will go into the creation of corporate bank accounts and holdings. Preincorporation agreements are important because they fall into a different classification than other contracts. Because the corporation has not yet been formed, these agreements are not binding on the corporation. If they are not binding on the corporation, what happens when someone wishes to enforce the agreement? If the corporation is not a party to the agreement, how can it be compelled to honor contractual obligations? The simple answer is that the corporation usually ratifies or adopts the contract after it has been officially created. Assuming the contractual liability is one way to make the corporation a party to the contract. One of the most important areas of preincorporation agreements involves promoters.

preincorporation agreement An agreement entered into among the persons who will form a corporation, including how and when the corporation will be formed and the responsibilities of the various parties.

promoter The person or persons who take responsibility for creating and organizing a business into a corporation.

Promoters

In corporation law, a **promoter** is an individual who comes up with the idea of creating a corporation. The promoter is a person who investigates the laws, brings together the individuals, and seeks funding for the new business enterprise. Because there is no corporation at this point, a promoter is not protected by limited liability. Working as a promoter can be a risky undertaking. However, the flip side to the risk is the compensation. Promoters can be paid, sometimes quite lucratively, for bringing together the ingredients to form a corporation. Sometimes this compensation comes in the form of shares in the new corporation. Promoters often sell property to the newly formed corporation and pocket the profit as part of their compensation package.[15]

Promoters fall into an unusual classification. They are working on behalf of an entity that does not exist yet. What is their ethical obligation under these circumstances? Can promoters take advantage of the disorganization and chaos that often occurs prior to the creation of a company to personally enrich themselves? The courts have answered with an emphatic no. Promoters are fiduciaries, which means that they have ethical and legal obligations to the new company, even though it hasn't come into official form yet. Therefore, promoters must deal honestly and fairly with the corporation, keeping the best interests of the corporation foremost in their minds.

 ## ARTICLES OF INCORPORATION

articles of incorporation The document that frames the creation, organization, day-to-day operation, sale of assets, identity of registered agent, and dissolution of a corporation.

One of the most important steps in creating a corporation is the drafting of the **articles of incorporation**. This one document creates the rights, duties, and obligations of all parties involved in the new corporate venture, from shareholders and officers to the board of directors.

GETTING TO THE BASICS

The rights of the stockholders are created in the articles of incorporation.[16]

Given the fact that this document is so important to the fledgling corporation, it is interesting to note that there is no preset formula of words, or even particular phrases, that must be used to create the articles. What is required is that the individuals involved show evidence that they intended to take advantage of the corporate structure as authorized by statute.[17] They must indicate their clear intention to create a corporation that will be recognized by state law and receive the benefit of limited liability protection. Along with the rights and obligations of the corporate members, the articles must comply with the state law.[18]

Most states provide that there are only three or four mandatory provisions that must be contained in all articles of incorporation filed with the state secretary of state's office. They include:

- the name of the corporation
- the number of shares issued by the new corporation
- the registered office of incorporation and the name and address of the registered agent
- the names and addresses of the incorporators

Although there is no requirement to include additional information on the articles of incorporation, many companies provide additional information about certain topics, including:

- names and addresses of directors of the newly formed corporation
- the purpose of the corporation (if not purpose is listed, and the corporation can engage in any lawful business)
- classification of shares (There are a wide variety of classifications of shares that can be issued by newly formed corporation. Depending on where the company plans to run the business, it might decide to issue different types of shares. Voting rights associated with the shares should also be clarified in the articles incorporation.)
- procedure for filling vacancies and removing directors
- assumption of personal liability (If any of the shareholders opt to surrender some or all of their limited liability protection, this must be listed in the articles of incorporation.)

See Exhibits 8–5 and 8–6.

ERRORS OR OMISSIONS IN THE ARTICLES OF INCORPORATION

What effect do errors or omissions in the articles of incorporation have on the filing with the state? Although there is authority for the state to refuse to acknowledge the business's standing as a corporation and instead treat it as a sole proprietorship or as a general partnership, most states do not opt for such drastic measures. If the corporation can show substantial compliance with state law, the business will still be recognized as a corporation. Minor defects, such as clerical errors or typographical errors, will result in a ruling that the corporation is in substantial compliance with state law and will be recognized as a corporation.[19]

FILING ISSUES

The general method of incorporating business is by filing one or more copies of the corporation's articles of incorporation with the state secretary of state's office, along with the official form and a filing fee. If the documents have been submitted in their proper form, with no fatal errors in the paperwork, the corporation is recognized as coming into existence the moment

Exhibit 8–5. State of Minnesota Articles of Incorporation form

STATE OF MINNESOTA
SECRETARY OF STATE

ARTICLES OF INCORPORATION
Business and Nonprofit Corporations

PLEASE TYPE OR PRINT LEGIBLY IN BLACK INK.

Please read the directions on the reverse side before completing this form. All information on this form is public information.

The undersigned incorporator(s) is an (are) individual(s) 18 years of age or older and adopt the following articles of incorporation to form a (mark ONLY one):

☐ FOR-PROFIT BUSINESS CORPORATION (Chapter 302A)   ☐ NONPROFIT CORPORATION (Chapter 317A)

ARTICLE I   NAME

The name of the corporation is:

_____

(Business Corporation names must include a corporate designation such as Incorporated, Corporation, Company, Limited or an abbreviation of one of those words.)

ARTICLE II   REGISTERED OFFICE ADDRESS AND AGENT

The registered office address of the corporation is:

_____

(A complete street address or rural route and rural route box number is required; the address cannot be a P.O. Box) City State Zip

The registered agent at the above address is:

_____

Name (**Note**: You are not required to have a registered agent.)

ARTICLE III   SHARES

The corporation is authorized to issue a total of _____ shares.
(If you are a business corporation you must authorize at least one share. Nonprofit corporations are not required to have shares.)

ARTICLE IV   INCORPORATORS

I (We), the undersigned incorporator(s) certify that I am (we are) authorized to sign these articles and that the information in these articles is true and correct. I (We) also understand that if any of this information is intentionally or knowingly misstated that criminal penalties will apply as if I (we) had signed these articles under oath. (Provide the name and address of each incorporator. Each incorporator must sign below. List the incorporators on an additional sheet if you have more than two incorporators.)

_____

| Name | Street | City | State | Zip | Signature |

_____

| Name | Street | City | State | Zip | Signature |

Print name and phone number of person to be contacted if there is a question about the filing of these articles.

_____   (_____)_____

Name   Phone Number

bus 3   Rev. 3-03

Exhibit 8–6. Articles of incorporation Arkansas*

> (a) The articles of incorporation must set forth:
> (1) a corporate name for the corporation that satisfies the requirements of § 4-27-401;
> (2) the number of shares the corporation is authorized to issue and, if such shares are to consist of one (1) class only, the par value of each of such shares, or a statement that all of such shares are without par value; or, if such shares are to be divided into classes, the number of shares of each class, and a statement of the par value of the shares of each such class or that such shares are without par value;
> (3) the street address of the corporation's initial registered office and the name of its initial registered agent at that office;
> (4) the name and address of each incorporator; and
> (5) the primary purpose or purposes for which the corporation is organized, which is provided to the Secretary of State for informational purposes and shall not, unless specifically stated in the articles of incorporation, limit the broad purposes provided in § 4-27-301.

*Ark. Code Ann. § 4-27-204 (Michie, 2006).

that the paperwork is stamped "filed" with the secretary of state's office. The stamp satisfies the conditions precedent for creating a corporation.

Once filed, the articles of incorporation become the central document in the day-to-day functioning of the business. They are the first document that a court will review when litigation arises about the corporation, and they are also important in establishing other rights and responsibilities, not the least of which concerns the incorporators themselves.

INCORPORATORS

The **incorporators** are the people who form the corporation. We have already seen that in order to create a corporate business entity, the business must meet certain minimum requirements. This is also true of the incorporators. For instance, the people who create the corporation must have the contractual capacity to do so. We have already come across the concept of contractual capacity in previous chapters. Capacity refers to an individual's ability to know and understand the obligations involved in creating a contract. In order to form a corporation, a person must have contractual capacity, which means that he or she cannot have any impediment, such as being under the influence of alcohol or drugs, being under the legal age, or any of the other conditions that can result in a person being declared incapable. State statutes might also restrict a person's ability to form a corporation, such as preventing people who are classed as "alien enemies," residing in another country that is in open conflict with the United States.[20] See Exhibit 8–7.

incorporator The person or persons who form the corporation.

> **Sidebar**
>
> Although minors may be barred from working as incorporators, there is generally no prohibition that prevents them from owning stock in a corporation.[21]

Exhibit 8–7. Articles of incorporation form, Commonwealth of Massachusetts

The Commonwealth of Massachusetts

William Francis Galvin
Secretary of the Commonwealth
One Ashburton Place, Boston, Massachusetts 02108-1512

Articles of Organization
(General Laws Chapter 156D, Section 2.02; 950 CMR 113.16)

ARTICLE I
The exact name of the corporation is:

ARTICLE II
Unless the articles of organization otherwise provide, all corporations formed pursuant to G.L. Chapter 156D have the purpose of engaging in any lawful business. Please specify if you want a more limited purpose:

ARTICLE III
State the total number of shares and par value, * if any, of each class of stock that the corporation is authorized to issue. All corporations must authorize stock. If only one class or series is authorized, it is not necessary to specify any particular designation.

WITHOUT PAR VALUE		WITH PAR VALUE		
TYPE	NUMBER OF SHARES	TYPE	NUMBER OF SHARES	PAR VALUE

*G.L. Chapter 156D eliminates the concept of par value, however a corporation may specify par value in Article III. See G.L. Chapter 156D, Section 6.21, and the comments relative thereto.

P.C.

c156ds202950c11316 01/13/05

(continued)

Exhibit 8–7. Articles of incorporation form, Commonwealth of Massachusetts *(continued)*

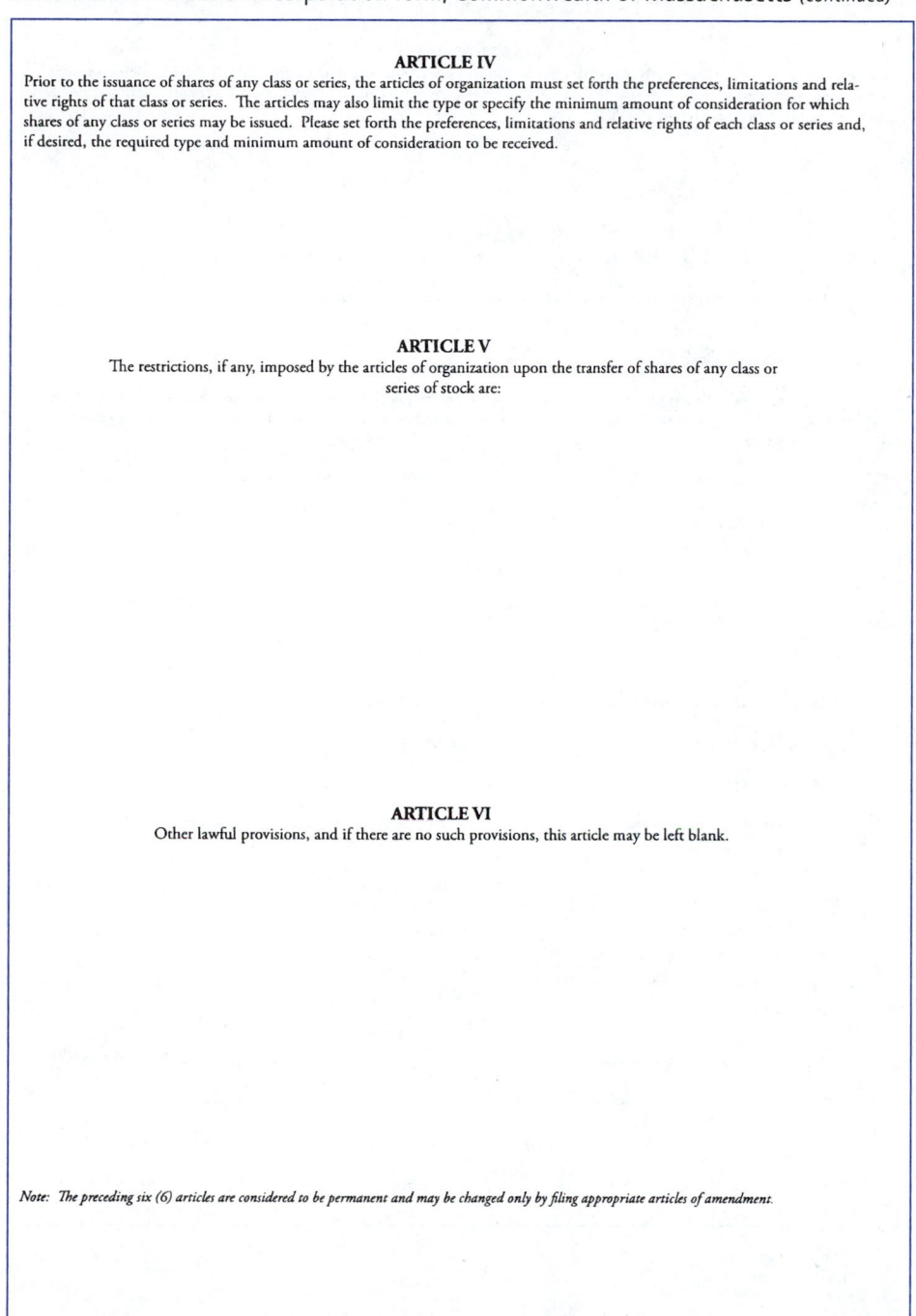

ARTICLE IV

Prior to the issuance of shares of any class or series, the articles of organization must set forth the preferences, limitations and relative rights of that class or series. The articles may also limit the type or specify the minimum amount of consideration for which shares of any class or series may be issued. Please set forth the preferences, limitations and relative rights of each class or series and, if desired, the required type and minimum amount of consideration to be received.

ARTICLE V

The restrictions, if any, imposed by the articles of organization upon the transfer of shares of any class or series of stock are:

ARTICLE VI

Other lawful provisions, and if there are no such provisions, this article may be left blank.

Note: The preceding six (6) articles are considered to be permanent and may be changed only by filing appropriate articles of amendment.

(continued)

Exhibit 8–7. Articles of incorporation form, Commonwealth of Massachusetts *(continued)*

ARTICLE VII

The effective date of organization of the corporation is the date and time the articles were received for filing if the articles are not rejected within the time prescribed by law. If a later effective date is desired, specify such date, which may not be later than the 90th day after the articles are received for filing:

ARTICLE VIII

The information contained in this article is not a permanent part of the articles of organization.

    a.   The street address of the initial registered office of the corporation in the commonwealth:

    b.   The name of its initial registered agent at its registered office:

    c.   The names and addresses of the individuals who will serve as the initial directors, president, treasurer and secretary of the corporation (an address need not be specified if the business address of the officer or director is the same as the principal office location):

President:

Treasurer:

Secretary:

Director(s):

    d.   The fiscal year end of the corporation:

    e.   A brief description of the type of business in which the corporation intends to engage:

    f.   The street address of the principal office of the corporation:

    g.   The street address where the records of the corporation required to be kept in the commonwealth are located is:

_____ , which is

(number, street, city or town, state, zip code)

☐ its principal office;

☐ an office of its transfer agent;

☐ an office of its secretary/assistant secretary;

☐ its registered office.

Signed this _____ day of _____ , _____ by the incorporator(s):

Signature: _____

Name: _____

Address: _____

Some states also limit incorporators to "natural persons." Under this definition, an existing corporation cannot organize the new corporation. People, not companies, must do this. See Exhibit 8–8.

KEY POINT

An incorporator is someone who is a member of the corporation, who may be either a stockholder or an officer. Many states have restricted the category of incorporator to "natural persons."[22]

Exhibit 8–8. Qualifying as an Incorporator (New York).

One or more natural persons at least eighteen years of age may act as incorporators of a corporation to be formed under this chapter.*

*N.Y.Corp. Law §401 (McKinney, 2006).

NUMBER AND TYPE OF AUTHORIZED SHARES

Shares are ownership interests in the company. There are different types of shares, and these different classifications give rise to different levels of participation in the company. For instance, some shares give the owners voting rights in the company's decision making, while others do not. The articles of incorporation are where the company decides on the type and variety of shares that it will issue. The articles must also specify any limitations on the shares, including voting rights. When a company is privately owned, statutes restrict how many shares it can issue and also prevent the company from selling its shares on the open market. We will discuss shares in greater detail in a later chapter.

shares Ownership interests in a corporation.

REGISTERED OFFICE

Most states require that the company identify its principal place of business, or at least the place where the company records will be located. This provision is similar to the registered office requirement we have seen with limited liability companies and limited partnerships.

Does a corporation have a domicile or a residence? Most authorities argue that a corporation cannot have a residence and can maintain a domicile, or home state, only in the strictly metaphorical sense. As such, a corporation is not a citizen of a particular state, but may have a base of operations in a particular place.[23]

REGISTERED AGENT

In addition to a registered office, the corporation must also have a **registered agent**. This is the person on whom lawsuits and other official notices will be filed. Service on this person equates to service on the corporation and triggers the time periods in civil suits.

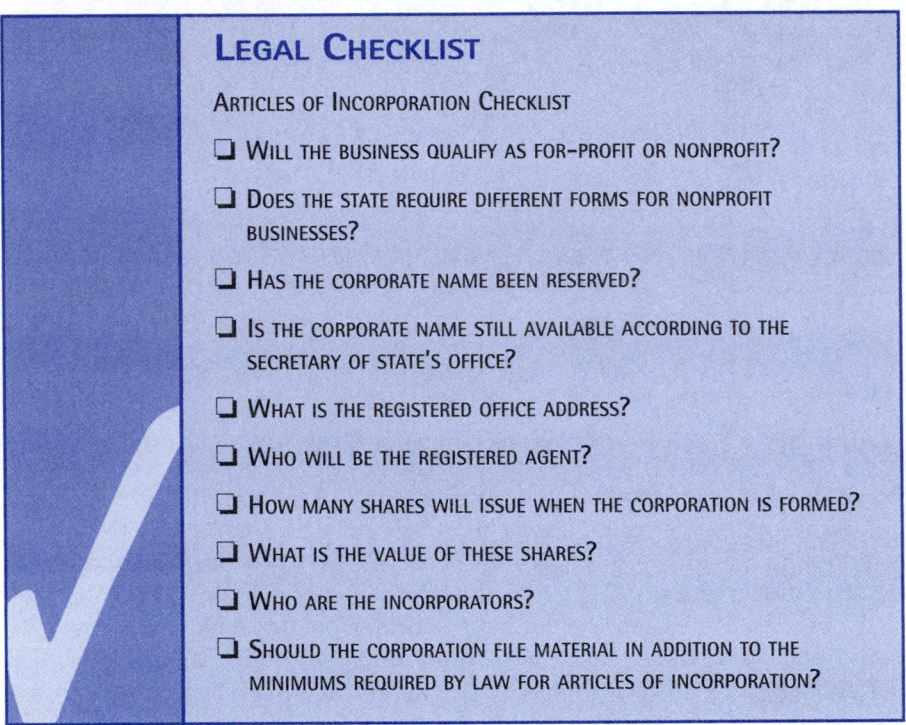

LEGAL CHECKLIST

ARTICLES OF INCORPORATION CHECKLIST

❏ WILL THE BUSINESS QUALIFY AS FOR-PROFIT OR NONPROFIT?

❏ DOES THE STATE REQUIRE DIFFERENT FORMS FOR NONPROFIT BUSINESSES?

❏ HAS THE CORPORATE NAME BEEN RESERVED?

❏ IS THE CORPORATE NAME STILL AVAILABLE ACCORDING TO THE SECRETARY OF STATE'S OFFICE?

❏ WHAT IS THE REGISTERED OFFICE ADDRESS?

❏ WHO WILL BE THE REGISTERED AGENT?

❏ HOW MANY SHARES WILL ISSUE WHEN THE CORPORATION IS FORMED?

❏ WHAT IS THE VALUE OF THESE SHARES?

❏ WHO ARE THE INCORPORATORS?

❏ SHOULD THE CORPORATION FILE MATERIAL IN ADDITION TO THE MINIMUMS REQUIRED BY LAW FOR ARTICLES OF INCORPORATION?

▶ THE FINAL STEPS IN ORGANIZING THE CORPORATION

Once the articles of incorporation have been filed, some additional steps must be followed to complete proper organization of the newly formed business. They include:

- initial organizational meeting
- creation and adoption of corporate bylaws
- election of corporate officers
- approval of shareholders agreements
- election of directors not named in the articles of incorporation
- banking resolution and fiscal year provisions
- issuance of shares
- annual reports

ORGANIZATIONAL MEETING

The **organizational meeting**, or initial meeting, is the first official business of the newly formed corporation. The purpose of this meeting is to bring together the various members of the corporation and adopt bylaws, vote on officers, and take care of the other clerical work that must be done to officially launch the corporation. In many states, the minutes of this meeting must be filed with the state, and the failure to do so may result in a finding that the corporation is a nullity. One of the most important duties at the organizational meeting is the adoption of corporate bylaws. See Exhibit 8–9.

organizational meeting The statutorily required first meeting of a newly formed corporation where directors are elected and shares are issued.

Exhibit 8–9. The organization meeting.

(a) After the corporate existence has begun, an organization meeting of the initial directors, or, if directors are not designated in the certificate of incorporation, of the incorporator or incorporators, shall be held within or without this state, for the purpose of adopting by-laws, electing directors to hold office as provided in the certificate of incorporation or the by-laws, and the transaction of such other business as may come before the meeting.*

*N.Y. Corporate Law §405 (McKinney, 2006).

CORPORATE BYLAWS

Bylaws usually contain guidelines for how the business will be run. The usual practice is to adopt corporate bylaws at the initial organizational meeting of the corporation. Although there is a certain degree of flexibility in the content of corporate bylaws, there are some mandatory provisions. For instance, the bylaws should make provisions for the following:

bylaws Rules adopted by a business entity to regulate its internal policies and actions.

- date and place of the annual shareholder meeting
- the number of directors
- the authority, duties, and titles of corporate officers

The bylaws must be consistent with the articles of incorporation. Obviously, the bylaws cannot contain provisions that run counter to state or federal laws or attempt to exclude corporate responsibility from applicable law. Many courts have defined bylaws as the essential contract between shareholders and the corporation.

Emergency Bylaw Provisions

Corporations are authorized to create emergency bylaws vesting power in a single individual to conduct business on behalf of the entire corporation. These emergency bylaws usually contain provisions outlining how and when an emergency meeting of the board of directors can be called, what constitutes a quorum during such an emergency meeting, and who can be designated as an emergency officer or member of the board of directors.

ELECTION OF CORPORATE OFFICERS

Members of the corporation who have shares entitling them to vote can decide among themselves who they would like to elect to the board of directors. These directors will set the policies for the corporation and handle many other important decisions, including the payment of taxes and franchise fees and change in corporate procedures.

APPROVAL OF SHAREHOLDER AGREEMENTS

shareholder agreement An agreement between the members of a corporation, setting out issues such as who can own shares and how these shares affect rights within the corporation.

Although we will discuss **shareholder agreements** in a later chapter, the organizational meeting is where these agreements are made official. Shareholder agreements are the contracts among the incorporators that set out a wide variety of issues, such as:

- Who can be a shareholder in the company?
- Who is permitted to serve on the board of directors?
- How will shares be distributed in the event of a shareholder's death or declaration of bankruptcy?
- What is the value of the shares?

BANKING RESOLUTIONS

The organizational meeting also has some clerical duties to consider. Among these duties is the adoption of banking resolutions that authorize the creation and maintenance of corporate bank accounts. These resolutions will limit who has access to the accounts, who is permitted to sign corporate checks, who is allowed to oversee the accounts, and how account reports will be made to the shareholders.

ISSUANCE OF SHARES

The organizational meeting is also the point where the company shares are officially distributed to the various members.

ANNUAL REPORTS

Corporations are required to file an annual report with the secretary of state's office listing the names and addresses of the officers and directors. Corporations are also obligated to follow tax laws on both the state and federal level. See Exhibit 8–10.

Exhibit 8–10. Annual report for domestic and foreign corporations, Commonwealth of Massachusetts

D F

The Commonwealth of Massachusetts

William Francis Galvin
Secretary of the Commonwealth
One Ashburton Place, Boston, Massachusetts 02108-1512

Filing Fee: $125.00
Late Fee: $25.00

**Annual Report for Domestic
and Foreign Corporations**
(General Laws Chapter 156D, Section 16.22; 950 CMR 113.57)

(1) Exact name of the corporation: _____

(2) Jurisdiction of incorporation: _____

(3) Street address of the corporation's registered office in the commonwealth:

_____
(number, street, city or town, state, zip code)

(4) Name of the registered agent at the registered office: _____

(5) Street address of the corporation's principal office:

_____
(number, street, city or town, state, zip code)

(6) Provide the names and addresses of the corporation's board of directors and its president, treasurer, secretary, and if different, its chief executive officer and chief financial officer.

	NAME	ADDRESS
President:		
Treasurer:		
Secretary:		
Chief Executive Officer:		
Chief Financial Officer:		
Directors:		

(7) Briefly describe the business of the corporation: _____

(8-9) Capital stock of each class and series:

CLASS OF STOCK	TOTAL AUTHORIZED BY ARTICLES OF ORGANIZA-TION OR AMENDMENTS Number of Shares	TOTAL ISSUED AND OUTSTANDING Number of Shares
COMMON		
PREFERRED		

(10) Check if the stock of the corporation is publicly traded. ☐

(11) Report is filed for fiscal year ending: _____ / _____ / _____
         (month)   *(day)*   *(year)*

Signed by: _____

☐ Chairman of the board of directors   ☐ President   ☐ Other officer   ☐ Court-appointed fiduciary

on this _____ day of _____ , _____ .

c156ds1622950c11357 01/13/05

CORPORATE "SEALS"

In the past, corporations adopted official seals that officers and directors would then use to sign official documents. However, corporate seals are no longer required in most states. Instead, the officer authorized to sign on behalf of the corporation (usually the president) can simply write the word "seal" beside his or her signature.[24]

Ethics File: Researching Corporate Databases

Although it might seem to be an unusual feature to raise in a section on ethics, being able to sift through corporate database filings is an important legal (and ethical) skill. Many states now provide Internet-based databases that permit anyone with Web access to check on a wide variety of corporate filings. Because corporations can face dire consequences for failing to keep up with record keeping, it is often up to the legal professional to help corporations keep abreast of the filing requirements, and to double check that filings, such as the minutes of initial meetings and annual reports, actually make it to the right office. If you have the opportunity, spend a little time reviewing the Web sites provided at the end of this chapter and see how much information you can gather about a particular company.

CASE LAW: *When a Corporation Owns Real Estate*

Matter of Servo Systems, Inc.[25]
Burton R. Lifland, Bankruptcy Judge.

The debtor, on the morning of a scheduled State Court mortgage foreclosure sale, filed a petition under Chapter 11 of the Bankruptcy Code. It additionally sought and obtained a stay order directed against the scheduled sale. The order was ignored despite actual notice to the participants at the sale. Within weeks of the commencement of the case, the debtor's attorney, who was also its sole operating officer and active board of directors member, died. At this unforeseen, crucial stage of the proceedings, while the debtor was devitalized and without supervision or guidance, counsel for Larchmont Federal Savings and Loan Association ("Larchmont") sought dismissal.

After focusing on the myriad serious and nonserious issues raised by Larchmont, it is clear that continued refuge by the debtor in Chapter 11 depends upon the determination of a surpassing single issue: did this debtor have an interest in the foreclosed upon property on the dates relevant to the New York State mortgage foreclosure proceeding? In summary,

the debtor, a Florida corporation, claims ownership to the subject real property located in this state as its sole valuable asset. Its interest, if any, is based upon a deed delivered to the debtor by its parent corporate grantor during a hiatus between the execution of its articles of incorporation and their subsequent filing by the Florida Secretary of State. Ownership of the property is essential to the debtor's reorganization.

The debtor is a Florida corporation whose articles of incorporation were executed on March 21, 1980, but not filed until July 10, 1980. Proceeding from this state (New York) counsel for the incorporators utilized a nationwide corporate service company to handle the mechanical aspects of the incorporation process (i. e.: to supply the necessary form documentation and make the proper filings with the State of Florida). Evidently, the need to procure a registered agent in compliance with Florida's General Corporation Act s 607.037, delayed the necessary filing.

Under New York's law of deeds, a valid grant may be made to a corporation that can hold either in its own right or as trustee. Grants may not be made to lesser formalized groups, combinations or associations who are not accorded positive legal status. In Schein v. Erasmus Realty Co., 194 A.D. 38, 184 N.Y.S. 840, 841 (1920) the court was unequivocal in proclaiming that a mere association, which failed to qualify as a juridical entity, is incapable of holding title. Where such a transfer is attempted, no legal title passes and title remains in the grantor. For a deed to be operative as a conveyance, the law requires that a designated, legally recognized, grantee, be it a natural or artificial person, be in existence at the time of the conveyance and be capable of taking title. A fortiori, an unincorporated enterprise that intends to become a corporation, but fails to achieve corporate status in law or in fact at the time of a grant, does not receive title to real property, even if it achieves corporate status at some later date, because there is no grantee in existence capable of holding title to the property when the parties attempt the transfer.

While a corporation may be capable of taking title to real property, a foreign corporation such as the debtor, has no inherent right to hold property in New York. Foreign corporations are, however, permitted to do so by statute. And, while under this section foreign corporations may acquire and hold real property in this state, it is clear that this right is an exercise of comity and that the enactment does not change, modify, or enlarge the powers of corporations given by the state which created them. Implicitly, foreign corporations are subject to applicable domestic law, and may not engage in acts prohibited by local laws or against local public policy.

The Florida General Corporation Act, added by Laws 1975 c. 75-250, effective January 1, 1976, contains 3 sections bearing upon the debtor's attainment of corporate status. In pertinent part they provide:

607.164 Articles of incorporation; execution; content; delivery and filing

The articles of incorporation shall be delivered to the Department of State. If the Department of State finds that the articles of incorporation conform to law, it shall, when all fees have been paid as prescribed in this chapter, file the articles of incorporation in accordance with this chapter.

607.167 Commencement of corporate existence

The date when corporate existence shall commence shall be upon the filing of the articles of incorporation by the Department of State. . . .

607.171 Effect of certificate of incorporation

The certificate of incorporation shall be conclusive evidence that all conditions precedent required to be performed by the incorporators have been complied with and that the corporation has been incorporated under this chapter, except as against this state in a proceeding to cancel or revoke the certificate of incorporation or for involuntary dissolution of the corporation.

Clearly, the debtor had not satisfied these provisions and was acting outside the regular course at the time it received its deed to the property. A defect or other irregularity in the process of creating or organizing a corporation is not, however, necessarily fatal to a finding of corporate presence.

Under some circumstances a state will attribute corporate incidents to an enterprise despite its failure to comply with all statutory prerequisites. Such a corporation is labeled "de facto" and, although it is not a true corporation, for reasons of public policy, it is vulnerable only to attack by the sovereign state of its domicile. Corporate status is granted by the very fact of its acting like one. For all intents and purposes it functions as would a "de jure" corporation, which is a corporation regularly created in full compliance with all legal requirements, whose corporate franchise is not subject to attack by anyone.

Both the states of Florida and New York have recognized the de facto doctrine on various occasions and both have approved a de facto corporation's right to hold and transfer real property.

The kinds of infirmities or defects in the incorporation process that result in de facto corporate status

(continued)

CASE LAW: *When a Corporation Owns Real Estate* (continued)

are not readily susceptible to precise definitions. As pointed out quite candidly by Professor Hornstein, sympathetic judges are often influenced in their decision by the realization of the consequences.

As pertains to filing, as opposed to not filing, of articles of incorporation, Florida case law is silent. Generally, whether the filing or recording, or both, of the articles of incorporation is a condition precedent to any corporate existence depends mainly upon the statutory scheme and the terms of the governing statutes relating to filing or recording. The various states, whose statutes vary considerably, are understandably not in agreement.

Reviewing the relevant Florida General Corporation Act provisions set out above, this court concludes that the terms of the statute and the statutory scheme evidence an intent by Florida's legislature to make the filing of the articles of incorporation mandatory to the inception of any corporate existence. Section 607.171 states the certificate of incorporation shall be conclusive evidence that all conditions precedent have been performed. It does not state that the filing of the articles of incorporation shall be conclusive evidence of the performance of conditions precedent because the filing is of itself an important condition precedent. Section 607.171 must also be read together with s 607.167, which specifies that corporate existence shall commence upon the filing of the articles of incorporation by the Department of State. Thus, once the Department of State has reviewed the articles, as it must under s 607.164, and has filed them, the corporation springs to life and is subject to attack only by the state and no other under s 607.171. Beforehand, there is nothing.

In retrospect, one must recognize that the entire process is artificial, finding substance in fictions of creation. Essentials of the formulative process cannot be overlooked or omitted.

Moreover, in this case, absent the legislative demise of the de facto doctrine in Florida, I would conclude that no de facto corporation had arisen.

The Florida cases detail four essential elements for a de facto corporation:

1. A law or charter providing for the organization of the corporation of the kind attempted to be organized.
2. An attempted good-faith compliance with statutory requirements intended as conditions precedent.
3. An unintentional omission of some legal requirement.
4. The exercise of good faith of corporate functions by which it is intended to carry out the purpose and object of the attempted incorporation under the law.

As stated in Part II, apparently, the debtor's delay in consummating the incorporation process was its need to procure a registered agent. At the time of the attempted conveyance, debtor's incorporator, who was also the transferor of the property, obviously knew full well that the articles of incorporation had not been filed. Nonetheless, according to testimony by a Unicorn witness, because of certain regulations pertaining to conduct of its own business, debtor's incorporator/transferor had to pass the property posthaste. Given these circumstances, this court cannot see how the failure to file was unintentional, or how there was an attempt, or an exercise of good faith, to see that the articles were duly filed. The debtor has not asserted that this is a case where the debtor's articles of incorporation were delivered to the Department of State and the Department of State lost or misplaced the articles of incorporation or for some other reason neglected to file the articles. In fact, the Florida Department of State was duty bound not to file the articles of incorporation until the debtor's incorporator complied fully with applicable law.

To achieve de facto status more is required than the mere signing of articles of incorporation, or the giving of instructions to an attorney, or an attorney's giving of instructions to a corporate service company, to incorporate. There must be a bona fide attempt or colorable compliance with the statutory scheme; or, as expounded by the Florida courts, an attempted, good faith compliance combined with an unintentional omission. This effort simply was not present.

Occasionally, courts are tempted, with the benefit of hindsight, to strain and find compliance with the prerequisites to the de facto doctrine, especially since, where, as here, the ultimate filing resulted in de jure status. But it is impossible to conclude that there was corporate existence at the time of the attempted grant. In fact, casting further doubt, it was not until four months after the grant from Unicorn that the debtor's articles of incorporation were finally filed and compliance achieved. Moreover, there is clearly a lack of equity here for finding in favor of the debtor. This is not a case where the court has to protect an innocent third party mortgage. Nor can the court bootstrap and sidestep the issue by finding express or implied ratification of a promoter's contract. A deed to a grantee not in existence is not susceptible to this theory. Finally, this is not a case where a holding adverse to alleged corporate existence exposes shareholders to liability beyond that of their intended capital contribution.

On the basis of Florida law, divined with the help of the authorities, the court concludes that at the time of the grant to the debtor, the debtor was neither a corporation de jure or de facto. The grant was made to a nul tiel corporation incapable under New York law of taking title to property, and thus the deed did not pass title and is void. Accordingly, this case under Chapter 11 is dismissed for cause including the absence of a reasonable likelihood of rehabilitation.

CASE QUESTIONS

1. According to the court, what is the main issue in this case?

2. Under New York law, can property be conveyed to an unincorporated business? Why or why not?

3. How does Florida's corporate law bear on this dispute?

4. Why does the judge determine that no de facto corporation existed in this case?

5. What effect does the judge's decision on the corporate status of Servo Systems have on the underlying issues in the case?

SUMMARY

Creating a corporation involves painstaking attention to detail. Corporations are creatures of state statutes, and these laws must be complied with in order to create corporation. Statutes dictate the steps involved in creating a corporation. When a corporation fails to meet all of the statutory obligations, it may be classified as a de facto corporation. A corporation that fails to meet its statutory obligations may also have its charter revoked. The secretary of state's office maintains records on all corporations for each corporation organized within the state. When a business wishes to incorporate, it files appropriate paperwork in the state secretary of state's office. The most important document that must be filed there is the articles of incorporation. The articles of incorporation provide basic information about corporations, including the principal office address, the identity of the registered agent, and the number and quality of shares issued by the corporation. The final steps in creating a corporation consist of conducting the organizational meeting, where corporate bylaws are adopted and directors and officers are elected. Following the organizational meeting, corporations are required to submit annual reports to the secretary of state's office.

HELPFUL WEB SITES

California Secretary of State
http://www.ss.ca.gov/business/business.htm

Securities and Exchange Commission Filings and Forms
http://www.sec.gov/edgar.shtml

Florida Department of State
http://www.sunbiz.org/

South Carolina Secretary of State
http://www.scsos.com/corporations.htm

New York Secretary of State
http://www.dos.state.ny.us/

KEY TERMS

articles of incorporation	preincorporation agreement
bylaws	promoter
de facto	registered agent
incorporator	shareholder agreement
organizational meeting	shares

APPLYING CHAPTER CONCEPTS

Contact your state's secretary of state's office and inquire about the forms necessary to form a corporation. Request a package explaining the process of creating a corporation, including the filing of articles of incorporation and reserving a corporate name. Choose a name that you might wish to use for your corporation, and then see if you can discover whether another corporation in your state has already used that name.

REVIEW QUESTIONS

1. Why is the choice of corporate structure so important?
2. What role does the state secretary of state's office play in creating a corporation?
3. What rules and regulations must individuals follow if they plan to create a corporation under state law?
4. What limitations are placed on the name that a newly formed corporation can take?

5. What are articles of incorporation?

6. What information must articles of incorporation contain?

7. What provisions must articles of incorporation make toward naming a registered agent?

8. What are incorporators?

9. What liability do incorporators have for contracts negotiated on behalf of the newly formed corporation?

10. What are promoters?

11. What role do promoters have in creating a corporation?

12. What is the difference between preferred stock and common stock?

13. What is the purpose of the initial meeting?

14. What function do the bylaws serve for a newly formed corporation?

QUESTIONS FOR REFLECTION

Are corporations forced to give up too much information or too little? For instance, if a terrorist were considering damaging the American economy, destroying some corporate headquarters might seem like a worthwhile goal. On the other hand, it was the disguising and outright concealment of information that led to economic disasters like Enron, World Com, and others. How much or how little should corporations be forced to tell the public about their businesses?

ENDNOTES

[1]*Andover Savings Bank v. Commissioner of Revenue,* 439 N.E.2d 282, 387 Mass. 229 (1982).

[2]*Shreveport Traction Co. v. Kansas City, S. & G.R. Co.,* 44 So. 457, 119 La. 759 (1907).

[3]*W. L. Wells Co. v. Gastonia Cotton Mfg. Co.,* N.C., 25 S.Ct. 640, 198 U.S. 177, 49 L.Ed. 1003 (1902).

[4]*Lurie v. Arizona Fertilizer & Chemical Co.,* 421 P.2d 330, 101 Ariz. 482 (1966).

[5]*Kaszubowksi v. Buffalo Telegram Corp.,* 227 N.Y.S. 435, 131 Misc. 563 (1928).

[6]*Cunnyngham v. Shelby,* 136 Tenn. 176, 181, 188 S.W. 1147 (1916).

[7]*Matter of Servo Systems, Inc.,* Bkrtcy. S.D.N.Y., 11 B.R. 879 (1981).

[8]Slip Copy, 2005 WL 1413183 (D.Conn, 2005).

[9]*Debs Memorial Radio Fund, Inc. v. Lomenzo,* 269 N.Y.S.2d 632, 50 Misc.2d 51 (1966).

[10]*Guptill Holding Corp. v. State,* 3 Dept., 307 N.Y.S.2d 970, 33 A.D.2d 362 (1970).

[11]CJS Corporations § 28. (2005)

[12]CJS Corporations § 28. (2005)

[13]*Farrell v. Winchester Avenue R. Co.*, 61 Conn. 127, 130, 23 A. 757 (1891).

[14]*Westport Stone Co. v. Thomas*, 175 Ind. 319, 94 N.E. 406, 410 (1911).

[15]*Bivens v. Watkins*, 313 S.C. 228, 437 S.E.2d 132 (Ct. App. 1993).

[16]*Berger v. Amana Society*, 250 Iowa 1060, 95 N.W.2d 909, 70 A.L.R.2d 830, 838 (1959).

[17]*Nedeau v. United Petroleum*, 232 N.W. 202, 251 Mich. 673 (1930).

[18]*B & H Warehouse, Inc. v. Atlas Van Lines, Inc.*, C.A.Tex., 490 F.2d 818 (N.D. Tex, 1972).

[19]*Owensboro Wagon Co. v. Bliss*, 31 So. 81, 132 Ala. 253 (1901).

[20]*Hangar v. Abbott*, Ark., 73 U.S. 532, 18 L.Ed. 939 (1867).

[21]*In re Globe Mut. Ben. Ass'n,* 17 N.Y.S. 852, 63 Hun 263, affirmed 32 N.E. 122, 135 N.Y. 280 (1892).

[22]*Mark Twain Cape Girardeau Bank v. State Banking Bd.,* 528 S.W.2d 443 (1975).

[23]*People v. Barker*, 39 N.Y.S. 88, 16 Misc. 252 (1896).

[24]*Avery v. Kane Gas Light & Heating Co.*, 403 F.Supp. 14 (D.C.Pa.).

[25]11 B.R. 879 (Bkrtcy. N.Y., 1981).

Chapter 9

The Participants in the Corporation

Chapter Objectives

Upon completion of this chapter, you should be able to:

- List the various participants in a corporation.
- Explain the rights that shareholders enjoy under the corporate organizational model.
- Define the duties of corporate officers.
- Explain the function of corporate directors.
- Describe the interrelationships between shareholders, officers, and directors.

▶ INTRODUCTION

In this chapter, we will examine the three types of individuals who are essential to the corporation: shareholders, directors, and officers. Each of these categories has rules that apply to it only, and each classification has some impact on the other two. We have already seen that corporations are considered to be artificial persons, but this legal designation can take a business only so far. The artificial person needs real people to carry out its business. It is these individuals we will discuss in this chapter.

KEY POINT

A corporation is composed of three different classes of individuals: shareholders, directors, and officers. They all have their own rights and duties.

▶ SHAREHOLDERS

In previous chapters, we examined the statutes that authorize the creation of corporations. Statutes also define the roles of the various participants. When examining the rights of shareholders, officers, or directors, a legal professional should always begin with state statutes. See Exhibit 9–1.

Exhibit 9–1. Shareholder rights

> (a) Meetings of shareholders may be held at such place within or without this state as may be stated in or fixed in accordance with the bylaws. If no other place is stated or so fixed, shareholder meetings shall be held at the principal executive office of the corporation.
>
> (b) An annual meeting of shareholders shall be held for the election of directors on a date and at a time stated in or fixed in accordance with the bylaws. Any other proper business may be transacted at the annual meeting.*

*California Corporation Code § 600 (West, 2006).

shareholder a person who owns shares in a corporation.

A **shareholder** is someone who owns a percentage of a corporation. In this case, a share is literally the physical representation of a predetermined amount of the business. When a corporation is formed, one of the first orders of business is to determine how many shares to issue. If the company decides to issue 1,000 shares and distribute these shares among four people, each would own 25 percent of the business. Share ownership is often distributed among a much larger group of people, and the initial amount of shares authorized may also be much larger, but the general principle still applies.

Ownership of shares in a corporation brings with it two fundamental rights: the right to participate in the control of the corporation by voting and the right to share in the profits of the business. The right to vote is considered to be one of the more fundamental rights that a shareholder enjoys. All shareholders are the owners of the corporation, although they do not have some of the rights we often associate with ownership. For instance, shareholders are not authorized to sell corporate property, negotiate contracts on behalf of the corporation, or take individual action to hire and fire employees. Shareholders are protected by limited liability, and with this protection comes specific limitations.

A person does not become a shareholder simply because he or she was involved in the original action to create the corporation. Directors, incorporators, and promoters do not automatically become stockholders.[1]

The articles of incorporation create the rights, duties, and obligations of shareholders, directors, and officers. Other features of the relationship between these individuals are found in the bylaws and any shareholder agreements.[2]

NATURE OF A SHAREHOLDER

A shareholder is someone who owns part of a corporation.[3] The symbol of that ownership is a share. In order to qualify as a shareholder, a person must have the right to possess stock and to exercise the rights normally associated with share ownership. A shareholder can be a natural person or even another corporation. When it comes to the aspect of stock ownership, courts are often very liberal in permitting a wide range of individuals to possess stock. Consider Scenario 9–1.

> **Scenario 9–1. The Will**
>
> Alfred owned 1,000 shares in XYZ corporation. On his death, his will stipulated that all of his property should be transferred to his wife, Martha.
>
> There are ten other shareholders in XYZ corporation, and Martha has made it very clear that she doesn't like any of them. When the other shareholders learn that Martha will receive Alfred's shares, they decide to hold a special meeting and vote to change the rules so that Martha cannot receive the shares. Will they be successful?
>
> **Answer:** No. Alfred was within his rights to transfer his shares as he saw fit. The fact that the other shareholders don't like Martha will not affect this transfer. Martha is a shareholder, and the others must learn to live with it or try to buy her out.

Qualification to Be a Shareholder

Although the rules about recognizing stock ownership in corporations are liberally construed, there is one prerequisite that cannot be ignored. A person must consent to becoming a shareholder in a corporation. No one can be forced to own stock or can receive stock without knowledge.[4] Stock ownership in a corporation is actually a contract: the person agrees to take on the duties of being a shareholder in exchange for a vote on corporate matters and a share of the profits in the business. Because consent is a necessary component in any contractual relationship, a person must voluntarily become a shareholder. Consider Scenario 9–2.

> **Scenario 9–2. Skullduggery Inc.**
>
> Matt owns 48 percent of the stock in WXY Corporation, but he wants to become a majority stockholder so that he can have a greater impact on corporate policy and also can receive a greater proportion of corporate profits. He convinces another shareholder, Myron, to transfer some of his stock to "a poor widow who could really use the income." Myron agrees and transfers the stock to "Kathy O'Leary." Ms. O'Leary is Matt's third-grade teacher and has no knowledge of any of these matters. Matt accepts the stock for Ms. O'Leary and then promptly forges her name on the documents to transfer the stocks to himself. Was Ms. O'Leary ever an actual shareholder in this corporation?

Answer: No. If this had been an actual transaction, Ms. O'Leary would have had the option of accepting the shares and making herself a shareholder. Because she was never given this option, there was never a point in this fraudulent transaction where she was a shareholder. (Under the laws of all states, once this transaction was discovered, a court would invalidate it and transfer the shares back to their original owner. Matt may also be facing criminal charges for forging Ms. O'Leary's signature.)

Unlike other business models, a corporation is a distinct legal entity, separate from the identity of its individual shareholders. The practical result of this arrangement is that describing shareholders as the "owners" of the corporation is not technically correct. Shareholders are entitled to vote in corporate proceedings, to receive a share of corporate profits, and also to receive preferential treatment in receiving corporate assets if the corporation should ever be dissolved. Individual shareholders are not the equivalent of sole proprietors. They more closely resemble the members of a limited liability company, or the limited partners in a limited liability partnership. In fact, stock ownership has often been described as a willing arrangement between the corporation and the individual shareholders where the shareholders surrender many of their rights to the corporation in exchange for business profits.[5] This contract is not found in any one document. Instead, the agreement between shareholders and the corporation is scattered across the articles of incorporation, the corporate bylaws, statements on stock certificates, and shareholder agreements.[6]

KEY POINT

The relationship between a corporation and its stockholders is a contract: the stockholders surrender certain rights in exchange for guarantees, such as profits and limited liability.

Even when the government becomes a stockholder in a corporation, such as when a person dies without recognizable heirs, the government must abide by the terms of stock ownership in exactly the same way as a private individual would.

 ### GETTING TO THE BASICS

The shareholder/corporation relationship is a contract. The shareholder surrenders certain rights to the corporation (the right to take an active role in the business, the right to make hiring and firing decisions, etc.) in exchange for priority in receiving corporate profits.[7]

QUALIFICATIONS FOR BECOMING A SHAREHOLDER

The typical way to become a shareholder is to receive shares as one of the founding members of a corporation or by purchasing them from others. As a general rule, anyone can own shares in a corporation. Shareholders have the right to refuse to sell their stock to particular individuals, but they do not have the right to control what current shareholders do with their stock. Participants in professional corporations can limit stock ownership to membership in a particular profession.[8] For instance, if a professional corporation has been formed by a group of lawyers, the articles of incorporation can prevent transfer of sales to anyone who is not a member of the state bar.

Although we have said that share ownership is similar to a contract, it is interesting to note that individuals who normally cannot enter into contracts are permitted to own shares. Minors, for example, who are barred from entering into most types of contracts, are permitted to own shares in a corporation and to receive the same benefits of this ownership as any other shareholder.[9] When a person is wrongfully excluded from stock ownership, he or she can sue to have shareholder rights restored.[10] Consider Scenario 9–3.

> **Scenario 9–3. Excluding Members**
>
> CDE Corporation's stock is freely sold on exchanges across the country. One day, Manny decides to buy 100 shares of CDE Corporation. Manny is the owner of DEF Company, which is in the same business as CDE, Inc., and Manny has often stated his desire to destroy CDE by any legal means he can find. The board of directors doesn't want to have anything to do with Manny, and certainly doesn't want him to have voting rights in the corporation. Can they stop him?
>
> **Answer:** No. As long as Manny meets the minimum qualifications of share ownership, the corporation has no power to prevent him from buying the shares.[11]

Some stock is bought and sold on markets, like the New York Stock Exchange and NASDAQ (discussed in the next chapter). Shares in private corporations are held by a small group of individuals and are not traded on stock exchanges. The stocks can be transferred, but the pool of potential buyers is much more limited and the transaction may not fall under the regulations set out by the Securities and Exchange Commission. (We will discuss the SEC and stock exchanges in the next chapter).

Registered Ownership

Interestingly enough, ownership of stock doesn't necessarily mean physical possession of the actual stock certificates. The certificates may be in someone else's possession or even held at corporate headquarters. The certificates are only the symbols of ownership; the real power comes from the rights they represent, not the possession of the certificates themselves.[12] The documents that confer shareholder rights are in the articles of incorporation, the bylaws, and any shareholder agreements.

stock certificates Printed documents
that indicate share ownership.

Stock Certificates

Even if the **stock certificates** are not properly issued, or there is some incorrect procedure at the initial meeting, courts will still recognize stock ownership. This is true even if the directors never actually authorized the issuance of the stock originally proposed in the articles of incorporation.[13]

What is important for stockholders is not possession of stock certificates, but whether or not the stockholder is registered. Because most jurisdictions require registration or some type of documentation that shows that an individual is a stockholder in a particular corporation, this registration entitles the person to recognition as a stockholder, but does not determine whether the person possesses stock certificates.[14] The fact that stock certificates have not been printed does not determine a person's status as a stockholder. This status comes from the legal rights he or she has acquired in the corporation, not through possession of stock certificates.[15]

 GETTING TO THE BASICS

> Stock ownership is evidenced by registration, not the mere possession of a stock certificate.

SHAREHOLDER RIGHTS

Among the rights granted to shareholders are:

- the right to vote on management issues
- the right to a percentage of corporate earnings
- the right to corporate assets if the company should be dissolved[16]
- the right to elect directors

Of these rights, the right to vote on corporate issues is considered to be one of the most important. Shareholders have specific rights, but they cannot, by their initiative, sell off corporate property. They are not owners in that sense. Instead, shareholders have specific entitlements as a direct result of share ownership. See Exhibit 9–2.

KEY POINT

> Corporate bylaws create the basic framework of the corporation and its operating rules.

Exhibit 9–2. Excerpt from corporate bylaws detailing voting rights for shareholders

---

Article I

The corporation shall be known as Happy Bee, Inc.

Article II

The corporation shall commence business as soon as a certificate is issued by the Secretary of State of the State of Iowa, and shall continue for a period of twenty (20) years, with power of renewal, unless sooner dissolved by the vote of a majority of the voting stock then outstanding.

Article III

The voting power shall be vested exclusively in the Class A common stock, and each share of Class A common stock shall be entitled to one vote in person or by written proxy at all annual or special meetings of the Corporation, or on matters in which the stockholders are entitled to vote. At all meetings of the stockholders of the Corporation or on any matter in which the stockholders are required or permitted to give consent, a majority of the common stock outstanding are entitled to vote as aforesaid. Except with reference to voting rights, Class A common stock and Class B common stock shall in all respects be of equal rank and priority.

Article IV

The stockholders entitled to vote at the annual meeting, or whenever a board of directors is to be lawfully elected, shall determine the number of directors to be elected, within the limits hereinbefore set out. The directors of the Corporation, who need not be stockholders thereof, shall be elected at the annual meeting of the stockholders, as hereinafter provided.

Article V

Special meetings may be called by the president or the board of directors, or by a majority of the voting stock by written consent and on twenty (20) days' written notice.

Article VI

Stockholders holding a majority of voting stock of the corporation outstanding and entitled to vote may make an adjudication in respect to indemnification granted to directors against certain liabilities when directors not incurring liability do not constitute a majority of the board.

(continued)

Exhibit 9–2. Excerpt from corporate bylaws detailing voting rights for shareholders. *(continued)*

> ### Article VII
> The private property of the stockholders of this corporation shall not be liable for corporate debts, and this Article shall not be amended or changed except by the unanimous consent of all the stockholders of the corporation in writing.
>
> ### Article VIII
> These Articles of Incorporation may be amended at any time by a vote of a majority of the voting stock of the corporation outstanding, at any regular meeting of the stockholders or any special meeting called for that purpose.*

*Adapted from *DuVall v. Moore*, 276 F.Supp. 674 (D.C. Iowa 1967).

Voting Trusts

voting trust An agreement between shareholders to vote in a certain way.

Shareholders have the right to form **voting trusts** or groups that vote together on specific issues. Such voting agreements have been upheld on appeal in numerous cases.[17] Of course, the shareholders cannot enter into an agreement to ignore the applicable law. Any result from such an agreement would be void. See Exhibit 9–3.

Proxy Voting

In addition to forming voting agreements, shareholders can also temporarily transfer their voting rights to one individual and allow that individual to vote

Exhibit 9–3. Voting trusts and other voting agreements.

> (a) One stockholder or 2 or more stockholders may by agreement in writing deposit capital stock of an original issue with or transfer capital stock to any person or persons, or entity or entities authorized to act as trustee, for the purpose of vesting in such person or persons, entity or entities, who may be designated voting trustee, or voting trustees, the right to vote thereon for any period of time determined by such agreement, upon the terms and conditions stated in such agreement. The agreement may contain any other lawful provisions not inconsistent with such purpose.*

*Del. Code Ann. titl, 8 §218 (2006).

all the shares in one way. **Proxy** voting has a long history and allows corporate members a method to exercise greater control over the corporation. There are, however, some rules that limit how and when proxies can be used. See Exhibit 9–4.

proxy A temporary transfer of voting rights to another person or voting trust.

Exhibit 9–4. Federal legislation relevant to proxy voting

> **Proxies**
> (a) Solicitation of proxies in violation of rules and regulations
> It shall be unlawful for any person, by the use of the mails or by any means or instrumentality of interstate commerce or of any facility of a national securities exchange or otherwise, in contravention of such rules and regulations as the Commission may prescribe as necessary or appropriate in the public interest or for the protection of investors, to solicit or to permit the use of his name to solicit any proxy or consent or authorization in respect of any security (other than an exempted security) registered pursuant to section 78l of this title.
> (b) Giving or refraining from giving proxy in respect of any security carried for account of customer Securities Exchange Act of 1934.*

*15 U.S.C.A. § 78n.

 GETTING TO THE BASICS

In a "proxy fight" groups of shareholders have pledged their votes to a particular individual who uses this as leverage to attempt to change corporate policy, or even to remove a director.

SHAREHOLDER MEETINGS

Shareholders come together at least once a year in an annual shareholders' meeting, where they vote on any of a number of issues, including corporate policies and the election of corporate board of directors. This meeting is where the shareholders are permitted to make their voices heard by voting on corporate policies, profit sharing, management issues, and perhaps the most important right: the election of individuals who compose the board of directors. The directors play an important role in the management of the corporation. See Exhibit 9–5.

Exhibit 9–5. Meetings of stockholders

> (a)(1) Meetings of stockholders may be held at such place, either within or without this State as may be designated by or in the manner provided in the certificate of incorporation or bylaws, or if not so designated, as determined by the board of directors. If, pursuant to this paragraph or the certificate of incorporation or the bylaws of the corporation, the board of directors is authorized to determine the place of a meeting of stockholders, the board of directors may, in its sole discretion, determine that the meeting shall not be held at any place, but may instead be held solely by means of remote communication as authorized by paragraph (a)(2) of this section.*

*Del. Code Ann, titl 8, § 211 (2006).

CASE LAW: *Judicial Dissolution of a Corporation*

Herbert v. Porter[18]
Bryant, J.

Defendant-Appellant, Janice Porter, appeals a Seneca County Common Pleas Court judgment, granting Plaintiff-Appellee's, Sue Herbert, motion for judicial dissolution of Professional Restaffing of Ohio ("PRO"). Porter contends that the trial court's judgment ordering judicial dissolution was contrary to law. Finding the dissolution of PRO was permissible under R.C. 1701.91(A)(4), we affirm the judgment of the trial court.

Porter and Herbert, along with Sue Herbert's husband, Larry Herbert (hereinafter jointly referred to as "Herberts"), were the co-owners of PRO, an Ohio corporation located in Tiffin, Ohio. PRO was incorporated in 1988 and served as a temporary staffing agency. The Herberts each held twenty-five percent of PRO's shares, while Porter owned the remaining fifty percent of the shares. From 1988 until 2003, PRO profited; however, the working relationship between the Herberts and Porter was strained. The Herberts dissatisfaction ultimately culminated when Porter drew two twenty thousand dollar checks from PRO's line of credit for herself and her husband.

In November of 2002, the Herberts filed their initial complaint against Porter, alleging conversion of funds, breach of fiduciary duties, breach of contract and quantum meruit. The Herberts also sought an injunction preventing Porter from drawing any additional PRO funds. In May of 2003, the Herberts amended their complaint to include judicial dissolution of PRO, pursuant to R.C. 1701.91.

On August 1, 2003, the Herberts notified Porter of a shareholder's meeting to be held on August 18, 2003, to elect directors. At the August 18, 2003 meeting, the Herberts attended with their attorneys and Porter attended with her attorney by phone. No objections to service of notice for the meeting were raised. During the meeting, both Porter and Sue Herbert were elected as directors. However, the third director seat remained vacant, because the Herberts voted for Larry Herbert and Porter voted for her husband.

On September 2, 2003, the dissolution hearing was held. Both Porter and Herbert testified to the event that took place during the August 18, 2003 meeting. Based on the evidence presented, the court granted the order for PRO's dissolution pursuant to R.C. 1701.91(A)(4). It is from this judgment Porter appeals, presenting the following sole assignment of error for our review.

The trial court erred as a matter of law by ordering a judicial dissolution of the corporation, Professional Restaffing of Ohio, Inc., ("Pro") under R.C. 1701.91(A)(4).

In her sole assignment of error, Porter asserts that the trial court erred as a matter of law in ordering that PRO be dissolved under R.C. 1701.91(A)(4). Specifically, Porter argues that the court erred in ordering PRO's dissolution, because she was never served with proper notice of the August 18, 2003 shareholder's meeting, the court did not make a finding that PRO was deadlocked before granting the dissolution, the court did not explore other available remedies prior to granting the dissolution and a unilateral increase in compensation was not cause for deadlock.

Upon a review of the record, we find that the Porter's arguments are without merit and that court properly granted dissolution pursuant to R.C. 1701.91(A)(4).

R.C. 1701.91 provides for judicial dissolution, stating in pertinent part:

(A) A corporation may be dissolved judicially and its affairs wound up:

(4) By order of the court of common pleas of the county in this state in which the corporation has its principal office, in an action brought by one-half of the directors when there is an even number of directors or by the holders of shares entitling them to exercise one-half of the voting power, when it is established that the corporation has an even number of directors who are deadlocked in the management of the corporate affairs and the shareholders are unable to break the deadlock, or when it is established that the corporation has an

uneven number of directors and that the shareholders are deadlocked in voting power and unable to agree upon or vote for the election of directors as successors to directors whose terms normally would expire upon the election of their successors. Under these circumstances, dissolution of the corporation shall not be denied on the grounds that the business of the corporation has been or could be conducted at a profit.

In her first argument, Porter argues that the she did not receive proper service of notice for the August 18, 2003 meeting. However, Porter failed to raise an objection at the hearing before the trial court. Furthermore, she attended the August 18, 2003 meeting and fully participated without objection. Accordingly, Porter has waived her right to raise this issue on appeal.

Next, Porter argues that the trial court failed to make the proper statutory findings, in that the court failed to establish that PRO was deadlocked prior to ordering dissolution. Here, the trial court, in its journal entry found that the parties were "moving and acting in a deadlocked manner." While Porter argues there has been no finding that PRO was deadlocked, we do not find the court's language to be defective. Furthermore, upon a review of the entire record we find that there is sufficient evidence to support a finding of deadlock under R.C. 1701.91(A)(4). Here, PRO had an uneven number of directors and as of the August 18, 2003 meeting, the shareholders were deadlocked in their voting power. While the shareholders were able to agree on two directors, they were deadlocked as to the third director. Janice Porter had nominated her husband, while Sue Herbert nominated Larry Herbert. Porter, with her fifty percent of the shares, voted for her husband, and Sue Herbert and Larry Herbert, who each held twenty-five percent of the shares, voted for Larry Herbert. Accordingly, the PRO shareholders were clearly "deadlocked in voting power and unable to agree upon or vote for the election of directors." R.C. 1701.91(A)(4). Finding PRO's situation to be exactly the type of situation R.C. 1701.91(A)(4) provides for, the trial court's determination granting dissolution was clearly proper.

(continued)

CASE LAW: *Judicial Dissolution of a Corporation* (continued)

Finally, Porter argues that the trial court failed to explore other remedies and that a unilateral increase in compensation is not cause for the court to find deadlock. There is no statutory requirement that the trial court explore alternative remedies. Additionally, based on the foregoing, we find there is clear statutory authority to support the court's judgment, ordering PRO's dissolution.

Finding the court had clear authority under R.C. 1701.91(A)(4) to grant the order for PRO's dissolution, Porter's assignment of error is overruled.

Having found no error prejudicial to the appellant herein, in the particulars assigned and argued, we affirm the judgment of the trial court.

Judgment affirmed.

CASE QUESTIONS

1. What are the allegations that the Herberts brought against Porter?
2. What error does Porter claim the trial court committed?
3. When, and under what circumstances, can a corporation be judicially dissolved?
4. How does the court handle Porter's claim that she was not given sufficient notice of the corporate meeting?
5. What is the appellate court's ruling concerning whether the trial court was correct in dissolving the corporation?

▶ DIRECTORS

The shareholders elect the directors, usually at the annual corporate meeting.[19] Once elected, the directors are the only group to speak on behalf of the corporation or to make statements about corporate policy or liability.[20] The directors manage the business of the corporation.[21] Directors are responsible for administrative issues arising in the corporate business. They also control the business and delegate duties to officers to put policy into practice.[22] The corporation always owns its own assets, but the control and management of those assets is vested in the officers and directors. See Exhibit 9–6.

Exhibit 9–6. Election of directors by shareholders

> If the articles of incorporation authorize dividing the shares into classes, the articles may also authorize the election of all or a specified number of directors by the holders of one (1) or more authorized classes of shares. Each class (or classes) of shares entitled to elect one (1) or more directors is a separate voting group for purposes of the election of directors.*

*Ind. Code §23-1-33-4 (2006).

DUTIES

Corporations do not owe any fiduciary duties to their shareholders, but directors do. We have discussed fiduciary duties in other contexts already. As we saw in earlier chapters, a fiduciary is someone who has ethical, moral, and financial duties to act in the best interests of another. The directors owe fiduciary duties to the corporation and, by extension, the shareholders.[23]

Individual corporate directors are not the corporation's agents. They are not authorized, for example, to negotiate contracts on behalf of the corporation, without the knowledge of the other directors, officers, and shareholders. Directors owe fiduciary duties to the corporation.[24] See Exhibit 9–7 and 9–8.

Exhibit 9–7. Statute authorizing corporate directors

> (a) The business and affairs of every corporation organized under this chapter shall be managed by or under the direction of a board of directors, except as may be otherwise provided in this chapter or in its certificate of incorporation. If any such provision is made in the certificate of incorporation, the powers and duties conferred or imposed upon the board of directors by this chapter shall be exercised or performed to such extent and by such person or persons as shall be provided in the certificate of incorporation.
>
> (b) The board of directors of a corporation shall consist of 1 or more members, each of whom shall be a natural person. The number of directors shall be fixed by, or in the manner provided in, the bylaws, unless the certificate of incorporation fixes the number of directors, in which case a change in the number of directors shall be made only by amendment of the certificate. Directors need not be stockholders unless so required by the certificate of incorporation or the bylaws. The certificate of incorporation or bylaws may prescribe other qualifications for directors. Each director shall hold office until such director's successor is elected and qualified or until such director's earlier resignation or removal.*

*Del. Code Ann. titl 8, §141 (2006)

Exhibit 9–8. Duties directors owe their corporations

> ❏ duty of care
> ❏ duty of loyalty
> ❏ duty to exercise independent judgment*
> ❏ duty to avoid conflicts of interest

*Cede & Co. v. Technicolor, Inc., 634 A.2d 345 (Del. 1995).

Conflicts of Interest

In some instances, directors are referred to as corporate trustees and in others, as corporate agents. The truth is that they are neither. The obligation imposed on corporate directors is similar to an agency or trust relationship, but is actually independent of both. It makes more sense to refer to directors as fiduciaries of the corporation.[25]

Whether or not a director has breached a fiduciary duty is something that must be decided on a case-by-case basis.[26] The fiduciary duty imposed on directors is straightforward: they owe the corporation an undivided loyalty that prohibits them from self-dealing and conflicts of interest.[27] Directors have a duty to refrain from doing anything in their capacity as director of a corporation that would injure corporate interests, deprive the corporation of profit, or take personal advantage of corporate information.[28] They are not permitted to use their position to further their own selfish interests. Consider Scenario 9–4.

Scenario 9–4. The Director's Land

Darrel Director has been on the board of directors of GHI, Inc., for ten years. At a recent board meeting, he learned that the corporation must buy a specific tract of land near the airport to build a new facility. Without this purchase, the corporation will not be able to expand its operations. Shortly after the meeting, Darrel contacted the landowner and purchased the property for $20,000. He then contacted the board and offered the land for $200,000. Is this a violation of Darrel's fiduciary duties to GHI, Inc.?

Answer: Yes. Darrel has clearly engaged in a conflict of interest. He has also used information gleaned from a corporate meeting to personally enrich himself. The shareholders would be justified in bringing action against Darrel for breach of his ethical duties.

Generally, the decision of the board of directors is presumed to be for the corporation's benefit unless proven otherwise.[29] We will discuss the ramifications of this presumption, such as the "business judgment rule," in the next chapter.

Scenario 9–5. The Director's Gift

Darrel Director wants to make amends for his previous breach of ethical rules and hopes that the shareholders won't vote to remove him. He knows that the corporation is considering a joint venture with Venture, LLP. He approaches the general partner who handles business for the limited partnership and offers him some of the expensive office furniture to modernize the partner's office. When the partner asks if Darrel has authority to give away corporate property, Darrel responds, "Of course, I'm a director." Is he right?

Answer: No. Directors do not have the right to give away corporate property, unless on approval of the entire board.[30]

LIMITATIONS ON DIRECTORS

The articles of incorporation can place additional limits on who can qualify as a director.[31] For instance, the corporation might impose a limitation that only someone who owns shares in the corporation can qualify as a director. The bylaws that authorize the position of director may also set the conditions for removing one. For instance, a director may be removed by vote of the shareholders. Other provisions might automatically disqualify a director from seeking another term when certain preconditions are not met, such as failure to hold a specific number of shares in the company, or when the director has been charged with a crime. Consider 9–6.

Shareholder Control of Directors

We have already seen that shareholders elect the directors, so it should not be any surprise to learn that they also have the power to remove them. They have the right to remove a director for "good cause," such as a proven allegation of fraud or embezzlement.[32] If the articles of incorporation contain the provision, they can even remove a director for "any cause."

> ### Scenario 9–6. "Pleading the Fifth"
>
> Darrel Director has been subpoenaed to appear before the local grand jury. When he takes the stand, he is questioned about his financial actions purportedly on behalf of GHI, Inc. Darrel invokes his rights under the U.S. Constitution to refuse to answer any questions that might incriminate him. He answers each and every question by "pleading the fifth." Later, when the shareholders learn of his actions, they vote to remove him from the board. Is this action legal?
>
> **Answer:** Yes, depending on the wording of the articles of incorporation and corporate bylaws, the shareholders are permitted to remove directors under this situation. After all, the amendment was designed to protect people from criminal investigations, not to help them keep their position on a corporate board of directors.[33]

▶ OFFICERS

The final category of individuals associated with corporations is the **officer**. The officers are the persons who are empowered to carry out specific activities for the corporation. The corporate president, for example, is empowered to sign agreements and contracts on behalf of the corporation, while the corporate secretary maintains records and keeps the corporate seal. The board of directors selects the individuals who will act as the corporate officers. Officers derive their power from corporate mandates, not from simply holding a specific title. An officer who acts without approval, or without the directors' knowledge and acquiescence, has exceeded his or her power and can be held personally liable for the resulting monetary damage to the corporation.[34] Officers are not protected by unlimited liability.

Most corporations have the following classifications of officers:

- president
- vice president
- treasurer
- secretary

officer An individual hired or selected by a board of directors who has specific authority, such as the ability to bind the corporation to contracts and other agreements.

PRESIDENT

In many ways, the president is the human face of the corporation. The corporate president is the person empowered to act as the agent for the corporation.[35] The president is not the alter ego of the corporation. The corporation and the president are separate and distinct entities, and the practical result of this relationship is that there are times when a president can take an action that is not authorized and can be disavowed by the corporation (through the board of directors or the shareholders). The president of a corporation does not occupy a position that is analogous to the President of the United States. The President has sweeping powers, such as the ability to veto legislation and to act as Commander in Chief. A corporate president, on the other hand, has the power to sign contracts and enter into negotiations on behalf of the corporation. In fact, a corporate president has no greater power than any of the directors. Most corporate presidents act as chief executive officer, giving them the power to decide whom to hire and fire, how to manage the business, and the power to oversee other employees. But the president clearly lacks any authority not granted to him or her in the articles of incorporation or by statute.

VICE PRESIDENT

Corporate vice presidents have very little to do with the day-to-day function of a corporation. Usually, they are authorized to take action only in specific situations, such as when the corporate president is unavailable. However, in large corporations, the president may delegate power to any of a number of vice presidents, who are then responsible for specific facets of the corporation. One vice president might preside over advertising and marketing, while another oversees employment and labor issues. However, all of these positions owe their activities to powers delegated to them by the corporate president.[36]

TREASURER

The treasurer is the person responsible for maintaining records of the corporation's finances. The treasurer "keeps the books." Essentially, the treasurer's role is clerical; he or she is responsible for ensuring that all corporate checking accounts, revenues, and accounts receivable are accurate and up-to-date.

SECRETARY

The corporate secretary is responsible for maintaining nonmonetary records for the corporation. The secretary keeps the corporate seal, if there is one. The secretary keeps records of all shareholder and directors' meetings and also ensures that proper documentation is filed with the state secretary of state's office.

DIFFERENCE BETWEEN OFFICER AND AGENT

"Agent" is a broad term encompassing any individual who works, even temporarily, for another's interest. A corporate officer, on the other hand, is narrowly defined as an individual who functions for a specific corporation. When in doubt about a particular person's status, consider the person's relationship with the business, not the specific actions carried out. Agency relationships are created through contractual relationships and often have a specific agenda. Officers, who are employees of the corporation, have general duties.

"INSIDER TRADING"

Insider trading is a term that is often used to describe unethical—or illegal—activity by a corporate officer. However, not all insider trading is illegal. Corporate officers frequently buy and sell their own company's stock. When they do, they must report these transactions to the Securities and Exchange Commission. Some forms of insider trading are illegal, however. Because officers are privy to confidential information about a corporation's activities, such as proposed sales, mergers, and other actions, this information has the potential to earn a corporate officer a great deal of money. When a corporate officer uses secret information to personally enrich themself or others, this is illegal insider trading and constitutes a violation of the Securities and Exchange Act. Violators may be subject to civil and criminal sanctions. Consider Scenario 9–7.

> **insider trading** Buying or selling stocks in breach of fiduciary duty while in possession of nonpublic, nondisclosed information about a company.

> ### Scenario 9–7. Insider Training
>
> Marva Sturgeon owns 1,000 shares in I.M. Clone, Inc. IMC has developed a wonder drug that is supposed to help people suffering from high blood pressure. Unfortunately, the Food and Drug Administration has decided not to approve the drug for use. This is going to have a dramatic effect on IMC's stock. Sam Wannabe, who is a vice president for IMC, calls his friend Marva and tells her about the FDA denial. He encourages her to sell her shares before the public becomes aware of the denial. Sam also sells his stock. The following day, when news of the FDA action reaches the public, the price of the stock plummets, leaving those individuals who purchased the stock at its much higher price facing a substantial monetary loss. Is this a case of insider trading?
>
> **Answer:** Yes. Sam can certainly be cited for insider trading because he used his position as a corporate officer to personally enrich himself and to assist a friend to earn a substantial profit on the stocks. Marva, who is not a corporate officer, may be charged as an accessory to the crime of insider trading.

Case Law: *Shareholder Derivative Suit*

Fisher v. State Mut. Ins. Co.[37]
Barkett, Circuit Judge.

Marvin L. Fisher, Randy J. Cosby, Tom A. Carden, and Philip M. Cavender (for convenience, "Fisher") brought a shareholder derivative suit against State Mutual Insurance Company ("State Mutual"), North American Financial Services, Inc. ("North American"), State Mutual Directors Delos H. Yancey, Jr. and Delos H. Yancey III ("the Yanceys"), a shareholder of North American named Rodney Hale, and the corporate secretary of State Mutual, Ann Rogers (collectively, "Defendants"), alleging that Defendants engaged in improper self-dealing. Specifically, Fisher alleged that, during their tenure with State Mutual, the Yanceys, along with Hale and Rogers, formed a separate shell company to which they sold one of State Mutual's principal assets at an unreasonably low price, generating a substantial loss for State Mutual and correlative profit for the shell company and the other defendants. The trial court granted summary judgment in favor of the Defendants on the basis of Georgia's "safe harbor" law, O.G.C.A. § 14-2-862, which insulates certain self-interested transactions from judicial scrutiny. Fisher now appeals, and we affirm.

BACKGROUND

Delos H. Yancey, Jr. and Delos H. Yancey III were, at times material to this case, directors of State Mutual. Ann Rogers was State Mutual's corporate secretary. In 1993, while working for State Mutual, they formed North American together with Rodney Hale, who was neither an officer nor a director of State Mutual. The Yanceys and Hale served on North American's board of directors and Rogers served as its corporate secretary (thus, the Yanceys were simultaneously directors of both State Mutual and North American).

Prior to the formation of North American, State Mutual bought a company called Atlas Life Insurance Company ("Atlas") for $13.9 million. Approximately one year after the formation of North American, State Mutual decided to sell Atlas. Several months into the process, North American expressed an interest in purchasing Atlas, which it ultimately did for approximately $8.7 million. State Mutual sustained a loss of $5.2 million on the sale. Two years later, North American re-sold Atlas for approximately $31.5 million, making a profit of approximately $22.6 million.

Fisher brought this derivative suit to recover North American's $22.6 million profit, alleging that State Mutual's sale of Atlas to North American was void as an interested transaction. The Defendants responded that the Yanceys had recused themselves from State Mutual's decision to sell Atlas to North

American, and, in so doing, had complied with the relevant provisions of Georgia's safe harbor law such that the transaction was valid and immune to judicial review.

In granting summary judgment for the Defendants, the district court found the following facts to be undisputed: In 1995, State Mutual decided to sell a subsidiary called Home Federal, which was expected to generate a significant tax liability. In order to offset this liability, State Mutual considered the possibility of selling Atlas, which was expected to generate a tax loss. Several months into the process, North American formed an interest in purchasing Atlas. Prior to North American's engaging in any negotiations with State Mutual, however, the Yanceys disclosed to State Mutual's Board of Directors their affiliation with North American and their resulting conflict of interest. Thereafter, the Yanceys abstained from any proceedings or negotiations regarding the proposed Atlas transaction.

Following the Yanceys' notice, State Mutual's Board of Directors formed a Special Committee consisting of three disinterested directors to review, evaluate, and negotiate the Atlas transaction. The Board authorized the Special Committee "to retain such advisors as it deems necessary to assist it in determining the value of Atlas, the fairness of the proposed transaction, and compliance with all legal requirements applicable to the proposed transaction." Accordingly, the Committee retained Larry Warnock, an actuarial consultant, Peter Mattingly, an investment banker, and James L. Smith III, an attorney, to assist with the valuation of Atlas, and to provide financial and legal advice regarding the potential transaction. Based upon the report of the retained experts, the Special Committee negotiated a sale of Atlas to North American for $8.7 million, which the full State Mutual Board approved. The Yanceys recused themselves from the Board's discussions and vote. In accordance with Georgia law, State Mutual then sought and received approval of the Atlas sale from the Georgia Insurance Commissioner.

Based on these facts, the district court held that the Yanceys had complied with the requirements of the Georgia safe harbor law. Therefore, the court held that the transaction was insulated from judicial review and granted summary judgment in favor of the Defendants. We review the district court's grant of summary judgment de novo, viewing the record and drawing all inferences in favor of the non-moving party. See Arrington v. Cobb County, 139 F.3d 865, 871 (11th Cir. 1998).

DISCUSSION

Fisher first contends that the district court erred in finding that the Yanceys complied with the requirements of the safe harbor, O.C.G.A § 14-2-862, and therefore, that the Atlas transaction was immune to judicial review. Second, Fisher argues that the plain language of O.C.G.A § 14-2-861(b) only shields from judicial scrutiny transactions that are challenged "on the ground of an interest in the transaction of the director," whereas his complaint challenges the Atlas transaction on grounds other than "an interest in the transaction of the director," specifically, corporate waste, fraud, usurpation of corporate opportunity, and breach of fiduciary duty. We first consider the language of O.C.G.A § 14-2-861(b) and O.C.G.A § 14-2-862, which together constitute the safe harbor.

O.C.G.A § 14-2-861(b), provides in relevant part:

(b) A director's conflicting interest transaction may not be enjoined, set aside, or give rise to an award of damages or other sanctions, in an action by a shareholder or by or in the right of the corporation, on the ground of an interest in the transaction of the director or any person with whom or which he has a personal, economic, or other association, if:

(1) Directors' action respecting the transaction was at any time taken in compliance with Code Section 14-2-862...

(3) The transaction, judged in the circumstances at the time of commitment, is established to have been fair to the corporation. O.G.C.A. § 14-2-862, in turn, provides:

(a) Directors' action respecting a transaction is effective for purposes of paragraph (1) of subsection (b) of Code Section 14-2-861 if the

(continued)

CASE LAW: *Shareholder Derivative Suit* (continued)

transaction received the affirmative vote of a majority (but not less than two) of those qualified directors on the board of directors or on a duly empowered committee thereof who voted on the transaction after either required disclosure to them (to the extent the information was not known by them) or compliance with subsection (b) of this Code section.

(b) If a director has a conflicting interest respecting a transaction, but neither he nor a related person of the director specified in subparagraph (a) of paragraph (3) of Code Section 14-2-860 is a party thereto, and if the director has a duty under law or a professional cannon, or a duty of confidentiality to another person, respecting information relating to the transaction such that the director cannot, consistent with that duty, make the disclosure contemplated by Subparagraph (B) of paragraph (4) of Code Section 14-2-860 [required disclosure], then disclosure is sufficient for purposes of subsection (a) of this Code section if the director:

(1) Discloses to the directors voting on the transaction the existence and nature of his conflicting interest and informs them of the character of and limitations imposed by that duty prior to their vote on the transactions; and

(2) Plays no part, directly or indirectly in their deliberations or vote.

Under these provisions, the Yanceys were required either (a) to disclose to State Mutual any and all knowledge that they may have had regarding the Atlas transaction as a result of their affiliation with North American, or, (b) if they had a conflicting fiduciary duty to North American, to advise State Mutual's disinterested directors of the existence and nature of their conflicting interest (and the character of, and limitations imposed upon them by, that conflicting interest), and then to refrain from playing any part, directly or indi-

rectly, in State Mutual's deliberations and vote on the Atlas sale.

The district court accepted the Defendants' contentions that § 14-2-862(a) was inapplicable because they had a fiduciary duty to North American, and, therefore, that they had to comply with the safe harbor by giving notice to State Mutual of their conflicting interest and abstaining from participating in the Atlas transaction, on behalf of State Mutual, thereafter. The court then held that Defendants had complied with O.G.C.A. § 14-2-862(b)(1) and (2) by advising the disinterested directors of State Mutual that they were directors of North American and recusing themselves from direct or indirect participation in State Mutual's decision to sell Atlas to North American. Fisher contends that the Yanceys should have complied with § 14-2-862(a) because they did not actually have a fiduciary duty to North American that prevented them from making any disclosures required by O.G.C.A. § 14-2-862(a); they merely had a "fabricated" fiduciary duty which they themselves created (by forming North American) for the sole purpose of "getting around" the disclosure requirement. Alternatively, Fisher argues, even assuming the Yanceys did have a genuine fiduciary duty to North American, the district court erred in finding that the Yanceys abstained from direct or indirect participation in the proceedings because, Fisher claims, the Yanceys "orchestrated" the entire Atlas sale from behind the scenes.

With respect to his first claim, Fisher argues that the Yanceys were under no "real" duty to North American because North American (1) "had no confidential information or competitive secrets"; (2) "conducted no business prior to its acquisition of Atlas Life"; and (3) was a "mere shell corporation." We find that none of these characteristics demonstrates that the Yanceys did not owe a fiduciary duty to North American. Georgia law clearly establishes, without exception, that as directors of North American, the Yanceys owed duties of confidentiality and loyalty to that company irrespective of its specific characteristics or history. It is settled law that corporate officers and directors occupy a fiduciary relationship to the corporation and its shareholders, and are held to the standard of utmost good faith and loyalty. Accordingly, the commentary to the alternative disclosure provision of § 14-2-862(b) specifically recognizes that "[t]he most frequent use of subsection (b) . . . will undoubtedly be in connection with common directors who find themselves in a position of dual fiduciary obligations that clash." Fisher has not pointed to anything in Georgia law that establishes an exception to the normal fiduciary rule for "shell corporations" or corporations that have not transacted business prior to the occasion in question. Instead, the safe harbor unambiguously provides that if a director has a fiduciary duty to another corporation, he or she may comply with that provision through the notice-plus-non-participation procedures of O.C.G.A. § 14-2-862(b). In any event, the Yanceys testified in their depositions that they do not recall any facts concerning Atlas that they could have disclosed to State Mutual, but did not, and Fisher has not produced any evidence to the contrary.

In sum, because Georgia law clearly establishes that the Yanceys, as directors of a bona fide corporation (i.e., North American), were subject to a fiduciary duty that conflicted with their duty to State Mutual, the district court did not err in holding that Defendants were obligated to comply with the safe harbor by giving notice of their conflicting interest and abstaining thereafter from all participation on behalf of State Mutual in the Atlas transaction.

Because it is undisputed that the Yanceys notified State Mutual of their conflict of interest, we turn to Fisher's argument that the Yanceys failed to comply with § 14-2-862(b)(1) and (2) because they did not in fact abstain from all participation in the Atlas transaction, but rather "orchestrated" it behind the scenes. We must reject this contention because there is insufficient record evidence to support it. Fisher asserts that the evidence of direct involvement can first be found in Yancey, Jr.'s participation in choosing the members of the Special Committee. Although Yancey, Jr. did chair the May 8, 1995 meeting at which

three disinterested directors were selected to constitute the Special Committee, and may have cast a vote selecting them, there is no indication that he exerted any improper or special influence over this selection. Regardless, Georgia does not require that a corporate special committee be selected wholly by disinterested directors.

Finally, Fisher contends that the Yancey, Jr. and Hale "hand picked" the independent advisers retained by the Special Committee to evaluate the proposed transaction. First, we note that Hale was not an officer or director of State Mutual, and thus, did not have any obligation to State Mutual. Second, we find no error in the district court's determination that the evidence is insufficient to support Fisher's contention.

In sum, while Yancey, Jr. and Hale's involvement in hiring the experts ultimately retained by the Special Committee is somewhat troubling, Fisher has simply not produced sufficient evidence to show that the Yanceys were directly or indirectly involved in the Atlas transaction such that the transaction should be deprived of its statutory immunity. Even viewing the facts in the light most favorable to Fisher, therefore, we cannot conclude that he adduced sufficient evidence to overcome summary judgment on this basis.

Finally, Fisher argues alternatively that even if the Defendants complied with the requirements of the safe harbor law, his complaint is not barred because, in addition to challenging the Atlas transaction on the basis of the Yanceys' self-interest, the complaint alleges corporate waste, fraud, breach of fiduciary duty, and usurpation of corporate opportunity, and such claims are not barred by the safe harbor. However, these allegations are not independent of Fisher's essential claim of self-dealing, but are totally interrelated. The complaint does mention fraud, waste, mismanagement, and usurpation of corporate opportunity. However, it does so only in the context of detailing the nature of Defendants' alleged self-dealing, which is the essence of Fisher's claims for relief. In this regard, we note that Fisher has sued only State Mutual itself, North American, the Yanceys, Rogers, and Hale, and not the disinterested members

(continued)

CASE LAW: *Shareholder Derivative Suit* (continued)

of State Mutual's Board of Directors who actually voted on the Atlas sale. Simply put, the Yanceys did not vote on the sale of Atlas, Hale and Rogers were not members of the State Mutual Board, and North American, obviously, is a separate company.

With regard to Fisher's claim that the complaint alleged "usurpation of a corporate opportunity," we note that the facts of this case preclude such an allegation. Under Georgia law, the paradigmatic "usurpation of a corporate opportunity" claim arises when a corporate director or officer is presented with a business opportunity that could benefit the corporation, but the director conceals the opportunity from the corporation in order to avail himself of it personally. It is undisputed that State Mutual's Board knew of the Atlas sale and had a full opportunity to evaluate the proposed transaction. In such circumstances, a "usurpation" claim is simply not available. In this regard, we note that Fisher's complaint does not make any reference to O.C.G.A. § 14-2-831(a)(1)(C), which authorizes shareholders to bring a derivative action against directors to seek relief for "[t]he appropriation, in violation of his duties, of any business opportunity of the corporation," and which has been recognized by the Georgia courts as the only basis for a "usurpation" claim.

The simple fact is, regardless of how Fisher now seeks to characterize his cause of action, the entire complaint in this case is premised on the allegation that the Atlas sale was tainted by the Yanceys' dual roles as directors of both State Mutual and North American. In substance, therefore, the complaint seeks damages on a theory of self-dealing and therefore falls within the purview of the safe harbor law. The district court correctly determined that Fisher's lawsuit is barred.

CONCLUSION

For the foregoing reasons, the district court's grant of summary judgment in favor of the Defendants is
AFFIRMED.

CASE QUESTIONS

1. What allegations did the shareholders raise against the corporate directors and secretary?

2. What amount of money were the shareholders seeking to recover, and what was the basis of their claim?

3. How does a director's recusal trigger the "safe harbor" rule?

4. What fiduciary duties did the directors have to the various corporations involved in this case?

5. Did the directors protect themselves under state law by giving appropriate notice of their conflict of interest between the corporations? Why or why not?

SUMMARY

There are three different classes of members in a corporation: shareholders, officers, and directors. Shareholders often organize themselves into voting groups or trusts in order to maximize the effect of their individual votes. Although shareholders can vote on management issues, they have no say in the day-to-day operation of the business. That duty falls to corporate officers. The officers carry out the business of the corporation. They are responsible for paying bills, ensuring that the product is manufactured, and double-checking to make sure that payments have been received. They are also responsible for marketing and advertising the business. Corporate officers work under the direction of the board of directors. The board of directors consists of individuals who are responsible for the management of the business. Directors hire and fire employees, including corporate officers. Directors have a fiduciary responsibility to shareholders, and that responsibility is reflected in the various duties imposed upon them. Corporate directors must always act in the best interests of the shareholders and avoid conflicts of interest and other ethical dilemmas that might put their own personal interests ahead of those of shareholders.

HELPFUL WEB SITES

Securities and Exchange Commission—Insider trading
http://www.sec.gov/answers/insider.htm

Legal Information Institute—Corporate Law
http://www.law.cornell.edu/topics/corporations.html

Oregon Secretary of State
http://www.sos.state.or.us/

Louisiana Secretary of State
http://www.sos.louisiana.gov/

New Hampshire Secretary of State
http://www.sos.nh.gov/index.html

KEY TERMS

fiduciary	share
insider trading	shareholder
officer	stock certificates
proxy	voting trust

APPLYING CHAPTER CONCEPTS

Based on the explanation of fiduciary duties that corporate directors owe their shareholders, as explained in this chapter, prepare a handout listing the do's and don'ts of ethical behavior that could be given to newly created boards of directors.

REVIEW QUESTIONS

1. What is the definition of a corporate shareholder?
2. What voting rights does share ownership confer?
3. What is voting by proxy?
4. What is cumulative voting?
5. What is a shareholder agreement?
6. What is the purpose of a shareholders meeting?
7. What are some of the limitations placed on shareholders when they wish to transfer ownership in their shares?
8. What rights do shareholders normally enjoy?
9. How does corporate law define the role of directors?
10. What are the duties of corporate directors?
11. Do corporate directors face personal liability? Explain your answer.
12. Are corporate directors fiduciaries for the corporation? Explain.
13. What are corporate officers?
14. Give some examples of the titles held by various corporate officers.
15. What are the duties of corporate officers?
16. Are corporate officers protected by limited liability?
17. What is "insider trading"?

QUESTION FOR REFLECTION

Should the rules about who can hold shares be more relaxed or more stringent? Justify your answer.

ENDNOTES

[1]*Jernigan v. State*, 589 S.W.2d 681 (Tex. Crim. App. 1979).

[2]*Appeal of Two Crow Ranch, Inc.*, 159 Mont. 16, 494 P.2d 915 (1972).

[3]*Valley Intern. Properties, Inc. v. Los Campeones, Inc.*, 568 S.W.2d 680 (Tex. Civ. App. Corpus Christi 1978).

[4]*Pink v. A. A. A. Highway Express*, 191 Ga. 502, 13 S.E.2d 337.

[5]*Noble v. Farmers Union Trading Co.*, 123 Mont. 518, 216 P.2d 925 (1950).

[6]*DuVall v. Moore*, 276 F.Supp. 674 (D.C. Iowa 1967).

[7]*Bishop v. Middle States Utilities Co.*, 225 Iowa 941, 282 N.W. 305.

[8]Am. Jur Corporations § 610.

[9]*Wuller v. Chuse Grocery Co.*, 241 Ill. 398, 89 N.E. 796 (1909).

[10]Am. Jur. Corporations § 788.

[11]*Meyers v. Lux*, 76 S.D. 182, 75 N.W.2d 533 (1956).

[12]*De Loach v. Bennett*, 156 Ga. 633, 119 S.E. 592 (1923).

[13]*Zinger v. Gattis*, 382 So. 2d 379 (Fla. Dist. Ct. App. 5th Dist. 1980).

[14]18 CJS Corporations, § 475.

[15]*Rocha Toussier y Asociados, S.C. v. Rivero*, 184 A.D.2d 397, 585 N.Y.S.2d 384 (1st Dep't 1992).

[16]Am. Jur. Corporations § 622.

[17]*Thompson v. J. D. Thompson Carnation Co.*, 116 N.E. 648, 279 Ill. 54.

[18]2004 WL 765116, 3 (Ohio App. 3 Dist. 2004).

[19]*Duffy v. Loft, Inc.*, 17 Del. Ch. 376, 152 A. 849 (1930).

[20]*Campbell v. Loew's, Inc.*, 36 Del. Ch. 563, 134 A.2d 852 (1957).

[21]*Olson Bros. v. Englehart*, 42 Del. Ch. 348, 211 A.2d 610 (1965), aff'd, 245 A.2d 166 (Del. 1968).

[22]*Cahall v. Lofland*, 12 Del. Ch. 299, 114 A. 224 (1921), aff'd, 13 Del. Ch. 384, 118 A. 1 (1922).

[23]*Harden v. Eastern States Pub. Serv. Co.*, 14 Del. Ch. 156, 122 A. 705 (1923).

[24]*Arnold v. Society for Savs. Bancorp.*, 678 A.2d 533 (Del. 1996).

[25]*Bowen v. Imperial Theatres, Inc.*, 13 Del. Ch. 120, 115 A. 918 (1922).

[26]*Kors v. Carey*, 39 Del. Ch. 47, 158 A.2d 136 (1960).

[27]*Talo-Petro. Corp. of Am. v. Hannigan*, 40 Del. 534, 14 A.2d 401 (1940).

[28]*Guth v. Loft, Inc.*, 23 Del. Ch. 255, 5 A.2d 503 (1939), aff'd, 25 Del. Ch. 363, 19 A.2d 721 (1941).

[29]*Karasik v. Pacific E. Corp.*, 21 Del. Ch. 81, 180 A. 604 (1935).

[30]*Taussig v. Wellington Fund, Inc.*, 187 F. Supp. 179 (D. Del. 1960), aff'd, 313 F.2d 472 (3d Cir.), cert. denied, 374 U.S. 806, 83 S. Ct. 1693, 10 L. Ed. 2d 1031 (1963).

[31]*Stroud v. Milliken Enters., Inc.*, 585 A.2d 1306 (Del. Ch. 1988), appeal dismissed, 552 A.2d 476 (Del. 1989).

[32]*Campbell v. Loew's, Inc.*, 36 Del. Ch. 563, 134 A.2d 852 (1957).

[33]*Hollinger Int'l, Inc. v. Black,* 844 A.2d 1022 (Del. Ch. 2004).

[34]*Anderson-Tully Co. v. Gillett Lumber Co.,* 244 S.W. 26, 155 Ark. 224.

[35]*Joseph Greenspon's Sons Iron & Steel Co. v. Pecos Valley Gas Co.,* 34 Del. 567, 156 A. 350 (1931).

[36]*DeKalb Realty Co. v. McColgan,* 147 Ga.App. 696, 250 S.E.2d 29.

[37]290 F.3d 1256 (C.A.11 Ga. 2002).

Chapter 10

FINANCING THE CORPORATION

Chapter Objectives

Upon completion of this chapter, you should be able to:

- Explain the basics of corporate financing.
- Define the differences between common and preferred stock.
- Describe the function of the various stock exchanges.
- Explain the financial disclosures that publicly traded companies must make.
- Define the role of the Securities and Exchange Commission in publicly traded companies.

▶ INTRODUCTION

In this chapter, we will discuss the role that financing plays in creating and running a corporation. Capital is the lifeblood of businesses, and this is as true for sole proprietorships as it is for huge, multinational corporations. Selling stock is among the methods that companies use to acquire the cash that they need. We will discuss not only how companies sell stock, but also the markets where investors purchase it and the role that the Securities and Exchange Commission plays in monitoring corporations.

▶ FINANCING OF THE CORPORATION

Throughout this chapter, we will address how corporations raise capital for their business activities. Although there are numerous ways that a corporation could raise money, such as through bank loans, the primary method is by selling shares in the corporation. The money that the corporation generates by the sale of shares gives it the capital that it needs to function. The sale is actually a contract between the corporation and the shareholder. The corporation receives money in exchange for the promise to abide by the terms of the particular sale. In many circumstances, this promise could be as simple as sharing profits with the shareholder. However, as we will see throughout this chapter, generating capital has become a very complex business, and corporations have created a wide variety of vehicles to generate additional capital. However, before we address the complexities of the rights and burdens created by corporate financing, we must first address a more fundamental issue: What are shares?

NATURE OF SHARES

share ownership interests in a corporation.

A **share** is the smallest unit that represents corporate ownership. Under this definition, the total value of a corporation is broken down into units, called shares. These units can represent as little as one dollar or as high as any value the corporation wishes to set. Let's suppose that the total value of all corporate assets is $1 million. The corporation wants to issue 10,000 shares. What is the value of an individual share? If we take $1 million and divide by 10,000 we come up with a total value of $100 per share.

Comparing Shares to Stock

Before we begin discussing the various types of stock that a corporation can create, we must first address an issue of terminology: What is the difference between shares and stocks? The simple answer is that "share" is a generic term, while "stock" is a specific term. However, that definition does not clear up the distinction between the two terms. Share is the general term used to describe how the corporation is financed. Stock, on the other hand, represents a stockholder's financial interests and voting rights.[1] There are many different types of stock, some of which can be valued higher or lower than the individual share price. Some stock gives the stockholder the right to receive dividends, while other stock does not. We will discuss the various types of stock available as we proceed through this chapter.

STOCK

stock an ownership interest in a corporation that gives the holder specific rights, also known as equity.

Stock represents ownership interest in a company. Whether or not a corporation can actually issue stock depends on the wording in its articles of incorporation, its bylaws, and the state statutes that govern corporations. Statutes control not only whether or not a corporation can issue stock, but also the type of stock and the identity of the officer or director who is authorized to issue it.[2]

 GETTING TO THE BASICS

The articles of incorporation and corporate bylaws specifically control who can issue stock.

Corporations are free to create different classes of stock. In the absence of any provision specifying differences, all shares of stock are created equal and have the same rights. Most states allow corporations to create two or more classes of stocks that have different voting powers and other restrictions. The two most common classifications are common stock and preferred stock.

Common Stock

Common stock is a classification that entitles the holder to receive dividends when the company declares a profit. The shareowners are entitled to receive dividends based on their percentage of ownership. If the corporation declares profits for a year, it will issue a specific profit per share. For instance, the corporation might declare a dividend of $0.25 per share. A shareholder who owns 50 shares would receive $12.50.

Owners of common stock have the right to receive dividends and can take advantage of the appreciation in stock price by selling stock to others. However, common stock has certain limitations. For instance, if a person owns common stock in a corporation, it means that in the event the corporation is dissolved, the common stockholder will receive only whatever assets are left over after bondholders and preferred stockholders have been paid. Owners of common stock typically receive one vote per share. However, different types of stock can confer different types of voting rights. For instance, some types of stock confer greater than one vote per share. See Exhibit 10–1.

common stock Stock that provides its owner with voting rights and a share of the corporation's profits in the form of dividends or capital appreciation in the value of stock.

Exhibit 10–1. Authorizing different classifications of shares

The VWX Corporation hereby authorizes the issuance of 2,000 shares, to be classified as follows:
❏ 1,000 shares in common stock
❏ 1,000 shares in preferred stock
Neither classification of stock shall have a par value.

preemptive rights The right of common-stock holders to purchase newly issued stock to maintain their overall percentage of ownership in a company.

Common-stock owners also have **preemptive rights.** This means that if the corporation should decide to issue new stock, common-stock holders can purchase the new stock to maintain their proportional ownership in the company. Consider Scenario 10–1.

> **Scenario 10–1. Stockholder's Preemptive Rights**
> CDE Corporation is planning on issuing new shares of common stock. Sally, who owns 1,000 shares of common stock in CDE, is worried that with the issuance of these stocks, the value of her stock will correspondingly decrease. After all, the larger the pool of stock, the less the worth of her individual shares. Sally uses her preemptive rights to purchase enough stock to maintain her overall percentage of ownership.

Common stock is the stock that a company issues in order to raise capital. This stock is sold on stock exchanges around the world. The stock price is based partly on the base value of the stock (called the par value) and the perceived wealth of the company. Holders of common stock are entitled to dividend payments (if the corporation declares a dividend for a particular year). Common-stock owners can exert authority and control over the corporation by electing particular members to the board of directors and by their votes on corporate agenda and policy.

Although common-stock ownership does confer numerous rights, it also has specific limitations. The downside to common-stock ownership is that if the corporation declares bankruptcy, these stockholders will receive compensation only after all creditors and preferred stockholders have received their compensation.

KEY POINT

Common stock is usually a straightforward proposition. Unlike other types of stock that have complex features, such as convertibility to other forms of stock, common stock simply provides the rights to receive dividends and to vote on corporate matters.

Preferred Stock

preferred stock A class of stock that entitles the holder priority if the corporation is liquidated.

Holders of **preferred stock** may or may not receive a fixed dividend, but they do enjoy a priority status when it comes to liquidating the corporation. In that event, holders of preferred stock will be first in line to receive the liquidated assets, based on the amount of shares that they own. However, with this advantage comes a disadvantage: Preferred stockholders do not have voting rights in the corporation. Without voting rights, they cannot vote to remove directors or seek to affect corporate policy.

GETTING TO THE BASICS

Preferred stock usually does not provide voting rights to its owners.

Other Types of Stock

Although common and preferred stock are the two most common types of stock categories, corporations are free to create a dizzying variety of shares with all manner of limitations, rights, and obligations. As long as their articles of incorporation and state statutes permit it, a corporation can create nearly any type of stock category that it wishes. However, no matter how many different classes of shares a corporation creates, there are some basic guidelines. For instance, all of the shares within a particular class must have the same rights. This means that if the corporation creates class-C shares, everyone who holds class-C shares must have the same rights. Although a corporation can establish different classes of shares, there is no distinction made between the rights of small shareholders and large shareholders. Share ownership is what confers these rights, not the quantity of shares.[3] Some classifications refer to specific investment vehicles created to generate income for a corporation, while other stock classifications are designations to explain a stock's features. See Exhibit 10–2 for a sample of the different classifications of stock that exist.

CASE LAW: *Rights of Stockholders Who Possess Different Classes of Stock*

DuVall v. Moore[4]
MEMORANDUM AND ORDER
HANSON, District Judge.

This ruling is predicated upon a motion by the defendants for summary judgment. Jurisdiction of the instant case is grounded upon diversity of citizenship. The complaint was filed by certain minority shareholders in relation to a purported amendment to the Articles of Incorporation of Midwest Limestone Co., Incorporated, hereinafter called Midwest, which sought to give the corporation perpetual existence.

Certain facts are without dispute. Defendant Midwest filed its Articles of Incorporation and was issued its license by the State of Iowa on February 2, 1953. The Articles provided that the life of the Corporation was twenty years which meant it would end on or about February 2, 1973. Pursuant to the Articles, two types of common stock, Class A and Class B, were issued by Midwest. The two types of capital stock were allocated as follows:

The defendants, G. E. Moore and James E. Scherrman, individually and as Trustees of the Midwest Employees' Profit Sharing Trust, were the owners of 690 shares of Class A stock and 2,430

(continued)

CASE LAW: *Rights of Stockholders Who Possess Different Classes of Stock* (continued)

shares of Class B stock. These amounts constituted a majority of both classes of stock. The plaintiffs and the other stockholders own a minority of the stock in interest.

On or about November 28, 1966, the defendants G. E. Moore, as President, and James E. Scherrman, as Secretary, caused a 'Notice of Annual Meeting of Stockholders' to be sent to all the shareholders of Midwest. The Notice contained a proposal that the Articles be amended to provide for the perpetual existence of the Corporation. The annual meeting was held on December 8, 1966, at the home office of Midwest in Gilmore City, Iowa. A written objection to the perpetual duration proposal in the form of a 'Notice of Dissent' was filed with the President and Secretary of Midwest. It was signed by Thomas O. DuVall, Lucille C. DuVall, and Ben C. Birdsall, Plaintiffs, and John A. Cloos. Birdsall and Cloos were personally present at the meeting. Birdsall filed a proxy at the beginning of the meeting which gave him authority to vote all of DuVall's stock, Class A and Class B. The Chairman of the meeting ruled that the Class B stock could not vote. Plaintiffs and John A. Cloos objected to the ruling and stated that it was their position that the Class B stock was entitled to vote on the proposed renewal. The objection was overruled by defendant Moore, the Chairman. Moore then called for a vote on the resolution, announcing that only Class A stock was entitled to vote. Plaintiffs and Cloos again objected and filed a document purporting to show their vote if they had been permitted to vote. The minutes show that the resolution passed by a vote of 690 to 310.

The complaint consists of two Counts. In Count I of the complaint, plaintiffs appear to be asserting a number of theories. In Paragraph 18, plaintiffs allege that the amendment to secure perpetual existence was in bad faith and for the purpose of depriving them of their property rights. In Paragraph 26 of the complaint, it is alleged that the plaintiffs and defendants are unable to agree as to the value of the stock owned by plaintiffs and the obligations of defendants in relation thereto. Plaintiffs claim that the defendants are obligated to purchase all their stock and that of John A. Cloos under Iowa Code Section 491.25. Finally, plaintiffs allege that Section 491.25 is unconstitutional if it is construed to exclude the Class B stock owned by plaintiffs.

Plaintiffs pray, inter alia, for a declaration that defendants are obligated to purchase all of plaintiffs' stock, Class A and Class B, and for the Court to determine the real value thereof. In addition, plaintiffs seek recovery 'for the costs of this action and for such other, further and different relief as to the Court may seem just and equitable in the premises.'

Count II relates to an alleged agreement that both Class A and Class B stock were to vote on the proposed resolution to renew the Corporation.

The major issues which have been framed for the Court's consideration by the Motion for Summary Judgment and the briefs of the parties are: (1) Whether plaintiffs can have any recovery in the cause as pleaded; (2) Whether the Class B stock was entitled to vote upon the resolution to amend the Articles of Midwest to provide for perpetual existence; (3) Whether Iowa Code Section 491.25 is unconstitutional; (4) Whether the complaint is sufficient in its allegations of bad faith on the part of defendants; and (5) Whether Count II, relating to the voting agreement, can withstand the Motion for Summary Judgment.

As to the first issue presented for the Court's determination, the defendants contend that the plaintiffs have sought only a declaration that defendants are obligated to purchase all of the plaintiffs' stock and that they are not entitled to such relief regardless of whether or not the Class B stock was entitled to vote. The argument runs as follows: If the Class B stock was entitled to vote and if the Court were to deem that such stock was voted against the renewal, the resolution would have failed to pass by a vote of 1510 to 690; on the other hand, if the Court were to determine that the Class B stock was entitled to vote and the votes were not cast against the extension, there would similarly be no obligation of defendants to purchase plaintiffs' stock as Section 491.25 applies only to 'stock voted against such renewal.'

The premise from which defendants' argument flows is fallacious. Plaintiffs pray not only for appraisal but also general equitable relief. A prayer for general equitable relief must be liberally construed. Alcorn v. Linke, 257 Iowa 630, 133 N.W.2d 89 (1965). An equity court will grant relief under such a prayer when it is raised by the issues and supported by the evidence apart from other relief requested. Baldwin v. Equitable Life Assurance Society, 252 Iowa 639, 108 N.W.2d 66 (1961); 27 Am.Jur.2d 813.

Deprivation of a stockholder's right to vote takes away an essential attribute of his property.

It would seem that for the sake of clarity and to avoid confusion, the Court should first determine whether or not plaintiffs are entitled to an injunction against the operation of the amendment providing for renewal. Injunction is the only remedy if defendants have transgressed Section 491.25 by their action in disallowing Class B stock votes on the proposal because the acceptance thereof would be void. Thus, there will be no right to appraisal for either the Class A or Class B shares in the present action. If they have violated such a statutory mandate, the Court will, however, be concerned with whether or not appraisal rights will accrue to the Class B shareholders upon another renewal vote. Both plaintiffs and defendants are imbued with the notion that the Court can presume the outcome of such a revote. As already mentioned, if plaintiffs were entitled to vote, the acceptance of the amendment is void and no appraisal rights can accrue thereon. Also, the Court does not have the right to vote the Class B stock of the parties. In any event, defendants' conclusion that the measure would have failed by a vote of 1510 to 690 is unwarranted. Defendants assume that all plaintiffs' Class A and Class B stock would have been cast against the measure and do not include their own Class B shares in the vote. The Court cannot be at liberty to presume how defendants would have voted their Class B stock, but if they had voted against it, the amendment would probably have passed as they were the holders of a majority of both Class A and Class B shares.

If defendants have not unlawfully taken away plaintiffs' voting rights, the Court will turn its attention to whether defendants' motion will be allowed as to the issues of whether the conduct of defendants was in bad faith and whether defendants are bound by an alleged voting agreement.

The plaintiffs contend that extension of corporate life is a fundamental change and cannot be made without the consent of all shareholders. The defendants have no quarrel with the principle as stated. The cardinal rule upon the shareholder's right to vote was established in Berger v. Amana Society, supra, 95 N.W.2d at pp. 913, 914:

We think the true rule is thus expressed in 18 C.J.S. Corporations § 496, page 1174: 'A radical and fundamental change in the objects, purposes, or business of the corporation interferes with the contract rights of each stockholder with the corporation and cannot be made without the consent of all stockholders, except by virtue of some act of legislation which may be read into the contract of incorporation.' Our problem here is to determine whether the amendments attempted in 1955 are within the class permitted by the provisions of the charter or the corporation laws of Iowa.'

The relation between a corporation and its shareholders is contractual. In determining the agreement, the statutes governing corporations, their organization, and all of the provisions of the charter are a part of the contract.

The plaintiffs contend that the Articles of Midwest do not expressly state that Class B stock cannot vote on renewal. The portions of the Articles of Midwest material to the contractual arrangement must be set out. Article V provides that:

(continued)

CASE LAW: *Rights of Stockholders Who Possess Different Classes of Stock* (continued)

'The voting power shall be vested exclusively in the Class A common stock and each share of Class A common stock shall be entitled to one vote in person or by written proxy at all annual or special meetings of the Corporation, or on matters in which the stockholders are entitled to vote. At all meetings of the stockholders of the Corporation or on any matter in which the stockholders are required or permitted to give consent, a majority of the common stock outstanding and entitled to vote as aforesaid shall constitute a quorum . . . unless otherwise herein specifically provided. Except with reference to voting rights, Class A common stock and Class B common stock shall in all respects be of equal rank and priority.'

Article VI provides:

'The stockholders entitled to vote at the annual meeting, or whenever a board of directors is to be lawfully elected, shall determine the number of directors to be elected, within the limits hereinbefore set out. The directors of the Corporation, who need not be stockholders thereof, shall be elected at the annual meeting of the stockholders, as hereinafter provided.'

Article VII declares that:

'Special meetings may be called by the President or the board of directors, or by a majority of the voting stock by written consent and on twenty (20) days' written notice.'

Article IX proclaims that the stockholders holding a 'majority of voting stock of the corporation outstanding and entitled to vote' may make an 'adjudication' in respect to indemnification granted to directors against certain liabilities when directors not incurring liability do not constitute a majority of the board.

Article X determines that:

'The private property of the stockholders of this corporation shall not be liable for corporate debts,

and this Article shall not be amended or changed except by the unanimous consent of all the stockholders of the corporation in writing.'

Article XI makes provision for amendment of the Articles by stating that:

'These Articles of incorporation, except Article X may be amended at any time by a vote of a majority of the voting stock of the corporation outstanding, at any regular meeting of the stockholders or any special meeting called for that purpose.'

Article II reads as follows:

'The corporation shall commence business as soon as a certificate is issued by the Secretary of State of the State of Iowa, and shall continue for a period of twenty (20) years, with power of renewal, unless sooner dissolved by the vote of a majority of the voting stock then outstanding.'

The issue is 'the intent of the parties in making the contract which the plaintiffs hold with the corporation.' It is manifest from the Articles that the intent of the parties was to bestow voting rights only upon the holders of Class A stock except as to Article X relating to personal liability of shareholders.

Article V is unambiguous in vesting voting rights exclusively in Class A stock with one vote per share 'at all annual or special meetings of the corporation, or on matters in which the stockholders are entitled to vote.' Article V then provides that a 'majority of the common stock outstanding and entitled to vote' constitutes a quorum on matters in which the stockholders 'are required or permitted to give consent unless otherwise herein specifically provided.' The plain inference of the latter provision is that because only stockholders entitled to vote can constitute a quorum, only their shares may vote at all unless otherwise provided. Such a provision is typical of articles limiting voting rights. The exception to the exclusive quorum and voting rights provisions for Class A stock is Article X. Also, Class A common stock and Class B common stock are stated to be exactly the same except they are specifically differentiated as to voting rights by Article V.

As if any further clarification of the Articles were needed upon this matter, Article XI provides that 'These Articles' may be amended by a majority vote of the 'voting stock' with the exception of Article X. Thus, it is plainly contemplated that only voting shares may vote on amendments to the Articles with the above exception.

Plaintiffs seek to draw comfort from the fact that Article II does not mention 'by the vote of a majority of the voting stock' after providing for renewal as it does in the case of dissolution in Article II, issuance of additional stock in Article V, indemnification in Article IX, and amendment of the Articles in Article XI. It is fruitless to urge such a proposition in light of the foregoing discussion. The exception is the situation in which Class B stock has a right to vote. The Articles expressly provide that Class A shares have sole voting privileges upon all matters, including amendments to the Articles. It would be utterly inconsistent and a mastication of the plain words of the Articles to say that stock which always has exclusive voting rights is denied such rights merely because such rights are not mentioned as to the specific matter. It is equally implausible to say that Class B stock which never has voting rights is granted such rights as to a proposal due to failure to mention that the Class A stock has exclusive voting rights as to the specific subject.

Moreover, renewal necessitates an amendment to the Articles. Amendments to the Articles are already covered in a separate Article. The matters pointed out by plaintiffs are effectuated without amendment. Each subject is covered in only one place in the Articles. The draftsmen of the Articles were entirely reasonable to draft one Article as to voting rights on all amendments but to take the precautionary measure of directing attention to such rights as to each one of these other matters.

In summary, the Articles of Midwest expressly deprive Class B stock of voting rights as to extension of the corporation's activity beyond the stated period.

It is definitely the judgment of this Court that the motion in its entirety and in its separate components should be overruled. It seems that further statement need not be made as it relates to the issues which are dispositive of this case. The facts necessary for the determination of whether the Board's action in denying Class B stock the right to vote are not in dispute. It is here decided that the resolution must be voided. In general, it is the law that when one party is entitled to summary judgment as a matter of law on a single issue which is dispositive of the case, other issues become immaterial. However, in this cause of action, it would seem that it would be the better practice for the Court to confine itself merely to ruling upon the motion for summary judgment and not taking affirmative action until requested.

Accordingly, it is hereby ordered that defendants' motion for summary judgment is overruled.

CASE QUESTIONS

1. For what length of time was the corporation originally created?

2. What is the primary difference between Class A stock and Class B stock?

3. Explain the plaintiff's contention that amending the corporate existence beyond 20 years was in bad faith.

4. According to the court, what are the major issues in this case?

5. What role do the articles of incorporation play in this case?

6. Explain why the court rules that owners of Class B stock could not vote on corporate matters.

Exhibit 10–2. Other types of stock

> Among the various other types of stock there are
> ❑ capital
> ❑ control
> ❑ convertible
> ❑ registered

Although we will not address all of the various types of stock that a corporation can create, it is important to point out some of the differences found in these various classifications. What, for instance is the difference between capital stock and controlling stock?

Capital Stock

"Capital stock" is the term used to describe all stock issued to capitalize the corporation. It represents the total financial commitment by all shareholders. The stock is the financial bedrock upon which the corporation is built.[5]

Registered Stock

As we will see later in this chapter, there is no requirement that a stockholder actually possess a stock certificate to be considered a stockholder. In fact, there are several good reasons why a person would not want his or her stock ownership signified by a printed share certificate. However, a person would want to be a registered stockholder. "Registered stock" refers to the fact that an individual investor's rights are recorded with the company. The investor's name appears on the company's ledgers as an owner of record, and this confers the stockholder rights that are so important to investors.

Controlling Stock

"Controlling stock" refers to the stock owned by a specific stockholder that amounts to a majority interest in the corporation. When an investor owns more than 50 percent of a corporation's outstanding stock, this puts the investor in a strong position when it comes to voting on corporate director positions and management issues. Consider Scenario 10–2.

Scenario 10–2.51 Percent Ownership

Mario currently owns 49 percent of the outstanding shares of FGH Corporation. If he can pull together enough money to purchase 100 more shares, his percentage of ownership will increase to 51 percent. What will that entitle Mario to do?

Answer: As controlling stockholder, Mario can have a significant impact on the composition of the board of directors. After all, these individuals are elected by shareholders, with one vote going for every share owned. With 51 percent ownership, Mario will have a majority of the votes.

Convertible Stock

Convertible stocks give the owner the right to change the stock into another category. For instance, one type of convertible stock might allow a holder to convert the stock from preferred to common. However, convertible-stock rules generally require the conversion process to go in one direction: from the more complex to the less. Fully convertible stocks can be exchanged to Series A (which gives the owner the right to a specific dividend), to Series C (which gives the owner general dividend rights, but no voting rights), or to common stock (which gives the owner all of the typical common-stock rights, but no rights as a preferred stockholder).

PAR VALUE

A corporation is permitted to set a minimal or base amount for the value of its shares. This is referred to as **par value,** and it is often used to calculate the percent of ownership held by stockholders and to provide a comparison of par value against the actual capital held by the corporation. Because par value is often set at $1 per share, the value usually does not reflect the true financial position of the company.

par value An arbitrary value set on the price of an individual share.

The origin of par value lies in the idea that there should be an untouchable corpus of funds acting as a reserve for the corporation. The source of funds was represented by the number of shares issued and the par value assigned to these shares. The idea was that the shares represented a pool of funds that formed the operating capital of the corporation. Under the old rules, a corporation could declare a dividend only when its income had met or exceeded the par value of all outstanding stocks.

Of course, the reality of corporate financing is completely different from the theory suggested by something as arbitrary as par value. In recent years, theory has given way to pragmatism, and with it the idea of par value, or nominal value of shares, has gradually eroded. In many states, for example, the legal significance of par value has been eliminated. Corporations can still assign a par value to their shares by listing that value in the articles of incorporation, but many corporations now list shares without any par value at all.[6] If there is no par value for stock, stock value can be set by the stockholders or by the board of directors.

STOCK DIVIDENDS

A stock **dividend** is the payment made to stockholders that allots a specific profit per stock held. Some publicly held companies, such as utilities, routinely pay stock dividends to their stockholders. Other corporations, especially those in need of additional financing for research and development, may declare dividends only periodically or not at all.

dividend A share of profits or property; usually a payment per share of the corporation's stock, often paid on a quarterly basis.

record date The date upon which specific stockholder rights are fixed; for example, all stockholders owning stock as of the record date are entitled to receive a dividend.

When a company decides to declare a dividend, it sets a **record date.** All persons who owned stock on that particular date are entitled to receive the dividend. If a person buys the stock after that record date, but before the dividend checks are mailed, he or she is not entitled to receive a dividend check. The record date is also important because it determines other stockholder rights. For instance, the record date determines who will be sent financial reports, proxy statements, and other material directly related to stockholder rights. Dividends are not always in the form of cash. A corporation might decide to issue additional stock as a type of dividend. Consider Scenario 10–3.

Sidebar

A good source for information about dividends—and record dates—for companies is Standard and Poor's Dividend Record Binder.

Scenario 10–3. Who Gets the Dividend?

Maria owned shares of Acme, Inc., stock on the record date. However, the following business day, she sold it to Mark. Mark was the owner of the stock on the day that the dividend was sent. Who is entitled to receive the dividend check?

Answer: Maria. Because she was the owner as of the record date, that fixes her rights to the dividend. The fact that she later sold it to Mark will not affect her right to receive the dividend.

Sidebar

A stock split is a procedure where the number of shares held by a specific individual is multiplied without increasing or diminishing the overall value of the stock.

SHARE CERTIFICATES

The share certificate is simply the physical form that represents stock ownership. Most states have provisions that provide that stock ownership is perfectly valid without any stock certificates. In those cases, being a registered stockholder is the only significant data. A registered stockholder is entitled to all of the rights granted by the stock. If a stock certificate exists, it must bear the name of the issuing corporation and state under whose laws it is organized. Stocks certificates must also contain:

- the name of the person to whom the certificate is issued
- the number of shares that the certificate represents
- the class of stock

When a stock sale is recorded only on company ledgers, or on company computer files, it is referred to as **book entry.** In this situation, the stock holder does not receive a printed certificate.

book entry A stock that is registered under a stockholder's name and for which no stock certificate issues.

▶ FINANCIAL DISCLOSURES

We have already discussed the difference between publicly held and privately held corporations in chapter 7, but a word about them is also important here. A publicly held company is one whose stock is bought and sold on the open market. Later in this chapter, we will see that an entire industry has arisen for the express purpose of bringing buyers and sellers of stock together. Publicly held stock is stock that the public is free to buy. It is traded on stock markets, and this public status brings with it several responsibilities not seen with privately held corporations. Among these responsibilities is the obligation to file financial information with the appropriate authorities.

FINANCIAL STATEMENTS

Financial statements primarily show the status of corporate assets. They record the source of corporate financing and the way this money was spent. Financial statements consist of four main reports.

- balance sheets
- income statements
- cash flow statements
- statement of shareholder equity

KEY POINT

The annual report contains all of the accounting information required to understand the operations of the company; it is also required by the SEC.

Balance Sheets

Balance sheets provide a snapshot of corporate assets as of a particular date. They show how the corporation has made money and where this money has gone.

Balance Sheet Entries

The basic entries found in a balance sheet consist of assets, liabilities, and shareholder equity.

Assets

Assets consist of anything of value that the corporation owns. They can consist of real property or personal property, such as trucks, inventory, or services. Assets also consist of intangibles, such as copyrights, trademarks, and patents owned by the corporation.

Liabilities

Liabilities consist of bills that the corporation must pay out to others. Examples of liabilities include loan payments, bonds, taxes, rent, employee payroll, and the like.

Shareholder Equity

The category of shareholder equity is an accounting entry that lists the difference between everything the corporation owns and everything the corporation owes. If you deduct the total value of all assets from the total value of all liabilities, the final amount is the shareholder equity. This is what the shareholders would be entitled to receive if the company were liquidated.

Income Statements

Income statements show how the corporation made and spent money over a particular period of time, such as the fiscal year. These reports show income and any costs associated with that income and provide a grand total, or "bottom line," showing the company's net earnings (or losses) for the fiscal year.

Cash Flow Statements

Cash flow statements show how the corporation used its capital during a specific time period. This statement shows all of the money that both came in and went out of the company's accounts. Cash flow statements are important because they show whether or not the company has money on hand. This differentiates between a company's net earnings and the extra money that a company needs to purchase new inventory or to meet unexpected financial demands. A company could easily show a net profit for the year and still have negative cash flow. This statement helps investors discern whether the company is managing its money well.

Statement of Shareholder Equity

The statement of shareholder equity details the ebb and flow of the shareholders' stock possession over time. As the corporation earns money, shareholder equity gradually increases. Shareholder equity is the amount that would be left over if everything the corporation owned were sold. There are numerous, and very complicated, financial equations that can go into creating an annual report, but there is one simple equation that applies to all corporate financing: Total Assets = Total Liabilities + Shareholder Equity.

 GETTING TO THE BASICS

Balance sheets are set up like any accounting model, with assets on the left side and liabilities on the right. Just like a checking account statement. In the end, the two columns must balance.

ANNUAL REPORTS

Financial disclosures all come together in the company's annual report. This report, more like a printed brochure, is sent to all stockholders. It contains balance sheets, cash flow statements, and a wealth of additional information. There are companies that take this information and prepare it for investors.

Individuals interested in becoming stockholders in particular companies can read these publications, like Moody's or Standard & Poor's, for not only an overview of a particular company, but also information about how this company compares to others in the same industry. Investors can also get this information by contacting the companies directly, or by going through their stockbrokers. Information about small companies is another matter entirely. If a company has less then $10 million in assets, it is not required to file as much information with the government. The issue of corporate annual reports, corporate investing, and the information that an investor needs to make informed decisions can, and often does, take up entire books.

◢ SALES OF STOCK

One of the primary ways that a corporation raises money is by selling stock. As we have seen, both private and publicly held corporations issue stock to raise money for their operations. However, when a company moves from privately held to publicly held, some important issues arise. A corporation's first public sale of stock is referred to as "going public."

KEY POINT

A corporation is authorized to sell its own stock, as long as it acts in good faith. Examples of bad faith include selling stock to avoid creditors or judgments that have been assessed against the corporation.

GOING PUBLIC

When a corporation decides on **going public,** it must go through several steps before it will be authorized to sell stock to the general public. Corporations that decide to go public often rely on investment banking firms to publicize the stock to investors. Before the stock can be offered, it must be underwritten. Underwriters thoroughly investigate the company, especially its financial structure and assets. This investigation also encompasses the industry that the corporation is part of, its competitors, its economic outlook, and a myriad of other factors. Eventually, an **initial public offering (IPO)** will be held, where investors can get in on the ground floor of a new corporation by buying the first stocks issued. Obviously, these investors believe that the corporation will prosper and that this prosperity will be reflected in either hefty dividends or a dramatic increase in the stock price. Investors can either keep the stock and receive dividend checks or sell the stocks at a higher price. Of course, it is just as likely that the business may not do well, that no

going public Carrying out an initial public offering of stock.

initial public offering (IPO) The first public sale of a corporation's stock.

dividends will be declared and the value of the stock will plummet. At that point, investors can either sell the stock at a loss or, if no buyers can be found, retain the stock in what has become an essentially worthless company. Because of the risks involved in initial public offerings, only savvy investors should be involved in them.

An Example of an IPO

The history of the initial public offering for Priceline.com is a good example of what can happen in the topsy-turvy world of buying and selling stocks. When the company originally filed for registration, the estimated price of its stock stood at seven dollars. Had the company sold every one of its shares at that price, it would have made $1.15 billion. However, by the time the stock was ready for sale, it was trading at $16 per share. On trading day, it was selling at $81 per share. Two months later, the shares were selling for more than $150 per share. However, within three months, price per share had dropped to two dollars. Investors who purchased the stock on trading day or in the months that followed lost huge amounts of money in another example of the dot-com bust.[7]

GOING PRIVATE

The reverse process of going public is when a corporation decides to "go private." This occurs when a corporation buys up all outstanding stocks and decides to stop offering its stock on the public market. A company might decide to go private when it needs to do substantial restructuring, such as occurs when the company has been in financial trouble or the industry has gone through dramatic changes in a relatively short period of time.

SECURITIES

security A share of stock, a bond, a note, or one of many different kinds of documents showing a share in a company or a debt owed by a company or a government.

A **security** is broadly defined as a share of stock, a bond, a note, or any other investment vehicle. A security is an investment that is bought and sold by investors. Because securities form such an important part of the economy, they have been regulated in this country for over a century.

We have already drawn a distinction between shares and stocks; now it is time to consider the relationship of stocks to securities. Although stocks are considered to be a vehicle for raising additional capital for a business, they are also investments. As an investment, they fall into the broad category of securities. This category includes corporate and government bonds, annuities, mutual funds, debts, and stocks. This means that stocks have a dual nature: they are created by the authority of an individual corporate charter, but they are also bought and sold as securities in an enormous financial market. More importantly, securities fall under the jurisdiction of the Securities and Exchange Commission.

GETTING TO THE BASICS

> A security is an investment device, such as a stock, fixed annuity, or corporate or government bond.

The Securities and Exchange Commission

The Securities and Exchange Commission (SEC) has been a potent force in the securities field since its inception. Today, it polices stock exchanges, brokers, investment advisors, financial institutions, and publicly traded companies. On average, the SEC brings about 500 actions per year for behavior as diverse as insider trading, fraud, and giving false information to investors or government agencies.

The SEC's Division of Corporation Finance is responsible for ensuring that investors receive the information necessary to make informed decisions about stocks and other securities. The DCF requires information from companies not only during their initial public offering, but also continually through the life of the corporation—at least as long as the stock is offered publicly.

Although securities fall under the jurisdiction of various state laws, they fall under federal law as well. This was not always the case. Prior to the stock market crash in 1929, securities law was almost exclusively a state law issue. However, with the tremendous financial losses that occurred after that financial disaster, the federal government passed a series of statutes governing the securities field, with the result that this topic falls under both state and federal jurisdiction. See Exhibit 10–3.

Exhibit 10–3. SEC definition of securities

> The Securities Exchange Act of 1934 defines a security as "Any note, stock, treasury stock, bond, debenture, certificate of interest or participation in any profit-sharing agreement or in any oil, gas, or other mineral royalty or lease, any collateral trust certificate, preorganization certificate or subscription, transferable share, investment contract, voting-trust certificate, certificate of deposit, for a security, any put, call, straddle, option, or privilege on any security, certificate of deposit, or group or index of securities (including any interest therein or based on the value thereof), or any put, call, straddle, option, or privilege entered into on a national securities exchange relating to foreign currency, or in general, any instrument commonly known as a

(continued)

Exhibit 10–3. SEC definition of securities *(continued)*

> 'security'; or any certificate of interest or participation in, temporary or interim certificate for, receipt for, or warrant or right to subscribe to or purchase, any of the foregoing; but shall not include currency or any note, draft, bill of exchange, or banker's acceptance which has a maturity at the time of issuance of not exceeding nine months, exclusive of days of grace, or any renewal thereof the maturity of which is likewise limited."*

*Securities Act of 1993.

Federal Laws That Apply to Securities

The first federal laws that regulated securities came about because of the financial disaster of the Great Depression. The first of these was the Securities Act of 1933. This act provided, among other things, that investors must receive complete and accurate financial information about companies that offer their securities for public sale, and it authorized penalties for fraudulent and deceitful practices on the part of stockbrokers, financial institutions, and companies. The Securities Act was quickly followed by the Securities Exchange Act of 1934, which created the Securities and Exchange Commission. See Exhibit 10–4.

Exhibit 10–4. Securities Act of 1933

> Section 6—Registration of Securities and Signing of Registration Statement
>
> Any security may be registered with the Commission under the terms and conditions hereinafter provided, by filing a registration statement in triplicate, at least one of which shall be signed by each issuer, its principal executive officer or officers, its principal financial officer, its comptroller or principal accounting officer, and the majority of its board of directors or persons performing similar functions (or, if there is no board of directors or persons performing similar functions, by the majority of the persons or board having the power of management of the issuer). Signatures of all such persons when written on the said registration statements shall be presumed to have been so written by authority of the person whose signature is so affixed and the burden of proof, in the event such authority shall be denied, shall be upon the party denying the same. The affixing of any signature without the authority of the purported signer shall constitute a violation of this title. A registration statement shall be deemed effective only as to the securities specified therein as proposed to be offered. Securities Act of 1933.

Registration with the SEC

One of the primary methods that the SEC uses to ensure that companies abide by its rules is by making the information public. Investors who discover fraud in publicly filed documents can easily point it out to the SEC. Under SEC rules, a company must register before it can sell any type of security, including stocks. SEC registration information requires

- the company name, its business, and basic features
- the security being offered for sale
- a description of the company's management
- financial statements that support the filings

Public Access to SEC Information

One of the most helpful features of the SEC is its database of information about companies, securities, and financial information. The SEC maintains all of this information in a public-access database called EDGAR. This database can be accessed directly from the SEC's Web page at *http://www.sec.gov.*

STOCK EXCHANGES

There are two main national stock exchanges: the New York Stock Exchange and the National Association of Securities Dealers Quotation System, otherwise known as NASDAQ. These stock exchanges, along with numerous other smaller and regional stock exchanges, provide a marketplace for people who wish to buy or sell stock in particular companies. The brokers who work in these exchanges charge commissions for the purchase or sale of stock. They also maintain a listing of the share price of all publicly traded stocks. Rather than discuss the nuances and complexities of stock exchanges, which have been the subject of thousands of books, suffice it to say that these stock exchanges provide a vehicle for investors and corporations to buy and sell shares. The stock market is a huge and vital component of the American and global economies.

There is a market for stocks, just as there is a market for appliances, automobiles, and virtually every other item. However, the stock market has specific limitations. Because of the potential risks, individuals who wish to buy and sell stocks must do so through a broker. A stockbroker functions in much the same way that a real estate broker does. A real estate broker is in the business of putting buyers and sellers together, and a real estate broker has access to information and sources that are not accessible to the general public. When a real estate broker arranges a sale, he or she is entitled to a commission, which is a percentage of the overall sale price. However, the analogy between real estate brokers and stockbrokers begins to break down at the point of sale. For instance, homeowners can always sell their own homes, simply by putting a "for sale" sign in the front yard. Individual investors must work through brokers and are not allowed to post their stocks for sale.

Sidebar

The Dow Jones Industrial Average (DJIA) is a listing of 30 "blue chip" stocks. The average sale prices of the stocks in this average are posted daily. If the "Dow" has gained five percent, it means that, on average, the stock prices for these listings have gained in value by five percent. Whether or not this presents an accurate picture of the rest of the economy is an open question.

bond An investment that resembles a loan; an investor buys a bond for a specific amount and then is repaid over a period of time, at a specific interest rate.

Stockbrokers are in the business of arranging sales between individuals wishing to sell stock and individuals wishing to buy it. Although they provide a wide range of services, the foundation of a stockbroker's practice is charging a commission on the sale or purchase of stocks. How a person becomes a stockbroker is a topic that is too broad to cover in this chapter. Suffice it to say that becoming a broker involves not only a great deal of training and education, but also testing and certification. Once a person is a fully fledged stockbroker, he or she can charge a commission on sales and purchases of stocks.

Despite the fact that investors must use brokers to arrange for sales, the actual prices for stocks are available to all investors, whether they have a broker or not. In fact, you could argue that stock prices are the most widely available information for any item. You can find a list of the sale prices of individual stocks in the financial section of major newspapers every day. The various market indices are published there, and are also available on television and the Internet.

▶ CORPORATE BONDS

Issuing stock is not the only method that a company can use to raise money. Another method is to issue **bonds** to investors. A bond is essentially a loan made by an investor to the corporation. Under this loan agreement, the corporation agrees to make regular payments on this loan over a specific period. The return on this loan is often much higher than the rate that the investor could make by simply depositing that same amount of money in a savings account. However, it may not be as much as the investor could make if he or she bought the company's stock. Bonds offer dependability and lower risk, but the downside is that the bond's return will always remain the same. If the company develops a new product, or the company stock rises dramatically, the bond payment will remain the same. Of course, the opposite situation is also true. If the corporation's stock price drops dramatically, the bond holder will continue to receive the same amount of money. Of course, not all bonds are created equal. Bonds from companies that are undercapitalized, or that suffer from other financial trouble, may be riskier.

When an investor purchases a bond, he or she puts up a specific sum of money, such as $100,000, and the company begins making payments on the bond. The payments may come quarterly and will have fixed amounts. A bond might have a provision, for example, that it will be repaid in increments over a twenty-year period. During this time, the corporation's payments will include repayment of the principal plus a set interest rate.

Many investors opt for a portfolio that contains a combination of stocks and bonds, tailored to their individual level of risk tolerance. The more daring will weight their portfolio towards stocks, while the more cautious will opt for a higher proportion of bonds.

Case Law: *Insider Trading*

U.S. v. Mooney[9]
Before MURPHY, LAY, and BRIGHT, Circuit Judges.

PER CURIAM:

Michael Alan Mooney was convicted by a jury of eight counts of mail fraud, four counts of securities fraud, and five counts of money laundering. The district court sentenced him to 42 months, and Mooney appeals. He seeks a judgment of acquittal because of insufficient evidence, a new trial because of evidentiary error, or resentencing. We affirm Mooney's conviction but remand for further proceedings in respect to his sentence.

Mooney was formerly vice president of underwriting for United Healthcare Corporation (United). United is one of the largest health care management service companies in the country, and its stock trades on the New York Stock Exchange. Mooney opened a margin account in 1990 at the brokerage house Recom which he used solely to invest in United stock. Recom extended him a line of credit equal to half the value of the securities he maintained in the account. If the value of his securities were to fall below half the account's total value, Recom would make a margin call. Mooney would then have to make a deposit to restore equity in the account or Recom could sell assets of his to restore the 50% margin.

As part of United's strategy to acquire health insurance companies, it approached privately owned MetraHealth (Metra) in early 1995 and entered into negotiations with it in February. At that time Metra provided health insurance to more individuals than United, and it also had a substantial indemnity business. If United were to succeed in acquiring Metra, it would become the largest health care services company in the United States. It would have more than 40 million people enrolled in a variety of health care programs, with projected annual revenue of more than $8 billion. Mooney received stock options from time to time as part of his compensation at United, and on April 13 he exercised his right to purchase 20,000 shares of United stock for $36,000. The market value on that day for that amount of stock was $917,500.

During the 1995 negotiations, United and Metra conducted due diligence inquiries which involved confidential meetings at the headquarters of each company. Mooney had attended many such meetings on behalf of United in the past, and he and other senior representatives of United went to Metra's Virginia headquarters on May 11, 1995 for due diligence meetings. They spent four days looking through Metra's financial records, membership projections, cost data, and confidential Book of Business. United's corporate counsel reminded the participants in the meetings not to trade in stock during the due diligence period and to protect the secrecy of the proceedings by referring to the proposed merger transaction as "Project Fjord" and to Metra as "Musky."

(continued)

CASE LAW: *Insider Trading* (continued)

United has a written policy on insider trading which prohibits United employees from trading in its stock in two situations: (1) during the blackout period at the end of each quarter before the United earnings report is released, and (2) when an employee possesses material nonpublic information. The insider trading policy defines material nonpublic information as information that a reasonable investor would use in deciding whether to invest. It also states that information about proposed mergers and acquisitions by United is material. United's policy was frequently published in employee newsletters and mentioned in oral reminders at due diligence meetings.

After Mooney returned from the meetings at Metra's Virginia headquarters, he contacted his stockbroker on May 17, 1995 to sell the 20,000 shares of United common stock he had purchased in April. The sale cleared on May 24, and Mooney used part of the $775,500 proceeds to purchase call options in United stock. The call options were purchased between May 24 and June 14 for a total price of $258,283.03. They gave him the right to buy a total of 40,000 shares of United stock at $35 a share in the following months of September, December, and January. Both the sale of his United shares and his purchases of the United call options occurred before the end of the due diligence period in the Metra transaction.

Mooney subsequently sold his call options at a profit. On July 14, 1995 he sold the September options, and early in October he sold the December and January options. His total return on these sales was $532,482.49, and between August 3 and November 20, 1995 he deposited $428,000 into an account he had at Firstar Bank. These deposits were made by five checks drawn on his account at Recom Securities.

The first media mention of the acquisition appeared on June 21, 1995 in the *New York Times*, which reported that United was in advanced discussions with Metra. United issued a press release on the same day, confirming the ongoing discussions. The daily volume of trade in United shares increased markedly, and the stock price rose 5%. On June 22 the *Wall Street Journal* reported speculation about United's approaching acquisition of Metra, and United common stock rose another 6%. Then on June 26 United announced its agreement to acquire Metra for $1.65 billion in cash and stock. On June 20, the day before the first national media story, United stock had traded at $40.125. By July 15 the price was $44.50 a share, and by October 5 it was over $49.00. Shortly after the public announcement of United's acquisition of Metra, stock market surveillance officials notified the Securities and Exchange Commission (SEC) about bullish positions taken in United call options prior to the announcement of the acquisition. The SEC asked United to investigate whether Mooney had engaged in prohibited securities trading. Although Mooney denied it to United's corporate counsel, the SEC filed a civil action against him on August 2, 1999, alleging that the options were purchased while he had material nonpublic information regarding United's plan to acquire MetraHealth. The SEC sought an injunction, disgorgement of his gains, and a civil penalty. Shortly thereafter on August 9, United suspended Mooney for violating its insider trading policy. He later resigned. The SEC's civil action was stayed after he was indicted in this case.

The indictment charged Mooney with eight counts of mail fraud in violation of 18 U.S.C. §§ 1341 and 1346; four counts of securities fraud in violation of 15 U.S.C. §§ 78j(b), 78ff(a), and 17 C.F.R. § 240.10b-5; and five counts of money laundering in violation of 18 U.S.C. § 1957. The mail fraud counts referenced eight separate mailings of confirmation slips, for his May 17 sale of United common stock and for his subsequent call option transactions. The securities fraud counts covered his four separate purchases of call options. The money laundering counts were based on his deposits of five checks from Recom into his Firstar Bank account during August, October, and November 1995; the indictment alleged that these funds were derived from his securities and mail fraud.

Mooney was found guilty by a jury on all counts and required to forfeit $70,000. The district court denied his motions for judgment of acquittal or new trial and sentenced him to 42 months in prison and a $150,000 fine. Mooney appeals from the judgment, alleging insufficient evidence, abuse of discretion in an evidentiary ruling, and sentencing error.

In reviewing the sufficiency of the evidence in a case such as this, the evidence is considered in the light most favorable to the government, evidentiary conflicts are resolved in its favor, and all reasonable inferences are drawn from the evidence in support of the jury's verdict. We will reverse only if no reasonable jury could have found the accused guilty beyond a reasonable doubt.

Mooney argues that the government did not prove a scheme to defraud beyond a reasonable doubt. The government alleged that Mooney acquired material, nonpublic information relating to United's acquisition of MetraHealth and that he breached the duty of trust he owed to United and its shareholders by purchasing the call options as part of a fraudulent scheme. Mooney's securities fraud charges alleged the use of manipulative and deceptive devices in connection with the purchase or sale of securities, and false and misleading statements willfully made. Fraudulent intent need not be proven directly, but can be inferred from the facts and circumstances surrounding the defendant's actions.

Mooney contends that there was insufficient evidence to prove that he used material nonpublic information in violation of the securities laws. Mooney argues that his case differs from the typical insider trading case. He claims that an inside trader ordinarily knows to a greater degree of certainty how the stock price will be affected by the release of nonpublic information. He argues that it was not certain that the United stock price would increase because of the merger with Metra. The legal test is not whether the price would certainly rise, however, but whether the inside information used was material. A fact is material in the securities fraud context if there is a substantial likelihood that a reasonable investor would consider it important in making an investment decision.

There was more than enough evidence here for a reasonable jury to find that Mooney's inside information was material. He exercised employee stock options to purchase United stock on April 13 after negotiations with Metra had begun. As soon as he returned home from the May due diligence meetings, he began to purchase call options for United stock. The jury could infer that Mooney sought to capitalize on his nonpublic information and anticipated he could profit by purchasing call options that could later be sold at a higher price. Mooney also had access to information that the acquisition of Metra was likely to present new growth opportunities for United. Because of his participation in high level confidential meetings, Mooney knew that the due diligence review had not derailed negotiations and that United would only proceed with acquisitions that were expected to increase earnings. He also knew that United would grow considerably in size, programs, and projected revenue. All of this information would have been of interest to a reasonable investor, and the jury could have found a substantial likelihood that it would have been considered important in making investment decisions.

Mooney also argues that any rational investor who observed the seasonal trends in the price of United stock would have made similar investment decisions. Whether or not that might be true, there was sufficient evidence for a reasonable jury to find Mooney's sale of common stock was part of a fraudulent scheme to use the sale proceeds to purchase the United call options, that these transactions were based on his use of material nonpublic information, and that there was sufficient evidence on all elements of the securities fraud counts.

Mooney argues that the government did not prove beyond a reasonable doubt that the mails were used to carry out the fraudulent scheme. A mail fraud conviction under 18 U.S.C. § 1341 requires proof that the defendant voluntarily and intentionally devised or participated in a scheme to defraud,

(continued)

CASE LAW: *Insider Trading* (continued)

that he entered into the scheme with the intent to defraud, that he knew that it was reasonably foreseeable that the mails would be used, and that he used the mails in furtherance of the scheme. *See United States v. Bearden*, 265 F.3d 732, 736 (8th Cir.2001).

Experienced investors such as Mooney expect confirmation slips to confirm their transactions, and Mooney could have anticipated that his buy and sell orders would result in the mailing of confirmation slips. Confirmation slips are integral to an investor's contract relationship with his broker. Because the broker's use of the mails is attributable to the investor's buy or sell order, it is sufficient to satisfy the requirement of use of the mails in furtherance of a fraudulent scheme. These slips recorded the sale of Mooney's United stock and the number of call options he purchased and sold, at what price and date, their expiration dates, and details of their sale. The jury could reasonably find that these mailed records aided Mooney in his scheme to defraud. The jury was entitled to consider the confirmation slips in deciding whether the mails had been used as part of Mooney's fraudulent scheme, and we conclude there was sufficient evidence to satisfy the mailing element of the mail fraud counts.

Mooney also challenges the sufficiency of the evidence for his money laundering convictions under 18 U.S.C. § 1957. Money laundering is defined in the statute as knowingly engaging in, or attempting to engage in, a monetary transaction in criminally derived property that is valued at more than $10,000. Mooney argues that the money laundering counts must fail if the predicate offenses of securities fraud and mail fraud were not established, but as already discussed there was sufficient evidence to support his convictions for those offenses.

Mooney argues that there was insufficient evidence to prove that the funds deposited into his Firstar Bank account were proceeds of insider trading. The evidence showed that the deposits consisted of five withdrawals from the Recom account Mooney used for transactions in United stock. He contends that there was enough United common stock or "clean money" in the account to cover the deposit checks. There was thus insufficient evidence he argues, to show that the deposits were from proceeds of the sale of his call options or "dirty money." The government contends that the issue is unreviewable because Mooney did not raise this commingled funds theory in his motion for acquittal. The point is well taken, but we note in any event that the government need not trace each dollar to a criminal source to prove a violation of 18 U.S.C. § 1957.

Mooney's theory would allow wrongdoers to evade prosecution for money laundering simply by commingling criminal proceeds with legitimate funds. Moreover, the jury could reasonably find from the evidence that Mooney was only able to withdraw the funds from his Recom account without going below his margin limit because the account contained the proceeds from the sale of his call options. We conclude that there was sufficient evidence to support Mooney's convictions for illegal monetary transactions.

In summary, we conclude that Mooney is not entitled to prevail on any of his arguments for judgment of acquittal or new trial and we affirm his conviction.

CASE QUESTIONS

1. How did Mooney take advantage of information he gathered in his position as vice president for United Healthcare Corporation?

2. What suggestions did United Healthcare's attorney propose to safeguard sensitive information?

3. When did Mooney sell his stock, and what did he do with the profits?

4. How did Mooney come to the attention of the SEC?

5. Explain the basis of the money laundering charge against Mooney.

SUMMARY

A company can raise money in any of a number of ways, but the most common is to issue stock. Stock comes in many different forms, from common stock, which gives the owner voting rights in the corporation and entitles the holder to a dividend, to preferred stock, which provides for priority when the corporation is liquidated, but does not provide any voting rights. Corporations can be authorized to issue an almost endless variety of stock. When a company is publicly traded, it must make specific financial disclosures. The Securities and Exchange Commission was originally created to monitor publicly traded stocks and to insist on the accuracy of the financial data that is given to the public.

HELPFUL WEB SITES

NASDAQ
http://www.nasdaq.com

Scripophily.com
http://www.scripophily.com

A company that researches old stock or bond certificates to see if they are still valuable.

Moody's Investor Services
http://www.moodys.com

A company that offers extensive research, profiles, and data on publicly traded companies.

KEY TERMS

bond	preemptive rights
book entry	preferred stock
common stock	record date
dividend	security
going public	share
initial public offering	stock
par value	

APPLYING CHAPTER CONCEPTS

Visit the SEC site *(http://www.sec.gov)* and locate information on a well known company, such as Coca-Cola or Microsoft. What kind of information is available on these companies?

REVIEW QUESTIONS

1. How is the sale of stock comparable to a contract between the stockholder and the corporation?
2. How does the term "share" compare with the term "stock"?
3. What rights does stock ownership confer on the owner?
4. What is common stock?
5. What is preferred stock, and how does it compare to common stock?
6. What are preemptive rights?
7. What is capital stock?
8. What is registered stock?
9. What is controlling stock, and how does it compare to capital stock?
10. Explain convertible stock.
11. What is par value?
12. What is the significance of stock dividends?
13. What is a record date, and how does it relate to stock dividends?
14. Is a share certificate the only way to possess stocks? Explain.
15. What is book entry, and what relationship does it have to stock ownership?
16. What are the elements commonly found in balance sheets?
17. What is the difference between an income statement and a cash flow statement?
18. What is the Securities and Exchange Commission, and what role does it play in publicly traded stocks?
19. What is "going public"?
20. What are bonds, and how do they compare to stocks?

QUESTIONS FOR REFLECTION

Given recent scandals involving companies such as Enron and WorldCom, is the SEC doing enough to ensure that companies are filing correct information? Should the SEC be given additional powers? According to the SEC Web site, what types of enforcement tools does it have to force companies to comply with existing regulations?

ENDNOTES

[1]*Wright v. Georgia Railroad & Banking Co., Ga.*, 30 S.Ct. 242, 216 U.S. 420, 54 L.Ed. 544.

[2]*Dunham v. Chemical Bank & Trust Co.*, 71 P.2d 468, 180 Okl. 537.

[3]*Coaxial Communications, Inc. v. CNA Fin. Corp.*, 367 A.2d 994 (Del. 1976).

[4]276 F.Supp. 674 (D.C. Iowa 1967).

[5]CJS CORPORATNS § 122.

[6]*Randle v. Winona Coal Co.*, 89 So. 790, 206 Ala. 254.

[7]Source: NASDAQ.

[8]Securities Act of 1933.

[9]401 F.3d 940 (C.A.8 Minn. 2005).

Chapter 11

CORPORATE LIABILITY

Chapter Objectives

Upon completion of this chapter, you should be able to:

- Describe the types of personal liability that corporate directors or officers may face.
- Explain the significance of the business judgment rule.
- Define the importance of the concept of "piercing the corporate veil."
- Explain the basis of corporate criminal liability.
- Describe shareholder derivative suits.

◗ INTRODUCTION

Because a corporation is an artificial person, it can be both civilly and criminally liable for actions carried out on its behalf. A corporation can also be punished, by being forced to pay fines or civil judgments or even by being judicially dissolved. In this chapter we will examine the issue of corporate liability and determine how corporate officers and directors can also be liable for their actions.

KEY POINT

Corporations can sue and be sued.

▶ CIVIL ACTIONS AGAINST CORPORATE OFFICERS AND DIRECTORS

We saw in chapter 9 that directors have specific duties and obligations to the corporation and the corporate shareholders. Among these duties is the requirement to use due care and diligence in business matters. What happens when shareholders believe that the directors have not met their obligations? Can shareholders sue directors for what they believe to be bad business decisions? In most cases, the answer is no. See Exhibit 11–1.

Exhibit 11–1. "Who sues whom?" (Source: Civil Trial Cases and Verdicts in Large Counties, 2001. Bureau of Justice Statistics, page 3)

Who sues whom?

The most common type of civil trial involved an individual suing either another individual (42%) or a business (31%). Businesses sued each other in about 11% of all civil trials (table 4). Among bench trials, a larger proportion of businesses were more likely to be plaintiffs suing either businesses (27%) or individuals (14%) (not shown in a table).

LIABILITY OF CORPORATE OFFICERS AND DIRECTORS

When officers or directors breach the duties that they owe the corporation, they may find themselves civilly liable to the corporation. Directors are personally liable for breaches of their duties and any economic injuries to the corporation that result from their negligence.[1]

Directors must exercise ordinary care and diligence in their actions on behalf of the corporation. What is "ordinary care"? Courts define it as the care that an ordinary, prudent person would use in conducting his or her own affairs.[2] All courts agree that directors must act in good faith and in the best interests of the corporation.[3] They are not, however, insurers against catastrophes and financial problems. A director does not become liable simply because he or she was on the board when business conditions deteriorated. They are also not liable for clerical errors or "slight omissions." They are, however, liable for gross negligence.[4]

Officers and directors are liable for any action that falls below the minimum standards of care and prudence imposed on all corporate officers. When they commit acts of gross negligence, such as failing to carry out their duties, failing to check on financial and other records before they are released, or generally ignoring their duties to shareholders, they may become personally liable for their failures. In such a case, shareholders could institute a lawsuit against them under the theory of derivative actions. We will discuss derivative actions in greater detail later in this chapter.

▶ **GETTING TO THE BASICS**

Although shareholders are protected by limited liability, officers and directors can be personally liable for their actions when they engage in gross negligence and dereliction of their duties.

The premise behind officer and director liability rests in agency law. Because these positions resemble, in many ways, the relationship of agents to principals, discussed in chapter 2, courts have treated officers and directors who mismanage corporate affairs, engage in negligent conduct, or violate their ethical duties, as agents who have acted against the interests of their principals. In many ways, the punishment is the same. The officers and directors, like agents, must **indemnify** the shareholders for the economic loss to the corporation.[5]

indemnify To compensate for business losses or expenses tied to an individual's conduct.

Indemnification

Indemnification refers to the payment by an offending party of all losses that flow directly from negligent or harmful conduct. The indemnity payments would be made to the shareholders to compensate them for their losses. Indemnification can be a complicated issue. What, for instance, is the actual dollar value of an officer's gross negligence? Is the loss limited to the officer's salary during the period that he or she ignored his duties, or can it be expanded to the potential profits that would have come from business dealings had the officer been acting with diligence? Shareholders who seek losses for business deals that never materialized must prove that the failure to consummate the deal rests squarely with the negligent officer before the court will entertain any action for indemnification for possible lost profits.

Directors are also required to stay informed about business matters and the general activities that the corporation is engaged in. As far as the courts are concerned, a director's failure to know about particular activities that hurt shareholder interests is just as bad as knowingly engaging in them.[6] Under this theory, directors have an affirmative duty to know and understand the financial activities carried on in their companies. They cannot claim, for instance, that they were mere figureheads with no understanding of the underlying corporate situation. Consider Scenario 11–1.

> **Scenario 11–1. Duties of Unpaid Directors**
>
> The board of directors at QPR, Inc., do not receive a salary for their participation on the board. When shareholders bring a claim of gross negligence against the members, is it a defense for directors to claim that because they were not paid, they did not owe the same level of duties as members who are paid?
>
> **Answer:** No. The duties of directors remain, regardless of whether or not they are paid board members.[7]

Courts have come up with several tests to help determine when a corporate officer or director has breached a duty to the corporation. One test is to determine whether the individual had a personal stake in the decision. If the officer or director will be personally enriched by the business decision, courts are more likely to rule that the individual breached a duty and is liable to the corporation.

Another test that courts use to determine whether an officer or director has breached a duty to the corporation is to inquire about the relationship between the director and some other party who is engaging in unauthorized practices or actually breaking the law. If this person is controlling the director, the law will presume that the director has breached a duty as well.[8]

Although the courts have come up with several different tests to determine officer and director liability, there is one that outweighs all others. The most important doctrine that the courts have created to fix the boundaries of corporate liability is the business judgment rule.

▶ BUSINESS JUDGMENT RULE

business judgment rule A rule that protects corporate officers and directors from liability for business decisions made in good faith.

The **business judgment rule** originated under old common law, but has been recognized in all states.[9] The rule essentially creates a presumption that directors acted in good faith and with the corporation's best interests in mind, even if their decision later turns out to be wrong. The core responsibility of directors is to weigh risk against reward. This is an art, not a science. Courts have been reluctant to second-guess such decisions, reasoning that the directors were the best judges of the circumstances as they existed at the time. After all, the directors were acquainted with the facts, knew their company's financial situation, and had an obligation to act in the company's best interests. A negotiation that might seem favorable months or even years later might not have been as attractive when it was actually negotiated. As long as the directors can show they acted in good faith and in accordance with their corporate duties, the business judgment rule prevents the courts from becoming backseat drivers to corporate business decisions. It also prevents shareholders from bringing actions against directors when the shareholders are not fully familiar with the details surrounding the circumstances and are unable to objectively evaluate all of the factors.

Officers and directors are shielded against civil liability from their business decisions when they can show that:

1. they acted in good faith
2. they were not acting to further their personal interests over those of the corporation
3. their actions were reasonable under the circumstances
4. they reasonably believed that the decision was in the best interests of the corporation

GETTING TO THE BASICS

The business judgment rule protects corporate officers and directors from being sued when their business judgments turn out to be incorrect.

The four-prong test for the business judgment rule is not difficult to prove. Officers and directors routinely interpose the business judgment rule against the anger of shareholders who do not like the decisions—or outcomes—from particular business decisions.

The business judgment rule not only insulates officers and directors from lawsuits from shareholders, it also keeps courts out of the business of monitoring business decisions. If irate shareholders could bring civil suits every time something happened that they did not like, the courts would be swamped with litigation. The business judgment rule holds back a tide of lawsuits that would overwhelm an already overworked court system.

Persons Protected by the Business Judgment Rule

The business judgment rule protects officers and directors. It also protects the actions of majority or controlling stockholders[10] and directors in nonprofit corporations. However, the rule does not apply when a director or officer is shown to be grossly negligent in his or her duties or has committed fraud or where the individual has a personal interest in the transaction in question.[11] In any of these situations, the officer or director would not be acting in good faith and would therefore not come under the first protection offered by the business judgment rule.

LEGAL CHECKLIST

SHAREHOLDERS CAN OVERCOME THE PRESUMPTION IN THE BUSINESS JUDGMENT BY PRESENTING ANY OF THE FOLLOWING:

❏ A DIRECTOR HAD A FINANCIAL STAKE IN THE BUSINESS DECISION.

❏ AN OFFICER/DIRECTOR WAS GROSSLY NEGLIGENT IN MAKING THE DECISION.

❏ AN OFFICER/DIRECTOR WAS ENGAGED IN SELF-DEALING.

❏ AN OFFICER/DIRECTOR ACTED FRAUDULENTLY.

❏ THE ACTION WAS ILLEGAL.[12]

Justification for the Business Judgment Rule

The business judgment rule acknowledges that directors must be given wide latitude in their decisions. Without this protection, directors might become shell shocked by frequent lawsuits and refuse to take any risks. In business, the rule is simple: the greater the risk, the greater the potential reward. Without the business judgment rule, shareholders could challenge any risky venture, and the practical result would be boards of directors that would take no risks at all.[13] Courts have traditionally been reluctant to second-guess business decisions and even more reluctant to become embroiled in weighing possibilities and probabilities in business affairs. As a result, they have continued to urge the business judgment rule as a defense against shareholders' wrath against corporate directors.

 GETTING TO THE BASICS

> Under the business judgment rule, officers and directors are not liable to shareholders for errors or mistakes in judgment.

Reliance on Others

Directors are permitted to rely on statements of the individuals who have specific corporate responsibility. The law does not impose on them the requirement to investigate the detailed reports created by specialists. This means that if the directors rely, in good faith, on financial reports from the treasurer or chief financial officer, they will be protected by the business judgment rule. See Exhibit 11–2.

> #### Scenario 11–2. Business Judgment
>
> Last year, the board of directors for LM-N, Inc., received a report from their chief financial officer that the corporation had earned $10.5 million for that fiscal year. Based on that report, the board issued an annual report to its stockholders providing that information. They also used that report as the basis to seek further funding to buy new facilities and expand its research and development section. Sales of stock in LM-N jumped dramatically. This year, an investigation by the SEC revealed that the chief financial officer had used the income statements of subsidiary companies that actually did not exist to bolster the financial information for last year's income. It turns out that LM-N, Inc. actually lost $2.4 million last year and is well on its way to losing even more this year. Shareholders and others wish to file suit, naming not only the chief financial officer, but also the board of directors. Is the board protected by the business judgment rule?
>
> **Answer:** Yes. As long as the board can show that it relied in good faith on the reports, and had no reason to be suspicious of them, they will be protected by the business judgment rule.

KEY POINT

One fact that goes a long way towards invoking the business judgment rule is that the director did not gain personally from the bad decision.

Exhibit 11–2. Commercial defendants and money laundering

Commercial defendants and money laundering

Businesses comprised less than 2% of all money laundering-related defendants adjudicated during 2001. The 22 businesses charged with money laundering as the most serious offense included auto dealerships, grocery stores, banks, furniture stores, restaurants, physicians' offices, construction firms, beauty shops, and research firms.

Of the 22 charged, 15 were convicted (68.2%); 13 received probation (with an average term of 38.8 months), and 8 were fined (an average of $68,454).

Individuals comprised at least 98% of defendants charged with money laundering offenses, 1994-2001

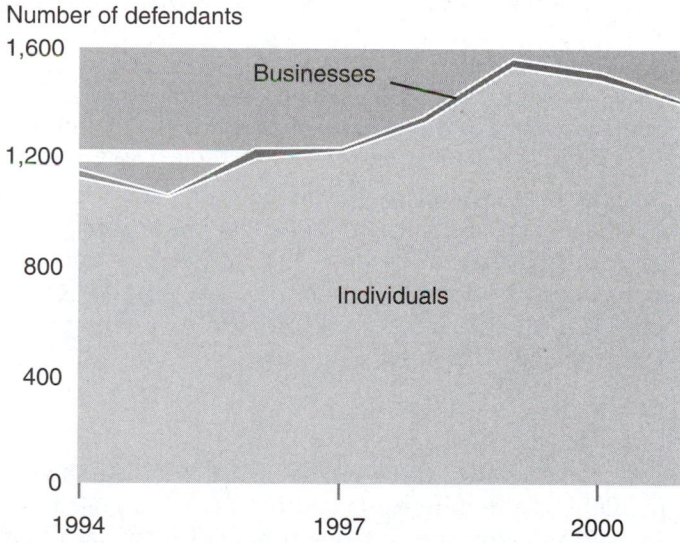

Number of defendants

Money laundering was the most serious offense filed.

Source: Administrative Office of the U.S. Courts, criminal master file.

(Source: Federal Justice Statistics Program, Bureau of Justice Statistics, page 10).

Limitations of the Business Judgment Rule

Scenario 11–2 points out an important limitation on the business judgment rule. The business judgment rule is not a complete bar to all actions against the board of directors and officers. Instead, it requires that those individuals exercise good judgment and act in good faith. Courts will not invoke the rule to protect directors when it is obvious that they were negligent in their duties or when a reasonably prudent person would have had suspicions about specific information relayed to the board. Consider Scenario 11–3.

KEY POINT

The business judgment rule applies when officers and directors act in good faith, not when they commit fraud or negligence.

Scenario 11-3. Business Judgment, Part 2

This involves the same basic facts as Scenario 11–2, with one important exception. Several members of the board have made inquiries about the subsidiary companies' income. One has even pointed out that she cannot find any evidence that these companies exist and has requested additional information about them. Despite this, when the CFO gives his report, the board takes the actions. Does the business judgment rule protect the entire board now?

Answer: No. The business judgment rule no longer protects any member of the board, even those that made inquiries. The individual directors had an obligation to follow up on their suspicions, and their failure to do so results in a decision that the business judgment rule does not apply.[15]

Of course, the business judgment rule will not protect directors or officers who have acted in bad faith or those who have committed fraud or crimes in the course of their duties for a corporation. There are other important limitations on the business judgment rule. For instance, federal legislation has chipped away at some of the protections of the rule. One such example is the Sarbanes-Oxley Act.

The Sarbanes-Oxley Act

Passed in 2002, the **Sarbanes-Oxley Act** (15 U.S.C.A. §7245) made sweeping revisions in SEC filing requirements and the duties imposed on corporate directors and officers who certify the accuracy of financial reports. Under Sarbanes, when the president or CEO signs off on an annual report, his or her signature indicates that the CEO has reviewed the financial records contained in the report and is attesting to their accuracy. If later investigation reveals that these documents were false or misleading, the CEO may be personally liable under Sarbanes.

Sarbanes-Oxley Act An act that made sweeping revisions to SEC filing requirements by publicly traded companies.

Sarbanes-Oxley contains many other provisions that limit corporate activities, such as extending personal loans to corporate officers, and that create additional protections for whistleblowers, as well as requirements for archiving data showing compliance. But the Sarbanes-Oxley Act is not the only limitation imposed on the business judgment rule. The rule has been held not to apply to ultra vires actions.

ULTRA VIRES ACTIONS

When corporate officers or directors exceed their authority, the business judgment rule no longer protects them. Such acts are deemed to be **ultra vires.** The term literally means "beyond the power," and this is an excellent description of the legal principle involved. Ultra vires acts are those that are beyond the powers expressly or impliedly granted to a corporation.[16] Some courts have described ultra vires actions as those that are "foreign to the nature and design" of the corporation.[17]

ultra vires (Latin) "beyond the power." An action carried out by an officer or director of a corporation that is not authorized by the corporate charter.

 GETTING TO THE BASICS

An ultra vires action is one that the corporation is not authorized to take.

There is an important distinction to make here. An ultra vires action is one that a corporation has no power to carry out. A corporation chartered with the express purpose of functioning as a nonprofit business is not authorized to carry on activities that earn a profit. They are also not authorized to make distributions to shareholders. But ultra vires not only applies to what a particular corporation can do, it also applies to the actions of individual officers. A corporation may have the power to carry out an action, while a particular officer may not. The corporation's treasurer, for example, is authorized to maintain all financial records, but if this person were to negotiate a contract on behalf of the corporation, the action would be deemed ultra vires. Treasurers do not have this power. In such a situation, the act would be deemed void. An officer or director who commits an ultra vires action cannot seek ratification of the act later. We first encountered the term "ratification" in the section on agency law. There are times when an agent exceeds his or her authority and then seeks approval, or ratification, of the act after it has been completed. Although that is an option for agents, it is not available for officers. The action was not authorized, and asking the board to approve it later does not change the fact.[18] There is another reason to deprive officers of the option of seeking ratification for unauthorized acts: it prevents many officers from engaging in questionable practices in the first place.

Scenario 11–4. An Improper Relationship?

Cal works on the board of directors for X-YZ Corporation and is involved in a romantic relationship with Stella, a local real estate agent. Stella knows that the corporation is considering buying a warehouse and purchases one that meets all of the corporation's needs (as she has learned them from Cal). She approaches Cal and offers to sell X-YZ, Inc. the warehouse. She doesn't mention that she will earn a 50 percent profit on the sale. Cal presents the offer to the board. Cal will not personally gain from the sale, but when the shareholders discover the transaction, they bring action against Cal, alleging breach of duty and requesting that Cal pay the difference between the fair market value of the warehouse and the amount that the corporation actually spent. Will the shareholders be successful?

Answer: Even when a director does not personally benefit from a transaction, his or her actions can be questioned when shareholders can show that because of a relationship with a third party, the director's judgment was clouded.[19] In this case, Cal may be ordered to indemnify the corporate shareholders for the amount the corporation spent on the warehouse that was above fair market value.

CASE LAW: *What Is an Ultra Vires Action?*

Beyer v. F & R Oilfield Contractors, Inc.[20]
LABORDE, Judge.

This is a suit by the minority shareholders of a corporation against the corporation and its directors and officers. Allen Beyer, Laura Beyer, Claven Frederick and Shirley Frederick (plaintiffs) filed suit against F & R Oilfield Contractors, Inc. (F & R), Dalton Fremin, Roy Fremin, and Roland Breaux (defendants), seeking to recover damages sustained through the defendants' fraudulent and ultra vires acts. The defendants filed an exception of no right of action alleging that plaintiffs have no right of action to recover individually for the damages alleged; that recovery must be had through a shareholder's derivative action to bring the allegedly illegal dispersed funds back into the corporation. The trial court sustained the exception and dismissed the suit. From this decision, the plaintiffs have perfected this appeal. We affirm.

The sole issue on appeal is whether or not shareholders of a corporation can directly recover damages from the officers and directors of that corporation for alleged illegal and ultra vires acts.

The plaintiffs are stockholders in F & R Oilfield Contractors, Inc. (F & R). The defendants are officers and directors of F & R. The plaintiffs' petition alleges that they have suffered damages due to the defendants' illegal and ultra vires acts which improperly raised the expenses of the corporation. These complained of acts of defendants are: the defendants paid themselves excessive salaries and bonuses; the defendants have denied plaintiffs access to the corporate books and have improperly maintained the corporate books; the defendants have failed to properly insure corporate property; the defendants have given excessive credit to poor credit risks; the defendants have improperly obtained loans from the corporation, depleting the working capital; the defendants have claimed fictitious loans to the corporation; and the defendants have illegally removed the plaintiffs from the board of directors.

The defendants filed an exception of no right of action. The trial court held that the cause of action asserted by plaintiffs is one belonging solely to the corporation and the proper procedural vehicle is a shareholder's derivative action and not a suit by the individual shareholders in their own behalf. However, the trial court did hold that the plaintiffs have a right of action in their own behalf to gain access to the corporation's books and records.

We agree with the trial court that the right of action asserted by the plaintiffs, i.e., one to bring the illegally dispersed funds back into the corporation, can only be asserted through the corporation by a shareholder's derivative suit. Such an action for mismanagement or fraud belongs to the corporation, not the stockholders. The right to recover for such losses was explained in Orlando v. Nix, supra:

"As the Reliance Homestead Association is a body corporate its assets belong to it, and no individual stockholder has a property right in them. If the corporation sustains a loss by reason of mismanagement or fraud upon the part of its officials, the right to recover for the loss is an asset of the corporation, and not of the stockholders. It is only in extreme cases that a stockholder is permitted to sue for damage done a corporation, and even then the right does not arise until an ineffectual demand has been made on the corporation to institute the suit, and the suit, when brought, must be brought in behalf of the corporation, which alone is entitled to the amount recovered."

Likewise in the instant case, as an asset of the corporation, such a right to recover loss for mismanagement or fraud may only be asserted secondarily by a shareholder through a shareholder's derivative suit.

The plaintiffs contend that the above cited cases are not controlling because they were decided prior to the 1968 amendment of the corporate code (LSA-R.S. 12:1 et seq.) and that such a right of action against directors is conferred by LSA-R.S. 12:91 which reads:

"Officers and directors shall be deemed to stand in a fiduciary relation to the corporation and its shareholders, and shall discharge the duties of their respective positions in good faith, and with that diligence, care, judgment and skill which ordinarily prudent men would exercise under similar circumstances in like positions. Nothing herein contained shall derogate from any indemnification authorized by R.S. 12:83."

Although this statute extends the officers' and directors' fiduciary relationship to the shareholders, it does not extend a direct right of action by the shareholders against the officers and directors. The comments under LSA-R.S. 12:91 explain that an action to recover from an officer or director for such a breach of a fiduciary duty is secondary and must be asserted through a shareholder's derivative suit:

"Committee Comment-1968

The fiduciary relationship has been expressly extended to shareholders. The second sentence of this Section is new. Articles 591-611 of the Code of Civil Procedure contain procedural provisions applicable to shareholders' secondary actions, which are also subject to the provisions of R.S. 13:3201-3207."

Articles 591-611 of the Code of Civil Procedure deal solely with class and secondary actions. Counsel for the plaintiff cites no authority which allows the plaintiffs to recover directly from the officers and directors of a corporation for losses sustained by the corporation due to the officers' and directors' mismanagement or fraud.

We hold that the plaintiffs' sole remedy is through a shareholder's derivative suit.

For the above and foregoing reasons, the decision of the trial court, dismissing without prejudice plaintiffs' suit except the plaintiffs' demands to inspect the books and records of the corporation, is affirmed. All costs are taxed to plaintiffs-appellants.

AFFIRMED.

CASE QUESTIONS

1. Who are the plaintiffs in this action?

2. What allegations concerning ultra vires actions did the plaintiffs raise in this case?

3. Explain the court's reasoning concerning whether this case can be brought by individual plaintiffs or must be brought as a derivative action.

4. How do the plaintiffs counter the court's argument that only a shareholder derivative suit can be the basis of a claim?

5. Does the statute cited by the plaintiffs give the individual shareholders an individual right of action against the corporation?

Limitations of Ultra Vires

There are limits to the use of an ultra vires action. For example, courts will not allow the action where it will actually result in an injustice to the parties. After all, the doctrine was created to prevent injustice and to force officers and directors to live up to their corporate obligations. Allowing them to use it to avoid those actions would run counter to the whole reason for the doctrine in the first place.[21] An officer could not, for instance, negotiate the sale of corporate property, obtain payment, and then refuse to carry out the contract on the basis that he or she was acting beyond an officer's authorized duties. In such a situation, the contract might be voided, and the other party, as well as the shareholders, would be permitted to bring suit against the officer. He or she would not be authorized to interpose ultra vires as a defense. Only shareholders or others who have a direct interest in the corporation can raise a claim of ultra vires. Members of the general public who do not own stock in the corporation have no standing to bring such actions. Because ultra vires challenges are raised on behalf of the financial interests of shareholders, members of the general public are barred from bringing such a claim. They have no financial stake in the litigation; therefore they have no standing to maintain an action.

Standing

standing A showing that the plaintiff has personal stake in the litigation; his or her personal rights, financial interests, property rights, or other legally recognized rights will be impacted by the lawsuit.

Before any person can bring a civil action, he or she must establish **standing.** In a civil action, standing refers to the potential injury to property or financial interests. When a person has no potential loss to property, finances, ownership, or other legally recognized claim, he or she lacks standing. In such a situation, the court will dismiss the suit. However, the rules about standing and corporate actions are relatively simple: shareholders usually have standing to challenge almost all of the officer and director's actions. After all, they obviously have a financial interest in the corporation's affairs.

Consequences of Ultra Vires Actions

Ultra vires actions are not necessarily illegal, just unauthorized. An officer or director who acts without express or implied authority, on behalf of the corporation, has committed an ultra vires act. The consequences of the act can be serious. If the court determines that a particular action was ultra vires, the corporation will not be bound by it. However, the party who acted without authority may be. In such a case, the officer or director might be called upon to pay damages to either the corporation, the third party, or both.[22] For instance, when a contract is based on an ultra vires act, most jurisdictions rule that it is void.

The principle of ultra vires may also apply not only to actions that exceed corporate authority, but also to actions that are illegal or that violate public policy.[23]

Scenario 11–5. Excessive Interest Rates

RST Real Estate Corporation has recently opened a sideline venture: It is now advertising a service to make small term loans to consumers. The interest rate for these transactions, which is contained in small print on the last page of the loan documents, is 422 percent. Is RST's action ultra vires?

Answer: Yes. Even if there were no statutes regulating interest rates on short-term loans, such an arrangement would most likely be seen as void for public policy reasons.

 GETTING TO THE BASICS

"Ultra vires" refers to an action that is beyond the powers granted to the corporation, either through the articles of incorporation or by statute.

PIERCING THE CORPORATE VEIL

Another form of corporate liability lies in a court's power to disregard the corporate existence entirely and allow actions against shareholders and others who created or run the corporation. This is referred to as "**piercing the corporate veil**" and is a drastic remedy. After all, one of the most attractive features of a corporation is the fact that it is protected by limited liability. There are circumstances, however, where a court can terminate limited liability. Piercing the corporate veil is not an action that a court can take lightly. In fact, it runs counter to centuries of legal decisions that clearly state that a corporation is a separate legal entity and its owners are not legally responsible for debts or judgments against it.[24] In fact, appellate courts have ruled that the decision is one that can be made only on a case-by-case method and should be used with "reluctance and caution."[25]

piercing the corporate veil A rule that allows courts to disregard corporate protections and allow suits against corporate creators and shareholders.

KEY POINT

Piercing the corporate veil means that the corporate existence is considered null and void and the corporate owners are no longer protected by limited liability.

When a court determines that corporate existence should be ignored, it never does so for the benefit of the corporation or its shareholders. The only decision that would protect them would be a finding that the corporation should remain intact. Piercing the corporate veil is a judicial order that is invoked when the corporation has been set up as a sham or an artifice to shield shareholder assets.

Justification for Piercing the Corporate Veil

A court can disregard the existence of the corporation only in specific instances. A court can order that the corporation is no longer protected by limited liability when:

- the shareholders engaged in fraud in creating or maintaining the corporation.[26]
- the corporation is actively involved in criminal enterprises.
- the corporation was set up to evade specific laws, such as income tax rules and regulations or environmental regulations.[27]
- the shareholders created the corporation to divert funds for their personal use.[28]
- the corporation is an alter ego of its creators.

Although most of the grounds set out above to justify piercing the corporate veil are self-explanatory, the last one requires further discussion. A corporation that is the alter ego of its incorporators is one where the shareholders make no distinction between their personal assets and corporate assets. They routinely use corporate accounts for personal expenses, and the corporation has no separate existence. In this situation, a court might rule that the corporation is a sham, and it would be justified in a decision to pierce the corporate veil.

SHAREHOLDER DERIVATIVE ACTIONS

derivative suit A lawsuit brought by shareholders in the name of and on behalf of the corporation.

When shareholders wish to bring suit against their own corporation, they do so in a **derivative suit.** The action bears this name because the shareholders' right to bring the action derives from the powers granted to the corporation. In essence, shareholders claim that they are looking after the best interests of the corporation by bringing suit in its name against the officers or directors. The most common reason for a derivative suit is that shareholders are dissatisfied with the actions or policies of corporate management that have caused harm to the corporation. The first step in bringing such an action is to request that the corporation file the action on their behalf. Only when the corporation refuses are the shareholders allowed to proceed in the name of the business. In such cases, the corporation may need to hire outside counsel because of the potential conflicts of using corporate counsel. It raises far too many ethical issues to have the same attorneys who regularly advise the board of directors to then represent the shareholders in a derivative action against those same directors. See Exhibit 11–3.

PERSONAL LIABILITY OF OFFICER OR DIRECTOR

So far, our discussion has focused on the corporation's liability for certain actions. But do corporate officers and directors face personal liability for actions taken on behalf of the corporation? The answer is yes. When officers

Exhibit 11–3. Federal Rule of Civil Procedure 23.1. Derivative actions by shareholders

> In a derivative action brought by one or more shareholders or members to enforce a right of a corporation or of an unincorporated association, the corporation or association having failed to enforce a right which may properly be asserted by it, the complaint shall be verified and shall allege (1) that the plaintiff was a shareholder or member at the time of the transaction of which the plaintiff complains or that the plaintiff's share or membership thereafter devolved on the plaintiff by operation of law, and (2) that the action is not a collusive one to confer jurisdiction on a court of the United States which it would not otherwise have. The complaint shall also allege with particularity the efforts, if any, made by the plaintiff to obtain the action the plaintiff desires from the directors or comparable authority and, if necessary, from the shareholders or members, and the reasons for the plaintiff's failure to obtain the action or for not making the effort. The derivative action may not be maintained if it appears that the plaintiff does not fairly and adequately represent the interests of the shareholders or members similarly situated in enforcing the right of the corporation or association. The action shall not be dismissed or compromised without the approval of the court, and notice of the proposed dismissal or compromise shall be given to shareholders or members in such manner as the court directs.*

*Federal Rules of Civil Procedure Rule 23.1 (2006).

KEY POINT

A shareholder derivative suit is authorized only after the corporation refuses the shareholders' request to bring a civil action. Only then can they bring it themselves.

or directors take actions that are clearly beyond their power or authority, they can be personally liable for the losses sustained by the corporation. Courts can order them to pay for the loss out of personal funds.[29] If directors or officers use corporate funds for their own purposes, courts can order them to make full restitution to the corporation.[30]

On the other hand, if the directors and officers are acting within their authority and make bad business decisions, the business judgment rule may protect them. However, we have already seen that the business judgment rule was never designed to protect officers and directors who engage in criminal or tortuous acts. In those situations, they would also be personally liable for their actions. See Exhibit 11–4.

Exhibit 11–4. *SEC v. Credit Suisse First Boston*

U.S. Securities and Exchange Commission

UNITED STATES DISTRICT COURT
SOUTHERN DISTRICT OF NEW YORK

SECURITIES AND EXCHANGE COMMISSION,

Plaintiff,

-against-   Civil Action No.

CREDIT SUISSE FIRST BOSTON LLC, F/K/A
CREDIT SUISSE FIRST BOSTON CORPORATION,

Defendant.

FINAL JUDGMENT AS TO DEFENDANT
CREDIT SUISSE FIRST BOSTON LLC, F/K/A
CREDIT SUISSE FIRST BOSTON CORPORATION

Plaintiff Securities and Exchange Commission ("Commission") having filed a Complaint in this action ("Complaint") and Defendant Credit Suisse First Boston LLC, f/k/a Credit Suisse First Boston Corporation ("Defendant"), having (a) entered a general appearance, (b) consented to the Court's jurisdiction over Defendant and the subject matter of this action, (c) consented to entry of this Final Judgment without admitting or denying the allegations of the Complaint (except as to jurisdiction), (d) waived findings of fact and conclusions of law, and (e) waived any right to appeal from this Final Judgment; and the Commission having agreed that, on the basis of this Final Judgment, it will not institute a proceeding against Defendant pursuant to Sections 15(b), 15B, 15C, or 19(h) of the Securities Exchange Act of 1934 (the "Exchange Act"):

I.
Injunctive Relief

IT IS HEREBY ORDERED, ADJUDGED AND DECREED that:

A. Defendant, Defendant's officers, agents, servants, employees, attorneys, and all persons in active concert or participation with them who receive actual notice of this Final Judgment by personal service or otherwise are permanently restrained and enjoined from violating Section 15(c) of the Exchange Act and Rule 15c1-2 promulgated thereunder [15 U.S.C. §_78o (c) and 17 C.F.R. § 240.15c1-2] by making use of the mails or any means or instrumentality of interstate commerce to effect any transaction in, or to induce or attempt to induce the purchase or sale of, any security by means of any act, practice, or course of business which operates or would operate as a fraud or deceit upon any person.

CORPORATE CRIMINAL RESPONSIBILITY

All jurisdictions recognize that a corporation can be guilty of a crime.[31] However, by their very nature, corporations act through human agents, and it is the actions of these persons that make the corporation liable. In any investigation of corporate criminality, there are two approaches: the corporation and the individual corporate agents can both be prosecuted.[32] The general rule about corporate criminal liability is that the corporation is responsible for the actions of its directors, officers, and agents, if these persons are acting on behalf of the business. This is true even when the corporate charter did not specifically authorize the act, although there are some states that require management approval of the action before the corporation can be charged with the crime.[33] In those jurisdictions, the prosecution must show that the board of directors or officers approved of the illegal action.

In some instances, a corporation can be criminally responsible for the actions of its employees, even if the employees were acting for their own interests and not those of the corporation. Here the theory is that the corporate officers and directors should have discovered what was going on and put a stop to it. Examples of situations where a corporation is liable for actions of its employees acting on their own would be the following:

- use of corporate facilities to transport narcotics
- use of corporate buildings to conduct illegal gambling activities
- use of corporate accounts to launder money from criminal enterprises[34]

The reason that a corporation can be criminally liable, separate and distinct from the actions of its employees, officers, or directors, arises from the legal artifice that gives the corporation such sweeping powers in the first place. The corporation is an artificial person, and that status gives it not only the right to own property and pay taxes, but also the burden of facing criminal charges.[35]

CRIMINAL PENALTIES AGAINST CORPORATIONS

Prosecuting corporations carries some obvious limitations. For instance, there is no way to actually punish a corporation. The company cannot be incarcerated, and short of judicially dissolving the franchise, the only method left open to prosecutors and judges is to seek fines against the corporation. Various criminal statues also authorize seizure of some or all of the corporate assets.[36]

TORT LIABILITY AND CORPORATIONS

A tort is an action brought by one individual against another for negligence or intentional harm. The most common example of a tort action is a personal injury case where one person causes harm to another through negligence.

Personal injury car-wreck cases are some of the most common lawsuits in the United States. We have already seen that a corporation can be criminally liable, so it should come as no surprise to learn that a corporation can also be civilly liable under tort theory. Here again the corporation becomes liable through the actions of its directors, officers, or employees. When an employee commits a tort against another, both the employee and the corporation may be liable. If a corporation can be held criminally liable for the actions of its employees, then it should not be difficult to create a theory of civil liability for employees. But civil liability under these circumstances raises some interesting questions.

Why should a corporation be liable for the actions of its employees? If an employee is engaging in negligent actions, away from the direct supervision of his or her employers, why should the corporation bear the responsibility for his actions? The answer is found in the theory of respondeat superior.

RESPONDEAT SUPERIOR

respondeat superior (Latin) "let the master respond." A legal theory that imposes legal liability on an employer for the actions of the employee when the employee is carrying out his duties for the employer.

Respondeat superior is an ancient theory based on a premise that employers should be responsible for the actions carried out by their employee as long as the employee is acting within the scope of his or her employment. It is based on an original theory that made slaveholders liable for the actions of their slaves, but was later modified to include employers and employees.

Limitations of Respondeat Superior
A corporate employer is not liable for all actions carried out by an employee. For instance, if the employee is not on his job, there is no liability imputed to the corporation for the employee's actions. The employee must be acting within the scope of his or her employment. There are also other important limitations on the doctrine.

Frolic and Detour
When an employee is taking care of personal business, such as running an errand, respondeat superior does not apply. This is classified as frolic (conducting personal errands). Another exception to respondeat superior deals with detours. When an employee is on company business, but deviates from his job to go to some other place, he is on a detour, and the corporation will not be liable for any actions he carries out. Only when the employee returns to his business duties will his actions be imputed to the corporation. Consider Scenario 11–6.

> **Scenario 11–6. Respondeat Superior and Employee's Negligence**
> Ingrid is driving to work one day and stops at a red light. A large delivery van, emblazoned with the company logo "Cook's Cola" is in the same lane and fails to stop in time. The van rear-ends Ingrid, causing her severe injuries. The driver, Dan, is delivering cola to local stores, but over the last few weeks, he has opted for a different route. The traffic patterns around the city are such that he makes his last scheduled delivery first

and then backtracks from there. Does respondeat superior apply in this situation?

Answer: Yes, Ingrid can sue both Dan and Cook's Cola. She can sue Dan for negligence for failing to stop at the red light, and she can sue Cook's Cola because Dan is an employee and acting on behalf of the corporation. The fact that Dan has altered his route does not change the fact that, at the time of the wreck, he was on company business. His deviation from the planned route does not qualify as frolic or detour.

Independent Contractors

Respondeat superior also does not apply to independent contractors. An independent contractor is someone who makes his or her own decisions about what work to perform and how it should be carried out. Independent contractors have little or no supervision by the company; as a result, the corporation is not responsible for their actions.

Ethics File: Conflicts of Interest for Corporate Counsel

One of the most important ethical concerns in corporate law concerns conflicts of interest. Because corporate representation can involve interactions with so many different individuals, including shareholders, directors, and officers, it is sometimes a temptation for corporate counsel and corporate paralegals to forget where their professional duties lie. Attorneys and paralegals who represent corporations owe their duties first and foremost to the corporation, not the individuals within it. It is a conflict of interest for a legal professional to provide legal services for individuals against the corporate client. This could occur in situations where corporate officers seek advice about how best to shield their income, personal loans, accounting errors, and other questionable practices from shareholders.

Ethical concerns have become even more important with recent accounting and financial scandals at major corporations. Corporate officers have been prosecuted for defrauding their corporations. Public attitudes about corporations show that a vast majority distrust corporations and the individuals who work for them.

Section 307 of the Sarbanes-Oxley Act, found in 15 U.S.C. §7245, requires that the Securities and Exchange Commission must create minimum ethical standards for attorneys who practice before the SEC. These new requirements, in addition to the ethical rules already imposed on attorneys and paralegals through their professional associations, are all good reasons for legal professionals to know, understand, and strive to implement all ethical rules regarding corporate practice.[37]

CASE LAW: *The Limits of Ultra Vires*

Central New York Bridge Ass'n, Inc. v. American Contract Bridge League, Inc.[38]

The petitioners Central New York Bridge Association, Inc. (Central N.Y.) and Upper New York State Regional Conference, Inc. (Regional Conference) and the respondent American Contract Bridge League, Inc. (ACBL) are New York Not-For-Profit corporations. The petitioners, sibling organizations of the respondent, have brought a proceeding under Article 78, CPLR to set aside a resolution of the respondent's Board of Directors for being arbitrary, capricious and ultra vires. The respondent ACBL moves now for summary judgment.

(continued)

CASE LAW: *The Limits of Ultra Vires* (continued)

Since it was not raised as an issue, we shall not consider whether a decision of the Board of Directors of ACBL is a determination of a 'body or officer' which may be reviewed under Article 78 (but see 8 Weinstein-Korn-Miller, New York Civil Practice, par. 7802.01). The petitioners' argument seems to confuse ultra vires with arbitrariness and capriciousness by saying that, because an action is ultra vires, it must be arbitrary and capricious even though it otherwise would not be. Actually they are different types of invalid action.

In a claim of arbitrariness and capriciousness, which may be asserted through Article 78, the petitioners must make a factual showing that the Board of Directors has acted "contrary to natural justice" or 'inconsistent with' fair play." Otherwise they are 'bound by the decisions, interpretations, rules and laws of the national organization, and that in the absence of fraud or corruption the courts will not interfere in the internal affairs of membership corporations. Organizations have the right to govern themselves within the framework of their Constitutions.' The question for the court is simply and wholly whether the case was so bare of evidence to sustain the decision that no honest mind could reach the (same) conclusion . . .

Whether a corporation's actions are arbitrary and capricious or not, they may still be in excess of its granted powers, that is, ultra vires and this may be asserted in opposition to them (Not-For-Profit Corporation Law, s 203). Whether the assertion must be made by application for injunction, as the section would seem to indicate, or by Article 78 is beside the point here. Either way, without supportive facts to the contrary, a corporation's acts are presumed to be valid. ACBL, the parent organization, was formed to promote the playing of competitive bridge among its individual members and to provide them a ranking of their skill through a system of point awards at recognized tournaments. It operates through separately chartered 'Units' to which it assigns territorial juris-

diction, with each ACBL member belonging to the Unit within whose territory he resides.

The petitioner Central N.Y. is a chartered corporation composed of the ACBL members resident in the latter's Unit 112, a geographical section running north and south through the center of New York State. Its eastern boundary runs roughly from where the Delaware enters Sullivan County to where the St. Lawrence enters Franklin County. Its western boundary excludes the counties of Niagara, Erie, Chautauqua, Cattaraugus and Allegany. Its certificate of incorporation recognizes its subservience to ACBL's authority.

The respondent ACBL's bylaws provide for contiguous units being grouped into 'Districts,' each District to contain at least 4000 ACBL members, and each District to supply one representative who collectively constitute ACBL's Board of Directors. For some time past Unit 112 (Central N.Y.) has been a part of District 2, an area including most of the Province of Ontario and all of New York north of the Sullivan-Ulster-Columbia county line, excluding Chautauqua, Cattaraugus and Allegany counties.

Historically ACBL has encouraged inter-unit bridge tournaments (in fact they are necessary for advanced status as we shall see), and this prompted the formation of the petitioner Regional Conference. This corporation's members belong to ACBL and thus to some unit, either in or around Unit 112. It holds tournaments in and outside of Unit 112, specifically in Albany, Schenectady, Syracuse, Rochester, Binghamton and Buffalo. Such regional organizations as Regional Conference are recognized by ACBL's bylaws and Regional Conference's certificate of incorporation acknowledges the hegemony of ACBL.

To maintain equal representation on its Board of Directors, ACBL's bylaws require that every five years it must review and adjust the grouping of units into districts and, by extension, adjust the territorial jurisdiction of units, if that be necessary. Its Redistricting Committee commenced such a review in

1970, and, in July, 1971, presented a redistricting plan to the Board of Directors. The plan broke up old District 2 and, in doing so, divided old Unit 112.

The new plan made a new District 2 composed of units located wholly in Canada. Niagara and Erie counties, formerly in old District 2 but not in old Unit 112, were put in a new District 5. Monroe, Orleans, Genesee, Wyoming and Livingston counties were taken from old Unit 112 and were also put in new District 5. The balance of old Unit 112 remained intact and was put in a new District 4.

New District 5 was to consist of western New York, western Pennsylvania, eastern Ohio, northern West Virginia and the panhandle of Maryland. New District 4 would be composed of central New York from north to south, eastern Pennsylvania, southern New Jersey and all of Delaware.

Considering the huge size of the Province of Ontario compared with these small eastern states, we suspect that each of new Districts 4 and 5 is much smaller in area than old District 2. Certainly the new districts are more equitably proportioned in ACBL memberships, even though the new Canadian districts may not reach the average size. But the petitioners were not happy with the new deal, and with some underlying justification. The redistricting made them remote in their district from the center of bridge activity, which will now be located in Pittsburgh in new District 5 and Philadelphia in new District 4. In old District 2, they were in the center of activity, the Buffalo-Rochester-Syracuse-Albany axis.

The Court tends to sympathize with the petitioners because we have seen other reapportionments made from map outlines which ignore historic traffic-flow patterns. The petitioners argue with considerable persuasion that in their area customary travel is east and west, not north and south. (We can imagine, though, that for years the Toronto and Ottawa members of old District 2 were making the same argument in vain.) But justifiable unhappiness with a given result is not to say that it is contrary to natural justice, inconsistent with fair play, fraudulent or corrupt.

When the redistricting plan was presented to ACBL's Board of Directors, the petitioner Central

N.Y. did not throw in its hand and concede the game. It voiced its dissatisfaction by having its representative, one of its officers who is a New York attorney, appear and object in detail. He asked that old Unit 112 be kept whole, and, if not put in a district entirely within New York State, that it be put in new District 5. The Board of Directors considered the objections, overrode them, adopted the Redistricting Committee's plan, but made a concession by adding that the new plan would not affect the petitioner Regional Conference's tournaments nor the validity of points that could be won at them.

Central N.Y., now joined by Regional Conference, pressed its objections and to hear them, ACBL, according to its procedure for such matters, convened as Administrative Board of Review. After a hearing on January 22, 1972, the objectors and the Review Board agreed: that the Review Board would recommend to the ACBL Board of Directors at its next meeting, which would commence on March 13th, that old Unit 112 should remain intact and be put in new District 4 (not 5); that the objectors would present this recommendation for their members' approval on February 14th, and report their decision as soon after that as possible.

The ACBL Board of Directors commenced its meeting on March 13th with no word from Central N.Y. and Regional Conference. On March 14th, still no one had heard, and so the Review Board made its recommendation anyway. Despite the recommendation (or perhaps because the Board of Directors had not heard any approval of it from the petitioners) the Board, on March 14th, reaffirmed its approval of the redistricting plan, again with the saving clause for Regional Conference's tournaments.

Following this the petitioners commenced the Article 78 proceeding by show cause order of this Court which stayed the respondent ACBL from carrying out its redistricting plan pending resolution of the controversy. Some of the petitioners' trump were finessed, however, by the action of the respondent's Board of Directors at its 1972 summer meeting. There it rescinded its splitting of old Unit 112 and adopted the recommendation of the Board of Review that it be

(continued)

CASE LAW: *The Limits of Ultra Vires* (continued)

placed in its entirety in District 4, this to take effect if and when the Court's stay is lifted. With that done, the respondent brought on this motion for summary judgment to dismiss the proceeding.

The relief they have been given by ACBL is not the relief the petitioners want. True they have been kept intact, but they also seek to be put in an all-New York District or in new District 5. The reasons they feel that ACBL has treated them in an arbitrary, capricious and ultra vires manner, are alleged in their petition.

There is one more complaint: that the redistricting plan, as it affects the petitioners, was motivated solely by the desire of ACBL to put Canadian units in all-Canadian districts; that ACBL's sanctioning even Canadian units, to say nothing of Canadian districts, is ultra vires beyond ACBL's authority. In short, the petitioners assert that ACBL is authorized to act only in the United States of America.

The reasoning behind this complaint is disclosed by the linked allegation that, if ACBL had not been motivated to segregate the Canadian units, Unit 112 could then have been placed in an all-New York district and failure of the ACBL to do this was arbitrary and unreasonable. There are no facts supplied to support this leap in logic.

Let us assume that ACBL was not motivated to segregate the Canadian units and the petitioners are correct that their sanctioning is ultra vires. The petitioners have not shown that the result would have been any different than what it is that Unit 112 would go either into District 4 or District 5, neither of them all-New York. Trying it the other way and assuming that ACBL was not motivated to segregate the Canadian units and their sanctioning is not ultra vires—the petitioners have not shown that they would still not be in old District 2. That was not all-New York but included most of the Province of Ontario. So, to say that, if ACBL had not been motivated to segregate the Canadian units, it would have put Unit 112 in an all-New York district, is an unwarranted con-

clusion. To say that it could have, is only to state a possibility, a frustrated desire. Absent facts, it does not condemn the contrary as arbitrary or unreasonable, especially since both petitioners acknowledge ACBL's authority over territorial jurisdictions, and ACBL was acting to accomplish a proper corporate purpose, proportionate representation on its Board of Directors.

The ultra vires complaint, then, no matter how it is resolved, cannot give the petitioners an all-New York district, nor even restore old District 2. Nonetheless, we see no reason why members of a corporation, with nothing personally at stake, cannot protest their corporation's acts as being ultra vires solely for an altruistic reason, simply because they do not want their corporation to act extra-legally.

The petitioners claim that ACBL's sanctioning of Canadian units is ultra vires because its certificate of incorporation declares it to be a 'national organization' whose relationship internationally is only to 'cooperate with other bodies of similar character in other countries for mutual legislation and the conduct and government of international competitions.' There is no doubt that ACBL has indulged for years in substantial corporate action in Canada (and also in Mexico and the Bermudas; see In re Stone v. American Contract Bridge League, New York Law Journal, March 6, 1959, p. 13, col. 1). But the question is to be determined, not by an estoppel of history, but by the statutes, certificate and bylaws.

The enabling statute does not restrict New York Not-For-Profit corporations to operating in New York or in the United States. Rather, it permits one '(t)o conduct the activities of the corporation and have offices and exercise the powers granted by this chapter in any jurisdiction within or without the United States' (Not-For-Profit Corporation Law, s 202, subd. (a), par. (11)).

Looking at the certificate, we notice first that the corporation is not the United States Contract Bridge League but the American Contract Bridge League.

Surely the petitioners are not among those provincialists who would exclude every country in the western hemisphere from being American except the United States.

ACBL's bylaws make membership open to all without restriction of country of residence or citizenship and they are likewise free of any language which would suggest that its operations were confined to the United States. In consequence we find that there is nothing in the statutes, certificate of incorporation or ACBL's bylaws which would forbid the exercise of the Board of Directors' power to sanction Canadian units or districts.

We must conclude: that there has been no showing that ACBL has acted contrary to natural justice, inconsistent with fair play, fraudulently or corruptly; that its actions were within the framework of its constitution; that this Court cannot interfere with its internal management.

The Article 78 proceeding presents no issue of fact. Summary judgment dismissing it and lifting the stay order must be granted.

CASE QUESTIONS

1. According to this case, how are claims of arbitrariness and capriciousness different from claims of ulta vires actions?

2. What presumption guides the courts when it considers the actions of a corporation?

3. What provisions in ACBL's bylaws guarantee equal representation on its board of directors?

4. Why were the petitioners objecting to the redistricting plan?

5. Does the enabling statute restrict not-for-profit corporations from operating outside the state?

SUMMARY

Because corporations are artificial persons, they not only benefit from many of the same rights that natural persons have, but they also face the same types of obligations. The corporation can be both civilly and criminally liable. Corporate officers and directors can also be personally liable for the decisions that they make on behalf of the corporation. However, there are limits to the extent of civil liability when it comes to officers and directors. For example, the business judgment rule was created specifically to insulate officers and directors from civil actions by shareholders or others when these individuals make business decisions in good faith. When a corporation carries out an action that is not authorized by the corporate charter or by state law, the action is said to be ultra vires. Such actions are void and can result in personal liability for the individuals who carry them out. Shareholders who wish to enforce rights or protect the corporation are entitled to bring shareholder derivative suits against corporate officers and directors. A corporation can also be criminally liable. It is possible to prosecute a corporation for a crime; however, the only possible sanction that can be brought against the corporation is to assess it with a fine. Corporate officers and directors, on the other hand, can be both fined and imprisoned for their criminal actions. Corporations can also be liable under tort law for the actions carried out by employees or others on the corporation's behalf.

HELPFUL WEB SITES

Corporate Law Basics
http://www.legal-database.com/corporationlaw.htm

Investor Words
www.investorwords.com

Legal Definitions
www.legaldefinitions.com

Find Law (numerous articles on business judgment rule and shareholder derivative suits)
www.findlaw.com/casecode/index.html

Securities and Exchange Commission
http://www.sec.gov/

KEY TERMS

business judgment rule	respondeat superior
derivative suit	Sarbanes-Oxley Act
indemnify	standing
piercing the corporate veil	ultra vires

APPLYING CHAPTER CONCEPTS

Locate examples of criminal actions brought against corporations. What were the allegations? How was the corporation tried? What was the verdict? If applicable, how was the corporation punished?

REVIEW QUESTIONS

1. Why is a corporation liable to be sued in its own right?
2. How can corporate officers and directors become personally liable in their corporate duties?
3. What is the business judgment rule?
4. Provide two arguments for the business judgment rule.
5. What is the four-prong test of the business judgment rule?
6. When does a corporate officer's reliance on others shield the officer from liability?
7. What are some of the limitations of the business judgment rule?

8. What are ultra vires actions?

9. What are the legal consequences of entering into an ultra vires contract?

10. Explain the concept of piercing the corporate veil.

11. When and under what circumstances can a corporation be guilty of a crime?

12. What type of criminal penalties can be brought against a corporation?

13. Can a corporation be liable in a tort action? Explain.

14. What is the doctrine of respondeat superior, and how does it apply to corporations?

15. What are "frolic" and "detour" as they apply to respondeat superior?

16. How does respondeat superior affect independent contractors?

17. What are shareholder derivative actions?

18. What are some of the ethical concerns faced by corporate counsel?

QUESTIONS FOR REFLECTION

1. Should the rules for piercing the corporate veil be more lenient or more stringent? Justify your answer.

2. Do you think that Sarbanes-Oxley will help improve the public's attitude towards corporations? Explain.

ENDNOTES

[1]*Fausett v. American Resources Management Corp.*, 542 F. Supp. 1234 (D. Utah 1982).

[2]*Stamp v. Touche Ross & Co.*, 263 Ill. App. 3d 1010, 201 Ill. Dec. 184, 636 N.E.2d 616 (1st Dist. 1993).

[3]*Great Rivers Co-op. of Southeastern Iowa v. Farmland Industries, Inc.*, 198 F.3d 685, 45 Fed. R. Serv. 3d 833 (8th Cir. 1999).

[4]*Stern v. Lucy Webb Hayes Nat. Training School for Deaconesses and Missionaries*, 381 F. Supp. 1003 (D.D.C. 1974).

[5]*Wilshire Oil Co. of Tex. v. Riffe*, 409 F.2d 1277, 37 A.L.R.3d 1341 (10th Cir. 1969).

[6]*Ashby v. Peters*, 128 Neb. 338, 258 N.W. 639, 99 A.L.R. 843 (1935).

[7]*Weidner v. Engelhart*, 176 N.W.2d 509 (N.D. 1970).

[8]*Pace v. Jordan*, 999 S.W.2d 615 (Tex. App. Houston 1st Dist. 1999).

[9]*United Artists Theatre Co. v. Walton*, 315 F.3d 217 (3d Cir. 2003).

[10]*Solar-West, Inc. v. Falk*, 141 Ariz. 414, 687 P.2d 939 (Ct. App. Div. 2 1984).

[11]*Cookies Food Products, Inc., by Rowedder v. Lakes Warehouse Distributing, Inc.,* 430 N.W.2d 447 (Iowa 1988).

[12]*Simon Property Group, Inc. v. Taubman Centers, Inc.,* 261 F. Supp. 2d 919 (E.D. Mich. 2003).

[13]*Reget v. Paige,* 242 Wis. 2d 278, 2001 WI. App. 73, 626 N.W.2d 302 (Ct. App. 2001).

[14]*Resolution Trust Corp. v. Acton,* 844 F. Supp. 307 (N.D. Tex. 1994), aff'd, 49 F.3d 1086 (5th Cir. Texas 1995).

[15]*Cornell v. Seddinger,* 237 Pa. 389, 85 A. 446 (1912).

[16]*Faw, Casson & Co. v. Everngam,* 616 A.2d 426, 436, 94 Md. App. 129, 150 (1992).

[17]*Bank One, Arizona v. Rouse,* 181 Ariz. 36, 887 P.2d 566 Ariz. App. Div. 1 (1994).

[18]*Sammis v. Stafford,* 48 Cal. App. 4th 1935, 56 Cal. Rptr. 2d 589 (4th Dist. 1996).

[19]*Shapiro v. Greenfield,* 136 Md. App. 1, 764 A.2d 270 (2000).

[20]407 So.2d 15 (La. App. 1981).

[21]*Vermont Dept. of Public Service v. Massachusetts Mun. Wholesale Elec. Co.,* 151 Vt. 73, 558 A.2d 215 (1988).

[22]*Greenbelt Homes, Inc. v. Nyman Realty, Inc.,* 48 Md. App. 42, 426 A.2d 394 (1981).

[23]*Staacke v. Routledge,* 111 Tex. 489, 241 S.W. 994 (1922).

[24]*Morris v. N.Y.S. Dep't. of Taxation & Fin.,* 82 N.Y. 2d 135, 623 N.E. 2d 1157 (1993).

[25]*C.M. Corp. v. Oberer Development Co.,* 631 F.2d 536 (1980).

[26]*Dole Food Co. v. Patrickson,* 538 U.S. 468, 123 S.Ct 1655 (2003).

[27]*Dept. of Environmental Protection v. Ventron Corp.,* 94 N.J. 473 468 A.2d 150 (1983).

[28]*U.S. v. Van Diviner,* 822 F.2d 960 (1987).

[29]*Commercial Fire Ins. Co. v. Board of Revenue,* 99 Ala. 1, 14 S. 490 (1892).

[30]*Garner v. First Nat. City Bank,* 465 F.Supp. 372 (1979).

[31]*State v. CECOS Intern. Inc.,* 38 3d 120, 526 N.E. 2d 807 (1988).

[32]*U.S. v. Cincotta,* 689 F. 2d 238 (1st Cir. 1982).

[33]*U.S. v. Bi-Co Pavers, Inc.,* 741 F. 2d 730 (5th Cir. 1984); *Morris v. Ameritech Illinois,* 337 Ill. App. 3d. 40, 785 N.E.2d 62 (2003).

[34]*Huffman v. Poore,* 6 Neb. App. 43, 569 N.W. 2d 549 (1997).

[35]*Commonwealth v. J.P. Mascaro & Sons, Inc.*, 266 Pa. 402, A.2d 1050 (1979).

[36]*State v. Compassionate Home Care, Inc.*, 354 N.W. 2d. 17 (Minn. 1984).

[37]*In re Implementation of Standards of Professional Conduct for Attorneys*, 2003 WL 193527, 1; 17 Geo. J. Legal Ethics 715.

[38]72 Misc. 2d 271, 339 N.Y.S.2d 438 (Supp. 1972).

Chapter 12

TERMINATING CORPORATE EXISTENCE

Chapter Objectives

Upon completion of this chapter, you should be able to:

- Explain the significance of corporate dissolution and termination.
- Describe the process involved in administrative dissolution of a corporation.
- Explain the role that majority shareholders play in the voluntary dissolution of a corporation.
- Define the significance of winding up of corporate affairs.
- Describe the factors that can contribute to the decision to dissolve a corporation.

▶ INTRODUCTION

In this chapter we will examine the issues surrounding the dissolution of a corporation. Businesses terminate for a wide variety of reasons, but when a corporation seeks to end its legal existence, there are special rules that must be complied with. It should be no surprise to learn that, as with every other phase of corporate life, statutes control the final phase of a corporation's existence.

▶ PERPETUAL EXISTENCE OF CORPORATIONS

In previous chapters we saw that a corporation has perpetual existence. In most situations, corporations do not exist for a set time period. Instead, corporations can exist for centuries, long outliving the individuals who created them. However, simply because a corporation can last forever does not necessarily mean that it will. There are numerous reasons why a corporation would terminate. The corporation might go bankrupt, or the officers and shareholders might reach a consensus that the corporate structure no longer serves a useful purpose. A corporation might also be judicially dissolved. When the corporation does cease to exist, the corporate charter, the articles of incorporation, and any other document related to the corporation's existence cease to have any legal significance.[1]

 ## GETTING TO THE BASICS

Unless otherwise stated, corporations have perpetual existence.

Termination, or dissolution, of a corporation can be a complicated affair. Unlike some of the simpler business models we discussed at the beginning of this book, terminating a corporation involves several distinct steps, all of which are controlled by state statutes. Even after the corporation has been dissolved, there is an additional time period in which any claims for or against the corporation can be resolved. However, before we can address the issue of what corporate dissolution is, we must first examine what it is not.

Corporations do not cease to exist simply because the company is no longer carrying out a particular business. As we have seen in previous chapters, corporations are artificial persons, and they have the freedom to change the direction of their business ventures or even to temporarily suspend their activities. None of these decisions results in an automatic dissolution of a corporation. The law allows for the possibility that the corporation's business may resume at some point in the future. During temporary suspensions of business activities, the corporation continues to enjoy a legal existence.

A corporation also does not cease to exist on the death of individual corporate shareholders. The death of shareholders, officers, or directors has no effect on the continued existence of the corporate entity. In fact, this is one of the most attractive features of a corporate business structure. The corporation may continue even when the natural persons who created it have died. However, there are some important exceptions to this rule. Professional corporations, for example, who are bereft of any member legally qualified to practice the profession must be dissolved. In most circumstances, however, corporations continue to exist no matter what members of the company have died.

When a shareholder dies, his or her shares pass through normal probate procedures. Stock can be left to specific individuals as a bequest in a will, and it can also be distributed when a shareholder dies intestate (without a will). The corporation does not dissolve even when all of its officers have died and the corporation is insolvent. Corporations with no money and no assets are still legally recognized as corporations. Even when a corporation files for bankruptcy protection, it does not mean that the corporation is terminated. Instead, the corporation continues to exist until state statutes have been complied with that officially dissolve the corporation.[2] These rules apply to all types of corporations, large or small. Consider Scenario 12–1.

Scenario 12–1. Dissolution of a Small Corporation

FGE, Inc., is a small, closely held corporation. All of the shareholders, directors, and officers come from the same family. After a family meeting, they decide to dissolve the corporation and simply divide up the assets. Is there any requirement that this corporation must go through the same statutory dissolution process as a large corporation?

Answer: Yes. The rules apply to all corporations, large or small. Simply because the corporation is closely held does not excuse it from following applicable state law.[3]

KEY POINT

A corporation is not dissolved by the death of shareholders, or even a complete change in ownership. One hundred percent transfer of all shares to other individuals has no effect on the existence of the corporation.

◗ DISSOLVING A CORPORATION

Now that we have seen what events do not result in a termination of corporate existence, we will examine exactly how a corporation is dissolved. When we use the term "dissolution" to describe the process of terminating the corporation, we are not talking about something as simple as turning a switch. Dissolving a corporation can take months or even years. The first step is usually the filing of articles of dissolution, but even after this document is a matter of public record, there may be a lengthy period of winding up corporate affairs before corporate existence is finally terminated. During this time, all of the corporation's assets will be distributed to creditors and shareholders.[4] Like every other phase of corporate existence, state statutes provide the framework for dissolution.

Among the methods that can be employed to dissolve a corporation are:

- voluntary dissolution
- dissolution by specific terms in the articles of incorporation
- administrative dissolution
- judicial dissolution

VOLUNTARY DISSOLUTION

There is nothing prohibiting the corporation's owners from deciding to terminate the corporation. This decision might be reached for any of a number of reasons. Corporate assets may have increased in value to such a degree that the corporation's property is worth more than the revenue generated by the business. Commerce may have changed, and a formerly thriving business might easily contract to such a point that the shareholders realize that the company will not recover. In any event, the shareholders have the right to vote to dissolve the corporation and divide up the assets among themselves. see Exhibit 12–1.

Exhibit 12–1. Authorization of dissolution

> (a) A corporation may be dissolved under this article. Such dissolution shall be authorized at a meeting of shareholders by (i) for corporations the certificate of incorporation of which expressly provides such or corporations incorporated after the effective date of paragraph (b) of this section, a majority of the votes of all outstanding shares entitled to vote thereon or (ii) for other corporations, two-thirds of the votes of all outstanding shares entitled to vote thereon, except, in either case, as otherwise provided under section 1002 (Dissolution under provision in certificate of incorporation).
>
> (b) Any corporation may adopt an amendment of the certificate of incorporation providing that such dissolution shall be authorized at a meeting of shareholders by a specified proportion of votes of all outstanding shares entitled to vote thereon, provided that such proportion may not be less than a majority.*

N.Y. Corporate Law § 1001 (McKinney, 2006).

 GETTING TO THE BASICS

Shareholders must agree, usually by simple majority vote, to dissolve the corporation.

Numerous elements are involved in voluntarily dissolving a corporation. Although these steps can vary from state to state, in general the following steps must take place to satisfy state statutes:

- Shareholders agree to dissolve the corporation.
- Creditors are notified.

- Outstanding debts are paid from corporate assets.
- Remaining assets are distributed to the shareholders.
- The corporation submits articles of dissolution (certificate of dissolution) to the state secretary of state's office.[5]

Shareholders Agree to Dissolve the Corporation

Before a corporation can be voluntarily dissolved, the shareholders must agree. The board of directors does not have the power to initiate a **liquidation** of the corporation; only the shareholders can approve such an action. Most states provide that a minimum percentage of the shareholders must agree before the action can be taken. For instance, some states require a two-third majority vote for dissolution before the process can begin. Other states allow a simple majority. However, the right to dissolve the corporation rests with the shareholders because they are the owners of the corporation and are entitled to vote on business matters, including terminating corporate existence.[6] When one person is the majority shareholder, he or she can initiate a corporate dissolution without the need for any other shareholders to agree.[7]

When dealing with voluntary dissolution, the majority rules. As long as the majority shareholders act in accordance with state law, they can dissolve the corporation over the protests of the minority stockholders. This does not mean, however, that the rights of the minority shareholders can be overlooked. They continue to have voting rights and rights to corporate assets, even though they have objected to the dissolution of the corporation in the first place. There is no authorization for a **freeze out** of minority shareholders.

Once the majority has made the decision to dissolve the corporation, there is very little that minority stockholders can do about it. Courts, for instance, are traditionally reluctant to become involved in a legal battle between majority and minority shareholders and routinely refuse to interfere in corporate proceedings, absent a showing that the majority is not acting in good faith, is ignoring minority stockholder rights, or is engaging in fraud. Courts will not interfere with a voluntary dissolution even when the motives of the majority are questionable. Consider Scenario 12–2.

> ### Scenario 12–2. Rights of minority shareholders
>
> Gordon Glutton is in the business of buying stock in a company until he amasses a majority interest and then votes to dissolve the corporation. He has become rich by liquidating the assets of dozens of corporations. When he buys a majority of shares in FGH Corporation, minority shareholders file suit, asking the court to bar Gordon from any action to dissolve the corporation. Although they will gain financially by his actions, they want the corporation to continue in existence. Will their suit be successful?
>
> **Answer:** No. Gordon's motives are irrelevant. As long as he abides by state law and does not disregard the rights of minority stockholders, he is free to use his majority interest to initiate dissolution of the corporation.[8]

The other side of majority rule is that minority shareholders cannot vote to dissolve the corporation over the wishes of the majority. If they disagree

liquidation The selling off of assets and distribution of the cash obtained.

freeze out The process of dissolving a business over the objection and to the detriment of the rights of minority stockholders.

with the way that the corporation is being run, they can vote for new members on the board of directors, but they cannot force the majority to dissolve the corporation. There are some exceptions to this general rule.

KEY POINT

A minority of shareholders cannot vote to voluntarily dissolve a corporation; only a majority can take such an action.

Minority stockholders can bring suit and request a court to dissolve a corporation, but only in limited circumstances. Examples of situations that would qualify for such a ruling include:

- corporate insolvency
- corporate mismanagement
- fraud
- shareholder deadlock
- failure of corporate purpose

Failure of Corporate Purpose

Although the situations set out in the previous paragraph are self-explanatory, the last one, failure of corporate purpose, deserves some further attention. An example of a corporation that is unable to fulfill its purpose is one that was established to do business with a foreign government and then war is declared between the two countries. In such a situation, the original purpose for the creation of the corporation has been frustrated. Another example is that a corporation is created with a specific business purpose in mind and then that business proves to be impossible to conduct. Consider Scenario 12–3.

Scenario 12–3. Fulfillment of Purpose

Actress Annette Biting entered into a contract last year with Binge Productions to license her name to promote Binge's product line. Later, Ms. Biting formed a corporation called Biting Binge, Inc., which had an exclusive contract with Binge. Ms. Biting was a minority stockholder in this corporation. After some harsh words between Ms. Biting and Harold Binge, of Binge Productions, Ms. Biting severed all business dealings with Binge Productions. Now, she has filed suit to have the corporation dissolved. She alleges that because there is no longer any contract with Binge, Biting Binge, Inc. can no longer fulfill its purpose and should be dissolved. Is this grounds for a court to order that the corporation should be dissolved?

Answer: Yes. Because there is no contract between Binge Productions and Ms. Biting, and because the corporation was specifically designed to implement this agreement, there is no possibility of conducting any further business. Therefore, the corporation can be dissolved.[9]

Notification of Creditors

When a corporation is considering dissolution, it must notify its creditors of its intention. This notification provides the creditors with the opportunity to file any claims and pursue payment on any outstanding debts, judgments, bills, or other encumbrances. Notice is usually given in the form of a legal classified ad in the local newspaper. For details of notice required under the law, see Exhibit 12–2.

Exhibit 12–2. Notice to creditors; filing or barring claims

(a) At any time after dissolution, the corporation may give a notice requiring all creditors and claimants, including any with unliquidated or contingent claims and any with whom the corporation has unfulfilled contracts, to present their claims in writing and in detail at a specified place and by a specified day, which shall not be less than six months after the first publication of such notice. Such notice shall be published at least once a week for two successive weeks in a newspaper of general circulation in the county in which the office of the corporation was located at the date of dissolution. On or before the date of the first publication of such notice, the corporation shall mail a copy thereof, postage prepaid and addressed to his last known address, to each person believed to be a creditor of or claimant against the corporation whose name and address are known to or can with due diligence be ascertained by the corporation. The giving of such notice shall not constitute a recognition that any person is a proper creditor or claimant, and shall not revive or make valid, or operate as a recognition of the validity of, or a waiver of any defense or counterclaim in respect of any claim against the corporation, its assets, directors, officers or shareholders, which has been barred by any statute of limitations or become invalid by any cause, or in respect of which the corporation, its directors, officers or shareholders, has any defense or counterclaim.*

*N.Y. Corporation Law § 1001 (McKinney, 2006).

 GETTING TO THE BASICS

Creditors must be notified of a corporation's plans to dissolve.

CASE LAW: *When Can Shareholders Voluntarily Dissolve a Corporation?*

Ovadia v. Abdullah[10]
WOODS (A. M.), P. J.

This appeal is from a judgment that required Anwar Abdullah and Jamil Abdullah (Anwar, Jamil or appellants) to sell their stock in West Coast Laboratories, Inc., a family-owned corporation, back to the corporation pursuant to the provisions of Corporations Code section 2000. Respondents are appellants' brothers, Maurice Ovadia and Naim Abdullah (Maurice, Naim or respondents), who initiated proceedings under section 2000.

West Coast Laboratories, Inc., (West Coast) is a pharmaceutical manufacturing company begun in 1967 by the parties, each of whom held 25 percent of the corporation's stock. Without here relating the various charges and countercharges that the parties have levied at each other, suffice it to say that relations between the brothers were not harmonious.

On September 12, 1991, respondents filed a petition to avoid voluntary dissolution of West Coast under section 2000. In the unverified petition, respondents alleged that "at a series of meetings . . . Anwar Abdullah and Jamil Abdullah Shad stated that their shares were being voted either to sell the Corporation to a third person, and not to respondents, or to dissolve the Corporation." In support of this allegation, respondents submitted the declaration of their attorney and their own declarations. In his declaration, their attorney stated that he was asked by respondents "to consult with them concerning the decision of their brothers, . . . , to vote their 50% ownership interest in West Coast Laboratories, Inc. in favor of dissolving and winding up the corporation." He also stated he discussed the matter with appellants' attorney with respect to obtaining an appraisal of appellants' stock.

Maurice's declaration stated: ". . . Naim and I realized it was impossible to continue to work as before because our relationship with appellants had deteriorated considerably. Naim and I called a meeting for

the four of us, and Naim and I offered Jamil and Anwar the following: Either they buy our shares from us after an appraisal or we buy their shares from them after an appraisal, or we sell the whole company to a third party.

Jamil and Anwar replied that they agree to sell the company to a third party providing that neither me nor Naim would remain working for the buyer, even if it was on a consulting basis and for a short time. Naim and I told Jamil and Anwar that it would be difficult to find a buyer who would accept these terms. Anwar and Jamil then said they want the assets of the company to be sold and money or left-over assets divided among the four of us and then everyone goes his own way."

Along with the petition, appellants' filed a motion for appointment of appraisers to ascertain the fair value of the corporate shares.

On March 9, 1992, appellants moved to strike the petition asserting that a suit for a voluntary or involuntary dissolution was not pending. They also filed an opposition to respondents' motion for appointment of appraisers on the same ground.

In their reply, respondents submitted the further declaration of their attorney who stated that he had been negotiating with appellants' counsel who had "assured" him that appellants "want to dissolve the corporation and take their one-half share of the proceeds."

Appellants' counsel promptly filed a declaration denying this statement and characterizing it as "false." He submitted correspondence with respondents' counsel to show that "there has never been a vote for dissolution of any kind."

At the hearing on the petition and the motion, appellants' counsel, in response to the court's asking why it should not appoint an appraiser, said, "Because there is no proceeding for a voluntary dissolution made by the appellants. Under 601A and under 601F there has to be a written notice of the meeting, and under 601F, if there is no such meeting, if there is no such written notice, your Honor-

"The Court: So, are you telling me-

"Mr. Grunfeld:-or written waiver, it invalidates the shareholders meeting.

"The Court: Are you telling me, counsel, that everything's fine with this corporation?

"Mr. Grunfeld: No, your Honor, I am not.

"The Court: And that there's no possible dissolution of this corporation, and that everything, and nobody's attempting to buy out the other side?

"Mr. Grunfeld: Your Honor, there are clearly negotiations going on, or which have gone on, between and among the brothers. That is not tantamount to a voluntary dissolution proceeding being filed by these respondents. As I started to say, your Honor, under 601A, under 601F, a failure to have a written notice or the failure to have a written waiver specifically invalidates any action taken at a meeting of the shareholders; even if there were one that ever took place. We contend that there is not."

At a later point in the hearing, the court asked appellants' counsel: "So there is a dispute, then?"

"Mr. Grunfeld: Disputes are not tantamount to a voluntary proceeding for dissolution which is the issue here as to whether there is a proceeding under 2000.

"The Court: Well, let's see what the Court of Appeals [*sic*] says, if you feel it's necessary."

The court granted the petition and appointed the appraisers. Respondents were instructed to prepare the order.

On March 23, 1992, respondents filed their opposition to appellants' motion to strike the petition. They argued that a voluntary proceeding for dissolution had been proven by their declarations regarding appellants' statements that they wanted to sell the company, divide the assets and each go his separate way. Further, respondents asserted that West Coast was a small company, "run informally," and thus the meetings referred to in their declarations were sufficient to satisfy the procedural requirements.

On March 26, 1992, appellants filed a motion for reconsideration of the order granting the petition and appointing appraisers, or, in the alternative, for a new trial. In connection with this motion, both appellants filed declarations. Regarding respondents' claim that at an informal meeting appellants had voted to dissolve the corporation, Jamil declared: "While there were discussions between the brothers, there were never any formal meetings. I never received notice of any such meetings, never signed a unanimous written consent to any conduct of action at those meetings, and never attended a meeting where either my brother Anwar or myself requested or demanded that the corporation be voluntarily dissolved. The accusation that Anwar and I decided to dissolve the company is absolutely false."

Anwar's declaration made the same point: ". . . I was never accorded any notice of any meetings of shareholders or directors in 1990 and 1991 where Jamil or myself requested a corporate dissolution. Similarly, I never signed any written consent to such action by shareholders. Finally, neither my brother Jamil nor myself ever requested or demanded that the corporation be voluntarily dissolved."

The three court-appointed appraisers concluded that West Coast was worth $1.6 million. On July 30, 1992, respondents filed a petition to confirm the award. On August 4, 1992, appellants responded by filing an at-issue memorandum for a trial on the issue of whether dissolution proceedings were pending. On August 19, 1992, they filed their opposition to the petition to confirm the award in which they demanded an evidentiary hearing on whether a voluntary dissolution had occurred.

The petition was set for August 26, 1992. The hearing was continued to September 18, 1992, because the parties had apparently reached an agreement to settle the case. The following day, however, respondents withdrew from the agreement.

On September 18, 1992, the court granted the petition to confirm the award permitting respondents 30 days within which to purchase appellants' stock for $800,000. The court denied appellants' request for an evidentiary hearing. Appellants' counsel raised

(continued)

CASE LAW: *When Can Shareholders Voluntarily Dissolve a Corporation?* (continued)

the issue of whether a dissolution had occurred. Ultimately, the court stated: "It says to me that no matter what happens, there's no settlement, no agreement, and there never will be. Therefore, this court is being forced into a situation where it must rule, and it is willing to do so, and it has ruled. Tentative stands."

On October 16, 1992, appellants filed their notice of appeal. We reverse.

I

In our review of the record in this case, it is clear that the trial judge, faced with the seemingly intractable conflict between the parties, attempted to fashion a fair and workable solution. While we commend him for his efforts, we must reverse the judgment on the grounds that the purported voluntary dissolution of West Coast, which set these proceedings in motion, was procedurally invalid and not supported by the evidence.

"There is no independent right on the part of one or more stockholders in a corporation to compel the sale to them of the shares of stock of another." (*Cubalevic v. Superior Court* (1966) 240 Cal.App.2d 557, 562 .) *Cubalevic* was decided under the predecessor statute to section 2000. The reviewing court issued a writ to prohibit the superior court from proceeding with a hearing to determine the fair cash value of stock in a corporation on a cross-complaint to stay the involuntary dissolution of the corporation where the complaint to dissolve it had been dismissed. "There being no such independent right to compel the sale of stock it must follow that there could be no cause of action stated to compel such a sale whether by way of cross-complaint or counter-claim which would survive after dismissal of the action for involuntary dissolution of the corporation in which the remedy of purchase is given."

By parity of reasoning, there can be no action under section 2000 to avoid the *voluntary* dissolution of

a corporation through purchase of the initiating shareholders' stock unless they have, in fact, initiated a voluntary dissolution. Whether this has happened is both a question of procedure and a question of fact.

Section 1900, subdivision (a) provides: "Any corporation may elect voluntarily to wind up and dissolve by the vote of shareholders holding shares representing 50 percent or more of the voting power." (§ 1900, subd. (a).) Under section 1903, subdivision (a), "Voluntary proceedings for winding up the corporation commenced upon the adoption of the resolution of shareholders or directors of the corporation electing to wind up and dissolve, or upon the filing with the corporation of a written consent of shareholders thereto." (§ 1903, subd. (a).)

Furthermore, section 601, subdivision (f), in the chapter of the code that discusses shareholder meetings and consents, states, in relevant part: "Any shareholder approval at a meeting, other than unanimous approval by those entitled to vote, pursuant to Section . . . 1900 . . . *shall* be valid only if the general nature of the proposal so approved was stated in the notice of meeting or in any written waiver of notice." (§ 601, subd. (f), italics added.)

Appellants argue that the failure of West Coast to have followed the motion/waiver requirement set out in section 601, subdivision (f) renders that alleged dissolution invalid. Based on the plain language of the statute, we must agree.

The word "shall" expresses a mandatory intent unless the legislative history of the statute where it occurs shows otherwise. The legislative history of section 601, subdivision (f) is set forth in the Legislative Committee comment to the statute: "Certain matters presented for action to shareholders are of such fundamental importance that specific notice of their proposed consideration at any meeting, including the annual meeting, is required by this subdivision."

Respondents do not contend either that the required notice was given or that a written waiver was signed but instead advance the following arguments: the waiver by attendance provision of section 601, subdivision (e) applies; compliance with subdivision (f) was excused because West Coast is a small, family-held corporation that has always been informally run; and the notice, if any was due, should have been given by appellants since they were the ones who wanted to dissolve the corporation and thus they are estopped from objecting to the noncompliance with subdivision (f). None of these arguments has any merit.

Section 601, subdivision (e) provides in relevant part: "Attendance of a person at a meeting shall constitute a waiver of notice of and presence at such meeting, except when the person objects, at the beginning of the meeting, to the transaction of any business because the meeting is not lawfully called or convened and except that attendance at a meeting is not a waiver of any right to object to the consideration of matters required by this division to be included in the notice but not so included, if such objection is expressly made at the meeting. Neither the business to be transacted at nor the purpose of any regular or special meeting of shareholders need be specified in any written waiver of notice, consent to the holding of the meeting or approval of the minutes thereof, unless otherwise provided in the articles or bylaws, *except as provided in subdivision (f)."* (§ 601, subd. (e), italics added.)

In short, there was a total and inexcusable failure to comply with the notice/waiver requirements that are a prerequisite to a valid voluntary dissolution of a corporation and, therefore, the judgment must be reversed.

The judgment is reversed and remanded for further proceeding consistent with this opinion. Appellants to have their costs on appeal.

CASE QUESTIONS

1. Explain the corporate structure of West Coast Laboratories, Inc.

2. Was a petition for voluntary dissolution of the corporation ever filed? Explain.

3. Does the fact that this corporation is small and family-owned mean that the parties can follow a certain informality in dissolving it? Why or why not?

4. Can one group of stockholders force another group to "sell out"? Why or why not?

5. How do the California corporate notice provisions affect the final decision in this case?

Payment of Outstanding Debts from Corporate Assets

Following notification of corporate creditors, the corporation liquidates its assets and uses the cash to pay off all outstanding debts. As we will see later in this chapter, statutes require that creditors receive higher priority than corporate shareholders when it comes to distributing corporate assets. In fact, only after all corporate creditors are paid will shareholders be entitled to receive any remaining corporate assets.

Articles of Dissolution (Certificate of Dissolution)

The final step in a voluntary dissolution is the filing of articles of dissolution. Referred to as a certificate of dissolution in some jurisdictions, this document sets out the corporate shareholders' desire to dissolve the corporation. A certificate of dissolution also makes the following assertions:

■ Corporate assets have been fully distributed.
■ Corporate liabilities have been satisfied.

- The decision to dissolve the corporation was made and voted on by the shareholders.[11]

The articles of dissolution are filed with the secretary of state's office. When received, they are made a matter of public record, and the date determines other activities, such as the length of time that the corporation is allotted to wind up all business. See Exhibits 12–3 and 12–4.

KEY POINT

Once the certificate of dissolution has been filed, the corporation ceases to exist, except for the limited purposes of winding up corporate affairs.[12]

Official Date of Dissolution

The official date of the dissolution of the corporation is the date that the certificate of dissolution is signed and issued by the state.[13] Filing the articles is vital because the date of filing determines other time periods and is also the method to determine the exact date of final dissolution. The articles of dissolution are normally filed with the secretary of state's office.[14]

DISSOLUTION BY SPECIFIC TERMS IN ARTICLES OF INCORPORATION

If the articles of incorporation contain a specific date upon which the corporation will be dissolved, then the expiration of that time period will result in a voluntary dissolution of the corporation. This rule is as true for nonprofit corporations as it is for corporations created to generate profits. However, most corporations do not have such a provision, and dissolving a corporation by this method is not common.[15]

ADMINISTRATIVE DISSOLUTION

Corporations can also be dissolved by state action. After all, a corporation receives its authority to exist from state law, and the same state law has the authority to take away a corporation's charter. Of course, there must be a specific reason for the state to intercede in a corporation and dissolve it.[16] States have the power to institute administrative dissolution of a corporation for a variety of reasons including fraud, misuse of corporate purpose, and the commission of crimes. See Exhibit 12–5.

For corporations that function in several different states, which state has authority to dissolve the corporate structure? The answer is whatever state the corporation is domiciled in. All corporations are founded under the laws

Exhibit 12–3. Certificate of dissolution, Connecticut

CERTIFICATE OF DISSOLUTION
STOCK CORPORATION
Office of the Secretary of the State
30 Trinity Street / P.O. Box 150470 / Hartford, CT 06115-0470 /Rev. 07/01/2003

See reverse for instruction

Space For Office Use Only	Filing Fee $25.00

1. NAME OF CORPORATION

2. DATE ON WHICH DISSOLUTION WAS AUTHORIZED _____ / _____ / _____

3. Complete Block (A) if Dissolution was authorized by incorporators or initial directors or block (B) if Dissolution was authorized by directors and shareholders.

(A) Place a check mark next to either 1 or 2 as appropriate:

_____ **1. None of the corporation's shares have been issued**   _____ **2. The corporation has not commenced business**

The undersigned makes the following assertions in connection with the selection made under section (A) of this form: that no debt of the corporation remains unpaid; that if shares were issued, the net assets of the corporation remaining after winding up have been distributed to the shareholders; and that a majority of the incorporators or initial directors authorized the dissolution.

(B) _____ **The proposal to dissolve was duly approved by the shareholders in the manner required by sections 33-600 to 33-998 (inclusive) of the Connecticut General Statutes, and by the Certificate of Incorporation.**

4. EXECUTION

Dated this _____ day of _____ , 20 _____ .

Print or type name of signatory	Capacity of signatory	Signature

NOTE: A corporation may only revoke its dissolution within 120 days following the effective date of such dissolution.

Exhibit 12–4. Articles of dissolution, Florida

ARTICLES OF DISSOLUTION

Pursuant to section 607.1401, Florida Statutes, this Florida profit corporation submits the following Articles of Dissolution:

FIRST:　　　The name of the corporation as currently filed with the Florida Department of State:

_____

SECOND:　　The document number of the corporation (if known):_____

THIRD:　　　The file date of the articles of incorporation: _____

FOURTH:　　(CHECK AT LEAST ONE BOX)

　　　　　　❑　None of the corporation's shares have been issued.

　　　　　　❑　The corporation has not commenced business.

FIFTH:　　　No debt of the corporation remains unpaid.

SIXTH:　　　The net assets of the corporation remaining after winding up have been distributed to the shareholders, if shares were issued.

SEVENTH:　　Adoption of Dissolution　(CHECK ONE)

　　　　　　❑　A majority of the incorporators authorized the dissolution.

　　　　　　❑　A majority of the directors authorized the dissolution.

Signed this _____ day of _____, _____.

Signature:_____
　　　　　　　(By a director, president or other officer - if directors or officers have not been selected, by an incorporator - if
　　　　　　　in the hands of a receiver, trustee, or other court appointed fiduciary, by that fiduciary.)

_____
(Typed or printed name of person signing)

_____
(Title of person signing)

Filing Fee: $35

(continued)

Exhibit 12–4. Articles of dissolution, Florida *(continued)*

ARTICLES OF DISSOLUTION

Pursuant to section 607.1403, Florida Statutes, this Florida profit corporation submits the following Articles of Dissolution:

FIRST: The name of the corporation as currently filed with the Florida Department of State:

_____

SECOND: The document number of the corporation (if known):_____

THIRD: The date dissolution was authorized: _____

Effective date of dissolution <u>if applicable</u>: _____
(no more than 90 days after dissolution file date)

FOURTH: Adoption of Dissolution (CHECK ONE)

❑ Dissolution was approved by the shareholders. The number of votes cast for dissolution was sufficient for approval.

❑ Dissolution was approved by of the shareholders through voting groups.

The following statement must be separately provided for each voting group entitled to vote separately on the plan to dissolve:

The number of votes cast for dissolution was sufficient for approval by

_____
. (voting group)

Signed this _____ day of _____, _____.

Signature: _____
(By a director, president or other officer - if directors or officers have not been selected, by an incorporator - if in the hands of a receiver, trustee, or other court appointed fiduciary, by that fiduciary)

_____
(Typed or printed name of person signing)

_____
(Title of person signing)

Filing Fee: $35

(continued)

Exhibit 12–4. Articles of dissolution, Florida *(continued)*

Notice of Corporate Dissolution

This notice is submitted by the dissolved corporation named below for resolution of payment of unknown claims against this corporation as provided in s. 607.1407, F.S.

This "*Notice of Corporate Dissolution*" is optional and is not required when filing a voluntary dissolution.

Name of Corporation:_____

Date of dissolution will be the date the dissolution is filed with the Department of State or as specified in the *Articles of Dissolution*.

Description of information that must be included in a claim:

_____

_____

_____

_____

_____

Mailing address where claims can be sent: (Claims cannot be sent to the Division of Corporations)

_____

_____

_____

_____

A claim against the above named corporation will be barred unless a proceeding to enforce the claim is commenced within 4 years after the filing of this notice.

_____   _____
Printed Name of the Person Filing   Signature of the Person Filing

No charge if included with Articles of Dissolution. If filed separately $35.00

(continued)

Exhibit 12–4. Articles of dissolution, Florida *(continued)*

Articles of Dissolution

Business Corporations Act
Sections 211 and 212

1. **Name of Corporation**

2. **Corporate Access Number**

3. **The Corporation has:** *(check the appropriate box)*

(a) ☐ not issued any shares, has no property and no liabilities

(b) ☐ no property and no liabilities

(c) ☐ liabilities

(d) ☐ not sent a statement of revocation of intent to dissolve

4. **If the Corporation is being dissolved under Section 212 of the Business Corporations Act, the following question must be answered:**

Has this Corporation complied with Section 212(7) of the Act? ☐ Yes ☐ No

5. **Documents and records of the Corporation shall be kept for six years from the date of dissolution by:**

Name *(First, Initial, Last)*

Business Address | City / Town | Province | Postal Code

_____ | _____ | _____
Authorized Signature | Name of Person Authorizing *(please print)* | Date
(applicable for societies only)

_____ | _____
Identification | Title *(please print)*
(not applicable for societies)

This information is being collected for the purposes of corporate registry records in accordance with the Business Corporations Act. Questions about the collection of this information can be directed to the Freedom of Information and Protection of Privacy Coordinator for Alberta Registries, Box 3140, Edmonton, Alberta T5J 2G7, (780) 427-7013.

REG 3038 (Rev. 2003/05)

Exhibit 12–5. Statute authorizing administrative dissolution

§ 1801. Action by attorney general; grounds; conditions precedent; notice to correct; authority of court; service of process; publication of notice

(a) The Attorney General may bring an action against any domestic corporation or purported domestic corporation in the name of the people of this state, upon the Attorney General's own information or upon complaint of a private party, to procure a judgment dissolving the corporation and annulling, vacating or forfeiting its corporate existence upon any of the following grounds:

(1) The corporation has seriously offended against any provision of the statutes regulating corporations.

(2) The corporation has fraudulently abused or usurped corporate privileges or powers.

(3) The corporation has violated any provision of law by any act or default which under the law is a ground for forfeiture of corporate existence.*

*California Corp. Code §1801 (2006).

of a particular state, even if they later conduct business in others. The law of that original, domicile state controls when it comes to the issue of dissolving the corporation. Under this theory, courts in one state cannot dissolve a corporation organized under the laws of another state.[17]

Most states have a provision that allows the state attorney general to institute an action to administratively dissolve a corporation. Grounds for administrative dissolution can include any of the following:

- fraud by the incorporators in creating the corporation
- filing of false or misleading articles of incorporation
- creating a corporation for an unlawful purpose[18]

Other reasons that justify the administrative dissolution of a corporation include the failure to file annual reports or to make other necessary financial disclosures or to pay taxes. However, jurisdictions are split on the question of whether a corporation can be administratively dissolved because it does not hold its required meetings or issue any stock.[19]

Statutory Steps Required to Dissolve a Corporation

When the state seeks to dissolve a corporation, it must follow the prescribed method set out in state law. For an example of such a statute, see Exhibit 12–6. If the statutory method is not followed, the corporation is not dissolved and continues to exist. Consider Scenario 12–4.

Sidebar

A "de facto dissolution" refers to a corporation's insolvency and complete liquidation of all assets.[20]

Scenario 12–4. Dissolution and State Law

BCD Corporation sells all of its assets, settles its affairs, and divides the surplus cash among its shareholders. Has BCD corporation officially dissolved?

Answer: No. Although these actions will go a long way towards establishing a de facto dissolution, the corporation is not officially dissolved until it has complied with state law.[21]

JUDICIAL DISSOLUTION

The power to dissolve a corporation is not limited to state agencies. Judges also have this power, at least in some circumstances. For instance, some states give the state Supreme Court power to dissolve a corporation. See Exhibit 12–6.

Exhibit 12–6. Petition for dissolution of a corporation in supreme judicial court

A petition for dissolution of a corporation may be filed in the supreme judicial court in the following cases:—

(a) A corporation which desires to close its affairs may authorize the filing of such a petition by a vote of a majority of each class of its stock outstanding and entitled to vote thereon;

(b) Such a petition may be filed by the holder or holders of not less than forty per cent of all the shares of its stock outstanding and entitled to vote thereon, treating all classes of stock entitled to vote as a single class for the purpose of determining whether the petition is brought by the holders of not less than forty per cent of the outstanding shares as aforesaid, if:

  (1) the directors are deadlocked in the management of corporate affairs, and the shareholders are unable to break the deadlock; or

  (2) the shareholders are deadlocked in voting powers and have failed to elect successors to directors whose terms have expired or would have expired upon the election of their successors.*

*Mass. Gen. Laws Ann. ch156B, §99 (West, 2006).

> **Sidebar**
>
> Other grounds that justify the judicial dissolution of a corporation are when management has engaged in illegal conduct, gross mismanagement, or fraud.

However, in the states that authorize courts to dissolve corporations, there are strict limits on the circumstances that can justify such an action. All of these jurisdictions have cases that stand for the proposition that judicial dissolution of a corporation should be used only as a last resort. Courts are encouraged to find some other remedy short of declaring that the corporation is terminated.[22] Part of the judicial reluctance stems from the fact that there are statutes authorizing the state attorney general's or secretary of state's office to institute proceedings to dissolve the corporation under statutory authority. The other reason for the judiciary to take a cautionary approach to dissolving corporations is that it does not wish to be in the business of litigating disagreements between shareholders. Courts cannot declare judicial termination of a corporation simply because the current management is sustaining financial losses or because the shareholders disagree with the direction or policy of the board of directors. Similarly, the courts cannot order dissolution because the corporation has not declared a dividend.[23] Corporate dissolution is not authorized for management disputes. If shareholders believe that there has been financial mismanagement, they are entitled to bring a derivative suit, not an action to dissolve the corporation.[24] See Exhibit 12–7.

Exhibit 12–7. Grounds for judicial dissolution

> A circuit court may dissolve a corporation or order such other remedy as provided in § 607.1434:
> (1)(a) In a proceeding by the Department of Legal Affairs if it is established that:
> 1. The corporation obtained its articles of incorporation through fraud; or
> 2. The corporation has continued to exceed or abuse the authority conferred upon it by law.*

*Fla. Stat. Ann §607.1430 (West, 2006).

On the other hand, shareholders cannot seek to create a bulletproof corporation, or one that can never be judicially dissolved. For instance, if the incorporators insert a provision in the articles of incorporation declaring that the corporation can never be dissolved by judicial action, the provision will not be enforced. Such a clause is void for public policy reasons.[26] Courts routinely negate provisions in agreements that deny parties access to the court system.

Judicial Dissolution of a Closely Held Corporation

The rules for judicial dissolution can vary depending on the type of corporation involved in the litigation. For instance, a shareholder who is seeking to dissolve a closely held corporation has different elements to prove than those seeking a court order to dissolve other types of corporations. A shareholder filing suit to dissolve a closely held corporation must show the following:

- He or she had expectations about the corporation that were understood by other shareholders.
- Those expectations have been frustrated or completely ignored.
- The frustration of his or her expectations was not caused by the shareholder.
- The circumstances justify some type of relief.[27]

LIQUIDATION OF CORPORATE ASSETS

Once the decision has been reached that the corporation must be dissolved, the next step involves actually liquidating corporate assets. This step is necessary whether the majority stockholders voted to dissolve the corporation voluntarily, a court made the decision, or the state sought the dissolution.

The purpose of liquidating a corporation is to distribute all of the company's assets to those individuals and businesses that have claims against the corporation.[28] A liquidator will be appointed and will collect all information about outstanding claims, prioritize the payment of those claims, and transfer all corporate assets until nothing of the corporation is left. See Exhibit 12–8.

Exhibit 12–8. Procedure after dissolution

(a) After dissolution:
   (1) The corporation shall carry on no business except for the purpose of winding up its affairs.
   (2) The corporation shall proceed to wind up its affairs, with power to fulfill or discharge its contracts, collect its assets, sell its assets for cash at public or private sale, discharge or pay its liabilities, and do all other acts appropriate to liquidate its business.
   (3) After paying or adequately providing for the payment of its liabilities:
      (A) The corporation, if authorized at a meeting of shareholders by a majority of the votes of all outstanding shares entitled to vote thereon may sell its remaining assets, or any part thereof, for shares, bonds or other securities or partly for cash and partly for shares, bonds or other securities, and distribute the same among the shareholders according to their respective rights.*

*N.Y. Corporation Law §1006 (McKinney, 2006).

APPOINTMENT OF A LIQUIDATOR

liquidator A person appointed, usually by a court, to collect and distribute assets on behalf of others.

receiver Also known as liquidator; a person who collects and distributes assets on behalf of others; "receiver" is a term often applied in bankruptcy proceedings.

In some states, after the filing of articles of dissolution, the directors automatically become trustees for the shareholders and supervise the liquidation of corporate assets.[29] In other states, a **liquidator** is appointed. Also known as a **receiver**, this person is responsible for the orderly disposition of the corporation's affairs, including paying creditors and distributing the remaining assets to the shareholders. Liquidators also have the right to make demands for payments due to the corporation for unpaid invoices, to collect and sue for outstanding payments, and to settle any claims currently pending against the corporation.[30] See Exhibit 12–9.

Exhibit 12–9. Appointment of receiver to liquidate corporate assets

> If, at the time of the filing of a complaint for involuntary dissolution or at any time thereafter, the court has reasonable grounds to believe that unless a receiver of the corporation is appointed the interest of the corporation and its shareholders will suffer pending the hearing and determination of the complaint, upon the application of the plaintiff, and after a hearing upon such notice to the corporation as the court may direct and upon the giving of security pursuant to Sections 566 and 567 of the Code of Civil Procedure, the court may appoint a receiver to take over and manage the business and affairs of the corporation and to preserve its property pending the hearing and determination of the complaint for dissolution.*

*Cal. Corp. Code §1803 (West, 2006).

Liquidators have extensive powers to wind up a corporation's business affairs, but they do have important limitations. For instance, they cannot engage in any new business on behalf of the corporation. Their duties are closely proscribed by state law or judicial decisions. Liquidators routinely perform the following tasks:

- settling claims pending brought by or against the corporation
- transferring title to corporate property
- assigning corporate assets to another entity
- negotiating foreclosure
- paying taxes
- releasing claims

PRIORITIZATION OF CLAIMS

Priority is an important issue when it comes to liquidating corporate assets. When we say that someone has priority it means that he or she has the right to receive payment before others. When it comes to dissolving corporations, creditors always have priority over shareholders. Among the shareholders, there are also different levels of priority, based on the different classes of stock held by shareholders. Some states also have statutes that forbid the payment of any assets to the corporation when the company is insolvent and cannot meet the full burden of its debts to creditors.

There are even different ranks of creditors, with secured lenders receiving priority over nonsecured creditors. When the corporation's assets are insufficient to meet the claims of all the creditors, those in the same category divide up the assets equally. In some cases, the creditors receive an identical percentage of the corporate assets. For instance, all creditors might receive 90 percent of their outstanding claims, rather than a payout of 100 percent of some creditors' claims and only 10 percent or less of other claims.

 ## GETTING TO THE BASICS

Shareholders are entitled to whatever corporate assets are left over after corporate creditors have been paid.

Prioritization among Shareholders

Once all creditors have been paid, the remainder of the corporate assets can be divided up among the shareholders. The amount that any one shareholder receives depends on the number of shares he or she owns and the classification of the shares. See Exhibit 12–10.

Exhibit 12–10. Payment of assets to shareholders

> (1) Any net assets remaining after paying or adequately providing for the payment of all debts and liabilities of the corporation, including all costs and expenses of the liquidation and any and all contingent liabilities of which the liquidator has knowledge, shall be paid by the liquidator to the shareholders according to their respective rights and preferences. The share of any shareholder who cannot be found shall be delivered to the administrator of the Uniform Unclaimed Property Act of 1997.*

*LSA-R.S. 12:145 (2006).

Common Stock and Preferred Stock Revisited

As we saw in a previous chapter, different classifications of stock give the stockholder different rights. Preferred stockholders have a higher priority to receive corporate assets during liquidation than common stockholders. In fact, common stockholders receive distribution only once all creditors and preferred stockholders have been paid. If there is no money left after these disbursements, then common stockholders receive nothing. However, these are general rules. Preferred stock comes in a wide variety of forms, with some giving priority during liquidation, while others give preferred status only to dividend payments. In the absence of set preferences related to liquidation, the stockholders share the assets on the basis of the number of their shares. See Exhibit 12–11.

Exhibit 12–11. Holders of preferred stock

> (d) The holders of the preferred or special stock of any class or of any series thereof shall be entitled to such rights upon the dissolution of, or upon any distribution of the assets of, the corporation as shall be stated in the certificate of incorporation or in the resolution or resolutions providing for the issue of such stock adopted by the board of directors as hereinabove provided.*

*Del. Code Ann. tit. §§151 (2006).

The Trust Doctrine

When courts dissolve a corporation, they often employ a legal fiction referred to as the "trust doctrine." Under this theory, the corporate profits that come from divestiture are held in trust for the shareholders. Once corporate debts are paid out of these funds, the remainder becomes the legal property of the shareholders as a kind of trust.[31] Corporate officers must hold this money for the benefit of the shareholders in the same way that a trustee would be obligated to hold, and account for, funds received on behalf of another.

KEY POINT

Any assets remaining after creditor claims have been satisfied must be distributed to the shareholders on the basis of their number and type of shares.

Escheat

escheat The transfer of ownership rights to the government when no other legally qualified person can be located to take ownership of the property.

If some of the stockholders cannot be located so that they can receive their share of the corporate assets, then the corporation must set up a trust to hold it for them until such time that they can be located.[32] States set varying time periods in which these stockholders must come forward to claim their shares or they will **escheat** to the state. Escheat is the process of transferring legal title to unclaimed property to the state. If the shareholders fail to come forward, the state will eventually receive the shares and may use the money from the sale of the stocks.

▶ "WINDING UP" CORPORATE AFFAIRS

Whatever method is used to dissolve incorporation, there is always a time period following the stated intention to dissolve and the official dissolution of the corporation. During this period, which varies from state to state, but can be as long as three years, a corporation can still sue and be sued. However, once this statutory period has passed, the corporation is entirely dissolved and no further lawsuits can be brought either for it or against it.

Liquidation and **winding up** are two terms closely intertwined. Liquidation refers to the process of divesting all corporate assets, while winding up refers to the process of concluding all corporate business.[33]

During the winding up process, statutes give specific time periods during which the corporation can continue to conduct business, bring suits, and take many other actions necessary to dispose of all corporate business. This time period also gives anyone with a claim against the corporation the opportunity to come forward.

winding up The process of settling all outstanding legal and financial obligations for a company.

Sidebar

Once a corporation has sought voluntary dissolution, it does have the right to petition the state for full reinstatement as a viable corporation.

LEGAL CHECKLIST

DISSOLVING A CORPORATION

- ❑ HAVE A MAJORITY OF SHAREHOLDERS AUTHORIZED DISSOLUTION?
  - ▪ WERE MINORITY SHAREHOLDERS ALLOWED TO VOTE?
  - ▪ ARE MINORITY INTERESTS ADEQUATELY PROTECTED?

- ❑ HAS NOTICE TO CORPORATE CREDITORS BEEN GIVEN, INDICATING THAT THE CORPORATION IS DISSOLVING?

- ❑ HAVE ALL CORPORATE ASSETS BEEN CATALOGED?

- ❑ IS THERE A COMPLETE LIST OF ALL OUTSTANDING CLAIMS, BILLS, JUDGMENTS, AND OTHER ACCOUNTS PAYABLE?

- ❑ HAS A DETERMINATION OF SHAREHOLDER PRIORITY BEEN MADE?

- ❑ HAS THE CORPORATION FILED ARTICLES OF DISSOLUTION?
  - ▪ WHAT IS THE DATE OF THIS FILING?

- ❑ WHAT IS THE PERIOD FOR WINDING UP CORPORATE BUSINESS?

THE LEGAL EFFECT OF DISSOLUTION

The legal effect of dissolution is to terminate the corporation's existence. It does not, however, eliminate a corporation's debts. Those may still have a life that extends beyond the limit of the corporation. Corporate debts may, in some circumstances, be assessed against the corporation's former stockholders.[34]

Ethics File: The Importance of Ethics

Throughout this text, we have seen that ethical practices are vitally important for corporate legal professionals. This is as true for corporate paralegals as it is for corporate attorneys. Recent national scandals such as the Enron or WorldCom corporate accounting frauds have served to bring ethical standards into even higher relief. As lawsuits and criminal prosecutions continue to evolve, so too will the ethical rules governing all aspects of corporate legal practice. Anyone practicing in this area should be aware of the swiftly changing, and enhanced, duties, and must stay abreast of changes in ethical rules governing a broad range of corporate practices.

CASE LAW: *Majority Control of the Minority Shareholders*

Allen v. Royale 16, Inc.[35]
BARRY, Judge.

Plaintiffs appeal the dismissal of their consolidated cases which involve the purchase and sale of a hotel and its management through a closely held corporation.

In early August, 1980 plaintiff Norman Allen was approached by French Market Homestead (FMH) regarding the management or purchase of The Noble Arms Hotel in New Orleans. On August 14 FMH acquired the property at foreclosure and the next day Allen and the defendants, Sherri Dazet, Kathleen and Nuncion Falcone began managing the hotel. On September 9 these individuals incorporated Royale "16", Inc. On September 15 the group purchased the hotel from FMH for $520,000 with $52,000 down paid equally by Allen, Dazet, and the Falcones and a note for the balance endorsed by all parties. On November 18 the group sold the hotel to Royale "16", Inc. By letter dated January 30, 1981 attorney Michael Ogden (drafter of Royale "16", Inc.) informed Dazet and the Falcones that Allen had been issued all 1200 shares in Royale "16", Inc. and recommended a meeting to clarify their interests. On March 11 the Board of Royale "16", Inc. (composed of all the parties) reissued the stock: 400 shares to Allen, 400 shares to Dazet, and 400 shares to the Falcones. Allen and his wife were removed from the Board and he was ousted as President. Allen sued his associates to rescind the hotel sale to the corporation and asked for management fees, then sued to dissolve Royale "16", Inc. and asked that a receiver be appointed. Defendants reconvened for attorney's and accountant's expenses for defense of the lawsuits. All demands were dismissed. We affirm.

RESCISSION OF THE SALE

Plaintiffs argue the trial court erred by refusing to rescind the sale due to Allen's error as to the nature of the contract, LSA-C.C. Art. 1841. Allen claims the intent of all parties was for the hotel (and corporation) to be managed and operated by unanimous consent and incorporation was only intended to limit liability. He states shortly after the hotel was transferred to the corporation the defendants "conspired to gain control" and prevent him from participating in the management. Allen argues he erred as to the nature of the corporate articles (which provide for majority control): if the incorporation was invalid, then the hotel's transfer was void.

Allen points to Ogden's testimony which indicates the articles were "boiler plate" from a memory typewriter in the attorney's office. He claims there was no discussion as to the corporate structure and the defendants' testimony indicates there was no agreement as to majority versus unanimous control. However, it is uncontested that the parties purchased equal ownership in the hotel and it was their intent (including Allen's) that each would own one-third of the stock.

Ogden, who was Allen's attorney, testified he did not recall an instruction from Allen to include a provision in the articles for unanimous consent. He stated the articles were drafted as he had done for Allen in the past and if there had been a request for unanimity it would have been provided.

The defendants' testimony, as stated by the trial judge, is that a majority would control.

Agreements legally entered into have the effect of law on those who form them. LSA-C.C. Art. 1901. One who signs a contract is presumed to know its terms and cannot avoid its provisions, absent fraud or error, simply because he fails to read or understand it.

There is no allegation of fraud. The articles were signed by Allen and drafted at his request. The party alleging error, advice of consent, bears the burden of proving it. The articles were executed on September 9, 1980 and Allen did not raise any question until January, 1981. Apparently the articles were drafted hastily, but there was adequate time between their execution and the sale by the individuals to the corporation (November 18, 1980) for Allen to read and make any necessary changes or correct errors.

Any change in the Charter must conform to the Louisiana Corporation Law, LSA-R.S. 12:31. Shareholders and others dealing with the corporation must rely on the articles as they appear in the Charter Books of the State. Otherwise one could not enter an act of sale or deal with the corporation for fear that a minority shareholder could have the transaction rescinded by claiming the articles are invalid.

The articles clearly provide for majority control. Plaintiffs' allegations of error are unsupported and the trial judge properly refused to rescind the sale.

INVOLUNTARY DISSOLUTION

Plaintiffs complain the trial court erred by refusing to order the involuntary dissolution of the corporation.

LSA-R.S. 12:143 provides in part:

A. The court may entertain a proceeding for involuntary dissolution under its supervision when it is made to appear that:

(1) The corporate assets are insufficient to pay all just demands for which the corporation is liable, or to afford reasonable security to those who may deal with it; or

(2) The objects of the corporation have wholly failed, or are entirely abandoned, or their accomplishment is impracticable; or

(3) It is beneficial to the interests of the shareholders that the corporation should be liquidated and dissolved, or . . .

(7) The corporation has been guilty of gross and persistent ultra vires acts;

Plaintiffs claim the corporation was several months behind in paying its hotel-motel taxes and had overdrawn its bank account four or five times during 1982. "The objects of the corporation have wholly failed, or are entirely abandoned or their accomplishment is impracticable" because the corporation never made a profit and Allen never received funds from the corporation. Allen argues it would be "beneficial to the interests of the shareholders that the corporation be liquidated and dissolved" because the accounting procedures used by the corporation are inadequate and improper and are endangering the interests of the shareholders. Plaintiffs allege the

(continued)

CASE LAW: *Majority Control of the Minority Shareholders* (continued)

following deficiencies in the corporation's bookkeeping practices:

- The bookkeeper was six months behind in posting cash receipts.
- No quarterly statements were prepared and loans were not on the corporation's balance sheet.
- The bank statements were not reconciled.
- Bank account overdrafts cost penalties.
- Tax returns were filed late resulting in penalties.
- 16% of the room cards, were missing.
- There was minimum internal control over cash and no separation of duties regarding receiving and accounting for cash.
- There was no listing of capital purchases and no way to calculate depreciation.
- Room deposits were not accounted for.

Plaintiffs also claim "the corporation has been guilty of gross and persistent ultra vires acts" citing Gooding v. Millet, 430 So.2d 742 (La.App. 5th Cir. 1983). As in Gooding, Allen asserts there have been no shareholder or board meetings since March, 1981. He alleges the corporation failed to give him annual reports, refused to allow inspection of the books and records contrary to LSA-R.S. 12:103, and Dazet resided in the hotel for five weeks.

LSA-R.S. 12:103(D) provides in part:

Upon at least five days' written demand, any shareholder, except a business competitor, who has been the holder of record of at least two per cent of all outstanding shares of the corporation for at least six months, shall have the right to examine, in person or by agent or attorney, at any reasonable time, for any proper and reasonable purpose, any and all of the records and accounts of the corporation, and to make extracts therefrom.

Louisiana courts are reluctant to apply the drastic remedy of involuntary dissolution and the statutory grounds are limited and specific.

The evidence does not prove that the assets are insufficient to pay the debts and the corporation is insolvent. The first mortgage was current. According to Mrs. Falcone and Ms. Dazet the corporation was meeting its obligations. The testimony of a CPA concerning the corporation's inability to pay its debts was based on its 1981 tax return. Ms. Dazet explained that a large amount of the loss was due to scheduled depreciation on the property. She testified the corporation would break even in 1982 and stated the only borrowed money in 1982 was $1300 which was loaned by her and the Falcones.

The evidence also does not show that the "objects of the corporation have wholly failed, or are entirely abandoned, or their accomplishment is impracticable." The corporation at the time of trial was only two years old. When the parties took over the hotel it was failing. Ms. Dazet testified that initially she and Mrs. Falcone took care of everything, from housekeeping to bookkeeping. In 1981 they loaned the corporation $15,000 and in 1982 the additional $1300 was required. They were not paid for their work.

Lack of profit is a consideration to determine if the objects of a corporation have failed, but it is not determinative here. The hotel's operation is improving and defendants appear to be making the business profitable.

We do not believe dissolution would be beneficial to the shareholders. The litany of accounting deficiencies cited by plaintiff are not persuasive.

- The daily cash ledger was posted daily and current;
- Bank statements were reconciled monthly;
- Overdrafts did occur but infrequently;
- The tax returns were filed late due to a mix-up with the accountant.

Defendants have since engaged another accounting firm.

Plaintiffs' CPA was most concerned with the missing room cards which he felt reflected inadequate internal controls and could represent missing cash. Ms. Dazet testified (and this was confirmed by the CPA) that she had not been asked to explain or locate the missing cards and there was no indication this was a problem. The CPA was unable to state that any cash was missing. He testified the books and records were in "fairly" good order but could not say the management and bookkeeping procedures constituted gross mismanagement.

We do not find that the defendants/majority shareholders and the board are guilty of ultra vires acts. In Gruenberg v. Goldmine Plantation, Inc., 360 So.2d 884 (La.App. 4th Cir. 1978) we quoted 58 Fletcher Cyclopedia Corporations 5821:

Unless it clearly appears that the act is an abuse of discretion, intra vires, legal and good faith acts of the board of directors, other corporate officers, or the majority stockholders, i.e., acts pertaining to the internal management, of the corporation, where they are not fraudulent or unfair to minority stockholders, will not be interfered with or remedied at the instance of minority stockholders, regardless of whether such acts are wise or expedient. In other words, to warrant the interposition of a court in favor of the minority shareholders in a corporation, as against the contemplated action of the majority, where such action is within the corporate powers, a case must be made out which plainly shows that such action is so far opposed to the true interests of the corporation itself as to lead to the clear inference that no one thus acting could have been influenced by any honest desire to secure such interests, but that he must have acted with an intent to subserve some outside purpose, regardless of the consequences to the company and in a manner inconsistent with its interests. This is the unavoidable result of the fundamental principle that the majority can regulate and control the lawful exercise of the powers conferred upon a corporation by its character. The wisdom of the action taken or threatened will not be considered. It is only when the corporate acts are so unjust as to be evidence of fraud and intentional wrong that the internal management will be interfered with. Courts cannot compel corporate officers to act wisely but they can compel them to act honestly.

Plaintiff's reliance on Gooding, supra, is misplaced. The situation in Gooding was longstanding (approximately ten years) and corporate formalities were totally disregarded. The Fifth Circuit commented:

To hold otherwise would be to condone the way the Saints Oil Corporation has been managed and, more significantly, to allow the majority stockholders to come to court virtually empty-handed with regard to corporate records and contend that the acts complained of were not ultra vires.

Gooding is not remotely similar to this case. Admittedly, no meetings were held since March, 1981, but suit was filed May 18, 1981 and the parties have been at odds since. There were several meetings between September, 1980 and March, 1981.

The fact that the majority of the shareholders (defendants) removed Allen from the Board and as President is insufficient to justify involuntary dissolution. The actions of the majority were within the corporate powers and not ultra vires. There is no legal basis to order involuntary dissolution of the corporation.

APPOINTMENT OF A RECEIVER

In the alternative, plaintiff requests appointment of a receiver pursuant to LSA-R.S. 12:151 which provides in part:

A. The court may, after trial, appoint a receiver to take charge of the corporation's property when it is made to appear, in a proceeding instituted against the corporation:

(1) By any shareholder or creditor, that the directors or officers of the corporation are jeopardizing the rights of its shareholders or creditors by grossly mismanaging the business, or by committing gross and persistent ultra vires acts, or by wasting, misusing or misapplying the assets of the corporation; or . . .

(5) By any shareholder, that a majority of the shareholders are violating the rights of minority shareholders and endangering their interests

Plaintiff relies on the same allegations discussed above.

(continued)

CASE LAW: *Majority Control of the Minority Shareholders* (continued)

Fincher v. Claiborne Butane Co., 349 So.2d 1014 (La.App. 2d Cir. 1977) sets forth the applicable legal principles:

The appointment of a receiver is not mandatory but is subject to sound judicial discretion. In determining whether or not the facts justify and make advisable a receivership, in the absence of a clear showing of fraud or breach of trust the courts are slow to interfere, will order the appointment of a receiver only when it is manifest that it should be made, and are influenced by a consideration of whether such action would serve a useful purpose. This court will not disturb the ruling of the trial judge in his refusal to appoint a receiver except in a case where it clearly appears that the interest of the minority of stockholders are in imminent danger. . . . receivership of a corporation, as a remedy, looks only to the prevention of future injuries rather than to the redress of past grievances. . . . The effect of appointing a receiver being to take the property of the corporation out of the control of its own officers to whom it has been entrusted by its stockholders, the courts proceed with extreme caution in the exercise if so summary a power, and in construing such statutes they are inclined to give them a strict construction. A minority of the stockholders of a corporation is not entitled to a receiver because of dissatisfaction with the policy and management of a majority of the officers and directors in the absence of any showing of fraud or insolvency.

Receivership is granted in cases where there is imminent danger of the rights of minority stockholders being destroyed by a fraudulent or illegal practice intentionally designed to dissipate the assets of the corporation.

Plaintiff has not shown that the corporation is insolvent nor that the defendants intend to dissipate its assets. Plaintiffs' CPA stated there was no waste, misuse or misapplication of assets and the defendants had not committed ultra vires acts. Plaintiffs' other CPA testified the corporate expenses were normal, but filing late tax returns was a waste of assets. However, this is not the sort of "wasting" envisioned by the legislature to justify appointment of a receiver. As fully stated above, plaintiffs' other allegations are unsupported by the record.

Receivership is proper only where mismanagement is "wilful and its purpose is to ruin the corporation . . . where the facts disclose a scheme on the part of the . . . majority stockholder to wreck the corporation and dissipate its assets." West v. Certified Credit Corporation, 162 So.2d 589, 595 (La.App. 2d Cir. 1964). The lower court concluded there has been no such showing and we find no error in the trial judge's refusal to appoint a receiver.

The judgment of the District Court is affirmed at plaintiffs' cost.

AFFIRMED.

CASE QUESTIONS

1. What contention does Allen raise about the "error" in the creation of the articles of incorporation?

2. What claim does Allen make about his attorney's practice in creating the articles of incorporation?

3. What legal presumptions weigh against the plaintiff in this case?

4. According to the court, is this a case of involuntary dissolution? Why or why not?

5. What specific facts does the plaintiff refer to in his contention that dissolution of the corporation is the best course?

SUMMARY

There are a variety of ways that a corporation's existence can be terminated. Majority shareholders can vote to dissolve the corporation, even over the objections of minority shareholders. Corporations can also be dissolved by administrative action, initiated either by the state attorney general's office or by the secretary of state. Grounds for administrative dissolution include the failure to file appropriate paperwork and the corporation's having been created for an illegal or fraudulent purpose. Courts are also permitted to dissolve corporations in certain circumstances. Judicial dissolution of the corporation can be based on any of a number of factors, including the fact that the corporation is now incapable of carrying out its original purpose. The consequence of dissolution is that the corporation can no longer carry out any new business. Once the corporation has filed articles of dissolution with the state, the only business it is allowed to conduct is the winding up of its affairs. This includes paying off any outstanding claims, court judgments, liquidating corporate assets, and distributing them to shareholders. Once dissolution is complete, the corporation's legal significance is at an end.

HELPFUL WEB SITES

Ohio Secretary of State's Office
http://www.sos.state.oh.us/

Florida Department of State
http://www.dos.state.fl.us/

Texas Secretary of State
http://www.sos.state.tx.us/

National Association of Secretaries of State
http://www.nass.org/sos/sosflags.html

KEY TERMS

escheat	liquidator
freeze out	receiver
liquidation	winding up

APPLYING CHAPTER CONCEPTS

Visit your secretary of state's Web site and locate articles of dissolution. Does your secretary of state provide information on corporations that have been administratively or judicially dissolved? If so, what information can you glean from the site? Does the site provide legal forms that relate to corporate dissolution and termination?

REVIEW QUESTIONS

1. What is judicial dissolution?
2. How does administrative dissolution compare to judicial dissolution?
3. What is the legal significance of corporate dissolution?
4. What are the priority rights of shareholders in liquidating corporate assets?
5. Can majority shareholders dissolve the corporation over the objection of the minority shareholders? Explain your answer.
6. When it comes to liquidating corporate assets, who has greater priority, creditors or shareholders? Explain your answer.
7. What is the "trust doctrine" as that term applies to liquidating a corporation's assets?
8. Explain how members of a corporation's board of directors can become trustees during corporate liquidation.
9. How does a corporation prioritize who will receive its assets after it terminates existence?
10. What impact do state laws have on the dissolution of a corporation?
11. What are articles of dissolution?
12. What are the duties of a liquidator?
13. Who has greater priority in receiving corporate assets during a corporate dissolution, preferred shareholders or common shareholders? Explain your answer.
14. Can a corporation declare bankruptcy? Explain.
15. What are some of the methods through which a corporation can terminate?

QUESTIONS FOR REFLECTION

1. Do the laws concerning dissolution of a corporation make it more or less likely that a corporation that should be terminated actually will be?
2. Should a minority of shareholders have the power to force a corporation into voluntary dissolution? Why or why not?

[1]*Gast Monuments, Inc. v. Rosehill Cemetery Co.*, 207 Ill. App. 3d 901, 152 Ill. Dec. 800, 566 N.E.2d 487 (1st Dist. 1990).

[2]*State v. Dyer,* 145 Tex. 586, 200 S.W.2d 813 (1947).

[3]*Ovadia v. Abdullah,* 24 Cal. App. 4th 1100, 29 Cal. Rptr. 2d 527 (2d Dist. 1994).

[4]*Craddock-Terry Co. v. Powell,* 181 Va. 417, 25 S.E.2d 363 (1943).

[5]*Andrews v. Arisco,* 2002 WL 1164152 (Tex. App. Houston 1st Dist. 2002).

[6]*Sutter v. Sutter Ranching Corp.,* 2000 OK 84, 14 P.3d 58 (Okla. 2000).

[7]*Berger v. Levin,* 231 So. 2d 875 (Fla. Dist. Ct. App. 3d Dist. 1970).

[8]*Gabhart v. Gabhart,* 267 Ind. 370, 370 N.E.2d 345 (1977).

[9]*Reynolds v. Special Projects, Inc.,* 260 Cal. App. 2d 496, 67 Cal. Rptr. 374 (2d Dist. 1968).

[10]24 Cal.App.4th 1100 (Cal. App. Dist. 2., 1994).

[11]*Catalina Investments, Inc. v. Jones,* 98 Cal. App. 4th 1, 119 Cal. Rptr. 2d 256 (2d Dist. 2002), review denied, (Aug. 21, 2002).

[12]*Greene v. Stevenson,* 295 Ky. 832, 175 S.W.2d 519 (1943).

[13]*Licht v. Association Services, Inc.,* 236 Neb. 616, 463 N.W.2d 566 (1990).

[14]*Multilist Service of Cape Girardeau, Missouri, Inc. v. Wilson,* 14 S.W.3d 110 (Mo. Ct. App. E.D. 2000).

[15]*Eagle Pass Realty Co. v. Esparza,* 474 S.W.2d 624 (Tex. Civ. App. San Antonio 1971).

[16]*Leventhal v. Atlantic Finance Corp.,* 316 Mass. 194, 55 N.E.2d 20, 154 A.L.R. 260 (1944).

[17]Am. Jur. 2d, Foreign Corporations § 413 (2006).

[18]*New Orleans Debenture Redemption Co. of Louisiana v. State of Louisiana,* 180 U.S. 320, 21 S. Ct. 378, 45 L.Ed. 550 (1901).

[19]*Warthan v. Midwest Consol. Ins. Agencies, Inc.,* 450 N.W.2d 145 (Minn. Ct. App. 1990).

[20]*Fulton Paper Co., Inc. v. Reeves,* 212 Ga. App. 314, 441 S.E.2d 881 (1994).

[21]*Dunning v. Firemen's Ins. Co. of Newark,* N. J., 194 S.C. 98, 8 S.E.2d 318 (1940).

[22]*Scott v. Trans-System, Inc.,* 148 Wash. 2d 701, 64 P.3d 1 (2003).

[23]*Long v. Norwood Hills Corp.,* 380 S.W.2d 451 (Mo. Ct. App. 1964).

[24]*Gimpel v. Bolstein*, 125 Misc. 2d 45, 477 N.Y.S.2d 1014 (Sup 1984).

[25]*Wall & Beaver Street Corp. v. Munson Line*, 58 F.Supp. 101, 107 (D.Md.1943).

[26]*Schimel v. Berkun*, 264 A.D.2d 725, 696 N.Y.S.2d 49 (2d Dep't 1999).

[27]*Stumpf v. C.E. Stumpf & Sons, Inc.*, 47 Cal. App. 3d 230, 120 Cal. Rptr. 671 (1st Dist. 1975).

[28]*In re Commissioner of Banks and Real Estate*, 327 Ill. App. 3d 441, 261 Ill. Dec. 775, 764 N.E.2d 66 (1st Dist. 2001), appeal denied, 198 Ill. 2d 592, 262 Ill. Dec. 619, 766 N.E.2d 239 (2002).

[29]*Scott v. Seek Lane Venture, Inc.*, 91 Md. App. 668, 605 A.2d 942 (1992).

[30]*Leader Buick, GMC Trucks, Inc. v. Weinmann*, 841 So. 2d 34 (La. Ct. App. 4th Cir. 2003).

[31]*Friendly Home, Inc. v. Shareholders and Creditors of Royal Homestead Land Co.*, 477 A.2d 934 (R.I. 1984).

[32]*Price v. State*, 79 Ill. App. 3d 143, 34 Ill. Dec. 690, 398 N.E.2d 365 (1st Dist. 1979).

[33]*W & K Farms, Inc. v. Walter*, 235 Neb. 952, 458 N.W.2d 230 (1990).

[34]*Alpine Property Owners Ass'n, Inc. v. Mountaintop Development Co.*, 179 W. Va. 12, 365 S.E.2d 57 (1987).

[35]449 So.2d 1365 (La.App. 4 Cir. 1984).

APPENDIX A
UNIFORM PARTNERSHIP ACT (1997)

Drafted by the

NATIONAL CONFERENCE OF COMMISSIONERS
ON UNIFORM STATE LAWS

and by it

APPROVED AND RECOMMENDED FOR ENACTMENT
IN ALL THE STATES

at its

ANNUAL CONFERENCE
MEETING IN ITS ONE-HUNDRED-AND-FIFTH YEAR
SAN ANTONIO, TEXAS
JULY 12 - JULY 19, 1996

WITH PREFATORY NOTE AND COMMENTS

Copies of this Act may be obtained from:

NATIONAL CONFERENCE OF COMMISSIONERS
ON UNIFORM STATE LAWS
211 E. Ontario Street, Suite 1300
Chicago, Illinois 60611
312/915-0195

UNIFORM PARTNERSHIP ACT (1997)

PREFATORY NOTE

The National Conference of Commissioners on Uniform State Laws first considered a uniform law of partnership in 1902. Although early drafts had proceeded along the mercantile or "entity" theory of partnerships, later drafts were based on the common-law "aggregate" theory. The resulting Uniform Partnership Act ("UPA"), which embodied certain aspects of each theory, was finally approved by the Conference in 1914. The UPA governs general partnerships, and also governs limited partnerships except where the limited partnership statute is inconsistent. The UPA has been adopted in every State other than Louisiana and has been the subject of remarkably few amendments in those States over the past 80 years.

In January of 1986, an American Bar Association subcommittee issued a detailed report that recommended extensive revisions to the UPA. See UPA Revision Subcommittee of the Committee on Partnerships and Unincorporated Business Organizations, Section of Business Law, American Bar Association, *Should the Uniform Partnership Act be Revised?*, 43 Bus. Law. 121 (1987) ("ABA Report"). The ABA Report recommended that the entity theory "should be incorporated into any revision of the UPA whenever possible." *Id.* at 124.

In 1987, the Conference appointed a Drafting Committee to Revise the Uniform Partnership Act and named a Reporter. The Committee held its initial meeting in January of 1988 and a first reading of the Committee's draft was begun at the Conference's 1989 Annual Meeting in Kauai, Hawaii. The first reading was completed at the 1990 Annual Meeting in Milwaukee. The second reading was begun at Naples, Florida, in 1991 and completed at San Francisco in 1992. The Revised Uniform Partnership Act (1992) was adopted unanimously by a vote of the States on August 6, 1992. The following year, in response to suggestions from various groups, including an American Bar Association subcommittee and several state bar associations, the Drafting Committee recommended numerous revisions to the Act. Those were adopted at the Charleston, South Carolina, Annual Meeting in 1993, and the Act was restyled as the Uniform Partnership Act (1993). Subsequently, a final round of changes was incorporated, and the Conference unanimously adopted the Uniform Partnership Act (1994) at its 1994 Annual Meeting in Chicago. The Revised Act was approved by the American Bar Association House of Delegates in August, 1994.

The Uniform Partnership Act (1994) ("Revised Act" or "RUPA") gives supremacy to the partnership agreement in almost all situations. The Revised Act is, therefore, largely a series of "default rules" that govern the relations among partners in situations they have not addressed in a partnership agreement. The primary focus of RUPA is the small, often informal, partnership. Larger partnerships generally have a partnership agreement addressing, and often modifying, many of the provisions of the partnership act.

The Revised Act enhances the entity treatment of partnerships to achieve simplicity for state law purposes, particularly in matters concerning title to partnership property. RUPA does not, however, relentlessly apply the entity approach. The aggregate approach is retained for some purposes, such as partners' joint and several liability.

The Drafting Committee spent significant effort on the rules governing partnership breakups. RUPA's basic thrust is to provide stability for partnerships that have continuation agreements. Under the UPA, a partnership is dissolved every time a member leaves. The Revised Act provides that there are many departures or "dissociations" that do not result in a dissolution.

Under the Revised Act, the withdrawal of a partner is a "dissociation" that results in a dissolution of the partnership only in certain limited circumstances. Many dissociations result merely in a buyout of the withdrawing partner's interest rather than a winding up of the partnership's business. RUPA defines both the substance and procedure of the buyout right.

Article 6 of the Revised Act covers partner dissociations; Article 7 covers buyouts; and Article 8 covers dissolution and the winding up of the partnership business. *See generally* Donald J. Weidner & John W. Larson, *The Revised Uniform Partnership Act: The Reporters' Overview,* 49 Bus. Law. 1 (1993).

The Revised Act also includes a more extensive treatment of the fiduciary duties of partners. Although RUPA continues the traditional rule that a partner is a fiduciary, it also makes clear that a partner is not required to be a disinterested trustee. Provision is made for the legitimate pursuit of self-interest, with a counterbalancing irreducible core of fiduciary duties.

Another significant change introduced by RUPA is provision for the public filing of statements containing basic information about a partnership, such as the agency authority of its partners. Because of the informality of many partnerships, and the inadvertence of some, mandatory filings were eschewed in favor of a voluntary regime. It was the Drafting Committee's belief, however, that filings would become routine for sophisticated partnerships and would be required by lenders and others for major transactions.

Another innovation is found in Article 9. For the first time, the merger of two or more partnerships and the conversion of partnerships to limited partnerships (and the reverse) is expressly authorized, and a "safe harbor" procedure for effecting such transactions is provided.

One final change deserves mention. Partnership law no longer governs limited partnerships pursuant to the provisions of RUPA itself. First, limited partnerships are not "partnerships" within the RUPA definition. Second, UPA Section 6(2), which provides that the UPA governs limited partnerships in cases not provided for in the Uniform Limited Partnership Act (1976) (1985) ("RULPA") has been deleted. No substantive change in result is intended, however. Section 1105 of RULPA already provides that the UPA governs in any case not provided for in RULPA, and thus the express linkage in RUPA is unnecessary. Structurally, it is more appropriately left to RULPA to determine the applicability of RUPA to limited partnerships. It is contemplated that the Conference will review the linkage question carefully, although no changes in RULPA may be necessary despite the many changes in RUPA.

Finally, the Drafting Committee wishes to express its deep appreciation for the extraordinary time and effort that has been devoted to this project by its Reporter, Donald J. Weidner, Dean of the Florida State University College of Law; by its Assistant Reporter, Professor John W. Larson of the Florida State University College of Law; by its American Bar Association Advisors Allan G. Donn, of Norfolk, Virginia (ABA Section of Taxation and later the ABA Advisor, and a member of the original ABA subcommittee that recommended revising the UPA), Harry J. Haynsworth, Dean of the Southern Illinois University School of Law (the original ABA Advisor until he became a Commissioner and member of the Drafting Committee in 1992 and who was also a member of the original ABA subcommittee), S. Stacy Eastland, of Houston, Texas (Probate and Trust Division of the ABA Section of Real Property, Probate and Trust Law), and Caryl B. Welborn, of San Francisco, California (Real Property Division of the ABA Section of Real Property, Probate and Trust Law); and by a number of other advisors and observers without whose assistance the successful completion of this project would not have been possible: Edward S. Merrill of Walnut Creek, California, Gregory P.L. Pierce of Chicago, Illinois, Paul L. Lion, III, of San Jose, California, Professor Robert W. Hillman of the University of California at Davis School of Law, John Goode of Richmond, Virginia, Ronald H. Wilcomes of New York, New York, Professor Gary S. Rosin of the South Texas College of Law, James F. Fotenos of San Francisco, California, and Joel S. Adelman of Detroit, Michigan (who also was a member of the original ABA subcommittee). The Drafting Committee also would like to express its appreciation to the members of the ABA Committee on Partnerships and Unincorporated Business Organizations, and its chairs, Thurston R. Moore of Richmond, Virginia, and John H. Small of Wilmington, Delaware, for all the time and effort they devoted to this project, and to that Committee's special Subcommittee on the Revised Uniform Partnership Act, the chairs of that subcommittee, Lauris G.L. Rall of New York, New York, and Gerald V. Niesar of San Francisco, California, and its members, in particular, Robert R. Keatinge of Denver, Colorado, Professor Larry E. Ribstein of the

George Mason University School of Law, and Anthony van Westrum of Denver, Colorado. Each of these individuals added immeasurably to the Drafting Committee's discussion and consideration of both the major policy issues and the technical drafting issues raised by the Act.

ADDENDUM

In 1995, the Conference appointed a Drafting Committee to add provisions to RUPA authorizing the creation of a new form of general partnership called a limited liability partnership (LLP). At the time RUPA was first approved in 1992, only two states had adopted limited liability partnership legislation. By the time the LLP amendments to RUPA were approved by the Conference at the 1996 Annual Meeting, over forty states had adopted limited liability partnership provisions to their general partnership statutes.

The LLP amendments to RUPA deal with four major issues: (1) scope of a partner's liability shield; (2) the voting requirement to become an LLP; (3) the effect of becoming an LLP on the partnership agreement; and (4) the annual filing requirement.

1.   Scope of a Partner's Liability Shield

The amendments to add LLP provisions to RUPA include a new Section 306(c) providing for a corporate-styled liability shield which protects partners from vicarious personal liability for all partnership obligations incurred while a partnership is a limited liability partnership. The complete liability shield comports with the modern trend among the states. Most states, however, have adopted a partial liability shield protecting the partners only from vicarious personal liability for all partnership obligations arising from negligence, wrongful acts or misconduct, whether characterized as tort, contract or otherwise, committed while the partnership is an LLP. The Act does not alter a partner's liability for personal misconduct and does not alter the normal partnership rules regarding a partner's right to indemnification from the partnership (Section 401(c)). Therefore, the primary effect of the new liability shield is to sever a partner's personal liability to make contributions to the partnership when partnership assets are insufficient to cover its indemnification obligation to a partner who incurs a partnership obligation in the ordinary course of the partnership's business.

2.   Voting Requirement to Become an LLP

The Act includes a new Section 1001(b) which provides that the decision to become an LLP is a major partnership event equivalent to an amendment of the partnership agreement. Therefore, the required vote equals the vote required to amend the partnership agreement. When the agreement is silent on these matters, the required vote would be unanimous. Where the agreement includes several amendment votes depending on the nature of the amendment, the required vote is that which considers contribution obligations since those obligations are the most affected by the amendments. Most states currently consider the required vote to become a limited liability partnership to be an ordinary partnership decision requiring only a majority consent.

In becoming an LLP, each partner should consider a personal liability calculus. Where partnership assets are insufficient to indemnify a partner for an LLP obligation, each partner forfeits a right to receive contributions from other partners in exchange for being relieved of the obligation to contribute to the personal liability of other partners. This calculus will be different for each partner and will vary, for example, depending on the size and business of the partnership, the number of partners, the amount of insurance, and the relative risk of each partner's business practice compared to fellow partners. To adequately consider these varying interests, the Act adopts the vote required to amend the partnership agreement in special and general cases.

3. Effect of Becoming an LLP on the Partnership Agreement

The last sentence in new Section 306(c) provides that when a partnership becomes an LLP, the resulting liability shield applies notwithstanding inconsistent provisions of the partnership agreement existing immediately before the vote to become an LLP was taken. When the partners vote to become an LLP, they obviously intend to sever their personal responsibility to make contributions to the partnership when partnership assets are insufficient to cover partnership indemnification obligations to a partner. A partner's contribution obligation may be enforced not only by a partner (Sections 401 and 405) but also by a partner's creditors (Section 807(f)). In essence, the new Section 306(c) automatically "amends" the partnership agreement to remove personal liability for contribution obligations that may exist under the terms of the partnership agreement as it exists immediately before the vote. However, the partners are not prohibited from thereafter amending the partnership agreement again to reestablish contribution obligations (see Section 103(b)).

4. Annual Filing Requirement

The Act includes new Section 1001(d) which provides that a partnership's status as an LLP remains effective until it is revoked by a vote of the partners or is canceled by the Secretary of State under new Section 1003(c) for the failure to file an annual report or pay the required annual fees. Most states provide that unless an LLP timely files an annual registration statement, its LLP status is "automatically" terminated but may be resurrected prospectively only with a subsequent corrective filing. Under this view, an operating partnership may have significant "gaps" in its shield which is further complicated by sourcing rules necessary to determine when a partnership obligation belongs to the shielded LLP or the unshielded partnership. As with corporations and limited liability companies, the Act preserves the LLP status and the partners' liability shield unless the LLP status is revoked by the partners or canceled by the Secretary of State. In the latter case, potential gaps in the liability shield are cured with a retroactive resurrection of the LLP status if a corrective filing is made within two years (Section 1003(e)).

The LLP Drafting Committee wishes to express its gratitude to the Reporter for this project, Professor Carter G. Bishop of Suffolk University Law School. Professor Bishop's comprehensive knowledge of partnership law and tax and his drafting expertise were instrumental in enabling the Drafting Committee to complete this project in one year. The Drafting Committee also wishes to thank the following advisors and observers, whose expertise and advice were very important to the success of this project: Elizabeth G. Hester of Richmond, Virginia (ABA Advisor); Lou Conti of Orlando, Florida (ABA Section of Business Law Advisor); Steven G. Frost of Chicago, Illinois (ABA Section of Taxation Advisor); Professor Thomas E. Geu of the University of South Dakota School of Law (ABA Section of Real Property, Probate and Trust Advisor); Sanford J. Liebschutz of Rochester, New York (ABA Section of Real Property, Probate and Trust Advisor and American College of Real Estate Lawyers Advisor); Robert A. Creamer of Chicago, Illinois (Attorneys' Liability Assurance Society, Inc.); R. Michael Duffy of Washington, D.C. (The Accountant's Coalition); Professor Philip Hablutzel of Chicago, Illinois (Illinois Secretary of State's Corporation Law Advisory Committee; Robert R. Keatinge of Denver, Colorado (ABA Business Law Section); Mark Lubin of San Francisco, California (California Bar Association); Professor Sandra Miller of Chester, Pennsylvania; and William R. Stein of Washington, D.C. (The Accountant's Coalition); and Ronald H. Wilcomes of Paramus, New Jersey (American College of Real Estate Lawyers).

UNIFORM PARTNERSHIP ACT (1997)

[ARTICLE] 1
GENERAL PROVISIONS

Section 101. Definitions.

In this [Act]:

(1) "Business" includes every trade, occupation, and profession.

(2) "Debtor in bankruptcy" means a person who is the subject of:
   (i) an order for relief under Title 11 of the United States Code or a comparable order under a successor statute of general application; or
   (ii) a comparable order under federal, state, or foreign law governing insolvency.

(3) "Distribution" means a transfer of money or other property from a partnership to a partner in the partner's capacity as a partner or to the partner's transferee.

(4) "Foreign limited liability partnership" means a partnership that:
    (i) is formed under laws other than the laws of this State; and
    (ii) has the status of a limited liability partnership under those laws.

(5) "Limited liability partnership" means a partnership that has filed a statement of qualification under Section 1001 and does not have a similar statement in effect in any other jurisdiction.

(6) "Partnership" means an association of two or more persons to carry on as co-owners a business for profit formed under Section 202, predecessor law, or comparable law of another jurisdiction.

(7) "Partnership agreement" means the agreement, whether written, oral, or implied, among the partners concerning the partnership, including amendments to the partnership agreement.

(8) "Partnership at will" means a partnership in which the partners have not agreed to remain partners until the expiration of a definite term or the completion of a particular undertaking.

(9) "Partnership interest" or "partner's interest in the partnership" means all of a partner's interests in the partnership, including the partner's transferable interest and all management and other rights.

(10) "Person" means an individual, corporation, business trust, estate, trust, partnership, association, joint venture, government, governmental subdivision, agency, or instrumentality, or any other legal or commercial entity.

(11) "Property" means all property, real, personal, or mixed, tangible or intangible, or any interest therein.

(12) "State" means a State of the United States, the District of Columbia, the Commonwealth of Puerto Rico, or any territory or insular possession subject to the jurisdiction of the United States.

(13) "Statement" means a statement of partnership authority under Section 303, a statement of denial under Section 304, a statement of dissociation under Section 704, a statement of dissolution under Section 805, a statement of merger under Section 907, a statement of qualification under Section 1001, a statement of foreign qualification under Section 1102, or an amendment or cancellation of any of the foregoing.

(14) "Transfer" includes an assignment, conveyance, lease, mortgage, deed, and encumbrance.

COMMENT

These Comments include the original Comments to the Revised Uniform Partnership Act (RUPA or the Act) and the new Comments to the Limited Liability Partnership Act Amendments to the Uniform Partnership Act (1994). The new Comments regarding limited liability partnerships are integrated into the RUPA Comments.

The RUPA continues the definition of "business" from Section 2 of the Uniform Partnership Act (UPA).

RUPA uses the more contemporary term "debtor in bankruptcy" instead of "bankrupt." The definition is adapted from the new Georgia Partnership Act, Ga. Code Ann. § 14-8-2(1). The definition does not distinguish between a debtor whose estate is being liquidated under Chapter 7 of the Bankruptcy Code and a debtor who is being rehabilitated under Chapter 11, 12, or 13 and includes both. The filing of a voluntary petition under Section 301 of the Bankruptcy Code constitutes an order for relief, but the debtor is entitled to notice and an opportunity to be heard before the entry of an order for relief in an involuntary case under Section 303 of the Code. The term also includes a debtor who is the subject of a comparable order under state or foreign law.

The definition of "distribution" is new and adds precision to the accounting rules established in Sections 401 and 807 and related sections. Transfers to a partner in the partner's capacity as a creditor, lessor, or employee of the partnership, for example, are not "distributions."

The definition of a "foreign limited liability partnership" includes a partnership formed under the laws of another State, foreign country, or other jurisdiction provided it has the status of a limited liability partnership in the other jurisdiction. Since the scope and nature of foreign limited liability partnership liability shields may vary in different jurisdictions, the definition avoids reference to similar or comparable laws. Rather, the definition incorporates the concept of a limited liability partnership in the foreign jurisdiction, however defined in that jurisdiction. The reference to formation "under laws other than the laws of this State" makes clear that the definition includes partnerships formed in foreign countries as well as in another State.

The definition of a "limited liability partnership" makes clear that a partnership may adopt the special liability shield characteristics of a limited liability partnership simply by filing a statement of qualification under Section 1001. A partnership may file the statement in this State regardless of where formed. When coupled with the governing law provisions of Section 106(b), this definition simplifies the choice of law issues applicable to partnerships with multi-state activities and contacts. Once a statement of qualification is filed, a partnership's internal affairs and the liability of its partners are determined by the law of the State where the statement is filed. See Section 106(b). The partnership may not vary this particular requirement. See Section 103(b)(9).

The reference to a "partnership" in the definition of a limited liability partnership makes clear that the RUPA definition of the term rather than the UPA concept controls for purposes of a limited liability partnership. Section 101(6) defines a "partnership" as "an association of two or more persons to carry on as co-owners a business for profit formed under Section 202, predecessor law, or comparable law of another jurisdiction." Section 202(b) further provides that "an association formed under a statute other than this [Act], a predecessor statute, or a comparable statute of another jurisdiction is not a partnership under this [Act]." This language was intended to clarify that a limited partnership is not a RUPA general partnership. It was not intended to preclude the application of any RUPA general partnership rules to limited partnerships where limited partnership law otherwise adopts the RUPA rules. See Comments to Section 202(b) and Prefatory Note.

The effect of these definitions leaves the scope and applicability of RUPA to limited partnerships to limited partnership law, not to sever the linkage between the two Acts in all cases. Certain provisions of RUPA will continue to govern limited partnerships by virtue of Revised Uniform Limited Partnership Act (RULPA) Section 1105 which provides that "in any case not provided for in this [Act] the provisions of the Uniform Partnership Act govern." The RUPA partnership definition includes partnerships formed under the UPA. Therefore, the limited liability partnership rules will govern limited partnerships "in any case not provided for" in RULPA. Since RULPA does not provide for any rules applicable to a limited partnership becoming a limited liability partnership, the limited liability partnership rules should apply to limited partnerships that file a statement of qualification.

Partner liability deserves special mention. RULPA Section 403(b) provides that a general partner of a limited partnership "has the liabilities of a partner in a partnership without limited partners." Thus limited partnership law expressly references general partnership law for general partner liability and does not separately consider the liability of such partners. The liability of a general partner of a limited partnership that becomes a LLLP would therefore be the liability of a general partner in an LLP and would be governed by Section 306. The liability of a limited partner in a LLLP is a more complicated matter. RULPA Section 303(a) separately considers the liability of a limited partner. Unless also a general partner, a limited partner is not liable for the obligations of a limited partnership unless the partner participates in the control of the business and then only to persons reasonably believing the limited partner is a general partner. Therefore, arguably limited partners in a LLLP will have the specific RULPA Section 303(c) liability shield while general partners will have a superior Section 306(c) liability shield. In order to clarify limited partner liability and other linkage issues, States that have adopted RUPA, these limited liability partnership rules, and RULPA may wish to consider an amendment to RULPA. A suggested form of such an amendment is:

Section 1107. Limited Liability Limited Partnership.

(a) A limited partnership may become a limited liability partnership by:

    (1) obtaining approval of the terms and conditions of the limited partnership becoming a limited liability limited partnership by the

vote necessary to amend the limited partnership agreement except, in the case of a limited partnership agreement that expressly considers contribution obligations, the vote necessary to amend those provisions;

(2) filing a statement of qualification under Section 1001(c) of the Uniform Partnership Act (1994); and

(3) complying with the name requirements of Section 1002 of the Uniform Partnership Act (1994).

(b) A limited liability limited partnership continues to be the same entity that existed before the filing of a statement of qualification under Section 1001(c) of the Uniform Partnership Act (1994).

(c) Sections 306(c) and 307(b) of the Uniform Partnership Act (1994) apply to both general and limited partners of a limited liability limited partnership.

"Partnership" is defined to mean an association of two or more persons to carry on as co-owners a business for profit formed under Section 202 (or predecessor law or comparable law of another jurisdiction), that is, a general partnership. Thus, as used in RUPA, the term "partnership" does not encompass limited partnerships, contrary to the use of the term in the UPA. Section 901(3) defines "limited partnership" for the purpose of Article 9, which deals with conversions and mergers of general and limited partnerships.

The definition of "partnership agreement" is adapted from Section 101(9) of RULPA. The RUPA definition is intended to include the agreement among the partners, including amendments, concerning either the affairs of the partnership or the conduct of its business. It does not include other agreements between some or all of the partners, such as a lease or loan agreement. The partnership agreement need not be written; it may be oral or inferred from the conduct of the parties.

Any partnership in which the partners have not agreed to remain partners until the expiration of a definite term or the completion of a particular undertaking is a "partnership at will." The distinction between an "at-will" partnership and a partnership for "a definite term or the completion of a particular undertaking" is important in determining the rights of dissociating and continuing partners following the dissociation of a partner. See Sections 601, 602, 701(b), 801(a), 802(b), and 803.

It is sometimes difficult to determine whether a partnership is at will or is for a definite term or the completion of a particular undertaking. Presumptively, every partnership is an at-will partnership. *See, e.g., Stone v. Stone*, 292 So. 2d 686 (La. 1974); *Frey v. Hauke*, 171 Neb. 852, 108 N.W.2d 228 (1961). To constitute a partnership for a term or a particular undertaking, the partners must agree (i) that the partnership will continue for a definite term or until a particular undertaking is completed **and** (ii) that they will remain partners until the expiration of the term or the completion of the undertaking. Both are necessary for a term partnership; if the partners have the unrestricted right, as distinguished from the power, to withdraw from a partnership formed for a term or particular undertaking, the partnership is one at will, rather than a term partnership.

To find that the partnership is formed for a definite term or a particular undertaking, there must be clear evidence of an agreement among the partners that the partnership (i) has a minimum or maximum duration or (ii) terminates at the conclusion of a particular venture whose time is indefinite but certain to occur. *See, e.g., Stainton v. Tarantino*, 637 F. Supp. 1051 (E.D. Pa. 1986) (partnership to dissolve no later than December 30, 2020); *Abel v. American Art Analog, Inc.*, 838 F.2d 691 (3d Cir. 1988) (partnership purpose to market an art book); *68th Street Apts., Inc. v. Lauricella*, 362 A.2d 78 (N.J. Super. Ct. 1976) (partnership purpose to construct an apartment building). A partnership to conduct a business which may last indefinitely, however, is an at-will partnership, even though there may be an obligation of the partnership, such as a mortgage, which must be repaid by a certain date, absent a specific agreement that no partner can rightfully withdraw until the obligation is repaid. *See, e.g., Page v. Page*, 55 Cal. 2d. 192, 359 P.2d 41 (1961) (partnership purpose to operate a linen supply business); *Frey v. Hauke, supra* (partnership purpose to contract and operate a bowling alley); *Girard Bank v. Haley*, 460 Pa. 237, 332 A.2d 443 (1975) (partnership purpose to maintain and lease buildings).

"Partnership interest" or "partner's interest in the partnership" is defined to mean all of a partner's interests in the partnership, including the partner's transferable interest and all management and other rights. A partner's "transferable interest" is a more limited concept and means only his share of the profits and losses and right to receive distributions, that is, the partner's economic interests. See Section 502 and Comment. Compare RULPA § 101(10) ("partnership interest" includes partner's economic interests only).

The definition of "person" is the usual definition used by the National Conference of Commissioners on Uniform State Laws (NCCUSL or the Conference). The definition includes other legal or commercial entities such as limited liability companies.

"Property" is defined broadly to include all types of property, as well as any interest in property.

The definition of "State" is the Conference's usual definition.

The definition of "statement" is new and refers to one of the various statements authorized by RUPA to enhance or limit the agency authority of a partner, to deny the authority or status of a partner, or to give notice of certain events, such as the dissociation of a partner or the dissolution of the partnership. See Sections 303, 304, 704, 805, and 907. Generally, Section 105 governs the execution, filing, and recording of all statements. The definition also makes clear that a statement of qualification under Section 1001 and a statement of foreign qualification under Section 1102 are considered statements. Both qualification statements are therefore subject to the execution, filing, and recordation rules of Section 105.

"Transfer" is defined broadly to include all manner of conveyances, including leases and encumbrances.

Section 102. Knowledge and Notice.

    (a) A person knows a fact if the person has actual knowledge of it.

    (b) A person has notice of a fact if the person:

        (1) knows of it;

        (2) has received a notification of it; or

        (3) has reason to know it exists from all of the facts known to the person at the time in question.

    (c) A person notifies or gives a notification to another by taking steps reasonably required to inform the other person in ordinary course, whether or not the other person learns of it.

    (d) A person receives a notification when the notification:

        (1) comes to the person's attention; or

        (2) is duly delivered at the person's place of business or at any other place held out by the person as a place for receiving communications.

    (e) Except as otherwise provided in subsection (f), a person other than an individual knows, has notice, or receives a notification of a fact for purposes of a particular transaction when the individual conducting the transaction knows, has notice, or receives a notification of the fact, or in any event when the fact would have been brought to the individual's attention if the person had exercised reasonable diligence. The person exercises reasonable diligence if it maintains reasonable routines for communicating significant information to the individual conducting the transaction and there is reasonable compliance with the routines. Reasonable diligence does not require an individual acting for the person to communicate information unless the communication is part of the individual's regular duties or the individual has reason to know of the transaction and that the transaction would be materially affected by the information.

    (f) A partner's knowledge, notice, or receipt of a notification of a fact relating to the partnership is effective immediately as knowledge by, notice to, or receipt of a notification by the partnership, except in the case of a fraud on the partnership committed by or with the consent of that partner.

COMMENT

The concepts and definitions of "knowledge," "notice," and "notification" draw heavily on Section 1-201(25) to (27) of the Uniform Commercial Code (UCC). The UCC text has been altered somewhat to improve clarity and style, but in general no substantive changes are intended from the UCC concepts. "A notification" replaces the UCC's redundant phrase, "a notice or notification," throughout the Act.

A person "knows" a fact only if that person has actual knowledge of it. Knowledge is cognitive awareness. That is solely an issue of fact. This is a change from the UPA Section 3(1) definition of "knowledge" which included the concept of "bad faith" knowledge arising from other known facts.

"Notice" is a lesser degree of awareness than "knows" and is based on a person's: (i) actual knowledge; (ii) receipt of a notification; or (iii) reason to know based on actual knowledge of other facts and the circumstances at the time. The latter is the traditional concept of inquiry notice.

Generally, under RUPA, statements filed pursuant to Section 105 do not constitute constructive knowledge or notice, except as expressly provided in the Act. *See* Section 301(1) (generally requiring knowledge of limitations on partner's apparent authority). Properly recorded statements of limitation on a partner's authority, on the other hand, generally constitute constructive knowledge with respect to the transfer of real property held in the partnership name. *See* Sections 303(d)(1), 303(e), 704(b), and 805(b). The other exceptions are Sections 704(c) (statement of dissociation effective 90 days after filing) and 805(c) (statement of dissolution effective 90 days after filing).

A person "receives" a notification when (i) the notification is delivered to the person's place of business (or other place for receiving communications) or (ii) the recipient otherwise actually learns of its existence.

The sender "notifies" or gives a notification by making an effort to inform the recipient, which is reasonably calculated to do so in ordinary course, even if the recipient does not actually learn of it.

The Official Comment to UCC Section 1-201(26), on which this subsection is based, explains that "notifies" is the word used when the essential fact is the proper dispatch of the notice, not its receipt. When the essential fact is the other party's receipt of the notice, that is stated.

A notification is not required to be in writing. That is a change from UPA Section 3(2)(b). As under the UCC, the time and circumstances under which a notification may cease to be effective are not determined by RUPA.

Subsection (e) determines when an agent's knowledge or notice is imputed to an organization, such as a corporation. In general, only the knowledge or notice of the agent conducting the particular transaction is imputed to the organization. Organizations are expected to maintain reasonable internal routines to insure that important information reaches the individual agent handling a transaction. If, in the exercise of reasonable diligence on the part of the organization, the agent should have known or had notice of a fact, or received a notification of it, the organization is bound. The Official Comment to UCC Section 1-201(27) explains:

This makes clear that reason to know, knowledge, or a notification, although "received" for instance by a clerk in Department A of an organization, is effective for a transaction conducted in Department B only from the time when it was or should have been communicated to the individual conducting that transaction.

Subsection (e) uses the phrase "person other than an individual" in lieu of the UCC term "organization."

Subsection (f) continues the rule in UPA Section 12 that a partner's knowledge or notice of a fact relating to the partnership is imputed to the partnership, except in the case of fraud on the partnership. Limited partners, however, are not "partners" within the meaning of RUPA. *See* Comment 4 to Section 202. It is anticipated that RULPA will address the issue of whether notice to a limited partner is imputed to a limited partnership.

SECTION 103. Effect of Partnership Agreement; Nonwaivable Provisions.

    (a) Except as otherwise provided in subsection (b), relations among the partners and between the partners and the partnership are governed by the partnership agreement. To the extent the partnership agreement does not otherwise provide, this [Act] governs relations among the partners and between the partners and the partnership.

    (b) The partnership agreement may not:

        (1) vary the rights and duties under Section 105 except to eliminate the duty to provide copies of statements to all of the partners;

        (2) unreasonably restrict the right of access to books and records under Section 403(b);

        (3) eliminate the duty of loyalty under Section 404(b) or 603(b)(3), but:

            (i) the partnership agreement may identify specific types or categories of activities that do not violate the duty of loyalty, if not manifestly unreasonable; or

      (ii) all of the partners or a number or percentage specified in the partnership agreement may authorize or ratify, after full disclosure of all material facts, a specific act or transaction that otherwise would violate the duty of loyalty;

(4) unreasonably reduce the duty of care under Section 404(c) or 603(b)(3);

(5) eliminate the obligation of good faith and fair dealing under Section 404(d), but the partnership agreement may prescribe the standards by which the performance of the obligation is to be measured, if the standards are not manifestly unreasonable;

(6) vary the power to dissociate as a partner under Section 602(a), except to require the notice under Section 601(1) to be in writing;

(7) vary the right of a court to expel a partner in the events specified in Section 601(5);

(8) vary the requirement to wind up the partnership business in cases specified in Section 801(4), (5), or (6);

(9) vary the law applicable to a limited liability partnership under Section 106(b); or

(10) restrict rights of third parties under this [Act].

COMMENT

1. The general rule under Section 103(a) is that relations among the partners and between the partners and the partnership are governed by the partnership agreement. *See* Section 101(5). To the extent that the partners fail to agree upon a contrary rule, RUPA provides the default rule. Only the rights and duties listed in Section 103(b), and implicitly the corresponding liabilities and remedies under Section 405, are mandatory and cannot be waived or varied by agreement beyond what is authorized. Those are the only exceptions to the general principle that the provisions of RUPA with respect to the rights of the partners *inter se* are merely default rules, subject to modification by the partners. All modifications must also, of course, satisfy the general standards of contract validity. See Section 104.

2. Under subsection (b)(1), the partnership agreement may not vary the requirements for executing, filing, and recording statements under Section 105, except the duty to provide copies to all the partners. A statement that is not executed, filed, and recorded in accordance with the statutory requirements will not be accorded the effect prescribed in the Act, except as provided in Section 303(d).

3. Subsection (b)(2) provides that the partnership agreement may not unreasonably restrict a partner or former partner's access rights to books and records under Section 403(b). It is left to the courts to determine what restric-

tions are reasonable. See Comment 2 to Section 403. Other information rights in Section 403 can be varied or even eliminated by agreement.

4. Subsection (b)(3) through (5) are intended to ensure a fundamental core of fiduciary responsibility. Neither the fiduciary duties of loyalty or care, nor the obligation of good faith and fair dealing, may be eliminated entirely. However, the statutory requirements of each can be modified by agreement, subject to the limitation stated in subsection (b)(3) through (5).

There has always been a tension regarding the extent to which a partner's fiduciary duty of loyalty can be varied by agreement, as contrasted with the other partners' consent to a particular and known breach of duty. On the one hand, courts have been loathe to enforce agreements broadly "waiving" in advance a partner's fiduciary duty of loyalty, especially where there is unequal bargaining power, information, or sophistication. For this reason, a very broad provision in a partnership agreement in effect negating any duty of loyalty, such as a provision giving a managing partner complete discretion to manage the business with no liability except for acts and omissions that constitute willful misconduct, will not likely be enforced. *See, e.g., Labovitz v. Dolan*, 189 Ill. App. 3d 403, 136 Ill. Dec. 780, 545 N.E.2d 304 (1989). On the other hand, it is clear that the remaining partners can "consent" to a particular conflicting interest transaction or other breach of duty, after the fact, provided there is full disclosure.

RUPA attempts to provide a standard that partners can rely upon in drafting exculpatory agreements. It is not necessary that the agreement be restricted to a particular transaction. That would require bargaining over every transaction or opportunity, which would be excessively burdensome. The agreement may be drafted in terms of types or categories of activities or transactions, but it should be reasonably specific.

A provision in a real estate partnership agreement authorizing a partner who is a real estate agent to retain commissions on partnership property bought and sold by that partner would be an example of a "type or category" of activity that is not manifestly unreasonable and thus should be enforceable under the Act. Likewise, a provision authorizing that partner to buy or sell real property for his own account without prior disclosure to the other partners or without first offering it to the partnership would be enforceable as a valid category of partnership activity.

Ultimately, the courts must decide the outer limits of validity of such agreements, and context may be significant. It is intended that the risk of judicial refusal to enforce manifestly unreasonable exculpatory clauses will discourage sharp practices while accommodating the legitimate needs of the parties in structuring their relationship.

5. Subsection (b)(3)(i) permits the partners, in their partnership agreement, to identify specific types or categories of partnership activities that do not violate the duty of loyalty. A modification of the statutory standard must not, however, be manifestly unreasonable. This is intended to discourage overreaching by a partner with superior bargaining power since the courts may refuse to enforce an overly broad exculpatory clause. *See, e.g., Vlases v. Montgomery Ward & Co.*, 377 F.2d 846, 850 (3d Cir. 1967) (limitation prohibits unconscionable agreements); *PPG Industries, Inc. v. Shell Oil Co.*, 919 F.2d 17, 19 (5th Cir. 1990) (apply limitation deferentially to agreements of sophisticated parties).

Subsection (b)(3)(ii) is intended to clarify the right of partners, recognized under general law, to consent to a known past or anticipated violation of duty and to waive their legal remedies for redress of that violation. This is intended to cover situations where the conduct in question is not specifically authorized by the partnership agreement. It can also be used to validate conduct that might otherwise not satisfy the "manifestly unreasonable" standard. Clause (ii) provides that, after full disclosure of all material facts regarding a specific act or transaction that otherwise would violate the duty of loyalty, it may be authorized or ratified by the partners. That authorization or ratification must be unanimous unless a lesser number or percentage is specified for this purpose in the partnership agreement.

6. Under subsection (b)(4), the partners' duty of care may not be unreasonably reduced below the statutory standard set forth in Section 404(d), that is, to refrain from engaging in grossly negligent or reckless conduct, intentional misconduct, or a knowing violation of law.

For example, partnership agreements frequently contain provisions releasing a partner from liability for actions taken in good faith and in the honest belief that the actions are in the best interests of the partnership and indemnifying the partner against any liability incurred in connection with the business of the partnership if the partner acts in a good faith belief that he has authority to act. Many partnership agreements reach this same result by listing various activities and stating that the performance of these activities is deemed not to constitute gross negligence or willful misconduct. These types of provisions are intended to come within the modifications authorized by subsection (b)(4). On the other hand, absolving partners of intentional misconduct is probably unreasonable. As with contractual standards of loyalty, determining the outer limit in reducing the standard of care is left to the courts.

The standard may, of course, be increased by agreement to one of ordinary care or an even higher standard of care.

7. Subsection (b)(5) authorizes the partners to determine the standards by which the performance of the obligation of good faith and fair dealing is to be measured. The language of subsection (b)(5) is based on UCC Section 1-102(3). The partners can negotiate and draft specific contract provisions tailored to their particular needs (*e.g.*, five days notice of a partners' meeting is adequate notice), but blanket waivers of the obligation are unenforceable. *See, e.g., PPG Indus., Inc. v. Shell Oil Co.*, 919 F.2d 17 (5th Cir. 1990); *First Security Bank v. Mountain View Equip. Co.*, 112 Idaho 158, 730 P.2d 1078 (Ct. App. 1986), *aff'd*, 112 Idaho 1078, 739 P.2d 377 (1987); *American Bank of Commerce v. Covolo*, 88 N.M. 405, 540 P.2d 1294 (1975).

8. Section 602(a) continues the traditional UPA Section 31(2) rule that every partner has the power to withdraw from the partnership at any time, which power can not be bargained away. Section 103(b)(6) provides that the partnership agreement may not vary the power to dissociate as a partner under Section 602(a), except to require that the notice of withdrawal under Section 601(1) be in writing. The UPA was silent with respect to requiring a written notice of withdrawal.

9. Under subsection (b)(7), the right of a partner to seek court expulsion of another partner under Section 601(5) can not be waived or varied (e.g., requiring a 90-day notice) by agreement. Section 601(5) refers to judicial expulsion on such grounds as misconduct, breach of duty, or impracticability.

10. Under subsection (b)(8), the partnership agreement may not vary the right of partners to have the partnership dissolved and its business wound up under Section 801(4), (5), or (6). Section 801(4) provides that the partnership must be wound up if its business is unlawful. Section 801(5) provides for judicial winding up in such circumstances as frustration of the firm's economic purpose, partner misconduct, or impracticability. Section 801(6) accords standing to transferees of an interest in the partnership to seek judicial dissolution of the partnership in specified circumstances.

11. Subsection (b)(9) makes clear that a limited liability partnership may not designate the law of a State other than the State where it filed its statement of qualification to govern its internal affairs and the liability of its partners. See Sections 101(5), 106(b), and 202(a). Therefore, the selection of a State within which to file a statement of qualification has important choice of law ramifications, particularly where the partnership was formed in another State. See Comments to Section 106(b).

12. Although stating the obvious, subsection(b)(10) provides expressly that the rights of a third party under the Act may not be restricted by an agreement among the partners to which the third party has not agreed. A

non-partner who is a party to an agreement among the partners is, of course, bound. *Cf.* Section 703(c) (creditor joins release).

13. The Article 9 rules regarding conversions and mergers are not listed in Section 103(b) as mandatory. Indeed, Section 907 states expressly that partnerships may be converted and merged in any other manner provided by law. The effect of compliance with Article 9 is to provide a "safe harbor" assuring the legal validity of such conversions and mergers. Although not immune from variation in the partnership agreement, noncompliance with the requirements of Article 9 in effecting a conversion or merger is to deny that "safe harbor" validity to the transaction. In this regard, Sections 903(b) and 905(c)(2) require that the conversion or merger of a limited partnership be approved by all of the partners, notwithstanding a contrary provision in the limited partnership agreement. Thus, in effect, the agreement can not vary the voting requirement without sacrificing the benefits of the "safe harbor."

Section 104. Supplemental Principles of Law.

(a) Unless displaced by particular provisions of this [Act], the principles of law and equity supplement this [Act].

(b) If an obligation to pay interest arises under this [Act] and the rate is not specified, the rate is that specified in [applicable statute].

COMMENT

The principles of law and equity supplement RUPA unless displaced by a particular provision of the Act. This broad statement combines the separate rules contained in UPA Sections 4(2), 4(3), and 5. These supplementary principles encompass not only the law of agency and estoppel and the law merchant mentioned in the UPA, but all of the other principles listed in UCC Section 1-103: the law relative to capacity to contract, fraud, misrepresentation, duress, coercion, mistake, bankruptcy, and other common law validating or invalidating causes, such as unconscionability. No substantive change from either the UPA or the UCC is intended.

It was thought unnecessary to repeat the UPA Section 4(1) admonition that statutes in derogation of the common law are not to be strictly construed. This principle is now so well established that it is not necessary to so state in the Act. No change in the law is intended. See the Comment to RUPA Section 1101.

Subsection (b) is new. It is based on the definition of "interest" in Section 14-8-2(5) of the Georgia act and establishes the applicable rate of interest in the absence of an agreement among the partners. Adopting States can select the State's legal rate of interest or other statutory interest rate, such as the rate for judgments.

Section 105. Execution, Filing, and Recording of Statements.

(a) A statement may be filed in the office of [the Secretary of State]. A certified copy of a statement that is filed in an office in another State may be filed in the office of [the Secretary of State]. Either filing has the effect provided in this [Act] with respect to partnership property located in or transactions that occur in this State.

(b) A certified copy of a statement that has been filed in the office of the [Secretary of State] and recorded in the office for recording transfers of real property has the effect provided for recorded statements in this [Act]. A recorded statement that is not a certified copy of a statement filed in the office of the [Secretary of State] does not have the effect provided for recorded statements in this [Act].

(c) A statement filed by a partnership must be executed by at least two partners. Other statements must be executed by a partner or other person authorized by this [Act]. An individual who executes a statement as, or on behalf of, a partner or other person named as a partner in a statement shall personally declare under penalty of perjury that the contents of the statement are accurate.

(d) A person authorized by this [Act] to file a statement may amend or cancel the statement by filing an amendment or cancellation that names the partnership, identifies the statement, and states the substance of the amendment or cancellation.

(e) A person who files a statement pursuant to this section shall promptly send a copy of the statement to every nonfiling partner and to any other person named as a partner in the statement. Failure to send a copy of a statement to a partner or other person does not limit the effectiveness of the statement as to a person not a partner.

(f) The [Secretary of State] may collect a fee for filing or providing a certified copy of a statement. The [officer responsible for recording transfers of real property] may collect a fee for recording a statement.

COMMENT

1. Section 105 is new. It mandates the procedural rules for the execution, filing, and recording of the various "statements" (see Section 101(11)) authorized by RUPA. Section 101(13) makes clear that a statement of qualification filed by a partnership to become a limited liability partnership is included in the definition of a statement. Therefore, the execution, filing, and recording rules of this section must be followed except that the decision to file the statement of qualification must be approved by the vote of the partners necessary to amend the partnership agreement as to contribution requirements. See Section 1001(b) and Comments.

No filings are mandatory under RUPA. In all cases, the filing of a statement is optional and voluntary. A system of mandatory filing and disclosure for partnerships, similar to that required for corporations and limited partnerships, was rejected for several reasons. First, RUPA is designed to accommodate the needs of small partnerships, which often have unwritten or sketchy agreements and limited resources. Furthermore, inadvertent partnerships are also governed by the Act, as the default form of business organization, in which case filing would be unlikely.

The RUPA filing provisions are, however, likely to encourage the voluntary use of partnership statements. There are a number of strong incentives for the partnership or the partners to file statements or for third parties, such as lenders or transferees of partnership property, to compel them to do so.

Only statements that are executed, filed, and, if appropriate (such as the authority to transfer real property), recorded in conformity with Section 105 have the legal consequences accorded statements by RUPA. The requirements of Section 105 cannot be varied in the partnership agreement, except the duty to provide copies of statements to all the partners. *See* Section 103(b)(1).

In most States today, the filing and recording of statements requires written documents. As technology advances, alternatives suitable for filing and recording may be developed. RUPA itself does not impose any requirement that statements be in writing. It is intended that the form or medium for filing and recording be left to the general law of adopting States.

2. Section 105(a) provides for a single, central filing of all statements, as is the case with corporations, limited partnerships, and limited liability companies. The expectation is that most States will assign to the Secretary of State the responsibility of maintaining the filing system for partnership statements. Since a partnership is an entity under RUPA, all statements should be indexed by partnership name, not by the names of the individual partners.

Partnerships transacting business in more than one State will want to file copies of statements in each State because subsection (a) limits the legal effect of filed statements to property located or transactions occurring within the State. The filing of a certified copy of a statement originally filed in another State is permitted, and indeed encouraged, in order to avoid inconsistencies between statements filed in different States.

3. Subsection (b), in effect, mandates the use of certified copies of filed statements for local recording in the real estate records by limiting the legal effect of recorded statements under the Act to those copies. The reason for recording only certified copies of filed statements is to eliminate the possibility of inconsistencies affecting the title to real property.

Subsection (c) requires that statements filed on behalf of a partnership, that is, the entity, be executed by at least two partners. Individual partners and other persons authorized by the Act to file a statement may execute it on their own behalf. To protect the partners and the partnership from unauthorized or improper filings, an individual who executes a statement as a partner must personally declare under penalty of perjury that the statement is accurate.

The amendment or cancellation of statements is authorized by subsection (d).

As a further safeguard against inaccurate or unauthorized filings, subsection (e) requires that a copy of every statement filed be sent to each partner, although the failure to do so does not limit the effectiveness of the statement. This requirement may, however, be eliminated in the partnership agreement. *See* Section 103(b)(1). Partners may also file a statement of denial under Section 304.

4. A filed statement may be amended or canceled by any person authorized by the Act to file an original statement. The amendment or cancellation must state the name of the partnership so that it can be properly indexed and found, identify the statement being amended or canceled, and the substance of the amendment or cancellation. An amendment generally has the same operative effect as an original statement. A cancellation of extraordinary authority terminates that authority. A cancellation of a limitation on authority revives a previous grant of authority. *See* Section 303(d). The subsequent filing of a statement similar in kind to a statement already of record is treated as an amendment, even if not so denominated. Any substantive conflict between filed statements operates as a cancellation of authority under Section 303.

Section 106. Governing Law.

(a) Except as otherwise provided in subsection (b), the law of the jurisdiction in which a partnership has its chief executive office governs relations among the partners and between the partners and the partnership.

(b) The law of this State governs relations among the partners and between the partners and the partnership and the liability of partners for an obligation of a limited liability partnership.

COMMENT

The subsection (a) internal relations rule is new. *Cf.* RULPA § 901 (internal affairs governed by law of State in which limited partnership organized).

RUPA looks to the jurisdiction in which a partnership's chief executive office is located to provide the law governing the internal relations among the partners and between the partners and the partnership. The concept of the partnership's "chief executive office" is drawn from UCC Section 9-103(3)(d). It was chosen in lieu of the State of organization because no filing is necessary to form a general partnership, and thus the situs of its organization is not always clear, unlike a limited partnership, which is organized in the State where its certificate is filed.

The term "chief executive office" is not defined in the Act, nor is it defined in the UCC. Paragraph 5 of the Official Comment to UCC Section 9-103(3)(d) explains:

"Chief executive office" . . . means the place from which in fact the debtor manages the main part of his business operations. . . . Doubt may arise as to which is the "chief executive office" of a multi-state enterprise, but it would be rare that there could be more than two possibilities. . . . [The rule] will be simple to apply in most cases. . . .

In the absence of any other clear rule for determining a partnership's legal situs, it seems convenient to use that rule for choice of law purposes as well.

The choice-of-law rule provided by subsection (a) is only a default rule, and the partners may by agreement select the law of another State to govern their internal affairs, subject to generally applicable conflict of laws requirements. For example, where the partners may not resolve a particular issue by an explicit provision of the partnership agreement, such as the rights and duties set forth in Section 103(b), the law chosen will not be applied if the partners or the partnership have no substantial relationship to the chosen State or other reasonable basis for their choice or if application of the law of the chosen State would be contrary to a fundamental policy of a State that has a materially greater interest than the chosen State. *See* Restatement (Second) of Conflict of Laws § 187(2) (1971). The partners must, however, select only one State to govern their internal relations. They cannot select one State for some aspects of their internal relations and another State for others.

Contrasted with the variable choice-of-law rule provided by subsection (a), the law of the State where a limited liability partnership files its statement of qualification applies to such a partnership and may not be varied by the agreement of the partners. See Section 103(b)(9). Also, a partnership that files a statement of qualification in another State is not defined as a limited liability partnership in this State. See Section 101(5). Unlike a general partnership which may be formed without any filing, a partnership may only become a limited liability partnership by filing a statement of qualification. Therefore, the situs of its organization is clear. Because it is often unclear where a general partnership is actually formed, the decision to file a statement of qualification in a particular State constitutes a choice-of-law for the partnership which cannot be altered by the partnership agreement. See

Comments to Section 103(b)(9). If the partnership agreement of an existing partnership specifies the law of a particular State as its governing law, and the partnership thereafter files a statement of qualification in another State, the partnership agreement choice is no longer controlling. In such cases, the filing of a statement of qualification "amends" the partnership agreement on this limited matter. Accordingly, if a statement of qualification is revoked or canceled for a limited liability partnership, the law of the State of filing would continue to apply unless the partnership agreement thereafter altered the applicable law rule.

Section 107. Partnership Subject to Amendment Or Repeal of [Act].

A partnership governed by this [Act] is subject to any amendment to or repeal of this [Act].

COMMENT

The reservation of power provision is new. It is adapted from Section 1.02 of the Revised Model Business Corporation Act (RMBCA) and Section 1106 of RULPA.

As explained in the Official Comment to the RMBCA, the genesis of those provisions is *Trustees of Dartmouth College v. Woodward*, 17 U.S. (4 Wheat) 518 (1819), which held that the United States Constitution prohibits the application of newly enacted statutes to existing corporations, while suggesting the efficacy of a reservation of power provision. Its purpose is to avoid any possible argument that a legal entity created pursuant to statute or its members have a contractual or vested right in any specific statutory provision and to ensure that the State may in the future modify its enabling statute as it deems appropriate and require existing entities to comply with the statutes as modified.

[ARTICLE] 2
NATURE OF PARTNERSHIP

Section 201. Partnership As Entity.

(a) A partnership is an entity distinct from its partners.
(b) A limited liability partnership continues to be the same entity that existed before the filing of a statement of qualification under Section 1001.

COMMENT

RUPA embraces the entity theory of the partnership. In light of the UPA's ambivalence on the nature of partnerships, the explicit statement provided by subsection (a) is deemed appropriate as an expression of the increased emphasis on the entity theory as the dominant model. *But see* Section 306 (partners' liability joint and several unless the partnership has filed a statement of qualification to become a limited liability partnership).

Giving clear expression to the entity nature of a partnership is intended to allay previous concerns stemming from the aggregate theory, such as the necessity of a deed to convey title from the "old" partnership to the "new" partnership every time there is a change of cast among the partners. Under RUPA, there is no "new" partnership just because of membership changes. That will avoid the result in cases such as *Fairway Development Co. v. Title Insurance Co.*, 621 F. Supp. 120 (N.D. Ohio 1985), which held that the "new" partnership resulting from a partner's death did not have standing to enforce a title insurance policy issued to the "old" partnership.

Subsection (b) makes clear that the explicit entity theory provided by subsection (a) applies to a partnership both before and after it files a statement of qualification to become a limited liability partnership. Thus, just as there is no "new" partnership resulting from membership changes, the filing of a statement of qualification does not create a "new" partnership. The filing partnership continues to be the same partnership entity that existed before the filing. Similarly, the amendment or cancellation of a statement of qualification under Section 105(d) or the revocation of a statement of qualification under Section 1003(c) does not terminate the partnership and create a "new" partnership. See Section 1003(d). Accordingly, a partnership remains the same entity regardless of a filing, cancellation, or revocation of a statement of qualification.

Section 202. Formation of Partnership.
- (a) Except as otherwise provided in subsection (b), the association of two or more persons to carry on as co-owners a business for profit forms a partnership, whether or not the persons intend to form a partnership.
- (b) An association formed under a statute other than this [Act], a predecessor statute, or a comparable statute of another jurisdiction is not a partnership under this [Act].
- (c) In determining whether a partnership is formed, the following rules apply:
  - (1) Joint tenancy, tenancy in common, tenancy by the entireties, joint property, common property, or part ownership does not by itself establish a partnership, even if the co-owners share profits made by the use of the property.
  - (2) The sharing of gross returns does not by itself establish a partnership, even if the persons sharing them have a joint or common right or interest in property from which the returns are derived.

(3) A person who receives a share of the profits of a business is presumed to be a partner in the business, unless the profits were received in payment:
    (i) of a debt by installments or otherwise;
    (ii) for services as an independent contractor or of wages or other compensation to an employee;
    (iii) of rent;
    (iv) of an annuity or other retirement or health benefit to a beneficiary, representative, or designee of a deceased or retired partner;
    (v) of interest or other charge on a loan, even if the amount of payment varies with the profits of the business, including a direct or indirect present or future ownership of the collateral, or rights to income, proceeds, or increase in value derived from the collateral; or
    (vi) for the sale of the goodwill of a business or other property by installments or otherwise.

COMMENT

1. Section 202 combines UPA Sections 6 and 7. The traditional UPA Section 6(1) "definition" of a partnership is recast as an operative rule of law. No substantive change in the law is intended. The UPA "definition" has always been understood as an operative rule, as well as a definition. The addition of the phrase, "whether or not the persons intend to form a partnership," merely codifies the universal judicial construction of UPA Section 6(1) that a partnership is created by the association of persons whose intent is to carry on as co-owners a business for profit, regardless of their subjective intention to be "partners." Indeed, they may inadvertently create a partnership despite their expressed subjective intention not to do so. The new language alerts readers to this possibility.

As under the UPA, the attribute of co-ownership distinguishes a partnership from a mere agency relationship. A business is a series of acts directed toward an end. Ownership involves the power of ultimate control. To state that partners are co-owners of a business is to state that they each have the power of ultimate control. See Official Comment to UPA § 6(1). On the other hand, as subsection (c)(1) makes clear, passive co-ownership of property by itself, as distinguished from the carrying on of a business, does not establish a partnership.

2. Subsection (b) provides that business associations organized under other statutes are not partnerships. Those statutory associations include corporations, limited partnerships, and limited liability companies. That continues the UPA concept that general partnership is the residual form of for profit business association, existing only if another form does not.

A limited partnership is not a partnership under this definition. Nevertheless, certain provisions of RUPA will continue to govern limited partnerships because RULPA itself, in Section 1105, so requires "in any case not provided for" in RULPA. For example, the rules applicable to a limited liability partnership will generally apply to limited partnerships. See Comment to Section 101(5) (definition of a limited liability partnership). In light of that RULPA Section 1105, UPA Section 6(2), which provides that limited partnerships are governed by the UPA, is redundant and has not been carried over to RUPA. It is also more appropriate that the applicability of RUPA to limited partnerships be governed exclusively by RULPA. For example, a RULPA amendment may clarify certain linkage questions regarding the application of the limited liability partnership rules to limited partnerships. See Comment to Section 101(5) for a suggested form of such an amendment.

It is not intended that RUPA change any common law rules concerning special types of associations, such as mining partnerships, which in some jurisdictions are not governed by the UPA.

Relationships that are called "joint ventures" are partnerships if they otherwise fit the definition of a partnership. An association is not classified as a partnership, however, simply because it is called a "joint venture."

An unincorporated nonprofit organization is not a partnership under RUPA, even if it qualifies as a business, because it is not a "for profit" organization.

3. Subsection (c) provides three rules of construction that apply in determining whether a partnership has been formed under subsection (a). They are largely derived from UPA Section 7, and to that extent no substantive change is intended. The sharing of profits is recast as a rebuttable presumption of a partnership, a more contemporary construction, rather than as prima facie evidence thereof. The protected categories, in which receipt of a share of the profits is not presumed to create a partnership, apply whether the profit share is a single flat percentage or a ratio which varies, for example, after reaching a dollar floor or different levels of profits.

Like its predecessor, RUPA makes no attempt to answer in every case whether a partnership is formed. Whether a relationship is more properly characterized as that of borrower and lender, employer and employee, or landlord and tenant is left to the trier of fact. As under the UPA, a person may function in both partner and nonpartner capacities.

Paragraph (3)(v) adds a new protected category to the list. It shields from the presumption a share of the profits received in payment of interest or other charges on a loan, "including a direct or indirect present or future ownership in the collateral, or rights to income, proceeds, or increase in value derived from the collateral." The quoted language is taken from Section 211 of the

Uniform Land Security Interest Act. The purpose of the new language is to protect shared-appreciation mortgages, contingent or other variable or performance-related mortgages, and other equity participation arrangements by clarifying that contingent payments do not presumptively convert lending arrangements into partnerships.

4. Section 202(e) of the 1993 Act stated that partnerships formed under RUPA are general partnerships and that the partners are general partners. That section has been deleted as unnecessary. Limited partners are not "partners" within the meaning of RUPA, however.

Section 203. Partnership Property.

Property acquired by a partnership is property of the partnership and not of the partners individually.

COMMENT

All property acquired by a partnership, by transfer or otherwise, becomes partnership property and belongs to the partnership as an entity, rather than to the individual partners. This expresses the substantive result of UPA Sections 8(1) and 25.

Neither UPA Section 8(1) nor RUPA Section 203 provides any guidance concerning when property is "acquired by" the partnership. That problem is dealt with in Section 204.

UPA Sections 25(2)(c) and (e) also provide that partnership property is not subject to exemptions, allowances, or rights of a partner's spouse, heirs, or next of kin. Those provisions have been omitted as unnecessary. No substantive change is intended. Those exemptions and rights inure to the property of the partners, and not to partnership property.

Section 204. When Property Is Partnership Property.

(a) Property is partnership property if acquired in the name of:

(1) the partnership; or

(2) one or more partners with an indication in the instrument transferring title to the property of the person's capacity as a partner or of the existence of a partnership but without an indication of the name of the partnership.

(b) Property is acquired in the name of the partnership by a transfer to:

(1) the partnership in its name; or

(2) one or more partners in their capacity as partners in the partnership, if the name of the partnership is indicated in the instrument transferring title to the property.

(c) Property is presumed to be partnership property if purchased with partnership assets, even if not acquired in the name of the partnership or of one or more partners with an indication in the instrument transferring title to the property of the person's capacity as a partner or of the existence of a partnership.

(d) Property acquired in the name of one or more of the partners, without an indication in the instrument transferring title to the property of the person's capacity as a partner or of the existence of a partnership and without use of partnership assets, is presumed to be separate property, even if used for partnership purposes.

COMMENT

1. Section 204 sets forth the rules for determining when property is acquired by the partnership and, hence, becomes partnership property. It is based on UPA Section 8(3), as influenced by the recent Alabama and Georgia modifications. The rules govern the acquisition of personal property, as well as real property, that is held in the partnership name. *See* Section 101(9).

2. Subsection (a) governs the circumstances under which property becomes "partnership property," and subsection (b) clarifies the circumstances under which property is acquired "in the name of the partnership." The concept of record title is emphasized, although the term itself is not used. Titled personal property, as well as all transferable interests in real property acquired in the name of the partnership, are covered by this section.

Property becomes partnership property if acquired (1) in the name of the partnership or (2) in the name of one or more of the partners with an indication in the instrument transferring title of either (i) their capacity as partners or (ii) of the existence of a partnership, even if the name of the partnership is not indicated. Property acquired "in the name of the partnership" includes property acquired in the name of one or more partners in their capacity as partners, but only if the name of the partnership is indicated in the instrument transferring title.

Property transferred to a partner is partnership property, even though the name of the partnership is not indicated, if the instrument transferring title indicates either (i) the partner's capacity as a partner or (ii) the existence of a partnership. This is consonant with the entity theory of partnership and resolves the troublesome issue of a conveyance to fewer than all the partners but which nevertheless indicates their partner status.

3. Ultimately, it is the intention of the partners that controls whether property belongs to the partnership or to one or more of the partners in their individual capacities, at least as among the partners themselves. RUPA sets

forth two rebuttable presumptions that apply when the partners have failed to express their intent.

First, under subsection (c), property purchased with partnership funds is presumed to be partnership property, notwithstanding the name in which title is held. The presumption is intended to apply if partnership credit is used to obtain financing, as well as the use of partnership cash or property for payment. Unlike the rule in subsection (b), under which property is **deemed** to be partnership property if the partnership's name or the partner's capacity as a partner is disclosed in the instrument of conveyance, subsection (c) raises only a **presumption** that the property is partnership property if it is purchased with partnership assets.

That presumption is also subject to an important caveat. Under Section 302(b), partnership property held in the name of individual partners, without an indication of their capacity as partners or of the existence of a partnership, that is transferred by the partners in whose name title is held to a purchaser without knowledge that it is partnership property is free of any claims of the partnership.

Second, under subsection (d), property acquired in the name of one or more of the partners, without an indication of their capacity as partners and without use of partnership funds or credit, is presumed to be the partners' separate property, even if used for partnership purposes. In effect, it is presumed in that case that only the use of the property is contributed to the partnership.

4. Generally, under RUPA, partners and third parties dealing with partnerships will be able to rely on the record to determine whether property is owned by the partnership. The exception is property purchased with partnership funds without any reference to the partnership in the title documents. The inference concerning the partners' intent from the use of partnership funds outweighs any inference from the State of the title, subject to the overriding reliance interest in the case of a purchaser without notice of the partnership's interest. This allocation of risk should encourage the partnership to eliminate doubt about ownership by putting title in the partnership.

5. UPA Section 8(4) provides, "A transfer to a partnership in the partnership name, even without words of inheritance, passes the entire estate or interest of the grantor unless a contrary intent appears." It has been omitted from RUPA as unnecessary because modern conveyancing law deems all transfers to pass the entire estate or interest of the grantor unless a contrary intent appears.

[ARTICLE] 3
RELATIONS OF PARTNERS TO PERSONS DEALING WITH PARTNERSHIP

Section 301. Partner Agent of Partnership.

Subject to the effect of a statement of partnership authority under Section 303:

(1) Each partner is an agent of the partnership for the purpose of its business. An act of a partner, including the execution of an instrument in the partnership name, for apparently carrying on in the ordinary course the partnership business or business of the kind carried on by the partnership binds the partnership, unless the partner had no authority to act for the partnership in the particular matter and the person with whom the partner was dealing knew or had received a notification that the partner lacked authority.

(2) An act of a partner which is not apparently for carrying on in the ordinary course the partnership business or business of the kind carried on by the partnership binds the partnership only if the act was authorized by the other partners.

COMMENT

1. Section 301 sets forth a partner's power, as an agent of the firm, to bind the partnership entity to third parties. The rights of the partners among themselves, including the right to restrict a partner's authority, are governed by the partnership agreement and by Section 401.

The agency rules set forth in Section 301 are subject to an important qualification. They may be affected by the filing or recording of a statement of partnership authority. The legal effect of filing or recording a statement of partnership authority is set forth in Section 303.

2. Section 301(1) retains the basic principles reflected in UPA Section 9(1). It declares that each partner is an agent of the partnership and that, by virtue of partnership status, each partner has apparent authority to bind the partnership in ordinary course transactions. The effect of Section 301(1) is to characterize a partner as a general managerial agent having both actual and apparent authority co-extensive in scope with the firm's ordinary business, at least in the absence of a contrary partnership agreement.

Section 301(1) effects two changes from UPA Section 9(1). First, it clarifies that a partner's apparent authority includes acts for carrying on in the ordinary course "business of the kind carried on by the partnership," not just the business of the particular partnership in question. The UPA is ambiguous on this point, but there is some authority for an expanded construction in accordance with the so-called English rule. *See, e.g., Burns v. Gonzalez,* 439 S.W.2d 128, 131 (Tex. Civ. App. 1969) (dictum); *Commercial Hotel Co. v. Weeks,* 254 S.W. 521 (Tex. Civ. App. 1923). No substantive change is intended by use of the more customary phrase "carrying on in the ordinary course" in lieu of the UPA phrase "in the usual way." The UPA and the case law use both terms without apparent distinction.

The other change from the UPA concerns the allocation of risk of a partner's lack of authority. RUPA draws the line somewhat differently from the UPA.

Under UPA Section 9(1) and (4), only a person with knowledge of a restriction on a partner's authority is bound by it. Section 301(1) provides that a person who has received a notification of a partner's lack of authority is also bound. The meaning of "receives a notification" is explained in Section 102(d). Thus, the partnership may protect itself from unauthorized acts by giving a notification of a restriction on a partner's authority to a person dealing with that partner. A notification may be effective upon delivery, whether or not it actually comes to the other person's attention. To that extent, the risk of lack of authority is shifted to those dealing with partners.

On the other hand, as used in the UPA, the term "knowledge" embodies the concept of "bad faith" knowledge arising from other known facts. As used in RUPA, however, "knowledge" is limited to actual knowledge. *See* Section 102(a). Thus, RUPA does not expose persons dealing with a partner to the greater risk of being bound by a restriction based on their purported reason to know of the partner's lack of authority from all the facts they did know. Compare Section 102(b)(3) (notice).

With one exception, this result is not affected even if the partnership files a statement of partnership authority containing a limitation on a partner's authority. Section 303(f) makes clear that a person dealing with a partner is not deemed to know of such a limitation merely because it is contained in a filed statement of authority. Under Section 303(e), however, all persons are deemed to know of a limitation on the authority of a partner to transfer real property contained in a recorded statement. Thus, a recorded limitation on authority concerning real property constitutes constructive knowledge of the limitation to the whole world.

3. Section 301(2) is drawn directly from UPA Section 9(2), with conforming changes to mirror the new language of subsection (1). Subsection (2) makes it clear that the partnership is bound by a partner's actual authority, even if the partner has no apparent authority. Section 401(j) requires the unanimous consent of the partners for a grant of authority outside the ordinary course of business, unless the partnership agreement provides otherwise. Under general agency principles, the partners can subsequently ratify a partner's unauthorized act. See Section 104(a).

4. UPA Section 9(3) contains a list of five extraordinary acts that require unanimous consent of the partners before the partnership is bound. RUPA omits that section. That leaves it to the courts to decide the outer limits of the agency power of a partner. Most of the acts listed in UPA Section 9(3) probably remain outside the apparent authority of a partner under RUPA, such as disposing of the goodwill of the business, but elimination of a statutory rule will afford more flexibility in some situations specified in UPA Section 9(3). In particular, it seems archaic that the submission of a partnership claim to arbitration always requires unanimous consent. *See* UPA § 9(3)(e).

5. Section 301(1) fully reflects the principle embodied in UPA Section 9(4) that the partnership is not bound by an act of a partner in contravention of a restriction on his authority known to the other party.

Section 302. Transfer of Partnership Property.

(a) Partnership property may be transferred as follows:

    (1) Subject to the effect of a statement of partnership authority under Section 303, partnership property held in the name of the partnership may be transferred by an instrument of transfer executed by a partner in the partnership name.

    (2) Partnership property held in the name of one or more partners with an indication in the instrument transferring the property to them of their capacity as partners or of the existence of a partnership, but without an indication of the name of the partnership, may be transferred by an instrument of transfer executed by the persons in whose name the property is held.

    (3) Partnership property held in the name of one or more persons other than the partnership, without an indication in the instrument transferring the property to them of their capacity as partners or of the existence of a partnership, may be transferred by an instrument of transfer executed by the persons in whose name the property is held.

(b) A partnership may recover partnership property from a transferee only if it proves that execution of the instrument of initial transfer did not bind the partnership under Section 301 and:

    (1) as to a subsequent transferee who gave value for property transferred under subsection (a)(1) and (2), proves that the subsequent transferee knew or had received a notification that the person who executed the instrument of initial transfer lacked authority to bind the partnership; or

    (2) as to a transferee who gave value for property transferred under subsection (a)(3), proves that the transferee knew or had received a notification that the property was partnership property and that

the person who executed the instrument of initial transfer lacked authority to bind the partnership.

(c) A partnership may not recover partnership property from a subsequent transferee if the partnership would not have been entitled to recover the property, under subsection (b), from any earlier transferee of the property.

(d) If a person holds all of the partners' interests in the partnership, all of the partnership property vests in that person. The person may execute a document in the name of the partnership to evidence vesting of the property in that person and may file or record the document.

COMMENT

1. Section 302 replaces UPA Section 10 and provides rules for the transfer and recovery of partnership property. The language is adapted in part from Section 14-8-10 of the Georgia partnership statute.

2. Subsection (a)(1) deals with the transfer of partnership property held in the name of the partnership and subsection (a)(2) with property held in the name of one or more of the partners with an indication either of their capacity as partners or of the existence of a partnership. Subsection (a)(3) deals with partnership property held in the name of one or more of the partners without an indication of their capacity as partners or of the existence of a partnership. Like the general agency rules in Section 301, the power of a partner to transfer partnership property under subsection (a)(1) is subject to the effect under Section 303 of the filing or recording of a statement of partnership authority. These rules are intended to foster reliance on record title.

UPA Section 10 covers only real property. Section 302, however, also governs the transfer of partnership personal property acquired by instrument and held in the name of the partnership or one or more of the partners.

3. Subsection (b) deals with the right of the partnership to recover partnership property transferred by a partner without authority. Subsection (b)(1) deals with the recovery of property held in either the name of the partnership or the name of one or more of the partners with an indication of their capacity as partners or of the existence of a partnership, while subsection (b)(2) deals with the recovery of property held in the name of one or more persons without an indication of their capacity as partners or of the existence of a partnership.

In either case, a transfer of partnership property may be avoided only if the partnership proves that it was not bound under Section 301 by the execution of the instrument of initial transfer. Under Section 301, the partnership is bound by a transfer in the ordinary course of business, unless the transferee actually knew or had received a notification of the partner's lack of authority. See Section 102(a) and (d). The reference to Section 301, rather than Section 301(1), is intended to clarify that a partner's actual authority is not revoked by Section 302. Compare UPA § 10(1) (refers to partner's authority under Section 9(1)).

The burden of proof is on the partnership to prove the partner's lack of authority and, in the case of a subsequent transferee, the transferee's knowledge or notification thereof. Thus, even if the transfer to the initial transferee could be avoided, the partnership may not recover the property from a subsequent purchaser or other transferee for value unless it also proves that the subsequent transferee knew or had received a notification of the partner's lack of authority with respect to the initial transfer. Since knowledge is required, rather than notice, a remote purchaser has no duty to inquire as to the authority for the initial transfer, even if he knows it was partnership property.

The burden of proof is on the transferee to show that value was given. Value, as used in this context, is synonymous with valuable consideration and means any consideration sufficient to support a simple contract.

The burden of proof on all other issues is allocated to the partnership because it is generally in a better position than the transferee to produce the evidence. Moreover, the partnership may protect itself against unauthorized transfers by ensuring that partnership real property is held in the name of the partnership and that a statement of partnership authority is recorded specifying any limitations on the partners' authority to convey real property. Under Section 303(e), transferees of real property held in the partnership name are conclusively bound by those limitations. On the other hand, transferees can protect themselves by insisting that the partnership record a statement specifying who is authorized to transfer partnership property. Under Section 303(d), transferees for value, without actual knowledge to the contrary, may rely on that grant of authority.

4. Subsection (b)(2) replaces UPA Section 10(3) and provides that partners who hold partnership property in their own names, without an indication in the record of their capacity as partners or of the existence of a partnership, may transfer good title to a transferee for value without knowledge or a notification that it was partnership property. To recover the property under this subsection, the partnership has the burden of proving that the transferee knew or had received a notification of the partnership's interest in the property, as well as of the partner's lack of authority for the initial transfer.

5. Subsection (c) is new and provides that property may not be recovered by the partnership from a remote transferee if any intermediate transferee of the property would have prevailed against the partnership. *Cf.* Uniform Fraud-

ulent Transfer Act, §§ 8(a) (subsequent transferee from bona fide purchaser protected), 8(b)(2) (same).

6. Subsection (d) is new. The UPA does not have a provision dealing with the situation in which all of the partners' interests in the partnership are held by one person, such as a surviving partner or a purchaser of all the other partners' interests. Subsection (d) allows for clear record title, even though the partnership no longer exists as a technical matter. When a partnership becomes a sole proprietorship by reason of the dissociation of all but one of the partners, title vests in the remaining "partner," although there is no "transfer" of the property. The remaining "partner" may execute a deed or other transfer of record in the name of the non-existent partnership to evidence vesting of the property in that person's individual capacity.

7. UPA Section 10(2) provides that, where title to real property is in the partnership name, a conveyance by a partner in his own name transfers the partnership's equitable interest in the property. It has been omitted as was done in Georgia and Florida. In this situation, the conveyance is clearly outside the chain of title and so should not pass title or any interest in the property. UPA Section 10(2) dilutes, albeit slightly, the effect of record title and is, therefore, inconsistent with RUPA's broad policy of fostering reliance on the record.

UPA Section 10(4) and (5) have also been omitted. Those situations are now adequately covered by Section 302(a).

Section 303. Statement of Partnership Authority.

(a) A partnership may file a statement of partnership authority, which:

    (1) must include:

        (i) the name of the partnership;

        (ii) the street address of its chief executive office and of one office in this State, if there is one;

        (iii) the names and mailing addresses of all of the partners or of an agent appointed and maintained by the partnership for the purpose of subsection (b); and

        (iv) the names of the partners authorized to execute an instrument transferring real property held in the name of the partnership; and

    (2) may state the authority, or limitations on the authority, of some or all of the partners to enter into other transactions on behalf of the partnership and any other matter.

(b) If a statement of partnership authority names an agent, the agent shall maintain a list of the names and mailing addresses of all of the partners and make it available to any person on request for good cause shown.

(c) If a filed statement of partnership authority is executed pursuant to Section 105(c) and states the name of the partnership but does not contain all of the other information required by subsection (a), the statement nevertheless operates with respect to a person not a partner as provided in subsections (d) and (e).

(d) Except as otherwise provided in subsection (g), a filed statement of partnership authority supplements the authority of a partner to enter into transactions on behalf of the partnership as follows:

(1) Except for transfers of real property, a grant of authority contained in a filed statement of partnership authority is conclusive in favor of a person who gives value without knowledge to the contrary, so long as and to the extent that a limitation on that authority is not then contained in another filed statement. A filed cancellation of a limitation on authority revives the previous grant of authority.

(2) A grant of authority to transfer real property held in the name of the partnership contained in a certified copy of a filed statement of partnership authority recorded in the office for recording transfers of that real property is conclusive in favor of a person who gives value without knowledge to the contrary, so long as and to the extent that a certified copy of a filed statement containing a limitation on that authority is not then of record in the office for recording transfers of that real property. The recording in the office for recording transfers of that real property of a certified copy of a filed cancellation of a limitation on authority revives the previous grant of authority.

(e) A person not a partner is deemed to know of a limitation on the authority of a partner to transfer real property held in the name of the partnership if a certified copy of the filed statement containing the limitation on authority is of record in the office for recording transfers of that real property.

(f) Except as otherwise provided in subsections (d) and (e) and Sections 704 and 805, a person not a partner is not deemed to know of a limitation on the authority of a partner merely because the limitation is contained in a filed statement.

(g) Unless earlier canceled, a filed statement of partnership authority is canceled by operation of law five years after the date on which the statement, or the most recent amendment, was filed with the [Secretary of State].

COMMENT

1. Section 303 is new. It provides for an optional statement of partnership authority specifying the names of the partners authorized to execute instruments transferring real property held in the name of the partnership. It may

also grant supplementary authority to partners, or limit their authority, to enter into other transactions on behalf of the partnership. The execution, filing, and recording of statements is governed by Section 105.

RUPA follows the lead of California and Georgia in authorizing the optional filing of statements of authority. Filing a statement of partnership authority may be deemed to satisfy the disclosure required by a State's fictitious name statute, if the State so chooses.

Section 105 provides for the central filing of statements, rather than local filing. However, to be effective in connection with the transfer of real property, a statement of partnership authority must also be recorded locally with the land records.

2. The most important goal of the statement of authority is to facilitate the transfer of real property held in the name of the partnership. A statement must specify the names of the partners authorized to execute an instrument transferring that property.

Under subsection (d)(2), a recorded grant of authority to transfer real property held in the name of the partnership is conclusive in favor of a transferee for value without actual knowledge to the contrary. A partner's authority to transfer partnership real property is affected by a recorded statement only if the property is held in the name of the partnership. A recorded statement has no effect on the partners' authority to transfer partnership real property that is held other than in the name of the partnership. In that case, by definition, the record will not indicate the name of the partnership, and thus the partnership's interest would not be disclosed by a title search. *See* Section 204. To be effective, the statement recorded with the land records must be a certified copy of the original statement filed with the Secretary of State. *See* Section 105(b).

The presumption of authority created by subsection (d)(2) operates only so long as and to the extent that a limitation on the partner's authority is not contained in another recorded statement. This is intended to condition reliance on the record to situations where there is no conflict among recorded statements, amendments, or denials of authority. See Section 304. If the record is in conflict regarding a partner's authority, transferees must go outside the record to determine the partners' actual authority. This rule is modified slightly in the case of a cancellation of a limitation on a partner's authority, which revives the previous grant of authority.

Under subsection (e), third parties are deemed to know of a recorded limitation on the authority of a partner to transfer real property held in the partnership name. Since transferees are bound under Section 301 by knowledge of a limitation on a partner's authority, they are bound by such a recorded limitation. Of course, a transferee with actual knowledge of a limitation on a partner's authority is bound under Section 301, whether or not there is a recorded statement of limitation.

3. A statement of partnership authority may have effect beyond the transfer of real property held in the name of the partnership. Under subsection (a)(2), a statement of authority may contain any other matter the partnership chooses, including a grant of authority, or a limitation on the authority, of some or all of the partners to enter into other transactions on behalf of the partnership. Since Section 301 confers authority on all partners to act for the partnership in ordinary matters, the real import of such a provision is to grant extraordinary authority, or to limit the ordinary authority, of some or all of the partners.

The effect given to such a provision is different from that accorded a provision regarding the transfer of real property. Under subsection (d)(1), a filed grant of authority is binding on the partnership, in favor of a person who gives value without actual knowledge to the contrary, unless limited by another filed statement. That is the same rule as for statements involving real property under subsection 301(d)(2). There is, however, no counterpart to subsection (e) regarding a filed limitation of authority. To the contrary, subsection (f) makes clear that filing a limitation of authority does **not** operate as constructive knowledge of a partner's lack of authority with respect to non-real property transactions.

Under Section 301, only a third party who knows or has received a notification of a partner's lack of authority in an ordinary course transaction is bound. Thus, a limitation on a partner's authority to transfer personal property or to enter into other non-real property transactions on behalf of the partnership, contained in a filed statement of partnership authority, is effective only against a third party who knows or has received a notification of it. The fact of the statement being filed has no legal significance in those transactions, although the filed statement is a potential source of actual knowledge to third parties.

4. It should be emphasized that Section 303 concerns the authority of partners to bind the partnership to third persons. As among the partners, the authority of a partner to take any action is governed by the partnership agreement, or by the provisions of RUPA governing the relations among partners, and is not affected by the filing or recording of a statement of partnership authority.

5. The exercise of the option to file a statement of partnership authority imposes a further disclosure obligation on the partnership. Under subsection (a)(1), a filed statement must include the street address of its chief ex-

ecutive office and of an office in the State (if any), as well as the names and mailing addresses of all of the partners or, alternatively, of an agent appointed and maintained by the partnership for the purpose of maintaining such a list. If an agent is appointed, subsection (b) provides that the agent shall maintain a list of all of the partners and make it available to any person on request for good cause shown. Under subsection (c), the failure to make all of the required disclosures does not affect the statement's operative effect, however.

6. Under subsection (g), a statement of authority is canceled by operation of law five years after the date on which the statement, or the most recent amendment, was filed.

7. Section 308(c) makes clear that a person does not become a partner solely because he is named as a partner in a statement of partnership authority filed by another person. See also Section 304 ("person named as a partner" may file statement of denial).

Section 304. Statement of Denial.
A partner or other person named as a partner in a filed statement of partnership authority or in a list maintained by an agent pursuant to Section 303(b) may file a statement of denial stating the name of the partnership and the fact that is being denied, which may include denial of a person's authority or status as a partner. A statement of denial is a limitation on authority as provided in Section 303(d) and (e).

COMMENT

Section 304 is new and complements Section 303. It provides partners (and persons named as partners) an opportunity to deny any fact asserted in a statement of partnership authority, including denial of a person's status as a partner or of another person's authority as a partner. A statement of denial must be executed, filed, and recorded pursuant to the requirements of Section 105.

Section 304 does not address the consequences of a denial of partnership. No adverse inference should be drawn from the failure of a person named as a partner to deny such status, however. See Section 308(c) (person not liable as a partner merely because named in statement as a partner).

A statement of denial operates as a limitation on a partner's authority to the extent provided in Section 303. Section 303(d) provides that a filed or recorded statement of partnership authority is conclusive, in favor of purchasers without knowledge to the contrary, so long as and to the extent that a limitation on that authority is not contained in another filed or recorded statement. A filed or recorded statement of denial operates as such a limitation on authority, thereby precluding reliance on an inconsistent grant of authority. Under Section 303(d), a filed or recorded cancellation of a statement of denial that operates as a limitation on authority revives the previous grant of authority.

Under Section 303(e), a recorded statement of denial of a partner's authority to transfer partnership real property held in the partnership name constitutes constructive knowledge of that limitation.

Section 305. Partnership Liable for Partner's Actionable Conduct.

(a) A partnership is liable for loss or injury caused to a person, or for a penalty incurred, as a result of a wrongful act or omission, or other actionable conduct, of a partner acting in the ordinary course of business of the partnership or with authority of the partnership.

(b) If, in the course of the partnership's business or while acting with authority of the partnership, a partner receives or causes the partnership to receive money or property of a person not a partner, and the money or property is misapplied by a partner, the partnership is liable for the loss.

COMMENT

Section 305(a), which is derived from UPA Section 13, imposes liability on the partnership for the wrongful acts of a partner acting in the ordinary course of the partnership's business or otherwise within the partner's authority. The scope of the section has been expanded by deleting from UPA Section 13, "not being a partner in the partnership." This is intended to permit a partner to sue the partnership on a tort or other theory during the term of the partnership, rather than being limited to the remedies of dissolution and an accounting. See also Comment 2 to Section 405.

The section has also been broadened to cover no-fault torts by the addition of the phrase, "or other actionable conduct."

The partnership is liable for the actionable conduct or omission of a partner acting in the ordinary course of its business or "with the authority of the partnership." This is intended to include a partner's apparent, as well as actual, authority, thereby bringing within Section 305(a) the situation covered in UPA Section 14(a).

The phrase in UPA Section 13, "to the same extent as the partner so acting or omitting to act," has been deleted to prevent a partnership from asserting a partner's immunity from liability. This is consistent with the general agency rule that a principal is not entitled to its agent's immunities. *See* Restatement (Second) of Agency § 217(b) (1957). The deletion is not intended to limit a partnership's contractual rights.

Section 305(b) is drawn from UPA Section 14(b), but has been edited to improve clarity. It imposes strict liability on the partnership for the misapplication of money or property received by a partner in the course of the partnership's business or otherwise within the scope of the partner's actual authority.

Section 306. Partner's Liability.

(a) Except as otherwise provided in subsections (b) and (c), all partners are liable jointly and severally for all obligations of the partnership unless otherwise agreed by the claimant or provided by law.

(b) A person admitted as a partner into an existing partnership is not personally liable for any partnership obligation incurred before the person's admission as a partner.

(c) An obligation of a partnership incurred while the partnership is a limited liability partnership, whether arising in contract, tort, or otherwise, is solely the obligation of the partnership. A partner is not personally liable, directly or indirectly, by way of contribution or otherwise, for such an obligation solely by reason of being or so acting as a partner. This subsection applies notwithstanding anything inconsistent in the partnership agreement that existed immediately before the vote required to become a limited liability partnership under Section 1001(b).

COMMENT

1. Section 306(a) changes the UPA rule by imposing joint and several liability on the partners for all partnership obligations where the partnership is not a limited liability partnership. Under UPA Section 15, partners' liability for torts is joint and several, while their liability for contracts is joint but not several. About ten States that have adopted the UPA already provide for joint and several liability. The UPA reference to "debts and obligations" is redundant, and no change is intended by RUPA's reference solely to "obligations."

Joint and several liability under RUPA differs, however, from the classic model, which permits a judgment creditor to proceed immediately against any of the joint and several judgment debtors. Generally, Section 307(d) requires the judgment creditor to exhaust the partnership's assets before enforcing a judgment against the separate assets of a partner.

2. RUPA continues the UPA scheme of liability with respect to an incoming partner, but states the rule more clearly and simply. Under Section 306(a), an incoming partner becomes jointly and severally liable, as a partner, for all partnership obligations, except as otherwise provided in subsection (b). That subsection eliminates an incoming partner's personal liability for partnership obligations incurred before his admission as a partner. In effect, a new

partner has no personal liability to existing creditors of the partnership, and only his investment in the firm is at risk for the satisfaction of existing partnership debts. That is presently the rule under UPA Sections 17 and 41(7), and no substantive change is intended. As under the UPA, a new partner's personal assets are at risk with respect to partnership liabilities incurred after his admission as a partner.

3. Subsection (c) alters classic joint and several liability of general partners for obligations of a partnership that is a limited liability partnership. Like shareholders of a corporation and members of a limited liability company, partners of a limited liability partnership are not personally liable for partnership obligations incurred while the partnership liability shield is in place solely because they are partners. As with shareholders of a corporation and members of a limited liability company, partners remain personally liable for their personal misconduct.

In cases of partner misconduct, Section 401(c) sets forth a partnership's obligation to indemnify the culpable partner where the partner's liability was incurred in the ordinary course of the partnership's business. When indemnification occurs, the assets of both the partnership and the culpable partner are available to a creditor. However, Sections 306(c), 401(b), and 807(b) make clear that a partner who is not otherwise liable under Section 306(c) is not obligated to contribute assets to the partnership in excess of agreed contributions to share the loss with the culpable partner. (See Comments to Sections 401(b) and 807(b). regarding a slight variation in the context of priority of payment of partnership obligations.) Accordingly, Section 306(c) makes clear that an innocent partner is not personally liable for specified partnership obligations, directly or indirectly, by way of contribution or otherwise.

Although the liability shield protections of Section 306(c) may be modified in part or in full in a partnership agreement (and by way of private contractual guarantees), the modifications must constitute an intentional waiver of the liability protections. See Sections 103(b), 104(a), and 902(b). Since the mere act of filing a statement of qualification reflects the assumption that the partners intend to modify the otherwise applicable partner liability rules, the final sentence of subsection (c) makes clear that the filing negates inconsistent aspects of the partnership agreement that existed immediately before the vote to approve becoming a limited liability partnership. The negation only applies to a partner's personal liability for future partnership obligations. The filing however has no effect as to previously created partner obligations to the partnership in the form of specific capital contribution requirements.

Inter se contribution agreements may erode part or all of the effects of the liability shield. For example, Section 807(f) provides that an assignee for the benefit of creditors of a partnership or a partner may enforce a partner's obligation to contribute to the partnership. The ultimate effect of such contribution obligations may make each partner jointly and severally liable for all partnership obligations - even those incurred while the partnership is a limited liability partnership. Although the final sentence of subsection (c) negates such provisions existing before a statement of qualification is filed, it will have no effect on any amendments to the partnership agreement after the statement is filed.

The connection between partner status and personal liability for partnership obligations is severed only with respect to obligations incurred while the partnership is a limited liability partnership. Partnership obligations incurred before a partnership becomes a limited liability partnership or incurred after limited liability partnership status is revoked or canceled are treated as obligations of an ordinary partnership. See Sections 1001 (filing), 1003 (revocation), and 1006 (cancellation). Obligations incurred by a partnership during the period when its statement of qualification is administratively revoked will be considered as incurred by a limited liability partnership provided the partnership's status as such is reinstated within two years under Section 1003(e). See Section 1003(f).

When an obligation is incurred is determined by other law. See Section 104(a). Under that law, and for the limited purpose of determining when partnership contract obligations are incurred, the reasonable expectations of creditors and the partners are paramount. Therefore, partnership obligations under or relating to a note, contract, or other agreement generally are incurred when the note, contract, or other agreement is made. Also, an amendment, modification, extension, or renewal of a note, contract, or other agreement should not affect or otherwise reset the time at which a partnership obligation under or relating to that note, contract, or other agreement is incurred, even as to a claim that relates to the subject matter of the amendment, modification, extension, or renewal. A note, contract, or other agreement may expressly modify these rules and fix the time a partnership obligation is incurred thereunder.

For the limited purpose of determining when partnership tort obligations are incurred, a distinction is intended between injury and the conduct causing that injury. The purpose of the distinction is to prevent unjust results. Partnership obligations under or relating to a tort generally are incurred when the tort conduct occurs rather than at the time of the actual injury or harm. This interpretation prevents a culpable partnership from engaging in wrongful conduct and then filing a statement of qualification to sever the vicarious responsibility of its partners for future injury or harm caused by conduct that occurred prior to the filing.

Section 307. Actions by and Against Partnership and Partners.

(a) A partnership may sue and be sued in the name of the partnership.

(b) An action may be brought against the partnership and, to the extent not inconsistent with Section 306, any or all of the partners in the same action or in separate actions.

(c) A judgment against a partnership is not by itself a judgment against a partner. A judgment against a partnership may not be satisfied from a partner's assets unless there is also a judgment against the partner.

(d) A judgment creditor of a partner may not levy execution against the assets of the partner to satisfy a judgment based on a claim against the partnership unless the partner is personally liable for the claim under Section 306 and:

(1) a judgment based on the same claim has been obtained against the partnership and a writ of execution on the judgment has been returned unsatisfied in whole or in part;

(2) the partnership is a debtor in bankruptcy;

(3) the partner has agreed that the creditor need not exhaust partnership assets;

(4) a court grants permission to the judgment creditor to levy execution against the assets of a partner based on a finding that partnership assets subject to execution are clearly insufficient to satisfy the judgment, that exhaustion of partnership assets is excessively burdensome, or that the grant of permission is an appropriate exercise of the court's equitable powers; or

(5) liability is imposed on the partner by law or contract independent of the existence of the partnership.

(e) This section applies to any partnership liability or obligation resulting from a representation by a partner or purported partner under Section 308.

COMMENT

1. Section 307 is new. Subsection (a) provides that a partnership may sue and be sued in the partnership name. That entity approach is designed to simplify suits by and against a partnership.

At common law, a partnership, not being a legal entity, could not sue or be sued in the firm name. The UPA itself is silent on this point, so in the absence of another enabling statute, it is generally necessary to join all the partners in an action against the partnership.

Most States have statutes or rules authorizing partnerships to sue or be sued in the partnership name. Many of those statutes, however, are found in the state provisions dealing with civil procedure rather than in the partnership act.

2. Subsection (b) provides that suit generally may be brought against the partnership and any or all of the partners in the same action or in separate actions. It is intended to clarify that the partners need not be named in an action against the partnership. In particular, in an action against a partnership,

it is not necessary to name a partner individually in addition to the partnership. This will simplify and reduce the cost of litigation, especially in cases of small claims where there are known to be significant partnership assets and thus no necessity to collect the judgment out of the partners' assets.

Where the partnership is a limited liability partnership, the limited liability partnership rules clarify that a partner not liable for the alleged partnership obligation may not be named in the action against the partnership unless the action also seeks to establish personal liability of the partner for the obligation. See subsections (b) and (d).

3. Subsection (c) provides that a judgment against the partnership is not, standing alone, a judgment against the partners, and it cannot be satisfied from a partner's personal assets unless there is a judgment against the partner. Thus, a partner must be individually named and served, either in the action against the partnership or in a later suit, before his personal assets may be subject to levy for a claim against the partnership.

RUPA leaves it to the law of judgments, as did the UPA, to determine the collateral effects to be accorded a prior judgment for or against the partnership in a subsequent action against a partner individually. See Section 60 of the Second Restatement of Judgments (1982) and the Comments thereto.

4. Subsection (d) requires partnership creditors to exhaust the partnership's assets before levying on a judgment debtor partner's individual property where the partner is personally liable for the partnership obligation under Section 306. That rule respects the concept of the partnership as an entity and makes partners more in the nature of guarantors than principal debtors on every partnership debt. It is already the law in some States.

As a general rule, a final judgment against a partner cannot be enforced by a creditor against the partner's separate assets unless a writ of execution against the partnership has been returned unsatisfied. Under subsection (d), however, a creditor may proceed directly against the partner's assets if (i) the partnership is a debtor in bankruptcy (see Section 101(2)); (ii) the partner has consented; or (iii) the liability is imposed on the partner independently of the partnership. For example, a judgment creditor may proceed directly against the assets of a partner who is liable independently as the primary tortfeasor, but must exhaust the partnership's assets before proceeding against the separate assets of the other partners who are liable only as partners.

There is also a judicial override provision in subsection (d)(4). A court may authorize execution against the partner's assets on the grounds that (i) the partnership's assets are clearly insufficient; (ii) exhaustion of the partnership's assets would be excessively burdensome; or (iii) it is otherwise equitable to do so. For example, if the partners who are parties to the action have assets located in the forum State, but the partnership does not, a court might find that exhaustion of the partnership's assets would be excessively burdensome.

5. Although subsection (d) is silent with respect to pre-judgment remedies, the law of pre-judgment remedies already adequately embodies the principle that partnership assets should be exhausted before partners' assets are attached or garnished. Attachment, for example, typically requires a showing that the partnership's assets are being secreted or fraudulently transferred or are otherwise inadequate to satisfy the plaintiff's claim. A showing of some exigent circumstance may also be required to satisfy due process. *See Connecticut v. Doehr*, 501 U.S. 1, 16 (1991).

6. Subsection (e) clarifies that actions against the partnership under Section 308, involving representations by partners or purported partners, are subject to Section 307.

Section 308. Liability of Purported Partner.

   (a) If a person, by words or conduct, purports to be a partner, or consents to being represented by another as a partner, in a partnership or with one or more persons not partners, the purported partner is liable to a person to whom the representation is made, if that person, relying on the representation, enters into a transaction with the actual or purported partnership. If the representation, either by the purported partner or by a person with the purported partner's consent, is made in a public manner, the purported partner is liable to a person who relies upon the purported partnership even if the purported partner is not aware of being held out as a partner to the claimant. If partnership liability results, the purported partner is liable with respect to that liability as if the purported partner were a partner. If no partnership liability results, the purported partner is liable with respect to that liability jointly and severally with any other person consenting to the representation.

   (b) If a person is thus represented to be a partner in an existing partnership, or with one or more persons not partners, the purported partner is an agent of persons consenting to the representation to bind them to the same extent and in the same manner as if the purported partner were a partner, with respect to persons who enter into transactions in reliance upon the representation. If all of the partners of the existing partnership consent to the representation, a partnership act or obligation results. If fewer than all of the partners of the existing partnership consent to the representation, the person acting and the partners consenting to the representation are jointly and severally liable.

(c) A person is not liable as a partner merely because the person is named by another in a statement of partnership authority.

(d) A person does not continue to be liable as a partner merely because of a failure to file a statement of dissociation or to amend a statement of partnership authority to indicate the partner's dissociation from the partnership.

(e) Except as otherwise provided in subsections (a) and (b), persons who are not partners as to each other are not liable as partners to other persons.

COMMENT

Section 308 continues the basic principles of partnership by estoppel from UPA Section 16, now more accurately entitled "Liability of Purported Partner." Subsection (a) continues the distinction between representations made to specific persons and those made in a public manner. It is the exclusive basis for imposing liability as a partner on persons who are not partners in fact. As under the UPA, there is no duty of denial, and thus a person held out by another as a partner is not liable unless he actually consents to the representation. See the Official Comment to UPA Section 16. Also see Section 308(c) (no duty to file statement of denial) and Section 308(d) (no duty to file statement of dissociation or to amend statement of partnership authority).

Subsection (b) emphasizes that the persons being protected by Section 308 are those who enter into transactions in reliance upon a representation. If all of the partners of an existing partnership consent to the representation, a partnership obligation results. Apart from Section 308, the firm may be bound in other situations under general principles of apparent authority or ratification.

If a partnership liability results under Section 308, the creditor must exhaust the partnership's assets before seeking to satisfy the claim from the partners. See Section 307.

Subsections (c) and (d) are new and deal with potential negative inferences to be drawn from a failure to correct inaccurate or outdated filed statements. Subsection (c) makes clear that an otherwise innocent person is not liable as a partner for failing to deny his partnership status as asserted by a third person in a statement of partnership authority. Under subsection (d), a partner's liability as a partner does not continue after dissociation solely because of a failure to file a statement of dissociation.

Subsection (e) is derived from UPA Section 7(1). It means that only those persons who are partners as among themselves are liable as partners to third parties for the obligations of the partnership, except for liabilities incurred by purported partners under Section 308(a) and (b).

[ARTICLE] 4
RELATIONS OF PARTNERS TO EACH OTHER
AND TO PARTNERSHIP

Section 401. Partner's Rights and Duties.

(a) Each partner is deemed to have an account that is:

   (1) credited with an amount equal to the money plus the value of any other property, net of the amount of any liabilities, the partner contributes to the partnership and the partner's share of the partnership profits; and

   (2) charged with an amount equal to the money plus the value of any other property, net of the amount of any liabilities, distributed by the partnership to the partner and the partner's share of the partnership losses.

(b) Each partner is entitled to an equal share of the partnership profits and is chargeable with a share of the partnership losses in proportion to the partner's share of the profits.

(c) A partnership shall reimburse a partner for payments made and indemnify a partner for liabilities incurred by the partner in the ordinary course of the business of the partnership or for the preservation of its business or property.

(d) A partnership shall reimburse a partner for an advance to the partnership beyond the amount of capital the partner agreed to contribute.

(e) A payment or advance made by a partner which gives rise to a partnership obligation under subsection (c) or (d) constitutes a loan to the partnership which accrues interest from the date of the payment or advance.

(f) Each partner has equal rights in the management and conduct of the partnership business.

(g) A partner may use or possess partnership property only on behalf of the partnership.

(h) A partner is not entitled to remuneration for services performed for the partnership, except for reasonable compensation for services rendered in winding up the business of the partnership.

(i) A person may become a partner only with the consent of all of the partners.

(j) A difference arising as to a matter in the ordinary course of business of a partnership may be decided by a majority of the partners. An act outside the ordinary course of business of a partnership and an amendment to the partnership agreement may be undertaken only with the consent of all of the partners.

(k) This section does not affect the obligations of a partnership to other persons under Section 301.

COMMENT

1. Section 401 is drawn substantially from UPA Section 18. It establishes many of the default rules that govern the relations among partners. All of these rules are, however, subject to contrary agreement of the partners as provided in Section 103.

2. Subsection (a) provides that each partner is deemed to have an account that is credited with the partner's contributions and share of the partnership profits and charged with distributions to the partner and the partner's share of partnership losses. In the absence of another system of partnership accounts, these rules establish a rudimentary system of accounts for the partnership. The rules regarding the settlement of the partners' accounts upon the dissolution and winding up of the partnership business are found in Section 807.

3. Subsection (b) establishes the default rules for the sharing of partnership profits and losses. The UPA Section 18(a) rules that profits are shared equally and that losses, whether capital or operating, are shared in proportion to each partner's share of the profits are continued. Thus, under the default rule, partners share profits per capita and not in proportion to capital contribution as do corporate shareholders or partners in limited partnerships. Compare RULPA Section 504. With respect to losses, the qualifying phrase, "whether capital or operating," has been deleted as inconsistent with contemporary partnership accounting practice and terminology; no substantive change is intended.

If partners agree to share profits other than equally, losses will be shared similarly to profits, absent agreement to do otherwise. That rule, carried over from the UPA, is predicated on the assumption that partners would likely agree to share losses on the same basis as profits, but may fail to say so. Of course, by agreement, they may share losses on a different basis from profits.

The default rules apply, as does UPA Section 18(a), where one or more of the partners contribute no capital, although there is case law to the contrary. *See, e.g., Kovacik v. Reed*, 49 Cal. 2d 166, 315 P.2d 314 (1957); *Becker v. Killarney*, 177 Ill. App. 3d 793, 523 N.E.2d 467 (1988). It may seem unfair that the contributor of services, who contributes little or no capital, should be obligated to contribute toward the capital loss of the large contributor who contributed no services. In entering a partnership with such a capital structure, the partners should foresee that application of the default rule may bring about unusual results and take advantage of their power to vary by agreement the allocation of capital losses.

Subsection (b) provides that each partner "is chargeable" with a share of the losses, rather than the UPA formulation that each partner shall "contribute" to losses. Losses are charged to each partner's account as provided in subsection (a)(2). It is intended to make clear that a partner is not obligated to contribute to partnership losses before his withdrawal or the liquidation of the partnership, unless the partners agree otherwise. In effect, unless related to an obligation for which the partner is not personally liable under Section 306(c), a partner's negative account represents a debt to the partnership unless the partners agree to the contrary. Similarly, each partner's share of the profits is credited to his account under subsection (a)(1). Absent an agreement to the contrary, however, a partner does not have a right to receive a current distribution of the profits credited to his account, the interim distribution of profits being a matter arising in the ordinary course of business to be decided by majority vote of the partners.

However, where a liability to contribute at dissolution and winding up relates to a partnership obligation governed by the limited liability rule of Section 306(c), a partner is not obligated to contribute additional assets even at dissolution and winding up. See Section 807(b). In such a case, although a partner is not personally liable for the partnership obligation, that partner's interest in the partnership remains at risk. See also Comment to Section 401(c) relating to indemnification.

In the case of an operating limited liability partnership, the Section 306 liability shield may be partially eroded where the limited liability partnership incurs both shielded and unshielded liabilities. Where the limited liability partnership uses its assets to pay shielded liabilities before paying unshielded liabilities, each partner's obligation to contribute to the limited liability partnership for that partner's share of the unpaid and unshielded obligations at dissolution and winding up remains intact. The same issue is less likely to occur in the context of the termination of a limited liability partnership since a partner's contribution obligation is based only on that partner's share of unshielded obligations and the partnership will ordinarily use the contributed assets to pay unshielded claims first as they were the basis of the contribution obligations. See Comments to Section 807(b).

4. Subsection (c) is derived from UPA Section 18(b) and provides that the partnership shall reimburse partners for payments made and indemnify them for liabilities incurred in the ordinary course of the partnership's business or for the preservation of its business or property. Reimbursement and indemnification is an obligation of the partnership. Indemnification may create a loss toward which the partners must contribute. Although the right to indemnification is usually enforced in the settlement of accounts among partners upon dissolution and winding up of the partnership business, the right accrues when the liability is incurred and thus may be enforced during the

term of the partnership in an appropriate case. *See* Section 405 and Comment. A partner's right to indemnification under this Act is not affected by the partnership becoming a limited liability partnership. Accordingly, partners continue to share partnership losses to the extent of partnership assets.

5. Subsection (d) is based on UPA Section 18(c). It makes explicit that the partnership must reimburse a partner for an advance of funds beyond the amount of the partner's agreed capital contribution, thereby treating the advance as a loan.

6. Subsection (e), which is also drawn from UPA Section 18(c), characterizes the partnership's obligation under subsection (c) or (d) as a loan to the partnership which accrues interest from the date of the payment or advance. See Section 104(b) (default rate of interest).

7. Under subsection (f), each partner has equal rights in the management and conduct of the business. It is based on UPA Section 18(e), which has been interpreted broadly to mean that, absent contrary agreement, each partner has a continuing right to participate in the management of the partnership and to be informed about the partnership business, even if his assent to partnership business decisions is not required. There are special rules regarding the partner vote necessary to approve a partnership becoming (or canceling its status as) a limited liability partnership. See Section 1001(b).

8. Subsection (g) provides that partners may use or possess partnership property only for partnership purposes. That is the edited remains of UPA Section 25(2)(a), which deals in detail with the incidents of tenancy in partnership. That tenancy is abolished as a consequence of the entity theory of partnerships. *See* Section 501 and Comments.

9. Subsection (h) continues the UPA Section 18(f) rule that a partner is not entitled to remuneration for services performed, except in winding up the partnership. Subsection (h) deletes the UPA reference to a "surviving" partner. That means any partner winding up the business is entitled to compensation, not just a surviving partner winding up after the death of another partner. The exception is not intended to apply in the hypothetical winding up that takes place if there is a buyout under Article 7.

10. Subsection (i) continues the substance of UPA Section 18(g) that no person can become a partner without the consent of all the partners.

11. Subsection (j) continues with one important clarification the UPA Section 18(h) scheme of allocating management authority among the partners. In the absence of an agreement to the contrary, matters arising in the ordinary course of the business may be decided by a majority of the partners. Amendments to

the partnership agreement and matters outside the ordinary course of the partnership business require unanimous consent of the partners. Although the text of the UPA is silent regarding extraordinary matters, courts have generally required the consent of all partners for those matters. *See, e.g., Paciaroni v. Crane*, 408 A.2d 946 (Del. Ch. 1989); *Thomas v. Marvin E. Jewell & Co.*, 232 Neb. 261, 440 N.W.2d 437 (1989); *Duell v. Hancock*, 83 A.D.2d 762, 443 N.Y.S.2d 490 (1981).

It is not intended that subsection (j) embrace a claim for an objection to a partnership decision that is not discovered until after the fact. There is no cause of action based on that after-the-fact second-guessing.

12. Subsection (k) is new and was added to make it clear that Section 301 governs partners' agency power to bind the partnership to third persons, while Section 401 governs partners' rights among themselves.

Section 402. Distributions In Kind.

A partner has no right to receive, and may not be required to accept, a distribution in kind.

COMMENT

Section 402 provides that a partner has no right to demand and receive a distribution in kind and may not be required to take a distribution in kind. That continues the "in kind" rule of UPA Section 38(l). The new language is suggested by RULPA Section 605.

This section is complemented by Section 807(a) which provides that, in winding up the partnership business on dissolution, any surplus after the payment of partnership obligations must be applied to pay in cash the net amount distributable to each partner.

Section 403. Partner's Rights and Duties with Respect to Information.

(a) A partnership shall keep its books and records, if any, at its chief executive office.

(b) A partnership shall provide partners and their agents and attorneys access to its books and records. It shall provide former partners and their agents and attorneys access to books and records pertaining to the period during which they were partners. The right of access provides the opportunity to inspect and copy books and records during ordinary business hours. A partnership may impose a reasonable charge, covering the costs of labor and material, for copies of documents furnished.

(c) Each partner and the partnership shall furnish to a partner, and to the legal representative of a deceased partner or partner under legal disability:

(1) without demand, any information concerning the partnership's business and affairs reasonably required for the proper exercise of the partner's rights and duties under the partnership agreement or this [Act]; and

(2) on demand, any other information concerning the partnership's business and affairs, except to the extent the demand or the information demanded is unreasonable or otherwise improper under the circumstances.

COMMENT

1. Subsection (a) provides that the partnership's books and records, if any, shall be kept at its chief executive office. It continues the UPA Section 19 rule, modified to include partnership records other than its "books," i.e., financial records. The concept of "chief executive office" comes from UCC Section 9-103(3)(d). See the Comment to Section 106.

Since general partnerships are often informal or even inadvertent, no books and records are enumerated as mandatory, such as that found in RULPA Section 105. Any requirement in UPA Section 19 that the partnership keep books is oblique at best, since it states merely where the books shall be kept, not that they shall be kept. Under RUPA, there is no liability to either partners or third parties for the failure to keep partnership books. A partner who undertakes to keep books, however, must do so accurately and adequately.

In general, a partnership should, at a minimum, keep those books and records necessary to enable the partners to determine their share of the profits and losses, as well as their rights on withdrawal. An action for an accounting provides an adequate remedy in the event adequate records are not kept. The partnership must also maintain any books and records required by state or federal taxing or other governmental authorities.

2. Under subsection (b), partners are entitled to access to the partnership books and records. Former partners are expressly given a similar right, although limited to the books and records pertaining to the period during which they were partners. The line between partners and former partners is not a bright one for this purpose, however, and should be drawn in light of the legitimate interests of a dissociated partner in the partnership. For example, a withdrawing partner's liability is ongoing for pre-withdrawal liabilities and will normally be extended to new liabilities for at least 90 days. It is intended that a former partner be accorded access to partnership books and records as reasonably necessary to protect that partner's legitimate interests during the period his rights and liabilities are being wound down.

The right of access is limited to ordinary business hours, and the right to inspect and copy by agent or attorney is made explicit. The partnership may impose a reasonable charge for furnishing copies of documents. *Accord,* RULPA § 105(b).

A partner's right to inspect and copy the partnership's books and records is not conditioned on the partner's purpose or motive. Compare RMBCA Section 16.02(c)(l) (shareholder must have proper purpose to inspect certain corporate records). A partner's unlimited personal liability justifies an unqualified right of access to the partnership books and records. An abuse of the right to inspect and copy might constitute a violation of the obligation of good faith and fair dealing for which the other partners would have a remedy. See Sections 404(d) and 405.

Under Section 103(b)(2), a partner's right of access to partnership books and records may not be unreasonably restricted by the partnership agreement. Thus, to preserve a partner's core information rights despite unequal bargaining power, an agreement limiting a partner's right to inspect and copy partnership books and records is subject to judicial review. Nevertheless, reasonable restrictions on access to partnership books and records by agreement are authorized. For example, a provision in a partnership agreement denying partners access to the compensation of other partners should be upheld, absent any abuse such as fraud or duress.

3. Subsection (c) is a significant revision of UPA Section 20 and provides a more comprehensive, although not exclusive, statement of partners' rights and duties with respect to partnership information other than books and records. Both the partnership and the other partners are obligated to furnish partnership information.

Paragraph (1) is new and imposes an affirmative disclosure obligation on the partnership and partners. There is no express UPA provision imposing an affirmative obligation to disclose any information other than the partnership books. Under some circumstances, however, an affirmative disclosure duty has been inferred from other sections of the Act, as well as from the common law, such as the fiduciary duty of good faith. Under UPA Section 18(e), for example, all partners enjoy an equal right in the management and conduct of the partnership business, absent contrary agreement. That right has been construed to require that every partner be provided with ongoing information concerning the partnership business. See Comment 7 to Section 401. Paragraph (1) provides expressly that partners must be furnished, without demand, partnership information reasonably needed for them to exercise their rights and duties as partners. In addition, a disclosure duty may, under some circumstances, also spring from the Section 404(d) obligation of good faith and fair dealing. See Comment 4 to Section 404.

Paragraph (2) continues the UPA rule that partners are entitled, on demand, to any other information concerning the partnership's business and affairs.

The demand may be refused if either the demand or the information demanded is unreasonable or otherwise improper. That qualification is new to the statutory formulation. The burden is on the partnership or partner from whom the information is requested to show that the demand is unreasonable or improper. The UPA admonition that the information furnished be "true and full" has been deleted as unnecessary, and no substantive change is intended.

The Section 403(c) information rights can be waived or varied by agreement of the partners, since there is no Section 103(b) limitation on the variation of those rights as there is with respect to the Section 403(b) access rights to books and records. *See* Section 103(b)(2).

Section 404. General Standards of Partner's Conduct.

(a) The only fiduciary duties a partner owes to the partnership and the other partners are the duty of loyalty and the duty of care set forth in subsections (b) and (c).

(b) A partner's duty of loyalty to the partnership and the other partners is limited to the following:

    (1) to account to the partnership and hold as trustee for it any property, profit, or benefit derived by the partner in the conduct and winding up of the partnership business or derived from a use by the partner of partnership property, including the appropriation of a partnership opportunity;

    (2) to refrain from dealing with the partnership in the conduct or winding up of the partnership business as or on behalf of a party having an interest adverse to the partnership; and

    (3) to refrain from competing with the partnership in the conduct of the partnership business before the dissolution of the partnership.

(c) A partner's duty of care to the partnership and the other partners in the conduct and winding up of the partnership business is limited to refraining from engaging in grossly negligent or reckless conduct, intentional misconduct, or a knowing violation of law.

(d) A partner shall discharge the duties to the partnership and the other partners under this [Act] or under the partnership agreement and exercise any rights consistently with the obligation of good faith and fair dealing.

(e) A partner does not violate a duty or obligation under this [Act] or under the partnership agreement merely because the partner's conduct furthers the partner's own interest.

(f) A partner may lend money to and transact other business with the partnership, and as to each loan or transaction the rights and obligations of the partner are the same as those of a person who is not a partner, subject to other applicable law.

(g) This section applies to a person winding up the partnership business as the personal or legal representative of the last surviving partner as if the person were a partner.

COMMENT

1. Section 404 is new. The title, "General Standards of Partner's Conduct," is drawn from RMBCA Section 8.30. Section 404 is both comprehensive and exclusive. In that regard, it is structurally different from the UPA which touches only sparingly on a partner's duty of loyalty and leaves any further development of the fiduciary duties of partners to the common law of agency. Compare UPA Sections 4(3) and 21.

Section 404 begins by stating that the **only** fiduciary duties a partner owes to the partnership and the other partners are the duties of loyalty and care set forth in subsections (b) and (c) of the Act. Those duties may not be waived or eliminated in the partnership agreement, but the agreement may identify activities and determine standards for measuring performance of the duties, if not manifestly unreasonable. *See* Sections 103(b)(3)-(5).

Section 404 continues the term "fiduciary" from UPA Section 21, which is entitled "Partner Accountable as a Fiduciary." Arguably, the term "fiduciary" is inappropriate when used to describe the duties of a partner because a partner may legitimately pursue self-interest (see Section 404(e)) and not solely the interest of the partnership and the other partners, as must a true trustee. Nevertheless, partners have long been characterized as fiduciaries. *See, e.g., Meinhard v. Salmon*, 249 N.Y. 458, 463, 164 N.E. 545, 546 (1928) (Cardozo, J.). Indeed, the law of partnership reflects the broader law of principal and agent, under which every agent is a fiduciary. *See* Restatement (Second) of Agency § 13 (1957).

2. Section 404(b) provides three specific rules that comprise a partner's duty of loyalty. Those rules are exclusive and encompass the entire duty of loyalty.

Subsection (b)(l) is based on UPA Section 21(1) and continues the rule that partnership property usurped by a partner, including the misappropriation of a partnership opportunity, is held in trust for the partnership. The express reference to the appropriation of a partnership opportunity is new, but merely codifies case law on the point. *See, e.g., Meinhard v. Salmon, supra; Fouchek v. Janicek*, 190 Ore. 251, 225 P.2d 783 (1950). Under a constructive trust theory, the partnership can recover any money or property in the partner's hands that can be traced to the partnership. *See, e.g., Yoder v. Hooper*, 695 P.2d 1182 (Colo. App. 1984), *aff'd*, 737 P.2d 852 (Colo. 1987); *Fortugno v. Hudson Manure Co.*, 51 N.J. Super. 482, 144 A.2d 207 (1958); *Harestad v. Weitzel*, 242 Or. 199, 536 P.2d 522 (1975). As a result, the partnership's claim is greater than that of an ordinary creditor. See Official Comment to UPA Section 21.

UPA Section 21(1) imposes the duty on partners to account for profits and benefits in all transactions connected with "the formation, conduct, or liquidation of the partnership." Reference to the "formation" of the partnership has been eliminated by RUPA because of concern that the duty of loyalty could be inappropriately extended to the pre-formation period when the parties are really negotiating at arm's length. *Compare Herring v. Offutt*, 295 A.2d 876 (Ct. App. Md. 1972), *with Phoenix Mutual Life Ins. Co. v. Shady Grove Plaza Limited Partnership*, 734 F. Supp. 1181 (D. Md. 1990), *aff'd*, 937 F.2d 603 (4th Cir. 1991). Once a partnership is agreed to, each partner becomes a fiduciary in the "conduct" of the business. Pre-formation negotiations are, of course, subject to the general contract obligation to deal honestly and without fraud.

Upon a partner's dissociation, Section 603(b)(3) limits the application of the duty to account for personal profits to those derived from matters arising or events occurring before the dissociation, unless the partner participates in winding up the partnership's business. Thus, after withdrawal, a partner is free to appropriate to his own benefit any new business opportunity thereafter coming to his attention, even if the partnership continues.

Subsection (b)(2) provides that a partner must refrain from dealing with the partnership as or on behalf of a party having an interest adverse to the partnership. This rule is derived from Sections 389 and 391 of the Restatement (Second) of Agency. Comment c to Section 389 explains that the rule is not based upon the harm caused to the principal, but upon avoiding a conflict of opposing interests in the mind of an agent whose duty is to act for the benefit of his principal.

Upon a partner's dissociation, Section 603(b)(3) limits the application of the duty to refrain from representing interests adverse to the partnership to the same extent as the duty to account. Thus, after withdrawal, a partner may deal with the partnership as an adversary with respect to new matters or events.

Section 404(b)(3) provides that a partner must refrain from competing with the partnership in the conduct of its business. This rule is derived from Section 393 of the Restatement (Second) of Agency and is an application of the general duty of an agent to act solely on his principal's behalf.

The duty not to compete applies only to the "conduct" of the partnership business; it does not extend to winding up the business, as do the other loyalty rules. Thus, a partner is free to compete immediately upon an event of dissolution under Section 801, unless the partnership agreement otherwise provides. A partner who dissociates without a winding up of the business resulting is also free to compete, because Section 603(b)(2) provides that the duty not to compete terminates upon dissociation. A dissociated partner is not, however, free to use confidential partnership information after dissocia-tion. *See* Restatement (Second) of Agency § 393 cmt. e (1957). Trade secret law also may apply. See the Uniform Trade Secrets Act.

Under Section 103(b)(3), the partnership agreement may not "eliminate" the duty of loyalty. Section 103(b)(3)(i) expressly empowers the partners, how-ever, to identify specific types or categories of activities that do not violate the duty of loyalty, if not manifestly unreasonable. As under UPA Section 21, the other partners may also consent to a specific act or transaction that otherwise violates one of the rules. For the consent to be effective under Section 103(b)(3)(ii), there must be full disclosure of all material facts regarding the act or transaction and the partner's conflict of interest. See Comment 5 to Sec-tion 103.

3. Subsection (c) is new and establishes the duty of care that partners owe to the partnership and to the other partners. There is no statutory duty of care under the UPA, although a common law duty of care is recognized by some courts. *See, e.g., Rosenthal v. Rosenthal*, 543 A.2d 348, 352 (Me. 1988) (duty of care limited to acting in a manner that does not constitute gross negligence or willful misconduct).

The standard of care imposed by RUPA is that of gross negligence, which is the standard generally recognized by the courts. *See, e.g., Rosenthal v. Rosen-thal, supra.* Section 103(b)(4) provides that the duty of care may not be elimi-nated entirely by agreement, but the standard may be reasonably reduced. See Comment 6 to Section 103.

4. Subsection (d) is also new. It provides that partners have an obligation of good faith and fair dealing in the discharge of all their duties, including those arising under the Act, such as their fiduciary duties of loyalty and care, and those arising under the partnership agreement. The exercise of any rights by a partner is also subject to the obligation of good faith and fair dealing. The obligation runs to the partnership and to the other partners in all matters re-lated to the conduct and winding up of the partnership business.

The obligation of good faith and fair dealing is a contract concept, imposed on the partners because of the consensual nature of a partnership. See Re-statement (Second) of Contracts § 205 (1981). It is not characterized, in RUPA, as a fiduciary duty arising out of the partners' special relationship. Nor is it a separate and independent obligation. It is an ancillary obligation that applies whenever a partner discharges a duty or exercises a right under the partner-ship agreement or the Act.

The meaning of "good faith and fair dealing" is not firmly fixed under pres-ent law. "Good faith" clearly suggests a subjective element, while "fair dealing" implies an objective component. It was decided to leave the terms un-defined in the Act and allow the courts to develop their meaning based on the experience of real cases. Some commentators, moreover, believe that good faith is more properly understood by what it excludes than by what it in-cludes. See Robert S. Summers, *"Good Faith" in General Contract Law and the Sales Provisions of the Uniform Commercial Code,* 54 Va. L. Rev. 195, 262 (1968):

Good faith, as judges generally use the term in matters contractual, is best un-derstood as an "excluder" - a phrase with no general meaning or meanings of its own. Instead, it functions to rule out many different forms of bad faith. It is hard to get this point across to persons used to thinking that every word must have one or more general meanings of its own - must be either univo-cal or ambiguous.

The UCC definition of "good faith" is honesty in fact and, in the case of a mer-chant, the observance of reasonable commercial standards of fair dealing in the trade. *See* UCC §§ 1-201(19), 2-103(b). Those definitions were rejected as too narrow or not applicable.

In some situations the obligation of good faith includes a disclosure component. Depending on the circumstances, a partner may have an affirmative disclosure obligation that supplements the Section 403 duty to render information.

Under Section 103(b)(5), the obligation of good faith and fair dealing may not be eliminated by agreement, but the partners by agreement may determine the standards by which the performance of the obligation is to be measured, if the standards are not manifestly unreasonable. See Comment 7 to Section 103.

5. Subsection (e) is new and deals expressly with a very basic issue on which the UPA is silent. A partner as such is not a trustee and is not held to the same standards as a trustee. Subsection (e) makes clear that a partner's conduct is not deemed to be improper merely because it serves the partner's own indi-vidual interest.

That admonition has particular application to the duty of loyalty and the ob-ligation of good faith and fair dealing. It underscores the partner's rights as an owner and principal in the enterprise, which must always be balanced against his duties and obligations as an agent and fiduciary. For example, a partner who, with consent, owns a shopping center may, under subsection (e), legitimately vote against a proposal by the partnership to open a com-peting shopping center.

6. Subsection (f) authorizes partners to lend money to and transact other business with the partnership and, in so doing, to enjoy the same rights and obligations as a nonpartner. That language is drawn from RULPA Section 107.

The rights and obligations of a partner doing business with the partnership as an outsider are expressly made subject to the usual laws governing those transactions. They include, for example, rules limiting or qualifying the rights and remedies of inside creditors, such as fraudulent transfer law, equitable subordination, and the law of avoidable preferences, as well as general debtor-creditor law. The reference to "other applicable law" makes clear that subsection (f) is not intended to displace those laws, and thus they are preserved under Section 104(a).

It is unclear under the UPA whether a partner may, for the partner's own account, purchase the assets of the partnership at a foreclosure sale or upon the liquidation of the partnership. Those purchases are clearly within subsection (f)'s broad approval. It is also clear under that subsection that a partner may purchase partnership assets at a foreclosure sale, whether the partner is the mortgagee or the mortgagee is an unrelated third party. Similarly, a partner may purchase partnership property at a tax sale. The obligation of good faith requires disclosure of the partner's interest in the transaction, however.

7. Subsection (g) provides that the prescribed standards of conduct apply equally to a person engaged in winding up the partnership business as the personal or legal representative of the last surviving partner, as if the person were a partner. This is derived from UPA Section 21(2), but now embraces the duty of care and the obligation of good faith and fair dealing, as well as the duty of loyalty.

Section 405. Actions by Partnership and Partners.

    (a) A partnership may maintain an action against a partner for a breach of the partnership agreement, or for the violation of a duty to the partnership, causing harm to the partnership.

    (b) A partner may maintain an action against the partnership or another partner for legal or equitable relief, with or without an accounting as to partnership business, to:

        (1) enforce the partner's rights under the partnership agreement;

        (2) enforce the partner's rights under this [Act], including:

            (i) the partner's rights under Sections 401, 403, or 404;

            (ii) the partner's right on dissociation to have the partner's interest in the partnership purchased pursuant to Section 701 or enforce any other right under [Article] 6 or 7; or

            (iii) the partner's right to compel a dissolution and winding up of the partnership business under or enforce any other right under [Article] 8; or

        (3) enforce the rights and otherwise protect the interests of the partner, including rights and interests arising independently of the partnership relationship.

    (c) The accrual of, and any time limitation on, a right of action for a remedy under this section is governed by other law. A right to an accounting upon a dissolution and winding up does not revive a claim barred by law.

COMMENT

1. Section 405(a) is new and reflects the entity theory of partnership. It provides that the partnership itself may maintain an action against a partner for any breach of the partnership agreement or for the violation of any duty owed to the partnership, such as a breach of fiduciary duty.

2. Section 405(b) is the successor to UPA Section 22, but with significant changes. At common law, an accounting was generally not available before dissolution. That was modified by UPA Section 22 which specifies certain circumstances in which an accounting action is available without requiring a partner to dissolve the partnership. Section 405(b) goes far beyond the UPA rule. It provides that, during the term of the partnership, partners may maintain a variety of legal or equitable actions, including an action for an accounting, as well as a final action for an accounting upon dissolution and winding up. It reflects a new policy choice that partners should have access to the courts during the term of the partnership to resolve claims against the partnership and the other partners, leaving broad judicial discretion to fashion appropriate remedies.

Under RUPA, an accounting is not a prerequisite to the availability of the other remedies a partner may have against the partnership or the other partners. That change reflects the increased willingness courts have shown to grant relief without the requirement of an accounting, in derogation of the so-called "exclusivity rule." *See, e.g., Farney v. Hauser,* 109 Kan. 75, 79, 198 Pac. 178, 180 (1921) ("[For] all practical purposes a partnership may be considered as a business entity"); *Auld v. Estridge,* 86 Misc. 2d 895, 901, 382 N.Y.S.2d 897, 901 (1976) ("No purpose of justice is served by delaying the resolution here on empty procedural grounds").

Under subsection (b), a partner may bring a direct suit against the partnership or another partner for almost any cause of action arising out of the conduct of the partnership business. That eliminates the present procedural barriers to suits between partners filed independently of an accounting action. In addition to a formal account, the court may grant any other appropriate legal or equitable remedy. Since general partners are not passive investors like limited partners, RUPA does not authorize derivative actions, as does RULPA Section 1001.

Subsection (b)(3) makes it clear that a partner may recover against the partnership and the other partners for personal injuries or damage to the property of the partner caused by another partner. *See, e.g., Duffy v. Piazza Construction Co.,* 815 P.2d 267 (Wash. App. 1991); *Smith v. Hensley,* 354 S.W.2d 744 (Ky. App.). One partner's negligence is not imputed to bar another partner's action. *See, e.g., Reeves v. Harmon,* 475 P.2d 400 (Okla. 1970); *Eagle Star Ins. Co. v. Bean,* 134 F.2d 755 (9th Cir. 1943) (fire insurance company not subrogated to claim against partners who negligently caused fire that damaged partnership property).

3. Generally, partners may limit or contract away their Section 405 remedies. They may not, however, eliminate entirely the remedies for breach of those duties that are mandatory under Section 103(b). See Comment 1 to Section 103.

4. Section 405(c) replaces UPA Section 43 and provides that other (i.e., non-partnership) law governs the accrual of a cause of action for which subsection (b) provides a remedy. The statute of limitations on such claims is also governed by other law, and claims barred by a statute of limitations are not revived by reason of the partner's right to an accounting upon dissolution, as they were under the UPA. The effect of those rules is to compel partners to litigate their claims during the life of the partnership or risk losing them. Because an accounting is an equitable proceeding, it may also be barred by laches where there is an undue delay in bringing the action. Under general law, the limitations periods may be tolled by a partner's fraud.

5. UPA Section 39 grants ancillary remedies to a person who rescinds his participation in a partnership because it was fraudulently induced, including the right to a lien on surplus partnership property for the amount of that person's interest in the partnership. RUPA has no counterpart provision to UPA Section 39, and leaves it to the general law of rescission to determine the rights of a person fraudulently induced to invest in a partnership. See Section 104(a).

Section 406. Continuation of Partnership Beyond Definite Term or Particular Undertaking.

    (a) If a partnership for a definite term or particular undertaking is continued, without an express agreement, after the expiration of the term or completion of the undertaking, the rights and duties of the partners remain the same as they were at the expiration or completion, so far as is consistent with a partnership at will.

    (b) If the partners, or those of them who habitually acted in the business during the term or undertaking, continue the business without any settlement or liquidation of the partnership, they are presumed to have agreed that the partnership will continue.

COMMENT

Section 406 continues UPA Section 23, with no substantive change. Subsection (a) provides that, if a term partnership is continued without an express agreement beyond the expiration of its term or the completion of the undertaking, the partners' rights and duties remain the same as they were, so far as is consistent with a partnership at will.

Subsection (b) provides that if the partnership is continued by the partners without any settlement or liquidation of the business, it is presumed that the partners have agreed not to wind up the business. The presumption is rebuttable. If the partnership is continued under this subsection, there is no dissolution under (2)(iii). As a partnership at will, however, the partnership may be dissolved under (1) at any time.

[ARTICLE] 5
TRANSFEREES AND CREDITORS OF PARTNER

Section 501. Partner not Co-Owner of Partnership Property.
A partner is not a co-owner of partnership property and has no interest in partnership property which can be transferred, either voluntarily or involuntarily.

COMMENT

Section 501 provides that a partner is not a co-owner of partnership property and has no interest in partnership property that can be transferred, either voluntarily or involuntarily. Thus, the section abolishes the UPA Section 25(1) concept of tenants in partnership and reflects the adoption of the entity theory. Partnership property is owned by the entity and not by the individual partners. See also Section 203, which provides that property transferred to or otherwise acquired by the partnership is property of the partnership and not of the partners individually.

RUPA also deletes the references in UPA Sections 24 and 25 to a partner's "right in specific partnership property," although those rights are largely defined away by the detailed rules of UPA Section 25 itself. Thus, it is clear that a partner who misappropriates partnership property is guilty of embezzlement the same as a shareholder who misappropriates corporate property.

Adoption of the entity theory also has the effect of protecting partnership property from execution or other process by a partner's personal creditors. That continues the result under UPA Section 25(2)(c). Those creditors may seek a charging order under Section 504 to reach the partner's transferable interest in the partnership.

RUPA does not interfere with a partner's exemption claim in nonpartnership property. As under the UPA, disputes over whether specific property belongs to the partner or to the firm will likely arise in the context of an exemption claim by a partner.

A partner's spouse, heirs, or next of kin are not entitled to allowances or other rights in partnership property. That continues the result under UPA Section 25(2)(e).

Section 502. Partner's Transferable Interest In Partnership.

The only transferable interest of a partner in the partnership is the partner's share of the profits and losses of the partnership and the partner's right to receive distributions. The interest is personal property.

COMMENT

Section 502 continues the UPA Section 26 concept that a partner's only transferable interest in the partnership is the partner's share of profits and losses and right to receive distributions, that is, the partner's financial rights. The term "distribution" is defined in Section 101(3). Compare RULPA Section 101(10) ("partnership interest").

The partner's transferable interest is deemed to be personal property, regardless of the nature of the underlying partnership assets.

Under Section 503(b)(3), a transferee of a partner's transferable interest has standing to seek judicial dissolution of the partnership business.

A partner has other interests in the partnership that may not be transferred, such as the right to participate in the management of the business. Those rights are included in the broader concept of a "partner's interest in the partnership." *See* Section 101(9).

Section 503. Transfer of Partner's Transferable Interest.

(a) A transfer, in whole or in part, of a partner's transferable interest in the partnership:

(1) is permissible;

(2) does not by itself cause the partner's dissociation or a dissolution and winding up of the partnership business; and

(3) does not, as against the other partners or the partnership, entitle the transferee, during the continuance of the partnership, to participate in the management or conduct of the partnership business, to require access to information concerning partnership transactions, or to inspect or copy the partnership books or records.

(b) A transferee of a partner's transferable interest in the partnership has a right:

    (1) to receive, in accordance with the transfer, distributions to which the transferor would otherwise be entitled;

    (2) to receive upon the dissolution and winding up of the partnership business, in accordance with the transfer, the net amount otherwise distributable to the transferor; and

    (3) to seek under (6) a judicial determination that it is equitable to wind up the partnership business.

(c) In a dissolution and winding up, a transferee is entitled to an account of partnership transactions only from the date of the latest account agreed to by all of the partners.

(d) Upon transfer, the transferor retains the rights and duties of a partner other than the interest in distributions transferred.

(e) A partnership need not give effect to a transferee's rights under this section until it has notice of the transfer.

(f) A transfer of a partner's transferable interest in the partnership in violation of a restriction on transfer contained in the partnership agreement is ineffective as to a person having notice of the restriction at the time of transfer.

COMMENT

1. Section 503 is derived from UPA Section 27. Subsection (a)(1) states explicitly that a partner has the right to transfer his transferable interest in the partnership. The term "transfer" is used throughout RUPA in lieu of the term "assignment." See Section 101(10).

Subsection (a)(2) continues the UPA Section 27(1) rule that an assignment of a partner's interest in the partnership does not of itself cause a winding up of the partnership business. Under Section 601(4)(ii), however, a partner who has transferred substantially all of his partnership interest may be expelled by the other partners.

Subsection (a)(3), which is also derived from UPA Section 27(l), provides that a transferee is not, as against the other partners, entitled (i) to participate in the management or conduct of the partnership business; (ii) to inspect the partnership books or records; or (iii) to require any information concerning or an account of partnership transactions.

2. The rights of a transferee are set forth in subsection (b). Under subsection (b)(1), which is derived from UPA Section 27(l), a transferee is entitled to receive, in accordance with the terms of the assignment, any distributions to which the transferor would otherwise have been entitled under the

partnership agreement before dissolution. After dissolution, the transferee is also entitled to receive, under subsection (b)(2), the net amount that would otherwise have been distributed to the transferor upon the winding up of the business.

Subsection (b)(3) confers standing on a transferee to seek a judicial dissolution and winding up of the partnership business as provided in Section 801(6), thus continuing the rule of UPA Section 32(2).

Section 504(b) accords the rights of a transferee to the purchaser at a sale foreclosing a charging order. The same rule should apply to creditors or other purchasers who acquire partnership interests by pursuing UCC remedies or statutory liens under federal or state law.

3. Subsection (c) is based on UPA Section 27(2). It grants to transferees the right to an account of partnership transactions, limited to the period since the date of the last account agreed to by all of the partners.

4. Subsection (d) is new. It makes clear that unless otherwise agreed the partner whose interest is transferred retains all of the rights and duties of a partner, other than the right to receive distributions. That means the transferor is entitled to participate in the management of the partnership and remains personally liable for all partnership obligations, unless and until he withdraws as a partner, is expelled under Section 601(4)(ii), or is otherwise dissociated under Section 601.

A divorced spouse of a partner who is awarded rights in the partner's partnership interest as part of a property settlement is entitled only to the rights of a transferee. The spouse may instead be granted a money judgment in the amount of the property award, enforceable by a charging order in the same manner as any other money judgment against a partner. In neither case, however, would the spouse become a partner by virtue of the property settlement or succeed to any of the partner's management rights. *See, e.g., Warren v. Warren*, 12 Ark. App. 260, 675 S.W.2d 371 (1984).

5. Subsection (e) is new and provides that the partnership has no duty to give effect to the transferee's rights until the partnership receives notice of the transfer. This is consistent with UCC Section 9-318(3), which provides that an "account debtor" is authorized to pay the assignor until the account debtor receives notification that the amount due or to become due has been assigned and that payment is to be made to the assignee. It further provides that the assignee, on request, must furnish reasonable proof of the assignment.

6. Subsection (f) is new and provides that a transfer of a partner's transferable interest in the partnership in violation of a restriction on transfer con-

tained in a partnership agreement is ineffective as to a person with timely notice of the restriction. Under Section 103(a), the partners may agree among themselves to restrict the right to transfer their partnership interests. Subsection (f) makes explicit that a transfer in violation of such a restriction is ineffective as to a transferee with notice of the restriction. See Section 102(b) for the meaning of "notice." RUPA leaves to general law and the UCC the issue of whether a transfer in violation of a valid restriction is effective as to a transferee without notice of the restriction.

Whether a particular restriction will be enforceable, however, must be considered in light of other law. *See* 11 U.S.C. § 541(c)(1) (property owned by bankrupt passes to trustee regardless of restrictions on transfer); UCC § 9-318(4) (agreement between account debtor and assignor prohibiting creation of security interest in a general intangible or requiring account debtor's consent is ineffective); *Battista v. Carlo,* 57 Misc. 2d 495, 293 N.Y.S.2d 227 (1968) (restriction on transfer of partnership interest subject to rules against unreasonable restraints on alienation of property) (dictum); *Tupper v. Kroc,* 88 Nev. 146, 494 P.2d 1275 (1972) (partnership interest subject to charging order even if partnership agreement prohibits assignments). *Cf. Tu-Vu Drive-In Corp. v. Ashkins,* 61 Cal. 2d 283, 38 Cal. Rptr. 348, 391 P.2d 828 (1964) (restraints on transfer of corporate stock must be reasonable). Even if a restriction on the transfer of a partner's transferable interest in a partnership were held to be unenforceable, the transfer might be grounds for expelling the partner-transferor from the partnership under Section 601(5)(ii).

7. Other rules that apply in the case of transfers include Section 601(4)(ii) (expulsion of partner who transfers substantially all of partnership interest); Section 601(6) (dissociation of partner who makes an assignment for benefit of creditors); and Section 801(6) (transferee has standing to seek judicial winding up).

Section 504. Partner's Transferable Interest Subject to Charging Order.

(a) On application by a judgment creditor of a partner or of a partner's transferee, a court having jurisdiction may charge the transferable interest of the judgment debtor to satisfy the judgment. The court may appoint a receiver of the share of the distributions due or to become due to the judgment debtor in respect of the partnership and make all other orders, directions, accounts, and inquiries the judgment debtor might have made or which the circumstances of the case may require.

(b) A charging order constitutes a lien on the judgment debtor's transferable interest in the partnership. The court may order a foreclosure of the interest subject to the charging order at any time. The purchaser at the foreclosure sale has the rights of a transferee.

(c) At any time before foreclosure, an interest charged may be redeemed:

    (1) by the judgment debtor;

    (2) with property other than partnership property, by one or more of the other partners; or

    (3) with partnership property, by one or more of the other partners with the consent of all of the partners whose interests are not so charged.

(d) This [Act] does not deprive a partner of a right under exemption laws with respect to the partner's interest in the partnership.

(e) This section provides the exclusive remedy by which a judgment creditor of a partner or partner's transferee may satisfy a judgment out of the judgment debtor's transferable interest in the partnership.

COMMENT

1. Section 504 continues the UPA Section 28 charging order as the proper remedy by which a judgment creditor of a partner may reach the debtor's transferable interest in a partnership to satisfy the judgment. Subsection (a) makes the charging order available to the judgment creditor of a transferee of a partnership interest. Under Section 503(b), the transferable interest of a partner or transferee is limited to the partner's right to receive distributions from the partnership and to seek judicial liquidation of the partnership. The court may appoint a receiver of the debtor's share of the distributions due or to become due and make all other orders that may be required.

2. Subsection (b) is new and codifies the case law under the UPA holding that a charging order constitutes a lien on the debtor's transferable interest. The lien may be foreclosed by the court at any time, and the purchaser at the foreclosure sale has the Section 503(b) rights of a transferee. For a general discussion of the charging order remedy, see *I Alan R. Bromberg & Larry E. Ribstein, Partnership* (1988), at 3:69.

3. Subsection (c) continues the UPA Section 28(2) right of the debtor or other partners to redeem the partnership interest before the foreclosure sale. Redemption by the partnership (i.e., with partnership property) requires the consent of all the remaining partners. Neither the UPA nor RUPA provide a statutory procedural framework for the redemption.

4. Subsection (d) provides that nothing in RUPA deprives a partner of his rights under the State's exemption laws. That is essentially the same as UPA Section 28(3).

5. Subsection (e) provides that the charging order is the judgment creditor's exclusive remedy. Although the UPA nowhere states that a charging order is the exclusive process for a partner's individual judgment creditor, the courts have generally so interpreted it. *See, e.g., Matter of Pischke*, 11 B.R. 913 (E.D. Va.

1981); *Baum v. Baum,* 51 Cal. 2d 610, 335 P.2d 481 (1959); *Atlantic Mobile Homes, Inc. v. LeFever,* 481 So. 2d 1002 (Fla. App. 1986).

Notwithstanding subsection (e), there may be an exception for the enforcement of family support orders. Some States have unique statutory procedures for the enforcement of support orders. In Florida, for example, a court may issue an "income deduction order" requiring any person or entity providing "income" to the obligor of a support order to remit to the obligee or a depository, as directed by the court, a specified portion of the income. Fla. Stat. § 61.1301 (1993). "Income" is broadly defined to include any form of payment to the obligor, including wages, salary, compensation as an independent contractor, dividends, interest, or other payment, regardless of source. Fla. Stat. § 61.046(4) (1993). That definition includes distributions payable to an obligor partner. A charging order under RUPA would still be necessary to reach the obligor's entire partnership interest, however.

[ARTICLE] 6
PARTNER'S DISSOCIATION

Section 601. Events Causing Partner's Dissociation.
A partner is dissociated from a partnership upon the occurrence of any of the following events:

(1) the partnership's having notice of the partner's express will to withdraw as a partner or on a later date specified by the partner;

(2) an event agreed to in the partnership agreement as causing the partner's dissociation;

(3) the partner's expulsion pursuant to the partnership agreement;

(4) the partner's expulsion by the unanimous vote of the other partners if:
  (i) it is unlawful to carry on the partnership business with that partner;
  (ii) there has been a transfer of all or substantially all of that partner's transferable interest in the partnership, other than a transfer for security purposes, or a court order charging the partner's interest, which has not been foreclosed;
  (iii) within 90 days after the partnership notifies a corporate partner that it will be expelled because it has filed a certificate of dissolution or the equivalent, its charter has been revoked, or its right to conduct business has been suspended by the jurisdiction of its incorporation, there is no revocation of the certificate of dissolution or no reinstatement of its charter or its right to conduct business; or
  (iv) a partnership that is a partner has been dissolved and its business is being wound up;

(5) on application by the partnership or another partner, the partner's expulsion by judicial determination because:

(i)   the partner engaged in wrongful conduct that adversely and ma-
      terially affected the partnership business;

(ii) the partner willfully or persistently committed a material breach
      of the partnership agreement or of a duty owed to the partner-
      ship or the other partners under Section 404; or

(iii) the partner engaged in conduct relating to the partnership busi-
      ness which makes it not reasonably practicable to carry on the
      business in partnership with the partner;

(6) the partner's:

(i)   becoming a debtor in bankruptcy;

(ii) executing an assignment for the benefit of creditors;

(iii) seeking, consenting to, or acquiescing in the appointment of a
      trustee, receiver, or liquidator of that partner or of all or substan-
      tially all of that partner's property; or

(iv) failing, within 90 days after the appointment, to have vacated or
      stayed the appointment of a trustee, receiver, or liquidator of the
      partner or of all or substantially all of the partner's property ob-
      tained without the partner's consent or acquiescence, or failing
      within 90 days after the expiration of a stay to have the appoint-
      ment vacated;

(7) in the case of a partner who is an individual:

(i)   the partner's death;

(ii) the appointment of a guardian or general conservator for the
      partner; or

(iii) a judicial determination that the partner has otherwise become
      incapable of performing the partner's duties under the partner-
      ship agreement;

(8) in the case of a partner that is a trust or is acting as a partner by virtue
     of being a trustee of a trust, distribution of the trust's entire transfer-
     able interest in the partnership, but not merely by reason of the sub-
     stitution of a successor trustee;

(9) in the case of a partner that is an estate or is acting as a partner by
     virtue of being a personal representative of an estate, distribution of
     the estate's entire transferable interest in the partnership, but not
     merely by reason of the substitution of a successor personal represen-
     tative; or

(10) termination of a partner who is not an individual, partnership, cor-
     poration, trust, or estate.

COMMENT

1. RUPA dramatically changes the law governing partnership breakups and
dissolution. An entirely new concept, "dissociation," is used in lieu of the
UPA term "dissolution" to denote the change in the relationship caused by a
partner's ceasing to be associated in the carrying on of the business. "Disso-

lution" is retained but with a different meaning. See Section 802. The entity theory of partnership provides a conceptual basis for continuing the firm itself despite a partner's withdrawal from the firm.

Under RUPA, unlike the UPA, the dissociation of a partner does not necessarily cause a dissolution and winding up of the business of the partnership. Section 801 identifies the situations in which the dissociation of a partner causes a winding up of the business. Section 701 provides that in all other situations there is a buyout of the partner's interest in the partnership, rather than a windup of the partnership business. In those other situations, the partnership entity continues, unaffected by the partner's dissociation.

A dissociated partner remains a partner for some purposes and still has some residual rights, duties, powers, and liabilities. Although Section 601 determines when a partner is dissociated from the partnership, the consequences of the partner's dissociation do not all occur at the same time. Thus, it is more useful to think of a dissociated partner as a partner for some purposes, but as a former partner for others. For example, see Section 403(b) (former partner's access to partnership books and records). The consequences of a partner's dissociation depend on whether the partnership continues or is wound up, as provided in Articles 6, 7, and 8.

Section 601 enumerates all of the events that cause a partner's dissociation. Section 601 is similar in approach to RULPA Section 402, which lists the events resulting in a general partner's withdrawal from a limited partnership.

2. Section 601(1) provides that a partner is dissociated when the partnership has notice of the partner's express will to withdraw as a partner, unless a later date is specified by the partner. If a future date is specified by the partner, other partners may dissociate before that date; specifying a future date does not bind the others to remain as partners until that date. See also Section 801(2)(i).

Section 602(a) provides that a partner has the power to withdraw at any time. The power to withdraw is immutable under Section 103(b)(6), with the exception that the partners may agree the notice must be in writing. This continues the present rule that a partner has the power to withdraw at will, even if not the right. See UPA Section 31(2). Since no writing is required to create a partner relationship, it was felt unnecessarily formalistic, and a trap for the unwary, to require a writing to end one. If a written notification is given, Section 102(d) clarifies when it is deemed received.

RUPA continues the UPA "express will" concept, thus preserving existing case law. Section 601(1) clarifies existing law by providing that the partnership must have notice of the partner's expression of will before the dissociation is effective. See Section 102(b) for the meaning of "notice."

3. Section 601(2) provides expressly that a partner is dissociated upon an event agreed to in the partnership agreement as causing dissociation. There is no such provision in the UPA, but that result has been assumed.

4. Section 601(3) provides that a partner may be expelled by the other partners pursuant to a power of expulsion contained in the partnership agreement. That continues the basic rule of UPA Section 31(1)(d). The expulsion can be with or without cause. As under existing law, the obligation of good faith under Section 404(d) does not require prior notice, specification of cause, or an opportunity to be heard. *See Holman v. Coie*, 11 Wash. App. 195, 522 P.2d 515, *cert. denied*, 420 U.S. 984 (1974).

5. Section 601(4) empowers the partners, by unanimous vote, to expel a partner for specified causes, even if not authorized in the partnership agreement. This changes the UPA Section 31(1)(d) rule that authorizes expulsion only if provided in the partnership agreement. A partner may be expelled from a term partnership, as well as from a partnership at will. Under Section 103(a), the partnership agreement may change or abolish the partners' power of expulsion.

Subsection (4)(i) is derived from UPA Section 31(3). A partner may be expelled if it is unlawful to carry on the business with that partner. Section 801(4), on the other hand, provides that the partnership itself is dissolved and must be wound up if substantially all of the business is unlawful.

Subsection (4)(ii) provides that a partner may be expelled for transferring substantially all of his transferable interest in the partnership, other than as security for a loan. (He may, however, be expelled upon foreclosure.) This rule is derived from UPA Section 31(1)(c). To avoid the presence of an unwelcome transferee, the remaining partners may dissolve the partnership under Section 801(2)(ii), after first expelling the transferor partner. A transfer of a partner's entire interest may, in some circumstances, evidence the transferor's intention to withdraw under Section 601(1).

Subsection (4)(iii) provides for the expulsion of a corporate partner if it has filed a certificate of dissolution, its charter has been revoked, or its right to conduct business has been suspended, unless cured within 90 days after notice. This provision is derived from RULPA Section 402(9). The cure proviso is important because charter revocation is very common in some States and partner status should not end merely because of a technical noncompliance with corporate law that can easily be cured. Withdrawal of a voluntarily filed notice of dissolution constitutes a cure.

Subsection (4)(iv) is the partnership analogue of paragraph (iii) and is suggested by RULPA Section 402(8). It provides that a partnership that is a partner may be expelled if it has been dissolved and its business is being wound up. It is intended that the right of expulsion not be triggered solely by the dissolution event, but only upon commencement of the liquidation process.

6. Section 601(5) empowers a court to expel a partner if it determines that the partner has engaged in specified misconduct. The enumerated grounds for judicial expulsion are based on the UPA Section 32(1) grounds for judicial dissolution. The application for expulsion may be brought by the partnership or any partner. The phrase "judicial determination" is intended to include an arbitration award, as well as any final court order or decree.

Subsection (5)(i) provides for the partner's expulsion if the court finds that the partner has engaged in wrongful conduct that adversely and materially affected the partnership business. That language is derived from UPA Section 32(1)(c).

Subsection (5)(ii) provides for expulsion if the court determines that the partner willfully or persistently committed a material breach of the partnership agreement or of a duty owed to the partnership or to the other partners under Section 404. That would include a partner's breach of fiduciary duty. Paragraph (ii), together with paragraph (iii), carry forward the substance of UPA Section 32(1)(d).

Subsection (5)(iii) provides for judicial expulsion of a partner who engaged in conduct relating to the partnership business that makes it not reasonably practicable to carry on the business in partnership with that partner. Expulsion for such misconduct makes the partner's dissociation wrongful under Section 602(a)(ii) and may also support a judicial decree of dissolution under Section 801(5)(ii).

7. Section 601(6) provides that a partner is dissociated upon becoming a debtor in bankruptcy or upon taking or suffering other action evidencing the partner's insolvency or lack of financial responsibility.

Subsection (6)(i) is derived from UPA Section 31(5), which provides for dissolution upon a partner's bankruptcy. *Accord* RULPA § 402(4)(ii). There is some doubt as to whether UPA Section 31(1) is limited to so-called "straight bankruptcy" under Chapter 7 or includes other bankruptcy relief, such as Chapter 11. Under RUPA Section 101(2), however, "debtor in bankruptcy" includes a person who files a voluntary petition, or against whom relief is ordered in an involuntary case, under any chapter of the Bankruptcy Code.

Initially, upon the filing of the bankruptcy petition, the debtor partner's transferable interest in the partnership will pass to the bankruptcy trustee as property of the estate under Section 541(a)(1) of the Bankruptcy Code, notwithstanding any restrictions on transfer provided in the partnership agreement. In most Chapter 7 cases, that will result in the eventual buyout of the partner's interest.

The application of various provisions of the federal Bankruptcy Code to Section 601(6)(i) is unclear. In particular, there is uncertainty as to the validity of UPA Section 31(5), and thus its RUPA counterpart, under Sections 365(e) and 541(c)(1) of the Bankruptcy Code. Those sections generally invalidate so-called *ipso facto* laws that cause a termination or modification of the debtor's contract or property rights because of the bankruptcy filing. As a consequence, RUPA Section 601(6)(i), which provides for a partner's dissociation by operation of law upon becoming a debtor in bankruptcy, may be invalid under the Supremacy Clause. *See, e.g., In the Matter of Phillips*, 966 F.2d 926 (5th Cir. 1992); *In re Cardinal Industries, Inc.*, 105 B.R. 385 (Bankr. S.D. Ohio 1989), 116 B.R. 964 (Bankr. S.D. Ohio 1990); *In re Corky Foods Corp.*, 85 B.R. 903 (Bankr. S.D. Fla. 1988). *But see, In re Catron*, 158 B.R. 629 (E.D. Va. 1993) (partnership agreement could not be assumed by debtor under Bankruptcy Code § 365(c)(1) because other partners excused by UPA from accepting performance by or rendering performance to party other than debtor and buyout option not invalid *ipso facto* clause under Code § 365 (e)), *aff'd per curiam*, 25 F.3d 1038 (4th Cir. 1994). RUPA reflects the policy choice, as a matter of state partnership law, that a partner be dissociated upon becoming a debtor in bankruptcy.

Subsection (6)(ii) is new and provides for dissociation upon a general assignment for the benefit of a partner's creditors. The UPA says nothing about an assignment for the benefit of creditors or the appointment of a trustee, receiver, or liquidator. Subsection (6)(iii) and (iv) cover the latter and are based substantially on RULPA Section 402(4) and (5).

8. UPA Section 31(4) provides for the dissolution of a partnership upon the death of any partner, although by agreement the remaining partners may continue the partnership business. RUPA Section 601(7)(i), on the other hand, provides for dissociation upon the death of a partner who is an individual, rather than dissolution of the partnership. That changes existing law, except in those States previously adopting a similar non-uniform provision, such as California, Georgia, and Texas. Normally, under RUPA, the deceased partner's transferable interest in the partnership will pass to his estate and be bought out under Article 7.

Section 601(7)(ii) replaces UPA Section 32(1)(a) and provides for dissociation upon the appointment of a guardian or general conservator for partner who is an individual. The appointment itself operates as the event of dissociation, and no further order of the court is necessary.

Section 601(7)(iii) is based on UPA Section 32(1)(b) and provides for dissociation upon a judicial determination that an individual partner has in any other way become incapable of performing his duties under the partnership agreement. The intent is to include physical incapacity.

9. Section 601(8) is new and provides for the dissociation of a partner that is a trust, or is acting as a partner by virtue of being a trustee of a trust, upon the distribution by the trust of its entire transferable interest in the partnership, but not merely upon the substitution of a successor trustee. The provision is inspired by RULPA Section 402(7).

10. Section 601(9) is new and provides for the dissociation of a partner that is an estate, or is acting as a partner by virtue of being a personal representative of an estate, upon the distribution of the estate's entire transferable interest in the partnership, but not merely the substitution of a successor personal representative. It is based on RULPA Section 402(10). Under Section 601(7), a partner is dissociated upon death, however, and the estate normally becomes a transferee, not a partner.

11. Section 601(10) is new and provides that a partner that is not an individual, partnership, corporation, trust, or estate is dissociated upon its termination. It is the comparable "death" analogue for other types of entity partners, such as a limited liability company.

Section 602. Partner's Power to Dissociate; Wrongful Dissociation.

(a) A partner has the power to dissociate at any time, rightfully or wrongfully, by express will pursuant to Section 601(1).

(b) A partner's dissociation is wrongful only if:

(1) it is in breach of an express provision of the partnership agreement; or

(2) in the case of a partnership for a definite term or particular undertaking, before the expiration of the term or the completion of the undertaking:

(i) the partner withdraws by express will, unless the withdrawal follows within 90 days after another partner's dissociation by death or otherwise under Section 601(6) through (10) or wrongful dissociation under this subsection;

(ii) the partner is expelled by judicial determination under Section 601(5);

(iii) the partner is dissociated by becoming a debtor in bankruptcy; or

        (iv) in the case of a partner who is not an individual, trust other than a business trust, or estate, the partner is expelled or otherwise dissociated because it willfully dissolved or terminated.

    (c) A partner who wrongfully dissociates is liable to the partnership and to the other partners for damages caused by the dissociation. The liability is in addition to any other obligation of the partner to the partnership or to the other partners.

COMMENT

1. Subsection (a) states explicitly what is implicit in UPA Section 31(2) and RUPA Section 601(1) - that a partner has the power to dissociate at any time by expressing a will to withdraw, even in contravention of the partnership agreement. The phrase "rightfully or wrongfully" reflects the distinction between a partner's **power** to withdraw in contravention of the partnership agreement and a partner's **right** to do so. In this context, although a partner can not be enjoined from exercising the power to dissociate, the dissociation may be wrongful under subsection (b).

2. Subsection (b) provides that a partner's dissociation is wrongful only if it results from one of the enumerated events. The significance of a wrongful dissociation is that it may give rise to damages under subsection (c) and, if it results in the dissolution of the partnership, the wrongfully dissociating partner is not entitled to participate in winding up the business under Section 804.

Under subsection (b), a partner's dissociation is wrongful if (1) it breaches an express provision of the partnership agreement or (2), in a term partnership, before the expiration of the term or the completion of the undertaking (i) the partner voluntarily withdraws by express will, except a withdrawal following **another** partner's wrongful dissociation or dissociation by death or otherwise under Section 601(6) through (10); (ii) the partner is expelled for misconduct under Section 601(5); (iii) the partner becomes a debtor in bankruptcy (see Section 101(2)); or (iv) a partner that is an entity (other than a trust or estate) is expelled or otherwise dissociated because its dissolution or termination was willful. Since subsection (b) is merely a default rule, the partnership agreement may eliminate or expand the dissociations that are wrongful or modify the effects of wrongful dissociation.

The exception in subsection (b)(2)(i) is intended to protect a partner's reactive withdrawal from a term partnership after the premature departure of another partner, such as the partnership's rainmaker or main supplier of capital, under the same circumstances that may result in the dissolution of the partnership under Section 801(2)(i). Under that section, a term partnership is dissolved 90 days after the bankruptcy, incapacity, death (or similar dissociation of a partner that is an entity), or wrongful dissociation of any partner, unless a majority in interest (see Comment 5(i) to Section 801 for a discussion of the term "majority in interest") of the remaining partners agree to continue the partnership. Under Section 602(b)(2)(i), a partner's exercise of the right of withdrawal by express will under those circumstances is rendered "rightful," even if the partnership is continued by others, and does not expose the withdrawing partner to damages for wrongful dissociation under Section 602(c).

A partner wishing to withdraw prematurely from a term partnership for any other reason, such as another partner's misconduct, can avoid being treated as a wrongfully dissociating partner by applying to a court under Section 601(5)(iii) to have the offending partner expelled. Then, the partnership could be dissolved under Section 801(2)(i) or the remaining partners could, by unanimous vote, dissolve the partnership under Section 801(2)(ii).

3. Subsection (c) provides that a wrongfully dissociating partner is liable to the partnership and to the other partners for any damages caused by the wrongful nature of the dissociation. That liability is in addition to any other obligation of the partner to the partnership or to the other partners. For example, the partner would be liable for any damage caused by breach of the partnership agreement or other misconduct. The partnership might also incur substantial expenses resulting from a partner's premature withdrawal from a term partnership, such as replacing the partner's expertise or obtaining new financing. The wrongfully dissociating partner would be liable to the partnership for those and all other expenses and damages that are causally related to the wrongful dissociation.

Section 701(c) provides that any damages for wrongful dissociation may be offset against the amount of the buyout price due to the partner under Section 701(a), and Section 701(h) provides that a partner who wrongfully dissociates from a term partnership is not entitled to payment of the buyout price until the term expires.

Under UPA Section 38(2)(c)(II), in addition to an offset for damages, the goodwill value of the partnership is excluded in determining the value of a wrongfully dissociating partner's partnership interest. Under RUPA, however, unless the partnership's goodwill is damaged by the wrongful dissociation, the value of the wrongfully dissociating partner's interest will include any goodwill value of the partnership. If the firm's goodwill is damaged, the amount of the damages suffered by the partnership and the remaining partners will be offset against the buyout price. See Section 701 and Comments.

Section 603. Effect of Partner's Dissociation.

(a) If a partner's dissociation results in a dissolution and winding up of the partnership business, [Article] 8 applies; otherwise, [Article] 7 applies.

(b) Upon a partner's dissociation:

(1) the partner's right to participate in the management and conduct of the partnership business terminates, except as otherwise provided in Section 803;

(2) the partner's duty of loyalty under Section 404(b)(3) terminates; and

(3) the partner's duty of loyalty under Section 404(b)(1) and (2) and duty of care under Section 404(c) continue only with regard to matters arising and events occurring before the partner's dissociation, unless the partner participates in winding up the partnership's business pursuant to Section 803.

COMMENT

1. Section 603(a) is a "switching" provision. It provides that, after a partner's dissociation, the partner's interest in the partnership must be purchased pursuant to the buyout rules in Article 7 **unless** there is a dissolution and winding up of the partnership business under Article 8. Thus, a partner's dissociation will always result in either a buyout of the dissociated partner's interest or a dissolution and winding up of the business.

By contrast, under the UPA, every partner dissociation results in the dissolution of the partnership, most of which trigger a right to have the business wound up unless the partnership agreement provides otherwise. *See* UPA § 38. The only exception in which the remaining partners have a statutory right to continue the business is when a partner wrongfully dissolves the partnership in breach of the partnership agreement. *See* UPA § 38(2)(b).

2. Section 603(b) is new and deals with some of the internal effects of a partner's dissociation. Subsection (b)(1) makes it clear that one of the consequences of a partner's dissociation is the immediate loss of the right to participate in the management of the business, unless it results in a dissolution and winding up of the business. In that case, Section 804(a) provides that all of the partners who have not wrongfully dissociated may participate in winding up the business.

Subsection (b)(2) and (3) clarify a partner's fiduciary duties upon dissociation. No change from current law is intended. With respect to the duty of loyalty, the Section 404(b)(3) duty not to compete terminates upon dissociation, and the dissociated partner is free immediately to engage in a competitive business, without any further consent. With respect to the partner's remaining loyalty duties under Section 404(b) and duty of care under Section 404(c), a withdrawing partner has a continuing duty after dissociation, but it is limited to matters that arose or events that occurred before the partner dissociated. For example, a partner who leaves a brokerage firm may immediately compete with the firm for new clients, but must exercise care in completing on-going client transactions and must account to the firm for any fees received from the old clients on account of those transactions. As the last clause makes clear, there is no contraction of a dissociated partner's duties under subsection (b)(3) if the partner thereafter participates in the dissolution and winding up the partnership's business.

[ARTICLE] 7
PARTNER'S DISSOCIATION WHEN BUSINESS NOT WOUND UP

Section 701. Purchase of Dissociated Partner's Interest.

(a) If a partner is dissociated from a partnership without resulting in a dissolution and winding up of the partnership business under Section 801, the partnership shall cause the dissociated partner's interest in the partnership to be purchased for a buyout price determined pursuant to subsection (b).

(b) The buyout price of a dissociated partner's interest is the amount that would have been distributable to the dissociating partner under Section 807(b) if, on the date of dissociation, the assets of the partnership were sold at a price equal to the greater of the liquidation value or the value based on a sale of the entire business as a going concern without the dissociated partner and the partnership were wound up as of that date. Interest must be paid from the date of dissociation to the date of payment.

(c) Damages for wrongful dissociation under Section 602(b), and all other amounts owing, whether or not presently due, from the dissociated partner to the partnership, must be offset against the buyout price. Interest must be paid from the date the amount owed becomes due to the date of payment.

(d) A partnership shall indemnify a dissociated partner whose interest is being purchased against all partnership liabilities, whether incurred before or after the dissociation, except liabilities incurred by an act of the dissociated partner under Section 702.

(e) If no agreement for the purchase of a dissociated partner's interest is reached within 120 days after a written demand for payment, the partnership shall pay, or cause to be paid, in cash to the dissociated partner the amount the partnership estimates to be the buyout price and accrued interest, reduced by any offsets and accrued interest under subsection (c).

(f) If a deferred payment is authorized under subsection (h), the partnership may tender a written offer to pay the amount it estimates to be the buyout price and accrued interest, reduced by any offsets under subsection (c), stating the time of payment, the amount and type of security for payment, and the other terms and conditions of the obligation.

(g) The payment or tender required by subsection (e) or (f) must be accompanied by the following:

(1) a statement of partnership assets and liabilities as of the date of dissociation;

(2) the latest available partnership balance sheet and income statement, if any;

(3) an explanation of how the estimated amount of the payment was calculated; and

(4) written notice that the payment is in full satisfaction of the obligation to purchase unless, within 120 days after the written notice, the dissociated partner commences an action to determine the buyout price, any offsets under subsection (c), or other terms of the obligation to purchase.

(h) A partner who wrongfully dissociates before the expiration of a definite term or the completion of a particular undertaking is not entitled to payment of any portion of the buyout price until the expiration of the term or completion of the undertaking, unless the partner establishes to the satisfaction of the court that earlier payment will not cause undue hardship to the business of the partnership. A deferred payment must be adequately secured and bear interest.

(i) A dissociated partner may maintain an action against the partnership, pursuant to Section 405(b)(2)(ii), to determine the buyout price of that partner's interest, any offsets under subsection (c), or other terms of the obligation to purchase. The action must be commenced within 120 days after the partnership has tendered payment or an offer to pay or within one year after written demand for payment if no payment or offer to pay is tendered. The court shall determine the buyout price of the dissociated partner's interest, any offset due under subsection (c), and accrued interest, and enter judgment for any additional payment or refund. If deferred payment is authorized under subsection (h), the court shall also determine the security for payment and other terms of the obligation to purchase. The court may assess reasonable attorney's fees and the fees and expenses of appraisers or other experts for a party to the action, in amounts the court finds equitable, against a party that the court finds acted arbitrarily, vexatiously, or not in good faith. The finding may be based on the partnership's failure to tender payment or an offer to pay or to comply with subsection (g).

COMMENT

1. Article 7 is new and provides for the buyout of a dissociated partner's interest in the partnership when the partner's dissociation does not result in a dissolution and winding up of its business under Article 8. *See* Section 603(a).

If there is no dissolution, the remaining partners have a right to continue the business and the dissociated partner has a right to be paid the value of his partnership interest. These rights can, of course, be varied in the partnership agreement. *See* Section 103. A dissociated partner has a continuing relationship with the partnership and third parties as provided in Sections 603(b), 702, and 703. See also Section 403(b) (former partner's access to partnership books and records).

2. Subsection (a) provides that, if a partner's dissociation does not result in a windup of the business, the partnership shall cause the interest of the dissociating partner to be purchased for a buyout price determined pursuant to subsection (b). The buyout is mandatory. The "cause to be purchased" language is intended to accommodate a purchase by the partnership, one or more of the remaining partners, or a third party.

For federal income tax purposes, a payment to a partner for his interest can be characterized either as a purchase of the partner's interest or as a liquidating distribution. The two have different tax consequences. RUPA permits either option by providing that the payment may come from either the partnership, some or all of the continuing partners, or a third party purchaser.

3. Subsection (b) provides how the "buyout price" is to be determined. The terms "fair market value" or "fair value" were not used because they are often considered terms of art having a special meaning depending on the context, such as in tax or corporate law. "Buyout price" is a new term. It is intended that the term be developed as an independent concept appropriate to the partnership buyout situation, while drawing on valuation principles developed elsewhere.

Under subsection (b), the buyout price is the amount that would have been distributable to the dissociating partner under Section 807(b) if, on the date of dissociation, the assets of the partnership were sold at a price equal to the greater of liquidation value or going concern value without the departing partner. Liquidation value is not intended to mean distress sale value. Under general principles of valuation, the hypothetical selling price in either case should be the price that a willing and informed buyer would pay a willing and informed seller, with neither being under any compulsion to deal. The notion of a minority discount in determining the buyout price is negated by valuing the business as a going concern. Other discounts, such as for a lack of marketability or the loss of a key partner, may be appropriate, however.

Since the buyout price is based on the value of the business at the time of dissociation, the partnership must pay interest on the amount due from the date of dissociation until payment to compensate the dissociating partner for the use of his interest in the firm. Section 104(b) provides that interest shall be at the legal rate unless otherwise provided in the partnership agreement. The

UPA Section 42 option of electing a share of the profits in lieu of interest has been eliminated.

UPA Section 38(2)(c)(II) provides that the good will of the business not be considered in valuing a wrongfully dissociating partner's interest. The forfeiture of good will rule is implicitly rejected by RUPA. See Section 602(c) and Comment 3.

The Section 701 rules are merely default rules. The partners may, in the partnership agreement, fix the method or formula for determining the buyout price and all of the other terms and conditions of the buyout right. Indeed, the very right to a buyout itself may be modified, although a provision providing for a complete forfeiture would probably not be enforceable. *See* Section 104(a).

4. Subsection (c) provides that the partnership may offset against the buyout price all amounts owing by the dissociated partner to the partnership, whether or not presently due, including any damages for wrongful dissociation under Section 602(c). This has the effect of accelerating payment of amounts not yet due from the departing partner to the partnership, including a long-term loan by the partnership to the dissociated partner. Where appropriate, the amounts not yet due should be discounted to present value. A dissociating partner, on the other hand, is not entitled to an add-on for amounts owing to him by the partnership. Thus, a departing partner who has made a long-term loan to the partnership must wait for repayment, unless the terms of the loan agreement provide for acceleration upon dissociation.

It is not intended that the partnership's right of setoff be construed to limit the amount of the damages for the partner's wrongful dissociation and any other amounts owing to the partnership to the value of the dissociated partner's interest. Those amounts may result in a net sum due to the partnership from the dissociated partner.

5. Subsection (d) follows the UPA Section 38 rule and provides that the partnership must indemnify a dissociated partner against all partnership liabilities, whether incurred before or after the dissociation, except those incurred by the dissociated partner under Section 702.

6. Subsection (e) provides that, if no agreement for the purchase of the dissociated partner's interest is reached within 120 days after the dissociated partner's written demand for payment, the partnership must pay, or cause to be paid, in cash the amount it estimates to be the buyout price, adjusted for any offsets allowed and accrued interest. Thus, the dissociating partner will receive in cash within 120 days of dissociation the undisputed minimum value of the partner's partnership interest. If the dissociated partner claims

that the buyout price should be higher, suit may thereafter be brought as provided in subsection (i) to have the amount of the buyout price determined by the court. This is similar to the procedure for determining the value of dissenting shareholders' shares under RMBCA Sections 13.20-13.28.

The "cause to be paid" language of subsection (a) is repeated here to permit either the partnership, one or more of the continuing partners, or a third-party purchaser to tender payment of the estimated amount due.

7. Subsection (f) provides that, when deferred payment is authorized in the case of a wrongfully dissociating partner, a written offer stating the amount the partnership estimates to be the purchase price should be tendered within the 120-day period, even though actual payment of the amount may be deferred, possibly for many years. See Comment 8. The dissociated partner is entitled to know at the time of dissociation what amount the remaining partners think is due, including the estimated amount of any damages allegedly caused by the partner's wrongful dissociation that may be offset against the buyout price.

8. Subsection (g) provides that the payment of the estimated price (or tender of a written offer under subsection (f)) by the partnership must be accompanied by (1) a statement of the partnership's assets and liabilities as of the date of the partner's dissociation; (2) the latest available balance sheet and income statement, if the partnership maintains such financial statements; (3) an explanation of how the estimated amount of the payment was calculated; and (4) a written notice that the payment will be in full satisfaction of the partnership's buyout obligation unless the dissociated partner commences an action to determine the price within 120 days of the notice. Subsection (g) is based in part on the dissenters' rights provisions of RMBCA Section 13.25(b).

Those disclosures should serve to identify and narrow substantially the items of dispute between the dissociated partner and the partnership over the valuation of the partnership interest. They will also serve to pin down the parties as to their claims of partnership assets and values and as to the existence and amount of all known liabilities. See Comment 4. Lastly, it will force the remaining partners to consider thoughtfully the difficult and important questions as to the appropriate method of valuation under the circumstances, and in particular, whether they should use going concern or liquidation value. Simply getting that information on the record in a timely fashion should increase the likelihood of a negotiated resolution of the parties' differences during the 120-day period within which the dissociated partner must bring suit.

9. Subsection (h) replaces UPA Section 38(2)(c) and provides a somewhat different rule for payment to a partner whose dissociation before the expiration of a definite term or the completion of a particular undertaking is wrongful

under Section 602(b). Under subsection (h), a wrongfully dissociating partner is not entitled to receive any portion of the buyout price before the expiration of the term or completion of the undertaking, unless the dissociated partner establishes to the satisfaction of the court that earlier payment will not cause undue hardship to the business of the partnership. In all other cases, there must be an immediate payment in cash.

10. Subsection (i) provides that a dissociated partner may maintain an action against the partnership to determine the buyout price, any offsets, or other terms of the purchase obligation. The action must be commenced within 120 days after the partnership tenders payment of the amount it estimates to be due or, if deferred payment is authorized, its written offer. This provision creates a 120-day "cooling off" period. It also allows the parties an opportunity to negotiate their differences after disclosure by the partnership of its financial statements and other required information.

If the partnership fails to tender payment of the estimated amount due (or a written offer, if deferred payment is authorized), the dissociated partner has one year after written demand for payment in which to commence suit.

If the parties fail to reach agreement, the court must determine the buyout price of the partner's interest, any offsets, including damages for wrongful dissociation, and the amount of interest accrued. If payment to a wrongfully dissociated partner is deferred, the court may also require security for payment and determine the other terms of the obligation.

Under subsection (i), attorney's fees and other costs may be assessed against any party found to have acted arbitrarily, vexatiously, or not in good faith in connection with the valuation dispute, including the partnership's failure to tender payment of the estimated price or to make the required disclosures. This provision is based in part on RMBCA Section 13.31(b).

Section 702. Dissociated Partner's Power to Bind and Liability to Partnership.

(a) For two years after a partner dissociates without resulting in a dissolution and winding up of the partnership business, the partnership, including a surviving partnership under [Article] 9, is bound by an act of the dissociated partner which would have bound the partnership under Section 301 before dissociation only if at the time of entering into the transaction the other party:

(1) reasonably believed that the dissociated partner was then a partner;

(2) did not have notice of the partner's dissociation; and

(3) is not deemed to have had knowledge under Section 303(e) or notice under Section 704(c).

(b) A dissociated partner is liable to the partnership for any damage caused to the partnership arising from an obligation incurred by the dissociated partner after dissociation for which the partnership is liable under subsection (a).

COMMENT

1. Section 702 deals with a dissociated partner's lingering apparent authority to bind the partnership in ordinary course partnership transactions and the partner's liability to the partnership for any loss caused thereby. It also applies to partners who withdraw incident to a merger under Article 9. *See* Section 906(e).

A dissociated partner has no **actual** authority to act for the partnership. *See* Section 603(b)(1). Nevertheless, in order to protect innocent third parties, Section 702(a) provides that the partnership remains bound, for two years after a partner's dissociation, by that partner's acts that would, before his dissociation, have bound the partnership under Section 301 if, and only if, the other party to the transaction reasonably believed that he was still a partner, did not have notice of the partner's dissociation, and is not deemed to have had knowledge of the dissociation under Section 303(e) or notice thereof under Section 704(c).

Under Section 301, every partner has **apparent** authority to bind the partnership by any act for carrying on the partnership business in the ordinary course, unless the other party knows that the partner has no actual authority to act for the partnership or has received a notification of the partner's lack of authority. Section 702(a) continues that general rule for two years after a partner's dissociation, subject to three modifications.

After a partner's dissociation, the general rule is modified, first, by requiring the other party to show reasonable reliance on the partner's status as a partner. Section 301 has no explicit reliance requirement, although the partnership is bound only if the partner purports to act on its behalf. Thus, the other party will normally be aware of the partnership and presumably the partner's status as such.

The second modification is that, under Section 702(a), the partnership is not bound if the third party has **notice** of the partner's dissociation, while under the general rule of Section 301 the partnership is bound unless the third party **knows** of the partner's lack of authority. Under Section 102(b), a person has "notice" of a fact if he knows or has reason to know it exists from all the facts that are known to him or he has received a notification of it. Thus, the partnership may protect itself by sending a notification of the dissociation to a third party, and a third party may, in any event, have a duty to inquire further based on what is known. That provides the partnership with greater protection from the unauthorized acts of a dissociated partner than from those of partners generally.

The third modification of the general apparent authority rule under Section 702(a) involves the effect of a statement of dissociation. Section 704(c) provides that, for the purposes of Sections 702(a)(3) and 703(b)(3), third parties are deemed to have notice of a partner's dissociation 90 days after the filing of a statement of dissociation. Thus, the filing of a statement operates as constructive notice of the dissociated partner's lack of authority after 90 days, conclusively terminating the dissociated partner's Section 702 apparent authority.

With respect to a dissociated partner's authority to transfer partnership real property, Section 303(e) provides that third parties are deemed to have knowledge of a limitation on a partner's authority to transfer real property held in the partnership name upon the proper recording of a statement containing such a limitation. Section 704(b) provides that a statement of dissociation operates as a limitation on the dissociated partner's authority for the purposes of Section 303(e). Thus, a properly recorded statement of dissociation operates as constructive knowledge of a dissociated partner's lack of authority to transfer real property held in the partnership name, effective immediately upon recording.

Under RUPA, therefore, a partnership should notify all known creditors of a partner's dissociation and may, by filing a statement of dissociation, conclusively limit to 90 days a dissociated partner's lingering agency power. Moreover, under Section 703(b), a dissociated partner's lingering liability for post-dissociation partnership liabilities may be limited to 90 days by filing a statement of dissociation. These incentives should encourage both partnerships and dissociating partners to file statements routinely. Those transacting substantial business with partnerships can protect themselves from the risk of dealing with dissociated partners, or relying on their credit, by checking the partnership records at least every 90 days.

2. Section 702(b) is a corollary to subsection (a) and provides that a dissociated partner is liable to the partnership for any loss resulting from an obligation improperly incurred by the partner under subsection (a). In effect, the dissociated partner must indemnify the partnership for any loss, meaning a loss net of any gain from the transaction. The dissociated partner is also personally liable to the third party for the unauthorized obligation.

Section 703. Dissociated Partner's Liability to Other Persons.

(a) A partner's dissociation does not of itself discharge the partner's liability for a partnership obligation incurred before dissociation. A dissociated partner is not liable for a partnership obligation incurred after dissociation, except as otherwise provided in subsection (b).

(b) A partner who dissociates without resulting in a dissolution and winding up of the partnership business is liable as a partner to the other party in a transaction entered into by the partnership, or a surviving partnership under [Article] 9, within two years after the partner's dissociation, only if the partner is liable for the obligation under Section 306 and at the time of entering into the transaction the other party:

    (1) reasonably believed that the dissociated partner was then a partner;

    (2) did not have notice of the partner's dissociation; and

    (3) is not deemed to have had knowledge under Section 303(e) or notice under Section 704(c).

  (c) By agreement with the partnership creditor and the partners continuing the business, a dissociated partner may be released from liability for a partnership obligation.

  (d) A dissociated partner is released from liability for a partnership obligation if a partnership creditor, with notice of the partner's dissociation but without the partner's consent, agrees to a material alteration in the nature or time of payment of a partnership obligation.

COMMENT

Section 703(a) is based on UPA Section 36(1) and continues the basic rule that the departure of a partner does not of itself discharge the partner's liability to third parties for any partnership obligation incurred before dissociation. The word "obligation" is used instead of "liability" and is intended to include broadly both tort and contract liability incurred before dissociation. The second sentence states affirmatively that a dissociating partner is not liable for any partnership obligation incurred after dissociation except as expressly provided in subsection (b).

Section 703(b) is new and deals with the problem of protecting third parties who extend credit to the partnership after a partner's dissociation, believing that he is still a partner. It provides that the dissociated partner remains liable as a partner for transactions entered into by the partnership within two years after departure, if the other party does not have notice of the partner's dissociation and reasonably believes when entering the transaction that the dissociated partner is still a partner. The dissociated partner is not personally liable, however, if the other party is deemed to know of the dissociation under Section 303(e) or to have notice thereof under Section 704(c). Also, a dissociated partner is not personally liable for limited liability partnership obligations for which the partner is not personally liable under Section 306.

Section 703(b) operates similarly to Section 702(a) in that it requires reliance on the departed partner's continued partnership status, as well as lack of notice. Under Section 704(c), a statement of dissociation operates conclusively as constructive notice 90 days after filing for the purposes of Section 703(b)(3) and, under Section 704(b), as constructive knowledge when recorded for the purposes of Section 303(d) and (e).

Section 703(c) continues the rule of UPA Section 36(2) that a departing partner can bargain for a contractual release from personal liability for a partnership obligation, but it requires the consent of both the creditor and the remaining partners.

Section 703(d) continues the rule of UPA Section 36(3) that a dissociated partner is released from liability for a partnership obligation if the creditor, with notice of the partner's departure, agrees to a material alteration in the nature or time of payment, without that partner's consent. This rule covers all partner dissociations and is not limited, as is the UPA rule, to situations in which a third party "agrees to assume the existing obligations of a dissolved partnership."

In general under RUPA, as a result of the adoption of the entity theory, relationships between a partnership and its creditors are not affected by the dissociation of a partner or by the addition of a new partner, unless otherwise agreed. Therefore, there is no need under RUPA, as there is under the UPA, for an elaborate provision deeming the new partnership to assume the liabilities of the old partnership. See UPA Section 41.

The "dual priority" rule in UPA Section 36(4) is eliminated to reflect the abolition of the "jingle rule," providing that separate debts have first claim on separate property, in order to conform to the Bankruptcy Code. See Comment 2 to Section 807. A deceased partner's estate, and thus all of his individual property, remains liable for partnership obligations incurred while he was a partner, however.

Section 704. Statement of Dissociation.

(a) A dissociated partner or the partnership may file a statement of dissociation stating the name of the partnership and that the partner is dissociated from the partnership.

(b) A statement of dissociation is a limitation on the authority of a dissociated partner for the purposes of Section 303(d) and (e).

(c) For the purposes of Sections 702(a)(3) and 703(b)(3), a person not a partner is deemed to have notice of the dissociation 90 days after the statement of dissociation is filed.

COMMENT

Section 704 is new and provides for a statement of dissociation and its effects. Subsection (a) authorizes either a dissociated partner or the partnership to file a statement of dissociation. Like other RUPA filings, the statement of dissociation is voluntary. Both the partnership and the departing partner have an incentive to file, however, and it is anticipated that those filings will become routine upon a partner's dissociation. The execution, filing, and recording of the statement is governed by Section 105.

Filing or recording a statement of dissociation has threefold significance:

(1) It is a statement of limitation on the dissociated partner's authority to the extent provided in Section 303(d) and (e). Under Section 303(d), a filed or recorded limitation on the authority of a partner destroys the conclusive effect of a prior grant of authority to the extent it contradicts the prior grant. Under Section 303(e), nonpartners are conclusively bound by a limitation on the authority of a partner to transfer real property held in the partnership name, if the statement is properly recorded in the real property records.

(2) Ninety days after the statement is filed, nonpartners are deemed to have notice of the dissociation and thus conclusively bound for purposes of cutting off the partner's apparent authority under Sections 301 and 702(a)(3).

(3) Ninety days after the statement is filed, third parties are conclusively bound for purposes of cutting off the dissociated partner's continuing liability under Section 703(b)(3) for transactions entered into by the partnership after dissociation.

Section 705. Continued Use of Partnership Name.

Continued use of a partnership name, or a dissociated partner's name as part thereof, by partners continuing the business does not of itself make the dissociated partner liable for an obligation of the partners or the partnership continuing the business.

COMMENT

Section 705 is an edited version of UPA Section 41(10) and provides that a dissociated partner is not liable for the debts of the continuing business simply because of continued use of the partnership name or the dissociated partner's name as a part thereof. That prevents forcing the business to forego the good will associated with its name.

[ARTICLE] 8
WINDING UP PARTNERSHIP BUSINESS

Section 801. Events Causing Dissolution and Winding
Up of Partnership Business.

A partnership is dissolved, and its business must be wound up, only upon the occurrence of any of the following events:

(1) in a partnership at will, the partnership's having notice from a partner, other than a partner who is dissociated under Section 601(2) through (10), of that partner's express will to withdraw as a partner, or on a later date specified by the partner;

(2) in a partnership for a definite term or particular undertaking:
   (i) within 90 days after a partner's dissociation by death or otherwise under Section 601(6) through (10) or wrongful dissociation under Section 602(b), the express will of at least half of the remaining partners to wind up the partnership business, for which purpose a partner's rightful dissociation pursuant to Section 602(b)(2)(i) constitutes the expression of that partner's will to wind up the partnership business;
   (ii) the express will of all of the partners to wind up the partnership business; or
   (iii) the expiration of the term or the completion of the undertaking;

(3) an event agreed to in the partnership agreement resulting in the winding up of the partnership business;

(4) an event that makes it unlawful for all or substantially all of the business of the partnership to be continued, but a cure of illegality within 90 days after notice to the partnership of the event is effective retroactively to the date of the event for purposes of this section;

(5) on application by a partner, a judicial determination that:
   (i) the economic purpose of the partnership is likely to be unreasonably frustrated;
   (ii) another partner has engaged in conduct relating to the partnership business which makes it not reasonably practicable to carry on the business in partnership with that partner; or
   (iii) it is not otherwise reasonably practicable to carry on the partnership business in conformity with the partnership agreement; or

(6) on application by a transferee of a partner's transferable interest, a judicial determination that it is equitable to wind up the partnership business:
   (i) after the expiration of the term or completion of the undertaking, if the partnership was for a definite term or particular undertaking at the time of the transfer or entry of the charging order that gave rise to the transfer; or
   (ii) at any time, if the partnership was a partnership at will at the time of the transfer or entry of the charging order that gave rise to the transfer.

COMMENT

1. Under UPA Section 29, a partnership is dissolved every time a partner leaves. That reflects the aggregate nature of the partnership under the UPA. Even if the business of the partnership is continued by some of the partners,

it is technically a new partnership. The dissolution of the old partnership and creation of a new partnership causes many unnecessary problems.

Under RULPA, limited partnerships dissolve far less readily than do general partnerships under the UPA. A limited partnership does not dissolve on the withdrawal of a limited partner, nor does it necessarily dissolve on the withdrawal of a general partner. *See* RULPA § 801(4).

RUPA's move to the entity theory is driven in part by the need to prevent a technical dissolution or its consequences. Under RUPA, not every partner dissociation causes a dissolution of the partnership. Only certain departures trigger a dissolution. The basic rule is that a partnership is dissolved, and its business must be wound up, only upon the occurrence of one of the events listed in Section 801. All other dissociations result in a buyout of the partner's interest under Article 7 and a continuation of the partnership entity and business by the remaining partners. *See* Section 603(a).

With only three exceptions, the provisions of Section 801 are merely default rules and may by agreement be varied or eliminated as grounds for dissolution. The first exception is dissolution under Section 801(4) resulting from carrying on an illegal business. The other two exceptions cover the power of a court to dissolve a partnership under Section 801(5) on application of a partner and under Section 801(6) on application of a transferee. *See* Comments 6-8 for further explanation of these provisions.

2. Under RUPA, "dissolution" is merely the commencement of the winding up process. The partnership continues for the limited purpose of winding up the business. In effect, that means the scope of the partnership business contracts to completing work in process and taking such other actions as may be necessary to wind up the business. Winding up the partnership business entails selling its assets, paying its debts, and distributing the net balance, if any, to the partners in cash according to their interests. The partnership entity continues, and the partners are associated in the winding up of the business until winding up is completed. When the winding up is completed, the partnership entity terminates.

3. Section 801 continues two basic rules from the UPA. First, it continues the rule that any member of an **at-will** partnership has the right to force a liquidation. Second, by negative implication, it continues the rule that the partners who wish to continue the business of a **term** partnership can not be forced to liquidate the business by a partner who withdraws prematurely in violation of the partnership agreement.

Those rules are gleaned from the separate UPA provisions governing dissolution and its consequences. Under UPA Section 31(1)(b), dissolution is caused by the express will of any partner when no definite term or particular undertaking is specified. UPA Section 38(1) provides that upon dissolution any partner has the right to have the business wound up. That is a default rule and applies only in the absence of an agreement affording the other partners a right to continue the business.

UPA Section 31(2) provides that a term partnership may be dissolved at any time, in contravention of the partnership agreement, by the express will of any partner. In that case, however, UPA Section 38(2)(b) provides that the nonbreaching partners may by unanimous consent continue the business. If the business is continued, they must buy out the breaching partner.

4. Section 801(1) provides that a partnership at will is dissolved and its business must be wound up upon the partnership's having notice of a partner's express will to withdraw as a partner, unless a later effective date is specified by the partner. A partner at will who has already been dissociated in some other manner, such as a partner who has been expelled, does not thereafter have a right to cause the partnership to be dissolved and its business wound up.

If, after dissolution, none of the partners wants the partnership wound up, Section 802(b) provides that, with the consent of all the partners, including the withdrawing partner, the remaining partners may continue the business. In that event, although there is a technical dissolution of the partnership and, at least in theory, a temporary contraction of the scope of the business, the partnership entity continues and the scope of its business is restored. See Section 802(b) and Comment 2.

5. Section 801(2) provides three ways in which a term partnership may be dissolved before the expiration of the term:

(i) Subsection (2)(i) provides for dissolution after a partner's dissociation by death or otherwise under Section 601(6) to (10) or wrongful dissociation under Section 602(b), if within 90 days after the dissociation at least half of the remaining partners express their will to dissolve the partnership. Thus if a term partnership had six partners and one of the partners dies or wrongfully dissociates before the end of the term, the partnership will, as a result of the dissociation, be dissolved only if three of the remaining five partners affirmatively vote in favor of dissolution within 90 days after the dissociation.[1]

This reactive dissolution of a term partnership protects the remaining partners where the dissociating partner is crucial to the successful continuation of the business. The corresponding UPA Section 38(2)(b) rule requires unanimous consent of the remaining partners to continue the business, thus giving each partner an absolute right to a reactive liquidation. Under UPA 1994, if the partnership is continued by the majority, any dissenting partner who wants to withdraw may do so rightfully under the exception to Section 602(b)(2)(i), in which case his interest in the partnership will be bought out under Article 7. By itself, however, a partner's vote not to continue the business is not necessarily an expression of the partner's will to withdraw, and a dissenting partner may still elect to remain a partner and continue in the business.

The Section 601 dissociations giving rise to a reactive dissolution are: (6) a partner's bankruptcy or similar financial impairment; (7) a partner's death or incapacity; (8) the distribution by a trust-partner of its entire partnership interest; (9) the distribution by an estate-partner of its entire partnership interest; and (10) the termination of an entity-partner. Any dissociation during the term of the partnership that is wrongful under Section 602(b), including a partner's voluntary withdrawal, expulsion or bankruptcy, also gives rise to a reactive dissolution. Those statutory grounds may be varied by agreement or the reactive dissolution may be abolished entirely.

Under Section 601(6)(i), a partner is dissociated upon becoming a debtor in bankruptcy. The bankruptcy of a partner or of the partnership is not, however, an event of dissolution under Section 801. That is a change from UPA Section 31(5). A partner's bankruptcy does, however, cause dissolution of a term partnership under Section 801(2)(i), unless a majority in interest of the remaining partners thereafter agree to continue the partnership. Affording the other partners the option of buying out the bankrupt partner's interest avoids the necessity of winding up a term partnership every time a partner becomes a debtor in bankruptcy.

Similarly, under Section 801(2)(i), the death of any partner will result in the dissolution of a term partnership, only if at least half of the remaining partners express their will to wind up the partnership's business. If dissolution does occur, the deceased partner's transferable interest in the partnership passes to his estate and must be bought out under Article 7. See Comment 8 to Section 601.

(ii) Section 801(2)(ii) provides that a term partnership may be dissolved and wound up at any time by the express will of all the partners. That is merely an expression of the general rule that the partnership agreement may override the statutory default rules and that the partnership agreement, like any contract, can be amended at any time by unanimous consent.

UPA Section 31(1)(c) provides that a term partnership may be wound up by the express will of all the partners whose transferable interests have not been assigned or charged for a partner's separate debts. That rule reflects the belief that the remaining partners may find transferees very intrusive. This provision has been deleted, however, because the liquidation is easily accomplished under Section 801(2)(ii) by first expelling the transferor partner under Section 601(4)(ii).

(iii) Section 801(2)(iii) is based on UPA Section 31(1)(a) and provides for winding up a term partnership upon the expiration of the term or the completion of the undertaking.

Subsection (2)(iii) must be read in conjunction with Section 406. Under Section 406(a), if the partners continue the business after the expiration of the term or the completion of the undertaking, the partnership will be treated as a partnership at will. Moreover, if the partners continue the business without any settlement or liquidation of the partnership, under Section 406(b) they are presumed to have agreed that the partnership will continue, despite the lack of a formal agreement. The partners may also agree to ratify all acts taken since the end of the partnership's term.

6. Section 801(3) provides for dissolution upon the occurrence of an event specified in the partnership agreement as resulting in the winding up of the partnership business. The partners may, however, agree to continue the business and to ratify all acts taken since dissolution.

7. Section 801(4) continues the basic rule in UPA Section 31(3) and provides for dissolution if it is unlawful to continue the business of the partnership, unless cured. The "all or substantially all" proviso is intended to avoid dissolution for insubstantial or innocent regulatory violations. If the illegality is cured within 90 days after notice to the partnership, it is effective retroactively for purposes of this section. The requirement that an uncured illegal business be wound up cannot be varied in the partnership agreement. *See* Section 103(b)(8).

8. Section 801(5) provides for judicial dissolution on application by a partner. It is based in part on UPA Section 32(1), and the language comes in part from RULPA Section 802. A court may order a partnership dissolved upon a judicial determination that: (i) the economic purpose of the partnership is likely to be unreasonably frustrated; (ii) another partner has engaged in conduct relating to the partnership business which makes it not reasonably practicable to carry on the business in partnership with that partner; or (iii) it is not otherwise reasonably practicable to carry on the partnership business in conformity with the partnership agreement. The court's power to wind up the partnership under Section 801(5) cannot be varied in the partnership agreement. *See* Section 103(b)(8).

RUPA deletes UPA Section 32(1)(e) which provides for dissolution when the business can only be carried on at a loss. That provision might result in a dissolution contrary to the partners' expectations in a start-up or tax shelter situation, in which case "book" or "tax" losses do not signify business failure. Truly poor financial performance may justify dissolution under subsection (5)(i) as a frustration of the partnership's economic purpose.

RUPA also deletes UPA Section 32(1)(f) which authorizes a court to order dissolution of a partnership when "other circumstances render a dissolution equitable." That provision was regarded as too open-ended and, given RUPA's expanded remedies for partners, unnecessary. No significant change in result is intended, however, since the interpretation of UPA Section 32(1)(f) is comparable to the specific grounds expressed in subsection (5). *See, e.g., Karber v. Karber,* 145 Ariz. 293, 701 P.2d 1 (Ct. App. 1985) (partnership dissolved on basis of suspicion and ill will, citing UPA §§ 32(1)(d) and (f)); *Fuller v. Brough,* 159 Colo. 147, 411 P.2d 18 (1966) (not equitable to dissolve partnership for trifling causes or temporary grievances that do not render it impracticable to carry on partnership business); *Lau v. Wong,* 1 Haw. App. 217, 616 P.2d 1031 (1980) (partnership dissolved where business operated solely for benefit of managing partner).

9. Section 801(6) provides for judicial dissolution on application by a transferee of a partner's transferable interest in the partnership, including the purchaser of a partner's interest upon foreclosure of a charging order. It is based on UPA Section 32(2) and authorizes dissolution upon a judicial determination that it is equitable to wind up the partnership business (i) after the expiration of the partnership term or completion of the undertaking or (ii) at any time, if the partnership were a partnership at will at the time of the transfer or when the charging order was issued. The requirement that the court determine that it is equitable to wind up the business is new. The rights of a transferee under this section cannot be varied in the partnership agreement. *See* Section 103(b)(8).

Section 802. Partnership Continues After Dissolution.

(a) Subject to subsection (b), a partnership continues after dissolution only for the purpose of winding up its business. The partnership is terminated when the winding up of its business is completed.

(b) At any time after the dissolution of a partnership and before the winding up of its business is completed, all of the partners, including any dissociating partner other than a wrongfully dissociating partner, may waive the right to have the partnership's business wound up and the partnership terminated. In that event:

(1) the partnership resumes carrying on its business as if dissolution had never occurred, and any liability incurred by the partnership or a partner after the dissolution and before the waiver is determined as if dissolution had never occurred; and

(2) the rights of a third party accruing under Section 804(1) or arising out of conduct in reliance on the dissolution before the third party knew or received a notification of the waiver may not be adversely affected.

COMMENT

1. Section 802(a) is derived from UPA Section 30 and provides that a partnership continues after dissolution only for the purpose of winding up its business, after which it is terminated. RUPA continues the concept of "termination" to mark the completion of the winding up process. Since no filing or other formality is required, the date will often be determined only by hindsight. No legal rights turn on the partnership's termination or the date thereof. Even after termination, if a previously unknown liability is asserted, all of the partners are still liable.

2. Section 802(b) makes explicit the right of the remaining partners to continue the business after an event of dissolution if all of the partners, including the dissociating partner or partners, waive the right to have the business wound up and the partnership terminated. Only those "dissociating" partners whose dissociation was the immediate cause of the dissolution must waive the right to have the business wound up. The consent of wrongfully dissociating partners is not required.

3. Upon waiver of the right to have the business wound up, Paragraph (1) of the subsection provides that the partnership entity may resume carrying on its business as if dissolution had never occurred, thereby restoring the scope of its business to normal. "Resumes" is intended to mean that acts appropriate to winding up, authorized when taken, are in effect ratified, and the partnership remains liable for those acts, as provided explicitly in paragraph (2).

If the business is continued following a waiver of the right to dissolution, any liability incurred by the partnership or a partner after the dissolution and before the waiver is to be determined as if dissolution had never occurred. That has the effect of validating transactions entered into after dissolution that might not have been appropriate for winding up the business, because, upon waiver, any liability incurred by either the partnership or a partner in those transactions will be determined under Sections 702 and 703, rather than Sections 804 and 806.

As to the liability for those transactions among the partners themselves, the partners by agreement may provide otherwise. Thus, a partner who, after dissolution, incurred an obligation appropriate for winding up, but **not** appropriate for continuing the business, may protect himself by conditioning his consent to the continuation of the business on the ratification of the transaction by the continuing partners.

Paragraph (2) of the subsection provides that the rights of third parties accruing under Section 804(1) before they knew (or were notified) of the waiver may not be adversely affected by the waiver. That is intended to mean the partnership is bound, notwithstanding a subsequent waiver of dissolution and resumption of its business, by a transaction entered into after dissolution that was appropriate for winding up the partnership business, even if **not** appropriate for continuing the business. Similarly, any rights of a third party arising out of conduct in reliance on the dissolution are protected, absent knowledge (or notification) of the waiver. Thus, for example, a partnership loan, callable upon dissolution, that has been called is not reinstated by a subsequent waiver. If the loan has not been called before the lender learns (or is notified) of the waiver, however, it may not thereafter be called because of the dissolution. On the other hand, a waiver does not reinstate a lease that is terminated by the dissolution itself.

Section 803. Right to Wind Up Partnership Business.

    (a) After dissolution, a partner who has not wrongfully dissociated may participate in winding up the partnership's business, but on application of any partner, partner's legal representative, or transferee, the [designate the appropriate court], for good cause shown, may order judicial supervision of the winding up.

    (b) The legal representative of the last surviving partner may wind up a partnership's business.

    (c) A person winding up a partnership's business may preserve the partnership business or property as a going concern for a reasonable time, prosecute and defend actions and proceedings, whether civil, criminal, or administrative, settle and close the partnership's business, dispose of and transfer the partnership's property, discharge the partnership's liabilities, distribute the assets of the partnership pursuant to Section 807, settle disputes by mediation or arbitration, and perform other necessary acts.

COMMENT

Section 803(a) is drawn from UPA Section 37. It provides that the partners who have not wrongfully dissociated may participate in winding up the partnership business. Wrongful dissociation is defined in Section 602. On application of any partner, a court may for good cause judicially supervise the winding up.

Section 803(b) continues the rule of UPA Section 25(2)(d) that the legal representative of the last surviving partner may wind up the business. It makes clear that the representative of the last surviving partner will not be forced to go to court for authority to wind up the business. On the other hand, the legal representative of a deceased partner, other than the last surviving partner, has only the rights of a transferee of the deceased partner's transferable interest. See Comment 8 to Section 601.

Section 803(c) is new and provides further guidance on the powers of a person who is winding up the business. It is based on Delaware Laws, Title 6, Section 17-803. The powers enumerated are not intended to be exclusive.

Subsection (c) expressly authorizes the preservation of the partnership's business or property as a going concern for a reasonable time. Some courts have reached that result without benefit of statutory authority. *See, e.g., Paciaroni v. Crane,* 408 A.2d 946 (Del. Ch. 1979). An agreement to continue the partnership business in order to preserve its going-concern value until sale is not a waiver of a partner's right to have the business liquidated.

The authorization of mediation and arbitration implements Conference policy to encourage alternative dispute resolution.

A partner's fiduciary duties of care and loyalty under Section 404 extend to winding up the business, except as modified by Section 603(b).

Section 804. Partner's Power to Bind Partnership After Dissolution.

Subject to Section 805, a partnership is bound by a partner's act after dissolution that:

(1) is appropriate for winding up the partnership business; or

(2) would have bound the partnership under Section 301 before dissolution, if the other party to the transaction did not have notice of the dissolution.

COMMENT

Section 804 is the successor to UPA Sections 33(2) and 35, which wind down the authority of partners to bind the partnership to third persons.

Section 804(1) provides that partners have the authority to bind the partnership after dissolution in transactions that are appropriate for winding-up the partnership business. Section 804(2) provides that partners also have the power after dissolution to bind the partnership in transactions that are inconsistent with winding up. The partnership is bound in a transaction not appropriate for winding up, however, only if the partner's act would have bound the partnership under Section 301 before dissolution and the other party to the transaction did not have notice of the dissolution. *See* Section 102(b) (notice). Compare Section 301(1) (partner has apparent authority unless other party knows or has received a notification of lack of authority).

Section 804(2) attempts to balance the interests of the partners to terminate their mutual agency authority against the interests of outside creditors who have no notice of the partnership's dissolution. Even if the partnership is not bound under Section 804, the faithless partner who purports to act for the partnership after dissolution may be liable individually to an innocent third party under the law of agency. See Section 330 of the Restatement (Second) of Agency (agent liable for misrepresentation of authority), applicable under RUPA as provided in Section 104(a).

RUPA eliminates the special and confusing UPA rules limiting the authority of partners after dissolution. The special protection afforded by UPA Section 35(1)(b)(I) to former creditors and the lesser special protection afforded by UPA Section 35(1)(b)(II) to other parties who knew of the partnership before dissolution are both abolished. RUPA eschews these cumbersome notice provisions in favor of the general apparent authority rules of Section 301, subject to the effect of a filed or recorded statement of dissolution under Section 805. This enhances the protection of innocent third parties and imposes liability on the partnership and the partners who choose their fellow partner-agents and are in the best position to protect others by providing notice of the dissolution.

Also deleted are the special rules for unknown partners in UPA Section 35(2) and for certain causes of dissolution in UPA Section 35(3). Those, too, are inconsistent with RUPA's policy of adhering more closely to the general agency rules of Section 301.

Section 804 should be contrasted with Section 702, which winds down the power of a partner being bought out. The power of a dissociating partner is limited to transactions entered into within two years after the partner's dissociation. Section 804 has no time limitation. However, the apparent authority of partners in both situations is now subject to the filing of a statement of dissociation or dissolution, as the case may be, which operates to cut off such authority after 90 days.

Section 805. Statement of Dissolution.

(a) After dissolution, a partner who has not wrongfully dissociated may file a statement of dissolution stating the name of the partnership and that the partnership has dissolved and is winding up its business.

(b) A statement of dissolution cancels a filed statement of partnership authority for the purposes of Section 303(d) and is a limitation on authority for the purposes of Section 303(e).

(c) For the purposes of Sections 301 and 804, a person not a partner is deemed to have notice of the dissolution and the limitation on the partners' authority as a result of the statement of dissolution 90 days after it is filed.

(d) After filing and, if appropriate, recording a statement of dissolution, a dissolved partnership may file and, if appropriate, record a statement of partnership authority which will operate with respect to a person not a partner as provided in Section 303(d) and (e) in any transaction, whether or not the transaction is appropriate for winding up the partnership business.

COMMENT

1. Section 805 is new. Subsection (a) provides that, after an event of dissolution, any partner who has not wrongfully dissociated may file a statement of dissolution on behalf of the partnership. The filing and recording of a statement of dissolution is optional. The execution, filing, and recording of the statement is governed by Section 105. The legal consequences of filing a statement of dissolution are similar to those of a statement of dissociation under Section 704.

2. Subsection (b) provides that a statement of dissolution cancels a filed statement of partnership authority for the purposes of Section 303(d), thereby terminating any extraordinary grant of authority contained in that statement.

A statement of dissolution also operates as a limitation on authority for the purposes of Section 303(e). That section provides that third parties are deemed to know of a limitation on the authority of a partner to transfer real property held in the name of the partnership if a certified copy of the statement containing the limitation is recorded with the real estate records. In effect, a properly recorded statement of dissolution restricts the authority of all partners to real property transfers that are appropriate for winding up the business. Thus, third parties must inquire of the partnership whether a contemplated real property transfer is appropriate for winding up. After dissolution, the partnership may, however, file and record a new statement of authority that will bind the partnership under Section 303(d).

3. Subsection (c) operates in conjunction with Sections 301 and 804 to wind down partners' apparent authority after dissolution. It provides that, for purposes of those sections, 90 days after the filing of a statement of dissolution nonpartners are deemed to have notice of the dissolution and the corresponding limitation on the authority of all partners. Sections 301 and 804 provide that a partner's lack of authority is binding on persons with notice thereof. Thus, after 90 days the statement of dissolution operates as constructive notice conclusively limiting the apparent authority of partners to transactions that are appropriate for winding up the business.

4. Subsection (d) provides that, after filing and, if appropriate, recording a statement of dissolution, the partnership may file and record a new statement of partnership authority that will operate as provided in Section 303(d). A grant of authority contained in that statement is conclusive and may be relied upon by a person who gives value without knowledge to the contrary, whether or not the transaction is appropriate for winding up the partnership

business. That makes the partners' record authority conclusive after dissolution, and precludes going behind the record to inquire into whether or not the transaction was appropriate for winding up.

Section 806. Partner's Liability to Other Partners After Dissolution.

(a) Except as otherwise provided in subsection (b) and Section 306, after dissolution a partner is liable to the other partners for the partner's share of any partnership liability incurred under Section 804.

(b) A partner who, with knowledge of the dissolution, incurs a partnership liability under Section 804(2) by an act that is not appropriate for winding up the partnership business is liable to the partnership for any damage caused to the partnership arising from the liability.

COMMENT

Section 806 is the successor to UPA Sections 33(1) and 34, which govern the rights of partners among themselves with respect to post-dissolution liability.

Subsection (a) provides that, except as provided in Section 306(a) and subsection (b), after dissolution each partner is liable to the other partners by way of contribution for his share of any partnership liability incurred under Section 804. That includes not only obligations that are appropriate for winding up the business, but also obligations that are inappropriate if within the partner's apparent authority. Consistent with other provisions of this Act, Section 806(a) makes clear that a partner does not have a contribution obligation with regard to limited liability partnership obligations for which the partner is not liable under Section 306. *See* Comments to Section 401(b).

Subsection (a) draws no distinction as to the cause of dissolution. Thus, as among the partners, their liability is treated alike in all events of dissolution. That is a change from UPA Section 33(l).

Subsection (b) creates an exception to the general rule in subsection (a). It provides that a partner, who with knowledge of the winding up nevertheless incurs a liability binding on the partnership by an act that is inappropriate for winding up the business, is liable to the partnership for any loss caused thereby.

Section 806 is merely a default rule and may be varied in the partnership agreement. *See* Section 103(a).

Section 807. Settlement of Accounts and Contributions Among Partners.

(a) In winding up a partnership's business, the assets of the partnership, including the contributions of the partners required by this section, must be applied to discharge its obligations to creditors, including, to the extent permitted by law, partners who are creditors. Any surplus must be applied to pay in cash the net amount distributable to partners in accordance with their right to distributions under subsection (b).

(b) Each partner is entitled to a settlement of all partnership accounts upon winding up the partnership business. In settling accounts among the partners, profits and losses that result from the liquidation of the partnership assets must be credited and charged to the partners' accounts. The partnership shall make a distribution to a partner in an amount equal to any excess of the credits over the charges in the partner's account. A partner shall contribute to the partnership an amount equal to any excess of the charges over the credits in the partner's account but excluding from the calculation charges attributable to an obligation for which the partner is not personally liable under Section 306.

(c) If a partner fails to contribute the full amount required under subsection (b), all of the other partners shall contribute, in the proportions in which those partners share partnership losses, the additional amount necessary to satisfy the partnership obligations for which they are personally liable under Section 306. A partner or partner's legal representative may recover from the other partners any contributions the partner makes to the extent the amount contributed exceeds that partner's share of the partnership obligations for which the partner is personally liable under Section 306.

(d) After the settlement of accounts, each partner shall contribute, in the proportion in which the partner shares partnership losses, the amount necessary to satisfy partnership obligations that were not known at the time of the settlement and for which the partner is personally liable under Section 306.

(e) The estate of a deceased partner is liable for the partner's obligation to contribute to the partnership.

(f) An assignee for the benefit of creditors of a partnership or a partner, or a person appointed by a court to represent creditors of a partnership or a partner, may enforce a partner's obligation to contribute to the partnership.

COMMENT

1. Section 807 provides the default rules for the settlement of accounts and contributions among the partners in winding up the business. It is derived in part from UPA Sections 38(1) and 40.

2. Subsection (a) continues the rule in UPA Section 38(l) that, in winding up the business, the partnership assets must first be applied to discharge partnership liabilities to creditors. For this purpose, any required contribution by the partners is treated as an asset of the partnership. After the payment of all

partnership liabilities, any surplus must be applied to pay in cash the net amount due the partners under subsection (b) by way of a liquidating distribution.

RUPA continues the "in-cash" rule of UPA Section 38(1) and is consistent with Section 402, which provides that a partner has no right to receive, and may not be required to accept, a distribution in kind, unless otherwise agreed. The in-cash rule avoids the valuation problems that afflict unwanted in-kind distributions.

The partnership must apply its assets to discharge the obligations of partners who are creditors on a parity with other creditors. *See* Section 404(f) and Comment 6. In effect, that abolishes the priority rules in UPA Section 40(b) and (c) which subordinate the payment of inside debt to outside debt. Both RULPA and the RMBCA do likewise. *See* RULPA § 804; RMBCA §§ 6.40(f), 14.05(a). Ultimately, however, a partner whose "debt" has been repaid by the partnership is personally liable, as a partner, for any outside debt remaining unsatisfied, unlike a limited partner or corporate shareholder. Accordingly, the obligation to contribute sufficient funds to satisfy the claims of outside creditors may result in the equitable subordination of inside debt when partnership assets are insufficient to satisfy all obligations to non-partners.

RUPA in effect abolishes the "dual priority" or "jingle" rule of UPA Section 40(h) and (i). Those sections gave partnership creditors priority as to partnership property and separate creditors priority as to separate property. The jingle rule has already been preempted by the Bankruptcy Code, at least as to Chapter 7 partnership liquidation proceedings. Under Section 723(c) of the Bankruptcy Code, and under RUPA, partnership creditors share pro rata with the partners' individual creditors in the assets of the partners' estates.

3. Subsection (b) provides that each partner is entitled to a settlement of all partnership accounts upon winding up. It also establishes the default rules for closing out the partners' accounts. First, the profits and losses resulting from the liquidation of the partnership assets must be credited or charged to the partners' accounts, according to their respective shares of profits and losses. Then, the partnership must make a final liquidating distribution to those partners with a positive account balance. That distribution should be in the amount of the excess of credits over the charges in the account. Any partner with a negative account balance must contribute to the partnership an amount equal to the excess of charges over the credits in the account provided the excess relates to an obligation for which the partner is personally liable under Section 306. The partners may, however, agree that a negative account does not reflect a debt to the partnership and need not be repaid in settling the partners' accounts.

Section 807(b) makes clear that a partner's contribution obligation to a partnership in dissolution only considers the partner's share of obligations for which the partner was personally liable under Section 306 ("unshielded obligations"). See Comments to Section 401(b) (partner contribution obligation to an operating partnership). Properly determined under this Section, the total required partner contributions will be sufficient to satisfy the partnership's total unshielded obligations. In special circumstances where a partnership has both shielded and unshielded obligations and the partner required contributions are used to first pay shielded partnership obligations, the partners may be required to make further contributions to satisfy the partnership unpaid unshielded obligations. The proper resolution of this matter is left to debtor-creditor law as well as the law governing the fiduciary obligations of the partners. See Section 104(a).

RUPA eliminates the distinction in UPA Section 40(b) between the liability owing to a partner in respect of capital and the liability owing in respect of profits. Section 807(b) speaks simply of the right of a partner to a liquidating distribution. That implements the logic of RUPA Sections 401(a) and 502 under which contributions to capital and shares in profits and losses combine to determine the right to distributions. The partners may, however, agree to share "operating" losses differently from "capital" losses, thereby continuing the UPA distinction.

4. Subsection (c) continues the UPA Section 40(d) rule that solvent partners share proportionately in the shortfall caused by insolvent partners who fail to contribute their proportionate share. The partnership may enforce a partner's obligation to contribute. *See* Section 405(a). A partner is entitled to recover from the other partners any contributions in excess of that partner's share of the partnership's liabilities. *See* Section 405(b)(iii).

5. Subsection (d) provides that, after settling the partners' accounts, each partner must contribute, in the proportion in which he shares losses, the amount necessary to satisfy partnership obligations that were not known at the time of the settlement. That continues the basic rule of UPA Section 40(d) and underscores that the obligation to contribute exists independently of the partnership's books of account. It specifically covers the situation of a partnership liability that was unknown when the partnership books were closed.

6. Under subsection (e), the estate of a deceased partner is liable for the partner's obligation to contribute to partnership losses. That continues the rule of UPA Section 40(g).

7. Subsection (f) provides that an assignee for the benefit of creditors of the partnership or of a partner (or other court appointed creditor representative) may enforce any partner's obligation to contribute to the partnership. That continues the rules of UPA Sections 36(4) and 40(e).

[ARTICLE] 9
CONVERSIONS AND MERGERS

Section 901. Definitions.

In this [article]:

(1) "General partner" means a partner in a partnership and a general partner in a limited partnership.

(2) "Limited partner" means a limited partner in a limited partnership.

(3) "Limited partnership" means a limited partnership created under the [State Limited Partnership Act], predecessor law, or comparable law of another jurisdiction.

(4) "Partner" includes both a general partner and a limited partner.

COMMENT

1. Article 9 is new. The UPA is silent with respect to the conversion or merger of partnerships, and thus it is necessary under the UPA to structure those types of transactions as asset transfers. RUPA provides specific statutory authority for conversions and mergers. It provides for continuation of the partnership entity, thereby simplifying those transactions and adding certainty to the legal consequences.

A number of States currently authorize the merger of limited partnerships, and some authorize them to merge with other business entities such as corporations and limited liability companies. A few States currently authorize the merger of a general and a limited partnership or the conversion of a general to a limited partnership.

2. As Section 908 makes clear, the requirements of Article 9 are not mandatory, and a partnership may convert or merge in any other manner provided by law. Article 9 is merely a "safe harbor." If the requirements of the article are followed, the conversion or merger is legally valid. Since most States have no other established procedure for the conversion or merger of partnerships, it is likely that the Article 9 procedures will be used in virtually all cases.

3. Article 9 does not restrict the provisions authorizing conversions and mergers to domestic partnerships. Since no filing is required for the creation of a partnership under RUPA, it is often unclear where a partnership is domiciled. Moreover, a partnership doing business in the State satisfies the definition of a partnership created under this Act since it is an association of two or more co-owners carrying on a business for profit. Even a partnership clearly domiciled in another State could easily amend its partnership agreement to provide that its internal affairs are to be governed by the laws of a jurisdiction that has enacted Article 9 of RUPA. No harm is likely to result from extending to foreign partnerships the right to convert or merge under local law.

4. Because Article 9 deals with the conversion and merger of both general and limited partnerships, Section 901 sets forth four definitions distinguishing between the two types of partnerships solely for the purposes of Article 9. "Partner" includes both general and limited partners, and "general partner" includes general partners in both general and limited partnerships.

Section 902. Conversion of Partnership to Limited Partnership.

(a) A partnership may be converted to a limited partnership pursuant to this section.

(b) The terms and conditions of a conversion of a partnership to a limited partnership must be approved by all of the partners or by a number or percentage specified for conversion in the partnership agreement.

(c) After the conversion is approved by the partners, the partnership shall file a certificate of limited partnership in the jurisdiction in which the limited partnership is to be formed. The certificate must include:

(1) a statement that the partnership was converted to a limited partnership from a partnership;

(2) its former name; and

(3) a statement of the number of votes cast by the partners for and against the conversion and, if the vote is less than unanimous, the number or percentage required to approve the conversion under the partnership agreement.

(d) The conversion takes effect when the certificate of limited partnership is filed or at any later date specified in the certificate.

(e) A general partner who becomes a limited partner as a result of the conversion remains liable as a general partner for an obligation incurred by the partnership before the conversion takes effect. If the other party to a transaction with the limited partnership reasonably believes when entering the transaction that the limited partner is a general partner, the limited partner is liable for an obligation incurred by the limited partnership within 90 days after the conversion takes effect. The limited partner's liability for all other obligations of the limited partnership incurred after the conversion takes effect is that of a limited partner as provided in the [State Limited Partnership Act].

COMMENT

Section 902(a) authorizes the conversion of a "partnership" to a "limited partnership." Section 202(b) limits the usual RUPA definition of "partnership" to general partnerships. That definition is applicable to Article 9. If a limited partnership is contemplated, Article 9 uses the term "limited partnership." See Section 901(3).

Subsection (b) provides that the terms and conditions of the conversion must be approved by all the partners, unless the partnership agreement specifies otherwise for a conversion.

Subsection (c) provides that, after approval, the partnership must file a certificate of limited partnership which includes the requisite information concerning the conversion.

Subsection (d) provides that the conversion takes effect when the certificate is filed, unless a later effective date is specified.

Subsection (e) establishes the partners' liabilities following a conversion. A partner who becomes a limited partner as a result of the conversion remains fully liable as a general partner for any obligation arising before the effective date of the conversion, both to third parties and to other partners for contribution. Third parties who transact business with the converted partnership unaware of a partner's new status as a limited partner are protected for 90 days after the conversion. Since RULPA Section 201(a)(3) requires the certificate of limited partnership to name all of the general partners, and under RUPA Section 902(c) the certificate must also include a statement of the conversion, parties transacting business with the converted partnership can protect themselves by checking the record of the State where the limited partnership is formed (the State where the conversion takes place). A former general partner who becomes a limited partner as a result of the conversion can avoid the lingering 90-day exposure to liability as a general partner by notifying those transacting business with the partnership of his limited partner status.

Although Section 902 does not expressly provide that a partner's withdrawal upon a term partnership's conversion to a limited partnership is rightful, it was assumed that the unanimity requirement for the approval of a conversion would afford a withdrawing partner adequate opportunity to protect his interest as a condition of approval. This question is left to the partnership agreement if it provides for conversion without the approval of all the partners.

Section 903. Conversion of Limited Partnership to Partnership.
  (a) A limited partnership may be converted to a partnership pursuant to this section.
  (b) Notwithstanding a provision to the contrary in a limited partnership agreement, the terms and conditions of a conversion of a limited partnership to a partnership must be approved by all of the partners.
  (c) After the conversion is approved by the partners, the limited partnership shall cancel its certificate of limited partnership.

    (d) The conversion takes effect when the certificate of limited partnership is canceled.

    (e) A limited partner who becomes a general partner as a result of the conversion remains liable only as a limited partner for an obligation incurred by the limited partnership before the conversion takes effect. Except as otherwise provided in Section 306, the partner is liable as a general partner for an obligation of the partnership incurred after the conversion takes effect.

COMMENT

Section 903(a) authorizes the conversion of a limited partnership to a general partnership.

Subsection (b) provides that the conversion must be approved by all of the partners, even if the partnership agreement provides to the contrary. That includes all of the general and limited partners. *See* Section 901(4). The purpose of the unanimity requirement is to protect a limited partner from exposure to personal liability as a general partner without clear and knowing consent at the time of conversion. Despite a general voting provision to the contrary in the partnership agreement, conversion to a general partnership may never have been contemplated by the limited partner when the partnership investment was made.

Subsection (c) provides that, after approval of the conversion, the converted partnership must cancel its certificate of limited partnership. *See* RULPA § 203.

Subsection (d) provides that the conversion takes effect when the certificate of limited partnership is canceled.

Subsection (e) provides that a limited partner who becomes a general partner is liable as a general partner for all partnership obligations for which a general partner would otherwise be personally liable for if incurred after the effective date of the conversion, but still has only limited liability for obligations incurred before the conversion.

Section 904. Effect of Conversion; Entity Unchanged.

    (a) A partnership or limited partnership that has been converted pursuant to this [article] is for all purposes the same entity that existed before the conversion.

    (b) When a conversion takes effect:

        (1) all property owned by the converting partnership or limited partnership remains vested in the converted entity;

(2) all obligations of the converting partnership or limited partnership continue as obligations of the converted entity; and

(3) an action or proceeding pending against the converting partnership or limited partnership may be continued as if the conversion had not occurred.

COMMENT

Section 904 sets forth the effect of a conversion on the partnership. Subsection (a) provides that the converted partnership is for all purposes the same entity as before the conversion.

Subsection (b) provides that upon conversion: (1) all partnership property remains vested in the converted entity; (2) all obligations remain the obligations of the converted entity; and (3) all pending legal actions may be continued as if the conversion had not occurred. The term "entity" as used in Article 9 refers to either or both general and limited partnerships as the context requires.

Under subsection (b)(1), title to partnership property remains vested in the converted partnership. As a matter of general property law, title remains vested without further act or deed and without reversion or impairment.

Section 905. Merger of Partnerships.

(a) Pursuant to a plan of merger approved as provided in subsection (c), a partnership may be merged with one or more partnerships or limited partnerships.

(b) The plan of merger must set forth:

(1) the name of each partnership or limited partnership that is a party to the merger;

(2) the name of the surviving entity into which the other partnerships or limited partnerships will merge;

(3) whether the surviving entity is a partnership or a limited partnership and the status of each partner;

(4) the terms and conditions of the merger;

(5) the manner and basis of converting the interests of each party to the merger into interests or obligations of the surviving entity, or into money or other property in whole or part; and

(6) the street address of the surviving entity's chief executive office.

(c) The plan of merger must be approved:

(1) in the case of a partnership that is a party to the merger, by all of the partners, or a number or percentage specified for merger in the partnership agreement; and

    (2) in the case of a limited partnership that is a party to the merger,
        by the vote required for approval of a merger by the law of the
        State or foreign jurisdiction in which the limited partnership is or-
        ganized and, in the absence of such a specifically applicable law,
        by all of the partners, notwithstanding a provision to the contrary
        in the partnership agreement.

(d) After a plan of merger is approved and before the merger takes effect,
    the plan may be amended or abandoned as provided in the plan.

(e) The merger takes effect on the later of:

    (1) the approval of the plan of merger by all parties to the merger, as
        provided in subsection (c);

    (2) the filing of all documents required by law to be filed as a condi-
        tion to the effectiveness of the merger; or

    (3) any effective date specified in the plan of merger.

COMMENT

Section 905 provides a "safe harbor" for the merger of a general partnership
and one or more general or limited partnerships. The surviving entity may be
either a general or a limited partnership.

The plan of merger must set forth the information required by subsection (b),
including the status of each partner and the manner and basis of converting
the interests of each party to the merger into interests or obligations of the
surviving entity.

Subsection (c) provides that the plan of merger must be approved: (1) by all
the partners of each general partnership that is a party to the merger, unless
its partnership agreement specifically provides otherwise for mergers; and
(2) by all the partners, including both general and limited partners, of each
limited partnership that is a party to the merger, notwithstanding a contrary
provision in its partnership agreement, unless specifically authorized by the
law of the jurisdiction in which that limited partnership is organized. Like
Section 902(b), the purpose of the unanimity requirement is to protect limited
partners from exposure to liability as general partners without their clear and
knowing consent.

Subsection (d) provides that the plan of merger may be amended or abandoned at any time before the merger takes effect, if the plan so provides.

Subsection (e) provides that the merger takes effect on the later of: (1) approval by all parties to the merger; (2) filing of all required documents; or
(3) the effective date specified in the plan. The surviving entity must file all
notices and documents relating to the merger required by other applicable
statutes governing the entities that are parties to the merger, such as articles

of merger or a certificate of limited partnership. It may also amend or cancel a statement of partnership authority previously filed by any party to the merger.

Section 906. Effect of Merger.

(a) When a merger takes effect:

    (1) the separate existence of every partnership or limited partnership that is a party to the merger, other than the surviving entity, ceases;

    (2) all property owned by each of the merged partnerships or limited partnerships vests in the surviving entity;

    (3) all obligations of every partnership or limited partnership that is a party to the merger become the obligations of the surviving entity; and

    (4) an action or proceeding pending against a partnership or limited partnership that is a party to the merger may be continued as if the merger had not occurred, or the surviving entity may be substituted as a party to the action or proceeding.

(b) The [Secretary of State] of this State is the agent for service of process in an action or proceeding against a surviving foreign partnership or limited partnership to enforce an obligation of a domestic partnership or limited partnership that is a party to a merger. The surviving entity shall promptly notify the [Secretary of State] of the mailing address of its chief executive office and of any change of address. Upon receipt of process, the [Secretary of State] shall mail a copy of the process to the surviving foreign partnership or limited partnership.

(c) A partner of the surviving partnership or limited partnership is liable for:

    (1) all obligations of a party to the merger for which the partner was personally liable before the merger;

    (2) all other obligations of the surviving entity incurred before the merger by a party to the merger, but those obligations may be satisfied only out of property of the entity; and

    (3) except as otherwise provided in Section 306, all obligations of the surviving entity incurred after the merger takes effect, but those obligations may be satisfied only out of property of the entity if the partner is a limited partner.

(d) If the obligations incurred before the merger by a party to the merger are not satisfied out of the property of the surviving partnership or limited partnership, the general partners of that party immediately before the effective date of the merger shall contribute the amount necessary to satisfy that party's obligations to the surviving entity, in the manner provided in Section 807 or in the [Limited Partnership

Act] of the jurisdiction in which the party was formed, as the case may be, as if the merged party were dissolved.

(e) A partner of a party to a merger who does not become a partner of the surviving partnership or limited partnership is dissociated from the entity, of which that partner was a partner, as of the date the merger takes effect. The surviving entity shall cause the partner's interest in the entity to be purchased under Section 701 or another statute specifically applicable to that partner's interest with respect to a merger. The surviving entity is bound under Section 702 by an act of a general partner dissociated under this subsection, and the partner is liable under Section 703 for transactions entered into by the surviving entity after the merger takes effect.

COMMENT

Section 906 states the effect of a merger on the partnerships that are parties to the merger and on the individual partners.

Subsection (a) provides that when the merger takes effect: (1) the separate existence of every partnership that is a party to the merger (other than the surviving entity) ceases; (2) all property owned by the parties to the merger vests in the surviving entity; (3) all obligations of every party to the merger become the obligations of the surviving entity; and (4) all legal actions pending against a party to the merger may be continued as if the merger had not occurred or the surviving entity may be substituted as a party. Title to partnership property vests in the surviving entity without further act or deed and without reversion or impairment.

Subsection (b) makes the Secretary of State the agent for service of process in any action against the surviving entity, if it is a foreign entity, to enforce an obligation of a domestic partnership that is a party to the merger. The purpose of this rule is to make it more convenient for local creditors to sue a foreign surviving entity when the credit was extended to a domestic partnership that has disappeared as a result of the merger.

Subsection (c) provides that a general partner of the surviving entity is liable for (1) all obligations for which the partner was personally liable before the merger; (2) all other obligations of the surviving entity incurred before the merger by a party to the merger, which obligations may be satisfied only out of the surviving entity's partnership property; and (3) all obligations incurred by the surviving entity after the merger, limited to the surviving entity's property in the case of limited partners and also limited to obligations of the partnership for which the partner was personally liable under Section 306.

This scheme of liability is similar to that of an incoming partner under Section 306(b). Only the surviving partnership itself is liable for all obligations, including obligations incurred by every constituent party before the merger. A general partner of the surviving entity is personally liable for obligations of the surviving entity incurred before the merger by the partnership of which he was a partner and those incurred by the surviving entity after the merger. Thus, a general partner of the surviving entity is liable only to the extent of his partnership interest for obligations incurred before the merger by a constituent party of which he was not a general partner.

Subsection (d) requires general partners to contribute the amount necessary to satisfy all obligations for which they were personally liable before the merger, if such obligations are not satisfied out of the partnership property of the surviving entity, in the same manner as provided in Section 807 or the limited partnership act of the applicable jurisdiction, as if the merged party were then dissolved. *See* RULPA §§ 502, 608.

Subsection (e) provides for the dissociation of a partner of a party to the merger who does not become a partner in the surviving entity. The surviving entity must buy out that partner's interest in the partnership under Section 701 or other specifically applicable statute. If the state limited partnership act has a dissenter's rights provision providing a different method of determining the amount due a dissociating limited partner, it would apply, rather than Section 701, since the two statutes should be read *in pari materia*.

Although subsection (e) does not expressly provide that a partner's withdrawal upon the merger of a term partnership is rightful, it was assumed that the unanimity requirement for the approval of a merger would afford a withdrawing partner adequate opportunity to protect his interest as a condition of approval. This question is left to the partnership agreement if it provides for merger without the approval of all the partners.

Under subsection (e), a dissociating general partner's lingering agency power is wound down, pursuant to Section 702, the same as in any other dissociation. Moreover, a dissociating general partner may be liable, under Section 703, for obligations incurred by the surviving entity for up to two years after the merger. A dissociating general partner can, however, limit to 90 days his exposure to liability by filing a statement of dissociation under Section 704.

Section 907. Statement of Merger.

(a) After a merger, the surviving partnership or limited partnership may file a statement that one or more partnerships or limited partnerships have merged into the surviving entity.

(b) A statement of merger must contain:

(1) the name of each partnership or limited partnership that is a party to the merger;

     (2) the name of the surviving entity into which the other partnerships or limited partnership were merged;

     (3) the street address of the surviving entity's chief executive office and of an office in this State, if any; and

     (4) whether the surviving entity is a partnership or a limited partnership.

(c) Except as otherwise provided in subsection (d), for the purposes of Section 302, property of the surviving partnership or limited partnership which before the merger was held in the name of another party to the merger is property held in the name of the surviving entity upon filing a statement of merger.

(d) For the purposes of Section 302, real property of the surviving partnership or limited partnership which before the merger was held in the name of another party to the merger is property held in the name of the surviving entity upon recording a certified copy of the statement of merger in the office for recording transfers of that real property.

(e) A filed and, if appropriate, recorded statement of merger, executed and declared to be accurate pursuant to Section 105(c), stating the name of a partnership or limited partnership that is a party to the merger in whose name property was held before the merger and the name of the surviving entity, but not containing all of the other information required by subsection (b), operates with respect to the partnerships or limited partnerships named to the extent provided in subsections (c) and (d).

COMMENT

Section 907(a) provides that the surviving entity may file a statement of merger. The execution, filing, and recording of the statement are governed by Section 105.

Subsection (b) requires the statement to contain the name of each party to the merger, the name and address of the surviving entity, and whether it is a general or limited partnership.

Subsection (c) provides that, for the purpose of the Section 302 rules regarding the transfer of partnership property, all personal and intangible property which before the merger was held in the name of a party to the merger becomes, upon the filing of the statement of merger with the Secretary of State, property held in the name of the surviving entity.

Subsection (d) provides a similar rule for real property, except that real property does not become property held in the name of the surviving entity until a certified copy of the statement of merger is recorded in the office for recording transfers of that real property under local law.

Subsection (e) is a savings provision in the event a statement of merger fails to contain all of the information required by subsection (b). The statement will have the operative effect provided in subsections (c) and (d) if it is executed and declared to be accurate pursuant to Section 105(e) and correctly states the name of the party to the merger in whose name the property was held before the merger, so that it would be found by someone searching the record. Compare Section 303(c) (statement of partnership authority).

Section 908. Nonexclusive.
This [article] is not exclusive. Partnerships or limited partnerships may be converted or merged in any other manner provided by law.

COMMENT

Section 908 provides that Article 9 is not exclusive. It is merely a "safe harbor." Partnerships may be converted or merged in any other manner provided by statute or common law. Existing statutes in a few States already authorize the conversion or merger of general partnerships and limited partnerships. See Comment 1 to Section 901. Those procedures may be followed in lieu of Article 9.

[ARTICLE] 10
LIMITED LIABILITY PARTNERSHIP

Section 1001. Statement of Qualification.

   (a) A partnership may become a limited liability partnership pursuant to this section.

   (b) The terms and conditions on which a partnership becomes a limited liability partnership must be approved by the vote necessary to amend the partnership agreement except, in the case of a partnership agreement that expressly considers obligations to contribute to the partnership, the vote necessary to amend those provisions.

   (c) After the approval required by subsection (b), a partnership may become a limited liability partnership by filing a statement of qualification. The statement must contain:

     (1) the name of the partnership;

     (2) the street address of the partnership's chief executive office and, if different, the street address of an office in this State, if any;

     (3) if the partnership does not have an office in this State, the name and street address of the partnership's agent for service of process;

(4) a statement that the partnership elects to be a limited liability partnership; and

(5) a deferred effective date, if any.

(d) The agent of a limited liability partnership for service of process must be an individual who is a resident of this State or other person authorized to do business in this State.

(e) The status of a partnership as a limited liability partnership is effective on the later of the filing of the statement or a date specified in the statement. The status remains effective, regardless of changes in the partnership, until it is canceled pursuant to Section 105(d) or revoked pursuant to Section 1003.

(f) The status of a partnership as a limited liability partnership and the liability of its partners is not affected by errors or later changes in the information required to be contained in the statement of qualification under subsection (c).

(g) The filing of a statement of qualification establishes that a partnership has satisfied all conditions precedent to the qualification of the partnership as a limited liability partnership.

(h) An amendment or cancellation of a statement of qualification is effective when it is filed or on a deferred effective date specified in the amendment or cancellation.

COMMENT

Any partnership may become a limited liability partnership by filing a statement of qualification. See Comments to Sections 101(6) and 202(b) regarding a limited partnership filing a statement of qualification to become a limited liability limited partnership. Section 1001 sets forth the required contents of a statement of qualification. The section also sets forth requirements for the approval of a statement of qualification, establishes the effective date of the filing (and any amendments) which remains effective until canceled or revoked, and provides that the liability of the partners of a limited liability partnership is not affected by errors or later changes in the statement information.

Subsection (b) provides that the terms and conditions on which a partnership becomes a limited liability partnership must be generally be approved by the vote necessary to amend the partnership agreement. This means that the act of becoming a limited liability partnership is equivalent to an amendment of the partnership agreement. Where the partnership agreement is silent as to how it may be amended, the subsection (b) vote requires the approval of every partner. Since the limited liability partnership rules are not intended to increase the vote necessary to amend the partnership agreement, where the partnership agreement specifically sets forth an amendment process, that process may be used. Where a partnership agreement sets forth several amendment procedures depending upon the nature of the amendment, the required vote will be that necessary to amend the contribution obligations of the partners. The specific "contribution" vote is preferred because the filing of the statement directly affects partner contribution obligations. Therefore, the language "considers contribution" should be broadly interpreted to include any amendment vote that indirectly affects any partner's contribution obligation such as a partner's obligation to "indemnify" other partners.

The unanimous vote default rule reflects the significance of a partnership becoming a limited liability partnership. In general, upon such a filing each partner is released from the personal contribution obligation imposed under this Act in exchange for relinquishing the right to enforce the contribution obligations of other partners under this Act. See Comments to Sections 306(c) and 401(b). The wisdom of this bargain will depend on many factors including the relative risks of the partners' duties and the assets of the partnership.

Subsection (c) sets forth the information required in a statement of qualification. The must include the name of the partnership which must comply with Section 1002 to identify the partnership as a limited liability partnership. The statement must also include the address of the partnership's chief executive office and, if different, the street address of any other office in this State. A statement must include the name and street address of an agent for service of process only if it does not have any office in this State.

As with other statements, a statement of qualification must be filed in the office of the Secretary of State. See Sections 101(13) and 105(a). Accordingly, a statement of qualification is executed, filed, and otherwise regarded as a statement under this Act. For example, a copy of a filed statement must be sent to every nonfiling partner unless otherwise provided in the partnership agreement. See Sections 105(e) and 103(b)(1). A statement of qualification must be executed by at least two partners under penalties of perjury that the contents of the statement are accurate. See Section 105(c). A person who files the statement must promptly send a copy of the statement to every nonfiling partner but failure to send the copy does not limit the effectiveness of the filed statement to a nonpartner. Section 105(e). The filing must be accompanied by the fee required by the Secretary of State. Section 105(f).

Subsection (d) makes clear that once a statement is filed and effective, the status of the partnership as a limited liability partnership remains effective until the partnership status is either canceled or revoked "regardless of changes in the partnership." Accordingly, a partnership that dissolves but whose business is continued under a business continuation agreement retains its status as a limited liability partnership without the need to refile a new statement. Also, limited liability partnership status remains even though a partnership may be dissolved, wound up, and terminated. Even after the termination of the partnership, the former partners of a terminated partnership would not be personally liable for partnership obligations incurred while the partnership was a limited liability partnership.

Subsection (d) also makes clear that limited liability partnership status remains effective until actual cancellation under Section 1003 or revocation under Section 105(d). Ordinarily the terms and conditions of becoming a limited liability partnership must be approved by the vote necessary to amend the partnership agreement. See Sections 1001(b), 306(c), and 401(j). Since the statement of cancellation may be filed by a person authorized to file the original statement of qualification, the same vote necessary to approve the filing of the statement of qualification must be obtained to file the statement of cancellation. See Section 105(d).

Subsection (f) provides that once a statement of qualification is executed and filed under subsection (c) and Section 105, the partnership assumes the status of a limited liability partnership. This status is intended to be conclusive with regard to third parties dealing with the partnership. It is not intended to affect the rights of partners. For example, a properly executed and filed statement of qualification conclusively establishes the limited liability shield described in Section 306(c). If the partners executing and filing the statement exceed their authority, the internal abuse of authority has no effect on the liability shield with regard to third parties. Partners may challenge the abuse of authority for purposes of establishing the liability of the culpable partners but may not effect the liability shield as to third parties. Likewise, third parties may not challenge the existence of the liability shield because the decision to file the statement lacked the proper vote. As a result, the filing of the statement creates the liability shield even when the required subsection (b) vote is not obtained.

Section 1002. Name.
The name of a limited liability partnership must end with "Registered Limited Liability Partnership", "Limited Liability Partnership", "R.L.L.P.", "L.L.P.", "RLLP," or "LLP".

COMMENT

The name provisions are intended to alert persons dealing with a limited liability partnership of the presence of the liability shield. Because many jurisdictions have adopted the naming concept of a "registered" limited liability partnership, this aspect has been retained. These name requirements also distinguish limited partnerships and general partnerships that become limited liability partnerships because the new name must be at the end of and in addition to the general or limited partnership's regular name. See Comments to Section 101(6). Since the name identification rules of this section do not alter the regular name of the partnership, they do not disturb historic notions of apparent authority of partners in both general and limited partnerships.

Section 1003. Annual Report.
(a) A limited liability partnership, and a foreign limited liability partnership authorized to transact business in this State, shall file an annual report in the office of the [Secretary of State] which contains:

(1) the name of the limited liability partnership and the State or other jurisdiction under whose laws the foreign limited liability partnership is formed;

(2) the street address of the partnership's chief executive office and, if different, the street address of an office of the partnership in this State, if any; and

(3) if the partnership does not have an office in this State, the name and street address of the partnership's current agent for service of process.

(b) An annual report must be filed between [January 1 and April 1] of each year following the calendar year in which a partnership files a statement of qualification or a foreign partnership becomes authorized to transact business in this State.

(c) The [Secretary of State] may revoke the statement of qualification of a partnership that fails to file an annual report when due or pay the required filing fee. To do so, the [Secretary of State] shall provide the partnership at least 60 days' written notice of intent to revoke the statement. The notice must be mailed to the partnership at its chief executive office set forth in the last filed statement of qualification or annual report. The notice must specify the annual report that has not been filed, the fee that has not been paid, and the effective date of the revocation. The revocation is not effective if the annual report is filed and the fee is paid before the effective date of the revocation.

(d) A revocation under subsection (c) only affects a partnership's status as a limited liability partnership and is not an event of dissolution of the partnership.

(e) A partnership whose statement of qualification has been revoked may apply to the [Secretary of State] for reinstatement within two years after the effective date of the revocation. The application must state:

(1) the name of the partnership and the effective date of the revocation; and

(2) that the ground for revocation either did not exist or has been corrected.

(f) A reinstatement under subsection (e) relates back to and takes effect as of the effective date of the revocation, and the partnership's status as a limited liability partnership continues as if the revocation had never occurred.

COMMENT

Section 1003 sets forth the requirements of an annual report that must be filed by all limited liability partnerships and any foreign limited liability partnership authorized to transact business in this State. See Sections 101(5)(definition of a limited liability partnership) and 101(4)(definition of a foreign limited liability partnership). The failure of a limited liability partnership to file an annual report is a basis for the Secretary of State to administratively revoke its statement of qualification. See Section 1003(c). A foreign limited liability partnership that fails to file an annual report may not maintain an action or proceeding in this State. See Section 1103(a).

Subsection (a) generally requires that an annual report contain the same information required in a statement of qualification. Compare Sections 1001(a) and 1003(a). The differences are that the annual report requires disclosure of the State of formation of a foreign limited liability partnership but deletes the delayed effective date and limited liability partnership election statement provisions of a statement of qualification. As such, the annual report serves to update the information required in a statement of qualification. Under subsection (b), the annual report must be filed between January 1 and April 1 of each calendar year following the year in which a statement of qualification was filed or a foreign limited liability partnership becomes authorized to transact business. This timing requirement means that a limited liability partnership must make an annual filing and may not prefile multiple annual reports in a single year.

Subsection (c) sets forth the procedure for the Secretary of State to administratively revoke a partnership's statement of qualification for the failure to file an annual report when due or pay the required filing fee. The Secretary of State must provide a partnership at least 60 days' written notice of the intent to revoke the statement. The notice must be mailed to the partnership at the address of its chief executive office set forth in the last filed statement or annual report and must state the grounds for revocation as well as the effective date of revocation. The revocation is not effective if the stated problem is cured before the stated effective date.

Under subsection (d), a revocation only terminates the partnership's status as a limited liability partnership but is not an event of dissolution of the partnership itself. Where revocation occurs, a partnership may apply for reinstatement under subsection (e) within two years after the effective date of the revocation. The application must state that the grounds for revocation either did not exist or have been corrected. The Secretary of State may grant the application on the basis of the statements alone or require proof of correction. Under subsection (f), when the application is granted, the reinstatement relates back to and takes effect as of the effective date of the revocation. The relation back doctrine prevents gaps in a reinstated partnership's liability shield. See Comments to Section 306(c).

[ARTICLE] 11
FOREIGN LIMITED LIABILITY PARTNERSHIP

Section 1101. Law Governing Foreign Limited Liability Partnership.
    (a) The law under which a foreign limited liability partnership is formed governs relations among the partners and between the partners and

the partnership and the liability of partners for obligations of the partnership.

(b) A foreign limited liability partnership may not be denied a statement of foreign qualification by reason of any difference between the law under which the partnership was formed and the law of this State.

(c) A statement of foreign qualification does not authorize a foreign limited liability partnership to engage in any business or exercise any power that a partnership may not engage in or exercise in this State as a limited liability partnership.

COMMENT

Section 1101 provides that the laws where a foreign limited liability partnership is formed rather than the laws of this State govern both the internal relations of the partnership and liability of its partners for the obligations of the partnership. See Section 101(4)(definition of a foreign limited liability partnership). Section 106(b) provides that the laws of this State govern the internal relations of a domestic limited liability and the liability of its partners for the obligations of the partnership. See Sections 101(5)(definition of a domestic limited liability partnership). A partnership may therefore chose the laws of a particular jurisdiction by filing a statement of qualification in that jurisdiction. But there are limitations on this choice.

Subsections (b) and (c) together make clear that although a foreign limited liability partnership may not be denied a statement of foreign qualification simply because of a difference between the laws of its foreign jurisdiction and the laws of this State, it may not engage in any business or exercise any power in this State that a domestic limited liability partnership may not engage in or exercise. Under subsection (c), a foreign limited liability partnership that engages in a business or exercises a power in this State that a domestic may not engage in or exercise, does so only as a ordinary partnership without the benefit of the limited liability partnership liability shield set forth in Section 306(c). In this sense, a foreign limited liability partnership is treated the same as a domestic limited liability partnership. Also, the Attorney General may maintain an action to restrain a foreign limited liability partnership from transacting an unauthorized business in this State. See Section 1105.

Section 1102. Statement of Foreign Qualification.

(a) Before transacting business in this State, a foreign limited liability partnership must file a statement of foreign qualification. The statement must contain:

(1) the name of the foreign limited liability partnership which satisfies the requirements of the State or other jurisdiction under whose law it is formed and ends with "Registered Limited Liability Partnership", "Limited Liability Partnership", "R.L.L.P.", "L.L.P.", "RLLP," or "LLP";

    (2) the street address of the partnership's chief executive office and, if different, the street address of an office of the partnership in this State, if any;

    (3) if there is no office of the partnership in this State, the name and street address of the partnership's agent for service of process; and

    (4) a deferred effective date, if any.

(b) The agent of a foreign limited liability company for service of process must be an individual who is a resident of this State or other person authorized to do business in this State.

(c) The status of a partnership as a foreign limited liability partnership is effective on the later of the filing of the statement of foreign qualification or a date specified in the statement. The status remains effective, regardless of changes in the partnership, until it is canceled pursuant to Section 105(d) or revoked pursuant to Section 1003.

(d) An amendment or cancellation of a statement of foreign qualification is effective when it is filed or on a deferred effective date specified in the amendment or cancellation.

COMMENT

Section 1102 provides that a foreign limited liability partnership must file a statement of foreign qualification before transacting business in this State. The section also sets forth the information required in the statement. As with other statements, a statement of foreign qualification must be filed in the office of the Secretary of State. See Sections 101(13), 105(a), and 1001(c). Accordingly, a statement of foreign qualification is executed, filed, and otherwise regarded as a statement under this Act. See Section 101(13)(definition of a statement includes a statement of foreign qualification).

Subsection (a) generally requires the same information in a statement of foreign qualification as is required in a statement of qualification. Compare Section 1001(c). The statement of foreign qualification must include a name that complies with the requirements for domestic limited liability partnership under Section 1002 and must include the address of the partnership's chief executive office and, if different, the street address of any other office in this State. If a foreign limited liability partnership does not have any office in this State, the statement of foreign qualification must include the name and street address of an agent for service of process.

As with a statement of qualification, a statement of foreign qualification (and amendments) is effective when filed or at a later specified filing date. Compare Sections 1102(b) and (c) with Sections 1001(e) and (h). Likewise, a statement of foreign qualification remains effective until canceled by the partnership or revoked by the Secretary of State, regardless of changes in the partnership. See Sections 105(d) (statement cancellation) and Section 1003 (revocation for failure to file annual report or pay annual filing fee) and Compare Sections 1102(b) and 1001(e). Statement of qualification provisions regarding the relationship of the status of a foreign partnership relative to its initial filing of a statement are governed by foreign law and are therefore omitted from this section. See Sections 1001(f)(effect of errors and omissions) and (g)(filing establishes all conditions precedent to qualification).

Section 1103. Effect of Failure to Qualify.

(a) A foreign limited liability partnership transacting business in this State may not maintain an action or proceeding in this State unless it has in effect a statement of foreign qualification.

(b) The failure of a foreign limited liability partnership to have in effect a statement of foreign qualification does not impair the validity of a contract or act of the foreign limited liability partnership or preclude it from defending an action or proceeding in this State.

(c) A limitation on personal liability of a partner is not waived solely by transacting business in this State without a statement of foreign qualification.

(d) If a foreign limited liability partnership transacts business in this State without a statement of foreign qualification, the [Secretary of State] is its agent for service of process with respect to a right of action arising out of the transaction of business in this State.

COMMENT

Section 1103 makes clear that the only consequence of a failure to file a statement of foreign qualification is that the foreign limited liability partnership will not be able to maintain an action or proceeding in this State. The partnership's contracts remain valid, it may defend an action or proceeding, personal liability of the partners is not waived, and the Secretary of State is the agent for service of process with respect to claims arising out of transacting business in this State. Sections 1103(b)-(d). Once a statement of foreign qualification is filed, the Secretary of State may revoke the statement for failure to file an annual report but the partnership has the right to cure the failure for two years. See Section 1003(c) and (e). Since the failure to file a statement of foreign qualification has no impact on the liability shield of the partners, a revocation of a statement of foreign qualification also has no impact on the liability shield created under foreign laws. Compare Sections 1103(c) and 1003(f) (revocation of the statement of qualification of a domestic limited liability partnership removes partner liability shield unless filing problems cured within two years).

Section 1104. Activities Not Constituting Transacting Business.

(a) Activities of a foreign limited liability partnership which do not constitute transacting business for the purpose of this [article] include:

(1) maintaining, defending, or settling an action or proceeding;

(2) holding meetings of its partners or carrying on any other activity concerning its internal affairs;

(3) maintaining bank accounts;

(4) maintaining offices or agencies for the transfer, exchange, and registration of the partnership's own securities or maintaining trustees or depositories with respect to those securities;

(5) selling through independent contractors;

(6) soliciting or obtaining orders, whether by mail or through employees or agents or otherwise, if the orders require acceptance outside this State before they become contracts;

(7) creating or acquiring indebtedness, with or without a mortgage, or other security interest in property;

(8) collecting debts or foreclosing mortgages or other security interests in property securing the debts, and holding, protecting, and maintaining property so acquired;

(9) conducting an isolated transaction that is completed within 30 days and is not one in the course of similar transactions; and

(10) transacting business in interstate commerce.

(b) For purposes of this [article], the ownership in this State of income-producing real property or tangible personal property, other than property excluded under subsection (a), constitutes transacting business in this State.

(c) This section does not apply in determining the contacts or activities that may subject a foreign limited liability partnership to service of process, taxation, or regulation under any other law of this State.

COMMENT

Because the Attorney General may restrain a foreign limited liability partnership from transacting an unauthorized business in this State and a foreign partnership may not maintain an action or proceeding in this State, the concept of "transacting business" in this State is important. To provide more certainty, subsection (a) sets forth ten separate categories of activities that do not constitute transacting business. Subsection (c) makes clear that the section only considers the definition of "transacting business" and as no impact on whether a foreign limited liability partnership's activities in this State subject it to service of process, taxation, or regulation under any other law of this State.

Section 1105. Action By [Attorney General].
The [Attorney General] may maintain an action to restrain a foreign limited liability partnership from transacting business in this State in violation of this [article].

COMMENT

Section 1105 makes clear that the Attorney General may restrain a foreign limited liability from transacting an unauthorized business in this State. As a threshold matter, a foreign limited liability partnership must be "transacting business" in this State within the meaning of Section 1104. Secondly, the business transacted in this State must be that which could not be engaged in by a domestic limited liability partnership. See Section 1101(c). The fact that a foreign limited liability partnership has a statement of foreign qualification does not permit it to engage in any unauthorized business in this State or impair the power of the Attorney General to restrain the foreign partnership from engaging in the unauthorized business. See Section 1101(c).

[ARTICLE] 12
MISCELLANEOUS PROVISIONS

Section 1201. Uniformity of Application and Construction.
This [Act] shall be applied and construed to effectuate its general purpose to make uniform the law with respect to the subject of this [Act] among States enacting it.

Section 1202. Short Title.
This [Act] may be cited as the Uniform Partnership Act (1997).

Section 1203. Severability Clause.
If any provision of this [Act] or its application to any person or circumstance is held invalid, the invalidity does not affect other provisions or applications of this [Act] which can be given effect without the invalid provision or application, and to this end the provisions of this [Act] are severable.

Section 1204. Effective Date.
This [Act] takes effect . . . .

COMMENT

The effective date of the Act established by an adopting State has operative effects under Section 1206, which defers mandatory application of the Act to existing partnerships.

Section 1205. Repeals.
Effective January 1, 199___, the following acts and parts of acts are repealed: [the State Partnership Act as amended and in effect immediately before the effective date of this [Act]].

COMMENT

This section repeals the adopting State's present general partnership act. The effective date of the repealer should not be any earlier than the date selected by that State in Section 1206(b) for the application of the Act to all partnerships.

Section 1206. Applicability.

(a) Before January 1, 199___, this [Act] governs only a partnership formed:

(1) after the effective date of this [Act], except a partnership that is continuing the business of a dissolved partnership under [Section 41 of the superseded Uniform Partnership Act]; and

(2) before the effective date of this [Act], that elects, as provided by subsection (c), to be governed by this [Act].

(b) On and after January 1, 199___, this [Act] governs all partnerships.

(c) Before January 1, 199___, a partnership voluntarily may elect, in the manner provided in its partnership agreement or by law for amending the partnership agreement, to be governed by this [Act]. The provisions of this [Act] relating to the liability of the partnership's partners to third parties apply to limit those partners' liability to a third party who had done business with the partnership within one year before the partnership's election to be governed by this [Act] only if the third party knows or has received a notification of the partnership's election to be governed by this [Act].

COMMENT

This section provides for a transition period in the applicability of the Act to existing partnerships, similar to that provided in the revised Texas partnership act. *See* Tex. Rev. Civ. Stat. Ann. art. 6132b-10.03 (Vernon Supp. 1994). Subsection (a) makes application of the Act mandatory for all partnerships formed after the effective date of the Act and permissive, by election, for existing partnerships. That affords existing partnerships and partners an opportunity to consider the changes effected by RUPA and to amend their partnership agreements, if appropriate.

Under subsection (b), application of the Act becomes mandatory for all partnerships, including existing partnerships that did not previously elect to be governed by it, upon a future date to be established by the adopting State. Texas, for example, deferred for five years mandatory compliance by existing partnerships.

Subsection (c) provides that an existing partnership may voluntarily elect to be governed by RUPA in the manner provided for amending its partnership agreement. Under UPA Section 18(h), that requires the consent of all the partners, unless otherwise agreed. Third parties doing business with the partnership must know or be notified of the election before RUPA's rules limiting a partner's liability become effective as to them. Those rules would include, for example, the provisions of Section 704 limiting the liability of a partner 90 days after the filing of a statement of dissociation. Without knowledge of the partnership's election, third parties would not be aware that they must check the record to ascertain the extent of a dissociated partner's personal liability.

Section 1207. Savings Clause.

This [Act] does not affect an action or proceeding commenced or right accrued before this [Act] takes effect.

COMMENT

This section continues the prior law after the effective date of the Act with respect to a pending action or proceeding or a right accrued at the time of the effective date. Since courts generally apply the law that exists at the time an action is commenced, in many circumstances the new law of this Act would displace the old law, but for this section.

Almost all States have general savings statutes, usually as part of their statutory construction acts. These are often very broad. Compare Uniform Statute and Rule Construction Act § 16(a) (narrow savings clause). As RUPA is remedial, the more limited savings provisions in Section 1207 are more appropriate than the broad savings provisions of the usual general savings clause. *See generally,* Comment to Uniform Statute and Rule Construction Act § 16.

Pending "action" refers to a judicial proceeding, while "proceeding" is broader and includes administrative proceedings. Although it is not always clear whether a right has "accrued," the term generally means that a cause of action has matured and is ripe for legal redress. *See, e.g., Estate of Hoover v. Iowa Dept. of Social Services,* 299 Iowa 702, 251 N.W.2d 529 (1977); *Nielsen v. State of Wisconsin,* 258 Wis. 1110, 141 N.W.2d 194 (1966). An inchoate right is not enough, and thus, for example, there is no accrued right under a contract until it is breached.

> *[Sections 1208 through 1211 are necessary only for jurisdictions adopting Uniform Limited Liability Partnership Act Amendments after previously adopting Uniform Partnership Act (1994)]*

Section 1208. Effective Date.

These [Amendments] take effect ....

Section 1209. Repeals.

Effective January 1, 199__, the following acts and parts of acts are repealed: [the Limited Liability Partnership amendments to the State Partnership Act as amended and in effect immediately before the effective date of these [Amendments]].

Section 1210. Applicability.

(a) Before January 1, 199__, these [Amendments] govern only a limited liability partnership formed:

    (1) on or after the effective date of these [Amendments], unless that partnership is continuing the business of a dissolved limited liability partnership; and

    (2) before the effective date of these [Amendments], that elects, as provided by subsection (c), to be governed by these [Amendments].

(b) On and after January 1, 199__, these [Amendments] govern all partnerships.

(c) Before January 1, 199__, a partnership voluntarily may elect, in the manner provided in its partnership agreement or by law for amending the partnership agreement, to be governed by these [Amendments]. The provisions of these [Amendments] relating to the liability of the partnership's partners to third parties apply to limit those partners' liability to a third party who had done business with the partnership within one year before the partnership's election to be governed by these [Amendments], only if the third party knows or has received a notification of the partnership's election to be governed by these [Amendments].

(d) The existing provisions for execution and filing a statement of qualification of a limited liability partnership continue until either the limited liability partnership elects to have this [Act] apply or January 1, 199__.

Section 1211. Savings Clause.

These [Amendments] do not affect an action or proceeding commenced or right accrued before these [Amendments] take effect.

1. Prior to August 1997, Section 801(2)(i) provided that upon the dissociation of a partner in a term partnership by death or otherwise under Section 601(6) through (10) or wrongful dissociation under 602(b) the partnership would dissolve unless "a majority in interest of the remaining partners (including partners who have rightfully dissociated pursuant to Section 602(b)(2)(i)) agree to continue the partnership." This language was thought to be necessary for a term partnership to lack continuity of life under the Internal Revenue Act tax classification regulations. These regulations were repealed effective January 1, 1997. The current language, approved at the 1997 annual meeting of the National Conference of Commissioners on Uniform State Laws, allows greater continuity in a term partnership than the prior version of this subsection and UPA Section 38(2)(b).

APPENDIX B
UNIFORM LIMITED PARTNERSHIP ACT (2001)

[ARTICLE] 1

GENERAL PROVISIONS

Section 101. Short Title.
This [Act] may be cited as the Uniform Limited Partnership Act [year of enactment].

Section 102. Definitions.
In this [Act]:

(1) "Certificate of limited partnership" means the certificate required by Section 201. The term includes the certificate as amended or restated.

(2) "Contribution", except in the phrase "right of contribution," means any benefit provided by a person to a limited partnership in order to become a partner or in the person's capacity as a partner.

(3) "Debtor in bankruptcy" means a person that is the subject of:

(A) an order for relief under Title 11 of the United States Code or a comparable order under a successor statute of general application; or

(B) a comparable order under federal, state, or foreign law governing insolvency.

(4) "Designated office" means:

(A) with respect to a limited partnership, the office that the limited partnership is required to designate and maintain under Section 114; and

(B) with respect to a foreign limited partnership, its principal office.

(5) "Distribution" means a transfer of money or other property from a limited partnership to a partner in the partner's capacity as a partner or to a transferee on account of a transferable interest owned by the transferee.

(6) "Foreign limited liability limited partnership" means a foreign limited partnership whose general partners have limited liability for the obligations of the foreign limited partnership under a provision similar to Section 404(c).

(7) "Foreign limited partnership" means a partnership formed under the laws of a jurisdiction other than this State and required by those laws to have one or more general partners and one or more limited partners. The term includes a foreign limited liability limited partnership.

(8) "General partner" means:

(A) with respect to a limited partnership, a person that:

(i) becomes a general partner under Section 401; or

(ii) was a general partner in a limited partnership when the limited partnership became subject to this [Act] under Section 1206(a) or (b); and

(B) with respect to a foreign limited partnership, a person that has rights, powers, and obligations similar to those of a general partner in a limited partnership.

(9) "Limited liability limited partnership", except in the phrase "foreign limited liability limited partnership", means a limited partnership whose certificate of limited partnership states that the limited partnership is a limited liability limited partnership.

(10) "Limited partner" means:

(A) with respect to a limited partnership, a person that:

(i) becomes a limited partner under Section 301; or

(ii) was a limited partner in a limited partnership when the limited partnership became subject to this [Act] under Section 1206(a) or (b); and

(B) with respect to a foreign limited partnership, a person that has rights, powers, and obligations similar to those of a limited partner in a limited partnership.

(11) "Limited partnership", except in the phrases "foreign limited partnership" and "foreign limited liability limited partnership", means an entity, having one or more general partners and one or more limited partners, which is formed under this [Act] by two or more persons or becomes subject to this [Act] under [Article] 11 or Section 1206(a) or (b). The term includes a limited liability limited partnership.

(12) "Partner" means a limited partner or general partner.

(13) "Partnership agreement" means the partners' agreement, whether oral, implied, in a record, or in any combination, concerning the limited partnership. The term includes the agreement as amended.

(14) "Person" means an individual, corporation, business trust, estate, trust, partnership, limited liability company, association, joint venture, government; governmental subdivision, agency, or instrumentality; public corporation, or any other legal or commercial entity.

(15) "Person dissociated as a general partner" means a person dissociated as a general partner of a limited partnership.

(16) "Principal office" means the office where the principal executive office of a limited partnership or foreign limited partnership is located, whether or not the office is located in this State.

(17) "Record" means information that is inscribed on a tangible medium or that is stored in an electronic or other medium and is retrievable in perceivable form.

(18) "Required information" means the information that a limited partnership is required to maintain under Section 111.

(19) "Sign" means:

   (A) to execute or adopt a tangible symbol with the present intent to authenticate a record; or

   (B) to attach or logically associate an electronic symbol, sound, or process to or with a record with the present intent to authenticate the record.

(20) "State" means a State of the United States, the District of Columbia, Puerto Rico, the United States Virgin Islands, or any territory or insular possession subject to the jurisdiction of the United States.

(21) "Transfer" includes an assignment, conveyance, deed, bill of sale, lease, mortgage, security interest, encumbrance, gift, and transfer by operation of law.

(22) "Transferable interest" means a partner's right to receive distributions.

(23) "Transferee" means a person to which all or part of a transferable interest has been transferred, whether or not the transferor is a partner.

Section 103. Knowledge and Notice.

   (a) A person knows a fact if the person has actual knowledge of it.

   (b) A person has notice of a fact if the person:

      (1) knows of it;

      (2) has received a notification of it;

      (3) has reason to know it exists from all of the facts known to the person at the time in question; or

      (4) has notice of it under subsection (c) or (d).

   (c) A certificate of limited partnership on file in the [office of the Secretary of State] is notice that the partnership is a limited partnership and the persons designated in the certificate as general partners are general partners. Except as otherwise provided in subsection (d), the certificate is not notice of any other fact.

(d) A person has notice of:

   (1) another person's dissociation as a general partner, 90 days after the effective date of an amendment to the certificate of limited partnership which states that the other person has dissociated or 90 days after the effective date of a statement of dissociation pertaining to the other person, whichever occurs first;

   (2) a limited partnership's dissolution, 90 days after the effective date of an amendment to the certificate of limited partnership stating that the limited partnership is dissolved;

   (3) a limited partnership's termination, 90 days after the effective date of a statement of termination;

   (4) a limited partnership's conversion under [Article] 11, 90 days after the effective date of the articles of conversion; or

   (5) a merger under [Article] 11, 90 days after the effective date of the articles of merger.

(e) A person notifies or gives a notification to another person by taking steps reasonably required to inform the other person in ordinary course, whether or not the other person learns of it.

(f) A person receives a notification when the notification:

   (1) comes to the person's attention; or

   (2) is delivered at the person's place of business or at any other place held out by the person as a place for receiving communications.

(g) Except as otherwise provided in subsection (h), a person other than an individual knows, has notice, or receives a notification of a fact for purposes of a particular transaction when the individual conducting the transaction for the person knows, has notice, or receives a notification of the fact, or in any event when the fact would have been brought to the individual's attention if the person had exercised reasonable diligence. A person other than an individual exercises reasonable diligence if it maintains reasonable routines for communicating significant information to the individual conducting the transaction for the person and there is reasonable compliance with the routines. Reasonable diligence does not require an individual acting for the person to communicate information unless the communication is part of the individual's regular duties or the individual has reason to know of the transaction and that the transaction would be materially affected by the information.

(h) A general partner's knowledge, notice, or receipt of a notification of a fact relating to the limited partnership is effective immediately as knowledge of, notice to, or receipt of a notification by the limited partnership, except in the case of a fraud on the limited partnership committed by or with the consent of the general partner. A limited partner's knowledge, notice, or receipt of a notification of a fact relating to the limited partnership is not effective as knowledge of, notice to, or receipt of a notification by the limited partnership.

Section 104. Nature, Purpose, and Duration of Entity.

(a) A limited partnership is an entity distinct from its partners. A limited partnership is the same entity regardless of whether its certificate states that the limited partnership is a limited liability limited partnership.

(b) A limited partnership may be organized under this [Act] for any lawful purpose.

(c) A limited partnership has a perpetual duration.

Section 105. Powers.

A limited partnership has the powers to do all things necessary or convenient to carry on its activities, including the power to sue, be sued, and defend in its own name and to maintain an action against a partner for harm caused to the limited partnership by a breach of the partnership agreement or violation of a duty to the partnership.

Section 106. Governing Law.

The law of this State governs relations among the partners of a limited partnership and between the partners and the limited partnership and the liability of partners as partners for an obligation of the limited partnership.

Section 107. Supplemental Principles of Law; Rate of Interest.

(a) Unless displaced by particular provisions of this [Act], the principles of law and equity supplement this [Act].

(b) If an obligation to pay interest arises under this [Act] and the rate is not specified, the rate is that specified in [applicable statute].

Section 108. Name.

(a) The name of a limited partnership may contain the name of any partner.

(b) The name of a limited partnership that is not a limited liability limited partnership must contain the phrase "limited partnership" or the abbreviation "L.P." or "LP" and may not contain the phrase "limited liability limited partnership" or the abbreviation "LLLP" or "L.L.L.P.".

(c) The name of a limited liability limited partnership must contain the phrase "limited liability limited partnership" or the abbreviation "LLLP" or "L.L.L.P." and must not contain the abbreviation "L.P." or "LP."

(d) Unless authorized by subsection (e), the name of a limited partnership must be distinguishable in the records of the [Secretary of State] from:

(1) the name of each person other than an individual incorporated, organized, or authorized to transact business in this State; and

(2) each name reserved under Section 109 [or other state laws allowing the reservation or registration of business names, including fictitious name statutes].

(e) A limited partnership may apply to the [Secretary of State] for authorization to use a name that does not comply with subsection (d). The [Secretary of State] shall authorize use of the name applied for if, as to each conflicting name:

(1) the present user, registrant, or owner of the conflicting name consents in a signed record to the use and submits an undertaking in a form satisfactory to the [Secretary of State] to change the conflicting name to a name that complies with subsection (d) and is distinguishable in the records of the [Secretary of State] from the name applied for;

(2) the applicant delivers to the [Secretary of State] a certified copy of the final judgment of a court of competent jurisdiction establishing the applicant's right to use in this State the name applied for; or

(3) the applicant delivers to the [Secretary of State] proof satisfactory to the [Secretary of State] that the present user, registrant, or owner of the conflicting name:
(A) has merged into the applicant;
(B) has been converted into the applicant; or
(C) has transferred substantially all of its assets, including the conflicting name, to the applicant.

(f) Subject to Section 905, this section applies to any foreign limited partnership transacting business in this State, having a certificate of authority to transact business in this State, or applying for a certificate of authority.

Section 109. Reservation of Name.

(a) The exclusive right to the use of a name that complies with Section 108 may be reserved by:

(1) a person intending to organize a limited partnership under this [Act] and to adopt the name;

(2) a limited partnership or a foreign limited partnership authorized to transact business in this State intending to adopt the name;

(3) a foreign limited partnership intending to obtain a certificate of authority to transact business in this State and adopt the name;

(4) a person intending to organize a foreign limited partnership and intending to have it obtain a certificate of authority to transact business in this State and adopt the name;

(5) a foreign limited partnership formed under the name; or

(6) a foreign limited partnership formed under a name that does not comply with Section 108(b) or (c), but the name reserved under this paragraph may differ from the foreign limited partnership's name only to the extent necessary to comply with Section 108(b) and (c).

(b) A person may apply to reserve a name under subsection (a) by delivering to the [Secretary of State] for filing an application that states the name to be reserved and the paragraph of subsection (a) which applies. If the [Secretary of State] finds that the name is available for use by the applicant, the [Secretary of State] shall file a statement of name reservation and thereby reserve the name for the exclusive use of the applicant for a 120 days.

(c) An applicant that has reserved a name pursuant to subsection (b) may reserve the same name for additional 120-day periods. A person having a current reservation for a name may not apply for another 120-day period for the same name until 90 days have elapsed in the current reservation.

(d) A person that has reserved a name under this section may deliver to the [Secretary of State] for filing a notice of transfer that states the reserved name, the name and street and mailing address of some other person to which the reservation is to be transferred, and the paragraph of subsection (a) which applies to the other person. Subject to Section 206(c), the transfer is effective when the [Secretary of State] files the notice of transfer.

Section 110. Effect of Partnership Agreement; Nonwaivable Provisions.

(a) Except as otherwise provided in subsection (b), the partnership agreement governs relations among the partners and between the partners and the partnership. To the extent the partnership agreement does not otherwise provide, this [Act] governs relations among the partners and between the partners and the partnership.

(b) A partnership agreement may not:

    (1) vary a limited partnership's power under Section 105 to sue, be sued, and defend in its own name;

    (2) vary the law applicable to a limited partnership under Section 106;

    (3) vary the requirements of Section 204;

    (4) vary the information required under Section 111 or unreasonably restrict the right to information under Sections 304 or 407, but the partnership agreement may impose reasonable restrictions on the availability and use of information obtained under those sections and may define appropriate remedies, including liquidated damages, for a breach of any reasonable restriction on use;

    (5) eliminate the duty of loyalty under Section 408, but the partnership agreement may:

        (A) identify specific types or categories of activities that do not violate the duty of loyalty, if not manifestly unreasonable; and

        (B) specify the number or percentage of partners which may authorize or ratify, after full disclosure to all partners of all material facts, a specific act or transaction that otherwise would violate the duty of loyalty;

(6) unreasonably reduce the duty of care under Section 408(c);

(7) eliminate the obligation of good faith and fair dealing under Sections 305(b) and 408(d), but the partnership agreement may prescribe the standards by which the performance of the obligation is to be measured, if the standards are not manifestly unreasonable;

(8) vary the power of a person to dissociate as a general partner under Section 604(a) except to require that the notice under Section 603(1) be in a record;

(9) vary the power of a court to decree dissolution in the circumstances specified in Section 802;

(10) vary the requirement to wind up the partnership's business as specified in Section 803;

(11) unreasonably restrict the right to maintain an action under [Article] 10;

(12) restrict the right of a partner under Section 1110(a) to approve a conversion or merger or the right of a general partner under Section 1110(b) to consent to an amendment to the certificate of limited partnership which deletes a statement that the limited partnership is a limited liability limited partnership; or

(13) restrict rights under this [Act] of a person other than a partner or a transferee.

Section 111. Required Information.

A limited partnership shall maintain at its designated office the following information:

(1) a current list showing the full name and last known street and mailing address of each partner, separately identifying the general partners, in alphabetical order, and the limited partners, in alphabetical order;

(2) a copy of the initial certificate of limited partnership and all amendments to and restatements of the certificate, together with signed copies of any powers of attorney under which any certificate, amendment, or restatement has been signed;

(3) a copy of any filed articles of conversion or merger;

(4) a copy of the limited partnership's federal, state, and local income tax returns and reports, if any, for the three most recent years;

(5) a copy of any partnership agreement made in a record and any amendment made in a record to any partnership agreement;

(6) a copy of any financial statement of the limited partnership for the three most recent years;

(7) a copy of the three most recent annual reports delivered by the limited partnership to the [Secretary of State] pursuant to Section 210;

(8) a copy of any record made by the limited partnership during the past three years of any consent given by or vote taken of any partner pursuant to this [Act] or the partnership agreement; and

(9) unless contained in a partnership agreement made in a record, a record stating:

    (A) the amount of cash, and a description and statement of the agreed value of the other benefits, contributed and agreed to be contributed by each partner;

    (B) the times at which, or events on the happening of which, any additional contributions agreed to be made by each partner are to be made;

    (C) for any person that is both a general partner and a limited partner, a specification of what transferable interest the person owns in each capacity; and

    (D) any events upon the happening of which the limited partnership is to be dissolved and its activities wound up.

Section 112. Business Transactions of Partner with Partnership.

A partner may lend money to and transact other business with the limited partnership and has the same rights and obligations with respect to the loan or other transaction as a person that is not a partner.

Section 113. Dual Capacity.

A person may be both a general partner and a limited partner. A person that is both a general and limited partner has the rights, powers, duties, and obligations provided by this [Act] and the partnership agreement in each of those capacities. When the person acts as a general partner, the person is subject to the obligations, duties and restrictions under this [Act] and the partnership agreement for general partners. When the person acts as a limited partner, the person is subject to the obligations, duties and restrictions under this [Act] and the partnership agreement for limited partners.

Section 114. Office and Agent for Service of Process.

(a) A limited partnership shall designate and continuously maintain in this State:

    (1) an office, which need not be a place of its activity in this State; and

    (2) an agent for service of process.

(b) A foreign limited partnership shall designate and continuously maintain in this State an agent for service of process.

(c) An agent for service of process of a limited partnership or foreign limited partnership must be an individual who is a resident of this State or other person authorized to do business in this State.

Section 115. Change of Designated Office or Agent for Service of Process.

(a) In order to change its designated office, agent for service of process, or the address of its agent for service of process, a limited partnership or a foreign limited partnership may deliver to the [Secretary of State] for filing a statement of change containing:

    (1) the name of the limited partnership or foreign limited partnership;

    (2) the street and mailing address of its current designated office;

    (3) if the current designated office is to be changed, the street and mailing address of the new designated office;

    (4) the name and street and mailing address of its current agent for service of process; and

    (5) if the current agent for service of process or an address of the agent is to be changed, the new information.

(b) Subject to Section 206(c), a statement of change is effective when filed by the [Secretary of State].

Section 116. Resignation of Agent for Service of Process.

(a) In order to resign as an agent for service of process of a limited partnership or foreign limited partnership, the agent must deliver to the [Secretary of State] for filing a statement of resignation containing the name of the limited partnership or foreign limited partnership.

(b) After receiving a statement of resignation, the [Secretary of State] shall file it and mail a copy to the designated office of the limited partnership or foreign limited partnership and another copy to the principal office if the address of the office appears in the records of the [Secretary of State] and is different from the address of the designated office.

(c) An agency for service of process is terminated on the 31st day after the [Secretary of State] files the statement of resignation.

Section 117. Service of Process.

(a) An agent for service of process appointed by a limited partnership or foreign limited partnership is an agent of the limited partnership or foreign limited partnership for service of any process, notice, or demand required or permitted by law to be served upon the limited partnership or foreign limited partnership.

(b) If a limited partnership or foreign limited partnership does not appoint or maintain an agent for service of process in this State or the agent for service of process cannot with reasonable diligence be found at the agent's address, the [Secretary of State] is an agent of the limited partnership or foreign limited partnership upon whom process, notice, or demand may be served.

(c) Service of any process, notice, or demand on the [Secretary of State] may be made by delivering to and leaving with the [Secretary of State] duplicate copies of the process, notice, or demand. If a process, notice, or demand is served on the [Secretary of State], the [Secretary of State] shall forward one of the copies by registered or certified mail, return receipt requested, to the limited partnership or foreign limited partnership at its designated office.

(d) Service is effected under subsection (c) at the earliest of:

  (1) the date the limited partnership or foreign limited partnership receives the process, notice, or demand;

  (2) the date shown on the return receipt, if signed on behalf of the limited partnership or foreign limited partnership; or

  (3) five days after the process, notice, or demand is deposited in the mail, if mailed postpaid and correctly addressed.

(e) The [Secretary of State] shall keep a record of each process, notice, and demand served pursuant to this section and record the time of, and the action taken regarding, the service.

(f) This section does not affect the right to serve process, notice, or demand in any other manner provided by law.

Section 118. Consent and Proxies of Partners.

Action requiring the consent of partners under this [Act] may be taken without a meeting, and a partner may appoint a proxy to consent or otherwise act for the partner by signing an appointment record, either personally or by the partner's attorney in fact.

[ARTICLE] 2

FORMATION; CERTIFICATE OF LIMITED PARTNERSHIP AND OTHER FILINGS

Section 201. Formation of Limited Partnership; Certificate of Limited Partnership.

(a) In order for a limited partnership to be formed, a certificate of limited partnership must be delivered to the [Secretary of State] for filing. The certificate must state:

  (1) the name of the limited partnership, which must comply with Section 108;

  (2) the street and mailing address of the initial designated office and the name and street and mailing address of the initial agent for service of process;

  (3) the name and the street and mailing address of each general partner;

    (4) whether the limited partnership is a limited liability limited partnership; and

    (5) any additional information required by [Article] 11.

(b) A certificate of limited partnership may also contain any other matters but may not vary or otherwise affect the provisions specified in Section 110(b) in a manner inconsistent with that section.

(c) If there has been substantial compliance with subsection (a), subject to Section 206(c) a limited partnership is formed when the [Secretary of State] files the certificate of limited partnership.

(d) Subject to subsection (b), if any provision of a partnership agreement is inconsistent with the filed certificate of limited partnership or with a filed statement of dissociation, termination, or change or filed articles of conversion or merger:

    (1) the partnership agreement prevails as to partners and transferees; and

    (2) the filed certificate of limited partnership, statement of dissociation, termination, or change or articles of conversion or merger prevail as to persons, other than partners and transferees, that reasonably rely on the filed record to their detriment.

Section 202. Amendment or Restatement of Certificate.

(a) In order to amend its certificate of limited partnership, a limited partnership must deliver to the [Secretary of State] for filing an amendment or, pursuant to [Article] 11, articles of merger stating:

    (1) the name of the limited partnership;

    (2) the date of filing of its initial certificate; and

    (3) the changes the amendment makes to the certificate as most recently amended or restated.

(b) A limited partnership shall promptly deliver to the [Secretary of State] for filing an amendment to a certificate of limited partnership to reflect:

    (1) the admission of a new general partner;

    (2) the dissociation of a person as a general partner; or

    (3) the appointment of a person to wind up the limited partnership's activities under Section 803(c) or (d).

(c) A general partner that knows that any information in a filed certificate of limited partnership was false when the certificate was filed or has become false due to changed circumstances shall promptly:

    (1) cause the certificate to be amended; or

    (2) if appropriate, deliver to the [Secretary of State] for filing a statement of change pursuant to Section 115 or a statement of correction pursuant to Section 207.

(d) A certificate of limited partnership may be amended at any time for any other proper purpose as determined by the limited partnership.

(e) A restated certificate of limited partnership may be delivered to the [Secretary of State] for filing in the same manner as an amendment.

(f) Subject to Section 206(c), an amendment or restated certificate is effective when filed by the [Secretary of State].

Section 203. Statement of Termination.

A dissolved limited partnership that has completed winding up may deliver to the [Secretary of State] for filing a statement of termination that states:

(1) the name of the limited partnership;

(2) the date of filing of its initial certificate of limited partnership; and

(3) any other information as determined by the general partners filing the statement or by a person appointed pursuant to Section 803(c) or (d).

Section 204. Signing of Records.

(a) Each record delivered to the [Secretary of State] for filing pursuant to this [Act] must be signed in the following manner:

(1) An initial certificate of limited partnership must be signed by all general partners listed in the certificate.

(2) An amendment adding or deleting a statement that the limited partnership is a limited liability limited partnership must be signed by all general partners listed in the certificate.

(3) An amendment designating as general partner a person admitted under Section 801(3)(B) following the dissociation of a limited partnership's last general partner must be signed by that person.

(4) An amendment required by Section 803(c) following the appointment of a person to wind up the dissolved limited partnership's activities must be signed by that person.

(5) Any other amendment must be signed by:

(A) at least one general partner listed in the certificate;

(B) each other person designated in the amendment as a new general partner; and

(C) each person that the amendment indicates has dissociated as a general partner, unless:

  (i) the person is deceased or a guardian or general conservator has been appointed for the person and the amendment so states; or

  (ii) the person has previously delivered to the [Secretary of State] for filing a statement of dissociation.

(6) A restated certificate of limited partnership must be signed by at least one general partner listed in the certificate, and, to the extent the restated certificate effects a change under any other paragraph

of this subsection, the certificate must be signed in a manner that satisfies that paragraph.

(7) A statement of termination must be signed by all general partners listed in the certificate or, if the certificate of a dissolved limited partnership lists no general partners, by the person appointed pursuant to Section 803(c) or (d) to wind up the dissolved limited partnership's activities.

(8) Articles of conversion must be signed by each general partner listed in the certificate of limited partnership.

(9) Articles of merger must be signed as provided in Section 1108(a).

(10) Any other record delivered on behalf of a limited partnership to the [Secretary of State] for filing must be signed by at least one general partner listed in the certificate.

(11) A statement by a person pursuant to Section 605(a)(4) stating that the person has dissociated as a general partner must be signed by that person.

(12) A statement of withdrawal by a person pursuant to Section 306 must be signed by that person.

(13) A record delivered on behalf of a foreign limited partnership to the [Secretary of State] for filing must be signed by at least one general partner of the foreign limited partnership.

(14) Any other record delivered on behalf of any person to the [Secretary of State] for filing must be signed by that person.

(b) Any person may sign by an attorney in fact any record to be filed pursuant to this [Act].

Section 205. Signing and Filing Pursuant to Judicial Order.

(a) If a person required by this [Act] to sign a record or deliver a record to the [Secretary of State] for filing does not do so, any other person that is aggrieved may petition the [appropriate court] to order:

(1) the person to sign the record;

(2) deliver the record to the [Secretary of State] for filing; or

(3) the [Secretary of State] to file the record unsigned.

(b) If the person aggrieved under subsection (a) is not the limited partnership or foreign limited partnership to which the record pertains, the aggrieved person shall make the limited partnership or foreign limited partnership a party to the action. A person aggrieved under subsection (a) may seek the remedies provided in subsection (a) in the same action in combination or in the alternative.

(c) A record filed unsigned pursuant to this section is effective without being signed.

Section 206. Delivery to and Filing of Records by [Secretary of State]; Effective Time and Date.

(a) A record authorized or required to be delivered to the [Secretary of State] for filing under this [Act] must be captioned to describe the record's purpose, be in a medium permitted by the [Secretary of State], and be delivered to the [Secretary of State]. Unless the [Secretary of State] determines that a record does not comply with the filing requirements of this [Act], and if all filing fees have been paid, the [Secretary of State] shall file the record and:

    (1) for a statement of dissociation, send:

        (A) a copy of the filed statement and a receipt for the fees to the person which the statement indicates has dissociated as a general partner; and

        (B) a copy of the filed statement and receipt to the limited partnership;

    (2) for a statement of withdrawal, send:

        (A) a copy of the filed statement and a receipt for the fees to the person on whose behalf the record was filed; and

        (B) if the statement refers to an existing limited partnership, a copy of the filed statement and receipt to the limited partnership; and

    (3) for all other records, send a copy of the filed record and a receipt for the fees to the person on whose behalf the record was filed.

(b) Upon request and payment of a fee, the [Secretary of State] shall send to the requester a certified copy of the requested record.

(c) Except as otherwise provided in Sections 116 and 207, a record delivered to the [Secretary of State] for filing under this [Act] may specify an effective time and a delayed effective date. Except as otherwise provided in this [Act], a record filed by the [Secretary of State] is effective:

    (1) if the record does not specify an effective time and does not specify a delayed effective date, on the date and at the time the record is filed as evidenced by the [Secretary of State's] endorsement of the date and time on the record;

    (2) if the record specifies an effective time but not a delayed effective date, on the date the record is filed at the time specified in the record;

    (3) if the record specifies a delayed effective date but not an effective time, at 12:01 a.m. on the earlier of:

        (A) the specified date; or

        (B) the 90th day after the record is filed; or

    (4) if the record specifies an effective time and a delayed effective date, at the specified time on the earlier of:

        (A) the specified date; or

        (B) the 90th day after the record is filed.

Section 207. Correcting Filed Record.

(a) A limited partnership or foreign limited partnership may deliver to the [Secretary of State] for filing a statement of correction to correct a record previously delivered by the limited partnership or foreign limited partnership to the [Secretary of State] and filed by the [Secretary of State], if at the time of filing the record contained false or erroneous information or was defectively signed.

(b) A statement of correction may not state a delayed effective date and must:

    (1) describe the record to be corrected, including its filing date, or attach a copy of the record as filed;

    (2) specify the incorrect information and the reason it is incorrect or the manner in which the signing was defective; and

    (3) correct the incorrect information or defective signature.

(c) When filed by the [Secretary of State], a statement of correction is effective retroactively as of the effective date of the record the statement corrects, but the statement is effective when filed:

    (1) for the purposes of Section 103(c) and (d); and

    (2) as to persons relying on the uncorrected record and adversely affected by the correction.

Section 208. Liability for False Information In Filed Record.

(a) If a record delivered to the [Secretary of State] for filing under this [Act] and filed by the [Secretary of State] contains false information, a person that suffers loss by reliance on the information may recover damages for the loss from:

    (1) a person that signed the record, or caused another to sign it on the person's behalf, and knew the information to be false at the time the record was signed; and

    (2) a general partner that has notice that the information was false when the record was filed or has become false because of changed circumstances, if the general partner has notice for a reasonably sufficient time before the information is relied upon to enable the general partner to effect an amendment under Section 202, file a petition pursuant to Section 205, or deliver to the [Secretary of State] for filing a statement of change pursuant to Section 115 or a statement of correction pursuant to Section 207.

(b) Signing a record authorized or required to be filed under this [Act] constitutes an affirmation under the penalties of perjury that the facts stated in the record are true.

Section 209. Certificate of Existence or Authorization.

(a)　The [Secretary of State], upon request and payment of the requisite fee, shall furnish a certificate of existence for a limited partnership if the records filed in the [office of the Secretary of State] show that the [Secretary of State] has filed a certificate of limited partnership and has not filed a statement of termination. A certificate of existence must state:

　(1)　the limited partnership's name;

　(2)　that it was duly formed under the laws of this State and the date of formation;

　(3)　whether all fees, taxes, and penalties due to the [Secretary of State] under this [Act] or other law have been paid;

　(4)　whether the limited partnership's most recent annual report required by Section 210 has been filed by the [Secretary of State];

　(5)　whether the [Secretary of State] has administratively dissolved the limited partnership;

　(6)　whether the limited partnership's certificate of limited partnership has been amended to state that the limited partnership is dissolved;

　(7)　that a statement of termination has not been filed by the [Secretary of State]; and

　(8)　other facts of record in the [office of the Secretary of State] which may be requested by the applicant.

(b)　The [Secretary of State], upon request and payment of the requisite fee, shall furnish a certificate of authorization for a foreign limited partnership if the records filed in the [office of the Secretary of State] show that the [Secretary of State] has filed a certificate of authority, has not revoked the certificate of authority, and has not filed a notice of cancellation. A certificate of authorization must state:

　(1)　the foreign limited partnership's name and any alternate name adopted under Section 905(a) for use in this State;

　(2)　that it is authorized to transact business in this State;

　(3)　whether all fees, taxes, and penalties due to the [Secretary of State] under this [Act] or other law have been paid;

　(4)　whether the foreign limited partnership's most recent annual report required by Section 210 has been filed by the [Secretary of State];

　(5)　that the [Secretary of State] has not revoked its certificate of authority and has not filed a notice of cancellation; and

　(6)　other facts of record in the [office of the Secretary of State] which may be requested by the applicant.

(c)　Subject to any qualification stated in the certificate, a certificate of existence or authorization issued by the [Secretary of State] may be relied upon as conclusive evidence that the limited partnership or foreign limited partnership is in existence or is authorized to transact business in this State.

Section 210. Annual Report for [Secretary of State].

(a) A limited partnership or a foreign limited partnership authorized to transact business in this State shall deliver to the [Secretary of State] for filing an annual report that states:

    (1) the name of the limited partnership or foreign limited partnership;

    (2) the street and mailing address of its designated office and the name and street and mailing address of its agent for service of process in this State;

    (3) in the case of a limited partnership, the street and mailing address of its principal office; and

    (4) in the case of a foreign limited partnership, the State or other jurisdiction under whose law the foreign limited partnership is formed and any alternate name adopted under Section 905(a).

(b) Information in an annual report must be current as of the date the annual report is delivered to the [Secretary of State] for filing.

(c) The first annual report must be delivered to the [Secretary of State] between [January 1 and April 1] of the year following the calendar year in which a limited partnership was formed or a foreign limited partnership was authorized to transact business. An annual report must be delivered to the [Secretary of State] between [January 1 and April 1] of each subsequent calendar year.

(d) If an annual report does not contain the information required in subsection (a), the [Secretary of State] shall promptly notify the reporting limited partnership or foreign limited partnership and return the report to it for correction. If the report is corrected to contain the information required in subsection (a) and delivered to the [Secretary of State] within 30 days after the effective date of the notice, it is timely delivered.

(e) If a filed annual report contains an address of a designated office or the name or address of an agent for service of process which differs from the information shown in the records of the [Secretary of State] immediately before the filing, the differing information in the annual report is considered a statement of change under Section 115.

[ARTICLE] 3

LIMITED PARTNERS

Section 301. Becoming Limited Partner.
A person becomes a limited partner:

    (1) as provided in the partnership agreement;

(2) as the result of a conversion or merger under [Article] 11; or

(3) with the consent of all the partners.

Section 302. No Right or Power as Limited Partner to Bind Limited Partnership.

A limited partner does not have the right or the power as a limited partner to act for or bind the limited partnership.

Section 303. No Liability as Limited Partner for Limited Partnership Obligations.

An obligation of a limited partnership, whether arising in contract, tort, or otherwise, is not the obligation of a limited partner. A limited partner is not personally liable, directly or indirectly, by way of contribution or otherwise, for an obligation of the limited partnership solely by reason of being a limited partner, even if the limited partner participates in the management and control of the limited partnership.

Section 304. Right of Limited Partner and Former Limited Partner to Information.

(a) On 10 days' demand, made in a record received by the limited partnership, a limited partner may inspect and copy required information during regular business hours in the limited partnership's designated office. The limited partner need not have any particular purpose for seeking the information.

(b) During regular business hours and at a reasonable location specified by the limited partnership, a limited partner may obtain from the limited partnership and inspect and copy true and full information regarding the state of the activities and financial condition of the limited partnership and other information regarding the activities of the limited partnership as is just and reasonable if:

(1) the limited partner seeks the information for a purpose reasonably related to the partner's interest as a limited partner;

(2) the limited partner makes a demand in a record received by the limited partnership, describing with reasonable particularity the information sought and the purpose for seeking the information; and

(3) the information sought is directly connected to the limited partner's purpose.

(c) Within 10 days after receiving a demand pursuant to subsection (b), the limited partnership in a record shall inform the limited partner that made the demand:

(1) what information the limited partnership will provide in response to the demand;

    (2) when and where the limited partnership will provide the information; and

    (3) if the limited partnership declines to provide any demanded information, the limited partnership's reasons for declining.

(d) Subject to subsection (f), a person dissociated as a limited partner may inspect and copy required information during regular business hours in the limited partnership's designated office if:

    (1) the information pertains to the period during which the person was a limited partner;

    (2) the person seeks the information in good faith; and

    (3) the person meets the requirements of subsection (b).

(e) The limited partnership shall respond to a demand made pursuant to subsection (d) in the same manner as provided in subsection (c).

(f) If a limited partner dies, Section 704 applies.

(g) The limited partnership may impose reasonable restrictions on the use of information obtained under this section. In a dispute concerning the reasonableness of a restriction under this subsection, the limited partnership has the burden of proving reasonableness.

(h) A limited partnership may charge a person that makes a demand under this section reasonable costs of copying, limited to the costs of labor and material.

(i) Whenever this [Act] or a partnership agreement provides for a limited partner to give or withhold consent to a matter, before the consent is given or withheld, the limited partnership shall, without demand, provide the limited partner with all information material to the limited partner's decision that the limited partnership knows.

(j) A limited partner or person dissociated as a limited partner may exercise the rights under this section through an attorney or other agent. Any restriction imposed under subsection (g) or by the partnership agreement applies both to the attorney or other agent and to the limited partner or person dissociated as a limited partner.

(k) The rights stated in this section do not extend to a person as transferee, but may be exercised by the legal representative of an individual under legal disability who is a limited partner or person dissociated as a limited partner.

Section 305. Limited Duties of Limited Partners.

(a) A limited partner does not have any fiduciary duty to the limited partnership or to any other partner solely by reason of being a limited partner.

(b) A limited partner shall discharge the duties to the partnership and the other partners under this [Act] or under the partnership agreement and exercise any rights consistently with the obligation of good faith and fair dealing.

(c) A limited partner does not violate a duty or obligation under this [Act] or under the partnership agreement merely because the limited partner's conduct furthers the limited partner's own interest.

Section 306. Person Erroneously Believing Self to Be Limited Partner.

(a) Except as otherwise provided in subsection (b), a person that makes an investment in a business enterprise and erroneously but in good faith believes that the person has become a limited partner in the enterprise is not liable for the enterprise's obligations by reason of making the investment, receiving distributions from the enterprise, or exercising any rights of or appropriate to a limited partner, if, on ascertaining the mistake, the person:

(1) causes an appropriate certificate of limited partnership, amendment, or statement of correction to be signed and delivered to the [Secretary of State] for filing; or

(2) withdraws from future participation as an owner in the enterprise by signing and delivering to the [Secretary of State] for filing a statement of withdrawal under this section.

(b) A person that makes an investment described in subsection (a) is liable to the same extent as a general partner to any third party that enters into a transaction with the enterprise, believing in good faith that the person is a general partner, before the [Secretary of State] files a statement of withdrawal, certificate of limited partnership, amendment, or statement of correction to show that the person is not a general partner.

(c) If a person makes a diligent effort in good faith to comply with subsection (a)(1) and is unable to cause the appropriate certificate of limited partnership, amendment, or statement of correction to be signed and delivered to the [Secretary of State] for filing, the person has the right to withdraw from the enterprise pursuant to subsection (a)(2) even if the withdrawal would otherwise breach an agreement with others that are or have agreed to become co-owners of the enterprise.

[ARTICLE] 4

GENERAL PARTNERS

Section 401. Becoming General Partner.
A person becomes a general partner:

(1) as provided in the partnership agreement:

(2) under Section 801(3)(B) following the dissociation of a limited partnership's last general partner;

(3) as the result of a conversion or merger under [Article] 11; or

(4) with the consent of all the partners.

Section 402. General Partner Agent of Limited Partnership.

(a) Each general partner is an agent of the limited partnership for the purposes of its activities. An act of a general partner, including the signing of a record in the partnership's name, for apparently carrying on in the ordinary course the limited partnership's activities or activities of the kind carried on by the limited partnership binds the limited partnership, unless the general partner did not have authority to act for the limited partnership in the particular matter and the person with which the general partner was dealing knew, had received a notification, or had notice under Section 103(d) that the general partner lacked authority.

(b) An act of a general partner which is not apparently for carrying on in the ordinary course the limited partnership's activities or activities of the kind carried on by the limited partnership binds the limited partnership only if the act was actually authorized by all the other partners.

Section 403. Limited Partnership Liable for General Partner's Actionable Conduct.

(a) A limited partnership is liable for loss or injury caused to a person, or for a penalty incurred, as a result of a wrongful act or omission, or other actionable conduct, of a general partner acting in the ordinary course of activities of the limited partnership or with authority of the limited partnership.

(b) If, in the course of the limited partnership's activities or while acting with authority of the limited partnership, a general partner receives or causes the limited partnership to receive money or property of a person not a partner, and the money or property is misapplied by a general partner, the limited partnership is liable for the loss.

Section 404. General Partner's Liability.

(a) Except as otherwise provided in subsections (b) and (c), all general partners are liable jointly and severally for all obligations of the limited partnership unless otherwise agreed by the claimant or provided by law.

(b) A person that becomes a general partner of an existing limited partnership is not personally liable for an obligation of a limited partnership incurred before the person became a general partner.

(c) An obligation of a limited partnership incurred while the limited partnership is a limited liability limited partnership, whether arising in contract, tort, or otherwise, is solely the obligation of the limited partnership. A general partner is not personally liable, directly or indirectly, by way of contribution or otherwise, for such an obligation solely by reason of being or acting as a general partner. This subsection applies despite anything inconsistent in the partnership agreement that existed immediately before the consent required to become a limited liability limited partnership under Section 406(b)(2).

Section 405. Actions by and Against Partnership and Partners.

(a) To the extent not inconsistent with Section 404, a general partner may be joined in an action against the limited partnership or named in a separate action.

(b) A judgment against a limited partnership is not by itself a judgment against a general partner. A judgment against a limited partnership may not be satisfied from a general partner's assets unless there is also a judgment against the general partner.

(c) A judgment creditor of a general partner may not levy execution against the assets of the general partner to satisfy a judgment based on a claim against the limited partnership, unless the partner is personally liable for the claim under Section 404 and:

    (1) a judgment based on the same claim has been obtained against the limited partnership and a writ of execution on the judgment has been returned unsatisfied in whole or in part;

    (2) the limited partnership is a debtor in bankruptcy;

    (3) the general partner has agreed that the creditor need not exhaust limited partnership assets;

    (4) a court grants permission to the judgment creditor to levy execution against the assets of a general partner based on a finding that limited partnership assets subject to execution are clearly insufficient to satisfy the judgment, that exhaustion of limited partnership assets is excessively burdensome, or that the grant of permission is an appropriate exercise of the court's equitable powers; or

    (5) liability is imposed on the general partner by law or contract independent of the existence of the limited partnership.

Section 406. Management Rights of General Partner.

(a) Each general partner has equal rights in the management and conduct of the limited partnership's activities. Except as expressly provided in this [Act], any matter relating to the activities of the limited partnership may be exclusively decided by the general partner or, if there is more than one general partner, by a majority of the general partners.

(b) The consent of each partner is necessary to:

    (1) amend the partnership agreement;

(2) amend the certificate of limited partnership to add or, subject to Section 1110, delete a statement that the limited partnership is a limited liability limited partnership; and

(3) sell, lease, exchange, or otherwise dispose of all, or substantially all, of the limited partnership's property, with or without the good will, other than in the usual and regular course of the limited partnership's activities.

(c) A limited partnership shall reimburse a general partner for payments made and indemnify a general partner for liabilities incurred by the general partner in the ordinary course of the activities of the partnership or for the preservation of its activities or property.

(d) A limited partnership shall reimburse a general partner for an advance to the limited partnership beyond the amount of capital the general partner agreed to contribute.

(e) A payment or advance made by a general partner which gives rise to an obligation of the limited partnership under subsection (c) or (d) constitutes a loan to the limited partnership which accrues interest from the date of the payment or advance.

(f) A general partner is not entitled to remuneration for services performed for the partnership.

Section 407. Right of General Partner and Former General Partner to Information.

(a) A general partner, without having any particular purpose for seeking the information, may inspect and copy during regular business hours:

(1) in the limited partnership's designated office, required information; and

(2) at a reasonable location specified by the limited partnership, any other records maintained by the limited partnership regarding the limited partnership's activities and financial condition.

(b) Each general partner and the limited partnership shall furnish to a general partner:

(1) without demand, any information concerning the limited partnership's activities and activities reasonably required for the proper exercise of the general partner's rights and duties under the partnership agreement or this [Act]; and

(2) on demand, any other information concerning the limited partnership's activities, except to the extent the demand or the information demanded is unreasonable or otherwise improper under the circumstances.

(c) Subject to subsection (e), on 10 days' demand made in a record received by the limited partnership, a person dissociated as a general partner may have access to the information and records described in subsection (a) at the location specified in subsection (a) if:

   (1) the information or record pertains to the period during which the person was a general partner;

   (2) the person seeks the information or record in good faith; and

   (3) the person satisfies the requirements imposed on a limited partner by Section 304(b).

(d) The limited partnership shall respond to a demand made pursuant to subsection (c) in the same manner as provided in Section 304(c).

(e) If a general partner dies, Section 704 applies.

(f) The limited partnership may impose reasonable restrictions on the use of information under this section. In any dispute concerning the reasonableness of a restriction under this subsection, the limited partnership has the burden of proving reasonableness.

(g) A limited partnership may charge a person dissociated as a general partner that makes a demand under this section reasonable costs of copying, limited to the costs of labor and material.

(h) A general partner or person dissociated as a general partner may exercise the rights under this section through an attorney or other agent. Any restriction imposed under subsection (f) or by the partnership agreement applies both to the attorney or other agent and to the general partner or person dissociated as a general partner.

(i) The rights under this section do not extend to a person as transferee, but the rights under subsection (c) of a person dissociated as a general may be exercised by the legal representative of an individual who dissociated as a general partner under Section 603(7)(B) or (C).

Section 408. General Standards of General Partner's Conduct.

(a) The only fiduciary duties that a general partner has to the limited partnership and the other partners are the duties of loyalty and care under subsections (b) and (c).

(b) A general partner's duty of loyalty to the limited partnership and the other partners is limited to the following:

   (1) to account to the limited partnership and hold as trustee for it any property, profit, or benefit derived by the general partner in the conduct and winding up of the limited partnership's activities or derived from a use by the general partner of limited partnership property, including the appropriation of a limited partnership opportunity;

   (2) to refrain from dealing with the limited partnership in the conduct or winding up of the limited partnership's activities as or on behalf of a party having an interest adverse to the limited partnership; and

(3) to refrain from competing with the limited partnership in the conduct or winding up of the limited partnership's activities.

(c) A general partner's duty of care to the limited partnership and the other partners in the conduct and winding up of the limited partnership's activities is limited to refraining from engaging in grossly negligent or reckless conduct, intentional misconduct, or a knowing violation of law.

(d) A general partner shall discharge the duties to the partnership and the other partners under this [Act] or under the partnership agreement and exercise any rights consistently with the obligation of good faith and fair dealing.

(e) A general partner does not violate a duty or obligation under this [Act] or under the partnership agreement merely because the general partner's conduct furthers the general partner's own interest.

[ARTICLE] 5

CONTRIBUTIONS AND DISTRIBUTIONS

Section 501. Form of Contribution.
A contribution of a partner may consist of tangible or intangible property or other benefit to the limited partnership, including money, services performed, promissory notes, other agreements to contribute cash or property, and contracts for services to be performed.

Section 502. Liability for Contribution.

(a) A partner's obligation to contribute money or other property or other benefit to, or to perform services for, a limited partnership is not excused by the partner's death, disability, or other inability to perform personally.

(b) If a partner does not make a promised non-monetary contribution, the partner is obligated at the option of the limited partnership to contribute money equal to that portion of the value, as stated in the required information, of the stated contribution which has not been made.

(c) The obligation of a partner to make a contribution or return money or other property paid or distributed in violation of this [Act] may be compromised only by consent of all partners. A creditor of a limited partnership which extends credit or otherwise acts in reliance on an obligation described in subsection (a), without notice of any compromise under this subsection, may enforce the original obligation.

Section 503. Sharing of Distributions.
A distribution by a limited partnership must be shared among the partners on the basis of the value, as stated in the required records when the limited

partnership decides to make the distribution, of the contributions the limited partnership has received from each partner.

Section 504. Interim Distributions.

A partner does not have a right to any distribution before the dissolution and winding up of the limited partnership unless the limited partnership decides to make an interim distribution.

COMMENT

Under Section 406(a), the general partner or partners make this decision for the limited partnership.

Section 505. No Distribution On Account of Dissociation.

A person does not have a right to receive a distribution on account of dissociation.

Section 506. Distribution In Kind.

A partner does not have a right to demand or receive any distribution from a limited partnership in any form other than cash. Subject to Section 812(b), a limited partnership may distribute an asset in kind to the extent each partner receives a percentage of the asset equal to the partner's share of distributions.

Section 507. Right to Distribution.

When a partner or transferee becomes entitled to receive a distribution, the partner or transferee has the status of, and is entitled to all remedies available to, a creditor of the limited partnership with respect to the distribution. However, the limited partnership's obligation to make a distribution is subject to offset for any amount owed to the limited partnership by the partner or dissociated partner on whose account the distribution is made.

Section 508. Limitations On Distribution.

    (a) A limited partnership may not make a distribution in violation of the partnership agreement.

    (b) A limited partnership may not make a distribution if after the distribution:

        (1) the limited partnership would not be able to pay its debts as they become due in the ordinary course of the limited partnership's activities; or

        (2) the limited partnership's total assets would be less than the sum of its total liabilities plus the amount that would be needed, if the limited partnership were to be dissolved, wound up, and terminated at the time of the distribution, to satisfy the preferential rights upon dissolution, winding up, and termination of partners whose preferential rights are superior to those of persons receiving the distribution.

(c) A limited partnership may base a determination that a distribution is not prohibited under subsection (b) on financial statements prepared on the basis of accounting practices and principles that are reasonable in the circumstances or on a fair valuation or other method that is reasonable in the circumstances.

(d) Except as otherwise provided in subsection (g), the effect of a distribution under subsection (b) is measured:

    (1) in the case of distribution by purchase, redemption, or other acquisition of a transferable interest in the limited partnership, as of the date money or other property is transferred or debt incurred by the limited partnership; and

    (2) in all other cases, as of the date:

        (A) the distribution is authorized, if the payment occurs within 120 days after that date; or

        (B) the payment is made, if payment occurs more than 120 days after the distribution is authorized.

(e) A limited partnership's indebtedness to a partner incurred by reason of a distribution made in accordance with this section is at parity with the limited partnership's indebtedness to its general, unsecured creditors.

(f) A limited partnership's indebtedness, including indebtedness issued in connection with or as part of a distribution, is not considered a liability for purposes of subsection (b) if the terms of the indebtedness provide that payment of principal and interest are made only to the extent that a distribution could then be made to partners under this section.

(g) If indebtedness is issued as a distribution, each payment of principal or interest on the indebtedness is treated as a distribution, the effect of which is measured on the date the payment is made.

Section 509. Liability for Improper Distributions.

(a) A general partner that consents to a distribution made in violation of Section 508 is personally liable to the limited partnership for the amount of the distribution which exceeds the amount that could have been distributed without the violation if it is established that in consenting to the distribution the general partner failed to comply with Section 408.

(b) A partner or transferee that received a distribution knowing that the distribution to that partner or transferee was made in violation of Section 508 is personally liable to the limited partnership but only to the extent that the distribution received by the partner or transferee exceeded the amount that could have been properly paid under Section 508.

(c) A general partner against which an action is commenced under subsection (a) may:

   (1) implead in the action any other person that is liable under subsection (a) and compel contribution from the person; and

   (2) implead in the action any person that received a distribution in violation of subsection (b) and compel contribution from the person in the amount the person received in violation of subsection (b).

(d) An action under this section is barred if it is not commenced within two years after the distribution.

[ARTICLE] 6

DISSOCIATION

Section 601. Dissociation as Limited Partner.

(a) A person does not have a right to dissociate as a limited partner before the termination of the limited partnership.

(b) A person is dissociated from a limited partnership as a limited partner upon the occurrence of any of the following events:

   (1) the limited partnership's having notice of the person's express will to withdraw as a limited partner or on a later date specified by the person;

   (2) an event agreed to in the partnership agreement as causing the person's dissociation as a limited partner;

   (3) the person's expulsion as a limited partner pursuant to the partnership agreement;

   (4) the person's expulsion as a limited partner by the unanimous consent of the other partners if:

      (A) it is unlawful to carry on the limited partnership's activities with the person as a limited partner;

      (B) there has been a transfer of all of the person's transferable interest in the limited partnership, other than a transfer for security purposes, or a court order charging the person's interest, which has not been foreclosed;

      (C) the person is a corporation and, within 90 days after the limited partnership notifies the person that it will be expelled as a limited partner because it has filed a certificate of dissolution or the equivalent, its charter has been revoked, or its right to conduct business has been suspended by the jurisdiction of its incorporation, there is no revocation of the certificate of dissolution or no reinstatement of its charter or its right to conduct business; or

      (D) the person is a limited liability company or partnership that has been dissolved and whose business is being wound up;

(5) on application by the limited partnership, the person's expulsion as a limited partner by judicial order because:

    (A) the person engaged in wrongful conduct that adversely and materially affected the limited partnership's activities;

    (B) the person willfully or persistently committed a material breach of the partnership agreement or of the obligation of good faith and fair dealing under Section 305(b); or

    (C) the person engaged in conduct relating to the limited partnership's activities which makes it not reasonably practicable to carry on the activities with the person as limited partner;

(6) in the case of a person who is an individual, the person's death;

(7) in the case of a person that is a trust or is acting as a limited partner by virtue of being a trustee of a trust, distribution of the trust's entire transferable interest in the limited partnership, but not merely by reason of the substitution of a successor trustee;

(8) in the case of a person that is an estate or is acting as a limited partner by virtue of being a personal representative of an estate, distribution of the estate's entire transferable interest in the limited partnership, but not merely by reason of the substitution of a successor personal representative;

(9) termination of a limited partner that is not an individual, partnership, limited liability company, corporation, trust, or estate;

(10) the limited partnership's participation in a conversion or merger under [Article] 11, if the limited partnership:

    (A) is not the converted or surviving entity; or

    (B) is the converted or surviving entity but, as a result of the conversion or merger, the person ceases to be a limited partner.

Section 602. Effect of Dissociation as Limited Partner.

(a) Upon a person's dissociation as a limited partner:

    (1) subject to Section 704, the person does not have further rights as a limited partner;

    (2) the person's obligation of good faith and fair dealing as a limited partner under Section 305(b) continues only as to matters arising and events occurring before the dissociation; and

    (3) subject to Section 704 and [Article] 11, any transferable interest owned by the person in the person's capacity as a limited partner immediately before dissociation is owned by the person as a mere transferee.

(b) A person's dissociation as a limited partner does not of itself discharge the person from any obligation to the limited partnership or the other partners which the person incurred while a limited partner.

Section 603. Dissociation as General Partner.
A person is dissociated from a limited partnership as a general partner upon the occurrence of any of the following events:

(1) the limited partnership's having notice of the person's express will to withdraw as a general partner or on a later date specified by the person;

(2) an event agreed to in the partnership agreement as causing the person's dissociation as a general partner;

(3) the person's expulsion as a general partner pursuant to the partnership agreement;

(4) the person's expulsion as a general partner by the unanimous consent of the other partners if:

    (A) it is unlawful to carry on the limited partnership's activities with the person as a general partner;

    (B) there has been a transfer of all or substantially all of the person's transferable interest in the limited partnership, other than a transfer for security purposes, or a court order charging the person's interest, which has not been foreclosed;

    (C) the person is a corporation and, within 90 days after the limited partnership notifies the person that it will be expelled as a general partner because it has filed a certificate of dissolution or the equivalent, its charter has been revoked, or its right to conduct business has been suspended by the jurisdiction of its incorporation, there is no revocation of the certificate of dissolution or no reinstatement of its charter or its right to conduct business; or

    (D) the person is a limited liability company or partnership that has been dissolved and whose business is being wound up;

(5) on application by the limited partnership, the person's expulsion as a general partner by judicial determination because:

    (A) the person engaged in wrongful conduct that adversely and materially affected the limited partnership activities;

    (B) the person willfully or persistently committed a material breach of the partnership agreement or of a duty owed to the partnership or the other partners under Section 408; or

    (C) the person engaged in conduct relating to the limited partnership's activities which makes it not reasonably practicable to carry on the activities of the limited partnership with the person as a general partner;

(6) the person's:

    (A) becoming a debtor in bankruptcy;

    (B) execution of an assignment for the benefit of creditors;

    (C) seeking, consenting to, or acquiescing in the appointment of a trustee, receiver, or liquidator of the person or of all or substantially all of the person's property; or

(D) failure, within 90 days after the appointment, to have vacated or stayed the appointment of a trustee, receiver, or liquidator of the general partner or of all or substantially all of the person's property obtained without the person's consent or acquiescence, or failing within 90 days after the expiration of a stay to have the appointment vacated;

(7) in the case of a person who is an individual:

(A) the person's death;

(B) the appointment of a guardian or general conservator for the person; or

(C) a judicial determination that the person has otherwise become incapable of performing the person's duties as a general partner under the partnership agreement;

(8) in the case of a person that is a trust or is acting as a general partner by virtue of being a trustee of a trust, distribution of the trust's entire transferable interest in the limited partnership, but not merely by reason of the substitution of a successor trustee;

(9) in the case of a person that is an estate or is acting as a general partner by virtue of being a personal representative of an estate, distribution of the estate's entire transferable interest in the limited partnership, but not merely by reason of the substitution of a successor personal representative;

(10) termination of a general partner that is not an individual, partnership, limited liability company, corporation, trust, or estate; or

(11) the limited partnership's participation in a conversion or merger under [Article] 11, if the limited partnership:

(A) is not the converted or surviving entity; or

(B) is the converted or surviving entity but, as a result of the conversion or merger, the person ceases to be a general partner.

Section 604. Person's Power to Dissociate as General Partner; Wrongful Dissociation.

(a) A person has the power to dissociate as a general partner at any time, rightfully or wrongfully, by express will pursuant to Section 603(1).

(b) A person's dissociation as a general partner is wrongful only if:

(1) it is in breach of an express provision of the partnership agreement; or

(2) it occurs before the termination of the limited partnership, and:
   (A) the person withdraws as a general partner by express will;
   (B) the person is expelled as a general partner by judicial determination under Section 603(5);
   (C) the person is dissociated as a general partner by becoming a debtor in bankruptcy; or

    (D) in the case of a person that is not an individual, trust other than a business trust, or estate, the person is expelled or otherwise dissociated as a general partner because it willfully dissolved or terminated.

  (c) A person that wrongfully dissociates as a general partner is liable to the limited partnership and, subject to Section 1001, to the other partners for damages caused by the dissociation. The liability is in addition to any other obligation of the general partner to the limited partnership or to the other partners.

Section 605. Effect of Dissociation as General Partner.

  (a) Upon a person's dissociation as a general partner:

    (1) the person's right to participate as a general partner in the management and conduct of the partnership's activities terminates;

    (2) the person's duty of loyalty as a general partner under Section 408(b)(3) terminates;

    (3) the person's duty of loyalty as a general partner under Section 408(b)(1) and (2) and duty of care under Section 408(c) continue only with regard to matters arising and events occurring before the person's dissociation as a general partner;

    (4) the person may sign and deliver to the [Secretary of State] for filing a statement of dissociation pertaining to the person and, at the request of the limited partnership, shall sign an amendment to the certificate of limited partnership which states that the person has dissociated; and

    (5) subject to Section 704 and [Article] 11, any transferable interest owned by the person immediately before dissociation in the person's capacity as a general partner is owned by the person as a mere transferee.

  (b) A person's dissociation as a general partner does not of itself discharge the person from any obligation to the limited partnership or the other partners which the person incurred while a general partner.

Section 606. Power to Bind and Liability to Limited Partnership Before Dissolution of Partnership of Person Dissociated as General Partner.

  (a) After a person is dissociated as a general partner and before the limited partnership is dissolved, converted under [Article] 11, or merged out of existence under [Article 11], the limited partnership is bound by an act of the person only if:

    (1) the act would have bound the limited partnership under Section 402 before the dissociation; and

    (2) at the time the other party enters into the transaction:

      (A) less than two years has passed since the dissociation; and

      (B) the other party does not have notice of the dissociation and reasonably believes that the person is a general partner.

(b) If a limited partnership is bound under subsection (a), the person dissociated as a general partner which caused the limited partnership to be bound is liable:

    (1) to the limited partnership for any damage caused to the limited partnership arising from the obligation incurred under subsection (a); and

    (2) if a general partner or another person dissociated as a general partner is liable for the obligation, to the general partner or other person for any damage caused to the general partner or other person arising from the liability.

Section 607. Liability to Other Persons of Person Dissociated as General Partner.

(a) A person's dissociation as a general partner does not of itself discharge the person's liability as a general partner for an obligation of the limited partnership incurred before dissociation. Except as otherwise provided in subsections (b) and (c), the person is not liable for a limited partnership's obligation incurred after dissociation.

(b) A person whose dissociation as a general partner resulted in a dissolution and winding up of the limited partnership's activities is liable to the same extent as a general partner under Section 404 on an obligation incurred by the limited partnership under Section 804.

(c) A person that has dissociated as a general partner but whose dissociation did not result in a dissolution and winding up of the limited partnership's activities is liable on a transaction entered into by the limited partnership after the dissociation only if:

    (1) a general partner would be liable on the transaction; and

    (2) at the time the other party enters into the transaction:

      (A) less than two years has passed since the dissociation; and

      (B) the other party does not have notice of the dissociation and reasonably believes that the person is a general partner.

(d) By agreement with a creditor of a limited partnership and the limited partnership, a person dissociated as a general partner may be released from liability for an obligation of the limited partnership.

(e) A person dissociated as a general partner is released from liability for an obligation of the limited partnership if the limited partnership's creditor, with notice of the person's dissociation as a general partner but without the person's consent, agrees to a material alteration in the nature or time of payment of the obligation.

[ARTICLE] 7

TRANSFERABLE INTERESTS AND RIGHTS OF TRANSFEREES AND CREDITORS

Section 701. Partner's Transferable Interest.
The only interest of a partner which is transferable is the partner's transferable interest. A transferable interest is personal property.

Section 702. Transfer of Partner's Transferable Interest.

(a) A transfer, in whole or in part, of a partner's transferable interest:

   (1) is permissible;

   (2) does not by itself cause the partner's dissociation or a dissolution and winding up of the limited partnership's activities; and

   (3) does not, as against the other partners or the limited partnership, entitle the transferee to participate in the management or conduct of the limited partnership's activities, to require access to information concerning the limited partnership's transactions except as otherwise provided in subsection (c), or to inspect or copy the required information or the limited partnership's other records.

(b) A transferee has a right to receive, in accordance with the transfer:

   (1) distributions to which the transferor would otherwise be entitled; and

   (2) upon the dissolution and winding up of the limited partnership's activities the net amount otherwise distributable to the transferor.

(c) In a dissolution and winding up, a transferee is entitled to an account of the limited partnership's transactions only from the date of dissolution.

(d) Upon transfer, the transferor retains the rights of a partner other than the interest in distributions transferred and retains all duties and obligations of a partner.

(e) A limited partnership need not give effect to a transferee's rights under this section until the limited partnership has notice of the transfer.

(f) A transfer of a partner's transferable interest in the limited partnership in violation of a restriction on transfer contained in the partnership agreement is ineffective as to a person having notice of the restriction at the time of transfer.

(g) A transferee that becomes a partner with respect to a transferable interest is liable for the transferor's obligations under Sections 502 and 509. However, the transferee is not obligated for liabilities unknown to the transferee at the time the transferee became a partner.

Section 703. Rights of Creditor of Partner or Transferee.

(a) On application to a court of competent jurisdiction by any judgment creditor of a partner or transferee, the court may charge the transferable interest of the judgment debtor with payment of the unsatisfied amount of the judgment with interest. To the extent so charged, the judgment creditor has only the rights of a transferee. The court may appoint a receiver of the share of the distributions due or to become due to the judgment debtor in respect of the partnership and make all other orders, directions, accounts, and inquiries the judgment debtor might have made or which the circumstances of the case may require to give effect to the charging order.

(b) A charging order constitutes a lien on the judgment debtor's transferable interest. The court may order a foreclosure upon the interest subject to the charging order at any time. The purchaser at the foreclosure sale has the rights of a transferee.

(c) At any time before foreclosure, an interest charged may be redeemed:

   (1) by the judgment debtor;

   (2) with property other than limited partnership property, by one or more of the other partners; or

   (3) with limited partnership property, by the limited partnership with the consent of all partners whose interests are not so charged.

(d) This [Act] does not deprive any partner or transferee of the benefit of any exemption laws applicable to the partner's or transferee's transferable interest.

(e) This section provides the exclusive remedy by which a judgment creditor of a partner or transferee may satisfy a judgment out of the judgment debtor's transferable interest.

Section 704. Power of Estate of Deceased Partner.
If a partner dies, the deceased partner's personal representative or other legal representative may exercise the rights of a transferee as provided in Section 702 and, for the purposes of settling the estate, may exercise the rights of a current limited partner under Section 304.

[ARTICLE] 8

DISSOLUTION

Section 801. Nonjudicial Dissolution.
Except as otherwise provided in Section 802, a limited partnership is dissolved, and its activities must be wound up, only upon the occurrence of any of the following:

   (1) the happening of an event specified in the partnership agreement;

(2) the consent of all general partners and of limited partners owning a majority of the rights to receive distributions as limited partners at the time the consent is to be effective;

(3) after the dissociation of a person as a general partner:

(A) if the limited partnership has at least one remaining general partner, the consent to dissolve the limited partnership given within 90 days after the dissociation by partners owning a majority of the rights to receive distributions as partners at the time the consent is to be effective; or

(B) if the limited partnership does not have a remaining general partner, the passage of 90 days after the dissociation, unless before the end of the period:

(i) consent to continue the activities of the limited partnership and admit at least one general partner is given by limited partners owning a majority of the rights to receive distributions as limited partners at the time the consent is to be effective; and

(ii) at least one person is admitted as a general partner in accordance with the consent;

(4) the passage of 90 days after the dissociation of the limited partnership's last limited partner, unless before the end of the period the limited partnership admits at least one limited partner; or

(5) the signing and filing of a declaration of dissolution by the [Secretary of State] under Section 809(c).

Section 802. Judicial Dissolution.

On application by a partner the [appropriate court] may order dissolution of a limited partnership if it is not reasonably practicable to carry on the activities of the limited partnership in conformity with the partnership agreement.

Section 803. Winding Up.

(a) A limited partnership continues after dissolution only for the purpose of winding up its activities.

(b) In winding up its activities, the limited partnership:

(1) may amend its certificate of limited partnership to state that the limited partnership is dissolved, preserve the limited partnership business or property as a going concern for a reasonable time, prosecute and defend actions and proceedings, whether civil, criminal, or administrative, transfer the limited partnership's property, settle disputes by mediation or arbitration, file a statement of termination as provided in Section 203, and perform other necessary acts; and

(2) shall discharge the limited partnership's liabilities, settle and close the limited partnership's activities, and marshal and distribute the assets of the partnership.

(c) If a dissolved limited partnership does not have a general partner, a person to wind up the dissolved limited partnership's activities may be appointed by the consent of limited partners owning a majority of the rights to receive distributions as limited partners at the time the consent is to be effective. A person appointed under this subsection:

(1) has the powers of a general partner under Section 804; and

(2) shall promptly amend the certificate of limited partnership to state:

(A) that the limited partnership does not have a general partner;

(B) the name of the person that has been appointed to wind up the limited partnership; and

(C) the street and mailing address of the person.

(d) On the application of any partner, the [appropriate court] may order judicial supervision of the winding up, including the appointment of a person to wind up the dissolved limited partnership's activities, if:

(1) a limited partnership does not have a general partner and within a reasonable time following the dissolution no person has been appointed pursuant to subsection (c); or

(2) the applicant establishes other good cause.

Section 804. Power of General Partner and Person Dissociated as General Partner to Bind Partnership After Dissolution.

(a) A limited partnership is bound by a general partner's act after dissolution which:

(1) is appropriate for winding up the limited partnership's activities; or

(2) would have bound the limited partnership under Section 402 before dissolution, if, at the time the other party enters into the transaction, the other party does not have notice of the dissolution.

(b) A person dissociated as a general partner binds a limited partnership through an act occurring after dissolution if:

(1) at the time the other party enters into the transaction:

(A) less than two years has passed since the dissociation; and

(B) the other party does not have notice of the dissociation and reasonably believes that the person is a general partner; and

(2) the act:

(A) is appropriate for winding up the limited partnership's activities; or

(B) would have bound the limited partnership under Section 402 before dissolution and at the time the other party enters into the transaction the other party does not have notice of the dissolution.

Section 805. Liability After Dissolution of General Partner and Person Dissociated as General Partner to Limited Partnership, Other General Partners, and Persons Dissociated as General Partner.

(a) If a general partner having knowledge of the dissolution causes a limited partnership to incur an obligation under Section 804(a) by an act that is not appropriate for winding up the partnership's activities, the general partner is liable:

    (1) to the limited partnership for any damage caused to the limited partnership arising from the obligation; and

    (2) if another general partner or a person dissociated as a general partner is liable for the obligation, to that other general partner or person for any damage caused to that other general partner or person arising from the liability.

(b) If a person dissociated as a general partner causes a limited partnership to incur an obligation under Section 804(b), the person is liable:

    (1) to the limited partnership for any damage caused to the limited partnership arising from the obligation; and

    (2) if a general partner or another person dissociated as a general partner is liable for the obligation, to the general partner or other person for any damage caused to the general partner or other person arising from the liability.

Section 806. Known Claims Against Dissolved Limited Partnership.

(a) A dissolved limited partnership may dispose of the known claims against it by following the procedure described in subsection (b).

(b) A dissolved limited partnership may notify its known claimants of the dissolution in a record. The notice must:

    (1) specify the information required to be included in a claim;

    (2) provide a mailing address to which the claim is to be sent;

    (3) state the deadline for receipt of the claim, which may not be less than 120 days after the date the notice is received by the claimant;

    (4) state that the claim will be barred if not received by the deadline; and

    (5) unless the limited partnership has been throughout its existence a limited liability limited partnership, state that the barring of a claim against the limited partnership will also bar any corresponding claim against any general partner or person dissociated as a general partner which is based on Section 404.

(c) A claim against a dissolved limited partnership is barred if the requirements of subsection (b) are met and:

    (1) the claim is not received by the specified deadline; or

(2) in the case of a claim that is timely received but rejected by the dissolved limited partnership, the claimant does not commence an action to enforce the claim against the limited partnership within 90 days after the receipt of the notice of the rejection.

(d) This section does not apply to a claim based on an event occurring after the effective date of dissolution or a liability that is contingent on that date.

Section 807. Other Claims Against Dissolved Limited Partnership.

(a) A dissolved limited partnership may publish notice of its dissolution and request persons having claims against the limited partnership to present them in accordance with the notice.

(b) The notice must:

(1) be published at least once in a newspaper of general circulation in the [county] in which the dissolved limited partnership's principal office is located or, if it has none in this State, in the [county] in which the limited partnership's designated office is or was last located;

(2) describe the information required to be contained in a claim and provide a mailing address to which the claim is to be sent;

(3) state that a claim against the limited partnership is barred unless an action to enforce the claim is commenced within five years after publication of the notice; and

(4) unless the limited partnership has been throughout its existence a limited liability limited partnership, state that the barring of a claim against the limited partnership will also bar any corresponding claim against any general partner or person dissociated as a general partner which is based on Section 404.

(c) If a dissolved limited partnership publishes a notice in accordance with subsection (b), the claim of each of the following claimants is barred unless the claimant commences an action to enforce the claim against the dissolved limited partnership within five years after the publication date of the notice:

(1) a claimant that did not receive notice in a record under Section 806;

(2) a claimant whose claim was timely sent to the dissolved limited partnership but not acted on; and

(3) a claimant whose claim is contingent or based on an event occurring after the effective date of dissolution.

(d) A claim not barred under this section may be enforced:

(1) against the dissolved limited partnership, to the extent of its undistributed assets;

(2) if the assets have been distributed in liquidation, against a partner or transferee to the extent of that person's proportionate share of the claim or the limited partnership's assets distributed to the partner or transferee in liquidation, whichever is less, but a person's total liability for all claims under this paragraph does not exceed the total amount of assets distributed to the person as part of the winding up of the dissolved limited partnership; or

(3) against any person liable on the claim under Section 404.

Section 808. Liability of General Partner and Person Dissociated as General Partner When Claim Against Limited Partnership Barred.

If a claim against a dissolved limited partnership is barred under Section 806 or 807, any corresponding claim under Section 404 is also barred.

Section 809. Administrative Dissolution.

(a) The [Secretary of State] may dissolve a limited partnership administratively if the limited partnership does not, within 60 days after the due date:

    (1) pay any fee, tax, or penalty due to the [Secretary of State] under this [Act] or other law; or

    (2) deliver its annual report to the [Secretary of State].

(b) If the [Secretary of State] determines that a ground exists for administratively dissolving a limited partnership, the [Secretary of State] shall file a record of the determination and serve the limited partnership with a copy of the filed record.

(c) If within 60 days after service of the copy the limited partnership does not correct each ground for dissolution or demonstrate to the reasonable satisfaction of the [Secretary of State] that each ground determined by the [Secretary of State] does not exist, the [Secretary of State] shall administratively dissolve the limited partnership by preparing, signing and filing a declaration of dissolution that states the grounds for dissolution. The [Secretary of State] shall serve the limited partnership with a copy of the filed declaration.

(d) A limited partnership administratively dissolved continues its existence but may carry on only activities necessary to wind up its activities and liquidate its assets under Sections 803 and 812 and to notify claimants under Sections 806 and 807.

(e) The administrative dissolution of a limited partnership does not terminate the authority of its agent for service of process.

Section 810. Reinstatement Following Administrative Dissolution.

(a) A limited partnership that has been administratively dissolved may apply to the [Secretary of State] for reinstatement within two years after the effective date of dissolution. The application must be delivered to the [Secretary of State] for filing and state:

(1) the name of the limited partnership and the effective date of its administrative dissolution;

(2) that the grounds for dissolution either did not exist or have been eliminated; and

(3) that the limited partnership's name satisfies the requirements of Section 108.

(b) If the [Secretary of State] determines that an application contains the information required by subsection (a) and that the information is correct, the [Secretary of State] shall prepare a declaration of reinstatement that states this determination, sign, and file the original of the declaration of reinstatement, and serve the limited partnership with a copy.

(c) When reinstatement becomes effective, it relates back to and takes effect as of the effective date of the administrative dissolution and the limited partnership may resume its activities as if the administrative dissolution had never occurred.

Section 811. Appeal from Denial of Reinstatement.

(a) If the [Secretary of State] denies a limited partnership's application for reinstatement following administrative dissolution, the [Secretary of State] shall prepare, sign and file a notice that explains the reason or reasons for denial and serve the limited partnership with a copy of the notice.

(b) Within 30 days after service of the notice of denial, the limited partnership may appeal from the denial of reinstatement by petitioning the [appropriate court] to set aside the dissolution. The petition must be served on the [Secretary of State] and contain a copy of the [Secretary of State's] declaration of dissolution, the limited partnership's application for reinstatement, and the [Secretary of State's] notice of denial.

(c) The court may summarily order the [Secretary of State] to reinstate the dissolved limited partnership or may take other action the court considers appropriate.

Section 812. Disposition of Assets; When Contributions Required.

(a) In winding up a limited partnership's activities, the assets of the limited partnership, including the contributions required by this section, must be applied to satisfy the limited partnership's obligations to creditors, including, to the extent permitted by law, partners that are creditors.

(b) Any surplus remaining after the limited partnership complies with subsection (a) must be paid in cash as a distribution.

(c) If a limited partnership's assets are insufficient to satisfy all of its obligations under subsection (a), with respect to each unsatisfied obligation incurred when the limited partnership was not a limited liability limited partnership, the following rules apply:

(1) Each person that was a general partner when the obligation was incurred and that has not been released from the obligation under Section 607 shall contribute to the limited partnership for the purpose of enabling the limited partnership to satisfy the obligation. The contribution due from each of those persons is in proportion to the right to receive distributions in the capacity of general partner in effect for each of those persons when the obligation was incurred.

(2) If a person does not contribute the full amount required under paragraph (1) with respect to an unsatisfied obligation of the limited partnership, the other persons required to contribute by paragraph (1) on account of the obligation shall contribute the additional amount necessary to discharge the obligation. The additional contribution due from each of those other persons is in proportion to the right to receive distributions in the capacity of general partner in effect for each of those other persons when the obligation was incurred.

(3) If a person does not make the additional contribution required by paragraph (2), further additional contributions are determined and due in the same manner as provided in that paragraph.

(d) A person that makes an additional contribution under subsection (c)(2) or (3) may recover from any person whose failure to contribute under subsection (c)(1) or (2) necessitated the additional contribution. A person may not recover under this subsection more than the amount additionally contributed. A person's liability under this subsection may not exceed the amount the person failed to contribute.

(e) The estate of a deceased individual is liable for the person's obligations under this section.

(f) An assignee for the benefit of creditors of a limited partnership or a partner, or a person appointed by a court to represent creditors of a limited partnership or a partner, may enforce a person's obligation to contribute under subsection (c).

[ARTICLE] 9

FOREIGN LIMITED PARTNERSHIPS

Section 901. Governing Law.

(a) The laws of the State or other jurisdiction under which a foreign limited partnership is organized govern relations among the partners of the foreign limited partnership and between the partners and the foreign limited partnership and the liability of partners as partners for an obligation of the foreign limited partnership.

(b) A foreign limited partnership may not be denied a certificate of authority by reason of any difference between the laws of the jurisdiction under which the foreign limited partnership is organized and the laws of this State.

(c) A certificate of authority does not authorize a foreign limited partnership to engage in any business or exercise any power that a limited partnership may not engage in or exercise in this State.

Section 902. Application for Certificate of Authority.

(a) A foreign limited partnership may apply for a certificate of authority to transact business in this State by delivering an application to the [Secretary of State] for filing. The application must state:

(1) the name of the foreign limited partnership and, if the name does not comply with Section 108, an alternate name adopted pursuant to Section 905(a).

(2) the name of the State or other jurisdiction under whose law the foreign limited partnership is organized;

(3) the street and mailing address of the foreign limited partnership's principal office and, if the laws of the jurisdiction under which the foreign limited partnership is organized require the foreign limited partnership to maintain an office in that jurisdiction, the street and mailing address of the required office;

(4) the name and street and mailing address of the foreign limited partnership's initial agent for service of process in this State;

(5) the name and street and mailing address of each of the foreign limited partnership's general partners; and

(6) whether the foreign limited partnership is a foreign limited liability limited partnership.

(b) A foreign limited partnership shall deliver with the completed application a certificate of existence or a record of similar import signed by the [Secretary of State] or other official having custody of the foreign limited partnership's publicly filed records in the State or other jurisdiction under whose law the foreign limited partnership is organized.

Section 903. Activities Not Constituting Transacting Business.

(a) Activities of a foreign limited partnership which do not constitute transacting business in this State within the meaning of this [article] include:

(1) maintaining, defending, and settling an action or proceeding;

(2) holding meetings of its partners or carrying on any other activity concerning its internal affairs;

(3) maintaining accounts in financial institutions;

(4) maintaining offices or agencies for the transfer, exchange, and registration of the foreign limited partnership's own securities or maintaining trustees or depositories with respect to those securities;

(5) selling through independent contractors;

(6) soliciting or obtaining orders, whether by mail or electronic means or through employees or agents or otherwise, if the orders require acceptance outside this State before they become contracts;

(7) creating or acquiring indebtedness, mortgages, or security interests in real or personal property;

(8) securing or collecting debts or enforcing mortgages or other security interests in property securing the debts, and holding, protecting, and maintaining property so acquired;

(9) conducting an isolated transaction that is completed within 30 days and is not one in the course of similar transactions of a like manner; and

(10) transacting business in interstate commerce.

(b) For purposes of this [article], the ownership in this State of income-producing real property or tangible personal property, other than property excluded under subsection (a), constitutes transacting business in this State.

(c) This section does not apply in determining the contacts or activities that may subject a foreign limited partnership to service of process, taxation, or regulation under any other law of this State.

Section 904. Filing of Certificate of Authority.

Unless the [Secretary of State] determines that an application for a certificate of authority does not comply with the filing requirements of this [Act], the [Secretary of State], upon payment of all filing fees, shall file the application, prepare, sign and file a certificate of authority to transact business in this State, and send a copy of the filed certificate, together with a receipt for the fees, to the foreign limited partnership or its representative.

Section 905. Noncomplying Name of Foreign Limited Partnership.

(a) A foreign limited partnership whose name does not comply with Section 108 may not obtain a certificate of authority until it adopts, for the purpose of transacting business in this State, an alternate name that complies with Section 108. A foreign limited partnership that adopts an alternate name under this subsection and then obtains a certificate of authority with the name need not comply with [fictitious name statute]. After obtaining a certificate of authority with an alternate name, a foreign limited partnership shall transact business in this

State under the name unless the foreign limited partnership is authorized under [fictitious name statute] to transact business in this State under another name.

(b) If a foreign limited partnership authorized to transact business in this State changes its name to one that does not comply with Section 108, it may not thereafter transact business in this State until it complies with subsection (a) and obtains an amended certificate of authority.

Section 906. Revocation of Certificate of Authority.

(a) A certificate of authority of a foreign limited partnership to transact business in this State may be revoked by the [Secretary of State] in the manner provided in subsections (b) and (c) if the foreign limited partnership does not:

(1) pay, within 60 days after the due date, any fee, tax or penalty due to the [Secretary of State] under this [Act] or other law;

(2) deliver, within 60 days after the due date, its annual report required under Section 210;

(3) appoint and maintain an agent for service of process as required by Section 114(b); or

(4) deliver for filing a statement of a change under Section 115 within 30 days after a change has occurred in the name or address of the agent.

(b) In order to revoke a certificate of authority, the [Secretary of State] must prepare, sign, and file a notice of revocation and send a copy to the foreign limited partnership's agent for service of process in this State, or if the foreign limited partnership does not appoint and maintain a proper agent in this State, to the foreign limited partnership's designated office. The notice must state:

(1) the revocation's effective date, which must be at least 60 days after the date the [Secretary of State] sends the copy; and

(2) the foreign limited partnership's failures to comply with subsection (a) which are the reason for the revocation.

(c) The authority of the foreign limited partnership to transact business in this State ceases on the effective date of the notice of revocation unless before that date the foreign limited partnership cures each failure to comply with subsection (a) stated in the notice. If the foreign limited partnership cures the failures, the [Secretary of State] shall so indicate on the filed notice.

Section 907. Cancellation of Certificate of Authority; Effect of Failure to Have Certificate.

(a) In order to cancel its certificate of authority to transact business in this State, a foreign limited partnership must deliver to the [Secretary of

State] for filing a notice of cancellation. The certificate is canceled when the notice becomes effective under Section 206.

(b) A foreign limited partnership transacting business in this State may not maintain an action or proceeding in this State unless it has a certificate of authority to transact business in this State.

(c) The failure of a foreign limited partnership to have a certificate of authority to transact business in this State does not impair the validity of a contract or act of the foreign limited partnership or prevent the foreign limited partnership from defending an action or proceeding in this State.

(d) A partner of a foreign limited partnership is not liable for the obligations of the foreign limited partnership solely by reason of the foreign limited partnership's having transacted business in this State without a certificate of authority.

(e) If a foreign limited partnership transacts business in this State without a certificate of authority or cancels its certificate of authority, it appoints the [Secretary of State] as its agent for service of process for rights of action arising out of the transaction of business in this State.

Section 908. Action by [Attorney General].
The [Attorney General] may maintain an action to restrain a foreign limited partnership from transacting business in this State in violation of this [article].

[ARTICLE] 10

ACTIONS BY PARTNERS

Section 1001. Direct Action by Partner.

(a) Subject to subsection (b), a partner may maintain a direct action against the limited partnership or another partner for legal or equitable relief, with or without an accounting as to the partnership's activities, to enforce the rights and otherwise protect the interests of the partner, including rights and interests under the partnership agreement or this [Act] or arising independently of the partnership relationship.

(b) A partner commencing a direct action under this section is required to plead and prove an actual or threatened injury that is not solely the result of an injury suffered or threatened to be suffered by the limited partnership.

(c) The accrual of, and any time limitation on, a right of action for a remedy under this section is governed by other law. A right to an accounting upon a dissolution and winding up does not revive a claim barred by law.

Section 1002. Derivative Action.

A partner may maintain a derivative action to enforce a right of a limited partnership if:

(1) the partner first makes a demand on the general partners, requesting that they cause the limited partnership to bring an action to enforce the right, and the general partners do not bring the action within a reasonable time; or

(2) a demand would be futile.

Section 1003. Proper Plaintiff.

A derivative action may be maintained only by a person that is a partner at the time the action is commenced and:

(1) that was a partner when the conduct giving rise to the action occurred; or

(2) whose status as a partner devolved upon the person by operation of law or pursuant to the terms of the partnership agreement from a person that was a partner at the time of the conduct.

Section 1004. Pleading.

In a derivative action, the complaint must state with particularity:

(1) the date and content of plaintiff's demand and the general partners' response to the demand; or

(2) why demand should be excused as futile.

Section 1005. Proceeds and Expenses.

(a) Except as otherwise provided in subsection (b):

(1) any proceeds or other benefits of a derivative action, whether by judgment, compromise, or settlement, belong to the limited partnership and not to the derivative plaintiff;

(2) if the derivative plaintiff receives any proceeds, the derivative plaintiff shall immediately remit them to the limited partnership.

(b) If a derivative action is successful in whole or in part, the court may award the plaintiff reasonable expenses, including reasonable attorney's fees, from the recovery of the limited partnership.

[ARTICLE] 11

CONVERSION AND MERGER

Section 1101. Definitions.

In this [article]:

(1) "Constituent limited partnership" means a constituent organization that is a limited partnership.

(2) "Constituent organization" means an organization that is party to a merger.

(3) "Converted organization" means the organization into which a converting organization converts pursuant to Sections 1102 through 1105.

(4) "Converting limited partnership" means a converting organization that is a limited partnership.

(5) "Converting organization" means an organization that converts into another organization pursuant to Section 1102.

(6) "General partner" means a general partner of a limited partnership.

(7) "Governing statute" of an organization means the statute that governs the organization's internal affairs.

(8) "Organization" means a general partnership, including a limited liability partnership; limited partnership, including a limited liability limited partnership; limited liability company; business trust; corporation; or any other person having a governing statute. The term includes domestic and foreign organizations whether or not organized for profit.

(9) "Organizational documents" means:

    (A) for a domestic or foreign general partnership, its partnership agreement;

    (B) for a limited partnership or foreign limited partnership, its certificate of limited partnership and partnership agreement;

    (C) for a domestic or foreign limited liability company, its articles of organization and operating agreement, or comparable records as provided in its governing statute;

    (D) for a business trust, its agreement of trust and declaration of trust;

    (E) for a domestic or foreign corporation for profit, its articles of incorporation, bylaws, and other agreements among its shareholders which are authorized by its governing statute, or comparable records as provided in its governing statute; and

    (F) for any other organization, the basic records that create the organization and determine its internal governance and the relations among the persons that own it, have an interest in it, or are members of it.

(10) "Personal liability" means personal liability for a debt, liability, or other obligation of an organization which is imposed on a person that co-owns, has an interest in, or is a member of the organization:

    (A) by the organization's governing statute solely by reason of the person co-owning, having an interest in, or being a member of the organization; or

    (B) by the organization's organizational documents under a provision of the organization's governing statute authorizing those documents to make one or more specified persons liable for all or specified debts, liabilities, and other obligations of the organization solely by reason of the person or persons co-owning, having an interest in, or being a member of the organization.

(11) "Surviving organization" means an organization into which one or more other organizations are merged. A surviving organization may preexist the merger or be created by the merger.

Section 1102. Conversion.

(a) An organization other than a limited partnership may convert to a limited partnership, and a limited partnership may convert to another organization pursuant to this section and Sections 1103 through 1105 and a plan of conversion, if:

(1) the other organization's governing statute authorizes the conversion;

(2) the conversion is not prohibited by the law of the jurisdiction that enacted the governing statute; and

(3) the other organization complies with its governing statute in effecting the conversion.

(b) A plan of conversion must be in a record and must include:

(1) the name and form of the organization before conversion;

(2) the name and form of the organization after conversion; and

(3) the terms and conditions of the conversion, including the manner and basis for converting interests in the converting organization into any combination of money, interests in the converted organization, and other consideration; and

(4) the organizational documents of the converted organization.

Section 1103. Action On Plan of Conversion by Converting Limited Partnership.

(a) Subject to Section 1110, a plan of conversion must be consented to by all the partners of a converting limited partnership.

(b) Subject to Section 1110 and any contractual rights, after a conversion is approved, and at any time before a filing is made under Section 1104, a converting limited partnership may amend the plan or abandon the planned conversion:

(1) as provided in the plan; and

(2) except as prohibited by the plan, by the same consent as was required to approve the plan.

Section 1104. Filings Required for Conversion; Effective Date.

(a) After a plan of conversion is approved:

(1) a converting limited partnership shall deliver to the [Secretary of State] for filing articles of conversion, which must include:

(A) a statement that the limited partnership has been converted into another organization;

(B) the name and form of the organization and the jurisdiction of its governing statute;

(C) the date the conversion is effective under the governing statute of the converted organization;

(D) a statement that the conversion was approved as required by this [Act];

(E) a statement that the conversion was approved as required by the governing statute of the converted organization; and

(F) if the converted organization is a foreign organization not authorized to transact business in this State, the street and mailing address of an office which the [Secretary of State] may use for the purposes of Section 1105(c); and

(2) if the converting organization is not a converting limited partnership, the converting organization shall deliver to the [Secretary of State] for filing a certificate of limited partnership, which must include, in addition to the information required by Section 201:

(A) a statement that the limited partnership was converted from another organization;

(B) the name and form of the organization and the jurisdiction of its governing statute; and

(C) a statement that the conversion was approved in a manner that complied with the organization's governing statute.

(b) A conversion becomes effective:

(1) if the converted organization is a limited partnership, when the certificate of limited partnership takes effect; and

(2) if the converted organization is not a limited partnership, as provided by the governing statute of the converted organization.

Section 1105. Effect of Conversion.

(a) An organization that has been converted pursuant to this [article] is for all purposes the same entity that existed before the conversion.

(b) When a conversion takes effect:

(1) all property owned by the converting organization remains vested in the converted organization;

(2) all debts, liabilities, and other obligations of the converting organization continue as obligations of the converted organization;

(3) an action or proceeding pending by or against the converting organization may be continued as if the conversion had not occurred;

(4) except as prohibited by other law, all of the rights, privileges, immunities, powers, and purposes of the converting organization remain vested in the converted organization;

(5) except as otherwise provided in the plan of conversion, the terms and conditions of the plan of conversion take effect; and

(6) except as otherwise agreed, the conversion does not dissolve a converting limited partnership for the purposes of [Article] 8.

(c) A converted organization that is a foreign organization consents to the jurisdiction of the courts of this State to enforce any obligation owed by the converting limited partnership, if before the conversion the converting limited partnership was subject to suit in this State on the obligation. A converted organization that is a foreign organization and not authorized to transact business in this State appoints the [Secretary of State] as its agent for service of process for purposes of enforcing an obligation under this subsection. Service on the [Secretary of State] under this subsection is made in the same manner and with the same consequences as in Section 117(c) and (d).

Section 1106. Merger.

(a) A limited partnership may merge with one or more other constituent organizations pursuant to this section and Sections 1107 through 1109 and a plan of merger, if:

(1) the governing statute of each the other organizations authorizes the merger;

(2) the merger is not prohibited by the law of a jurisdiction that enacted any of those governing statutes; and

(3) each of the other organizations complies with its governing statute in effecting the merger.

(b) A plan of merger must be in a record and must include:

(1) the name and form of each constituent organization;

(2) the name and form of the surviving organization and, if the surviving organization is to be created by the merger, a statement to that effect;

(3) the terms and conditions of the merger, including the manner and basis for converting the interests in each constituent organization into any combination of money, interests in the surviving organization, and other consideration;

(4) if the surviving organization is to be created by the merger, the surviving organization's organizational documents; and

(5) if the surviving organization is not to be created by the merger, any amendments to be made by the merger to the surviving organization's organizational documents.

Section 1107. Action On Plan of Merger by Constituent Limited Partnership.

(a) Subject to Section 1110, a plan of merger must be consented to by all the partners of a constituent limited partnership.

(b) Subject to Section 1110 and any contractual rights, after a merger is approved, and at any time before a filing is made under Section 1108, a constituent limited partnership may amend the plan or abandon the planned merger:

   (1) as provided in the plan; and

   (2) except as prohibited by the plan, with the same consent as was required to approve the plan.

Section 1108. Filings Required for Merger; Effective Date.

(a) After each constituent organization has approved a merger, articles of merger must be signed on behalf of:

   (1) each preexisting constituent limited partnership, by each general partner listed in the certificate of limited partnership; and

   (2) each other preexisting constituent organization, by an authorized representative.

(b) The articles of merger must include:

   (1) the name and form of each constituent organization and the jurisdiction of its governing statute;

   (2) the name and form of the surviving organization, the jurisdiction of its governing statute, and, if the surviving organization is created by the merger, a statement to that effect;

   (3) the date the merger is effective under the governing statute of the surviving organization;

   (4) if the surviving organization is to be created by the merger:
      (A) if it will be a limited partnership, the limited partnership's certificate of limited partnership; or
      (B) if it will be an organization other than a limited partnership, the organizational document that creates the organization;

   (5) if the surviving organization preexists the merger, any amendments provided for in the plan of merger for the organizational document that created the organization;

   (6) a statement as to each constituent organization that the merger was approved as required by the organization's governing statute;

   (7) if the surviving organization is a foreign organization not authorized to transact business in this State, the street and mailing address of an office which the [Secretary of State] may use for the purposes of Section 1109(b); and

   (8) any additional information required by the governing statute of any constituent organization.

(c) Each constituent limited partnership shall deliver the articles of merger for filing in the [office of the Secretary of State].

(d) A merger becomes effective under this [article]:

    (1) if the surviving organization is a limited partnership, upon the later of:

        (i) compliance with subsection (c); or

        (ii) subject to Section 206(c), as specified in the articles of merger; or

    (2) if the surviving organization is not a limited partnership, as provided by the governing statute of the surviving organization.

Section 1109. Effect of Merger.

(a) When a merger becomes effective:

    (1) the surviving organization continues or comes into existence;

    (2) each constituent organization that merges into the surviving organization ceases to exist as a separate entity;

    (3) all property owned by each constituent organization that ceases to exist vests in the surviving organization;

    (4) all debts, liabilities, and other obligations of each constituent organization that ceases to exist continue as obligations of the surviving organization;

    (5) an action or proceeding pending by or against any constituent organization that ceases to exist may be continued as if the merger had not occurred;

    (6) except as prohibited by other law, all of the rights, privileges, immunities, powers, and purposes of each constituent organization that ceases to exist vest in the surviving organization;

    (7) except as otherwise provided in the plan of merger, the terms and conditions of the plan of merger take effect; and

    (8) except as otherwise agreed, if a constituent limited partnership ceases to exist, the merger does not dissolve the limited partnership for the purposes of [Article] 8;

    (9) if the surviving organization is created by the merger:

        (A) if it is a limited partnership, the certificate of limited partnership becomes effective; or

        (B) if it is an organization other than a limited partnership, the organizational document that creates the organization becomes effective; and

    (10) if the surviving organization preexists the merger, any amendments provided for in the articles of merger for the organizational document that created the organization become effective.

(b) A surviving organization that is a foreign organization consents to the jurisdiction of the courts of this State to enforce any obligation owed by a constituent organization, if before the merger the constituent organization was subject to suit in this State on the obligation. A surviving organization that is a foreign organization and not authorized to transact business in this State appoints the [Secretary of State] as its agent for service of process for the purposes of enforcing an obligation under this subsection. Service on the [Secretary of State] under this subsection is made in the same manner and with the same consequences as in Section 117(c) and (d).

Section 1110. Restrictions on Approval of Conversions and Mergers and on Relinquishing LLLP Status.

(a) If a partner of a converting or constituent limited partnership will have personal liability with respect to a converted or surviving organization, approval and amendment of a plan of conversion or merger are ineffective without the consent of the partner, unless:

(1) the limited partnership's partnership agreement provides for the approval of the conversion or merger with the consent of fewer than all the partners; and

(2) the partner has consented to the provision of the partnership agreement.

(b) An amendment to a certificate of limited partnership which deletes a statement that the limited partnership is a limited liability limited partnership is ineffective without the consent of each general partner unless:

(1) the limited partnership's partnership agreement provides for the amendment with the consent of less than all the general partners; and

(2) each general partner that does not consent to the amendment has consented to the provision of the partnership agreement.

(c) A partner does not give the consent required by subsection (a) or (b) merely by consenting to a provision of the partnership agreement which permits the partnership agreement to be amended with the consent of fewer than all the partners.

Section 1111. Liability of General Partner after Conversion or Merger.

(a) A conversion or merger under this [article] does not discharge any liability under Sections 404 and 607 of a person that was a general partner in or dissociated as a general partner from a converting or constituent limited partnership, but:

(1) the provisions of this [Act] pertaining to the collection or discharge of the liability continue to apply to the liability;

(2) for the purposes of applying those provisions, the converted or surviving organization is deemed to be the converting or constituent limited partnership; and

(3) if a person is required to pay any amount under this subsection:

    (A) the person has a right of contribution from each other person that was liable as a general partner under Section 404 when the obligation was incurred and has not been released from the obligation under Section 607; and

    (B) the contribution due from each of those persons is in proportion to the right to receive distributions in the capacity of general partner in effect for each of those persons when the obligation was incurred.

(b) In addition to any other liability provided by law:

(1) a person that immediately before a conversion or merger became effective was a general partner in a converting or constituent limited partnership that was not a limited liability limited partnership is personally liable for each obligation of the converted or surviving organization arising from a transaction with a third party after the conversion or merger becomes effective, if, at the time the third party enters into the transaction, the third party:

(A) does not have notice of the conversion or merger; and

(B) reasonably believes that:

    (i) the converted or surviving business is the converting or constituent limited partnership;

    (ii) the converting or constituent limited partnership is not a limited liability limited partnership; and

    (iii) the person is a general partner in the converting or constituent limited partnership; and

(2) a person that was dissociated as a general partner from a converting or constituent limited partnership before the conversion or merger became effective is personally liable for each obligation of the converted or surviving organization arising from a transaction with a third party after the conversion or merger becomes effective, if:

(A) immediately before the conversion or merger became effective the converting or surviving limited partnership was a not a limited liability limited partnership; and

(B) at the time the third party enters into the transaction less than two years have passed since the person dissociated as a general partner and the third party:

    (i) does not have notice of the dissociation;

    (ii) does not have notice of the conversion or merger; and

    (iii) reasonably believes that the converted or surviving organization is the converting or constituent limited partnership, the converting or constituent limited partnership is not a limited liability limited partnership, and the person is a general partner in the converting or constituent limited partnership.

Section 1112. Power of General Partners and Persons Dissociated as General Partners to Bind Organization after Conversion or Merger.

(a) An act of a person that immediately before a conversion or merger became effective was a general partner in a converting or constituent limited partnership binds the converted or surviving organization after the conversion or merger becomes effective, if:

    (1) before the conversion or merger became effective, the act would have bound the converting or constituent limited partnership under Section 402; and

    (2) at the time the third party enters into the transaction, the third party:

        (A) does not have notice of the conversion or merger; and

        (B) reasonably believes that the converted or surviving business is the converting or constituent limited partnership and that the person is a general partner in the converting or constituent limited partnership.

(b) An act of a person that before a conversion or merger became effective was dissociated as a general partner from a converting or constituent limited partnership binds the converted or surviving organization after the conversion or merger becomes effective, if:

    (1) before the conversion or merger became effective, the act would have bound the converting or constituent limited partnership under Section 402 if the person had been a general partner; and

    (2) at the time the third party enters into the transaction, less than two years have passed since the person dissociated as a general partner and the third party:

        (A) does not have notice of the dissociation;

        (B) does not have notice of the conversion or merger; and

        (C) reasonably believes that the converted or surviving organization is the converting or constituent limited partnership and that the person is a general partner in the converting or constituent limited partnership.

(c) If a person having knowledge of the conversion or merger causes a converted or surviving organization to incur an obligation under subsection (a) or (b), the person is liable:

    (1) to the converted or surviving organization for any damage caused to the organization arising from the obligation; and

    (2) if another person is liable for the obligation, to that other person for any damage caused to that other person arising from the liability.

Section 1113. [Article] Not Exclusive.
This [article] does not preclude an entity from being converted or merged under other law.

[ARTICLE] 12

MISCELLANEOUS PROVISIONS

Section 1201. Uniformity of Application and Construction.
In applying and construing this Uniform Act, consideration must be given to the need to promote uniformity of the law with respect to its subject matter among States that enact it.

Section 1202. Severability Clause.
If any provision of this [Act] or its application to any person or circumstance is held invalid, the invalidity does not affect other provisions or applications of this [Act] which can be given effect without the invalid provision or application, and to this end the provisions of this [Act] are severable.

Section 1203. Relation to Electronic Signatures In Global and National Commerce Act.
This [Act] modifies, limits, or supersedes the federal Electronic Signatures in Global and National Commerce Act, 15 U.S.C. Section 7001 et seq., but this [Act] does not modify, limit, or supersede Section 101(c) of that Act or authorize electronic delivery of any of the notices described in Section 103(b) of that Act.

Section 1204. Effective Date.
This [Act] takes effect [effective date].

Section 1205. Repeals.
Effective [all-inclusive date] , the following acts and parts of acts are repealed: [the State Limited Partnership Act as amended and in effect immediately before the effective date of this [Act]].

Section 1206. Application to Existing Relationships.
- (a) Before [all-inclusive date], this [Act] governs only:
  - (1) a limited partnership formed on or after [the effective date of this [Act]]; and
  - (2) except as otherwise provided in subsections (c) and (d), a limited partnership formed before [the effective date of this [Act]] which elects, in the manner provided in its partnership agreement or by law for amending the partnership agreement, to be subject to this [Act].
- (b) Except as otherwise provided in subsection (c), on and after [all-inclusive date] this [Act] governs all limited partnerships.
- (c) With respect to a limited partnership formed before [the effective date of this [Act]], the following rules apply except as the partners otherwise elect in the manner provided in the partnership agreement or by law for amending the partnership agreement:

(1) Section 104(c) does not apply and the limited partnership has whatever duration it had under the law applicable immediately before [the effective date of this [Act]].

(2) the limited partnership is not required to amend its certificate of limited partnership to comply with Section 201(a)(4).

(3) Sections 601 and 602 do not apply and a limited partner has the same right and power to dissociate from the limited partnership, with the same consequences, as existed immediately before [the effective date of this [Act].

(4) Section 603(4) does not apply.

(5) Section 603(5) does not apply and a court has the same power to expel a general partner as the court had immediately before [the effective date of this [Act]].

(6) Section 801(3) does not apply and the connection between a person's dissociation as a general partner and the dissolution of the limited partnership is the same as existed immediately before [the effective date of this [Act]].

(d) With respect to a limited partnership that elects pursuant to subsection (a)(2) to be subject to this [Act], after the election takes effect the provisions of this [Act] relating to the liability of the limited partnership's general partners to third parties apply:

(1) before [all-inclusive date], to:

(A) a third party that had not done business with the limited partnership in the year before the election took effect; and

(B) a third party that had done business with the limited partnership in the year before the election took effect only if the third party knows or has received a notification of the election; and

(2) on and after [all-inclusive date], to all third parties, but those provisions remain inapplicable to any obligation incurred while those provisions were inapplicable under paragraph (1)(B).

Section 1207. Savings Clause.
This [Act] does not affect an action commenced, proceeding brought, or right accrued before this [Act] takes effect.

APPENDIX C
UNIFORM LIMITED LIABILITY COMPANY ACT (1996)

Drafted by the

NATIONAL CONFERENCE OF COMMISSIONERS
ON UNIFORM STATE LAWS

and by it

APPROVED AND RECOMMENDED FOR ENACTMENT
IN ALL THE STATES

at its

ANNUAL CONFERENCE
MEETING IN ITS ONE-HUNDRED-AND-FIFTH YEAR
SAN ANTONIO, TEXAS
JULY 12 - JULY 19, 1996

WITH PREFATORY NOTE AND COMMENTS

COPYRIGHT 1996
By
NATIONAL CONFERENCE OF COMMISSIONERS
ON UNIFORM STATE LAWS

UNIFORM LIMITED LIABILITY COMPANY ACT (1996)

The Committee that acted for the National Conference of Commissioners on Uniform State Laws in preparing the Uniform Limited Liability Company Act (1996) was as follows:

Edward I. Cutler, P.O. Box 3239, Tampa, FL 33601, *Chair*
Richard E. Ford, 203 West Randolph Street, Lewisburg, WV 24901
Harry J. Haynsworth, IV, William Mitchell College of Law,
875 Summit Avenue, St. Paul, MN 55105
Charles G. Kepler, P.O. Box 490, 1135 14th Street, Cody, WY 82414

Wayne C. Kreuscher, 1313 Merchants Bank Building, 11 South Meridian Street, Indianapolis, IN 46204

Reed L. Martineau, P.O. Box 45000, 10 Exchange Place, Salt Lake City, UT 84145

Richard F. Mutzebaugh, State Capitol Building, 200 East Colfax Avenue, Denver, CO 80203

Glee S. Smith, P.O. Box 360, 111 East 8th, Larned, KS 67550

Howard J. Swibel, Suite 1200, 120 South Riverside Plaza, Chicago, IL 60606

Carter G. Bishop, Suffolk University Law School, 41 Temple Street, Boston, MA 02114, *Reporter*

EX OFFICIO

Richard C. Hite, 200 West Douglas Avenue, Suite 600, Wichita, KS 67202, *President*

John P. Burton, P.O. Box 1357, Suite 101, 123 East Marcy Street, Santa Fe, NM 87501, *Chair, Division E*

Executive Director

Fred H. Miller, University of Oklahoma, College of Law, 300 Timberdell **Road, Norman,** OK 73019, *Executive Director*

Willam J. Pierce, 1505 Roxbury Road, Ann Arbor, MI 48104, *Executive Director Emeritus*

Review Committee

James M. Bush, Suite 2200, Two North Central Avenue, Phoenix, AZ 85004, *Chair*

Francis J. Pavetti, P.O. Box 829, Court House Square Building, New London, CT 06320

Donald Joe Willis, Suites 1600-1950, Pacwest Center, 1211 S.W. 5th Avenue, Portland, OR 97204

Advisors

Robert R. Keatinge, *American Bar Association*

Steven G. Frost, *American Bar Association, Section of Taxation*

Thomas Earl Geu, *American Bar Association, Section of Real Property, Probate and Trust Law, Probate and Trust Division*

James W. Reynolds, *American Bar Association, Section of Business Law*

Sanford J. Liebschutz, *American Bar Association, Section of Real Property, Probate and Trust Law, Real Property Division*

Copies of this Act may be obtained from:

National Conference of Commissioners on Univorm State Laws

676 North St. Clair Street, Suite 1700

Chicago, Illinois 60611

312/915-0195

Uniform Limited Liability Company Act (1996)

Table of Contents

UNIFORM LIMITED LIABILITY COMPANY ACT (1996)

PREFATORY NOTE

Borrowing from abroad, Wyoming initiated a national movement in 1977 by enacting this country's first limited liability company act. The movement started slowly as the Internal Revenue Service took more than ten years to announce finally that a Wyoming limited liability company would be taxed like a partnership. Since that time, every State has adopted or is considering its own distinct limited liability company act, many of which have already been amended one or more times.

The allure of the limited liability company is its unique ability to bring together in a single business organization the best features of all other business forms—properly structured, its owners obtain both a corporate-styled liability shield and the pass-through tax benefits of a partnership. General and limited partnerships do not offer their partners a corporate-styled liability shield. Corporations, including those having made a Subchapter Selection, do not offer their shareholders all the pass-through tax benefits of a partnership. All state limited liability company acts contain provisions for a liability shield and partnership tax status.

Despite these two common themes, state limited liability company acts display a dazzling array of diversity. Multistate activities of businesses are widespread. Recognition of out-of-state limited liability companies varies. Unfortunately, this lack of uniformity manifests itself in basic but fundamentally important questions, such as: may a company be formed and operated by only one owner; may it be formed for purposes other than to make a profit; whether owners have the power and right to withdraw from a company and receive a distribution of the fair value of their interests; whether a member's dissociation threatens a dissolution of the company; who has the apparent authority to bind the company and the limits of that authority; what are the fiduciary duties of owners and managers to a company and each other; how are the rights to manage a company allocated among its owners and managers; do the owners have the right to sue a company and its other owners in their own right as well as derivatively on behalf of the company; may general and limited partnerships be converted to limited liability companies and may limited liability companies merge with other limited liability companies and other business organizations; what is the law governing foreign limited liability companies; and are any or all of these and other rules simply default rules that may be modified by agreement or are they nonwaivable.

Practitioners and entrepreneurs struggle to understand the law governing limited liability companies organized in their own State and to understand the burgeoning law of other States. Simple questions concerning where to organize are increasingly complex. Since most state limited liability company acts are in their infancy, little if any interpretative case law exists. Even when case law develops, it will have limited precedential value because of the diversity of the state acts.

Accordingly, uniform legislation in this area of the law appeared to have become urgent.

After a Study Committee appointed by the National Conference of Commissioners in late 1991 recommended that a comprehensive project be undertaken, the Conference appointed a Drafting Committee which worked on a Uniform Limited Liability Company Act (ULLCA) from early 1992 until its adoption by the Conference at its Annual Meeting in August 1994. The Drafting Committee was assisted by a blue ribbon panel of national experts and other interested and affected parties and organizations. Many, if not all, of those assisting the Committee brought substantial experience from drafting limited liability company legislation in their own States. Many are also authors of leading treatises and articles in the field. Those represented in the drafting process included an American Bar Association (ABA) liaison, four advisors representing the three separate ABA Sections of Business Law, Taxation, and Real Property, Trust and Probate, the United States Treasury Department, the Internal Revenue Service, and many observers representing several other organizations, including the California Bar Association, the New York City Bar Association, the American College of Real Estate Lawyers, the National Association of Certified Public Accountants, the National Association of Secretaries of State, the Chicago and Lawyers Title Companies, the American Land Title Association, and several university law and business school faculty members.

The Committee met nine times and engaged in numerous national telephonic conferences to discuss policies, review over fifteen drafts, evaluate legal developments and consider comments by our many knowledgeable advisers and observers, as well as an ABA subcommittee's earlier work on a prototype. In examining virtually every aspect of each state limited liability company act, the Committee maintained a single policy vision—to draft a flexible act with a comprehensive set of default rules designed to substitute as the essence of the bargain for small entrepreneurs and others.

This Act is flexible in the sense that the vast majority of its provisions may be modified by the owners in a private agreement. Only limited and specific fundamental matters may not be altered by private agreement. To simplify, those nonwaivable provisions are set forth in a single subsection. Helped thereby, sophisticated parties will negotiate their own deal with the benefit of counsel.

The Committee also recognized that small entrepreneurs without the benefit of counsel should also have access to the Act. To that end, the great bulk of the Act sets forth default rules designed to operate a limited liability company without sophisticated agreements and to recognize that members may also modify the default rules by oral agreements defined in part by their own conduct. Uniquely, the Act combines two simple default structures which depend upon the presence of designations in the articles of organization. All default rules under the Act flow from these two designations.

First, unless the articles reflect that a limited liability company is a term company and the duration of that term, the company will be an at-will company. Generally, the owners of an at-will company may demand a payment of the fair value of their interests at any time. Owners of a term company must generally wait until the expiration of the term to obtain the value of their interests. Secondly, unless the articles reflect that a company will be managed by managers, the company will be managed by its members. This designation controls whether the members or managers have apparent agency authority, management authority, and the nature of fiduciary duties in the company.

In January of 1995 the Executive Committee of the Conference adopted an amendment to harmonize the Act with new and important Internal Revenue Service announcements, and the amendment was ratified by the National Conference at its Annual Meeting in August of 1995. Those Internal Revenue Service announcements generally provide that a limited liability company will not be taxed like a corporation regardless of its organizational structure. Freed from the old tax classification restraints, the amendment modifies the Act's dissolution provision by eliminating member dissociation as a dissolution event. This important amendment significantly increases the stability of a limited liability company and places greater emphasis on a limited liability company's required purchase of a dissociated member's interest.

The adoption of ULLCA will provide much needed consistency among the States, with flexible default rules, and multistate recognition of limited liability on the part of company owners. It will also promote the development of precedential case law.

UNIFORM LIMITED LIABILITY COMPANY ACT (1996)

[ARTICLE] 1

GENERAL PROVISIONS

Section 101. Definitions.
Section 102. Knowledge and Notice.
Section 103. Effect of Operating Agreement; Nonwaivable Provisions.
Section 104. Supplemental Principles of Law.
Section 105. Name.

Section 101. Definitions. In this [Act]:

(1) "Articles of organization" means initial, amended, and restated articles of organization and articles of merger. In the case of a foreign limited liability company, the term includes all records serving a similar function required to be filed in the office of the [Secretary of State] or other official having custody of company records in the State or country under whose law it is organized.

(2) "At-will company" means a limited liability company other than a term company.

(3) "Business" includes every trade, occupation, profession, and other lawful purpose, whether or not carried on for profit.

(4) "Debtor in bankruptcy" means a person who is the subject of an order for relief under Title 11 of the United States Code or a comparable order under a successor statute of general application or a comparable order under federal, state, or foreign law governing insolvency.

(5) "Distribution" means a transfer of money, property, or other benefit from a limited liability company to a member in the member's capacity as a member or to a transferee of the member's distributional interest.

(6) "Distributional interest" means all of a member's interest in distributions by the limited liability company.

(7) "Entity" means a person other than an individual.

(8) "Foreign limited liability company" means an unincorporated entity organized under laws other than the laws of this State which afford limited liability to its owners comparable to the liability under Section 303 and is not required to obtain a certificate of authority to transact business under any law of this State other than this [Act].

(9) "Limited liability company" means a limited liability company organized under this [Act].

(10) "Manager" means a person, whether or not a member of a manager-managed company, who is vested with authority under Section 301.

(11) "Manager-managed company" means a limited liability company which is so designated in its articles of organization.

(12) "Member-managed company" means a limited liability company other than a manager-managed company.

(13) "Operating agreement" means the agreement under Section 103 concerning the relations among the members, managers, and limited liability company. The term includes amendments to the agreement.

(14) "Person" means an individual, corporation, business trust, estate, trust, partnership, limited liability company, association, joint venture, government, governmental subdivision, agency, or instrumentality, or any other legal or commercial entity.

(15) "Principal office" means the office, whether or not in this State, where the principal executive office of a domestic or foreign limited liability company is located.

(16) "Record" means information that is inscribed on a tangible medium or that is stored in an electronic or other medium and is retrievable in perceivable form.

(17) "Sign" means to identify a record by means of a signature, mark, or other symbol, with intent to authenticate it.

(18) "State" means a State of the United States, the District of Columbia, the Commonwealth of Puerto Rico, or any territory or insular possession subject to the jurisdiction of the United States.

(19) "Term company" means a limited liability company in which its members have agreed to remain members until the expiration of a term specified in the articles of organization.

(20) "Transfer" includes an assignment, conveyance, deed, bill of sale, lease, mortgage, security interest, encumbrance, and gift.

COMMENT

Uniform Limited Liability Company Act ("ULLCA") definitions, like the rest of the Act, are a blend of terms and concepts derived from the Uniform Partnership Act ("UPA"), the Uniform Partnership Act (1994) ("UPA 1994", also previously known as the Revised Uniform Partnership Act or "RUPA"), the Revised Uniform Limited Partnership Act ("RULPA"), the Uniform Commercial Code ("UCC"), and the Model Business Corporation Act ("MBCA"), or their revisions from time to time; some are tailored specially for this Act.

"Business." A limited liability company may be organized to engage in an activity either for or not for profit. The extent to which contributions to a nonprofit company may be deductible for Federal income tax purposes is determined by federal law. Other state law determines the extent of exemptions from state and local income and property taxes.

"Debtor in bankruptcy." The filing of a voluntary petition operates immediately as an "order for relief." See Sections 601(7)(i) and 602(b)(2)(iii).

"Distribution." This term includes all sources of a member's distributions including the member's capital contributions, undistributed profits, and residual interest in the assets of the company after all claims, including those of third parties and debts to members, have been paid.

"Distributional interest." The term does not include a member's broader rights to participate in the management of the company. See Comments to Article 5.

"Foreign limited liability company." The term is not restricted to companies formed in the United States.

"Manager." The rules of agency apply to limited liability companies. Therefore, managers may designate agents with whatever titles, qualifications, and responsibilities they desire. For example, managers may designate an agent as "President."

"Manager-managed company." The term includes only a company designated as such in the articles of organization. In a manager-managed company agency authority is vested exclusively in one or more managers and not in the members. See Sections 101(10) (manager), 203(a)(6) (articles designation), and 301(b) (agency authority of members and managers).

"Member-managed limited liability company." The term includes every company not designated as "manager-managed" under Section 203(a)(6) in its articles of organization.

"Operating agreement." This agreement may be oral. Members may agree upon the extent to which their relationships are to be governed by writings.

"Principal office." The address of the principal office must be set forth in the annual report required under Section 211(a)(3).

"Record." This Act is the first Uniform Act promulgated with a definition of this term. The definition brings this Act in conformity with the present state of technology and accommodates prospective future technology in the communication and storage of information other than by human memory. Modern methods of communicating and storing information employed in commercial practices are no longer confined to physical documents.

The term includes any writing. A record need not be permanent or indestructible, but an oral or other unwritten communication must be stored or preserved on some medium to qualify as a record. Information that has not been retained other than through human memory does not qualify as a record. A record may be signed or may be created without the knowledge or intent of a particular person. Other law must be consulted to determine admissibility in evidence, the applicability of statute of frauds, and other questions regarding the use of records. Under Section 206(a), electronic filings may be permitted and even encouraged.

Section 102. Knowledge and Notice.

(a) A person knows a fact if the person has actual knowledge of it.

(b) A person has notice of a fact if the person:

    (1) knows the fact;

    (2) has received a notification of the fact; or

    (3) has reason to know the fact exists from all of the facts known to the person at the time in question.

(c) A person notifies or gives a notification of a fact to another by taking steps reasonably required to inform the other person in ordinary course, whether or not the other person knows the fact.

(d) A person receives a notification when the notification:

    (1) comes to the person's attention; or

    (2) is duly delivered at the person's place of business or at any other place held out by the person as a place for receiving communications.

(e) An entity knows, has notice, or receives a notification of a fact for purposes of a particular transaction when the individual conducting the transaction for the entity knows, has notice, or receives a notification of the fact, or in any event when the fact would have been brought to the individual's attention had the entity exercised reasonable diligence. An entity exercises reasonable diligence if it maintains reasonable routines for communicating significant information to the individual conducting the transaction for the entity and there is reasonable compliance with the routines. Reasonable diligence does not require an individual acting for the entity to communicate information unless the communication is part of the individual's regular duties or the individual has reason to know of the transaction and that the transaction would be materially affected by the information.

COMMENT

Knowledge requires cognitive awareness of a fact, whereas notice is based on a lesser degree of awareness. The Act imposes constructive knowledge under limited circumstances. See Comments to Sections 301(c), 703, and 704.

Section 103. Effect of Operating Agreement; Nonwaivable Provisions.

(a) Except as otherwise provided in subsection (b), all members of a limited liability company may enter into an operating agreement, which need not be in writing, to regulate the affairs of the company and the conduct of its business, and to govern relations among the members, managers, and company. To the extent the operating agreement does not otherwise provide, this [Act] governs relations among the members, managers, and company.

(b) The operating agreement may not:

(1) unreasonably restrict a right to information or access to records under Section 408;

(2) eliminate the duty of loyalty under Section 409(b) or 603(b)(3), but the agreement may:
   (i) identify specific types or categories of activities that do not violate the duty of loyalty, if not manifestly unreasonable; and
   (ii) specify the number or percentage of members or disinterested managers that may authorize or ratify, after full disclosure of all material facts, a specific act or transaction that otherwise would violate the duty of loyalty;

(3) unreasonably reduce the duty of care under Section 409(c) or 603(b)(3);

(4) eliminate the obligation of good faith and fair dealing under Section 409(d), but the operating agreement may determine the standards by which the performance of the obligation is to be measured, if the standards are not manifestly unreasonable;

(5) vary the right to expel a member in an event specified in Section 601(6);

(6) vary the requirement to wind up the limited liability company's business in a case specified in Section 801(3) or (4); or

(7) restrict rights of a person, other than a manager, member, and transferee of a member's distributional interest, under this [Act].

COMMENT

The operating agreement is the essential contract that governs the affairs of a limited liability company. Since it is binding on all members, amendments must be approved by all members unless otherwise provided in the agreement. Although many agreements will be in writing, the agreement and any amendments may be oral or may be in the form of a record. Course of dealing, course of performance and usage of trade are relevant to determine the meaning of the agreement unless the agreement provides that all amendments must be in writing.

This section makes clear that the only matters an operating agreement may not control are specified in subsection (b). Accordingly, an operating agreement may modify or eliminate any rule specified in any section of this Act except matters specified in subsection (b). To the extent not otherwise mentioned in subsection (b), every section of this Act is simply a default rule, regardless of whether the language of the section appears to be otherwise mandatory. This approach eliminates the necessity of repeating the phrase "unless otherwise agreed" in each section and its commentary.

Under subsection (b)(1), an operating agreement may not unreasonably restrict the right to information or access to any records under Section 408. This does not create an independent obligation beyond Section 408 to maintain any specific records. Under subsections (b)(2) to (4), an irreducible core of fiduciary responsibilities survive any contrary provision in the operating agreement. Subsection (b)(2)(i) authorizes an operating agreement to modify, but not eliminate, the three specific duties of loyalty set forth in Section 409(b)(1) to (3) provided the modification itself is not manifestly unreasonable, a question of fact. Subsection (b)(2)(ii) preserves the common law right of the members to authorize future or ratify past violations of the duty of loyalty provided there has been a full disclosure of all material facts. The authorization or ratification must be unanimous unless otherwise provided in an operating agreement, because the authorization or ratification itself constitutes an amendment to the agreement. The authorization or ratification of specific past or future conduct may sanction conduct that would have been manifestly unreasonable under subsection (b)(2)(i).

Section 104. Supplemental Principles of Law.

(a) Unless displaced by particular provisions of this [Act], the principles of law and equity supplement this [Act].

(b) If an obligation to pay interest arises under this [Act] and the rate is not specified, the rate is that specified in [applicable statute].

COMMENT

Supplementary principles include, but are not limited to, the law of agency, estoppel, law merchant, and all other principles listed in UCC Section 1-103, including the law relative to the capacity to contract, fraud, misrepresentation, duress, coercion, mistake, bankruptcy, and other validating and invalidating clauses. Other principles such as those mentioned in UCC Section 1-205 (Course of Dealing and Usage of Trade) apply as well as course of performance. As with UPA 1994 Section 104, upon which this provision is based, no substantive change from either the UPA or the UCC is intended. Section 104(b) establishes the applicable rate of interest in the absence of an agreement among the members.

Section 105. Name.

(a) The name of a limited liability company must contain "limited liability company" or "limited company" or the abbreviation "L.L.C.", "LLC", "L.C.", or "LC". "Limited" may be abbreviated as "Ltd.", and "company" may be abbreviated as "Co.".

(b) Except as authorized by subsections (c) and (d), the name of a limited liability company must be distinguishable upon the records of the [Secretary of State] from:

(1) the name of any corporation, limited partnership, or company incorporated, organized or authorized to transact business, in this State;

(2) a name reserved or registered under Section 106 or 107;

(3) a fictitious name approved under Section 1005 for a foreign company authorized to transact business in this State because its real name is unavailable.

(c) A limited liability company may apply to the [Secretary of State] for authorization to use a name that is not distinguishable upon the records of the [Secretary of State] from one or more of the names described in subsection (b). The [Secretary of State] shall authorize use of the name applied for if:

(1) the present user, registrant, or owner of a reserved name consents to the use in a record and submits an undertaking in form satisfactory to the [Secretary of State] to change the name to a name that is distinguishable upon the records of the [Secretary of State] from the name applied for; or

(2) the applicant delivers to the [Secretary of State] a certified copy of the final judgment of a court of competent jurisdiction establishing the applicant's right to use the name applied for in this State.

(d) A limited liability company may use the name, including a fictitious name, of another domestic or foreign company which is used in this State if the other company is organized or authorized to transact business in this State and the company proposing to use the name has:

(1) merged with the other company;

(2) been formed by reorganization with the other company; or

(3) acquired substantially all of the assets, including the name, of the other company.

Section 106. Reserved Name.

(a) A person may reserve the exclusive use of the name of a limited liability company, including a fictitious name for a foreign company whose name is not available, by delivering an application to the [Secretary of State] for filing. The application must set forth the name and address of the applicant and the name proposed to be reserved. If the [Secretary of State] finds that the name applied for is available, it must be reserved for the applicant's exclusive use for a nonrenewable 120-day period.

(b) The owner of a name reserved for a limited liability company may transfer the reservation to another person by delivering to the [Secretary of State] a signed notice of the transfer which states the name and address of the transferee.

COMMENT

A foreign limited liability company that is not presently authorized to transact business in the State may reserve a fictitious name for a nonrenewable

120-day period. When its actual name is available, a company will generally register that name under Section 107 because the registration is valid for a year and may be extended indefinitely.

Section 107. Registered Name.

(a) A foreign limited liability company may register its name subject to the requirements of Section 1005, if the name is distinguishable upon the records of the [Secretary of State] from names that are not available under Section 105(b).

(b) A foreign limited liability company registers its name, or its name with any addition required by Section 1005, by delivering to the [Secretary of State] for filing an application:

  (1) setting forth its name, or its name with any addition required by Section 1005, the State or country and date of its organization, and a brief description of the nature of the business in which it is engaged; and

  (2) accompanied by a certificate of existence, or a record of similar import, from the State or country of organization.

(c) A foreign limited liability company whose registration is effective may renew it for successive years by delivering for filing in the office of the [Secretary of State] a renewal application complying with subsection (b) between October 1 and December 31 of the preceding year. The renewal application renews the registration for the following calendar year.

(d) A foreign limited liability company whose registration is effective may qualify as a foreign company under its name or consent in writing to the use of its name by a limited liability company later organized under this [Act] or by another foreign company later authorized to transact business in this State. The registered name terminates when the limited liability company is organized or the foreign company qualifies or consents to the qualification of another foreign company under the registered name.

Section 108. Designated Office and Agent for Service of Process.

(a) A limited liability company and a foreign limited liability company authorized to do business in this State shall designate and continuously maintain in this State:

  (1) an office, which need not be a place of its business in this State; and

  (2) an agent and street address of the agent for service of process on the company.

(b) An agent must be an individual resident of this State, a domestic corporation, another limited liability company, or a foreign corporation or foreign company authorized to do business in this State.

COMMENT

Limited liability companies organized under Section 202 or authorized to transact business under Section 1004 are required to designate and continuously maintain an office in the State. Although the designated office need not be a place of business, it most often will be the only place of business of the company. The company must also designate an agent for service of process within the State and the agent's street address. The agent's address need not be the same as the company's designated office address. The initial office and agent designations must be set forth in the articles of organization, including the address of the designated office. See Section 203(a)(2) to (3). The current office and agent designations must be set forth in the company's annual report. See Section 211(a)(2). See also Section 109 (procedure for changing the office or agent designations), Section 110 (procedure for an agent to resign), and Section 111(b) (the filing officer is the service agent for the company if it fails to maintain its own service agent).

Section 109. Change of Designated Office or Agent for Service of Process.

A limited liability company may change its designated office or agent for service of process by delivering to the [Secretary of State] for filing a statement of change which sets forth:

(1) the name of the company;

(2) the street address of its current designated office;

(3) if the current designated office is to be changed, the street address of the new designated office;

(4) the name and address of its current agent for service of process; and

(5) if the current agent for service of process or street address of that agent is to be changed, the new address or the name and street address of the new agent for service of process.

Section 110. Resignation of Agent for Service of Process.

(a) An agent for service of process of a limited liability company may resign by delivering to the [Secretary of State] for filing a record of the statement of resignation.

(b) After filing a statement of resignation, the [Secretary of State] shall mail a copy to the designated office and another copy to the limited liability company at its principal office.

(c) An agency is terminated on the 31st day after the statement is filed in the office of the [Secretary of State].

Section 111. Service of Process.

(a) An agent for service of process appointed by a limited liability company or a foreign limited liability company is an agent of the company for service of any process, notice, or demand required or permitted by law to be served upon the company.

(b) If a limited liability company or foreign limited liability company fails to appoint or maintain an agent for service of process in this State or the agent for service of process cannot with reasonable diligence be found at the agent's address, the [Secretary of State] is an agent of the company upon whom process, notice, or demand may be served.

(c) Service of any process, notice, or demand on the [Secretary of State] may be made by delivering to and leaving with the [Secretary of State], the [Assistant Secretary of State], or clerk having charge of the limited liability company department of the [Secretary of State's] office duplicate copies of the process, notice, or demand. If the process, notice, or demand is served on the [Secretary of State], the [Secretary of State] shall forward one of the copies by registered or certified mail, return receipt requested, to the company at its designated office. Service is effected under this subsection at the earliest of:

   (1) the date the company receives the process, notice, or demand;

   (2) the date shown on the return receipt, if signed on behalf of the company; or

   (3) five days after its deposit in the mail, if mailed postpaid and correctly addressed.

(d) The [Secretary of State] shall keep a record of all processes, notices, and demands served pursuant to this section and record the time of and the action taken regarding the service.

(e) This section does not affect the right to serve process, notice, or demand in any manner otherwise provided by law.

COMMENT

Service of process on a limited liability company and a foreign company authorized to transact business in the State must be made on the company's agent for service of process whose name and address should be on file with the filing office. If for any reason a company fails to appoint or maintain an agent for service of process or the agent cannot be found with reasonable diligence at the agent's address, the filing officer will be deemed the proper agent.

Section 112. Nature of Business and Powers.

(a) A limited liability company may be organized under this [Act] for any lawful purpose, subject to any law of this State governing or regulating business.

(b) Unless its articles of organization provide otherwise, a limited liability company has the same powers as an individual to do all things necessary or convenient to carry on its business or affairs, including power to:

   (1) sue and be sued, and defend in its name;

(2) purchase, receive, lease, or otherwise acquire, and own, hold, improve, use, and otherwise deal with real or personal property, or any legal or equitable interest in property, wherever located;

(3) sell, convey, mortgage, grant a security interest in, lease, exchange, and otherwise encumber or dispose of all or any part of its property;

(4) purchase, receive, subscribe for, or otherwise acquire, own, hold, vote, use, sell, mortgage, lend, grant a security interest in, or otherwise dispose of and deal in and with, shares or other interests in or obligations of any other entity;

(5) make contracts and guarantees, incur liabilities, borrow money, issue its notes, bonds, and other obligations, which may be convertible into or include the option to purchase other securities of the limited liability company, and secure any of its obligations by a mortgage on or a security interest in any of its property, franchises, or income;

(6) lend money, invest and reinvest its funds, and receive and hold real and personal property as security for repayment;

(7) be a promoter, partner, member, associate, or manager of any partnership, joint venture, trust, or other entity;

(8) conduct its business, locate offices, and exercise the powers granted by this [Act] within or without this State;

(9) elect managers and appoint officers, employees, and agents of the limited liability company, define their duties, fix their compensation, and lend them money and credit;

(10) pay pensions and establish pension plans, pension trusts, profit sharing plans, bonus plans, option plans, and benefit or incentive plans for any or all of its current or former members, managers, officers, employees, and agents;

(11) make donations for the public welfare or for charitable, scientific, or educational purposes; and

(12) make payments or donations, or do any other act, not inconsistent with law, that furthers the business of the limited liability company.

COMMENT

A limited liability company may be organized for any lawful purpose unless the State has specifically prohibited a company from engaging in a specific activity. For example, many States require that certain regulated industries, such as banking and insurance, be conducted only by organizations that meet the special requirements. Also, many States impose restrictions on activities in which a limited liability company may engage. For example, the practice of certain professionals is often subject to special conditions.

A limited liability company has the power to engage in and perform important and necessary acts related to its operation and function. A company's power to enter into a transaction is distinguishable from the authority of an agent to enter into the transaction. See Section 301 (agency rules).

[ARTICLE] 2

ORGANIZATION

Section 201. Limited Liability Company as Legal Entity.
Section 202. Organization.
Section 203. Articles of Organization.
Section 204. Amendment or Restatement of Articles of Organization.
Section 205. Signing of Records.
Section 206. Filing in Office of [Secretary of State].
Section 207. Correcting Filed Record.
Section 208. Certificate of Existence or Authorization.
Section 209. Liability for False Statement in Filed Record.
Section 210. Filing By Judicial Act.
Section 211. Annual Report for [Secretary of State].

Section 201. Limited Liability Company as Legal Entity.
A limited liability company is a legal entity distinct from its members.

COMMENT

A limited liability company is legally distinct from its members who are not normally liable for the debts, obligations, and liabilities of the company. See Section 303. Accordingly, members are not proper parties to suits against the company unless an object of the proceeding is to enforce members' rights against the company or to enforce their liability to the company.

Section 202. Organization.

    (a) One or more persons may organize a limited liability company, consisting of one or more members, by delivering articles of organization to the office of the [Secretary of State] for filing.

    (b) Unless a delayed effective date is specified, the existence of a limited liability company begins when the articles of organization are filed.

    (c) The filing of the articles of organization by the [Secretary of State] is conclusive proof that the organizers satisfied all conditions precedent to the creation of a limited liability company.

COMMENT

Any person may organize a limited liability company by performing the ministerial act of signing and filing the articles of organization. The person need not be a member. As a matter of flexibility, a company may be organized and operated with only one member to enable sole proprietors to obtain the benefit of a liability shield. New and important Internal Revenue Service announcements clarify that a one-member limited liability company will not be taxed like a corporation. Nor will it be taxed like a partnership since it lacks at least two members. Rather, a one-member limited liability company is disregarded for Federal tax purposes and its operations are reported on the return of its single owner.

The existence of a company begins when the articles are filed. Therefore, the filing of the articles of organization is conclusive as to the existence of the limited liability shield for persons who enter into transactions on behalf of the company. Until the articles are filed, a firm is not organized under this Act and is not a "limited liability company" as defined in Section 101(9). In that case, the parties' relationships are not governed by this Act unless they have expressed a contractual intent to be bound by the provisions of the Act. Third parties would also not be governed by the provisions of this Act unless they have expressed a contractual intent to extend a limited liability shield to the members of the would-be limited liability company.

Section 203. Articles of Organization.

   (a) Articles of organization of a limited liability company must set forth:

      (1) the name of the company;

      (2) the address of the initial designated office;

      (3) the name and street address of the initial agent for service of process;

      (4) the name and address of each organizer;

      (5) whether the company is to be a term company and, if so, the term specified;

      (6) whether the company is to be manager-managed, and, if so, the name and address of each initial manager; and

      (7) whether one or more of the members of the company are to be liable for its debts and obligations under Section 303(c).

   (b) Articles of organization of a limited liability company may set forth:

      (1) provisions permitted to be set forth in an operating agreement; or

      (2) other matters not inconsistent with law.

   (c) Articles of organization of a limited liability company may not vary the nonwaivable provisions of Section 103(b). As to all other matters, if any provision of an operating agreement is inconsistent with the articles of organization:

      (1) the operating agreement controls as to managers, members, and members' transferees; and

(2) the articles of organization control as to persons, other than managers, members and their transferees, who reasonably rely on the articles to their detriment.

COMMENT

The articles serve primarily a notice function and generally do not reflect the substantive agreement of the members regarding the business affairs of the company. Those matters are generally reserved for an operating agreement which may be unwritten. Under Section 203(b), the articles may contain provisions permitted to be set forth in an operating agreement. Where the articles and operating agreement conflict, the operating agreement controls as to members but the articles control as to third parties. The articles may also contain any other matter not inconsistent with law. The most important is a Section 301(c) limitation on the authority of a member or manager to transfer interests in the company's real property.

A company will be at-will unless it is designated as a term company and the duration of its term is specified in its articles under Section 203(a)(5). The duration of a term company may be specified in any manner which sets forth a specific and final date for the dissolution of the company. For example, the period specified may be in the form of "50 years from the date of filing of the articles" or "the period ending on January 1, 2020." Mere specification of a particular undertaking of an uncertain business duration is not sufficient unless the particular undertaking is within a longer fixed period. An example of this type of designation would include "2020 or until the building is completed, whichever occurs first." When the specified period is incorrectly specified, the company will be an at-will company. Notwithstanding the correct specification of a term in the articles, a company will be an at-will company among the members under Section 203(c)(1) if an operating agreement so provides. A term company that continues after the expiration of its term specified in its articles will also be an at-will company.

A term company possesses several important default rule characteristics that differentiate it from an at-will company. An operating agreement may alter any of these rules. Generally, a member of an at-will company may rightfully dissociate at any time whereas a dissociation from a term company prior to the expiration of the specified term is wrongful. See Comments to Section 602(b). Accordingly, a dissociated member of an at-will company is entitled to have the company purchase that member's interest for its fair value determined as of the date of the member's dissociation. A dissociated member of a term company must generally await the expiration of the agreed term to withdraw the fair value of the interest determined at as of the date of the expiration of the agreed term. Thus, a dissociated member in an at-will company receives the fair value of their interest sooner than in a term compnay and also does not bear the risk of valuation changes for the remainder of the specified term. See Comments to Section 701(a).

A company will be member-managed unless it is designated as manager-managed under Section 203(a)(6). Absent further designation in the articles, a company will be a member-managed at-will company. The designation of a limited liability company as either member- or manager-managed is important because it defines who are agents and have the apparent authority to bind the company under Section 301. In a member-managed company, the members have the agency authority to bind the company. In a manager-managed company only the managers have that authority. New and important Internal Revenue Service announcements clarify that the agency structure of a limited liability company will not cause it to be taxed like a corporation. The agency designation relates only to agency and does not preclude members of a manager-managed company from participating in the actual management of company business. See Comments to Section 404(b).

Section 204. Amendment or Restatement of Articles of Organization.

(a) Articles of organization of a limited liability company may be amended at any time by delivering articles of amendment to the [Secretary of State] for filing. The articles of amendment must set forth the:

    (1) name of the limited liability company;

    (2) date of filing of the articles of organization; and

    (3) amendment to the articles.

(b) A limited liability company may restate its articles of organization at any time. Restated articles of organization must be signed and filed in the same manner as articles of amendment. Restated articles of organization must be designated as such in the heading and state in the heading or in an introductory paragraph the limited liability company's present name and, if it has been changed, all of its former names and the date of the filing of its initial articles of organization.

COMMENT

An amendment to the articles requires the consent of all the members unless an operating agreement provides for a lesser number. See Section 404(c)(3).

Section 205. Signing of Records.

(a) Except as otherwise provided in this [Act], a record to be filed by or on behalf of a limited liability company in the office of the [Secretary of State] must be signed in the name of the company by a:

    (1) manager of a manager-managed company;

    (2) member of a member-managed company;

    (3) person organizing the company, if the company has not been formed; or

    (4) fiduciary, if the company is in the hands of a receiver, trustee, or other court-appointed fiduciary.

(b) A record signed under subsection (a) must state adjacent to the signature the name and capacity of the signer.

(c) Any person may sign a record to be filed under subsection (a) by an attorney-in-fact. Powers of attorney relating to the signing of records to be filed under subsection (a) by an attorney-in-fact need not be filed in the office of the [Secretary of State] as evidence of authority by the person filing but must be retained by the company.

COMMENT

Both a writing and a record may be signed. An electronic record is signed when a person adds a name to the record with the intention to authenticate the record. See Sections 101(16) ("record" definition) and 101(17) ("signed" definition).

Other provisions of this Act also provide for the filing of records with the filing office but do not require signing by the persons specified in clauses (1) to (3). Those specific sections prevail.

Section 206. Filing in Office of [Secretary of State].

(a) Articles of organization or any other record authorized to be filed under this [Act] must be in a medium permitted by the [Secretary of State] and must be delivered to the office of the [Secretary of State]. Unless the [Secretary of State] determines that a record fails to comply as to form with the filing requirements of this [Act], and if all filing fees have been paid, the [Secretary of State] shall file the record and send a receipt for the record and the fees to the limited liability company or its representative.

(b) Upon request and payment of a fee, the [Secretary of State] shall send to the requester a certified copy of the requested record.

(c) Except as otherwise provided in subsection (d) and Section 207(c), a record accepted for filing by the [Secretary of State] is effective:

(1) at the time of filing on the date it is filed, as evidenced by the [Secretary of State's] date and time endorsement on the original record; or

(2) at the time specified in the record as its effective time on the date it is filed.

(d) A record may specify a delayed effective time and date, and if it does so the record becomes effective at the time and date specified. If a delayed effective date but no time is specified, the record is effective at the close of business on that date. If a delayed effective date is later than the 90th day after the record is filed, the record is effective on the 90th day.

COMMENT

The definition and use of the term "record" permits filings with the filing office under this Act to conform to technological advances that have been adopted by the filing office. However, since Section 206(a) provides that the filing "must be in a medium permitted by the [Secretary of State]", the Act simply conforms to filing changes as they are adopted.

Section 207. Correcting Filed Record.

(a) A limited liability company or foreign limited liability company may correct a record filed by the [Secretary of State] if the record contains a false or erroneous statement or was defectively signed.

(b) A record is corrected:

    (1) by preparing articles of correction that:

        (i) describe the record, including its filing date, or attach a copy of it to the articles of correction;

        (ii) specify the incorrect statement and the reason it is incorrect or the manner in which the signing was defective; and

        (iii) correct the incorrect statement or defective signing; and

    (2) by delivering the corrected record to the [Secretary of State] for filing.

(c) Articles of correction are effective retroactively on the effective date of the record they correct except as to persons relying on the uncorrected record and adversely affected by the correction. As to those persons, articles of correction are effective when filed.

Section 208. Certificate of Existence or Authorization.

(a) A person may request the [Secretary of State] to furnish a certificate of existence for a limited liability company or a certificate of authorization for a foreign limited liability company.

(b) A certificate of existence for a limited liability company must set forth:

    (1) the company's name;

    (2) that it is duly organized under the laws of this State, the date of organization, whether its duration is at-will or for a specified term, and, if the latter, the period specified;

    (3) if payment is reflected in the records of the [Secretary of State] and if nonpayment affects the existence of the company, that all fees, taxes, and penalties owed to this State have been paid;

    (4) whether its most recent annual report required by Section 211 has been filed with the [Secretary of State];

    (5) that articles of termination have not been filed; and

    (6) other facts of record in the office of the [Secretary of State] which may be requested by the applicant.

(c) A certificate of authorization for a foreign limited liability company must set forth:

    (1) the company's name used in this State;

    (2) that it is authorized to transact business in this State;

(3) if payment is reflected in the records of the [Secretary of State] and if nonpayment affects the authorization of the company, that all fees, taxes, and penalties owed to this State have been paid;

(4) whether its most recent annual report required by Section 211 has been filed with the [Secretary of State];

(5) that a certificate of cancellation has not been filed; and

(6) other facts of record in the office of the [Secretary of State] which may be requested by the applicant.

(d) Subject to any qualification stated in the certificate, a certificate of existence or authorization issued by the [Secretary of State] may be relied upon as conclusive evidence that the domestic or foreign limited liability company is in existence or is authorized to transact business in this State.

Section 209. Liability for False Statement in Filed Record.

If a record authorized or required to be filed under this [Act] contains a false statement, one who suffers loss by reliance on the statement may recover damages for the loss from a person who signed the record or caused another to sign it on the person's behalf and knew the statement to be false at the time the record was signed.

Section 210. Filing by Judicial Act.

If a person required by Section 205 to sign any record fails or refuses to do so, any other person who is adversely affected by the failure or refusal may petition the [designate the appropriate court] to direct the signing of the record. If the court finds that it is proper for the record to be signed and that a person so designated has failed or refused to sign the record, it shall order the [Secretary of State] to sign and file an appropriate record.

Section 211. Annual Report for [Secretary of State].

(a) A limited liability company, and a foreign limited liability company authorized to transact business in this State, shall deliver to the [Secretary of State] for filing an annual report that sets forth:

(1) the name of the company and the State or country under whose law it is organized;

(2) the address of its designated office and the name and address of its agent for service of process in this State;

(3) the address of its principal office; and

(4) the names and business addresses of any managers.

(b) Information in an annual report must be current as of the date the annual report is signed on behalf of the limited liability company.

(c) The first annual report must be delivered to the [Secretary of State] between [January 1 and April 1] of the year following the calendar year in which a limited liability company was organized or a foreign company was authorized to transact business. Subsequent annual reports must be delivered to the [Secretary of State] between [January 1 and April 1] of the ensuing calendar years.

(d) If an annual report does not contain the information required in subsection (a), the [Secretary of State] shall promptly notify the reporting limited liability company or foreign limited liability company and return the report to it for correction. If the report is corrected to contain the information required in subsection (a) and delivered to the [Secretary of State] within 30 days after the effective date of the notice, it is timely filed.

COMMENT

Failure to deliver the annual report within 60 days after its due date is a primary ground for administrative dissolution of the company under Section 809. See Comments to Sections 809 to 812.

[ARTICLE] 3

RELATIONS OF MEMBERS AND MANAGERS TO PERSONS DEALING WITH LIMITED LIABILITY COMPANY

Section 301. Agency of Members and Managers.
Section 302. Limited Liability Company Liable for Member's or Manager's Actionable Conduct.
Section 303. Liability of Members and Managers.

Section 301. Agency of Members and Managers.

(a) Subject to subsections (b) and (c):

(1) Each member is an agent of the limited liability company for the purpose of its business, and an act of a member, including the signing of an instrument in the company's name, for apparently carrying on in the ordinary course the company's business or business of the kind carried on by the company binds the company, unless the member had no authority to act for the company in the particular matter and the person with whom the member was dealing knew or had notice that the member lacked authority.

(2) An act of a member which is not apparently for carrying on in the ordinary course the company's business or business of the kind carried on by the company binds the company only if the act was authorized by the other members.

(b) Subject to subsection (c), in a manager-managed company:

(1) A member is not an agent of the company for the purpose of its business solely by reason of being a member. Each manager is an agent of the company for the purpose of its business, and an act of a manager, including the signing of an instrument in the company's name, for apparently carrying on in the ordinary course the company's business or business of the kind carried on by the company binds the company, unless the manager had no authority to act for the company in the particular matter and the person with whom the manager was dealing knew or had notice that the manager lacked authority.

(2) An act of a manager which is not apparently for carrying on in the ordinary course the company's business or business of the kind carried on by the company binds the company only if the act was authorized under Section 404.

(c) Unless the articles of organization limit their authority, any member of a member-managed company or manager of a manager-managed company may sign and deliver any instrument transferring or affecting the company's interest in real property. The instrument is conclusive in favor of a person who gives value without knowledge of the lack of the authority of the person signing and delivering the instrument.

COMMENT

Members of a member-managed and managers of manager-managed company, as agents of the firm, have the apparent authority to bind a company to third parties. Members of a manager-managed company are not as such agents of the firm and do not have the apparent authority, as members, to bind a company. Members and managers with apparent authority possess actual authority by implication unless the actual authority is restricted in an operating agreement. Apparent authority extends to acts for carrying on in the ordinary course the company's business and business of the kind carried on by the company. Acts beyond this scope bind the company only where supported by actual authority created before the act or ratified after the act.

Ordinarily, restrictions on authority in an operating agreement do not affect the apparent authority of members and managers to bind the company to third parties without notice of the restriction. However, the restriction may make a member or manager's conduct wrongful and create liability to the company for the breach. This rule is subject to three important exceptions. First, under Section 301(c), a limitation reflected in the articles of organization on the authority of any member or manager to sign and deliver an instrument affecting an interest in company real property is effective when filed, even to persons without knowledge of the agent's lack of authority. New and important Internal Revenue Service announcements clarify that the agency structure of a limited liability company will not cause it to be taxed like a corporation. Secondly, under Section 703, a dissociated member's apparent authority terminates two years after dissociation, even to persons without knowledge of the dissociation. Thirdly, under Section 704, a dissociated member's apparent authority may be terminated earlier than the two years by filing a statement of dissociation. The statement is effective 90 days after filing, even to persons without knowledge of the filing. Together, these three provisions provide constructive knowledge to the world of the lack of apparent authority of an agent to bind the company.

Section 302. Limited Liability Company Liable for Member's or Manager's Actionable Conduct.

A limited liability company is liable for loss or injury caused to a person, or for a penalty incurred, as a result of a wrongful act or omission, or other actionable conduct, of a member or manager acting in the ordinary course of business of the company or with authority of the company.

COMMENT

Since a member of a manager-managed company is not as such an agent, the acts of the member are not imputed to the company unless the member is acting under actual or apparent authority created by circumstances other than membership status.

Section 303. Liability of Members and Managers.

(a) Except as otherwise provided in subsection (c), the debts, obligations, and liabilities of a limited liability company, whether arising in contract, tort, or otherwise, are solely the debts, obligations, and liabilities of the company. A member or manager is not personally liable for a debt, obligation, or liability of the company solely by reason of being or acting as a member or manager.

(b) The failure of a limited liability company to observe the usual company formalities or requirements relating to the exercise of its company powers or management of its business is not a ground for imposing personal liability on the members or managers for liabilities of the company.

(c) All or specified members of a limited liability company are liable in their capacity as members for all or specified debts, obligations, or liabilities of the company if:

   (1) a provision to that effect is contained in the articles of organization; and

   (2) a member so liable has consented in writing to the adoption of the provision or to be bound by the provision.

COMMENT

A member or manager, as an agent of the company, is not liable for the debts, obligations, and liabilities of the company simply because of the agency. A member or manager is responsible for acts or omissions to the extent those acts or omissions would be actionable in contract or tort against the member or manager if that person were acting in an individual capacity. Where a member or manager delegates or assigns the authority or duty to exercise appropriate company functions, the member or manager is ordinarily not personally liable for the acts or omissions of the officer, employee, or agent if the member or manager has complied with the duty of care set forth in Section 409(c).

Under Section 303(c), the usual liability shield may be waived, in whole or in part, provided the waiver is reflected in the articles of organization and the member has consented in writing to be bound by the waiver. The importance and unusual nature of the waiver consent requires that the consent be evidenced by a writing and not merely an unwritten record. See Comments to Section 205. New and important Internal Revenue Service annuouncements clarify that the owner liability structure of a limited liability company (other than a foreign limited liability company formed outside the United States) will not cause it to be taxed like a corporation.

[ARTICLE] 4

RELATIONS OF MEMBERS TO EACH OTHER AND TO LIMITED LIABILITY COMPANY

Section 401. Form of Contribution.
Section 402. Member's Liability for Contributions.
Section 403. Member's and Manager's Rights to Payments and Reimbursement.
Section 404. Management of Limited Liability Company.
Section 405. Sharing of and Right to Distributions.
Section 406. Limitations on Distributions.
Section 407. Liability for Unlawful Distributions.
Section 408. Member's Right to Information.
Section 409. General Standards of Member's and Manager's Conduct.
Section 410. Actions by Members.
Section 411. Continuation of Term Company After Expiration of Specified Term.

Section 401. Form of Contribution.
A contribution of a member of a limited liability company may consist of tangible or intangible property or other benefit to the company, including money, promissory notes, services performed, or other agreements to contribute cash or property, or contracts for services to be performed.

COMMENT

Unless otherwise provided in an operating agreement, admission of a member and the nature and valuation of a would-be member's contribution are matters requiring the consent of all of the other members. See Section 404(c)(7). An agreement to contribute to a company is controlled by the operating agreement and therefore may not be created or modified without amending that agreement through the unanimous consent of all the members, including the member to be bound by the new contribution terms. See 404(c)(1).

Section 402. Member's Liability for Contributions.

(a) A member's obligation to contribute money, property, or other benefit to, or to perform services for, a limited liability company is not excused by the member's death, disability, or other inability to perform personally. If a member does not make the required contribution of property or services, the member is obligated at the option of the company to contribute money equal to the value of that portion of the stated contribution which has not been made.

(b) A creditor of a limited liability company who extends credit or otherwise acts in reliance on an obligation described in subsection (a), and without notice of any compromise under Section 404(c)(5), may enforce the original obligation.

COMMENT

An obligation need not be in writing to be enforceable. Given the informality of some companies, a writing requirement may frustrate reasonable expectations of members based on a clear oral agreement. Obligations may be compromised with the consent of all of the members under Section 404(c)(5), but the compromise is generally effective only among the consenting members. Company creditors are bound by the compromise only as provided in Section 402(b).

Section 403. Member's and Manager's Rights to Payments and Reimbursement.

(a) A limited liability company shall reimburse a member or manager for payments made and indemnify a member or manager for liabilities incurred by the member or manager in the ordinary course of the business of the company or for the preservation of its business or property.

(b) A limited liability company shall reimburse a member for an advance to the company beyond the amount of contribution the member agreed to make.

(c) A payment or advance made by a member which gives rise to an obligation of a limited liability company under subsection (a) or (b) constitutes a loan to the company upon which interest accrues from the date of the payment or advance.

(d) A member is not entitled to remuneration for services performed for a limited liability company, except for reasonable compensation for services rendered in winding up the business of the company.

COMMENT

The presence of a liability shield will ordinarily prevent a member or manager from incurring personal liability on behalf of the company in the ordinary course of the company's business. Where a member of a member-managed or a manager of a manager-managed company incurs such liabilities, Section 403(a) provides that the company must indemnify the member or manager where that person acted in the ordinary course of the company's business or the preservation of its property. A member or manager is therefore entitled to indemnification only if the act was within the member or manager's actual authority. A member or manager is therefore not entitled to indemnification for conduct that violates the duty of care set forth in Section 409(c) or for tortious conduct against a third party. Since members of a manager-managed company do not possess the apparent authority to bind the company, it would be more unusual for such a member to incur a liability for indemnification in the ordinary course of the company's business.

Section 404. Management of Limited Liability Company.

(a) In a member-managed company:

   (1) each member has equal rights in the management and conduct of the company's business; and

   (2) except as otherwise provided in subsection (c), any matter relating to the business of the company may be decided by a majority of the members.

(b) In a manager-managed company:

   (1) each manager has equal rights in the management and conduct of the company's business;

   (2) except as otherwise provided in subsection (c), any matter relating to the business of the company may be exclusively decided by the manager or, if there is more than one manager, by a majority of the managers; and

   (3) a manager:

      (i) must be designated, appointed, elected, removed, or replaced by a vote, approval, or consent of a majority of the members; and

      (ii) holds office until a successor has been elected and qualified, unless the manager sooner resigns or is removed.

(c) The only matters of a member or manager-managed company's business requiring the consent of all of the members are:

   (1) the amendment of the operating agreement under Section 103;

   (2) the authorization or ratification of acts or transactions under Section 103(b)(2)(ii) which would otherwise violate the duty of loyalty;

   (3) an amendment to the articles of organization under Section 204;

   (4) the compromise of an obligation to make a contribution under Section 402(b);

(5) the compromise, as among members, of an obligation of a member to make a contribution or return money or other property paid or distributed in violation of this [Act];

(6) the making of interim distributions under Section 405(a), including the redemption of an interest;

(7) the admission of a new member;

(8) the use of the company's property to redeem an interest subject to a charging order;

(9) the consent to dissolve the company under Section 801(b)(2);

(10) a waiver of the right to have the company's business wound up and the company terminated under Section 802(b);

(11) the consent of members to merge with another entity under Section 904(c)(1); and

(12) the sale, lease, exchange, or other disposal of all, or substantially all, of the company's property with or without goodwill.

(d) Action requiring the consent of members or managers under this [Act] may be taken without a meeting.

(e) A member or manager may appoint a proxy to vote or otherwise act for the member or manager by signing an appointment instrument, either personally or by the member's or manager's attorney-in-fact.

COMMENT

In a member-managed company, each member has equal rights in the management and conduct of the company's business unless otherwise provided in an operating agreement. For example, an operating agreement may allocate voting rights based upon capital contributions rather than the subsection (a) per capita rule. Also, member disputes as to any matter relating to the company's business may be resolved by a majority of the members unless the matter relates to a matter specified in subsection (c) (unanimous consent required). Regardless of how the members allocate management rights, each member is an agent of the company with the apparent authority to bind the company in the ordinary course of its business. See Comments to Section 301(a). A member's right to participate in management terminates upon dissociation. See Section 603(b)(1).

In a manager-managed company, the members, unless also managers, have no rights in the management and conduct of the company's business unless otherwise provided in an operating agreement. If there is more than one manager, manager disputes as to any matter relating to the company's business may be resolved by a majority of the managers unless the matter relates to a matter specified in subsection (c) (unanimous member consent required). Managers must be designated, appointed, or elected by a majority of the members. A manager need not be a member and is an agent of the company with the apparent authority to bind the company in the ordinary course of its business. See Sections 101(10) and 301(b).

To promote clarity and certainty, subsection (c) specifies those exclusive matters requiring the unanimous consent of the members, whether the company is member- or manager-managed. For example, interim distributions, including redemptions, may not be made without the unanimous consent of all the members. Unless otherwise agreed, all other company matters are to be determined under the majority of members or managers rules of subsections (a) and (b).

Section 405. Sharing of and Right to Distributions.

(a) Any distributions made by a limited liability company before its dissolution and winding up must be in equal shares.

(b) A member has no right to receive, and may not be required to accept, a distribution in kind.

(c) If a member becomes entitled to receive a distribution, the member has the status of, and is entitled to all remedies available to, a creditor of the limited liability company with respect to the distribution.

COMMENT

Recognizing the informality of many limited liability companies, this section creates a simple default rule regarding interim distributions. Any interim distributions made must be in equal shares and approved by all members. See Section 404(c)(6). The rule assumes that: profits will be shared equally; some distributions will constitute a return of contributions that should be shared equally rather than a distribution of profits; and property contributors should have the right to veto any distribution that threatens their return of contributions on liquidation. In the simple case where the members make equal contributions of property or equal contributions of services, those assumptions avoid the necessity of maintaining a complex capital account or determining profits. Where some members contribute services and others property, the unanimous vote necessary to approve interim distributions protects against unwanted distributions of contributions to service contributors. Consistently, Section 408(a) does not require the company to maintain a separate account for each member, the Act does not contain a default rule for allocating profits and losses, and Section 806(b) requires that liquidating distributions to members be made in equal shares after the return of contributions not previously returned. See Comments to Section 806(b).

Section 405(c) governs distributions declared or made when the company was solvent. Section 406 governs distributions declared or made when the company is insolvent.

Section 406. Limitations on Distributions.

  (a) A distribution may not be made if:

    (1) the limited liability company would not be able to pay its debts as they become due in the ordinary course of business; or

    (2) the company's total assets would be less than the sum of its total liabilities plus the amount that would be needed, if the company were to be dissolved, wound up, and terminated at the time of the distribution, to satisfy the preferential rights upon dissolution, winding up, and termination of members whose preferential rights are superior to those receiving the distribution.

  (b) A limited liability company may base a determination that a distribution is not prohibited under subsection (a) on financial statements prepared on the basis of accounting practices and principles that are reasonable in the circumstances or on a fair valuation or other method that is reasonable in the circumstances.

  (c) Except as otherwise provided in subsection (e), the effect of a distribution under subsection (a) is measured:

    (1) in the case of distribution by purchase, redemption, or other acquisition of a distributional interest in a limited liability company, as of the date money or other property is transferred or debt incurred by the company; and

    (2) in all other cases, as of the date the:
      (i) distribution is authorized if the payment occurs within 120 days after the date of authorization; or
      (ii) payment is made if it occurs more than 120 days after the date of authorization.

  (d) A limited liability company's indebtedness to a member incurred by reason of a distribution made in accordance with this section is at parity with the company's indebtedness to its general, unsecured creditors.

  (e) Indebtedness of a limited liability company, including indebtedness issued in connection with or as part of a distribution, is not considered a liability for purposes of determinations under subsection (a) if its terms provide that payment of principal and interest are made only if and to the extent that payment of a distribution to members could then be made under this section. If the indebtedness is issued as a distribution, each payment of principal or interest on the indebtedness is treated as a distribution, the effect of which is measured on the date the payment is made.

COMMENT

This section establishes the validity of company distributions, which in turn determines the potential liability of members and managers for improper distributions under Section 407. Distributions are improper if the company is insolvent under subsection (a) at the time the distribution is measured under subsection (c). In recognition of the informality of many limited liability companies, the solvency determination under subsection (b) may be made on the basis of a fair valuation or other method reasonable under the circumstances.

The application of the equity insolvency and balance sheet tests present special problems in the context of the purchase, redemption, or other acquisition of a company's distributional interests. Special rules establish the time of measurement of such transfers. Under Section 406(c)(1), the time for measuring the effect of a distribution to purchase a distributional interest is the date of payment. The company may make payment either by transferring property or incurring a debt to transfer property in the future. In the latter case, subsection (c)(1) establishes a clear rule that the legality of the distribution is tested when the debt is actually incurred, not later when the debt is actually paid. Under Section 406(e), indebtedness is not considered a liability for purposes of subsection (a) if the terms of the indebtedness itself provide that payments can be made only if and to the extent that a payment of a distribution could then be made under this section. The effect makes the holder of the indebtedness junior to all other creditors but senior to members in their capacity as members.

Section 407. Liability for Unlawful Distributions.

(a) A member of a member-managed company or a member or manager of a manager-managed company who votes for or assents to a distribution made in violation of Section 406, the articles of organization, or the operating agreement is personally liable to the company for the amount of the distribution which exceeds the amount that could have been distributed without violating Section 406, the articles of organization, or the operating agreement if it is established that the member or manager did not perform the member's or manager's duties in compliance with Section 409.

(b) A member of a manager-managed company who knew a distribution was made in violation of Section 406, the articles of organization, or the operating agreement is personally liable to the company, but only to the extent that the distribution received by the member exceeded the amount that could have been properly paid under Section 406.

(c) A member or manager against whom an action is brought under this section may implead in the action all:

(1) other members or managers who voted for or assented to the distribution in violation of subsection (a) and may compel contribution from them; and

(2) members who received a distribution in violation of subsection (b) and may compel contribution from the member in the amount received in violation of subsection (b).

(d) A proceeding under this section is barred unless it is commenced within two years after the distribution.

COMMENT

Whenever members or managers fail to meet the standards of conduct of Section 409 and vote for or assent to an unlawful distribution, they are personally liable to the company for the portion of the distribution that exceeds the maximum amount that could have been lawfully distributed. The recovery remedy under this section extends only to the company, not the company's creditors. Under subsection (a), members and managers are not liable for an unlawful distribution provided their vote in favor of the distribution satisfies the duty of care of Section 409(c).

Subsection (a) creates personal liability in favor of the company against members or managers who approve an unlawful distribution for the entire amount of a distribution that could not be lawfully distributed. Subsection (b) creates personal liability against only members who knowingly received the unlawful distribution, but only in the amount measured by the portion of the actual distribution received that was not lawfully made. Members who both vote for or assent to an unlawful distribution and receive a portion or all of the distribution will be liable, at the election of the company, under either but not both subsections.

A member or manager who is liable under subsection (a) may seek contribution under subsection (c)(1) from other members and managers who also voted for or assented to the same distribution and may also seek recoupment under subsection (c)(2) from members who received the distribution, but only if they accepted the payments knowing they were unlawful.

The two-year statute of limitations of subsection (d) is measured from the date of the distribution. The date of the distribution is determined under Section 406(c).

Section 408. Member's Right to Information.

(a) A limited liability company shall provide members and their agents and attorneys access to its records, if any, at the company's principal office or other reasonable locations specified in the operating agreement. The company shall provide former members and their agents and attorneys access for proper purposes to records pertaining to the period during which they were members. The right of access provides the opportunity to inspect and copy records during ordinary business hours. The company may impose a reasonable charge, limited to the costs of labor and material, for copies of records furnished.

(b) A limited liability company shall furnish to a member, and to the legal representative of a deceased member or member under legal disability:

    (1) without demand, information concerning the company's business or affairs reasonably required for the proper exercise of the member's rights and performance of the member's duties under the operating agreement or this [Act]; and

    (2) on demand, other information concerning the company's business or affairs, except to the extent the demand or the information demanded is unreasonable or otherwise improper under the circumstances.

(c) A member has the right upon written demand given to the limited liability company to obtain at the company's expense a copy of any written operating agreement.

COMMENT

Recognizing the informality of many limited liability companies, subsection (a) does not require a company to maintain any records. In general, a company should maintain records necessary to enable members to determine their share of profits and losses and their rights on dissociation. If inadequate records are maintained to determine those and other critical rights, a member may maintain an action for an accounting under Section 410(a). Normally, a company will maintain at least records required by state or federal authorities regarding tax and other filings.

The obligation to furnish access includes the obligation to insure that all records, if any, are accessible in intelligible form. For example, a company that switches computer systems has an obligation either to convert the records from the old system or retain at least one computer capable of accessing the records from the old system.

The right to inspect and copy records maintained is not conditioned on a member or former member's purpose or motive. However, an abuse of the access and copy right may create a remedy in favor of the other members as a violation of the requesting member or former member's obligation of good faith and fair dealing. See Section 409(d).

Although a company is not required to maintain any records under subsection (a), it is nevertheless subject to a disclosure duty to furnish specified information under subsection (b)(1). A company must therefore furnish to members, without demand, information reasonably needed for members to exercise their rights and duties as members. A member's exercise of these duties justifies an unqualified right of access to the company's records. The member's right to company records may not be unreasonably restricted by the operating agreement. See Section 103(b)(1).

Section 409. General Standards of Member's and Manager's Conduct.

(a) The only fiduciary duties a member owes to a member-managed company and its other members are the duty of loyalty and the duty of care imposed by subsections (b) and (c).

(b) A member's duty of loyalty to a member-managed company and its other members is limited to the following:

   (1) to account to the company and to hold as trustee for it any property, profit, or benefit derived by the member in the conduct or winding up of the company's business or derived from a use by the member of the company's property, including the appropriation of a company's opportunity;

   (2) to refrain from dealing with the company in the conduct or winding up of the company's business as or on behalf of a party having an interest adverse to the company; and

   (3) to refrain from competing with the company in the conduct of the company's business before the dissolution of the company.

(c) A member's duty of care to a member-managed company and its other members in the conduct of and winding up of the company's business is limited to refraining from engaging in grossly negligent or reckless conduct, intentional misconduct, or a knowing violation of law.

(d) A member shall discharge the duties to a member-managed company and its other members under this [Act] or under the operating agreement and exercise any rights consistently with the obligation of good faith and fair dealing.

(e) A member of a member-managed company does not violate a duty or obligation under this [Act] or under the operating agreement merely because the member's conduct furthers the member's own interest.

(f) A member of a member-managed company may lend money to and transact other business with the company. As to each loan or transaction, the rights and obligations of the member are the same as those of a person who is not a member, subject to other applicable law.

(g) This section applies to a person winding up the limited liability company's business as the personal or legal representative of the last surviving member as if the person were a member.

(h) In a manager-managed company:

   (1) a member who is not also a manager owes no duties to the company or to the other members solely by reason of being a member;

   (2) a manager is held to the same standards of conduct prescribed for members in subsections (b) through (f);

   (3) a member who pursuant to the operating agreement exercises some or all of the rights of a manager in the management and conduct of the company's business is held to the standards of conduct in subsections (b) through (f) to the extent that the mem-

ber exercises the managerial authority vested in a manager by this [Act]; and

(4) a manager is relieved of liability imposed by law for violation of the standards prescribed by subsections (b) through (f) to the extent of the managerial authority delegated to the members by the operating agreement.

COMMENT

Under subsections (a), (c), and (h), members and managers, and their delegatees, owe to the company and to the other members and managers only the fiduciary duties of loyalty and care set forth in subsections (b) and (c) and the obligation of good faith and fair dealing set forth in subsection (d). An operating agreement may not waive or eliminate the duties or obligation, but may, if not manifestly unreasonable, identify activities and determine standards for measuring the performance of them. See Section 103(b)(2) to (4).

Upon a member's dissociation, the duty to account for personal profits under subsection (b)(1), the duty to refrain from acting as or representing adverse interests under subsection (b)(2), and the duty of care under subsection (c) are limited to those derived from matters arising or events occurring before the dissociation unless the member participates in winding up the company's business. Also, the duty not to compete terminates upon dissociation. See Section 603(b)(3) and (b)(2). However, a dissociated member is not free to use confidential company information after dissociation. For example, a dissociated member of a company may immediately compete with the company for new clients but must exercise care in completing on-going client transactions and must account to the company for any fees from the old clients on account of those transactions. Subsection (c) adopts a gross negligence standard for the duty of care, the standard actually used in most partnerships and corporations.

Subsection (b)(2) prohibits a member from acting adversely or representing an adverse party to the company. The rule is based on agency principles and seeks to avoid the conflict of opposing interests in the mind of the member agent whose duty is to act for the benefit of the principal company. As reflected in subsection (f), the rule does not prohibit the member from dealing with the company other than as an adversary. A member may generally deal with the company under subsection (f) when the transaction is approved by the company.

Subsection (e) makes clear that a member does not violate the obligation of good faith under subsection (d) merely because the member's conduct furthers that member's own interest. For example, a member's refusal to vote for an interim distribution because of negative tax implications to that member does not violate that member's obligation of good faith to the other members. Likewise, a member may vote against a proposal by the company to open a shopping center that would directly compete with another shopping center in which the member owns an interest.

Section 410. Actions by Members.

(a) A member may maintain an action against a limited liability company or another member for legal or equitable relief, with or without an accounting as to the company's business, to enforce:

    (1) the member's rights under the operating agreement;

    (2) the member's rights under this [Act]; and

    (3) the rights and otherwise protect the interests of the member, including rights and interests arising independently of the member's relationship to the company.

(b) The accrual, and any time limited for the assertion, of a right of action for a remedy under this section is governed by other law. A right to an accounting upon a dissolution and winding up does not revive a claim barred by law.

COMMENT

During the existence of the company, members have under this section access to the courts to resolve claims against the company and other members, leaving broad judicial discretion to fashion appropriate legal remedies. A member pursues only that member's claim against the company or another member under this section. Article 11 governs a member's derivative pursuit of a claim on behalf of the company.

A member may recover against the company and the other members under subsection (a)(3) for personal injuries or damage to the member's property caused by another member. One member's negligence is therefore not imputed to bar another member's action.

Section 411. Continuation of Term Company After Expiration of Specified Term.

(a) If a term company is continued after the expiration of the specified term, the rights and duties of the members and managers remain the same as they were at the expiration of the term except to the extent inconsistent with rights and duties of members and managers of an at-will company.

(b) If the members in a member-managed company or the managers in a manager-managed company continue the business without any winding up of the business of the company, it continues as an at-will company.

Comment

A term company will generally dissolve upon the expiration of its term unless either its articles are amended before the expiration of the original specified term to provide for an additional specified term or the members or managers simply continue the company as an at-will company under this section. Amendment of the articles specifying an additional term requires the unanimous consent of the members. See Section 404(c)(3). Therefore, any member has the right to block the amendment. Absent an amendment to the articles, a company may only be continued under subsection (b) as an at-will company. The decision to continue a term company as an at-will company does not require the unanimous consent of the members and is treated as an ordinary business matter with disputes resolved by a simple majority vote of either the members or managers. See Section 404. In that case, subsection (b) provides that the members' conduct amends or becomes part of an operating agreement to "continue" the company as an at-will company. The amendment to the operating agreement does not alter the rights of creditors who suffer detrimental reliance because the company does not liquidate after the expiration of its specified term. See Section 203(c)(2).

Preexisting operating-agreement provisions continue to control the relationship of the members under subsection (a) except to the extent inconsistent with the rights and duties of members of an at-will company with an operating agreement containing the same provisions. However, the members could agree in advance that, if the company's business continues after the expiration of its specified term, the company continues as a company with a new specified term or that the provisions of its operating agreement survive the expiration of the specified term.

[Article] 5

Transferees and Creditors of Member

Section 501. Member's Distributional Interest.
Section 502. Transfer of Distributional Interest.
Section 503. Rights of Transferee.
Section 504. Rights of Creditor.

Section 501. Member's Distributional Interest.

(a) A member is not a co-owner of, and has no transferable interest in, property of a limited liability company.

(b) A distributional interest in a limited liability company is personal property and, subject to Sections 502 and 503, may be transferred in whole or in part.

(c) An operating agreement may provide that a distributional interest may be evidenced by a certificate of the interest issued by the limited liability company and, subject to Section 503, may also provide for the transfer of any interest represented by the certificate.

COMMENT

Members have no property interest in property owned by a limited liability company. A distributional interest is personal property and is defined under Section 101(6) as a member's interest in distributions only and does not include the member's broader rights to participate in management under Section 404 and to inspect company records under Section 408.

Under Section 405(a), distributions are allocated in equal shares unless otherwise provided in an operating agreement. Whenever it is desirable to allocate distributions in proportion to contributions rather than per capita, certification may be useful to reduce valuation issues. New and important Internal Revenue Service announcements clarify that certification of a limited liability company will not cause it to be taxed like a corporation.

Section 502. Transfer of Distributional Interest.

A transfer of a distributional interest does not entitle the transferee to become or to exercise any rights of a member. A transfer entitles the transferee to receive, to the extent transferred, only the distributions to which the transferor would be entitled.

COMMENT

Under Sections 501(b) and 502, the only interest a member may freely transfer is that member's distributional interest. A member's transfer of all of a distributional interest constitutes an event of dissociation. See Section 601(3). A transfer of less than all of a member's distributional interest is not an event of dissociation. A member ceases to be a member upon the transfer of all that member's distributional interest and that transfer is also an event of dissociation under Section 601(3). Relating the event of dissociation to the member's transfer of all of the member's distributional interest avoids the need for the company to track potential future dissociation events associated with a member no longer financially interested in the company. Also, all the remaining members may expel a member upon the transfer of "substantially all" the member's distributional interest. The expulsion is an event of dissociation under Section 601(5)(ii).

Section 503. Rights of Transferee.

(a) A transferee of a distributional interest may become a member of a limited liability company if and to the extent that the transferor gives the transferee the right in accordance with authority described in the operating agreement or all other members consent.

(b) A transferee who has become a member, to the extent transferred, has the rights and powers, and is subject to the restrictions and liabilities, of a member under the operating agreement of a limited liability company and this [Act]. A transferee who becomes a member also is liable for the transferor member's obligations to make contributions under Section 402 and for obligations under Section 407 to return unlawful distributions, but the transferee is not obligated for the transferor member's liabilities unknown to the transferee at the time the transferee becomes a member.

(c) Whether or not a transferee of a distributional interest becomes a member under subsection (a), the transferor is not released from liability to the limited liability company under the operating agreement or this [Act].

(d) A transferee who does not become a member is not entitled to participate in the management or conduct of the limited liability company's business, require access to information concerning the company's transactions, or inspect or copy any of the company's records.

(e) A transferee who does not become a member is entitled to:

(1) receive, in accordance with the transfer, distributions to which the transferor would otherwise be entitled;

(2) receive, upon dissolution and winding up of the limited liability company's business:
(i) in accordance with the transfer, the net amount otherwise distributable to the transferor;
(ii) a statement of account only from the date of the latest statement of account agreed to by all the members;

(3) seek under Section 801(5) a judicial determination that it is equitable to dissolve and wind up the company's business.

(f) A limited liability company need not give effect to a transfer until it has notice of the transfer.

COMMENT

The only interest a member may freely transfer is the member's distributional interest. A transferee may acquire the remaining rights of a member only by being admitted as a member of the company by all of the remaining members. New and important Internal Revenue Service announcements clarify that the transferability of membership interests of a limited liability company in excess of these default rules will not cause it to be taxed like a corporation. In many cases a limited liability company will be organized and operated with only a few members. These default rules were chosen in the interest of preserving the right of existing members in such companies to determine whether a transferee will become a member.

A transferee not admitted as a member is not entitled to participate in management, require access to information, or inspect or copy company records. The only rights of a transferee are to receive the distributions the transferor would otherwise be entitled, receive a limited statement of account, and seek a judicial dissolution under Section 801(a)(5).

Subsection (e) sets forth the rights of a transferee of an existing member. Although the rights of a dissociated member to participate in the future management of the company parallel the rights of a transferee, a dissociated member retains additional rights that accrued from that person's membership such as the right to enforce Article 7 purchase rights. See and compare Sections 603(b)(1) and 801(a)(4) and Comments.

Section 504. Rights of Creditor.

(a) On application by a judgment creditor of a member of a limited liability company or of a member's transferee, a court having jurisdiction may charge the distributional interest of the judgment debtor to satisfy the judgment. The court may appoint a receiver of the share of the distributions due or to become due to the judgment debtor and make all other orders, directions, accounts, and inquiries the judgment debtor might have made or which the circumstances may require to give effect to the charging order.

(b) A charging order constitutes a lien on the judgment debtor's distributional interest. The court may order a foreclosure of a lien on a distributional interest subject to the charging order at any time. A purchaser at the foreclosure sale has the rights of a transferee.

(c) At any time before foreclosure, a distributional interest in a limited liability company which is charged may be redeemed:

(1) by the judgment debtor;

(2) with property other than the company's property, by one or more of the other members; or

(3) with the company's property, but only if permitted by the operating agreement.

(d) This [Act] does not affect a member's right under exemption laws with respect to the member's distributional interest in a limited liability company.

(e) This section provides the exclusive remedy by which a judgment creditor of a member or a transferee may satisfy a judgment out of the judgment debtor's distributional interest in a limited liability company.

COMMENT

A charging order is the only remedy by which a judgment creditor of a member or a member's transferee may reach the distributional interest of a member or member's transferee. Under Section 503(e), the distributional interest of a member or transferee is limited to the member's right to receive distributions from the company and to seek judicial liquidation of the company.

[ARTICLE] 6

MEMBER'S DISSOCIATION

Section 601. Events Causing Member's Dissociation.
Section 602. Member's Power to Dissociate; Wrongful Dissociation.
Section 603. Effect of Member's Dissociation.

Section 601. Events Causing Member's Dissociation.
A member is dissociated from a limited liability company upon the occurrence of any of the following events:

(1) the company's having notice of the member's express will to withdraw upon the date of notice or on a later date specified by the member;

(2) an event agreed to in the operating agreement as causing the member's dissociation;

(3) upon transfer of all of a member's distributional interest, other than a transfer for security purposes or a court order charging the member's distributional interest which has not been foreclosed;

(4) the member's expulsion pursuant to the operating agreement;

(5) the member's expulsion by unanimous vote of the other members if:

    (i) it is unlawful to carry on the company's business with the member;

   (ii) there has been a transfer of substantially all of the member's distributional interest, other than a transfer for security purposes or a court order charging the member's distributional interest which has not been foreclosed;

  (iii) within 90 days after the company notifies a corporate member that it will be expelled because it has filed a certificate of dissolution or the equivalent, its charter has been revoked, or its right to conduct business has been suspended by the jurisdiction of its incorporation, the member fails to obtain a revocation of the certificate of dissolution or a reinstatement of its charter or its right to conduct business; or

  (iv) a partnership or a limited liability company that is a member has been dissolved and its business is being wound up;

(6) on application by the company or another member, the member's expulsion by judicial determination because the member:

    (i) engaged in wrongful conduct that adversely and materially affected the company's business;

   (ii) willfully or persistently committed a material breach of the operating agreement or of a duty owed to the company or the other members under Section 409; or

A member may be expelled from the company under paragraph (5)(ii) by the unanimous vote of the other members upon a transfer of "substantially all" of the member's distributional interest other than for a transfer as security for a loan. A transfer of "all" of the member's distributional interest is an event of dissociation under paragraph (3).

Although a member is dissociated upon death, the effect of the dissociation where the company does not dissolve depends upon whether the company is at-will or term. Only the decedent's distributional interest transfers to the decedent's estate which does not acquire the decedent member's management rights. See Section 603(b)(1). Unless otherwise agreed, if the company was at-will, the estate's distributional interest must be purchased by the company at fair value determined at the date of death. However, if a term company, the estate and its transferees continue only as the owner of the distributional interest with no management rights until the expiration of the specified term that existed on the date of death. At the expiration of that term, the company must purchase the interest of a dissociated member if the company continues for an additional term by amending its articles or simply continues as an at-will company. See Sections 411 and 701(a)(2) and Comments. Before that time, the estate and its transferees have the right to make application for a judicial dissolution of the company under Section 801(b)(5) as successors in interest to a dissociated member. See Comments to Sections 801, 411, and 701. Where the members have allocated management rights on the basis of contributions rather than simply the number of members, a member's death will result in a transfer of management rights to the remaining members on a proportionate basis. This transfer of rights may be avoided by a provision in an operating agreement extending the Section 701(a)(1) at-will purchase right to a decedent member of a term company.

Section 602. Member's Power to Dissociate; Wrongful Dissociation.

(a) Unless otherwise provided in the operating agreement, a member has the power to dissociate from a limited liability company at any time, rightfully or wrongfully, by express will pursuant to Section 601(1).

(b) If the operating agreement has not eliminated a member's power to dissociate, the member's dissociation from a limited liability company is wrongful only if:

(1) it is in breach of an express provision of the agreement; or

(2) before the expiration of the specified term of a term company:
   (i) the member withdraws by express will;
   (ii) the member is expelled by judicial determination under Section 601(6);
   (iii) the member is dissociated by becoming a debtor in bankruptcy; or

    (iii) engaged in conduct relating to the company's business which makes it not reasonably practicable to carry on the business with the member;

(7) the member's:
    (i) becoming a debtor in bankruptcy;
    (ii) executing an assignment for the benefit of creditors;
    (iii) seeking, consenting to, or acquiescing in the appointment of a trustee, receiver, or liquidator of the member or of all or substantially all of the member's property; or
    (iv) failing, within 90 days after the appointment, to have vacated or stayed the appointment of a trustee, receiver, or liquidator of the member or of all or substantially all of the member's property obtained without the member's consent or acquiescence, or failing within 90 days after the expiration of a stay to have the appointment vacated;

(8) in the case of a member who is an individual:
    (i) the member's death;
    (ii) the appointment of a guardian or general conservator for the member; or
    (iii) a judicial determination that the member has otherwise become incapable of performing the member's duties under the operating agreement;

(9) in the case of a member that is a trust or is acting as a member by virtue of being a trustee of a trust, distribution of the trust's entire rights to receive distributions from the company, but not merely by reason of the substitution of a successor trustee;

(10) in the case of a member that is an estate or is acting as a member by virtue of being a personal representative of an estate, distribution of the estate's entire rights to receive distributions from the company, but not merely the substitution of a successor personal representative; or

(11) termination of the existence of a member if the member is not an individual, estate, or trust other than a business trust.

COMMENT

The term "dissociation" refers to the change in the relationships among the dissociated member, the company and the other members caused by a member's ceasing to be associated in the carrying on of the company's business. Member dissociation from either an at-will or term company, whether member- or manager-managed is not an event of dissolution of the company unless otherwise specified in an operating agreement. See Section 801(a)(1). However, member dissociation will generally trigger the obligation of the company to purchase the dissociated member's interest under Article 7.

      (iv) in the case of a member who is not an individual, trust other than a business trust, or estate, the member is expelled or otherwise dissociated because it willfully dissolved or terminated its existence.

  (c) A member who wrongfully dissociates from a limited liability company is liable to the company and to the other members for damages caused by the dissociation. The liability is in addition to any other obligation of the member to the company or to the other members.

  (d) If a limited liability company does not dissolve and wind up its business as a result of a member's wrongful dissociation under subsection (b), damages sustained by the company for the wrongful dissociation must be offset against distributions otherwise due the member after the dissociation.

COMMENT

A member has the power to withdraw from both an at-will company and a term company although the effects of the withdrawal are remarkably different. See Comments to Section 601. At a minimum, the exercise of a power to withdraw enables members to terminate their continuing duties of loyalty and care. See Section 603(b)(2) to (3).

A member's power to withdraw by express will may be eliminated by an operating agreement. New and important Internal Revenue Service announcements clarify that alteration of a member's power to withdraw will not cause the limited liability company to be taxed like a corporation. An operating agreement may eliminate a member's power to withdraw by express will to promote the business continuity of an at-will company by removing member's right to force the company to purchase the member's distributional interest. See Section 701(a)(1). However, such a member retains the ability to seek a judicial dissolution of the company. See Section 801(a)(4).

If a member's power to withdraw by express will is not eliminated in an operating agreement, the withdrawal may nevertheless be made wrongful under subsection (b). All dissociations, including withdrawal by express will, may be made wrongful under subsection (b)(1) in both an at-will and term company by the inclusion of a provision in an operating agreement. Even where an operating agreement does not eliminate the power to withdraw by express will or make any dissociation wrongful, the dissociation of a member of a term company for the reasons specified under subsection (b)(2) is wrongful. The member is liable to the company and other members for damages caused by a wrongful dissociation under subsection (c) and, under subsection (d), the damages may be offset against all distributions otherwise due the member after the dissociation. Section 701(f) provides a similar rule permitting damages for wrongful dissociation to be offset against any company purchase of the member's distributional interest.

Section 603. Effect of Member's Dissociation.

    (a) Upon a member's dissociation:

        (1) in an at-will company, the company must cause the dissociated member's distributional interest to be purchased under [Article] 7; and

        (2) in a term company:

            (i) if the company dissolves and winds up its business on or before the expiration of its specified term, [Article] 8 applies to determine the dissociated member's rights to distributions; and

           (ii) if the company does not dissolve and wind up its business on or before the expiration of its specified term, the company must cause the dissociated member's distributional interest to be purchased under [Article] 7 on the date of the expiration of the term specified at the time of the member's dissociation.

    (b) Upon a member's dissociation from a limited liability company:

        (1) the member's right to participate in the management and conduct of the company's business terminates, except as otherwise provided in Section 803, and the member ceases to be a member and is treated the same as a transferee of a member;

        (2) the member's duty of loyalty under Section 409(b)(3) terminates; and

        (3) the member's duty of loyalty under Section 409(b)(1) and (2) and duty of care under Section 409(c) continue only with regard to matters arising and events occurring before the member's dissociation, unless the member participates in winding up the company's business pursuant to Section 803.

COMMENT

Member dissociation is not an event of dissolution of a company unless otherwise specified in an operating agreement. See Section 801(a)(1). Dissociation from an at-will company that does not dissolve the company causes the dissociated member's distributional interest to be immediately purchased under Article 7. See Comments to Sections 602 and 603. Dissociation from a term company that does not dissolve the company does not cause the dissociated member's distributional interest to be purchased under Article 7 until the expiration of the specified term that existed on the date of dissociation.

Subsection (b)(1) provides that a dissociated member forfeits the right to participate in the future conduct of the company's business. Dissociation does not however forfeit that member's right to enforce the Article 7 rights that accrue by reason of the dissociation. Similarly, where dissociation occurs by death, the decedent member's successors in interest may enforce that member's Article 7 rights. See and compare Comments to Section 503(e).

Dissociation terminates the member's right to participate in management, including the member's actual authority to act for the company under Section 301, and begins the two-year period after which a member's apparent authority conclusively ends. See Comments to Section 703. Dissociation also terminates a member's continuing duties of loyalty and care, except with regard to continuing transactions, to the company and other members unless the member participates in winding up the company's business. See Comments to Section 409.

[ARTICLE] 7

MEMBER'S DISSOCIATION WHEN BUSINESS NOT WOUND UP

Section 701. Company Purchase of Distributional Interest.

(a) A limited liability company shall purchase a distributional interest of a:

   (1) member of an at-will company for its fair value determined as of the date of the member's dissociation if the member's dissociation does not result in a dissolution and winding up of the company's business under Section 801; or

   (2) member of a term company for its fair value determined as of the date of the expiration of the specified term that existed on the date of the member's dissociation if the expiration of the specified term does not result in a dissolution and winding up of the company's business under Section 801.

(b) A limited liability company must deliver a purchase offer to the dissociated member whose distributional interest is entitled to be purchased not later than 30 days after the date determined under subsection (a). The purchase offer must be accompanied by:

   (1) a statement of the company's assets and liabilities as of the date determined under subsection (a);

   (2) the latest available balance sheet and income statement, if any; and

   (3) an explanation of how the estimated amount of the payment was calculated.

(c) If the price and other terms of a purchase of a distributional interest are fixed or are to be determined by the operating agreement, the price and terms so fixed or determined govern the purchase unless the purchaser defaults. If a default occurs, the dissociated member is entitled to commence a proceeding to have the company dissolved under Section 801(4)(iv).

(d) If an agreement to purchase the distributional interest is not made within 120 days after the date determined under subsection (a), the dissociated member, within another 120 days, may commence a proceeding against the limited liability company to enforce the purchase. The company at its expense shall notify in writing all of the remaining members, and any other person the court directs, of the commencement of the proceeding. The jurisdiction of the court in which the proceeding is commenced under this subsection is plenary and exclusive.

(e) The court shall determine the fair value of the distributional interest in accordance with the standards set forth in Section 702 together with the terms for the purchase. Upon making these determinations, the court shall order the limited liability company to purchase or cause the purchase of the interest.

(f) Damages for wrongful dissociation under Section 602(b), and all other amounts owing, whether or not currently due, from the dissociated member to a limited liability company, must be offset against the purchase price.

COMMENT

This section sets forth default rules regarding an otherwise mandatory company purchase of a distributional interest. Even though a dissociated member's rights to participate in the future management of the company are equivalent to those of a transferee of a member, the dissociation does not forfeit that member's right to enforce the Article 7 purchase right. Similarly, if the dissociation occurs by reason of death, the decedent member's successors in interest may enforce the Article 7 rights. See Comments to Sections 503(e) and 603(b)(1).

An at-will company must purchase a dissociated member's distributional interest under subsection (a)(1) when that member's dissociation does not result in a dissolution of the company under Section 801(a)(1). The purchase price is equal to the fair value of the interest determined as of the date of dissociation. Any damages for wrongful dissociation must be offset against the purchase price.

Dissociation from a term company does not require an immediate purchase of the member's interest but the operating agreement may specify that dissociation is an event of dissolution. See Section 801(a)(1). A term company must only purchase the dissociated member's distributional interest under subsection (a)(2) on the expiration of the specified term that existed on the date of the member's dissociation. The purchase price is equal to the fair value of the interest determined as of the date of the expiration of that specified term. Any damages for wrongful dissociation must be offset against the purchase price.

The valuation dates differ between subsections (a)(1) and (a)(2) purchases. The former is valued on the date of member dissociation whereas the latter is valued on the date of the expiration of the specified term that existed on the date of dissociation. A subsection (a)(2) dissociated member therefore assumes the risk of loss between the date of dissociation and the expiration of the then stated specified term. See Comments to Section 801 (dissociated member may file application to dissolve company under Section 801(a)(4)).

The default valuation standard is fair value. See Comments to Section 702. An operating agreement may fix a method or formula for determining the purchase price and the terms of payment. The purchase right may be modified. For example, an operating agreement may eliminate a member's power to withdraw from an at-will company which narrows the dissociation events contemplated under subsection (a)(1). See Comments to Section 602(a). However, a provision in an operating agreement providing for complete forfeiture of the purchase right may be unenforceable where the power to dissociate has not also been eliminated. See Section 104(a).

The company must deliver a purchase offer to the dissociated member within 30 days after the date determined under subsection (a). The offer must be accompanied by information designed to enable the dissociated member to evaluate the fairness of the offer. The subsection (b)(3) explanation of how the offer price was calculated need not be elaborate. For example, a mere statement of the basis of the calculation, such as "book value," may be sufficient.

The company and the dissociated member must reach an agreement on the purchase price and terms within 120 days after the date determined under subsection (a). Otherwise, the dissociated member may file suit within another 120 days to enforce the purchase under subsection (d). The court will then determine the fair value and terms of purchase under subsection (e). See Section 702. The member's lawsuit is not available under subsection (c) if the parties have previously agreed to price and terms in an operating agreement.

Section 702. Court Action to Determine Fair Value of Distributional Interest.

(a) In an action brought to determine the fair value of a distributional interest in a limited liability company, the court shall:

    (1) determine the fair value of the interest, considering among other relevant evidence the going concern value of the company, any agreement among some or all of the members fixing the price or specifying a formula for determining value of distributional interests for any other purpose, the recommendations of any appraiser appointed by the court, and any legal constraints on the company's ability to purchase the interest;

    (2) specify the terms of the purchase, including, if appropriate, terms for installment payments, subordination of the purchase obligation to the rights of the company's other creditors, security for a

          deferred purchase price, and a covenant not to compete or other restriction on a dissociated member; and

    (3) require the dissociated member to deliver an assignment of the interest to the purchaser upon receipt of the purchase price or the first installment of the purchase price.

(b) After the dissociated member delivers the assignment, the dissociated member has no further claim against the company, its members, officers, or managers, if any, other than a claim to any unpaid balance of the purchase price and a claim under any agreement with the company or the remaining members that is not terminated by the court.

(c) If the purchase is not completed in accordance with the specified terms, the company is to be dissolved upon application under Section 801(b)(5)(iv). If a limited liability company is so dissolved, the dissociated member has the same rights and priorities in the company's assets as if the sale had not been ordered.

(d) If the court finds that a party to the proceeding acted arbitrarily, vexatiously, or not in good faith, it may award one or more other parties their reasonable expenses, including attorney's fees and the expenses of appraisers or other experts, incurred in the proceeding. The finding may be based on the company's failure to make an offer to pay or to comply with Section 701(b).

(e) Interest must be paid on the amount awarded from the date determined under Section 701(a) to the date of payment.

COMMENT

The default valuation standard is fair value. Under this broad standard, a court is free to determine the fair value of a distributional interest on a fair market, liquidation, or any other method deemed appropriate under the circumstances. A fair market value standard is not used because it is too narrow, often inappropriate, and assumes a fact not contemplated by this section—a willing buyer and a willing seller.

The court has discretion under subsection (a)(2) to include in its order any conditions the court deems necessary to safeguard the interests of the company and the dissociated member or transferee. The discretion may be based on the financial and other needs of the parties.

If the purchase is not consummated or the purchaser defaults, the dissociated member or transferee may make application for dissolution of the company under subsection (c). The court may deny the petition for good cause but the proceeding affords the company an opportunity to be heard on the matter and avoid dissolution. See Comments to Section 801(a)(4).

The power of the court to award all costs and attorney's fees incurred in the suit under subsection (d) is an incentive for both parties to act in good faith. See Section 701(c).

Section 703. Dissociated Member's Power to Bind Limited Liability Company.

For two years after a member dissociates without the dissociation resulting in a dissolution and winding up of a limited liability company's business, the company, including a surviving company under [Article] 9, is bound by an act of the dissociated member which would have bound the company under Section 301 before dissociation only if at the time of entering into the transaction the other party:

(1) reasonably believed that the dissociated member was then a member;

(2) did not have notice of the member's dissociation; and

(3) is not deemed to have had notice under Section 704.

COMMENT

Member dissociation will not dissolve the company unless otherwise specified in an operating agreement. See Section 801(a)(1). A dissociated member of a member-managed company does not have actual authority to act for the company. See Section 603(b)(1). Under Section 301(a), a dissociated member of a member-managed company has apparent authority to bind the company in ordinary course transactions except as to persons who knew or had notice of the dissociation. This section modifies that rule by requiring the person to show reasonable reliance on the member's status as a member provided a Section 704 statement has not been filed within the previous 90 days. See also Section 804 (power to bind after dissolution).

Section 704. Statement of Dissociation.

(a) A dissociated member or a limited liability company may file in the office of the [Secretary of State] a statement of dissociation stating the name of the company and that the member is dissociated from the company.

(b) For the purposes of Sections 301 and 703, a person not a member is deemed to have notice of the dissociation 90 days after the statement of dissociation is filed.

[ARTICLE] 8

WINDING UP COMPANY'S BUSINESS

Section 801. Events Causing Dissolution and Winding Up of Company's Business.
Section 802. Limited Liability Company Continues After Dissolution.
Section 803. Right to Wind Up Limited Liability Company's Business.
Section 804. Member's or Manager's Power and Liability as Agent After Dissolution.
Section 805. Articles of Termination.
Section 806. Distribution of Assets in Winding Up Limited Liability Company's Business.

Section 801. Events Causing Dissolution and Winding Up of Company's Business.

A limited liability company is dissolved, and its business must be wound up, upon the occurrence of any of the following events:

(1) an event specified in the operating agreement;

(2) consent of the number or percentage of members specified in the operating agreement;

(3) an event that makes it unlawful for all or substantially all of the business of the company to be continued, but any cure of illegality within 90 days after notice to the company of the event is effective retroactively to the date of the event for purposes of this section;

(4) on application by a member or a dissociated member, upon entry of a judicial decree that:

   (i) the economic purpose of the company is likely to be unreasonably frustrated;

  (ii) another member has engaged in conduct relating to the company's business that makes it not reasonably practicable to carry on the company's business with that member;

 (iii) it is not otherwise reasonably practicable to carry on the company's business in conformity with the articles of organization and the operating agreement;

 (iv) the company failed to purchase the petitioner's distributional interest as required by Section 701; or

  (v) the managers or members in control of the company have acted, are acting, or will act in a manner that is illegal, oppressive, fraudulent, or unfairly prejudicial to the petitioner;

(5) on application by a transferee of a member's interest, a judicial determination that it is equitable to wind up the company's business:

  (i) after the expiration of the specified term, if the company was for a specified term at the time the applicant became a transferee by member dissociation, transfer, or entry of a charging order that gave rise to the transfer; or

 (ii) at any time, if the company was at will at the time the applicant became a transferee by member dissociation, transfer, or entry of a charging order that gave rise to the transfer; or

(6) the expiration of the term specified in the articles of organization.

COMMENT

The dissolution rules of this section are mostly default rules and may be modified by an operating agreement. However, an operating agreement may not modify or eliminate the dissolution events specified in subsection (a)(3) (illegal business) or subsection (a)(4) (member application). See Section 103(b)(6).

The relationship between member dissociation and company dissolution is set forth under subsection (a)(1). Unless member dissociation is specified as an event of dissolution in the operating agreement, such dissociation does not dissolve the company. New and important Internal Revenue Service announcements clarify that the failure of member dissociation to cause or threaten dissolution of a limited liability company will not cause the company to be taxed like a corporation.

A member or dissociated member whose interest is not required to be purchased by the company under Section 701 may make application under subsection (a)(4) for the involuntary dissolution of both an at-will company and a term company. A transferee may make application under subsection (a)(5). A transferee's application right, but not that of a member or dissociated member, may be modified by an operating agreement. See Section 103(b)(6). A dissociated member is not treated as a transferee for purposes of an application under subsections (a)(4) and (a)(5). See Section 603(b)(1). For example, this affords reasonable protection to a dissociated member of a term company to make application under subsection (a)(4) before the expiration of the term that existed at the time of dissociation. For purposes of a subsection (a)(4) application, a dissociated member includes a successor in interest, e.g., surviving spouse. See Comments to Section 601.

In the case of applications under subsections (a)(4) and (a)(5), the applicant has the burden of proving either the existence of one or more of the circumstances listed under subsection (a)(4) or that it is equitable to wind up the company's business under subsection (a)(5). Proof of the existence of one or more of the circumstances in subsection (a)(4), may be the basis of a subsection (a)(5) application. Even where the burden of proof is met, the court has the discretion to order relief other than the dissolution of the company. Examples include an accounting, a declaratory judgment, a distribution, the purchase of the distributional interest of the applicant or another member, or the appointment of a receiver. See Section 410.

A court has the discretion to dissolve a company under subsection (a)(4)(i) when the company has a very poor financial record that is not likely to improve. In this instance, dissolution is an alternative to placing the company in bankruptcy. A court may dissolve a company under subsections (a)(4)(ii), (a)(4)(iii), and (a)(4)(iv) for serious and protracted misconduct by one or more members. Subsection (a)(4)(v) provides a specific remedy for an improper squeeze-out of a member.

In determining whether and what type of relief to order under subsections (a)(4) and (a)(5) involuntary dissolution suits, a court should take into account other rights and remedies of the applicant. For example, a court should not grant involuntary dissolution of an at-will company if the applicant member has the right to dissociate and force the company to purchase that member's distributional interest under Sections 701 and 702. In other cases, involuntary dissolution or some other remedy such as a buy-out might be appropriate where, for example, one or more members have (i) engaged in fraudulent or unconscionable conduct, (ii) improperly expelled a member seeking an unfair advantage of a provision in an operating agreement that provides for a significantly lower price on expulsion than would be payable in the event of voluntary dissociation, or (iii) engaged in serious misconduct and the applicant member is a member of a term company and would not have a right to have the company purchase that member's distributional interest upon dissociation until the expiration of the company's specified term.

Section 802. Limited Liability Company Continues After Dissolution.

(a) Subject to subsection (b), a limited liability company continues after dissolution only for the purpose of winding up its business.

(b) At any time after the dissolution of a limited liability company and before the winding up of its business is completed, the members, including a dissociated member whose dissociation caused the dissolution, may unanimously waive the right to have the company's business wound up and the company terminated. In that case:

   (1) the limited liability company resumes carrying on its business as if dissolution had never occurred and any liability incurred by the company or a member after the dissolution and before the waiver is determined as if the dissolution had never occurred; and

   (2) the rights of a third party accruing under Section 804(a) or arising out of conduct in reliance on the dissolution before the third party knew or received a notification of the waiver are not adversely affected.

COMMENT

The liability shield continues in effect for the winding up period because the legal existence of the company continues under subsection (a). The company is terminated on the filing of articles of termination. See Section 805.

Section 803. Right to Wind Up Limited Liability Company's Business.

(a) After dissolution, a member who has not wrongfully dissociated may participate in winding up a limited liability company's business, but on application of any member, member's legal representative, or transferee, the [designate the appropriate court], for good cause shown, may order judicial supervision of the winding up.

(b) A legal representative of the last surviving member may wind up a limited liability company's business.

(c) A person winding up a limited liability company's business may preserve the company's business or property as a going concern for a reasonable time, prosecute and defend actions and proceedings, whether civil, criminal, or administrative, settle and close the company's business, dispose of and transfer the company's property, discharge the company's liabilities, distribute the assets of the company pursuant to Section 806, settle disputes by mediation or arbitration, and perform other necessary acts.

Section 804. Member's or Manager's Power and Liability as Agent After Dissolution.

(a) A limited liability company is bound by a member's or manager's act after dissolution that:

(1) is appropriate for winding up the company's business; or

(2) would have bound the company under Section 301 before dissolution, if the other party to the transaction did not have notice of the dissolution.

(b) A member or manager who, with knowledge of the dissolution, subjects a limited liability company to liability by an act that is not appropriate for winding up the company's business is liable to the company for any damage caused to the company arising from the liability.

COMMENT

After dissolution, members and managers continue to have the authority to bind the company that they had prior to dissolution provided that the third party did not have notice of the dissolution. See Section 102(b) (notice defined). Otherwise, they have only the authority appropriate for winding up the company's business. See Section 703 (agency power of member after dissociation).

Section 805. Articles of Termination.

(a) At any time after dissolution and winding up, a limited liability company may terminate its existence by filing with the [Secretary of State] articles of termination stating:

(1) the name of the company;

(2) the date of the dissolution; and

(3) that the company's business has been wound up and the legal existence of the company has been terminated.

(b) The existence of a limited liability company is terminated upon the filing of the articles of termination, or upon a later effective date, if specified in the articles of termination.

COMMENT

The termination of legal existence also terminates the company's liability shield. See Comments to Section 802 (liability shield continues in effect during winding up). It also ends the company's responsibility to file an annual report. See Section 211.

Section 806. Distribution of Assets In Winding Up Limited Liability Company's Business.

(a) In winding up a limited liability company's business, the assets of the company must be applied to discharge its obligations to creditors, including members who are creditors. Any surplus must be applied to pay in money the net amount distributable to members in accordance with their right to distributions under subsection (b).

(b) Each member is entitled to a distribution upon the winding up of the limited liability company's business consisting of a return of all contributions which have not previously been returned and a distribution of any remainder in equal shares.

Section 807. Known Claims Against Dissolved Limited Liability Company.

(a) A dissolved limited liability company may dispose of the known claims against it by following the procedure described in this section.

(b) A dissolved limited liability company shall notify its known claimants in writing of the dissolution. The notice must:

(1) specify the information required to be included in a claim;

(2) provide a mailing address where the claim is to be sent;

(3) state the deadline for receipt of the claim, which may not be less than 120 days after the date the written notice is received by the claimant; and

(4) state that the claim will be barred if not received by the deadline.

(c) A claim against a dissolved limited liability company is barred if the requirements of subsection (b) are met, and:

(1) the claim is not received by the specified deadline; or

(2) in the case of a claim that is timely received but rejected by the dissolved company, the claimant does not commence a proceeding to enforce the claim within 90 days after the receipt of the notice of the rejection.

(d) For purposes of this section, "claim" does not include a contingent liability or a claim based on an event occurring after the effective date of dissolution.

COMMENT

A known claim will be barred when the company provides written notice to a claimant that a claim must be filed with the company no later than at least 120 days after receipt of the written notice and the claimant fails to file the claim. If the claim is timely received but is rejected by the company, the claim is nevertheless barred unless the claimant files suit to enforce the claim within 90 days after the receipt of the notice of rejection. A claim described in subsection (d) is not a "known" claim and is governed by Section 808. This section does not extend any other applicable statutes of limitation. See Section 104. Depending on the management of the company, members or managers must discharge or make provision for discharging all of the company's known liabilities before distributing the remaining assets to the members. See Sections 806(a), 406, and 407.

Section 808. Other Claims Against Dissolved Limited Liability Company.

(a) A dissolved limited liability company may publish notice of its dissolution and request persons having claims against the company to present them in accordance with the notice.

(b) The notice must:

 (1) be published at least once in a newspaper of general circulation in the [county] in which the dissolved limited liability company's principal office is located or, if none in this State, in which its designated office is or was last located;

 (2) describe the information required to be contained in a claim and provide a mailing address where the claim is to be sent; and

 (3) state that a claim against the limited liability company is barred unless a proceeding to enforce the claim is commenced within five years after publication of the notice.

(c) If a dissolved limited liability company publishes a notice in accordance with subsection (b), the claim of each of the following claimants is barred unless the claimant commences a proceeding to enforce the claim against the dissolved company within five years after the publication date of the notice:

 (1) a claimant who did not receive written notice under Section 807;

 (2) a claimant whose claim was timely sent to the dissolved company but not acted on; and

 (3) a claimant whose claim is contingent or based on an event occurring after the effective date of dissolution.

(d) A claim not barred under this section may be enforced:

 (1) against the dissolved limited liability company, to the extent of its undistributed assets; or

 (2) if the assets have been distributed in liquidation, against a member of the dissolved company to the extent of the mem-

ber's proportionate share of the claim or the company's assets distributed to the member in liquidation, whichever is less, but a member's total liability for all claims under this section may not exceed the total amount of assets distributed to the member.

COMMENT

An unknown claim will be barred when the company publishes notice requesting claimants to file claims with the company and stating that claims will be barred unless the claimant files suit to enforce the claim within five years after the date of publication. The procedure also bars known claims where the claimant either did not receive written notice described in Section 807 or received notice, mailed a claim, but the company did not act on the claim.

Depending on the management of the company, members or managers must discharge or make provision for discharging all of the company's known liabilities before distributing the remaining assets to the members. See Comment to Section 807. This section does not contemplate that a company will postpone member distributions until all unknown claims are barred under this section. In appropriate cases, the company may purchase insurance or set aside funds permitting a distribution of the remaining assets. Where winding up distributions have been made to members, subsection (d)(2) authorizes recovery against those members. However, a claimant's recovery against a member is limited to the lesser of the member's proportionate share of the claim or the amount received in the distribution. This section does not extend any other applicable statutes of limitation. See Section 104.

Section 809. Grounds for Administrative Dissolution.

The [Secretary of State] may commence a proceeding to dissolve a limited liability company administratively if the company does not:

(1) pay any fees, taxes, or penalties imposed by this [Act] or other law within 60 days after they are due; or

(2) deliver its annual report to the [Secretary of State] within 60 days after it is due.

COMMENT

Administrative dissolution is an effective enforcement mechanism for a variety of statutory obligations under this Act and it avoids the more expensive judicial dissolution process. When applicable, administrative dissolution avoids wasteful attempts to compel compliance by a company abandoned by its members.

Section 810. Procedure for and Effect of Administrative Dissolution.

(a) If the [Secretary of State] determines that a ground exists for administratively dissolving a limited liability company, the [Secretary of

State] shall enter a record of the determination and serve the company with a copy of the record.

(b) If the company does not correct each ground for dissolution or demonstrate to the reasonable satisfaction of the [Secretary of State] that each ground determined by the [Secretary of State] does not exist within 60 days after service of the notice, the [Secretary of State] shall administratively dissolve the company by signing a certification of the dissolution that recites the ground for dissolution and its effective date. The [Secretary of State] shall file the original of the certificate and serve the company with a copy of the certificate.

(c) A company administratively dissolved continues its existence but may carry on only business necessary to wind up and liquidate its business and affairs under Section 802 and to notify claimants under Sections 807 and 808.

(d) The administrative dissolution of a company does not terminate the authority of its agent for service of process.

COMMENT

A company's failure to comply with a ground for administrative dissolution may simply occur because of oversight. Therefore, subsections (a) and (b) set forth a mandatory notice by the filing officer to the company of the ground for dissolution and a 60 day grace period for correcting the ground.

Section 811. Reinstatement Following Administrative Dissolution.

(a) A limited liability company administratively dissolved may apply to the [Secretary of State] for reinstatement within two years after the effective date of dissolution. The application must:

   (1) recite the name of the company and the effective date of its administrative dissolution;

   (2) state that the ground for dissolution either did not exist or have been eliminated;

   (3) state that the company's name satisfies the requirements of Section 105; and

   (4) contain a certificate from the [taxing authority] reciting that all taxes owed by the company have been paid.

(b) If the [Secretary of State] determines that the application contains the information required by subsection (a) and that the information is correct, the [Secretary of State] shall cancel the certificate of dissolution and prepare a certificate of reinstatement that recites this determination and the effective date of reinstatement, file the original of the certificate, and serve the company with a copy of the certificate.

(c) When reinstatement is effective, it relates back to and takes effect as of the effective date of the administrative dissolution and the company may resume its business as if the administrative dissolution had never occurred.

Section 812. Appeal from Denial of Reinstatement.

(a) If the [Secretary of State] denies a limited liability company's application for reinstatement following administrative dissolution, the [Secretary of State] shall serve the company with a record that explains the reason or reasons for denial.

(b) The company may appeal the denial of reinstatement to the [name appropriate] court within 30 days after service of the notice of denial is perfected. The company appeals by petitioning the court to set aside the dissolution and attaching to the petition copies of the [Secretary of State's] certificate of dissolution, the company's application for reinstatement, and the [Secretary of State's] notice of denial.

(c) The court may summarily order the [Secretary of State] to reinstate the dissolved company or may take other action the court considers appropriate.

(d) The court's final decision may be appealed as in other civil proceedings.

[ARTICLE] 9

CONVERSIONS AND MERGERS

Section 901. Definitions.
Section 902. Conversion of Partnership or Limited Partnership to Limited Liability Company.
Section 903. Effect of Conversion; Entity Unchanged.
Section 904. Merger of Entities.
Section 905. Articles of Merger.
Section 906. Effect of Merger.
Section 907. [Article] Not Exclusive.

Section 901. Definitions.
In this [article]:

(1) "Corporation" means a corporation under [the State Corporation Act], a predecessor law, or comparable law of another jurisdiction.

(2) "General partner" means a partner in a partnership and a general partner in a limited partnership.

(3) "Limited partner" means a limited partner in a limited partnership.

(4) "Limited partnership" means a limited partnership created under [the State Limited Partnership Act], a predecessor law, or comparable law of another jurisdiction.

(5) "Partner" includes a general partner and a limited partner.

(6) "Partnership" means a general partnership under [the State Partnership Act], a predecessor law, or comparable law of another jurisdiction.

(7) "Partnership agreement" means an agreement among the partners concerning the partnership or limited partnership.

(8) "Shareholder" means a shareholder in a corporation.

COMMENT

Section 907 makes clear that the provisions of Article 9 are not mandatory. Therefore, a partnership or a limited liability company may convert or merge in any other manner provided by law. However, if the requirements of Article 9 are followed, the conversion or merger is legally valid. Article 9 is not restricted to domestic business entities.

Section 902. Conversion of Partnership or Limited Partnership to Limited Liability Company.

(a) A partnership or limited partnership may be converted to a limited liability company pursuant to this section.

(b) The terms and conditions of a conversion of a partnership or limited partnership to a limited liability company must be approved by all of the partners or by a number or percentage of the partners required for conversion in the partnership agreement.

(c) An agreement of conversion must set forth the terms and conditions of the conversion of the interests of partners of a partnership or of a limited partnership, as the case may be, into interests in the converted limited liability company or the cash or other consideration to be paid or delivered as a result of the conversion of the interests of the partners, or a combination thereof.

(d) After a conversion is approved under subsection (b), the partnership or limited partnership shall file articles of organization in the office of the [Secretary of State] which satisfy the requirements of Section 203 and contain:

(1) a statement that the partnership or limited partnership was converted to a limited liability company from a partnership or limited partnership, as the case may be;

(2) its former name;

(3) a statement of the number of votes cast by the partners entitled to vote for and against the conversion and, if the vote is less than unanimous, the number or percentage required to approve the conversion under subsection (b); and

(4) in the case of a limited partnership, a statement that the certificate of limited partnership is to be canceled as of the date the conversion took effect.

(e) In the case of a limited partnership, the filing of articles of organization under subsection (d) cancels its certificate of limited partnership as of the date the conversion took effect.

(f) A conversion takes effect when the articles of organization are filed in the office of the [Secretary of State] or at any later date specified in the articles of organization.

(g) A general partner who becomes a member of a limited liability company as a result of a conversion remains liable as a partner for an obligation incurred by the partnership or limited partnership before the conversion takes effect.

(h) A general partner's liability for all obligations of the limited liability company incurred after the conversion takes effect is that of a member of the company. A limited partner who becomes a member as a result of a conversion remains liable only to the extent the limited partner was liable for an obligation incurred by the limited partnership before the conversion takes effect.

COMMENT

Subsection (b) makes clear that the terms and conditions of the conversion of a general or limited partnership to a limited liability company must be approved by all of the partners unless the partnership agreement specifies otherwise.

Section 903. Effect of Conversion; Entity Unchanged.

(a) A partnership or limited partnership that has been converted pursuant to this [article] is for all purposes the same entity that existed before the conversion.

(b) When a conversion takes effect:

(1) all property owned by the converting partnership or limited partnership vests in the limited liability company;

(2) all debts, liabilities, and other obligations of the converting partnership or limited partnership continue as obligations of the limited liability company;

(3) an action or proceeding pending by or against the converting partnership or limited partnership may be continued as if the conversion had not occurred;

(4) except as prohibited by other law, all of the rights, privileges, immunities, powers, and purposes of the converting partnership or limited partnership vest in the limited liability company; and

(5) except as otherwise provided in the agreement of conversion under Section 902(c), all of the partners of the converting partnership continue as members of the limited liability company.

COMMENT

A conversion is not a conveyance or transfer and does not give rise to claims of reverter or impairment of title based on a prohibited conveyance or transfer. Under subsection (b)(1), title to all partnership property, including real estate, vests in the limited liability company as a matter of law without reversion or impairment.

Section 904. Merger of Entities.

(a) Pursuant to a plan of merger approved under subsection (c), a limited liability company may be merged with or into one or more limited liability companies, foreign limited liability companies, corporations, foreign corporations, partnerships, foreign partnerships, limited partnerships, foreign limited partnerships, or other domestic or foreign entities.

(b) A plan of merger must set forth:

(1) the name of each entity that is a party to the merger;

(2) the name of the surviving entity into which the other entities will merge;

(3) the type of organization of the surviving entity;

(4) the terms and conditions of the merger;

(5) the manner and basis for converting the interests of each party to the merger into interests or obligations of the surviving entity, or into money or other property in whole or in part; and

(6) the street address of the surviving entity's principal place of business.

(c) A plan of merger must be approved:

(1) in the case of a limited liability company that is a party to the merger, by all of the members or by a number or percentage of members specified in the operating agreement;

(2) in the case of a foreign limited liability company that is a party to the merger, by the vote required for approval of a merger by the law of the State or foreign jurisdiction in which the foreign limited liability company is organized;

(3) in the case of a partnership or domestic limited partnership that is a party to the merger, by the vote required for approval of a conversion under Section 902(b); and

(4) in the case of any other entities that are parties to the merger, by the vote required for approval of a merger by the law of this State or of the State or foreign jurisdiction in which the entity is organized and, in the absence of such a requirement, by all the owners of interests in the entity.

(d) After a plan of merger is approved and before the merger takes effect, the plan may be amended or abandoned as provided in the plan.

(e) The merger is effective upon the filing of the articles of merger with the [Secretary of State], or at such later date as the articles may provide.

COMMENT

This section sets forth a "safe harbor" for cross-entity mergers of limited liability companies with both domestic and foreign: corporations, general and limited partnerships, and other limited liability companies. Subsection (c) makes clear that the terms and conditions of the plan of merger must be approved by all of the partners unless applicable state law specifies otherwise for the merger.

Section 905. Articles of Merger.

(a) After approval of the plan of merger under Section 904(c), unless the merger is abandoned under Section 904(d), articles of merger must be signed on behalf of each limited liability company and other entity that is a party to the merger and delivered to the [Secretary of State] for filing. The articles must set forth:

(1) the name and jurisdiction of formation or organization of each of the limited liability companies and other entities that are parties to the merger;

(2) for each limited liability company that is to merge, the date its articles of organization were filed with the [Secretary of State];

(3) that a plan of merger has been approved and signed by each limited liability company and other entity that is to merge;

(4) the name and address of the surviving limited liability company or other surviving entity;

(5) the effective date of the merger;

(6) if a limited liability company is the surviving entity, such changes in its articles of organization as are necessary by reason of the merger;

(7) if a party to a merger is a foreign limited liability company, the jurisdiction and date of filing of its initial articles of organization and the date when its application for authority was filed by the [Secretary of State] or, if an application has not been filed, a statement to that effect; and

(8) if the surviving entity is not a limited liability company, an agreement that the surviving entity may be served with process in this State and is subject to liability in any action or proceeding for the enforcement of any liability or obligation of any limited liability company previously subject to suit in this State which is to merge,

and for the enforcement, as provided in this [Act], of the right of members of any limited liability company to receive payment for their interest against the surviving entity.

(b) If a foreign limited liability company is the surviving entity of a merger, it may not do business in this State until an application for that authority is filed with the [Secretary of State].

(c) The surviving limited liability company or other entity shall furnish a copy of the plan of merger, on request and without cost, to any member of any limited liability company or any person holding an interest in any other entity that is to merge.

(d) Articles of merger operate as an amendment to the limited liability company's articles of organization.

Section 906. Effect of Merger.

(a) When a merger takes effect:

(1) the separate existence of each limited liability company and other entity that is a party to the merger, other than the surviving entity, terminates;

(2) all property owned by each of the limited liability companies and other entities that are party to the merger vests in the surviving entity;

(3) all debts, liabilities, and other obligations of each limited liability company and other entity that is party to the merger become the obligations of the surviving entity;

(4) an action or proceeding pending by or against a limited liability company or other party to a merger may be continued as if the merger had not occurred or the surviving entity may be substituted as a party to the action or proceeding; and

(5) except as prohibited by other law, all the rights, privileges, immunities, powers, and purposes of every limited liability company and other entity that is a party to a merger vest in the surviving entity.

(b) The [Secretary of State] is an agent for service of process in an action or proceeding against the surviving foreign entity to enforce an obligation of any party to a merger if the surviving foreign entity fails to appoint or maintain an agent designated for service of process in this State or the agent for service of process cannot with reasonable diligence be found at the designated office. Upon receipt of process, the [Secretary of State] shall send a copy of the process by registered or certified mail, return receipt requested, to the surviving entity at the address set forth in the articles of merger. Service is effected under this subsection at the earliest of:

(1) the date the company receives the process, notice, or demand;

(2) the date shown on the return receipt, if signed on behalf of the company; or

(3) five days after its deposit in the mail, if mailed postpaid and correctly addressed.

(c) A member of the surviving limited liability company is liable for all obligations of a party to the merger for which the member was personally liable before the merger.

(d) Unless otherwise agreed, a merger of a limited liability company that is not the surviving entity in the merger does not require the limited liability company to wind up its business under this [Act] or pay its liabilities and distribute its assets pursuant to this [Act].

(e) Articles of merger serve as articles of dissolution for a limited liability company that is not the surviving entity in the merger.

Section 907. [Article] Not Exclusive.
This [article] does not preclude an entity from being converted or merged under other law.

[ARTICLE] 10

FOREIGN LIMITED LIABILITY COMPANIES

Section 1001. Law Governing Foreign Limited Liability Companies.
Section 1002. Application for Certificate of Authority.
Section 1003. Activities Not Constituting Transacting Business.
Section 1004. Issuance of Certificate of Authority.
Section 1005. Name of Foreign Limited Liability Company.
Section 1006. Revocation of Certificate of Authority.
Section 1007. Cancellation of Authority.
Section 1008. Effect of Failure to Obtain Certificate of Authority.
Section 1009. Action by [Attorney General].

Section 1001. Law Governing Foreign Limited Liability Companies.

(a) The laws of the State or other jurisdiction under which a foreign limited liability company is organized govern its organization and internal affairs and the liability of its managers, members, and their transferees.

(b) A foreign limited liability company may not be denied a certificate of authority by reason of any difference between the laws of another jurisdiction under which the foreign company is organized and the laws of this State.

(c) A certificate of authority does not authorize a foreign limited liability company to engage in any business or exercise any power that a limited liability company may not engage in or exercise in this State.

COMMENT

The law where a foreign limited liability company is organized, rather than this Act, governs that company's internal affairs and the liability of its owners. Accordingly, any difference between the laws of the foreign jurisdiction and this Act will not constitute grounds for denial of a certificate of authority to transact business in this State. However, a foreign limited liability company transacting business in this State by virtue of a certificate of authority is limited to the business and powers that a limited liability company may lawfully pursue and exercise under Section 112.

Section 1002. Application for Certificate of Authority.

(a) A foreign limited liability company may apply for a certificate of authority to transact business in this State by delivering an application to the [Secretary of State] for filing. The application must set forth:

    (1) the name of the foreign company or, if its name is unavailable for use in this State, a name that satisfies the requirements of Section 1005;

    (2) the name of the State or country under whose law it is organized;

    (3) the street address of its principal office;

    (4) the address of its initial designated office in this State;

    (5) the name and street address of its initial agent for service of process in this State;

    (6) whether the duration of the company is for a specified term and, if so, the period specified;

    (7) whether the company is manager-managed, and, if so, the name and address of each initial manager; and

    (8) whether the members of the company are to be liable for its debts and obligations under a provision similar to Section 303(c).

(b) A foreign limited liability company shall deliver with the completed application a certificate of existence or a record of similar import authenticated by the secretary of state or other official having custody of company records in the State or country under whose law it is organized.

COMMENT

As with articles of organization, the application must be signed and filed with the filing office. See Sections 105, 107 (name registration), 205, 206, 209 (liability for false statements), and 1005.

Section 1003. Activities Not Constituting Transacting Business.

(a) Activities of a foreign limited liability company that do not constitute transacting business in this State within the meaning of this [article] include:

(1) maintaining, defending, or settling an action or proceeding;

(2) holding meetings of its members or managers or carrying on any other activity concerning its internal affairs;

(3) maintaining bank accounts;

(4) maintaining offices or agencies for the transfer, exchange, and registration of the foreign company's own securities or maintaining trustees or depositories with respect to those securities;

(5) selling through independent contractors;

(6) soliciting or obtaining orders, whether by mail or through employees or agents or otherwise, if the orders require acceptance outside this State before they become contracts;

(7) creating or acquiring indebtedness, mortgages, or security interests in real or personal property;

(8) securing or collecting debts or enforcing mortgages or other security interests in property securing the debts, and holding, protecting, and maintaining property so acquired;

(9) conducting an isolated transaction that is completed within 30 days and is not one in the course of similar transactions of a like manner; and

(10) transacting business in interstate commerce.

(b) For purposes of this [article], the ownership in this State of income-producing real property or tangible personal property, other than property excluded under subsection (a), constitutes transacting business in this State.

(c) This section does not apply in determining the contacts or activities that may subject a foreign limited liability company to service of process, taxation, or regulation under any other law of this State.

Section 1004. Issuance of Certificate of Authority.
Unless the [Secretary of State] determines that an application for a certificate of authority fails to comply as to form with the filing requirements of this [Act], the [Secretary of State], upon payment of all filing fees, shall file the application and send a receipt for it and the fees to the limited liability company or its representative.

Section 1005. Name of Foreign Limited Liability Company.

(a) If the name of a foreign limited liability company does not satisfy the requirements of Section 105, the company, to obtain or maintain a certificate of authority to transact business in this State, must use a fictitious name to transact business in this State if its real name is unavailable and it delivers to the [Secretary of State] for filing a copy of the resolution of its managers, in the case of a manager-managed company, or of its members, in the case of a member-managed company, adopting the fictitious name.

(b) Except as authorized by subsections (c) and (d), the name, including a fictitious name to be used to transact business in this State, of a foreign limited liability company must be distinguishable upon the records of the [Secretary of State] from:

    (1) the name of any corporation, limited partnership, or company incorporated, organized, or authorized to transact business in this State;

    (2) a name reserved or registered under Section 106 or 107; and

    (3) the fictitious name of another foreign limited liability company authorized to transact business in this State.

(c) A foreign limited liability company may apply to the [Secretary of State] for authority to use in this State a name that is not distinguishable upon the records of the [Secretary of State] from a name described in subsection (b). The [Secretary of State] shall authorize use of the name applied for if:

    (1) the present user, registrant, or owner of a reserved name consents to the use in a record and submits an undertaking in form satisfactory to the [Secretary of State] to change its name to a name that is distinguishable upon the records of the [Secretary of State] from the name of the foreign applying limited liability company; or

    (2) the applicant delivers to the [Secretary of State] a certified copy of a final judgment of a court establishing the applicant's right to use the name applied for in this State.

(d) A foreign limited liability company may use in this State the name, including the fictitious name, of another domestic or foreign entity that is used in this State if the other entity is incorporated, organized, or authorized to transact business in this State and the foreign limited liability company:

    (1) has merged with the other entity;

    (2) has been formed by reorganization of the other entity; or

    (3) has acquired all or substantially all of the assets, including the name, of the other entity.

(e) If a foreign limited liability company authorized to transact business in this State changes its name to one that does not satisfy the requirements of Section 105, it may not transact business in this State under the name as changed until it adopts a name satisfying the requirements of Section 105 and obtains an amended certificate of authority.

Section 1006. Revocation of Certificate of Authority.

(a) A certificate of authority of a foreign limited liability company to transact business in this State may be revoked by the [Secretary of State] in the manner provided in subsection (b) if:

(1) the company fails to:
   (i) pay any fees, taxes, and penalties owed to this State;
   (ii) deliver its annual report required under Section 211 to the [Secretary of State] within 60 days after it is due;
   (iii) appoint and maintain an agent for service of process as required by this [article]; or
   (iv) file a statement of a change in the name or business address of the agent as required by this [article]; or

(2) a misrepresentation has been made of any material matter in any application, report, affidavit, or other record submitted by the company pursuant to this [article].

(b) The [Secretary of State] may not revoke a certificate of authority of a foreign limited liability company unless the [Secretary of State] sends the company notice of the revocation, at least 60 days before its effective date, by a record addressed to its agent for service of process in this State, or if the company fails to appoint and maintain a proper agent in this State, addressed to the office required to be maintained by Section 108. The notice must specify the cause for the revocation of the certificate of authority. The authority of the company to transact business in this State ceases on the effective date of the revocation unless the foreign limited liability company cures the failure before that date.

Section 1007. Cancellation of Authority.

A foreign limited liability company may cancel its authority to transact business in this State by filing in the office of the [Secretary of State] a certificate of cancellation. Cancellation does not terminate the authority of the [Secretary of State] to accept service of process on the company for [claims for relief] arising out of the transactions of business in this State.

Section 1008. Effect of Failure to Obtain Certificate of Authority.

(a) A foreign limited liability company transacting business in this State may not maintain an action or proceeding in this State unless it has a certificate of authority to transact business in this State.

(b) The failure of a foreign limited liability company to have a certificate of authority to transact business in this State does not impair the validity of a contract or act of the company or prevent the foreign limited liability company from defending an action or proceeding in this State.

(c) Limitations on personal liability of managers, members, and their transferees are not waived solely by transacting business in this State without a certificate of authority.

(d) If a foreign limited liability company transacts business in this State without a certificate of authority, it appoints the [Secretary of State] as its agent for service of process for [claims for relief] arising out of the transaction of business in this State.

Section 1009. Action by [attorney General].

The [Attorney General] may maintain an action to restrain a foreign limited liability company from transacting business in this State in violation of this [article].

[ARTICLE] 11

DERIVATIVE ACTIONS

Section 1101. Right of Action.
Section 1102. Proper Plaintiff.
Section 1103. Pleading.
Section 1104. Expenses.

Section 1101. Right of Action.

A member of a limited liability company may maintain an action in the right of the company if the members or managers having authority to do so have refused to commence the action or an effort to cause those members or managers to commence the action is not likely to succeed.

COMMENT

A member may bring an action on behalf of the company when the members or managers having the authority to pursue the company recovery refuse to do so or an effort to cause them to pursue the recovery is not likely to succeed. See Comments to Section 411(a) (personal action of member against company or another member).

Section 1102. Proper Plaintiff.

In a derivative action for a limited liability company, the plaintiff must be a member of the company when the action is commenced; and:

(1) must have been a member at the time of the transaction of which the plaintiff complains; or

(2) the plaintiff's status as a member must have devolved upon the plaintiff by operation of law or pursuant to the terms of the operating agreement from a person who was a member at the time of the transaction.

Section 1103. Pleading.

In a derivative action for a limited liability company, the complaint must set forth with particularity the effort of the plaintiff to secure initiation of the action by a member or manager or the reasons for not making the effort.

Comment

There is no obligation of the company or its members or managers to respond to a member demand to bring an action to pursue a company recovery. However, if a company later decides to commence the demanded action or assume control of the derivative litigation, the member's right to commence or control the proceeding ordinarily ends.

Section 1104. Expenses.

If a derivative action for a limited liability company is successful, in whole or in part, or if anything is received by the plaintiff as a result of a judgment, compromise, or settlement of an action or claim, the court may award the plaintiff reasonable expenses, including reasonable attorney's fees, and shall direct the plaintiff to remit to the limited liability company the remainder of the proceeds received.

[ARTICLE] 12

MISCELLANEOUS PROVISIONS

Section 1201. Uniformity of Application and Construction.
Section 1202. Short Title.
Section 1203. Severability Clause.
Section 1204. Effective Date.
Section 1205. Transitional Provisions.
Section 1206. Savings Clause.

Section 1201. Uniformity of Application and Construction.

This [Act] shall be applied and construed to effectuate its general purpose to make uniform the law with respect to the subject of this [Act] among States enacting it.

Section 1202. Short Title.

This [Act] may be cited as the Uniform Limited Liability Company Act (1996).

Section 1203. Severability Clause.

If any provision of this [Act] or its application to any person or circumstance is held invalid, the invalidity does not affect other provisions or applications of this [Act] which can be given effect without the invalid provision or application, and to this end the provisions of this [Act] are severable.

Section 1204. Effective Date.
This [Act] takes effect [_____].

Section 1205. Transitional Provisions.

(a) Before January 1, 199__, this [Act] governs only a limited liability company organized:

(1) after the effective date of this [Act], unless the company is continuing the business of a dissolved limited liability company under [Section of the existing Limited Liability Company Act]; and

(2) before the effective date of this [Act], which elects, as provided by subsection (c), to be governed by this [Act].

(b) On and after January 1, 199__, this [Act] governs all limited liability companies.

(c) Before January 1, 199__, a limited liability company voluntarily may elect, in the manner provided in its operating agreement or by law for amending the operating agreement, to be governed by this [Act].

COMMENT

Under subsection (a)(1), the application of the Act is mandatory for all companies formed after the effective date of the Act determined under Section 1204. Under subsection (a)(2), the application of the Act is permissive, by election under subsection (c), for existing companies for a period of time specified in subsection (b) after which application becomes mandatory. This affords existing companies and their members an opportunity to consider the changes effected by this Act and to amend their operating agreements, if appropriate. If no election is made, the Act becomes effective after the period specified in subsection (b). The period specified by adopting States may vary, but a period of five years is a common period in similar cases.

Section 1206. Savings Clause.
This [Act] does not affect an action or proceeding commenced or right accrued before the effective date of this [Act].

APPENDIX D

SECRETARIES OF STATE OFFICE WEB SITES

Alabama
http://www.sos.state.al.us/

Alaska
http://www.gov.state.ak.us/ltgov/

Arizona
http://azsos.com

Arkansas
http://www.sosweb.state.ar.us/

California
http://www.ss.ca.gov/

Colorado
http://www.sos.state.co.us/

Connecticut
http://www.sots.state.ct.us/

Delaware
http://www.state.de.us/sos/default.shtml

District of Columbia
http://os.dc.gov/os/site/default.asp

Florida
http://www.dos.state.fl.us/

Georgia
http://www.sos.state.ga.us/default800.asp

Hawaii
http://www.hawaii.gov/ltgov

Idaho
http://www.idsos.state.id.us/

Illinois
http://www.sos.state.il.us/

Indiana
http://www.in.gov/sos/

Iowa
http://www.sos.state.ia.us/

Kansas
http://www.kssos.org/main.html

Kentucky
http://sos.ky.gov/

Louisiana
http://www.sec.state.la.us/

Maine
http://www.state.me.us/sos/

Maryland
http://www.sos.state.md.us/

Massachusetts
http://www.sec.state.ma.us/

Michigan
http://www.michigan.gov/sos

Minnesota
http://www.state.mn.us/

Mississippi
http://www.sos.state.ms.us/

Missouri
http://www.sos.mo.gov/

Montana
http://sos.state.mt.us/css/index.asp

Nebraska
http://www.sos.state.ne.us/

Nevada
http://sos.state.nv.us/

New Hampshire
http://www.sos.nh.gov/index.html

New Jersey
http://www.state.nj.us/state/

New Mexico
http://www.sos.state.nm.us/

New York
http://www.dos.state.ny.us/

North Carolina
http://www.secstate.state.nc.us/

North Dakota
http://www.nd.gov/sos/

Ohio
http://www.sos.state.oh.us/

Oklahoma
http://www.sos.state.ok.us/

Oregon
http://www.sos.state.or.us/

Pennsylvania
http://www.dos.state.pa.us/dos/site/default.asp

Puerto Rico
http://www.estado.gobierno.pr/

Rhode Island
http://www.state.ri.us/

South Carolina
http://www.scsos.com/

South Dakota
http://www.sdsos.gov/

Tennessee
http://state.tn.us/sos/

Texas
http://www.sos.state.tx.us/

Virgin Islands
http://www.ltg.gov.vi/

Utah
http://www.mycorporation.com/secretary-state/Utah.htm

Vermont
http://www.sec.state.vt.us/

Virginia
http://www.soc.state.va.us/

Washington
http://www.secstate.wa.gov/

West Virginia
http://www.wvsos.com/

Wisconsin
http://www.sos.state.wi.us/

Wyoming
http://soswy.state.wy.us/

GLOSSARY

A

actual authority   The authority legally conferred on the agent by the principal.

agency   A legally recognized, fiduciary relationship where one person acts on behalf of another. Agents act under the authority, consent, and control of principals.

agent   The person who acts for the principal; agents receive their authority to act from a principal and may undertake business relationships and commitments on behalf of the principal.

apparent authority   The authority created when a principal leaves another with the impression that someone is his or her agent, when, in fact, that is not true.

articles of dissolution   An official filing with the secretary of state requesting dissolution of a corporation.

articles of incorporation   The document that frames the creation, organization, day-to-day operation, sale of assets, identity of registered agent, and dissolution of a corporation.

articles of organization   The document that sets out the organization, powers, duration, day-to-day operation, and eventual dissolution of a limited liability company.

artificial person   An entity or "thing," especially a corporation, that the law gives some of the legal rights and duties of a person.

B

bond   An investment that resembles a loan; an investor buys a bond for a specific amount and then is repaid over a period of time, at a specific interest rate.

book entry   A stock that is registered under a stockholder's name and for which no stock certificate issues.

business judgment rule   A rule that protects corporate officers and directors from liability for business decisions made in good faith.

bylaws   Rules adopted by a business entity to regulate its internal policies and actions.

C

capacity   A person's ability to know and understand not only the terms of the contract, but also the legal obligation incurred.

closely held corporation   A small company owned and managed by shareholders.

common stock   Stock that provides its owner with voting rights and a share of the corporation's profits in the form of dividends or capital appreciation in the value of stock.

condition precedent   A condition, fact, or occurrence that must occur before a contractual obligation is triggered.

condition subsequent   If a certain future event happens, a right or obligation ends.

consideration   Bargained-for exchange in a contract; a requirement that all parties to a contract surrender something of value in exchange for receiving something of value.

constructive trust doctrine   The theory that a partner who acquires profits for his or her own enrichment holds such funds for the benefit of the company as a whole and can be ordered to return such funds to the other partners.

contract   An agreement between legally competent parties who have expressed intent to enter into agreement with one another in a form recognized by law.

contract of adhesion   A contract in which all the bargaining power favors one side.

contribution   The value of the limited partner's investment in the business; this determines the limited partner's percentage of profits and losses.

corporation   A creature of statute; corporations are considered to be artificial persons; investors enjoy limited liability; corporations may own property, pay taxes, and carry out many of the activities traditionally associated with natural persons.

counteroffer   A rejection of an offer and a new offer made back.

D

de facto   "In fact," an event that is true in fact, if not in law.

default judgment   A judgment for the full amount requested in the complaint when the defendant fails to file an answer to the complaint.

derivative suit   A lawsuit brought by shareholders in the name of and on behalf of the corporation.

detriment   The bargained for exchange in a contract, where the parties take on some responsibility that they are not legally obligated to undertake.

directors   Individuals who set policy and long-term goals for corporations.

discharge   To discharge a contract is to end the obligation by agreement or by carrying it out.

dissolution   The process of terminating corporate existence.

dividend   A share of profits or property; usually a payment per share of the corporation's stock.

E

escheat   The process of transferring title to the state for property for which no owner can be found.

express authority   The authority specifically conferred on the agent by the principal, either verbally or in writing.

F

fiduciary   A person who has an obligation to act with honesty, fair dealing, and trust for another.

fraud   Any kind of trickery used to cheat another of money or property.

freeze out   The process of dissolving a business over the objection and to the detriment of the rights of minority stockholders.

G

general partnership   An unincorporated business organization co-owned by two or more persons that is run for profit.

going public   Carrying out an initial public offering of stock.

I

implied authority   An agent's authority to act that is not expressed by the principal, but is assumed by both parties to be present.

incorporator   A person or persons who form the corporation.

initial public offering   The first public sale of a corporation's stock.

insider trading   Buying or selling stocks in breach of fiduciary duty while in possession of nonpublic, nondisclosed information about a company.

J

joint and several liability   When two or more persons are liable for the actions of either.

judicial dissolution   A court's determination that a company should be dissolved for the good of the partners, creditors, or because the business has engaged in illegal activities.

L

legality   The requirement that a contract have, as its purpose, a goal that is legitimate and not barred by any statute or common law provision.

limited liability   A legal concept that, when used in the context of business, refers to the protection of an investor's personal assets. Potential loss is limited to the total amount invested in the venture, not the investor's total personal assets.

limited liability company   A limited liability company is a cross between a partnership and a corporation, owned by members who may manage the company directly or delegate to officers or managers who are similar to a corporation's directors.

limited partnership   A partnership formed by general partners (who run the business and have liability for all partnership debts) and limited partners (who partly or fully finance the business, take no part in running it, and have no liability, for partnership debts beyond the money they put in or promise to put in).

limited partnership agreement   A contract between the general and limited partners setting out their rights, duties, and obligations.

liquidation   The process of collecting and selling off all corporate assets.

liquidator   A person whose function is to collect all corporate assets and debts, organize, and distribute them.

M

managers   The persons responsible for the day-to-day operation of a limited liability company.

material fact A critical fact in the contract or negotiations; one that, if truthfully revealed, might abort the transaction.

meeting of the minds Agreement among all persons entering into a deal on the basic meaning and legal effect of the contract.

members The persons who invest in a limited liability company.

minor A person who is under the age of full legal rights and duties.

monopoly A company's absolute, or near absolute, control over an industry or business area.

mutual assent The meeting of the minds of the parties to the contract; a general agreement as to the details of the arrangement between the contracting parties.

mutuality of obligation Describes the principle that, for a binding contract to exist, each side must have some obligation or duty to perform under the contract.

mutuality of remedy Under equity law, a principle that requires that both parties have a similar recourse through the courts.

N

negotiable instrument Any document that promises or orders the payment of money.

nonprofit corporation A corporation specifically created for a purpose other than generating income; for example, charity.

O

offer Make a proposal; present for acceptance or rejection.

officer An individual hired or selected by a board of directors who has specific authority, such as the ability to bind the corporation to contracts and other agreements.

operating agreement The general business agreement between members and managers as to the function of a limited liability company.

option A contract in which one person pays money for the right to buy something from, or sell something to, another person at a certain price and within a certain time period.

organizational meeting The statutorily required, first meeting of a newly formed corporation where directors are elected and shares are issued.

P

par value An arbitrary value set on the price of an individual share.

partial performance Carrying out some, but not all, of a contract, or doing something in reliance on another's promise.

partnership A form of business in which two or more persons conduct a business together, sharing both profits and losses.

partnership agreement The contract that sets out the duties, responsibilities, and benefits of the persons who have agreed to enter into a partnership with one another.

piercing the corporate veil A rule that allows courts to disregard corporate protections and allow suits against corporate creators and shareholders.

preemptive rights The right of common-stock holders to purchase newly issued stock to maintain their overall percentage of ownership in a company.

preferred stock A class of stock that entitles the holder to a stated dividend that must be paid before any dividend payment is made to holders of common stock. Holders of preferred stock generally do not have any voting rights in the corporation.

preincorporation agreement An agreement entered into among the persons who will form a corporation, including how and when the corporation will be formed and the responsibilities of the various parties.

principal The person for whom the agent acts; the principal receives the benefit of the agent's actions and is bound by the agent's actions on his or her behalf.

private corporation A corporation organized to carry out a private purpose, such as earning profits or administering a private charity.

professional corporation A special corporate structure reserved for individuals who can practice their profession only after receiving a license from the state.

promoter The person or persons who take responsibility for creating and organizing a business into a corporation.

proxy A temporary transfer of voting rights to another person or voting trust.

public corporation A corporation formed to carry out some function or service traditionally associated with state or federal government.

puffing Typical sales exaggerations about an item for sale; common sales statements that do not misrepresent material facts.

Q

quasi-public corporation A company that was originally created as a private corporation, but after taking on a governmental function, has been reclassified.

quid pro quo (Latin) "Something for something."

R

ratification Confirmation of a prior act that may not have been authorized, but to which the principal agrees to be bound.

record date The date upon which specific stockholder rights are fixed; for example, all stockholders owning stock as of the record date are entitled to receive a dividend.

registered agent An individual authorized to receive service of lawsuits and other notices on behalf of a business.

respondeat superior (Latin) "Let the master respond;" a legal theory that imposes legal liability on an employer for the actions of the employee when the employee is carrying out his duties for the employer.

S

Sarbanes-Oxley Act An act that made sweeping revisions to SEC filing requirements by publicly traded companies.

security A share of stock, a bond, a note, or one of many different kinds of documents showing a share in a company or a debt owned by a company or a government.

self-dealing   When persons put their own interests ahead of those of the business in which they are involved and in which they owe a fiduciary duty.

service of process   The service of a civil claim, such as a complaint for damages, on the defendant in the suit.

shareholder   A person who owns shares in a corporation.

shareholder agreement   An agreement between the members of a corporation, setting out issues such as who can own shares and how these shares affect rights within the corporation.

shares   Ownership interests in a corporation.

Sherman Anti-Trust Act   One of the first federal legislative attempts to regulate the power of corporations in the United States.

silent partner   A partner who takes no part in the management or day-to-day running of the general partnership.

sole proprietorship   One of the most basic business models; a business run by a single individual, in which all profits and losses are passed through on the individual's income tax returns and where the individual has little or no liability protection.

stock   An ownership interest in a corporation that gives the holder specific rights, also known as equity.

stock certificates   Printed documents that indicate share ownership.

U

ultra vires   (Latin) "Beyond the power." An action carried out by an officer or director of a corporation that is not authorized by the corporate charter.

under-capitalization   Lacking enough cash or short-term profit to stay in business.

unlimited liability   A concept that places all of a person's personal assets within reach of a civil judgment.

V

voting trust   An agreement between shareholders to vote in a certain way.

W

winding up   Concluding all corporate business and obligations.

INDEX